THE PAPERS OF

THOMAS JEFFERSON

RETIREMENT SERIES

THE PAPERS OF

Thomas Jefferson

RETIREMENT SERIES

Volume 6
11 March to 27 November 1813

J. JEFFERSON LOONEY, EDITOR

ROBERT F. HAGGARD, ASSOCIATE EDITOR

JULIE L. LAUTENSCHLAGER AND DEBORAH BECKEL,
ASSISTANT EDITORS

LISA A. FRANCAVILLA, MANAGING EDITOR

ELLEN C. HICKMAN AND PAULA VITERBO,
EDITORIAL ASSISTANTS

CATHERINE COINER CRITTENDEN, SENIOR DIGITAL TECHNICIAN

SUSAN SPENGLER, DIGITAL TECHNICIAN

PRINCETON AND OXFORD

PRINCETON UNIVERSITY PRESS

2009

Library of Congress Cataloging-in-Publication Data

Jefferson, Thomas, 1743–1826

The papers of Thomas Jefferson. Retirement series / J. Jefferson Looney, editor . . .

[et al.] p. cm.

Includes bibliographical references and index.

Contents: v. 1. 4 March to 15 November 1809

v. 2. 16 November 1809 to 11 August 1810

v. 3. 12 August 1810 to 17 June 1811

v. 4. 18 June 1811 to 30 April 1812

v. 5. 1 May 1812 to 10 March 1813

v. 6. 11 March to 27 November 1813

ISBN 978-0-691-13772-8 (cloth: v. 6: alk. paper)

1. Jefferson, Thomas, 1743–1826—Archives. 2. Jefferson, Thomas, 1743–1826—

Correspondence. 3. Presidents—United States—Archives. 4. Presidents—

United States—Correspondence. 5. United States—Politics and government—

1809–1817—Sources. 6. United States—Politics and government—1817–1825—

Sources.   I. Looney, J. Jefferson. II. Title. III. Title: Retirement series.

E302.J442 2004b

973.4'6'092—dc22   2004048327

DEDICATED TO THE MEMORY OF

ADOLPH S. OCHS

PUBLISHER OF THE NEW YORK TIMES

1896–1935

WHO BY THE EXAMPLE OF A RESPONSIBLE

PRESS ENLARGED AND FORTIFIED

THE JEFFERSONIAN CONCEPT

OF A FREE PRESS

ADVISORY COMMITTEE

THIS EDITION was made possible by a founding grant from The New York Times Company to Princeton University.

The Retirement Series is sponsored by the Thomas Jefferson Foundation, Inc., of Charlottesville, Virginia. It was created with a six-year founding grant from The Pew Charitable Trusts to the Foundation and to Princeton University, enabling the former to take over responsibility for the volumes associated with this period. Leading gifts from Richard Gilder, Mrs. Martin S. Davis, and Thomas A. Saunders III have assured the continuation of the Retirement Series. For these essential donations, and for other indispensable aid generously given by librarians, archivists, scholars, and collectors of manuscripts, the Editors record their sincere gratitude.

FOREWORD

THE 516 DOCUMENTS printed in this volume cover the period from 11 March to 27 November 1813. Although Thomas Jefferson assured his old friend George Logan on 3 October that "an entire confidence in the abilities and integrity of those now administering the government, has kept me from the inclination, as well as the occasion, of intermedling in the public affairs, even as a private citizen may justifiably do," he found it impossible to disassociate himself from politics completely. As the conflict with Great Britain dragged on, he recommended to President James Madison that gunboats be used to protect the Chesapeake Bay and wrote three long letters to his son-in-law John Wayles Eppes, the chairman of the Ways and Means Committee of the United States House of Representatives, urging the moral necessity of providing for the rapid repayment of the national debt and reining in a banking system he regarded as corrupt.

Despite his concern that the combined effect of the British naval blockade and the worst drought in half a century would ravage his personal finances, for the most part Jefferson remained active, optimistic, and healthy. As he commented to Abigail Adams on 22 August, except for recurring bouts of rheumatism "I have enjoyed general health; for I do not consider as a want of health the gradual decline & increasing debility which are the natural diathesis of age." The septuagenarian found it difficult to walk long distances, but his love of horseback riding remained undiminished, and during this period he traveled three times to his beloved Poplar Forest retreat. Jefferson also continued to entertain a steady stream of visitors at Monticello, including the noted Portuguese botanist José Corrêa da Serra, who made the first of many visits to the mountaintop in the summer of 1813. Such friendships aside, family remained a high priority for the ex-president. He happily supervised the education of his grandchildren and other relations, procured a gold watch for the seventeenth birthday of his granddaughter Ellen W. Randolph (Coolidge), and exchanged more letters than usual with his younger brother Randolph Jefferson, who lived nearby in Buckingham County.

The volume and diversity of Jefferson's other correspondence also showed no sign of abating. Pierre Samuel Du Pont de Nemours forwarded a French translation of the treatise on education in the United States that he had written at Jefferson's behest more than a decade earlier. Although he claimed to have little affinity for grammar, exchanges with John Waldo and John Wilson reveal Jefferson's love of neologisms and well-developed ideas about how to improve English orthography. The engineer and inventor Robert Fulton sent a detailed description of the military potential of submarine weaponry, and Fulton's business partner, the entrepreneur John Devereux DeLacy, requested Jefferson's endorsement of their plan to use steamboats to improve navigation along the Atlantic seaboard. In a 13 August letter to Isaac McPherson, Jefferson sought to restrict the scope of Oliver Evans's milling patents with an eloquent call for limits on government-sanctioned intellectual-property rights. Furthermore, Jefferson responded favorably when Paul Allen, who was in the process of preparing Nicholas Biddle's *History of the Expedition under the command of Captains Lewis and Clark* for publication, asked for biographical information about the two famed explorers. While he had little to offer Allen on William Clark, Jefferson supplied an account of Meriwether Lewis's life and career on 18 August that includes a penetrating study of Lewis's mental state leading up to his apparent suicide. Jefferson's narrative, which was printed in 1814 in the introductory section of Biddle's work, remains among the most frequently quoted primary-source documents regarding his former private secretary.

Finally, this volume contains the most intense period of communication between Jefferson and John Adams during their many years in retirement. Adams, who firmly believed, as he wrote on 15 July, that the two men "ought not to die, before We have explained ourselves to each other," sent Jefferson twenty-five letters between the latter part of May and the end of November, and Jefferson reciprocated with six lengthy replies. A few tense moments resulted when the older statesman read several decade-old letters from Jefferson to Joseph Priestley critical of Adams and his administration, which appeared without Jefferson's prior knowledge or permission in the recently published *Memoirs of the Late Reverend Theophilus Lindsey*. In general, however, Adams and Jefferson enjoyed considerable success in steering clear of recent political controversies. Instead, their letters abound with wide-ranging discussions of government, philosophy, religion, and a host of other topics. These exchanges, while sometimes threatening to degenerate into intellectual one-upmanship, provide real insight into their respective worldviews and their hopes and fears for the young nation they had done so much to create.

ACKNOWLEDGMENTS

MANY INDIVIDUALS and institutions provided aid and encouragement during the preparation of this volume. Those who helped us to locate and acquire primary and secondary sources and answered our research questions include our colleagues at the Thomas Jefferson Foundation, especially Anna Berkes, Eric D. M. Johnson, Jack Robertson, Leah Stearns, and Endrina Tay of the Jefferson Library; Robert H. Smith Director of Restoration William L. Beiswanger; Director of the Center for Historic Plants Peggy Cornett; Director of Gardens and Grounds Peter Hatch; Conservator of Architecture and Furniture Robert L. Self; Shannon Senior Research Historian Lucia C. Stanton; staff archaeologist Derek Wheeler; and Foundation historian Gaye Wilson. Also instrumental to our work were Valerie-Anne Lutz van Ammers and Charles Greifenstein from the American Philosophical Society; Lynne Harrell at Brown University Library; David S. Svahn at Christ Church, Cooperstown, New York; Joshua A. Lascell of Dartmouth College Library; Martha N. Noblick, Historic Deerfield Library, Deerfield, Massachusetts; Suzanne Porter from Duke University Medical Center Library; Ralph Ketchum; Leslie Jordanger of the Louisa County Historical Society; Karen Kravcov Malcolm; Inge Dupont, The Morgan Library & Museum, New York; Jack Gary, Travis C. McDonald, and Gail Pond at the Corporation for Jefferson's Poplar Forest; Presbyterian Cemetery, Lynchburg, Virginia; Christine W. Kitto and Daniel J. Linke from Princeton University; the South Carolina Department of Archives and History; Stephen G. Hague, Laura Keim, and Dennis Pickeral at Stenton, George Logan's home in Philadelphia; Pat O'Donnell of the Friends Historical Library, Swarthmore College; John J. McCusker, Trinity University, San Antonio, Texas; Rebecca Dobyns, William Luebke, and Patricia Ferguson Watkinson from the Library of Virginia; John McClure at the Virginia Historical Society; and Steve Bookman, Eileen O'Toole, Susan Riggs, Amy Schindler, Ute Schechter, and Chandi Singer of the College of William and Mary. As always, we received advice, assistance, and encouragement from a large number of our fellow documentary editors, including Margaret Hogan and Sara Martin from the Adams Papers; Mary Hackett and Angela Kreider from the Madison Papers; and Martha King, John Little and Linda Monaco from the Jefferson Papers in Princeton. Genevieve Moene and Roland H. Simon transcribed and translated the French letters included in this volume; David T. Gies, Jennifer McCune, and Pedro Alvarez de Miranda performed a similar service for those in Spanish; John F. Miller assisted us with Latin quotations; Jonathan T. Hine and Rosanna M. Giammanco Frongia provided aid with Italian; Peter S. Baker advised us on several words in Anglo-Saxon; and Coulter George helped us puzzle out passages in Greek. The maps of Jefferson's Virginia and Albemarle County were created by Rick Britton. The other illustrations that appear in this volume were assembled with the assistance of Barbara Bair and Bonnie Coles from the Library of Congress; Peter Drummey and Elaine Grublin at the Massachusetts Historical Society; Roy Eddey and Jill Slaight of the New-York Historical Society; Edward Gaynor, Margaret Hrabe, and Regina Rush from the Albert and Shirley Small Special Collections Library, University of Virginia; and Christina Deane and her colleagues at the University of Virginia's Rare Materials Digital Services. Stephen Perkins of Dataformat.com continued raising us to more sophisticated digital approaches. Our departing Retirement Series colleague Susan Holbrook Perdue contributed to this volume in a variety of ways, as did new arrival Andrea R. Gray. Finally, our colleagues and friends at Princeton University Press have gone the extra miles to keep this series and this edition at the highest level.

EDITORIAL METHOD AND APPARATUS

1. RENDERING THE TEXT

From its inception *The Papers of Thomas Jefferson* has insisted on high standards of accuracy in rendering text, but modifications in textual policy and editorial apparatus have been implemented as different approaches have become accepted in the field or as a more faithful rendering has become technically feasible. Prior discussions of textual policy appeared in Vols. 1:xxix–xxxiv, 22:vii–xi, 24:vii–viii, and 30:xiii–xiv of the First Series.

The textual method of the Retirement Series will adhere to the more literal approach adopted in Volume 30 of the parent edition. Original spelling, capitalization, and punctuation are retained as written. Such idiosyncrasies as Jefferson's failure to capitalize the beginnings of most of his sentences and abbreviations like "mr" are preserved, as are his preference for "it's" to "its" and his characteristic spellings of "knolege," "paiment," and "recieve." Modern usage is adopted in cases where intent is impossible to determine, an issue that arises most often in the context of capitalization. Some so-called slips of the pen are corrected, but the original reading is recorded in a subjoined textual note. Jefferson and others sometimes signaled a change in thought within a paragraph with extra horizontal space, and this is rendered by a three-em space. Blanks left for words and not subsequently filled by the authors are represented by a space approximating the length of the blank. Gaps, doubtful readings of illegible or damaged text, and wording supplied from other versions or by editorial conjecture are explained in the source note or in numbered textual notes. Foreign-language documents, the vast majority of which are in French during the retirement period, are transcribed in full as faithfully as possible, and followed by a full translation.

Two modifications from past practice bring this series still closer to the original manuscripts. Underscored text is presented as such rather than being converted to italics. Superscripts are also preserved rather than being lowered to the baseline. In most cases of superscripting, the punctuation that is below or next to the superscripted letters is dropped, since it is virtually impossible to determine what is a period or dash as opposed to a flourish under, over, or adjacent to superscripted letters.

Limits to the more literal method are still recognized, however, and readability and consistency with past volumes are prime considerations. In keeping with the basic design implemented in the first volume of the *Papers*, salutations and signatures continue to display in large and small capitals rather than upper- and lowercase letters. Expansion marks over abbreviations are silently omitted. With very rare exceptions, deleted text and information on which words were added during the process of composition is not displayed within the document transcription. Based on the Editors' judgment of their significance, such emendations are either described in numbered textual notes or ignored. Datelines for letters are consistently printed at the head of the text, with a comment in the descriptive note when they have been moved. Address information, endorsements, and dockets are quoted or described in the source note rather than reproduced in the document proper.

2. TEXTUAL DEVICES

The following devices are employed throughout the work to clarify the presentation of the text.

[...]	Text missing and not conjecturable. The size of gaps longer than a word or two is estimated in annotation.
[ ]	Number or part of number missing or illegible.
[roman]	Conjectural reading for missing or illegible matter. A question mark follows when the reading is doubtful.
[*italic*]	Editorial comment inserted in the text.
<*italic*>	Matter deleted in the manuscript but restored in our text.

3. DESCRIPTIVE SYMBOLS

The following symbols are employed throughout the work to describe the various kinds of manuscript originals. When a series of versions is included, the first to be recorded is the version used for the printed text.

Dft	draft (usually a composition or rough draft; multiple drafts, when identifiable as such, are designated "2d Dft," etc.)
Dupl	duplicate
MS	manuscript (arbitrarily applied to most documents other than letters)
PoC	polygraph copy

PrC   press copy
RC   recipient's copy
SC   stylograph copy

All manuscripts of the above types are assumed to be in the hand of the author of the document to which the descriptive symbol pertains. If not, that fact is stated. On the other hand, the following types of manuscripts are assumed not to be in the hand of the author, and exceptions will be noted:

FC   file copy (applied to all contemporary copies retained by the author or his agents)

Tr   transcript (applied to all contemporary and later copies except file copies; period of transcription, unless clear by implication, will be given when known)

4. LOCATION SYMBOLS

The locations of documents printed in this edition from originals in private hands and from printed sources are recorded in self-explanatory form in the descriptive note following each document. The locations of documents printed or referenced from originals held by public and private institutions in the United States are recorded by means of the symbols used in the *MARC Code List for Organizations* (2000) maintained by the Library of Congress. The symbols DLC and MHi by themselves stand for the collections of Jefferson Papers proper in these repositories. When texts are drawn from other collections held by these two institutions, the names of those collections are added. Location symbols for documents held by institutions outside the United States are given in a subjoined list. The lists of symbols are limited to the institutions represented by documents printed or referred to in this volume.

CSmH   Huntington Library, San Marino, California
          JF   Jefferson File
          JF-BA   Jefferson File, Bixby Acquisition
CtY   Yale University, New Haven, Connecticut
DeGH   Hagley Museum and Library, Greenville, Delaware
DeHi   Historical Society of Delaware, Wilmington
DLC   Library of Congress, Washington, D.C.
          TJ Papers   Thomas Jefferson Papers (this is assumed if not stated, but also given as indicated to furnish the precise location of an undated, misdated, or otherwise problematic document,

thus "DLC: TJ Papers, 213:38071–2" represents volume 213, folios 38071 and 38072 as the collection was arranged at the time the first microfilm edition was made in 1944–45. Access to the microfilm edition of the collection as it was rearranged under the Library's Presidential Papers Program is provided by the *Index to the Thomas Jefferson Papers* [1976])

DNA National Archives, Washington, D.C., with identifications of series (preceded by record group number) as follows:

CS	Census Schedules
LAR	Letters of Application and Recommendation
LRSW	Letters Received by the Secretary of War
MLRSN	Miscellaneous Letters Received by the Secretary of the Navy
NFMC	Notes to Foreign Ministers and Consuls
RWP	Revolutionary War Pension and Bounty-Land Warrant Application Files

DNT National Trust for Historic Preservation, Washington, D.C.

FTaSA Florida State Archives, Tallahassee

ICPRCU Polish Roman Catholic Union, Chicago, Illinois

L-Ar Louisiana State Archives, Baton Rouge

LNT Tulane University, New Orleans, Louisiana

MBCo Countway Library of Medicine, Boston, Massachusetts

MBPLi Boston Public Library, Boston, Massachusetts

MDeeP Pocumtuck Valley Memorial Association, Deerfield, Massachusetts

MdHi Maryland Historical Society, Baltimore

MH Harvard University, Cambridge, Massachusetts

MHi Massachusetts Historical Society, Boston

MoSHi Missouri History Museum, Saint Louis

TJC	Thomas Jefferson Collection
TJC-BC	Thomas Jefferson Collection, text formerly in Bixby Collection

MoSW	Washington University, Saint Louis, Missouri
NCaS	Saint Lawrence University, Canton, New York
NcD	Duke University, Durham, North Carolina
NHi	New-York Historical Society, New York City
NjMoHP	Morristown National Historical Park, New Jersey
NjP	Princeton University, Princeton, New Jersey
NN	New York Public Library, New York City
NNGL	Gilder Lehrman Collection, New York City
NNPM	Pierpont Morgan Library, New York City
PHC	Haverford College, Haverford, Pennsylvania
PHi	Historical Society of Pennsylvania, Philadelphia
PPAmP	American Philosophical Society, Philadelphia, Pennsylvania
PPGi	Girard College, Philadelphia, Pennsylvania
PPRF	Rosenback Foundation, Philadelphia, Pennsylvania
PSC-Hi	Friends Historical Library, Swarthmore College, Swarthmore, Pennsylvania
PU	University of Pennsylvania, Philadelphia
PWW	Washington and Jefferson College, Washington, Pennsylvania
ScCoAH	South Carolina, Department of Archives and History, Columbia
TxH	Houston Public Library, Houston, Texas
TxU	University of Texas, Austin
Vi	Library of Virginia, Richmond
ViCMRL	Thomas Jefferson Library, Thomas Jefferson Foundation, Inc., Charlottesville, Virginia
ViHi	Virginia Historical Society, Richmond
ViMtvL	Mount Vernon Ladies' Association, Mount Vernon, Virginia
ViU	University of Virginia, Charlottesville
	TJP	Thomas Jefferson Papers
	TJP-Ca	Thomas Jefferson Papers, text formerly in Cabell Papers
	TJP-CC	Thomas Jefferson Papers, text formerly in Carr-Cary Papers
	TJP-ER	Thomas Jefferson Papers, text formerly in Edgehill-Randolph Papers
	TJP-LBJM	Thomas Jefferson Papers, Thomas Jefferson's Legal Brief in

	Jefferson v. Michie, 1804–13, deposited by Mrs. Augustina David Carr Mills	
ViW	College of William and Mary, Williamsburg, Virginia	
	TC-JP	Jefferson Papers, Tucker-Coleman Collection
	TJP	Thomas Jefferson Papers
ViWn	Handley Regional Library, Winchester, Virginia	
VtMiM	Middlebury College, Middlebury, Vermont	

5. *OTHER ABBREVIATIONS AND SYMBOLS*

The following abbreviations and symbols are commonly employed in the annotation throughout the work.

Lb   Letterbook (used to indicate texts copied or assembled into bound volumes)

RG   Record Group (used in designating the location of documents in the Library of Virginia and the National Archives)

SJL   Jefferson's "Summary Journal of Letters" written and received for the period 11 Nov. 1783 to 25 June 1826 (in DLC: TJ Papers). This epistolary record, kept in Jefferson's hand, has been checked against the TJ Editorial Files. It is to be assumed that all outgoing letters are recorded in SJL unless there is a note to the contrary. When the date of receipt of an incoming letter is recorded in SJL, it is incorporated in the notes. Information and discrepancies revealed in SJL but not found in the letter itself are also noted. Missing letters recorded in SJL are accounted for in the notes to documents mentioning them, in related documents, or in an appendix

TJ   Thomas Jefferson

TJ Editorial Files   Photoduplicates and other editorial materials in the office of the Papers of Thomas Jefferson: Retirement Series, Jefferson Library, Thomas Jefferson Foundation, Charlottesville

d   Penny or denier

f   Florin

£   Pound sterling or livre, depending upon context (in doubtful cases, a clarifying note will be given)

s   Shilling or sou (also expressed as /)

₶   Livre Tournois

℞   Per (occasionally used for pro, pre)

6. SHORT TITLES

The following list includes short titles of works cited frequently in this edition. Since it is impossible to anticipate all the works to be cited in abbreviated form, the list is revised from volume to volume.

Acts of Assembly   *Acts of the General Assembly of Virginia* (cited by session; title varies over time)

ANB   John A. Garraty and Mark C. Carnes, eds., *American National Biography*, 1999, 24 vols.

Annals   *Annals of the Congress of the United States: The Debates and Proceedings in the Congress of the United States . . . Compiled from Authentic Materials*, Washington, D.C., Gales & Seaton, 1834–56, 42 vols. (all editions are undependable and pagination varies from one printing to another. Citations given below are to the edition mounted on the American Memory website of the Library of Congress and give the date of the debate as well as page numbers)

APS   American Philosophical Society

ASP   *American State Papers: Documents, Legislative and Executive, of the Congress of the United States*, 1832–61, 38 vols.

Axelson, *Virginia Postmasters*   Edith F. Axelson, *Virginia Postmasters and Post Offices, 1789–1832*, 1991

BDSCHR   Walter B. Edgar and others, eds., *Biographical Directory of the South Carolina House of Representatives*, 1974– , 5 vols.

Betts, *Farm Book*   Edwin M. Betts, ed., *Thomas Jefferson's Farm Book*, 1953 (in two separately paginated sections; unless otherwise specified, references are to the second section)

Betts, *Garden Book*   Edwin M. Betts, ed., *Thomas Jefferson's Garden Book, 1766–1824*, 1944

Biddle, *Lewis and Clark Expedition*   Nicholas Biddle, *History of the Expedition under the command of Captains Lewis and Clark to the Sources of the Missouri, thence across the Rocky Mountains and down the River Columbia to the Pacific Ocean. Performed during the years 1804–5–6. By order of the Government of the United States*, 2 vols., Philadelphia, 1814; Sowerby, no. 4168; Poor, *Jefferson's Library*, 7 (no. 370)

Biog. Dir. Cong.   *Biographical Directory of the United States Congress, 1774–1989*, 1989

Biographie universelle   *Biographie universelle, ancienne et moderne*, new ed., 1843–65, 45 vols.

Black's Law Dictionary   Bryan A. Garner and others, eds., *Black's Law Dictionary*, 7th ed., 1999

Brant, *Madison*   Irving Brant, *James Madison*, 1941–61, 6 vols.

Brigham, *American Newspapers*   Clarence S. Brigham, *History and Bibliography of American Newspapers, 1690–1820*, 1947, 2 vols.

Bruce, *University*   Philip Alexander Bruce, *History of the University of Virginia 1819–1919: The Lengthened Shadow of One Man*, 1920–22, 5 vols.

Brunck, *Gnomici Poetæ Græci*   Richard François Philippe Brunck, ed., *Ηθικη Ποιησις: Sive Gnomici Poetæ Græci*, Strasbourg, 1784; Sowerby, no. 4466; Poor, *Jefferson's Library*, 12 (no. 780); Adams's copy at MBPLi

Bush, *Life Portraits*   Alfred L. Bush, *The Life Portraits of Thomas Jefferson*, rev. ed., 1987

Callahan, *U.S. Navy*   Edward W. Callahan, *List of Officers of the Navy of the United States and of the Marine Corps from 1775 to 1900*, 1901, repr. 1969

Chambers, *Poplar Forest*   S. Allen Chambers, *Poplar Forest & Thomas Jefferson*, 1993

Chandler, *Campaigns of Napoleon*   David G. Chandler, *The Campaigns of Napoleon*, 1966

Claiborne, *Letter Books*   Dunbar Rowland, ed., *Official Letter Books of W. C. C. Claiborne, 1801–1816*, 1917, repr. 1972, 6 vols.

Clay, *Papers*   James F. Hopkins and others, eds., *The Papers of Henry Clay*, 1959–1992, 11 vols.

Connelly, *Napoleonic France*   Owen Connelly and others, eds., *Historical Dictionary of Napoleonic France, 1799–1815*, 1985

DAB   Allen Johnson and Dumas Malone, eds., *Dictionary of American Biography*, 1928–36, 20 vols.

DBF   *Dictionnaire de biographie française*, 1933– , 19 vols.

Destutt de Tracy, *Commentary and Review of Montesquieu's Spirit of Laws*   Antoine Louis Claude Destutt de Tracy, *A Commentary and Review of Montesquieu's Spirit of Laws. prepared for press from the Original Manuscript, in the hands of the Publisher. To which are annexed, Observations on the Thirty-First Book, by the late M. Condorcet; and Two Letters of Helvetius, on the merits of the same work*, Philadelphia, 1811; Sowerby, no. 2327; Poor, *Jefferson's Library*, 10 (no. 623)

Dexter, *Yale Biographies*   Francis Bowditch Dexter, *Biographical Sketches of the Graduates of Yale College*, 1885–1912, 6 vols.

DNB   Leslie Stephen and Sidney Lee, eds., *Dictionary of National Biography*, 1885–1901, 22 vols.

Dolley Madison, *Selected Letters*   David B. Mattern and Holly C. Shulman, eds., *The Selected Letters of Dolley Payne Madison*, 2003

DSB   Charles C. Gillispie, ed., *Dictionary of Scientific Biography*, 1970–80, 16 vols.

DVB   John T. Kneebone and others, eds., *Dictionary of Virginia Biography*, 1998– , 3 vols.

EG   Dickinson W. Adams and Ruth W. Lester, eds., *Jefferson's Extracts from the Gospels*, 1983, *The Papers of Thomas Jefferson*, Second Series

Fairclough, *Horace: Satires, Epistles, and Ars Poetica*   H. Rushton Fairclough, trans., *Horace: Satires, Epistles, and Ars Poetica*, Loeb Classical Library, 1926, repr. 1970

Fairclough, *Virgil*   H. Rushton Fairclough, trans., *Virgil*, ed. rev. by G. P. Goold, Loeb Classical Library, 1999–2000, 2 vols.

Ford   Paul Leicester Ford, ed., *The Writings of Thomas Jefferson*, Letterpress Edition, 1892–99, 10 vols.

Gaines, *Randolph*   William H. Gaines Jr., *Thomas Mann Randolph: Jefferson's Son-in-Law*, 1966

Gerber, *Greek Elegiac Poetry*   Douglas E. Gerber, trans., *Greek Elegiac Poetry from the Seventh to the Fifth Centuries BC*, Loeb Classical Library, 1999

Haggard, "Henderson Heirs"   Robert F. Haggard, "Thomas Jefferson v. The Heirs of Bennett Henderson, 1795–1818: A Case Study in Caveat Emptor," *MACH*, 63 (2005): 1–29

HAW   Henry A. Washington, ed., *The Writings of Thomas Jefferson*, 1853–54, 9 vols.

Heidler and Heidler, *War of 1812*   David S. Heidler and Jeanne T. Heidler, eds., *Encyclopedia of the War of 1812*, 1997

Heitman, *Continental Army*   Francis B. Heitman, comp., *Historical Register of Officers of the Continental Army during the War of the Revolution, April, 1775, to December, 1783*, rev. ed., 1914

Heitman, *U.S. Army*   Francis B. Heitman, comp., *Historical Register and Dictionary of the United States Army*, 1903, 2 vols.

Hening   William Waller Hening, ed., *The Statutes at Large; being a Collection of all the Laws of Virginia*, Richmond, 1809–23, 13 vols.

Hortus Third   Liberty Hyde Bailey, Ethel Zoe Bailey, and the staff of the Liberty Hyde Bailey Hortorium, Cornell University,

Hortus Third: A Concise Dictionary of Plants Cultivated in the United States and Canada, 1976

Jackson, *Letters of Lewis and Clark*   Donald Jackson, ed., *Letters of the Lewis and Clark Expedition with Related Documents, 1783–1854*, 2d ed., 1978, 2 vols.

Jackson, *Papers*   Sam B. Smith, Harold D. Moser, Daniel Feller, and others, eds., *The Papers of Andrew Jackson*, 1980– , 7 vols.

Jefferson Correspondence, Bixby   Worthington C. Ford, ed., *Thomas Jefferson Correspondence Printed from the Originals in the Collections of William K. Bixby*, 1916

JEP   *Journal of the Executive Proceedings of the Senate of the United States*

JHD   *Journal of the House of Delegates of the Commonwealth of Virginia*

JHR   *Journal of the House of Representatives of the United States*

JS   *Journal of the Senate of the United States*

JSV   *Journal of the Senate of Virginia*

Kimball, *Jefferson, Architect*   Fiske Kimball, *Thomas Jefferson, Architect*, 1916

L & B   Andrew A. Lipscomb and Albert E. Bergh, eds., *The Writings of Thomas Jefferson*, Library Edition, 1903–04, 20 vols.

Latrobe, *Papers*   John C. Van Horne and others, eds., *The Correspondence and Miscellaneous Papers of Benjamin Henry Latrobe*, 1984–88, 3 vols.

Lay, *Architecture*   K. Edward Lay, *The Architecture of Jefferson Country: Charlottesville and Albemarle County, Virginia*, 2000

LCB   Douglas L. Wilson, ed., *Jefferson's Literary Commonplace Book*, 1989, *The Papers of Thomas Jefferson*, Second Series

Leavitt, *Poplar Forest*   Messrs. Leavitt, *Catalogue of a Private Library . . . Also, The Remaining Portion of the Library of the Late Thomas Jefferson . . . offered by his grandson, Francis Eppes, of Poplar Forest, Va.*, 1873

Leonard, *General Assembly*   Cynthia Miller Leonard, comp., *The General Assembly of Virginia, July 30, 1619–January 11, 1978: A Bicentennial Register of Members*, 1978

List of Patents   *A List of Patents granted by the United States from April 10, 1790, to December 31, 1836*, 1872

Longworth's New York Directory   *Longworth's American Almanac, New-York Register, and City Directory*. New York, 1796–1842 (title varies; cited by year of publication)

MACH   *Magazine of Albemarle County History*, 1940– (title varies: issued until 1951 as *Papers of the Albemarle County Historical Society*)

Madison, *Papers*   William T. Hutchinson, Robert A. Rutland, John C. A. Stagg, and others, eds., *The Papers of James Madison*, 1962– , 31 vols.

    Congress. Ser., 17 vols.

    Pres. Ser., 6 vols.

    Sec. of State Ser., 8 vols

Malone, *Jefferson*   Dumas Malone, *Jefferson and his Time*, 1948–81, 6 vols.

Marshall, *Papers*   Herbert A. Johnson, Charles T. Cullen, Charles F. Hobson, and others, eds., *The Papers of John Marshall*, 1974–2006, 12 vols.

Mazzei, *Writings*   Margherita Marchione and others, eds., *Philip Mazzei: Selected Writings and Correspondence*, 1983, 3 vols.

MB   James A. Bear Jr. and Lucia C. Stanton, eds., *Jefferson's Memorandum Books: Accounts, with Legal Records and Miscellany, 1767–1826*, 1997, *The Papers of Thomas Jefferson*, Second Series

McCullough, *Adams*   David McCullough, *John Adams*, 2001

Memorial to Congress on Evans' Patent   *Memorial to Congress of sundry citizens of the United States, praying relief from the oppressive operation of Oliver Evans' Patent*, Baltimore, 1813

Notes, ed. Peden   Thomas Jefferson, *Notes on the State of Virginia*, ed. William Peden, 1955

OCD   Simon Hornblower and Antony Spawforth, eds., *The Oxford Classical Dictionary*, 2003

ODNB   H. C. G. Matthew and Brian Harrison, eds., *Oxford Dictionary of National Biography*, 2004, 60 vols.

OED   James A. H. Murray, J. A. Simpson, E. S. C. Weiner, and others, eds., *The Oxford English Dictionary*, 2d ed., 1989, 20 vols.

Papenfuse, *Maryland Public Officials*   Edward C. Papenfuse and others, eds., *An Historical List of Public Officials of Maryland*, 1990– , 1 vol.

Peale, *Papers*   Lillian B. Miller and others, eds., *The Selected Papers of Charles Willson Peale and His Family*, 1983– , 5 vols. in 6

Poor, *Jefferson's Library*   Nathaniel P. Poor, *Catalogue. President Jefferson's Library*, 1829

Priestley, *Heathen Philosophy*   Joseph Priestley, *The Doctrines of Heathen Philosophy compared with those of Revelation*, Northumberland, Pa., 1804; Sowerby, no. 1528

Princetonians   James McLachlan and others, eds., *Princetonians: A Biographical Dictionary*, 1976–90, 5 vols.

PTJ   Julian P. Boyd, Charles T. Cullen, John Catanzariti, Barbara B. Oberg, and others, eds., *The Papers of Thomas Jefferson*, 1950– , 34 vols.

PW   Wilbur S. Howell, ed., *Jefferson's Parliamentary Writings*, 1988, *The Papers of Thomas Jefferson*, Second Series

Randall, *Life*   Henry S. Randall, *The Life of Thomas Jefferson*, 1858, 3 vols.

Randolph, *Domestic Life*   Sarah N. Randolph, *The Domestic Life of Thomas Jefferson, Compiled from Family Letters and Reminiscences by His Great-Granddaughter*, 1871

Shackelford, *Descendants*   George Green Shackelford, ed., *Collected Papers to Commemorate Fifty Years of the Monticello Association of the Descendants of Thomas Jefferson*, 1965

Sibley's Harvard Graduates   John L. Sibley and others, eds., *Sibley's Harvard Graduates*, 1873– , 18 vols.

Sowerby   E. Millicent Sowerby, comp., *Catalogue of the Library of Thomas Jefferson*, 1952–59, 5 vols.

Sprague, *American Pulpit*   William B. Sprague, *Annals of the American Pulpit*, 1857–69, 9 vols.

Stagg, *Borderlines in Borderlands*   John C. A. Stagg, *Borderlines in Borderlands: James Madison and the Spanish-American Frontier, 1776–1821*, 2009

Stagg, *Madison's War*   John C. A. Stagg, *Mr. Madison's War: Politics, Diplomacy, and Warfare in the Early American Republic, 1783–1830*, 1983

Stein, *Worlds*   Susan R. Stein, *The Worlds of Thomas Jefferson at Monticello*, 1993

Terr. Papers   Clarence E. Carter and John Porter Bloom, eds., *The Territorial Papers of the United States*, 1934–75, 28 vols.

TJR   Thomas Jefferson Randolph, ed., *Memoir, Correspondence, and Miscellanies, from the Papers of Thomas Jefferson*, 1829, 4 vols.

True, "Agricultural Society"   Rodney H. True, "Minute Book of the Agricultural Society of Albemarle," *Annual Report of the American Historical Association for the Year 1918* (1921), 1:261–349

U.S. Reports   *Cases Argued and Decided in the Supreme Court of the United States*, 1790– (title varies; originally issued in distinct editions of separately numbered volumes with *U.S. Reports*

volume numbers retroactively assigned; original volume numbers here given parenthetically)

U.S. Statutes at Large   Richard Peters, ed., *The Public Statutes at Large of the United States . . . 1789 to March 3, 1845*, 1855–56, 8 vols.

Va. Reports   *Reports of Cases Argued and Adjudged in the Court of Appeals of Virginia*, 1798– (title varies; originally issued in distinct editions of separately numbered volumes with *Va. Reports* volume numbers retroactively assigned; original volume numbers here given parenthetically)

VMHB   *Virginia Magazine of History and Biography*, 1893–

Washington, *Papers*   W. W. Abbot, Dorothy Twohig, Philander D. Chase, Theodore J. Crackel, and others, eds., *The Papers of George Washington*, 1983– , 49 vols.

> *Colonial Ser.*, 10 vols.
> *Confederation Ser.*, 6 vols.
> *Pres. Ser.*, 14 vols.
> *Retirement Ser.*, 4 vols.
> *Rev. War Ser.*, 18 vols.

William and Mary Provisional List   *A Provisional List of Alumni, Grammar School Students, Members of the Faculty, and Members of the Board of Visitors of the College of William and Mary in Virginia. From 1693 to 1888*, 1941

WMQ   *William and Mary Quarterly*, 1892–

Woods, *Albemarle*   Edgar Woods, *Albemarle County in Virginia*, 1901, repr. 1991

CONTENTS

·◖❴ 1813 ❵◗·

CONTENTS

CONTENTS

CONTENTS

CONTENTS

CONTENTS

[xxx]

CONTENTS

CONTENTS

CONTENTS

CONTENTS

CONTENTS

CONTENTS

CONTENTS

MAPS

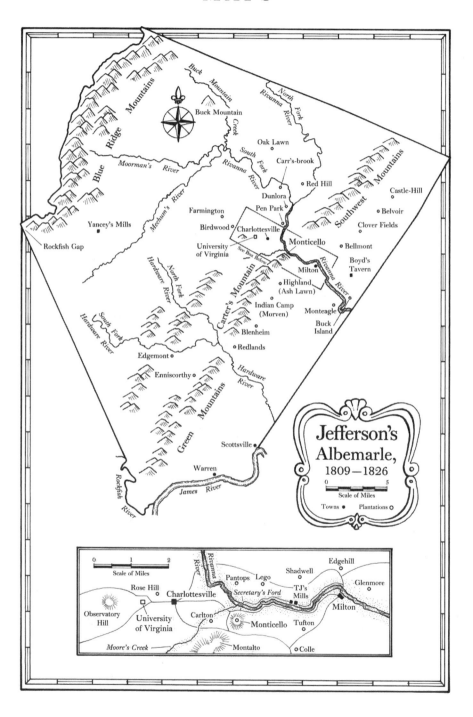

Jefferson's Albemarle, 1809–1826

0 5
Scale of Miles

Towns ● Plantations ○

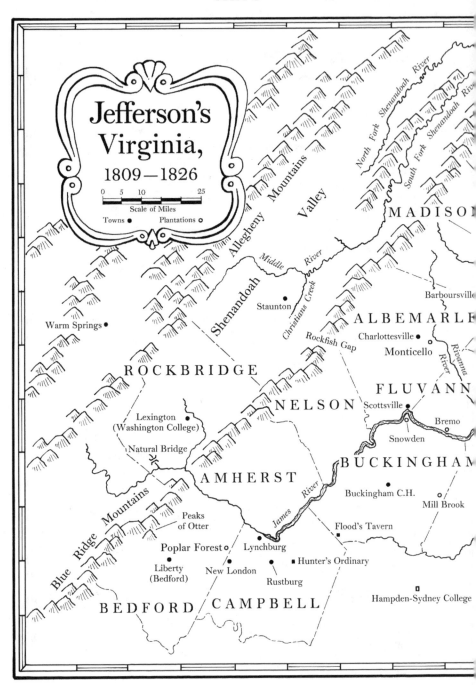

Jefferson's Virginia, 1809—1826

Scale of Miles

0 5 10 25

Towns ●   Plantations ○

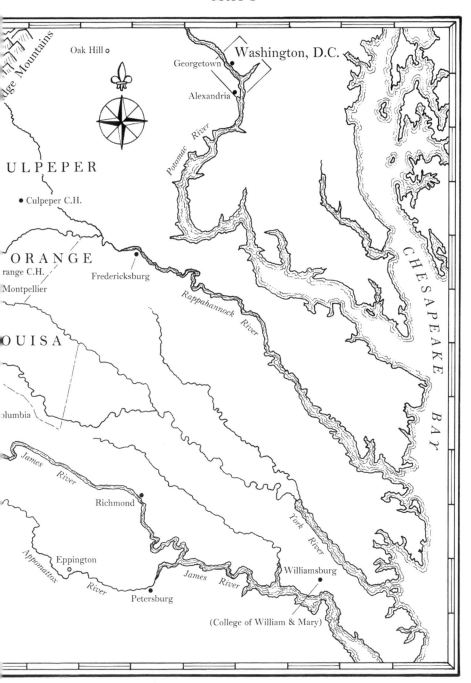

Blue Ridge Mountains

Oak Hill o

Washington, D.C.

Georgetown

Alexandria

Potomac River

CULPEPER

• Culpeper C.H.

ORANGE

Orange C.H.

Montpellier

Fredericksburg

Rappahannock River

LOUISA

Columbia

James River

Richmond

Appomattox River

Eppington

Petersburg

James River

York River

Williamsburg

(College of William & Mary)

CHESAPEAKE BAY

ILLUSTRATIONS

Following page 386

BIRD PEPPER (*Capsicum annuum glabriusculum*)

Dr. Samuel Brown, of Natchez, sent Jefferson the seed of the bird pepper in both October 1812 and May 1813. According to Brown, it proliferated "in very great abundance in the prairies west of the Sabine" River and was "with the Spaniards & Savages, an article in as great use as common salt is" among the people of the United States. The inhabitants of what is now Texas supposedly used the pepper both to spice up their dishes and for medicinal purposes. Jefferson forwarded some of the seeds to the Philadelphia horticulturist and nurseryman Bernard McMahon in June 1813 and planted others in his kitchen garden late the following March. Large numbers of small, red peppers grow on each compact, mound-like plant (Brown to TJ, 1 Oct. 1812, 25 May 1813; TJ to McMahon, 15 June 1813; Peter J. Hatch, "McMahon's Texas Bird Pepper: A Pretty Little Plant," *Twinleaf* [Jan. 1996]; Betts, *Garden Book*, 522).
Courtesy of the Thomas Jefferson Foundation, Inc.

JEFFERSON'S MILLS

FLOUR MILL

Jefferson's flour mill at Shadwell began operation in 1807. Jefferson initially leased it out to Jonathan and Isaac Shoemaker, but he replaced them with his son-in-law Thomas Mann Randolph and James McKinney four years later after the Shoemakers proved to be both incompetent and unable to keep up with their rent payments. McKinney retired, and Thomas Eston Randolph joined in the management of the concern in 1814. Thomas Mann Randolph stepped down soon thereafter, and Thomas Eston Randolph continued to direct the venture, both alone and in conjunction with Daniel Colclaser, until Jefferson's death. The combination of indifferent management and escalating repair and maintenance costs severely limited the return on Jefferson's initial investment of $10,000. In 1829 Thomas Jefferson Randolph and Martha Randolph sold the entire Shadwell mill complex and a small adjacent tract to James Magruder, John B. Magruder, and John Timberlake for $10,000. The photograph depicted was taken about 1870, not long before the building disappeared. An engraving of the mill was given in *Harper's New Monthly Magazine* in July 1853 (Betts, *Farm Book*, 342–3; *MB*, 2:1099, 1310 [engraving of 1853 reproduced opp. p. 1242]; K. Edward Lay, *The Architecture of Jefferson Country* [CD-ROM, 2000]; TJ to Charles L. Bankhead, 10 June 1811; TJ to Thomas Eston Randolph, 20 Jan. 1815; Albemarle Co. Deed Book, 28:116–7).
Courtesy of K. Edward Lay, photograph on deposit at the Albert and Shirley Small Special Collections Library, University of Virginia.

SAWMILL

Jefferson's sawmill was located roughly half a mile upriver from the Shadwell mills, on the opposite, or Monticello, side of the Rivanna River.

Completed by John Brown in 1813, it ultimately included a hominy beater and a hemp brake. Unfortunately, its operations were significantly hindered by an inadequate supply of water to power its machinery. To rectify this problem, Jefferson was forced to cut another canal from the river to the sawmill, which he completed in 1819. Jefferson's undated drawing shows the component parts of the sawmill, the canals and "tail race" that provided it with water, and its proximity to the Rivanna (Betts, *Farm Book*, 411; *MB*, 2:1285, 1291; TJ to Brown, 25 Apr. 1813; TJ to John H. Peyton, 17 Dec. 1819).

Courtesy of the Albert and Shirley Small Special Collections Library, University of Virginia.

OLIVER EVANS'S PATENT MACHINERY

Oliver Evans's book, *The Young Mill-wright & Miller's Guide* (Philadelphia, 1795, and many other editions; Sowerby, no. 1180), includes an illustration of his millworks in action among the plates printed at the end of the fourth part of the work. The engraving depicts his grain elevator (nos. 4–5 and elsewhere); his conveyor (nos. 15–6 and elsewhere); and his hopper-boy, a rake used to push meal over a hole in the floor (no. 25). Although he had received a federal patent for his machinery in 1790 and renewed it in 1808, questions were increasingly raised as to whether he was entitled to such protections. Jefferson, for his part, expressed strong doubts that the Evans elevator justified a patent. The lengthy letter that he wrote Isaac McPherson on the subject on 13 Aug. 1813 examines both Evans's pretensions and the importance of keeping frivolous patents in check (*List of Patents*, 4, 62).

Courtesy of the Albert and Shirley Small Special Collections Library, University of Virginia.

ROBERT FULTON

The engineer and inventor Robert Fulton (1765–1815) had never hesitated to bring his ideas to Jefferson's attention in the past, and 1813 proved to be no exception. His detailed examination of the possibility of using submarine weaponry to offset Britain's enormous naval advantage, which he sent to the ex-president in the early summer of 1813, is, like so many of his past productions, both thoughtful and thought-provoking. In addition to his other accomplishments, Fulton was no mean artist. The self-portrait he executed during the last decade of his life in Conté crayon, gray wash, black, white, and pink chalk, and white gouache on brown paper was inscribed by him as a gift to Henry Eckford, a prominent marine architect and shipbuilder (Cynthia Owen Philip, *Robert Fulton: a Biography* [1985], 313; *ODNB*).

Collection of the New-York Historical Society (negative #47765).

AMERICAN PHILOSOPHICAL SOCIETY MEMBERSHIP DIPLOMA

Jefferson joined the American Philosophical Society in 1780, and he served as one of its vice-presidents, 1791–94, and president, 1797–1814. During his seventeen years in the presidential chair, he affixed his signature to dozens of membership diplomas. The example reproduced here was dated 16 Apr. 1813 and awarded to Nicholas Biddle, a Philadelphia attorney, editor, politician, and future president of the Bank of the United States. After leaving Philadelphia for good in 1800, Jefferson presumably signed batches of blank certificates from time to time and sent them to the Society to be completed as needed (APS, Minutes [MS in PPAmP]; *PTJ*, 4:545–6n, 29:254; Biddle to TJ, 12 Dec. 1809, note; TJ to John Vaughan, 17 May 1813; TJ to Robert Patterson, 23 Nov. 1814; Silvio A. Bedini, *Jefferson and Science* [2002], 41).

Courtesy of the American Philosophical Society.

GREEK HANDWRITING OF JEFFERSON AND OF JOHN ADAMS

Thomas Jefferson and John Adams each received classical educations, which necessarily included intensive study of Greek language and literature, but an examination of their Greek script reveals a number of eccentricities. Both frequently omit accents and breathing marks. Adams occasionally replaces Greek letters—such as the iota, nu, and upsilon—with their Roman analog. Jefferson, for his part, routinely employs the terminal form of the sigma wherever it appears. Whatever the imperfections of their orthography, each man held Greek in high regard. Adams considered it the supreme language, while Jefferson wrote Joseph Priestley on 27 Jan. 1800 that to read "Greek authors in their original is a sublime luxury," and he thanked on his "knees him who directed my early education for having put into my possession this rich source of delight" (McCullough, *Adams*, 19; *PTJ*, 31:340).

Jefferson to Adams, 27 June 1813, *Courtesy of the Massachusetts Historical Society.*

Adams to Jefferson, [ca. 14] Aug. 1813, *Courtesy of the Library of Congress.*

THE HOUSE OF JOHN AND ABIGAIL ADAMS

The house in Quincy, Massachusetts, built by Major Leonard Vassall in about 1731 was purchased by John and Abigail Adams in 1787. It remained in the family's possession well into the twentieth century and was variously known as Peacefield, Montezillo, and the Old House. Eliza Susan Quincy (1798–1884), a distant relative of the Adams's and the daughter of Josiah Quincy, a mayor of Boston and president of Harvard University, included this watercolor in her two-volume unpublished memoir, which she donated to the Massachusetts Historical Society in 1870. Her depiction of the Adams home dates from 1822. It is painted en grisaille, or entirely in shades of gray, and employs dark washes for the foreground and light washes for the city of Boston, which is six miles distant (Eliza S. Quincy, *A Portfolio of Nine Watercolor Views, Relating to Certain Members of the Adams and Quincy Families and Their Quincy Houses and Environment Done in the Year 1822* [1975]; Lyman H. Butterfield, Richard Alan Ryerson, C. James Taylor, and others, eds., *Adams Family Correspondence* [1963–], 8:ix–x, xxv).

Courtesy of the Massachusetts Historical Society.

LETTER FROM JEFFERSON'S BROTHER RANDOLPH

Randolph Jefferson, Thomas Jefferson's younger brother, lived at Snowden in Buckingham County, just across the James River from Albemarle County. Although a dozen years and vastly different life experiences and personal interests separated the two men, they maintained a cordial relation-ship punctuated by occasional visits to each other's homes. Only thirty-two of the fifty or more letters that passed between them survive, nine of which appear in this volume. More than enough remain, however, to compare their orthography. Despite the fact that both men had received uncommonly good educations for their day, Randolph's limited vocabulary, somewhat phonetic spelling, lack of punctuation, and erratic hyphenation contrast strongly with that of his highly literate brother.

Courtesy of the Albert and Shirley Small Special Collections Library, University of Virginia.

Volume 6

11 March to 27 November 1813

JEFFERSON CHRONOLOGY

1743 · 1826

1743	Born at Shadwell, 13 April (New Style).
1760–1762	Studies at the College of William and Mary.
1762–1767	Self-education and preparation for law.
1769–1774	Albemarle delegate to House of Burgesses.
1772	Marries Martha Wayles Skelton, 1 January.
1775–1776	In Continental Congress.
1776	Drafts Declaration of Independence.
1776–1779	In Virginia House of Delegates.
1779	Submits Bill for Establishing Religious Freedom.
1779–1781	Governor of Virginia.
1782	Martha Wayles Skelton Jefferson dies, 6 September.
1783–1784	In Continental Congress.
1784–1789	In France on commission to negotiate commercial treaties and then as minister plenipotentiary at Versailles.
1790–1793	Secretary of State of the United States.
1797–1801	Vice President of the United States.
1801–1809	President of the United States.

RETIREMENT

1809	Attends James Madison's inauguration, 4 March.
	Arrives at Monticello, 15 March.
1810	Completes legal brief on New Orleans batture case, 31 July.
1811	Batture case dismissed, 5 December.
1812	Correspondence with John Adams resumed, 1 January.
	Batture pamphlet preface completed, 25 February; printed by 21 March.
1814	Named a trustee of Albemarle Academy, 25 March.
	Resigns presidency of American Philosophical Society, 23 November.
1815	Sells personal library to Congress, 29 April.
1816	Writes introduction and revises translation of Destutt de Tracy, *A Treatise on Political Economy* [1818].
	Named a visitor of Central College, 18 October.
1818	Attends Rockfish Gap conference to choose location of proposed University of Virginia, 1–4 August.
	Visits Warm Springs, 7–27 August.
1819	University of Virginia chartered, 25 January; named to Board of Visitors, 13 February; elected rector, 29 March.
	Debts greatly increased by bankruptcy of Wilson Cary Nicholas.
1820	Likens debate over slavery and Missouri statehood to "a fire bell in the night," 22 April.
1821	Writes memoirs, 6 January–29 July.
1823	Visits Poplar Forest for last time, 16–25 May.
1824	Lafayette visits Monticello, 4–15 November.
1825	University of Virginia opens, 7 March.
1826	Writes will, 16–17 March.
	Last recorded letter, 25 June.
	Dies at Monticello, 4 July.

THE PAPERS OF
THOMAS JEFFERSON

·⟨━━━━━⟩·

To Alrichs & Dixon

MESS^{RS} ALRICHS & DIXON   Monticello Mar. 11. 13.

I was much concerned to learn by a letter from Messrs Gibson & Jefferson of Richmond that they found difficulty in procuring a bill for the remittance I desired to be made to you. I immediately wrote to them to inclose you a hundred dollar bank bill of Richmond, which I doubted not you could have exchanged. the difference between this & the amount of your bill would be no more than a just compensation for the delay.   I am in expectation of recieving instructions from you as to the carding machine. I am the more encouraged to hope they will enable me to use it, by recieving information from mr Burwell that with that which you furnished him with he recieved from you such minute directions that he was able to set his to work himself without any difficulty. we are much retarded in our spinning for want of it. Accept my best wishes & respects.   TH: JEFFERSON

PoC (DLC); endorsed by TJ.

The day before TJ composed this let-ter, Alrichs & Dixon wrote him from Delaware acknowledging receipt of the BILL FOR THE REMITTANCE.

To Lewis Brown

SIR   Monticello Mar. 11. 13.

Your letter of Feb. 25. never got to my hands till last night. the purchase of the horse from you by mr Darnell was on my account, and the debt as much acknoleged as if a bond had been given. I had desired my merchant in Richmond, as soon as he could sell my flour from the Poplar Forest (which got down but lately) to remit a sum of money to mr Goodman, sufficient to pay your's and other debts there. but finding that the blockade of the Chesapeake has prevented the sale of my flour, I have this day authorised mr Goodman to recieve the money from a fund in Lynchburg which will become due on the 7th of the next month. you may count therefore on recieving what is due as[1] soon after that day, as mr Goodman can go to Lynchburg.

Accept my best wishes & respects.   TH: JEFFERSON

PoC (MHi); at foot of text: "Mr Lewis   [1] Word interlined in place of "very."
Brown"; endorsed by TJ.

To Patrick Gibson

DEAR SIR   Monticello Mar. 11. 13.

In my answer of the 7th to yours of the 3d of Mar. I omitted to note what you had stated as to the bargain for Mazzei's lot, to wit that the paiments were to be made within so many days after a sufficient title shall be made. I now expect daily an answer from mr Randolph after which there will be no delay in making what I deem a good title. but if mr Taylor should deem it otherwise, I take for granted, the bargain is relinquished on his part, & that we shall be free to sell to others. I have thought it necessary to say this much, until I recieve mr Randolph's answer that there may be no misunderstanding or disappointment on either side.

The objects of the remittance of 250.D. to Bedford, not admitting the delay of the sale of my flour, I have desired mr Harrison to pay that sum out of the fund in his hands, which supercedes the necessity of your remitting it out of the sales of the flour when that shall take place. Accept my friendly salutations.   TH: JEFFERSON

PoC (MHi); at foot of text: "Mr Gibson"; endorsed by TJ as a letter to Gibson & Jefferson and so recorded in SJL.

To Jeremiah A. Goodman

DR SIR   Monticello Mar. 11. 13.

The blockade of the Chesapeak having sunk the price of flour to 7. Dollars,[1] for which I am not disposed to sacrifice mine, and being desirous that my debts in your neighborhood therefore should not be put off for that sale, I have this day written to mr Harrison of Lynchburg to pay you 250.D. on the 7th of April, and I have countermanded the directions to mr Gibson which I had formerly given. Accept my best wishes.   TH: JEFFERSON

RC (PPRF); addressed: "Mr Jeremiah A. Goodman Poplar Forest near Lynchburg"; franked; postmarked Milton, 12 Mar. PoC (DeHi: Morse Autograph Collection); endorsed by TJ.

[1] Reworked from "Bar."

To Samuel J. Harrison

DEAR SIR   Mar. 11. 13

I wrote you on the 7th a request that the money for my tob° might be paid in Richmond. it now occurs that I have about 250.D. of debts to pay in the neighborhood of Poplar Forest which would be more conveniently done by what is in your hands, than by drawing it back again from Richm^d. you will oblige me therefore by paying that sum, when due, to Jeremiah A. Goodman, and having paiment made of the balance only at the counting house of Gibson & Jefferson in Richmond. Accept the assurance of my esteem & respect.

TH: JEFFERSON

PoC (MHi); at foot of text: "Mr Saml J. Harrison"; endorsed by TJ.

To John L. Thomas

SIR   Monticello Mar. 11. 13.

Your favor of the 1st has been recieved, and altho' it was incomprehensible to me what certificate the clerk of Henrico could want as to the deed to which you were a witness, yet I sent it to the clerk of Albemarle, who might know better. I reinclose you the deed with his answer. it is certain that the clerk of Henrico has taken a mistaken view of the subject, which I hope he will correct, and that you will be so good as to prove it at the next court day & return it to me by the post. the clerk may have been misled by observing that there are three instruments for the same land on the same paper. you are a witness to only one of them, and it is only your proof of that one, we ask to be recieved & certified by the court of Henrico. Accept the assurance of my esteem & respect.

TH: JEFFERSON

PoC (MHi); at foot of text: "Mr J. L. Thomas"; endorsed by TJ.

For the enclosed DEED, see TJ to Thomas, 23 Feb. 1813. TJ also enclosed the 10 Mar. 1813 answer from Alexander Garrett, the deputy CLERK OF ALBEMARLE, not found, but recorded in SJL as received 10 Mar. 1813 from Charlottesville.

To William Caruthers

Your letter of Feb. 3. has been recieved, and in answer to your enquiries respecting sheep, I will state that I have three distinct races which I keep at different places. 1. Merinos; of these I have but 2. ewes, and of course none to spare. President Madison has been more succesful, and sells some ram lambs, but not ewes. the Merino is a diminutive tender sheep, yielding very little wool, but that of extraordinary fineness, fit only for the finest broadcloths, but not at all for country use. I do not know mr Madison's prices, but in general the price of these rams is fallen to from 50. to 100.D. a piece. the wool sells high to the Northward to the hatters, but our hatters do not know how to use it.   2. I have the bigtail, or Barbary sheep. I raise it chiefly for the table, the meat being higher flavored than that of any other sheep, and easily kept fat. the tail is large, I have seen one 12.I. square & weighing 14.℔. they encumber the animal in getting out of the way of dogs, and are an obstacle to propagation without attentions which we do not pay to them. they are well sized, & well fleeced but the wool is apt to be coarse & hairy.   3. I have a Spanish race, the ram of which I recieved from Spain in 1794. I bred from him 7. years in and in, suffering no other ram on the place, and after his death I still selected the finest of his race to succeed him, so that the race may now be considered as pure as the original. they are above common size, finely formed, the hardiest race we have ever known, scarcely ever losing a lamb fully fleeced, the belly & legs down to the hoof covered with wool, & the wool of fine quality, some of it as fine as the half blood Merino. we consider it the finest race of[1] sheep ever known in this country. having never cut or killed a ram lamb of them, but given them out to those who wished them this part of the country is well stocked with them, and they sell at the public sales 50. per cent higher than the country sheep. I sent my flock of them to a place I have in Bedford, where they are beginning to be known & in great demand. if you should wish to get into this breed, and will accept of a pair of lambs the ensuing summer, you shall be welcome to them. my place is 3. miles from New London, on the road to Lynchburg. on your signifying your wish on this subject I will give directions to my manager there to deliver a pair to your order, and from my knolege of the country over the mountain I have no hesitation in pronouncing them the fittest sheep in the world for that country. if it should be more convenient to you to take them from here, mr Randolph, my son in law, who has raised them for a dozen years past, can furnish them. Accept the assurance of my esteem & respect. TH: JEFFERSON

PoC (DLC); at foot of first page: "Mr Caruthers"; endorsed by TJ.

On the ram TJ RECEIVED FROM SPAIN, see *PTJ*, 28:267–8, 375–6, and TJ to William Thornton, 27 [June] 1810. IN AND IN: to breed always with near relatives (*OED*).

^{1} Manuscript: "of of."

From John H. Cocke

SIR,   Bremo—March 12th 1813
   I have taken the liberty to order my Servant to call at Monticello and get (by your permission) a few plants of the scotch broom.— Yours respectfully   JN^o H. COCKE

RC (CSmH: JF); at foot of text: "Mr Jefferson"; endorsed by TJ as received 12 Mar. 1813 and so recorded in SJL.

To John H. Cocke

Monticello Mar. 12. 13.
   Th: Jefferson presents his compliments to mr Cocke, whose servant is desired to take as many Broom plants as he pleases, but having never found them to succeed by transplantation, he sends him some seed, which generally succeeds, altho sometimes it does not come up till the second spring.—he sends him also a little seed of the Sprout Kale, a plant he recieved from The National garden of France about 3. years ago, never before in this country. it is to be sown & managed as the Cabbage, but to stand in it's place thro' the winter uncovered. it's only use is to furnish sprouts, of which it will yield 2. or 3. crops of 6. or 8 I. long, in a winter, beginning in December & continuing thro' the whole winter, till the plant goes to seed in the spring. it is a tender & delicious winter vegetable. he salutes mr Cocke with esteem & respect.

RC (ViU: TJP); dateline at foot of text; addressed: "John H. Cocke esq."; endorsed by Cocke. Not recorded in SJL.

On 20 Mar. 1812 TJ recorded planting Scotch BROOM that had been sent to him from Edinburgh by James Ronaldson (Betts, *Garden Book*, 475).

From Margaret B. Bonneville

SIR   New York March 13. 1813 Barclay St^{rt} N° 8

From the time I inherited of T. Paine's manuscripts, papers &c. &c. my intention was to have the honor to write to you concerning your most valuable letters to him. The troublesome and dissagreeable affairs which have been suscited to me since his death: If not an excuse to negligence was the cause of my delay.

Family affairs require my presance in France I am waiting only[1] for a good opportunity.

Though the honor of Mr Paine has[2] heirs & executor is near to me, your letters are incontestably yours, and at your disposal; and as soon [as][3] you will be pleased to let me know your intention, I will punctually execute cheerfully your orders.

Permit me Sir to renew here my thanks for your favourable lettre to my friend Mercier concerning me, and my regret of not having had personally the advantage of presenting my respect to you

I am with high consideration & respect
Sir Your obd^{nt} Sv^{nt} B. BONNEVILLE

RC (DLC); dateline at foot of text; at head of text: "To the Honorable Thomas Jefferson"; endorsed by TJ as received 20 Mar. 1813 and so recorded in SJL.

Margaret B. Bonneville (ca. 1767–1846) was the wife of the French printer and revolutionary Nicolas de Bonneville. From 1797 until 1802 Thomas Paine lived with the Bonneville family in Paris. Shortly after Paine's return to the United States, Bonneville and her three sons joined him on his farm at New Rochelle, New York. Her husband having run afoul of Napoleon and being prevented from leaving France, Paine helped to support Bonneville and provided educational opportunities for her sons. She periodically resided with him, cared for him late in his life, inherited much of his estate, saw that his wishes for burial on his farm were carried out, and arranged for the posthumous publication of his work *On the Origin of Free-Masonry* [New York, 1810]. After Paine's death in 1809, New York journalist James Cheetham asserted in a biography that Paine had had an illicit relationship with Bonneville and fathered one of her sons. She promptly sued Cheetham and won a $150 libel judgment. Bonneville settled in Saint Louis about 1830 and lived there for the rest of her life (Bonneville to TJ, 12 Jan. 1809 [DLC]; Madison, *Papers, Sec. of State Ser.*, 4:151–2; David Freeman Hawke, *Paine* [1974], esp. 395–7, 399–401; Jack Fruchtman Jr., *Thomas Paine Apostle of Freedom* [1994], esp. 36, 275, 395, 411, 420; James Cheetham, *The Life of Thomas Paine* [New York, 1809]; New York *Public Advertiser*, 21 June 1810; John F. Darby, *Personal Recollections of Many Prominent People Whom I Have Known, and of Events—Especially of Those Relating to the History of St. Louis—During the First Half of the Present Century* [1880], 233–7).

SUSCITED: "raised from the dead" or "resuscitated," from a similar French term (*OED*). TJ included expressions FAVOURABLE to Bonneville in a 6 Feb. 1803 letter to Louis Sébastien Mercier (DLC).

[1] Word interlined.
[2] Thus in manuscript.
[3] Omitted word editorially supplied.

[8]

From William A. Burwell

D^R SIR,   march 13. 1813.

the only difficulty I can imagine with the aid of these directions is the
want of correspondent marks or letters on the different parts of your
machine, you may however without them soon discover them when
the machine is put in motion; I have added directions for the Drawing & Roving head, because it adds so much to the value of the Carding Engine, that you should lose no time in procuring one; the Roves
are made as fast as you can Card the cotton, they [are]¹ of uniform
Size, and will spin incomparably better than Roves made with hand
Cards, they are also made without any additional labor to that employd in Carding—I find new reason to be pleased with my machine,
with its aid <u>all</u> my people large & small have been clothed this winter
by one² woman, & 2 Girls—they have moreover made considerable
progress in the summer clothing—this is effected without trouble, &
if you find <u>one</u> Intelligent [&?] faithful Industrious woman, among
your people every thing [can be?] accomplishd in the spinning Department—If you had such a one in reach of me, I would take great
pleasure to instruct her—I should be very glad to get a spinning machine like the one you shewd me at your house, more for the benifit
of my neighbours than myself—there are men here who could make
them; could you have one made for me and sent to Bedford the first
[time]³ a boat passes with articles for you? I found my wife a little indisposed, but she is mending⁴ & I hope will soon recover, please to
remember us kindly to Mrs R. & the family, & believe me dr sir most
truly your friend   W. A BURWELL

RC (DLC); torn at seal; addressed:
"Mr Thomas Jefferson Milton Virginia
via Lynchburg"; stamped; postmarked
Brown's Store, Franklin County, 12 Mar.
1813, and Lynchburg, 21 Mar. 1813; endorsed by TJ as received 24 Mar. 1813
and so recorded in SJL.

M^{RS} R.: Martha Jefferson Randolph.

¹ Omitted word editorially supplied.
² Manuscript: "1 one."
³ Omitted word editorially supplied.
⁴ Manuscript: "minding."

ENCLOSURE

Instructions for the Use of a Carding Machine

Directions for using the Carding Engine

Make the feeding frame <u>fast</u> in front of the Engine, by means of the ∟ irons
and screw rod, and so placed that the cards on the main Cylinder will
just pass the fluted Rollers without touching them.—The upper fluted Roller

[9]

is kept down on the under one by two wires (⌒) hooked over the pivots of it at the ends, & under two small iron levers (◄▬) one end of which is put into a small wire staple in the frame of the Engine, and a weight hung on the other end. The small roller that has cards on it, and attached to the feeding, frame, is for keeping the fluted rollers clean, and must be so placed that it will pass as near as possible to the upper one, and to the cards on the main Cylinder without touching either. move the feeding rollers by a ✕ band from pully **B** on the doffer to pully **A** on[1] the under one. move the cleaning roller by an open band from pully **K** on the other end of the[2] doffer to pully **I** on it. Take out the funnel and board and the callender roller. **G** and the Engine ready for work. (all the other parts and bands being left in order by the maker) Begin by weighing $1\frac{1}{2}$ oz of clean cotton and spreading a part of it on[3] the feeding cloth as even as possible and within about two inches of the sides, (if the cotton is spread too wide on the feeding cloth it will cause the fleece to be so wide, that it will not go in between the sides of the frame, when it is to be carded again.) Set the Engine in motion And as soon as the comb begins to take any cotton off the Doffer, guide it between the callender roller & the Drum, & it adhere to the Drum and wrap round it; continue to feed on the $1\frac{1}{2}$ oz in about the time the Drum will turn round 10 times, when it is all fed on, leave a space of about 8 inches without cotton, then go on with the other $1\frac{1}{2}$ oz. and when that space is nearly out of sight tear the fleece on the drum straight across from one end of the drum to the other, roll it up carefully as the drum turns on, like a piece of cloth, untill it is all off, and lay to one side, for finishing; by this time the other $1\frac{1}{2}$ oz will begin to come through, guide it on the drum as before & guide it on thus till there is as much broke as convenient, Unhook the band that turns the board and put it on without crossing; replace the funnel and the board and callender roller **G** Turn down the arms **HH** and put the conveying[4] roller **F** into them, turn by an open band from a groove near the end of the callender roller **E** to the groove near the end of it; clean all the cotton out of the cards, both off the flats and main Cylinder. Open and Spread one end of fleece, carefully on the feeding cloth, & set the Engine in motion, take away the first cotton that the comb begins to take off the Doffer. till the sliver: begins to[5] come off the full thickness, then convey it through the funnel, between callender rollers, over the conveying roller **F** & into a large tin can. As the work goes on unroll the fleeces, carefully joining one to another on the cloth so that the place where[6] they are joined will be of the same thickness as other parts When the cards get loaded with dirty cotton & seeds, they must be cleaned, the flats must be cleaned often and may be done as the Engine turns round by taking off[7] one at a time. When the card teeth get dull they must be ground up sharp again, by the Emery boards, as follows, take off all the bands & flats & slip the doffer back, put the Emery board **R** in place of the flat marked II & III & regulate by means of the screw nuts so that the points of the teeth will just touch the emery from one end of the boards to the other, turn the Cylinder the <u>contrary</u> way from carding; screwing the emery board closer as the teeth are ground, off till they are all sharp again. The doffer may be ground by holding the emery board **S** carefully on it with the hands (but is better to fix it between the screw nuts on the goose-necks) turning the same way as when carding, but much faster, by an open band from pully **M** on the main cylinder to pully **K** on the doffer.

The flats are ground by the large Emery Roller fixed in the place of the Drum and turned by a band from pully **M**, out of the main cylinder to agree near the end of it (or if convenient in a turning leath) Hold them on lightly and carefully till sharp in fixing the Engine for carding again place the flat nearest the feeding rollers so that a cent would pass between it and the cards on the main cylinder, the next one[8] a little closer & so on & so on so that the last one will be just so close as not to touch; The doffer as <u>close as possible</u> not to touch, the Comb just so as to <u>touch the doffer</u> See that all the screws are tight and band not so tight as to cause engine to work hard, nor so slack as to slip.—When the Emery is worn off[9] the boards and roller it may be renewed by putting on a good coat of glue, and while wet, as much coarse Emery as will cover it completely, let it dry and brush off all the loose Emery & will be fit for use—

For the drawing and roving.[10]

See that all the weights, Levers, and Saddles, press fairly on the upper rollers, so as to keep them well down on the fluted ones (in the same manner that the spinning machine is fixed) Take two cans full of slivers from the carding Engine, put an end of each between the guide tins behind[11] the back roller, & between the fluted & covered rollers (one sliver to each boss nearest the end where the pullys are) turn the rollers so as to bring the ends through unite them and put them through the tin funnel, between the small callender roller & so into one of the smaller tin cans; drawing goes on, be carefull not to let one sliver go on without another and see that the cotton does not break or wrap round the rollers, instead of running through into the can, if it is intended for very coarse[12] yarn this one drawing may do, but if for fine it must be drauwn 2 3 or 4[13] in proportion to the quality wanted, uniting 2 3 or 4 of the first into one as convenient, taking it now to the roving boss, proceed as with the drawing, only running it into the twisting lanthorn instead of the can uniting 2 3 or 4 into one at pleasure, so as in some measure proportion the size of the rove to the size of the yarn wanted, being carefull to put the band that turns the lanthorn into proper groove so that the twist in the rove may suit its size, If the cotton,[14] is apt to wrap round the rollers (as it will sometimes in damp weather) a little very <u>fine</u> powderd Chalk may be used on them to advantage.
when the leather covering on the upper rollers gets loose or dirty it must be coverd anew with the same kind of leather or good Buckskin; the Drawing and Roving is drove by a Band from Pully **O** at the main Cylinder shaft of the Carding Engine to Pully **P**. on it—

MS (DLC: TJ Papers, 197:35161–3); in an unidentified hand; undated. The related drawing has not been found.

DOFFER: a comb or revolving cylinder in a carding machine that strips cotton or wool from cards. LEATH (lathe): a stand or supporting framework (*OED*).

[1] Manuscript: "one."
[2] Manuscript: "of the of the."
[3] Manuscript: "or."
[4] Manuscript: "coveying."
[5] Manuscript: "to to."
[6] Manuscript: "wher."
[7] Manuscript: "of," here and in the next sentence.
[8] Manuscript: "nex on."
[9] Manuscript: "of," here and further on in this sentence.
[10] Manuscript: "and roving and roving."

[11] Manuscript: "behing."
[12] Manuscript: "coare."
[13] Here "times" is canceled.

[14] Manuscript: "If the cotton, If the cotton."

From Dabney Carr

DEAR SIR.   Winchester. March 14th 1813

your letter of Feb. 27 was received by the last mail. Mr Randolph, was in this place, when I came to it last fall, & had resided here for some time previous; but soon after that, he left it, & has been since, as I am to be, with his son in law, Mr B. Taylor in Jefferson County, not far from the little village of Charleston: Being informed this morning, that Doctr Grayson, of this Town, was going immediately to Charleston, I have confided the letter to him; telling him, that it was on business of importance; & requesting that he would give it the speediest conveyance to Mr Randolph. I have no doubt he will attend to it—I enclosed the letter, in one from myself to Mr R. in which, without intimating that I was acquainted with the contents of your's I mentioned to him, your anxiety to hear from him, & my confidence, that he would not delay a reply.

I have heard that his mind is considerably strengthened of late; & I have very little doubt, that he will be quite well enough, to attend to your request.

Be pleased Sir, to mention me affectionately to your daughter & her family; & believe me truly & sincerely

yours &C   D CARR

RC (ViU: TJP-CC); endorsed by TJ as received 31 Mar. 1813 and so recorded in SJL.

From Sarah Grotjan

HONOURED SIR!   Philadelphia March 15th 1813.

Convinced that You will pardon an entire Stranger for intruding on Your time for a few minutes, when You become acquainted with the motives by which she is actuated, I solicit the favour of a few Lines in answer to the following Inquiry.

Accident has thrown in my way an unfortunate person by the name of Julia Bradley, whose maiden name as she informed me was Julia Webb, of Richmond Virginia. The distress in which she is at present,

and her engaging manners have interested me powerfully in her behalf. During a Conversation which I lately held with her she acciden-
taly informed me, that she had the honour to be known to You and
Your family.

Should this be really so, and her relations, perhaps from a false pride
on her part be unacquainted with her present distress, I should feel
the greatest Comfort of having been instrumental to promote her
relief.

I take this Step without her knowlledge, or that of her husbands,
who lives with her in this place, in a miserable abode, allmost deprived of the absolute necessaries of Life.

An Answer addressed to M\u207f Peter A. Grotjan in Philadelphia, will
reach

Your Obedient humble Servant   SARAH GROTJAN

RC (DLC); at head of text: "Thomas
Jefferson Esq:"; endorsed by TJ as re-
ceived 20 Mar. 1813 and so recorded in
SJL.

Sarah Fenimore Grotjan (ca. 1788–
1830) married Peter A. Grotjan, a Philadelphia newspaper publisher, in 1809.
She later named one of her children after
TJ and obtained a letter of advice from
him to the young boy (Peter A. Grotjan,
"Memoirs of an Early American," *Harper's Monthly Magazine* 172 [1936]:
168–9; Brigham, *American Newspapers*,
2:917; Grotjan to TJ, 1 Jan. 1824; TJ to
Grotjan and to Thomas Jefferson Grotjan, both 10 Jan. 1824; Philadelphia
Poulson's American Daily Advertiser, 29
July 1830).

From Benjamin Rush

MY DEAR SIR   Philadelphia march 15th 1813

soon After I became the Advocate of domestic Animals as far as related to thier diseases, in the lecture of which I sent you a copy, mr
Carver applied to me to become his advocate with our Citizens for the
purpose he has mentioned in his letter to you. His proposition at first
struck me as humane & praise worthy, but in a short time Afterwards
it appeared to me in the same light that it does to you. I gave him a
trifle to assist in paying[1] for his passage, & obtained for him a passport from m\u207f monroe. Here my Services to him ended. — After this information your line of Conduct will be an obvious One. — He is an
Englishman & has parents in England whom he has not seen for
many years. All this is inter nos. —

Alas! for the divided state of our citizens, and the distracted state
of the Councils of our country! — while I have uniformly considered
the War we are engaged in as just, I have lamented the manner

in which it has been conducted. The Attack upon Canada appears to involve in it too much of the conquering Spirit of the old world, and is contrary to the professions and interests of Republicans. Admit that we have conquered it,—shall We hold it as a province? or give it a representation in our national legislature?—If the latter,—by what means shall we eliminate British principles and habits from the representatives that will be sent by that British state to our Congress? Have we not evils eno' to contend with already from those principles and habits?—why then should we encrease them? But further,—is not the perpetuity of our Union and of our republican institutions intimately connected with our being constantly under the pressure of c̈ircumambient monarchical states?

In favor of defending our rights of Sovereignty upon the Ocean[2] exclusively, I have thought that as the outrages committed upon our national interests were upon the ocean, they ought to be vindicated there only,—that on the Ocean the resentments of our Citizens had arisen to the <u>war point,</u> but <u>no where else</u>; that our citizens, from the number of our bays, rivers & Creeks, and thier habits of living by Arts that render them familiar with the means of managing the waters, and by thier general knowledge of swimming, and Climbing, were better[3] prepared for a Sea, than a land war—that our ships could be manned by Volunteers only, and never by drafts from the farmers & mechanics of our Country, nor by Soldiers enlisted in a fit of intoxication,—that our inability to meet the force of Britain upon the Ocean would lessen every year, & that every Ship we built would require two or three ships of equal force to watch her, and that in this manner we might weaken the naval strength of Britain in the European and East India seas, without giving her an opportunity to lessen ours;—that in the winter months we could convoy our trade to and from our shores in spite of the whole navy of Britain, and that even this transient protection to our imports would supply our treasury with the means of defraying the expenses of our navy—and lastly that a navy would never be dangerous to liberty, & that it would transfer the Vices of war from our farmers and prevent women and Children from sharing <u>directly</u> in its calamities.

Our naval Victories are presages of what may be done by a free and incensed nation contending for the gift of god to all the inhabitants of the globe. The year 1812 will be memorable in the history of the world for having witnessed the first checks that have been given to the overgrown pride and power of France on land, & of Britain on the Ocean. many of the Crimes of Great Britain that remain yet "unwhipt by justice" to use the words of Shakespear, were perpetrated in

America. Our Country was settled by them. The jails and prison ships of new york, which were the theatres of[4] others of her Crimes,[5] during the revolutionary war have cried, for more than thirty years, to Heaven for retribution.[6] Those Cries have been echoed over & over by the Sailors who have been dragged from our merchentmen and compelled to shed thier blood in fighting against nations against whom they felt no hostility,[7] & in some instances against thier own Countrymen. Perhaps the time for punishing all those Crimes is now come, and as the Navy of Britain[8] has been the principal instrument of those Crimes, perhaps the long and much injured United states may be the means employed by a just Providence[9] setting bounds to the power of that navy, and the[re]by of rendering the ocean the safe & common high way of all nations.—Such an event would create a jubilee in all the maritime nations in the world.—Humanity & justice would for ever triumph in it.—

But whither has an attempt to reply to the latter part of your letter carried me? as an apology for it, I shall only add, that I am now in my 69th year,—that I seldom read any thing in a news paper but Articles of intelligence & that I loath political controversies above all things. From these declarations you have a right to infer that I have filled my paper with Nothing but the "bablings of a second Childhood."

I have lately published a volume of inquiries upon the diseases of the mind. They have been well received by the public. If you wish to look into them, I shall do myself the pleasure of sending you a copy of them.

The few Sands that remain [in][10] my glass urge me constantly to quicken my labors. my next work will be entitled "Hygiene, or Rules for the preservation of health accommodated to the climate, diet, manners & habits of the people of the United states."—all the imperfections of both these publications must be ascribed to a Conviction that my time in this world must necessarily be short. Had they been kept to the "novum annum," they would have had fewer faults.—

I enclosed in my last letter to you, a small book written by Bishop Porteus, as a present to mrs Randolph's Children. As you have not acknowledged the receipt of it in your letter, I fear it has not been received by you.

Mr Adams still does me the honor of favouring me now and then with a letter. In his last, he mentions your name with kindness, and speaks with surprise of the correctness of your Stile—of the Steadiness of your hand evidenced in your writing, and of your exploits on horseback, at your advanced stage of life.

From Dear Sir your sincere old friend of 1775.   Benjn Rush

PS: From the present Complexion of Affairs in our country Are you not disposed at times to repent of your Solicitude, and labors & Sacrifices[11] during our revolutionary strugg[le] for liberty and independance? Have you not been disappointed in the Conduct of both tories & whigs? Have not the former encreased in number not only by population, but by the accession of Englishmen, and the apostasy of many revolutionary Whigs? are not the sons of tories, nerone neronior? Have not our funding System, and its offspring, Banks like so many Delilahs robbed the whigs of thier revolutionary strength & virtue? War has its evils; so has a long peace. A field of battle covered with dead bodies putrefying in the open air, is an awful and distressing Spectacle, but a nation debased by the love of money, and exhibiting all the Vices and Crimes usually connected with that passion is a Spectacle far more awful, distressing and Offensive. Hince—hinc lacrymæ rerum!

RC (DLC); edge chipped; between signature and postscript: "Tho⁸ Jefferson Esquire"; endorsed by TJ as received 24 Mar. 1813 and so recorded in SJL.

Rush published his lecture on ANIMALS as "An Introductory Lecture to a Course of Lectures, upon the Institutes and Practice of Medicine, delivered in the University of Pennsylvania, on the 2nd of November, 1807; upon the duty and advantages of studying the Diseases of Domestic Animals, and the Remedies proper to remove them," *Memoirs of the Philadelphia Society for Promoting Agriculture* 1 (1808): xlix–lxv. In William Shakespeare's *King Lear*, act 3, scene 2, the title character speaks of "undivulged crimes" UNWHIPT BY JUSTICE. Rush had LATELY PUBLISHED *Medical Inquiries and Observations, upon the Diseases of the Mind* (Philadelphia, 1812). He died before his NEXT WORK was completed. NOVUM ANNUM: "new year." John ADAMS had written to Rush on 3 Feb. 1813 that "Jefferson is as tough as a lignum Vitæ Knot. He rides Journeys on Horseback. I have, within a few days a Letter from him, a very obliging one, written with all the precision of his best years. Not one Symptom of decay or decline can I discern in it" (RC in ViU: Albert H. Small Declaration of Independence Collection; FC in Lb in MHi: Adams Papers). NERONE NERONIOR: "more Nero-like than Nero himself." HINCE—HINC LACRYMÆ RERUM: "Here—here are tears for misfortune" alludes to Virgil, *Aeneid*, 1.462 (Fairclough, *Virgil*, 1:294–5).

[1] Preceding three words interlined in place of "pay."
[2] Manuscript: "Occean."
[3] Preceding two words interlined in place of "more."
[4] Manuscript: "of Of."
[5] Preceding nine words interlined.
[6] Word interlined in place of "<Venge> the punishment of those crimes."
[7] Manuscript: "hosility."
[8] Preceding two words interlined.
[9] Preceding five words interlined in place of "of restraining and."
[10] Omitted word editorially supplied.
[11] Rush here canceled "in the cause of Liberty and justice."

From André Thoüin

MONSIEUR ET VÉNÉRABLE COLLEGUE,   a Paris le 15 Mars 1813.

J'ai remis le 11 fevrier dernier, a M. Warden, Consul des Etâts unis a Paris, mon tribut annuel, que cet homme estimable S'est chargé avec empressement de vous faire passer par une voie Sure et prompte. Il est composé cette année de 270 Especes de graines d'arbres et de Plantes de toutes les divisions economiques et de fleurs d'ornemens pour les parterres & le Jardins de plaisance. Je Souhaitte que cet assortiment vous parvienne bientôt et qu'il vous Soit agréable et utile.

Si ce n'etait pas abuser de vos bontés, Je vous prirais, Monsieur, de vous interesser auprès de vos voyageurs pour me faire obtenir des Semences des végétaux indigênes entre les monts Aleghani et la mer du Sud. Ce Serait un grand bienfait dont je vous Serais infiniment reconnoissant.

Il vient de paraitre la Traduction d'un ouvrage Allement d'un grand interêt pour les grands proprietaires de biens ruraux. Ce Sont les Principes raisonnés d'agriculture de A. Thaer, Par E.V.B. Crud. Cet ouvrage est remarquable en ce que toutes Ses propositions Sont Soumises a l'analise et au calcul le plus exacte. fort différént des ouvrages qui L'ont précédé dans la plupart des quels on ne rencontre que des axiomes vagues et Supperficies. Ce livre merite d'etre connu et repandu en Amerique. Je vous le Signale a cet Effet.

Je vous renouvel toujours avec empressement

Monsieur et Venerable Collegue L'Expression de mon hommage tres respectueux   THOÜIN

nous désirerions bien voir dans nos annales quelques observations de vous, Monsieur?

EDITORS' TRANSLATION

SIR AND VENERABLE COLLEAGUE,   Paris 15 March 1813.

On 11 February I delivered my annual tribute to Mr. Warden, United States consul at Paris, and this estimable man willingly took charge of delivering it safely and promptly to you. This year it consists of 270 varieties of tree seeds, plants of every economic type, and ornamental flowers for parterres and pleasure gardens. I hope that this assortment reaches you soon and proves useful and pleasing to you.

Were it not an abuse of your good nature, I would ask you, Sir, to interest your explorers in procuring for me vegetable seeds indigenous to the region between the Allegheny Mountains and the Pacific Ocean. I would be infinitely grateful for this great kindness.

A recently published translation of a German work is of great interest to owners of large tracts of land. It is the *Principes raisonnés d'agriculture* of A. Thaer by E.V.B. Crud. This work is remarkable in that all of its propositions are submitted to analysis and the most accurate calculations. It varies greatly from works preceding it that, for the most part, contain only vague and superficial axioms. This book deserves to be known in America. I mention it to you for that reason.

As always, I renew with great eagerness

Sir and venerable colleague, the expression of my profound respect

THOÜIN

We would love to see some of your observations in our annals, Sir?

RC (DLC: TJ Papers, 197:35155); on printed letterhead of the "Muséum D'Histoire Naturelle," with Thoüin's handwritten identification of himself as "l'un des Professeurs-Administrateurs" ("one of the professors-administrators"); endorsed by TJ as a letter of 11 Mar. 1813 received 28 May 1813 and so recorded in SJL. Translation by Dr. Genevieve Moene. Enclosed in David Bailie Warden to TJ, 1 Apr. 1813.

Albrecht Daniel Thaer's OUVRAGE ALLEMENT was *Grundsätze der rationellen Landwirthschaft*, 4 vols. (Berlin, 1809–12). The French translation by Élie Victor Benjamin CRUD was *Principes raisonnés d'agriculture*, 4 vols. (Paris, 1811–16). An American edition did not appear until 1846.

Will of Thomas Mann Randolph

I Thomas Mann Randolph the elder of the county of Albemarle in the state of Virginia upon mature reflection and in the most deliberate manner do publish and declare this writing to be my last Will and Testament: Having from the experience of twenty three years full confidence in the understanding, judgement, honour and impartial Maternal feeling of my beloved Wife Martha and considering that her time of life precludes all reasonable apprehension of her contracting another marriage which I might nevertheless[1] have felt if I had not received from her frequently very solemn assurances to the contrary I give and bequeath to her my said Wife my whole estate real and personal to distribute among her children and retain for her own use as she may think fit after paying all my just debts according to such principles of settlement as I may have agreed to in my life time with the different parties as they will shew.

I recommend to her to sell the Varina estate to pay the debts but I advise her at the same time to reclaim all the tide land first by continuing the artificial Bank along the river from where I have stoped down to the lower corner on the river, and turning it across to the hill, then diging wide ditches with sufficient slope from the little rapid in the roundabout creek near the Fairhill gate of Varina to the river below Bollings orchard on the river bank; and if an agreement can be made for the purpose with Messrs Miller and Mosby, from the next little rapid in the same creek near where the line of the tract I got from Bullington crosses it around the foot of fair-hill and across the Back gate to the river immediately below the dam; the estate will by that operation be made worth 80 or 100.000$. and the work will be permanent if the creeks be stoped in the manner Wharves are made, with logs and alternate layers of gravel and mud, and the cost ought not to be over 1500$., with what work can be done from the farm without loss of the crop. Again I recommend to her to divide Edgehill as I have done into three separate farms after giving Jefferson the part allotted to him viz. from the mouth of the Chapel Branch to the mouth of that branch which runs into it at Chisholms Tobacco House, up the said Branch to the head spring of it, up the gulley to the line run along the back of the Chapel ridge by William Page and myself, by Martin Bakers Tobacco House to the back fence, along the back fence and along a line continuing its course to the great drain, up the great drain to the Lego line; and all the Wood land of McKenzies entry lying above a level line to be run from the narrow neck which joins the chapel ridge to the mountain around by the flat on the top of the piny spur to a very deep valley making down the mountain side by the said piny spur on the N.E. side thereof.[2] The first of the said three farms to be bounded by the chapel branch from Jeffersons line to the old three notched road where the said road departed from the branch toward where the Barn now stands, along the said road to the corner of the stable, from the corner of the stable across to the spring branch, from that junction up the spring branch leaving the spring close on the right, then up the branch runing down the valley by Nats house to the new fence which I laid off with Mr German and Mr Gooch, along that fence to the head of a certain valley shewn by me to Mr Gooch, down that valley to the dry branch and up the dry branch taking the Westernmost fork untill the East line of McKenzie's entry when continued Southward, shall join the said Branch. The other two of the said 3. farms to contain all the remainder of the tract and to be separated by a line along an old path leading out of the Hammocks gap road in the direction toward an old Tobacco house in the Wallnut field used by German for a stable untill the said path joins the branch on the east side of the Wallnut field, down the said branch to the fish dam, up the other branch leaving Brits-spring to the right untill a line runing from the road through Edgehill by the Wallnut tree and Ray's flat rock with as gentle a

slope as can be without too great a Curve shall meet the said Branch and along the road through to the junction of the new fence dividing Gooches from Germans place.
signed sealed published and declared before
BRICE HARLOW
MARTIN FIDDLER

TH: M. RANDOLPH
March 16. 1813,

MS (DLC: Randolph Family Miscellany); in Randolph's hand, signed by Randolph, Harlow, and Fiddler; endorsed by Randolph: "David Higinbotham Sept. 1813. Inclosure from"; with additional note by Randolph: "Mr Higinbotham is very particularly requested by his sincere friend Thomas Mann Randolph to take charge of this paper and put it into the hand of Mr Jefferson himself when they may first happen to be alone together."

This will was apparently never recorded in the Albemarle County Court, probably because at the time of his death in 1828, Randolph was no longer in posses-

sion either of VARINA, his property along the James River in Henrico County, or EDGEHILL, his Albemarle County farm. He gave control of both to his son Thomas Jefferson Randolph in a deed of trust dated 1 Apr. 1824. Over the next two years the younger Randolph sold both properties for the benefit of his father's creditors. In one of these sales Thomas Jefferson Randolph purchased Edgehill for himself (Gaines, *Randolph*, 148, 155–6, 161–2; Albemarle Co. Deed Book, 24:268–70).

[1] Word interlined.
[2] Preceding ten words interlined.

From Patrick Gibson

SIR   Richmond 17th March 1813

I have received your favors of the 7th & 11th with your note for $4300. and John Harvie's for $176.90 which Jno Brockenbrough has promised to pay to day—I remitted on the day I last wrote to you the $97 to Alricks and the $250 to J: A: Goodman, it was respecting the first sum only I apprehended any difficulty—no money has been paid by m^r Randolph since the 10th Novr last—m^r Darmsdatt requested me to say that if you want any fish this season, you would do well to speak for them immediately, as they will be very scarce, and no probability of procuring them from the Potomac so long as the present blockade continues, which I cannot agree with you in thinking is only as a shelter for their ships—every preparation seems to be making for an attack upon Norfolk, and no doubt an attempt will at the same time be made to destroy the Constellation, I am inform'd by major Preston that they have a disposable land force of upwards of 3000 men, which have been removed from the different ships on board

such, as are lying in the Roads—they are said to be waiting a reinforcement of eight ships of the line, which are daily expected—there
is literally nothing doing here flour is nominally 6$—I show'd your
letter of the 11ᵗʰ to Mʳ Taylor who is anxious that the papers relative
to mazzei's lot may be sent down he is of opinion the title is still in
Foster Webb's heir, if so, he will undertake to get young Webb, who
is just now of age to make the conveyance—   Respectfully I
am Your obᵗ Servᵗ   PATRICK GIBSON

RC (MHi); at head of text: "Thomas   THE ROADS: Hampton Roads.
Jefferson Esqʳᵉ"; endorsed by TJ as re-
ceived 19 Mar. 1813 and so recorded in
SJL.

From Charles Rogers

VENERABLE SIR,   [ca. 17 Mar. 1813]
    I am a man of no property—or hardly any name in society—I seek
not the honors—nor pleasures of the world—I could wish to be rich
tho', for I could thereby have an opportunity of extending my usefulness—yet I don't know what I might do if I were rich, for I don't
know myself, tho' I've been trying to study myself this twenty years—
still I do believe I should be the happiest man in the world if I could
only afford relief to the many needy objects I see & hear around me—
I might, by this means, multiply my existence, as it were, & live in the
life of every individual I had oblig'd—O! it would be the luxury of life
the very Soul of living to purpose!—But, it is time to let you into the
meaning of this strange note—If I have any design, Rever'd Sir, it
is to draw money from you—to Crave Alms—to <u>beg</u> in short—not for
<u>myself</u>—for I deserve nothing but destruction without mercy, having
for 35 years devoted my life to mere self-pleasing—but about six
years ago by the grace of God, starting from my loose reverie &
long—long night of dozing—I found I had no right to do as I pleas'd
unless I pleas'd to do right—& whereas I had before made <u>Self</u> the
supreme object thenceforth I have sought my happiness in the love of
God & in doing good to my fellow mortals—& may you too, most excellent Sir, obtain like precious faith—& believe it very possible with
God to assume our Nature & become man in order to reconcile
man to himself—In what, says Bourdaloue, a great French Divine of
the last century, 'In what consisted the offence against God?' In this
that man forgeting himself, proudly affected to be like God—"ye shall
be as Gods" & I says God-made-man, who am not only like to God,

[21]

but equal & consubstantial with him, thro' a very different kind of forgetfulness of myself will become the outcast of men "a worm & no man"—Is it possible, continues this eloquent & pious Divine, Is it possible to conceive a more effectual reparation!—Man, by revolting against God had shaken off the yoke of obedience, & violated the Commands of his Sovereign; & I says God-made-man, quite independent as I am of myself, will freely submit to the most painful humiliation

I will be obedient unto Death!—the Death of the Cross!!! But, to return—that benevolence which has heretofore been a prominent feature in your illustrious Character not doubting it remains the same with those other qualities with which God has so nobly distinguish'd You—<u>unimpaired</u> & <u>independant</u> & only wants a just occasion to exert itself, to be respected—to be honor'd—to be lov'd as well as ever—has induced the writer to solicit your Aid in behalf of suffering Virtue—A young Lady (Sarah Rogers) born in the interiour of New-Hampshire, of poor & simple parentage is now in the City philadelphia brought[1] thither by an affectionate Bro. whose discernment & feelings would not allow him to let her remain in obscurity & want &c.—but doom'd to part from her by indispensable obligations (his Father being at the point of Death) she now lies at the mercy of Strangers, with only a single relative, who can do little else than condole & participate in her penury—& what adds poignancy to the distressing scene—She owes money & <u>must pay it</u>—tho' without the use of hands or Feet!! & yet a kind Providence has made up the deficiency, by enabling her to perform with her mouth, the art of painting (which has hitherto been Consider'd as a property peculier to the hands)—a specimen of which accompanies this:—But tho' she has supported herself in this very wonderful[2] manner about six years—, & is still improving—still pressing with stubborn industry, thro' every obstacle—She is <u>now</u> in arrears for board to the Amount of 150 Doll[s] & what makes it doubly painful, she owes it to a worthy widow, very poor, very clever, & very industrious;—& at the same time she is so sensible of her own consequence that She will not apply to any one for relief,—nor is this so much owing to rank pride, as to a certain native delicacy which delights more in self-suffering than in troubling others,—&, is less wounded in feeling actual distress, than it would be in exposing itself to severe animadversion.—Now, Sir, tho' the moon, from its being so Commonly seen, is beheld without emotion is still an admirable object in itself—so, this Young Lady from being so often seen in this City for four years past, is beheld without incouragement—tho' she continues the same deserving—the same admirable object She ever has, & perhaps far more so:—The writer therefore, independantly of any person or thing, save only a simple wish to be obliged to You, Honor'd Sir, in preference to any other being on earth, presumes, in this way, to excite your attention towards one of the most extraordinary subjects of misfortune that ever God made use of to try the Charity of the Children of men Tho' the writer is aware that this simple statement requires a degree of faith & discernment, of which, the midling-sized soul, form'd upon & fitted to the customs & maxims of a suspicious world—untaught in the knowledge of genuine character, & unsusceptible of the simple marks of truth, can frame no ideas—yet he flatters himself that you, Rever'd Sir, will give Credence to it:—But, if after all, he should be disappointed in his expectations from <u>other</u> reasons (for he can't persuade himself he will be discredited)—it will be at least, a failure in 'noble daring'[3]—

—in the mean time, let the event turn as it may, he cannot be divested of the Consolation of being disappointed by Thomas Jefferson, who can never act, nor forbear to act without reason—From an Old, yet unknown Frd.   CHA. ROGERS

P.S.

<u>Any</u> Communication, under whatsoever restrictions,
directed to Sarah Rogers or Charles Rogers
                    philadelphia,
will be receiv'd with becoming gratitude
    & observ'd with the most mark'd attention

RC (MHi); undated; addressed: "Thomas Jefferson Esqr[e] Monticello, Virginia"; stamp canceled; franked; postmarked Belleville, 17 Mar.; endorsed by TJ as received 24 Mar. 1813 from Philadelphia and so recorded in SJL. Enclosure not found.

Rogers paraphrases from a sermon of Louis BOURDALOUE (Denis O'Mahony, *Great French Sermons from Bossuet, Bourdaloue, and Massillon* [1917], 17; Sowerby, no. 1570). YE SHALL BE AS GODS and A WORM & NO MAN are biblical quotations, from Genesis 3.5 and Psalms 22.6, respectively.

SARAH ROGERS (ca. 1788–1813) was born limbless. By 1807 she was staying at or near the Shakespeare Hotel in Philadelphia where, for an admission fee of twenty-five cents, onlookers could watch her as she "draws with a pencil, with delicacy and ease, paints landscapes and flowers, &c. She uses scissors, threads a needle and writes with facility." Rogers sold her works, including "Large Flowers fit for framing, and Gentleman's Watch Papers," and also traveled through the South, displaying her talents in Charleston, South Carolina, before her death in Philadelphia on 30 Oct. 1813 (*A Real Object of Charity* [Walpole, N.H., 1806]; Philadelphia *Aurora General Advertiser*, 11 Dec. 1807; Philadelphia *Poulson's American Daily Advertiser*, 26 July, 4 Nov. 1809, 2 Nov. 1813).

[1] Reworked from "this City brought."
[2] Manuscript: "wondeful."
[3] Omitted closing quotation mark editorially supplied.

From Alrichs & Dixon

Highly Esteemd Friend   Wilmington 18th 3 Mo 1813

we have to acknowledge thy[1] favour 11th current—; in our reply to thine, of 3rd Inst; (which we hope thou hast receivd;) we stated, what we supposd must be the cause of thy Carder not performing to satisfaction; and the way, we hoped, to remedy it.—we regret, exceeding, that thou has found so much dificulty; with thy machine;— we had tried it before we sent it on; and fully believed it would answer well—

the reduceing, and simplifying: of the Cotton Machinery; so as to introduce it into common domestic use; has been a subject, of much, and earnest, solicitude with us, we had a hope: that if they: could be so made; as to be used in private families; they might become so general, as to counteract; in this country: the groth of those <u>large</u> Manufacturing Establishments; which: we see are: in Europe: so distructive to all that ought, to be: Valuable to man—

If thy Machine should still not answer on trial of our last direction, we would be obliged if thou would write us perticularly how it is feed &c, we think it must and will perform well, and will most cheerfully do what is reasonable in our power toward makeing it

     we are with much Respect   ALRICHS & DIXON

RC (DLC); in Alrichs's hand; endorsed by TJ as received 24 Mar. 1813 and so recorded in SJL.

The earlier letter to TJ from Alrichs &

Dixon was dated 10 Mar. 1813, not the 3RD INST.

[1] Manuscript: "thy thy."

From Samuel J. Harrison

Dear Sir   Lynchbg mar 19–1813

I recd your Letter of the 7 Inst in due Course. I fear your Ideas as to the Intention of the Blockading Squadron will not be Realized— my opinion is that, it is intended, & will be permenant; except as to Bread Stuffs—and even as to that, unless they Should be necessitated abroad—which we have no right to believe will Shortly be the Case, as Various accounts from the Peninsula State the Quantity there to be great, & prices low—Besides we may now, expect Considerable Shipments will be made to them from the Baltick.

Mr Goodman has only Sent in 5 Hhds Tobo which being too high in Orders, has thrown him Considerably back, as he was obliged to

Exchange[1] a good deal, before it would be fit for prizing—He was with me yesterday, and Says he thinks there will be Rather over 20,000—but that I may Count Certainly upon that much—I have directed him to be Very particular about the order of the Balance; which may put off the last till perhaps, the middle of may—But wishing to Serve you—I here enclose you a Dft on my Friends Gibson & Jefferson for $1,000. at Ten Days Sight—which I Suspect will be about as much as the Crop will amount to, as the Hhds that are Rec[d] are much lighter than M[r] Goodman expected.

please acknowledge the Rec[t] of thro'

Y[r] M[o] ob Hb st   S J HARRISON

RC (MHi); endorsed by TJ as received 24 Mar. 1813 and so recorded in SJL. Enclosure not found.

THE PENINSULA: the Iberian Peninsula. HIGH IN ORDERS: tobacco in high order is too damp (*OED*).

TJ sent the enclosed draft for $1,000 to Patrick Gibson in a letter dated 25 Mar. 1813, not found but recorded in SJL (as a letter to Gibson & Jefferson) and extracted in the catalog for Sotheby Parke Bernet auction, New York City, 3 May 1977, item 68: "My tobacco in Bedford, being partly delivered to Mr. Harrison, he has enclosed me the within order for 1000D on account which I hasten to forward to you."

[1] Manuscript: "Echang."

List of 1812 Tobacco Crop Sold to Samuel J. Harrison, with Thomas Jefferson's Notes

Thomas Jefferson
N° 701 –170–1340
   702 –170–1344
   703 –170–1404
   788[1]–170–1354
   789 –170–1330
   705 –170–1050
   706 –170–1300
   985 –170–1412
   986 –170–1212
   987 –170–1276
   988 –170–1358 stemmed[2]
   989 –170–1051
   990[3]–170–1397
        16818[4]

Blackwater

[*Note by TJ in left margin:*]
16818
 1358   stemmed
15460   leaf @ 6.D   927.60
 1358 ⎤
 1500 ⎬
  944 ⎦
 3802. stemmed @ 5.D 190.10
                      1117.70

[*Note by TJ on verso:*]
Tobacco of 1812. sold to Saml J. Harrison
to wit 13. hhds leaf 15,542. @ 7.D = 932.52 D
     3. hhds stemm^d @ 5 D

MS (ViU: TJP-ER); written on a scrap in an unidentified hand, with additions in TJ's hand as indicated; undated, but evidently compiled after Harrison reported to TJ on 19 Mar. 1813 that Jeremiah A. Goodman had thus far sent in only five hogsheads of TJ's 1812 tobacco crop; endorsed by TJ: "Harrison Saml J."

George Cabell's BLACKWATER tobacco warehouse was located in Lynchburg.

The earlier negotiations for the sale of the 1812 Poplar Forest tobacco crop are documented in Harrison to TJ, 25 Dec. 1812, 17 Jan., 14 Feb. 1813; TJ to Harrison, 7, 31 Jan., 7 Mar. 1813; TJ to Goodman, 5 Feb. 1813; *MB*, 2:1287.

[1] Reworked from "704."
[2] Word added by TJ.
[3] Reworked from "980."
[4] The correct sum is 16,828.

George Poindexter to James Monroe

[before 20 Mar. 1813]

Mr Poindexter with his respects to M^r monroe asks the favor of him to convey the Guinea grass seed, sent herewith, to m^r Jefferson. Mr Poindexter regrets that through the carelessness of his servant the grass seed were mixed with some of another kind, and a quantity of them lost, by being loose in the Portmanteau. m^r P. however hopes that enough of them remain to make an experiment, of the utility of this discription of grass, in the Latitude of monticello. The Letter from Doct. Brown was also much worn, & the seal broken in the portmanteau, it having, been thrown by the boy among some silver. m^r P. hopes m^r Jefferson will have the goodness to excuse these accidents; they frequently occur in so long a journey, as that from Natchez to Washington.

RC (DLC: TJ Papers, 198:35222); undated; addressed: "The Honble James monroe." Enclosure: Samuel Brown to TJ, 1 Oct. 1812. Receipt by TJ on 20

Mar. 1813 acknowledged in TJ to Brown, 17 Apr. 1813.

George Poindexter (ca. 1779–1853), attorney and public official, was a native of Louisa County. He lacked formal schooling but read law with local attorneys and was admitted in 1798 to the Albemarle County bar. His early clients included Elizabeth Henderson, Bennett Henderson's widow. Poindexter moved to Mississippi Territory in 1802 and soon rose to prominence, serving as attorney general, as a member of the territorial legislature, and from 1807–13 as territorial delegate to the United States Congress. From 1813–17 he was federal district judge for the territory, and in the latter year he made important contributions to the drafting of the state's first constitution. Poindexter served from 1817–19 as the first Mississippi state member of the United States House of Representatives. He was governor from 1820–21, and during his tenure he began his codification of state law, which was completed in 1822 and adopted and published shortly thereafter as the *Revised Code of the Laws of Mississippi* (Natchez, 1824). Poindexter lost a race for a Congresssional seat in 1822 but served in the United States Senate, 1830–35. Initially a supporter of Andrew Jackson, he soon broke with the president and ran unsuccessfully as a states'-rights Whig for reelection to the Senate. Poindexter first retired to Kentucky but later returned to Mississippi and practiced law there until his death (*ANB*; *DAB*; Woods, *Albemarle*, 77, 110, 380; Poindexter to TJ, 7 Mar. 1808 [DLC]; *Terr. Papers*, vols. 5–6; Washington *Daily National Intelligencer*, 10 Sept. 1853).

From Benjamin Smith Barton

DEAR SIR,   March 23ᵈ 1813.

I find there is to be a "physician" general of the arm. of the U. States—I have the vanity to think, that I am not entirely unqualified for that important place, by my age, my experience in practise, & my long experience as a teacher of a "practical" branch of medicine. Perhaps, I have some claim upon the government, as a steady supporter, so far as I can go, of the measures of the executive. I add, I flatter myself, my appointment to the place would not be deemd an unpopular one: because, among other reasons, I have contributed essentially to the education of a very great number of the young physicians in the present army & navy of the U. States. For a considerable time past, my health has been good & firm: and I could go through many[1] of the fatigues[2] of the station which I solicit. I have written, on this subject, to the President: but I have not received any answer. I am confident that you could effect somewhat for me, if your opinion of my qualifications be favourable; & the views of the President be not quite fixed in another quarter. The place of physician general, & not of surgeon general, is what I ask.

I am, Sir, with very great respect Your obedient servant & affect. friend, &c., &c.,   BENJAMIN SMITH BARTON.

RC (DLC); dateline at foot of text; endorsed by TJ as received 31 Mar. 1813 and so recorded in SJL.

A provision in a 3 Mar. 1813 "Act for the better organization of the general staff of the Army of the United States" called for the appointment of both an apothecary general and a physician and surgeon GENERAL, "whose respective duties and powers shall be prescribed by the President of the United States," in order to insure the "better superintendence and management of the hospital and medical establishment of the army of the United States" (U.S. Statutes at Large, 2:819–20). The Senate subsequently confirmed President James Madison's nomination of James Tilton as "Physician and Surgeon General" and Francis Le Baron as apothecary general (JEP, 2:352, 353 [10, 11 June 1813]). No letter from Barton to THE PRESIDENT promoting his candidacy has been found. On 20 Apr. 1813 Barton asked Madison to consider appointing him treasurer of the United States Mint, a post left vacant by the death of Benjamin Rush (Madison, Papers, Pres. Ser., 6:224).

[1] Word interlined in place of "some."
[2] Manuscript: "fatigus."

From Thomas Lehré

DEAR SIR   Charleston (S° Cᵃ) Mar: 23ᵈ 1813

Presuming upon your goodness I have taken the liberty to mention to you the nature of an application I lately made to the President.   owing to the great sacrifices I have made for a number of years past to support the Republican cause in this State—The great increase of my family, and the pressure of the times, I have been induced, with the advice of my friends here, to offer my Services to the President, as a Candidate for any Civil office (within my capacity) that may be vacant.

It was currently reported a few days past, that the Federal Marshal of this District, is to be removed—as that is an office which I conceive myself, from my long experience in the Sheriffs office of this District, to be as competent to discharge the duties thereof, as any man in this State, I wrote a letter to the President respecting it—the enclosed is a true Copy of the same, since which I have not had the pleasure to hear from him.

It is well known here, from the Seaboard up to the mountains, that no man took a more firm, decisive, and active part throughout[1] this State, and in our Legislature, than I did, in the years 1796, 1800, and 1804, to promote your Election as President of the United States— and also, in the years 1808, and 1812, to promote Mʳ Madisons election (with which he is fully acquainted) to the same office, for which, I am well persuaded, your Political enemies, as well as the enemies of the present administration, have not, and will never[2] forgive me.   I should not have troubled you upon the present occasion had I not been well informed, that whenever the secret enemies of our Country, hear of any of your active, and particular friends, becoming a Candidate for any office under the United States, however well qualified they may be to fill the same, they (our secret enemies) instantly use every base art, means and intrigue in their power to prevent their getting into office to serve their Country. Therefore, as I am not personally known to the President, permit me Sir, to solicit the very great favor of you to drop him a line on my behalf, which will ever[3] be remembered by me with a lively sense of gratitude. Should the President think proper to appoint me to the above office, it will be highly gratifying to me, and to our Republican friends here, and he may be assured I shall (as I have always done in every office I have had the honor to fill in this State) discharge the duties thereof faithfully, and that he shall never have cause to say, he has served an ingrate.

I remain with the highest consideration
Dear Sir, Your very obedient and very humble Servant
THOMAS LEHRÉ

P.S. as the mails have been very irregular of late, can I with propriety request the favor of you to acknowledge the receipt of this letter.

RC (DLC: James Madison Papers); addressed: "Thomas Jefferson Late President of the U. States Monticello Virginia—Mail"; endorsed by TJ as received 3 Apr. 1813 and so recorded in SJL. Enclosure: Lehré to Madison, 16 Mar. 1813, requesting appointment as federal marshal for the South Carolina district, reporting that he has served twice as sheriff for this district, indicating that the state's congressional delegation and federal judges William Johnson and John Drayton will vouch for him, arguing that his exertions on behalf of the Republican party entitle him to consideration, and suggesting that during wartime the office needs to be filled by someone acquainted with the law and committed to enforcing it (RC in DLC: Madison Papers; Tr in DLC; in Lehré's hand; at head of text: "(Copy)"; printed in Madison, *Papers, Pres. Ser.*, 6:127–8). Enclosed in TJ to Madison, 10 Apr. 1813.

The FEDERAL MARSHAL for South Carolina was Robert E. Cochran.

[1] Word interlined in place of "in."
[2] Manuscript: "vever."
[3] Word interlined.

From Thomas Paine McMahon

SIR,   Phila March 24th 1813.

I take the liberty [of][1] addressing you on a request which I hope you will be kind enough to comply with.

I am [the?][2] son of Bernard McMahon of this city and Wish to get an appointment in the Navy or Army of the United States.

Knowing that you were good enough to corresspond With my father, I thought you would be so good as to give me a few lines of reccommendation to the secratary of the department you think I had better apply to.

I would prefer the Navy as I have been in the seafaring line before and have been to the East and West Inidies and several places in[3] south America. But I have been informed by Sam[1] Carswell Esq[r] of this place that he thought it would be useless to apply to the Navy Department, as there were so many applicants that there would be no probability of success: If so I would wish to get an appointment in the Army, and would prefer the peace Establishment, if there were any Vacancies.

Now is the time for those who are for their Country to come forward and support it; and I wish to be enrolled among the deffenders of their country and their Countries rights. I trust Sir, you will beleive me to be a republican in principal and practice, and rest assured that if you should think proper to grant my request, that I will neglect nothing on my part to prove myself deserving of your kindness. I am a young man about 22 years of age 6 feet high and I believe my Education is such as to quallify me for either the Army or Navy.

I hope Sir, you will be so good as to do me the honor of Writing to me at My fathers N° 39 South second st. As soon as it may be conveinent to you, and you will much Oblige Sir Yours &c.

With the greatest respect   TH: PAINE M^CMAHON.

RC (MoSHi: TJC-BC); at foot of text: "Th: Jefferson Esqr"; endorsed by TJ as received 31 Mar. 1813 and so recorded in SJL.

Thomas Paine McMahon (ca. 1791–1831) was born in Ireland before his father, the plant nurseryman Bernard McMahon, immigrated to Philadelphia in 1796. He was commissioned a third lieutenant in the 16th Infantry Regiment, United States Army, on 19 Apr. 1813. Promoted to second and first lieutenant effective 19 May 1813 and 1 Jan. 1814, respectively, he served as regimental quartermaster from May 1814 until his honorable discharge on 15 June 1815. McMahon was reinstated on 17 May 1816 as a second lieutenant with brevet rank of first lieutenant and resigned on 18 Apr. 1818. In 1819 and 1820 he published new editions of his father's book, *The American Gardener's Calendar*. McMahon was admitted to the Philadelphia bar on 29 July 1825 and was a notary public by 1827 (Heitman, *U.S. Army*, 1:676; *JEP*, 2:364, 380, 410, 435, 488, 503, 3:55, 62, 136 [18 June, 1, 28 July, 1 Aug. 1813, 17 Feb., 4 Mar. 1814, 10, 17 Dec. 1816, 17 Apr. 1818]; Baltimore *American Farmer*, 31 Dec. 1819; John Hill Martin, *Martin's Bench and Bar of Philadelphia* [1883], 291; McMahon to Stephen Girard, 13 July 1827 [PPGi: Girard Papers; PPAmP microfilm]; Philadelphia *Poulson's American Daily Advertiser*, 30 Aug. 1831).

[1] Omitted word editorially supplied.

[2] Omitted word editorially supplied.

[3] Preceding three words interlined in place of "North and."

From Samuel J. Harrison

Dear Sir   Lynchbg Mar 25. 1813
    Before the Rec^t of your Letter of the 10 Ins^t I had on the 19, En-
closed you a Dft on Messrs Gibson & Jefferson for $1000. Supposed
to be about as much as the Crop would amount to—But if the demand for the $250. at poplar Forest Should be pressing—you are
at Liberty to direct m^r Goodman to Call on me for that Sum; & you
Return it, if necessary, when you come up the last of april.
    I am Dear Sir Y^r M^o ob St   S J Harrison

RC (MHi); endorsed by TJ as received   TJ's letter to Harrison was actually
31 Mar. 1813 and so recorded in SJL.   dated 11 Mar. 1813.

From Robert Patterson

Sir   Philadelphia March 25th 1813.
    Your time-piece has been packed up, ready for shipment, in the
manner you directed, for a considerable time. But as soon as our river
had been rendered navigable, by the breaking up of the ice, it was
again stoped & still continues to be so,[1] by a British fleet. I am therefore, Sir, about to set it up at my own house, as it will be better to
keep it going than standing; & shall wait your further instructions
with respect to the manner in which you would have it sent on.
    I have the honour to be, with the most perfect esteem Your obed^t
Servt R. Patterson

RC (MHi); endorsed by TJ as received   [1] Preceding six words interlined.
31 Mar. 1813 and so recorded in SJL.

From William Caruthers

Sir   Lexington 26th Mar 1813
    Your Kind Offer of a pair of Lambs I Will accept With many
thanks I Will contrive Some Way to Get them Over & from your Discription of that Breed of Sheep I have Written to Mr Randof to Save
me all the Ewe Lambes he Will Spare, (for which I Will pay him his
price) I Wish to commence a flock this Summer and We have paid
no attention to improveing our Breed of Sheep in this country if I
Should Succeed in Getting a Marino Ram I Suppose a Cross of him
With your Old Spanish Breed Will Make Good Wool I Would be

{ 31 }

Glad to Get a Couple of Shepherds Doggs also as I purpose as Soon as my flock[1] is of Sufficient Size to Graze them in the mountain in Summer[2]

Accept My Best Respects[3]   W[M] CARUTHERS

RC (DLC); between dateline and salutation: "Tho[s] Jefferson Esq[r]"; mistakenly endorsed by TJ as a letter of 26 Nov. 1813 received 2 Apr. 1813 and recorded in SJL as a letter of 2 Apr. 1813 received that same date.

[1] Manuscript: "flouk."
[2] Manuscript: "Sumer."
[3] Manuscript: "Respets."

From John B. Colvin

SIR,   Washington City, March 26. 1813.

I beg you to accept the accompanying volume of "Historical Letters." I confess I am ashamed of the typographical execution of the work, the badness of which is chiefly to be attributed to its being published to the South of the Potomac. It is a reproach to that part of the United States that so useful an art as that of printing, should be there so much neglected, in point of embellishment, as it is. It is needless to say any thing to <u>you</u> of the orthographical errors, which arose from the distance between the author and printer; Your classical knowledge will easily enable you to correct those appertaining to the names of antiquity. All these inaccuracies might be avoided in a second edition. If your leisure will admit of it, I shall be much gratified by your candid opinion of the plan and execution of the work.

I have the Honor to be, Sir, with very great esteem and respect, Your mo. ob. ser.   J. B. COLVIN.

RC (DLC); at foot of text: "His Excellency Thomas Jefferson"; endorsed by TJ as received 31 Mar. 1813 and so recorded in SJL. Enclosure: Colvin, *Historical Letters; originally written for and published in the Virginia Argus: including a brief but general view of the History of the World, Civil, Military And Religious,* *from the earliest times to the Year of Our Lord, 1811* (Richmond, 1812; Sowerby, no. 138; Poor, *Jefferson's Library,* 3 [no. 3]).

The PRINTER and publisher was Samuel Pleasants.

From Louis Philippe Gallot de Lormerie

MONSIEUR   Philad^e 26 mars 1813—

Votre Equité, votre humanité, votre ançienne bienveillançe a mon Egard vous porteront sans doute a Excuser L'importunité a laquelle me forcent des circonstances impérieuses. . . . celle qui se présente aujourdhui et a laquelle vous m'avés recommandé vous même de Veiller, je veux dire LEnvoi d'un nouveau ministre en france justifiera je l'Espére la liberté que je prens de vous rapeller la promesse que vous a faité le secrétaire dEtat en août d^er pour moi.

Joffre s'il le faut de payer <u>en france</u> le fret des caisses &^c destinées pour le Museum impérial dhist: nat: de paris, et qui peuvent former Environ un Tonneau ordinaire de fret Je ferai Egalement pour mon passage tout le sacrifice qu'on Exigera malgré mon peu de fortune et la depense de plus de 400 dollars faite en attendant cette Occasion—Jai donc lieu dEsperer qu'au moins on ne me la refusera pas maintenant

Comme Membre de plusieurs sociétes Litteraires et n'Etant ni commerçant ni politique, ni militaire je ne puis compromettre l'Expédition et comme tel je suis muni d'un <u>Passeport</u> (ançien il est vrai) mais signé <u>par un mïnistre plenipotentiaire</u> de <u>la GB</u> dans <u>Les EU</u>, <u>pour moi</u>, <u>mon Bagâge et tous mes Effets</u>.—Juserai en outre de toute la Discrétion qu'on Exigera Vous priant de m'honorer d'une réponse au plutôt possible afin que je puisse savoir le tems et le lieu d'ou je dois partir, ou saisir <u>de suite</u> une autre Occasion, si finalement je ne puis joüir de celle qui vous avoit eté promise— . . . Daignés agréer les assurançes de mes trés respectueux Sentimens.   DE LORMERIE

P.s. LEugêne Navire français, un des plus beaux de l'Europe, est maintenant a N: york. c'est une Excellente Embarcation.

SIR   Philadelphia 26 March 1813—

Your fairness, humanity, and past kindnesses to me will surely induce you to excuse me for bothering you; pressing circumstances force me to do so. . . . you warned me to watch for the opportunity that presents itself today. The sending of a new minister to France will justify, I hope, the liberty I take in reminding you of the promise you made last August to the secretary of state concerning me.

I am offering, if necessary, to pay <u>in France</u> the freight on the boxes, etc., sent to the imperial museum of natural history in Paris, weighing about a ton. For my own passage I will make any additional sacrifice required, in spite of my meager financial resources and my expenditure of more than four hundred dollars while awaiting this opening—I have reason to hope, therefore, that this chance, at least, will not be denied me.

Being a member of several literary societies, and neither a merchant, politician, nor soldier, I cannot endanger the expedition. I have a <u>passport</u> (old it is true), signed <u>by a British minister plenipotentiary</u> to <u>the United States, for me, my baggage, and all my belongings.</u>—I will, moreover, be very discreet. I ask you kindly to honor me with a reply as soon as possible so that I may know the time and place from which I will depart or seize <u>immediately</u> another opportunity, if in the end I am unable to use that which had been promised to you— . . . Please accept my very respectful regards.

De Lormerie

P.S. The French ship Eugène, one of Europe's most beautiful, is now at New York. It is an excellent vessel.

RC (DLC); ellipses in original; between signature and postscript: "M. Thomas Jefferson Exprésident des E.U: Monticello"; endorsed by TJ as received 31 Mar. 1813 and so recorded in SJL. Translation by Dr. Genevieve Moene.

Robert Liston, Great Britain's ambassador extraordinary and minister plenipotentiary to the United States between 1796 and 1800, had issued Lormerie's PASSEPORT (Lormerie to TJ, 21 July 1812; *PTJ*, 30:223n, 33:190n).

Will of Anne Scott Marks

In the name of God Amen. I Anne S. Marks late of the county of Louisa, now of Albemarle, being in health of body and mind, make the following disposition of my estate real and personal after my death.

First it is my will that all the debts with which I am chargeable either on my own account or as executrice of my late husband Hastings Marks, be paid out of my whole estate. then I give the whole of the residue of my property real and personal to the children which shall be living at my death of my beloved niece Martha Randolph in consideration of the manifold and unceasing kindnesses & services which I have recieved and am constantly recieving at her hands: and I constitute her son, my great nephew, Thomas Jefferson Randolph my sole executor of this my will. In witness whereof I have signed this my will with my name this twenty sixth day of March one thousand eight hundred and thirteen. ANNE SCOTT MARKS

Attested by us the subscribers
who have subscribed our names
in presence of the testatrice.
WILLIAM M^CCLURE
HUGH CHISHOLM
E BACON

MS (ViU: TJP-ER); in TJ's hand, signed by Marks, McClure, Chisholm, and Bacon; endorsed by TJ: "Marks Anne S. her will."

Anne Scott Jefferson Marks (1755–1828), TJ's youngest sister and the twin of his only brother, Randolph Jefferson, married Hastings Marks in 1788. He died in 1811, after which the childless Marks resided at Monticello (Malone, *Jefferson*, 1:430, 6:154; *PTJ*, 9:397, 13:350–1, 15:93–4, 16:113, 115; TJ to Randolph Jefferson, 14 Jan. 1812; Will of Anne Scott Marks, 3 Aug. 1825).

This WILL was superseded by one dated 3 Aug. 1825, also in TJ's hand.

Conveyance of Part of Shadwell to Thomas Jefferson Randolph

This indenture made on the 26th day of March one thousand eight hundred & thirteen, between Thomas Jefferson of Monticello in the county of Albemarle on the one part, and Thomas Jefferson Randolph, his grandson of the same place and county on the other part witnesseth that the said Thomas Jefferson in consideration of the affection he bears to his said grandson Thomas Jefferson Randolph, & of the sum of one Dollar to him in hand paid, hath given granted bargained & sold unto the said Thomas Jefferson Randolph all that part of his tract of land called Shadwell in the same county which lies north of a line beginning on the river where it is nearest to the freestone quarry last opened (which quarry may be by guess twenty or thirty poles above the pier-head) and running thence round the quarry so as to include the same, & from it's upper side downwards to a point ten poles inland from the sd pierhead, thence downwards parallel to the canal & always ten poles from it to the Shadwell spring branch opposite to the great mill, thence downwards parallel with the river and always ten poles from it to the first deep gully about   below the mill & down that gully to the river, which grounds South of the said line are reserved for the convenience of the Shadwell mills, as is also a convenient breadth for a road from the beginning above mentioned upwards along the river bank to the Lego line, and from the ending at the gulley downwards along the river bank to the Edgehill line; which parcel North of the sd reserves, & intended to be conveyed by these presents is supposed to contain about three hundred & seventy five acres, be the same more or less, the whole tract being held for four hundred acres. to have & to hold the sd parcel of land north of the sd reserves to him the sd Thomas Jefferson Randolph and his heirs until a better provision shall be made for him out of the other estate of the sd Thomas Jefferson, on which event the estate hereby conveyed is to cease & determine, and revert ipso facto to the sd Thomas Jefferson & his heirs. In witness whereof he has hereto set his hand & seal on the day & year above written. TH: JEFFERSON

Signed, sealed ⎫ E BACON aug. 13
& delivered in ⎬ HUGH CHISHOLM 22 Oct. 1814
presence of ⎭ P^R CARR aug 13

MS (Forbes Magazine Collection, New York City, 2003); on indented paper; in TJ's hand, signed by TJ, Bacon, Chisholm, and Carr, with dates of witnesses' signatures in Alexander Garrett's hand; with seal affixed adjacent to TJ's signature; attested on verso: "At A court held for Albemarle county the 2^d August 1813 This Indenture was produced into court and proved by the oaths of Peter Carr and Edmund Bacon two of the witnesses thereto. and In the Office of said court 22^d October 1814 was fully proved by the oath of Hugh Chisholmn a third witness thereto. before me according to law. and thereupon admitted to record teste <John> Alex Garrett D C"; docketed: "Jefferson to Randolph} Deed 2^d Aug. 1813 proved by 2 Witnesses 22 Oct 1814 fully proved." Tr (Albemarle Co. Deed Book, 19:155–6); in Garrett's hand.

SHADWELL was in Randolph's possession at his death in 1875 (Shackelford, *Descendants*, 1:79).

Conveyance of Slaves to Thomas Jefferson Randolph

Know all men by these presents that I Thomas Jefferson of Monticello in the county of Albemarle in consideration of my affection to my grandson Thomas Jefferson Randolph of the same place & county have given to my said grandson four negro slaves to wit Thruston the son of Isabel, Bec daughter of Minerva, Lewis & Sally son & daughter of Jenny to hold the same in absolute property: in witness whereof I have delivered the said slaves into his actual possession, and have hereto set my hand & seal this 26th day of March 1813.
Witness TH: JEFFERSON
WILLIAM M^cCLURE
E BACON Aug 13
HUGH CHISHOLM 22 Oct. 1814
P^R CARR Aug 1813

MS (Mrs. William C. King, Richmond, 1979; photocopy in ViHi); in TJ's hand, except for signatures of witnesses in their hands and dates of their signatures in Alexander Garrett's hand; with seal affixed adjacent to TJ's signature; attested on verso: "At A court held for Albemarle county the 2^d August 1814 This Bill sale was produced into court and proved by the oaths of Peter Carr and Edmund Bacon two of the witnesses thereto and In the Office of the county court of Albemarle the 22^d October 1814 was fully proved by the oath of Hugh Chisholmn before me according to law and thereupon admitted to record teste Alex. Garrett D C"; docketed: "Jefferson to Randolph } Bill Sale 2ᵈ August 1813 proved by 2 Witnesses 22 Oct. 1814 fully proved" and "Recorded page 154 Examined." Tr (Albemarle Co. Deed Book, 19:154); in Garrett's hand.

A missing letter from TJ to Thomas Jefferson Randolph is recorded in SJL as written from Poplar Forest on 6 May 1813.

From Benjamin Waterhouse

DEAR SIR,   Boston 26ᵗʰ March 1813

Your letter of the 9ᵗʰ insᵗ opened[1] to my mind such a train of interesting ideas, that I could not resist writing you this, & enclosing you one of our Boston newspapers, containing a peice under the signature of an "Independent Whig." It will tend to confirm your opinion of our pretended _fautores_ of science. More than a dozen numbers have preceeded this, some of them calculated to expose the persecuting spirit of our priesthood. While these numbers have been read with avidity, they have stirred up the malice, & given additional venom to the persecution of the author.

Our college at Cambridge is under the absolute direction of the Essex Junto, at the head of which stands chief Justice Parsons, the Goliah of the Massachusetts Gentile-army, a man as cunning as Lucifer, & about half as good. This man is also at the head of the Corporation of the college. He is not only the soul of that body, but he is the evil councellor, the _Ahithophel_ of the high federal party, while H. G. Otis is the _Absalom_.

I rashly ventured to attack this champion[2] of the Phillistines. Nay, I told the Senate, the popular branch of the college government in so many words, in a memorial, that "I hoped to find a stone in the brook for the forehead of my enemy." The consequence has been that I have been secretly & slowly divested of every college emolument & office, under pretences purely jesuitiene. A medical combination joined this political & college party, & together they have treated me as a similar combination treated our friend Dʳ Rush, before Porcupine was driven from Philadelphia. This induced me to come forth with a plain narrative of facts in "the Boston Patriot"; and I have enclosed one of the papers, where you will see[3] the fate of my intended publication in London. all these things have perhaps wound up my mind to a pitch of resentment, that none but a rich man can express with safety.

The Medical Society of Massachusetts thwarted my efforts in diffusing vaccination, as early as 1803; & at the head of this opposition stood Dr Eustis. He did & said every thing to discourage the practice. The enmity of this gentleman was blown into rage when you gave me the marine-hospital, & this accounts for all that followed. The confluence of this medical & political enmity has formed a current too strong for me to stem. I cannot live in it; and therefore some of my friends have, without any solicitation on my part, written to President Madison, to know if something cannot be done for my relief: of these Mr Adams & Mr Gerry have been the most zealous. I have not had the courage myself to make any application to the President, from knowing that Dr Eustis had made an impression on his mind to my disadvantage. Still I am aware that if something be not done my enemies will triumph. When Dr Rush was encompassed by his enemies Mr Adams gave him the Treasury of the mint. By the help of this anchor he rode out the storm. Now I, & my friends are thoroughly convinced that unless I have some such anchor, the strong blast from the coast of Essex will drive me on a Bar where I may be wrecked. I never coveted money. I never wished to be rich. I never loved company or parade. I have devoted my time & powers to matters of public benefit rather than personal advantage. I began the medical school at Cambridge; & commenced & compleated their mineral cabinet. I introduced vaccination, & defended it, in its disputed march, through an host of enemies; & established it in America 30, or 40 years sooner than it would have been;—I reformed a marine hospital that was a sink [of]^4 filth, drunkenness & disorder; I rendered it a suitable pattern for all others in the country. I encreased the value of the hospital property, & made a saving to its funds of full half my salary annually. I never had a bill, that I approbated, ever refused payment; and yet I have been represented to President Madison as little better than a peculator; & treated accordingly. And now, in the 60th year of my^5 life, I find myself persecuted by the college, by my medical brethren here, and regarded unfavourably by the administration; that very administration, that I have defended unceasingly for four years past with my pen; while those whom it feeds & cloathest never moved a finger in its support! The federalists have scoffingly remarked these things to me & said— see Republican gratitude! To which I have replied—See how it is possible for a man to sacrifice his interest to his principles!—

Amidst^6 these trials, I have my consolations. My children are every thing a parent can wish; giving their parents a satisfaction beyond any thing that riches can procure. Another source of consolation is the correspondence of great^7 & good men. Among these is the Sage of Quincy, the venerable Adams. We exchange letters every week or two. In one received lately he says "your enemies are, in their hearts,

Rush's enemies; and for the same reasons medical & political. But you are both too fluent & dextrous[8] with your pens. They dare not attack you openly. They dare not meet you in the field of controversy[9] They have recourse to their sappers & miners. But for this cowardice, you[10] would soon see Rush's treatise, attacked from all quarters,[11] as well as your numbers of the Independent whig."[12]—He then adds— "I know no two characters more alike than Rush's & yours. I know not two more[13]—nor two better informed men: nor two better men: yet see the fortunes of you both! The Kingdom of virtue is not of this world: no! nor the Kingdom of science, nor the Kingdom of merit."— No production literary or philosophical is patronized in Boston, if not written by a federalist.[14]

We have but one good republican paper in Boston viz the <u>Patriot</u> and altho' we have several good writers among the Republicans, scarcely one of them will take the pen even to expose falsehood or repel scandal, or correct misrepresentation. I have, for 4, or 5 years past, endeavoured to pour a stream of republican principles upon the wheels of government. The piece signed "<u>Sallust</u>" which happens to be in the enclosed paper may serve as a specimen. We suffer at this head quarters of (<u>Hamilton's</u>) good principles for want of [a] good newspaper, constantly supplied with warm & glowing sentiments from the honest American heart; but we are in a degree smothered & overpowered by the English influence, which operates like a deleterious air on our senses.

I have never seen major Stoddert's book. It has never made its way to Boston. I was surprized to hear that you had so little to do, or say with the mountain of salt. It rested on my mind that it came from your pen. What reliance have we on past history, if the occurrences of our own days be thus involved in uncertainty?

Through all the changing[15] Scenes of my doubtful future life, to hear of your health & your happyness will be a cordial to your steady friend   BENJ[N] WATERHOUSE

RC (DLC); edge chipped; at foot of text: "Hon^be Thos Jefferson"; endorsed by TJ as received 7 Apr. 1813 and so recorded in SJL.

The enclosed newspaper was probably the *Boston Patriot*, 10 Mar. 1813, in which A PEICE penned by Waterhouse as INDE-PENDENT WHIG detailed his role in the assembling of a mineral collection in collaboration with John Coakley Lettsom, a British physician and fellow champion of smallpox vaccination, and its subsequent donation to Harvard University; described the disappearance of a large body of correspondence between the two men that had been intended for publication in London; and questioned the university's decision to move Waterhouse's lectures and collection from the philosophy chamber to the anatomical chamber. FAU-TORES: "supporters or patrons." In the Bible, David kills the Philistine champion Goliath (GOLIAH) with a stone (1 Samuel

17), and AHITHOPHEL and his unscrupulous partner ABSALOM later plot to overthrow him as king of Israel (2 Samuel 15). The Federalist newspapers conducted by William Cobbett as Peter PORCUPINE contained severe attacks on Benjamin Rush. Waterhouse quoted from a 16 Jan. 1813 letter RECEIVED LATELY from John Adams (RC in MHi: Adams-Waterhouse Collection; FC in Lb in MHi: Adams Papers). Waterhouse's PIECE SIGNED "SALLUST" in the *Boston Patriot* of 10 Mar. 1813 ruminated on a recent proclamation by the British governor of Bermuda related to the British Orders in Council of October 1812 authorizing the distribution of trading licenses to "friends and favorites dwelling in the ports" on the Eastern seaboard, concluding that both he and President James Madison would deem any American providing supplies to the enemy in time of war to be a traitor.

[1] Manuscript: "opended."
[2] Manuscript: "chanpion."
[3] Waterhouse here canceled "how it."
[4] Omitted word editorially supplied.
[5] Waterhouse here canceled "age."
[6] Manuscript: "Amidts."
[7] Manuscript: "grea."
[8] Preceding two words not in Adams-Waterhouse RC or FC.
[9] Preceding two words not in Adams-Waterhouse RC or FC.
[10] Manuscript: "cowardice, & you." Adams-Waterhouse RC and FC: "Cowardice you."
[11] Adams-Waterhouse RC and FC here add "as Refinement, Vision, Whim."
[12] Preceding nine words not in Adams-Waterhouse RC or FC.
[13] Adams-Waterhouse RC and FC here add "ingenious Men."
[14] Superfluous ending quotation mark editorially omitted.
[15] Manuscript: "chaning."

From Samuel & James Leitch

SIR,   Charlottesville Mar. 27[h] 1813

Agreeable to your request we have at length[1] procured you a Small pale of Fresh Butter for which we have given 1/3[d] it was more than we expected to have got it for but could not do better—we are in hopes the quality is Such as will meet your approbation

respectfully your Obd[t] Serv[ts]   SAM[L] & JA[S] LEITCH

P.S The Servant had better bring Something to Carry it in as the pale was reserved

RC (MHi); in Samuel Leitch's hand; addressed: "Tho[s] Jefferson Esqre Monticello"; endorsed by TJ.

[1] Manuscript: "lenght."

From John Waldo

SIR,   Georgetown (S.C.) March 27th 1813

Having, with much care and under peculiar difficulties, written a grammar of the English languag[e], my object is now to make the public acquainted with its real merits. But the present rage for publishing works of this kind, has rendered them so numerous as to destroy all curiosity to examine them; and the high repute in which Lindly Murray's is held, has also removed all expectation of material improvement in them. Whatever merit therefore a new work of this kind may possess it must, without the aid of the few who are free from prejudices, remain in obscurity[.] I have, therefore knowing your laudable zeal for the promotion of literature and your ability to judge of the merits of literary productions, and convinced also of the great influence your name would give its circulation taken the liberty of presenting you with a copy of my grammar and of requesting the favor of you to give it a thorough examination, if your other numerous and more important avocations, should not put it out of your power. I would not make this intrusion on your time, were I not convinced that the work possesses merit worthy the patronage of the public. In this opinion I am supported by some of the first literary characters in this state who have favoured me with their recommendations, with permission to publish them in the next edition. They all unite in its being highly philosophical,[1] while it possesses a simplicity that is well adapted to the capacity of children. I have also found from experience, that upon the plan I have there adapted that very young children acquire the first principles of grammar with remarkable facility.

If such are its merits it is a duty I owe not only to myself, but the rising generation and posterity, to use every proper exertion to make the public acquainted with it. The present edition consisting of only 500 copies, and being very incorrect,[2] I shall, as early as possible, have a new and correct one. I will therefore, should you find the work worthy of your patronage, one to which you would feel willing to lend the influence of your name, thank you to send me your opinion as early as you can make it convenient.

Your obd^t Servt   JOHN WALDO

RC (DLC); edge trimmed; endorsed by TJ as received 9 Apr. 1813 and so recorded in SJL. Enclosure: Waldo, *Rudiments of English Grammar; Designed for the Instruction of Youth of Different Ages or Capacities* (Georgetown, S.C., 1811; Sowerby, no. 4848).

John Waldo (1762–1826), educator, was a native of South Dover, Dutchess County, New York, who moved about 1793 to Georgetown, South Carolina. In the latter place he failed as a merchant and officiated briefly at the local Baptist church before establishing himself as the proprietor of an academy. Waldo wrote a number of English and Latin grammar textbooks (Waldo Lincoln, *Genealogy of the Waldo Family* [1902], 1:317; Leah Townsend, *South Carolina Baptists 1670–1805* [1974], 59, 60, 113, 120, 285–6; *Minutes of the Charleston Baptist Association . . . November 4, 1826* [1826], 1, 2–3; *Camden* [S.C.] *Journal*, 7 Oct. 1826).

The first American edition of Lindley

MURRAY'S *English Grammar, Adapted to the Different Classes of Learners* (York, Eng., 1795) appeared in Boston in 1800. Waldo had a NEW AND CORRECT edition of his own grammar printed in Philadel-phia and published in 1818 in Georgetown, South Carolina.

[1] Manuscript: "philosophiical."
[2] Prefix interlined.

From Edward Bolling

HON^D SIR   Buckingham March 29th 1813

This letter will be handed you by Mr Thos Roberts, who is anxious to obtain a commision in any of the military establishments now organizing, and in order to attain his wish, has solicited me to address you uppon that subject, and give you my opinion Respecting his qualifications &.c.

I shou'd be false to true friendship, was I to neglect him, where there was the smalest probability[1] of my Rendering him a service. I have had the pleasure of being acquainted with this Gent. several years, and it gives me great satisfaction, to find its in my power, to say he wants nothing but experience, (which can be acquired only by practice) to make him fully competent, to any commision his government may think proper to bestow upon him, or in other words any that he wou'd accept conscious as I am, that he wou,d receive no appointment, he thought himself incapable of conducting with the utmost propriety. Shou,d you think it expedient, to favor him with a letter of recommendation to the Honourable Secretary of war, I am convinced his friends, nor his government, will never have cause to complain, therefore in expectation of your assistance I remain with high consideration & respect

Yo^r Mo^t ob^t & very humble Servt   EDW^D BOLLING

RC (MHi); between dateline and salutation: "Thomas Jefferson Esqr"; endorsed by TJ as received 1 Apr. 1813 and so recorded in SJL.

Edward Bolling (d. 1835) was the son of John Bolling and TJ's sister Mary Jefferson Bolling. In 1800 he inherited property in Goochland County from his father. Bolling owned twenty-three slaves there a decade later. He subsequently moved to Buckingham County, and the 1820 census for that county credited him with the possession of eight slaves. In his capacity as executor of his father's estate, Bolling was a longtime debtor to TJ (Chesterfield Co. Will Book, 5:291–3; DNA: RG 29, CS, Goochland Co., 1810, Buckingham Co., 1820; TJ to James Lyle, 24 June 1811; Tarlton Saunders to TJ, 9 Apr. 1821; Louise Pecquet du Bellet, *Some Prominent Virginia Families* [1907], 309–10, 320; Wyndham Robertson and Robert A. Brock, *Pocahontas, Alias Matoaka, And Her Descendants* [1887], 35, 42).

[1] Manuscript: "brobability."

From Alexander Garrett

SIR   Charlottesville March 29th 1813

The bearer hereof Mr Li Pop a native of Italy wishes some advice how to become a citizen of the United States and several gentlemen have recommended to him to see you on the subject, he can state his situation to you. I have not the late act of Congress relative to Aliens, so as to point out to him the course he ought to pursue.

I am Sir Your Obdt Set   ALEX: GARRETT

RC (CSmH: JF); endorsed by TJ.

Joseph Lipop, coach ornamenter, was a native of Rome, Italy, who was living in Alexandria by 1811. He worked for French minister plenipotentiary Louis Barbé Charles Sérurier and was also employed by the Alexandria coachmaking firm of Evan P. Taylor before moving to Washington, D.C. By 1817 he had settled in Shenandoah County, where he lived until at least 1833 (*Alexandria Gazette & Daily Advertiser*, 7 Sept. 1819; T. Michael Miller, comp., *Artisans and Merchants of Alexandria, Virginia 1780–1820* [1991–92], 2:173; DNA: RG 29, CS, Shenandoah Co., 1820, 1830; John Walter Wayland, *A History of Shenandoah County, Virginia*, 2d ed. [1969; repr. 1980], 282).

A supplementary ACT OF CONGRESS RELATIVE TO ALIENS was not actually passed until 30 July 1813 (*U.S. Statutes at Large*, 3:53).

To Patrick Gibson

DEAR SIR   Monticello Mar. 29. 13.

I recieved the day before yesterday mr Edmund Randolph's answer that he would execute any deed I should desire for mr Mazzei which should[1] go to warrant only against himself & his heirs. I have thought it best to make a statement of the title which the purchaser may consider, and verify every material part of it for himself by the records at Richmond. he will see that the title is so short and clear as to need no other[2] warranty than the conveyance itself. I would have prepared a deed, but did not know how to describe the grounds. the purchaser therefore, as usual, will have a deed prepared, taking care that it be such an one as mr Randolph will sign. this had better be inclosed to me, and I will forward it to mr Randolph. I wish it to be done without delay, or an approaching visit to Bedford will cause a considerable suspension. I inclose the statement of title and tender you the assurance of my esteem & respect.

TH: JEFFERSON

PoC (MHi); at foot of text: "Mr Gibson"; endorsed by TJ as a letter to Gibson & Jefferson and so recorded in SJL. Enclosure not found.

EDMUND RANDOLPH'S ANSWER, not found, is recorded in SJL as received 26 Mar. 1813 from "Avon hill near Charlston. Virgª."

1 TJ here canceled "bind."
2 Word interlined.

From Rodolphus Dickinson

DEAR SIR,   Greenfield, Franklin County, (Mass.) March 30, 1813.

I am not flattered with the expectation that the little work enclosed will present you with any new views that will be interesting: but feel confident, whatever may be your decision, that this effort of youth will be regarded with indulgence.

I embrace the occasion, Sir, to tender you my most heartfelt respect and gratitude.   RODOLPHUS DICKINSON

RC (MHi); at foot of text: "Thomas Jefferson Esq."; endorsed by TJ as received 15 Apr. 1813 and so recorded in SJL. Enclosure: Dickinson, *A Geographical and Statistical View of Massachusetts Proper* (Greenfield, 1813).

Rodolphus Dickinson (1786–1862), attorney, author, and Episcopal minister, was born in Deerfield, Massachusetts, graduated from Yale College (later University) in 1805, and was admitted to the Massachusetts bar in 1808. He was clerk of the Franklin County courts from 1811 until 1819, when he accepted Episcopal orders and began serving two parishes in South Carolina. By 1832 Dickinson had returned to Deerfield, and he officiated at Trinity Parish in nearby Montague. His literary endeavors included geographical, legal, and religious works (Thomas W. Baldwin, *Vital Records of Deerfield Massachusetts, to the Year 1850* [1920], 55; *Catalogue of the Officers and Graduates of Yale University . . . 1701–1910* [1910], 83; David Willard, *Willard's History of Greenfield* [1838], 166; William Stevens Perry, ed., *Journals of General Conventions of the Protestant Episcopal Church, In the United States, 1785–1835* [1874], 2:502; George Sheldon, *A History of Deerfield Massachusetts* [1895–96; repr. 1972], 2:148–9; Greenfield *Gazette and Courier*, 3 Nov. 1862).

To Louis H. Girardin

Mar. 31: 13.

Th: Jefferson presents his compliments to mr Girardin & is sorry he cannot furnish him the Early York cabbage seed. he has ceased to cultivate it because the seed cannot be raised in this country. he sends him some green curled Savoy cabbage, the only kind he has. he sends him also some Malta Kale which he recieved from that island and finds preferable to either the Scotch or Delaware Kales. he sends him some Sprout Kale which he got from his friend Thouin, & is the most precious winter vegetable he knows. likewise Red Haricots which he recieved from M. Thouin, very delicate. he adds the best kind of

Snap he has ever seen in this country; Long Haricots sent him from Georgia, very delicious and a sowing of Ledman's Dwarf peas from Philadelphia which he thinks the very best of all the kinds of latter peas. it may be of some avail to mr Girardin to know that mr Price his neighbor of Milton is the best gardener of this neighborhood, is the most curious in cultivating the best species always, is a very kind honest man, and may be able to furnish mr Gerardin many kinds of seeds. if there are any other kinds in Th:J's stock which mr Girardin may need, they will be at his service. he salutes him with esteem & respect

RC (PPAmP: Thomas Jefferson Letters); dateline at foot of text; addressed: "Mr Girardin." Not recorded in SJL.

On this date TJ also recorded a payment of $3.50 to William McClure to settle a debt owed to Mary C. Oglesby (*MB*, 2:1287). On 16 Dec. 1812 Oglesby had written to McClure's wife that "I will thank you to send me the money for weaveing your Cloth, the sum is 21/ I am in want of it at this time" (RC in MoSHi: TJC-BC; written on a small scrap; endorsed by TJ: "Oglesby Mary C. 3.50 Mar. 31. 13. p^d to mr M^{c}lure").

From David Bailie Warden

DEAR SIR,   Paris—1 april, 1813.

on the 21st[1] of january last, I had the honor of writing to you, by Doctor Stephens, and of sending, for your acceptance, a copy of the civil, penal, and criminal codes of France. I also inclosed a letter from mr. mazzei. I have since forwarded to you, by mr. Breuil, of the schooner <u>Bellona</u>, bound to Philadelphia, a box of garden Seeds from mr. Thouin—I now inclose his letter on this subject—Senator Tracy is still without information concerning the <u>ms</u>, forwarded to you by mr. Barlow—It would give me great pleasure to write to you on political subjects; but, at present, there is great danger of my letter falling into the hands of the Enemy—I have not yet received instructions from our government in consequence of the ministers' death. All my time is occupied in supplying the Vacancy which it has made[2]—I pray you to present my respects to mr. and mrs Randolphe and to believe me your very[3] devoted Servt

DAVID BAILIE WARDEN

[*Postscript in Dupl only:*] P.S. Having ascertained that the Captain of the <u>Hornet</u> left several trunks and cases, at Cherburg, which he refused to take on board, belonging to the Philadelphia society &c and seeing that the Copy of Toulongeon's work to be forwarded by that opportunity was left at Cherburg, I send by mr. Hasler another Copy—the author died lately—much regretted—the Sudden departure of mr. Hasler does not allow me time to have it bound.

RC (DLC); at foot of text: "Thomas Jefferson Esquire"; lacks postscript; endorsed by TJ as received 28 May 1813 and so recorded in SJL. Dupl (DLC); at head of text: "Duplicate"; at foot of text: "the Hon^be Thomas Jefferson"; endorsed by TJ as received 17 Sept. 1813 and so recorded in SJL. FC (MdHi: Warden Letterbook); in Warden's hand; lacking postscript. Enclosure: André Thoüin to TJ, 15 Mar. 1813.

Although TJ probably never received Warden's letter of THE 21ST OF JANUARY LAST or its enclosed letter from Philip Mazzei, DOCTOR Alexander H. Stevens delivered him the COPY OF THE CIVIL, PENAL, AND CRIMINAL CODES OF FRANCE (Stevens to TJ, 10 Aug. 1813; TJ to Stevens, 23 Aug. 1813). Joel Barlow's recent DEATH had left vacant the position of United States minister plenipotentiary to France.

With the Dupl on 17 Sept. 1813 TJ received the WORK by François Emmanuel Vicomte de Toulongeon, *Histoire de France depuis la Révolution de 1789*, 7 vols. (Paris, 1801–10; Sowerby, no. 240; Poor, *Jefferson's Library*, 4 [no. 88]). In the note to Warden to TJ, 26 Jan. 1811, the Editors incorrectly asserted that TJ received no copy of this publication until 1815.

[1] RC and FC: "21st." Dupl: "24th." The earlier date is correct.

[2] Closing in Dupl: "Please to present my respects to Mr. and Mrs Randolph—I am, Dear Sir, with great respect, your most obed Sev^t." FC ends here with "my respects to the family."

[3] Manuscript: "every."

To Benjamin Smith Barton

DEAR SIR   Monticello Apr. 3. 13.

Yours of the 23^d Ult. has been duly recieved, and I shall place the subject of it before the President in a letter I am to write him immediately on another subject. nothing certainly can give me greater pleasure than to be useful to you on this and every other occasion. at the same time I am satisfied no stimulus can be wanting on the mind of the President. nobody better knows your qualifications for the office you desire, nor would be more disposed to do justice to them.

When shall we have your book on American botany, and when the 1st volume of Lewis & Clarke's travels? both of these works are of general expectation, and great interest, and to no one of more than to myself.   Accept the assurance of my constant esteem and respect.   TH: JEFFERSON

RC (PPAmP: Barton Papers, Violetta Delafield–Benjamin Smith Barton Collection); addressed: "Doct^r Benjamin S. Barton Philadelphia"; franked; postmarked Milton, 7 Apr. PoC (DLC); endorsed by TJ.

To Margaret B. Bonneville

SIR   Monticello Apr. 3. 13.

Your favor of Mar. 13. was long on the road, owing to the season
and my distance from the great post roads. I thank you for your polite attention on the subject of my letters to the late mr Paine. while
he lived, I thought it a duty, as well as a test of my own political principles to support him against the persecutions of an unprincipled faction. my letters to him therefore expressed the sincere effusions of my
heart. old now, and retired from the world, and anxious for tranquility, it is my wish that they should not be published during my life, as
they might draw on me renewed molestations from the irreconcilable
enemies of republican government. I would rather enjoy the remainder of life without disturbance from their buzzing. Accept my best
wishes for your safe and happy return to your native country, with
the assurance of my great esteem & respect.   TH: JEFFERSON

PoC (DLC); at foot of text: "M. de Bonneville"; endorsed by TJ.

To Sarah Grotjan

MADAM   Monticello Apr. 3. 13.

Your favor of Mar. 15. on the subject of mrs Julia Bradley formerly
Webb, has been duly recieved. I have in vain ransacked my own[1]
memory to recall any knolege of her which I might have had: but the
failure of that recollection is no proof against the fact, the multitude
of those occasionally made known to me having rendered a distinct
remembrance of them too much for my memory. I have therefore had
recourse to enquiry of others, & I learn that a miss Judith Webb formerly an inhabitant of Richmond, married a mr Bradley against the
advice & consent of her friends. she was a Fleming on the mother's
side, which family, as well as that of the Webbs, had been of respectable standing & property in this state. at present however both
are gone to entire decay not a single person of either name remaining
who is not in absolute penury. the nearest connection she has who are
any way at their ease, is the Tuckahoe branch of Randolphs, all of
whom now also are without property, except Colo Thos M. Randolph
commanding a regiment at Niagara, mrs Gouvernier Morris of N.
York, & a mrs Randolph in a distant part of this state. mrs Bradley
is the grandaughter of their aunt, and I learn that the multitude of

[47]

those of the same family with her, who stand nearer, or as near to these persons as she does, are more than sufficient to absorb all the aids which their limited circumstances can spare, and are more at hand to recieve them in the forms most convenient. while living in Richmond she was in the way of recieving some comforts from her friends there, which the unworthiness of her husband at length discouraged. this is the sum of what I learn from others. I wish it could have been more satisfactory to the kind dispositions which her situation has excited in yourself, or that it could have indicated more probable resources for her relief. Accept the assurance of my esteem & respect.   TH: JEFFERSON

PoC (DLC); at foot of text: "Mrs Sarah Grotjan"; endorsed by TJ.

JUDITH WEBB married Zenas Bradley in 1809. She was the daughter of Judith Fleming Webb and George Webb and granddaughter of Mary Randolph Flem-ing and Tarlton Fleming (Michael E. Pollock, *Marriage Bonds of Henrico County, Virginia 1782–1853* [1984], 20; Robert Isham Randolph, *The Randolphs of Virginia* [1936], 76).

[1] Word interlined.

To Samuel J. Harrison

DEAR SIR   Monticello Apr. 3. 13.

Your favor of Mar. 25. is recieved and I thank you for the offer it makes. I had desired mr Gibson on the reciept of my flour to remit 250.D. to Goodman as soon as he could make any sale. I found afterwards no sale could be made for a reasonable price, and therefore wrote the request to you to furnish that sum to Goodman, and countermanded my order on mr Gibson. in the mean time however he had remitted the money to Goodman. if you think the amount of the crop will cover one hundred dollars more, I would ask you to pay that sum to Nimrod Darnell who writes me word he is in want of it. but if it will not cover it, he must wait a little longer. I have about 450. barrels of flour in Richmond unsold. but having no doubt that the enemy will withdraw from the bay now that the equinoctial gales are over, I count on a speedy & good sale. they would certainly act against every principle of common sense or interest to remain there. for while they close the Chesapeake & Delaware not a barrel of flour can go to the W. Indies or the Peninsul., & they are starving too their favorites of Boston. New York had exported all her surplus beyond the wants of the army, so that no supplies can be had but from the Chesapeake & Delaware. Accept the assurance of my great[1] esteem & respect.
                                              TH: JEFFERSON

PoC (MHi); at foot of text: "Mr Saml J. Harrison"; endorsed by TJ.

Nimrod Darnil (Darnell) sent TJ WORD of his need for $100 in a missing letter of 12 Mar. recorded in SJL as re-ceived 24 Mar. 1813. TJ's 3 Apr. 1813 re-sponse to Darnil, not found, is also recorded in SJL.

[1] Manuscript: "greet."

To Louis Philippe Gallot de Lormerie

SIR   Monticello Apr. 3. 13.

Your letter of the 26th has been recieved, as had been that of the 5th. the preceding ones had been complied with by applications verbal and written to the members of the government, to which I could expect no specific answers, their whole time being due to the public, & employed on their concerns. had it been my good fortune to preserve at the age of seventy all the activity of body & mind which I enjoyed in earlier life, I should have employed it now, as then, in incessant labors to serve those to whom I could be useful. but the torpor of age is weighing heavily on me. the writing table is become my aversion, & it's drudgeries beyond my remaining powers. I have retired then of necessity from all correspondence not indispensably called for by some special duty, and I hope that this necessity will excuse me with you from further interference in obtaining your passage, to France, which requires sollicitations & exertions beyond what I am able to encounter. I request this the more freely, because I am sure of finding, in your candor & consideration, an acquiescence in the reasonableness of my desire to indulge the feeble remains of life in that state of ease & tranquility which my condition, physical & moral, require. accept then, with my Adieux, my best wishes for a safe & happy return to your native country & the assurances of my respect.   TH: JEFFERSON

PoC (DLC); at foot of text: "M. de Lormerie."

To Thomas Paine McMahon

SIR   Monticello Apr. 3. 13.

Your favor of Mar. 24. is recieved, and nothing could have been so pleasing to me as to have been able to comply with the request therein made, feeling especial motives to become useful to any person connected with mr McMahon. but I shall state to you the circumstances which controul my will, and rest on your candor their just estimate. when I retired from the government, 4. years ago, it was extremely my wish to withdraw myself from all concern with public affairs, and to enjoy with my fellow citizens the protection of government, under the auspices & direction of those to whom it was so worthily committed. sollicitations from my friends however to aid them in their applications for office drew from me an unwary compliance, till at length these became so numerous as to occupy a great portion of my time in writing letters to the President & heads of department, and altho' these were attended to by them with great indulgence, yet I was sensible they could not fail of being very embarrassing. they kept me at the same time standing for ever in the attitude of a suppliant before them, daily asking favors as humiliating & afflicting to my own mind, as they were unreasonable from their multitude. I was long sensible of the necessity of putting an end to these unceasing importunities, when a change in the heads of the two departments to which they were chiefly addressed, presented me an opportunity. I came to a resolution therefore, on that change, never to make another application. I have adhered to it strictly, and find that on it's rigid observance my own happiness and the friendship of the government too much depend for me to swerve from it in future. on consideration of these circumstances, I hope you will be sensible how much they import, both to the government and myself; and that you will do me the justice to be assured of the reluctance with which I decline an opportunity of being useful to one so nearly connected with mr McMahon, and that with the assurance of my regrets you will accept that of my best wishes for your success & of my great respect.

Th: Jefferson

PoC (DLC); at foot of text: "Mr Thomas Paine McMahon." The TWO DEPARTMENTS whose heads had recently changed were War and Navy.

To Craven Peyton

DEAR SIR   Monticello Apr. 3. 13.

As I presume you will go to court tomorrow, and I shall not, I must ask the favor of you to call on me. the perseverance and hostility of Capt Meriwether renders Hornsby's claim a very serious thing, and he will probably endeavor to engage the other two infant claimants to refuse their confirmation also. I wish to consult you on the best means of treating with those claimants & obtaining their confirmation. affectionately your's

TH: JEFFERSON

RC (ViMtvL); addressed: "Mr Craven Peyton Monteagle"; endorsed by Peyton. PoC (MHi); endorsed by TJ.

Albemarle attorney William D. MERIWETHER represented Thomas Hornsby and his wife, Frances Henderson Hornsby, in claiming that her rights, as well as those of the OTHER TWO INFANT CLAIMANTS, Lucy Henderson and Nancy C. Henderson, had been violated by Peyton's purchase of their patrimony from James L. Henderson, who was not their legally appointed guardian (TJ to Peyton, 12 May 1811; Haggard, "Henderson Heirs," 16–8).

From Isaac A. Coles

D^R SIR,   Leesburg April 4th 1813.

I take the liberty of introducing to your Acquaintance Lieut Peyton of the 20th Reg^t who has just been ordered to recruit at Charlottesville—He is an amiable & deserving Young officer—

The recent appointment of two Majors to our Reg^t, now with the army at Niagara, will have the effect, I fear, of keeping me in the recruiting for some time to come—

The appointment of Col: Randolph to the command of the 20th, has been particularly gratifying to all the officers of that Reg^t—I fear however that it may have been less acceptable to his family—

I hope in the course of four or five weeks to have it in my power to visit the different rendezvous in the upper Country, when I promise my self the happiness of Spending a day at Monticello—

with respectful attachm^t I am Dr Sir Y^r ob^{dt} Servt

I. A. COLES

RC (DLC); at foot of text: "Thomas Jefferson"; endorsed by TJ as received 15 Apr. 1813 and so recorded in SJL.

Bernard Peyton (1792–1854) entered the United States Army as a first lieutenant in May 1812, rose to the rank of captain in April 1813, and was honorably discharged in June 1815. By 1816 he had established a mercantile firm in Richmond. TJ soon charged him with making occasional purchases on his behalf. From about 1820 Peyton was also TJ's principal Richmond correspondent, endorsing and renewing bank loans, making payments and transferring funds, and selling his flour and tobacco. Peyton was a director of the Farmers' Bank in 1820, 1834, and 1835, and he was adjutant general of Virginia, 1823–41. TJ unsuccessfully recommended that he be appointed postmaster of Richmond in 1824, but he held that post from 1841–45. A member of the Virginia State Agricultural Society, Peyton bred and sold horses. By 1852 he had moved to Albemarle County, where he lived at Farmington (Horace Edwin Hayden, *A Genealogy of the Glassell Family of Scotland and Virginia* . . . [1891], 547; Peyton Society of Virginia, *The Peytons of*

Virginia II [2004], 2:433; Heitman, *U.S. Army*, 1:787; TJ to Peyton, 20 Jan. 1816, 25 Aug., 3 Sept. 1824; *MB*; *American Beacon and Norfolk & Portsmouth Daily Advertiser*, 12 Jan. 1820; *Richmond Enquirer*, 5 Mar. 1830, 16 Jan. 1834, 15 Jan. 1835; *American Turf Register and Sporting Magazine* 8 [1837]: 477; *JEP*, 5:372, 373, 6:444 [10 Mar. 1841, 14 Mar. 1845]; *Southern Planter* 1 [1841]: 148; 14 [1854]: 374; Lay, *Architecture*, 142; Albemarle Co. Will Book, 23:47; *Rich-*

mond Whig and Public Advertiser, 23 June 1854).

On this day Coles sent Thomas Mann RANDOLPH a letter introducing Peyton, reporting the recruitment of "about 400. men" for the 20th Infantry Regiment, and explaining that "As my return to active service will in all probability depend on my success in filling the Reg^t be assured that every effort will be made on my part to effect it" (RC in MHi).

To William Duane

DEAR SIR   Monticello Apr. 4. 13.

Your favor of Feb. 14. has been duly recieved, and the MS of the Commentary on Montesquieu is also safe at hand. I now forward to you the work of Tracy, which you will find a valuable supplement and corrective to those we already possess on political economy. it is a little unlucky that it's outset is of a metaphysical character, which may damp the ardor of perusal in some readers. he has been led to this by a desire to embody this work, as well as a future one he is preparing on Morals, with his former treatise on Ideology. by the bye, it is surely to this work that Bonaparte alludes in his answer to his council of state, published not long since, in which he scouts 'the dark & metaphysical doctrine of Ideology, which, diving into first causes, founds on this basis a legislation of the people E^{t}c.' if indeed this answer be not a forgery; for every thing is now forged, even to the fat of our beef & mutton. yet the speech is not unlike him, and affords scope for an excellent parody.   I wish you may succeed in getting the Commentary on Montesquieu reviewed by the Edinburgh Reviewers. I should expect from them an able & favorable Analysis of it. I sent a copy of it to a friend in England in the hope he would communicate it to them; not however expressing that hope, lest the source of it should have been made known. but the book will make it's way, and will become a standard work. a copy which I sent to France was under translation by one of the ablest men of that country.

It is true that I am tired of practical politics, and happier while reading the history of antient, than of modern times. the total banishment of all moral principle from the Code which governs the intercourse of nations, the melancholy reflection that after the mean, wicked and cowardly cunning of the Cabinets of the age of Machiavel had given place to the integrity and good faith which dignified the succeeding one of a Chatham and Turgot, that this is to be swept away again by the daring profligacy, and avowed destitution of all moral principle of a Cartouche and a Blackbeard, sickens my soul unto death. I turn from the contemplation with loathing, and take refuge in the histories of other times, where if they also furnished their Tarquins, their Catilines & Caligulas, their stories are handed to us under the brand of a Livy, a Sallust and a Tacitus, and we are comforted with the reflection that the condemnation of all succeeding generations has confirmed the censures of the historian, and consigned their memories to everlasting infamy, a solace we cannot have with the Georges & Napoleons, but by anticipation.

In surveying the scenes of which we make a part, I confess that three frigates taken by our gallant little navy, do not balance, in my mind, three armies lost by the treachery, cowardice, or incapacity of those to whom they were entrusted. I see that our men are good, and only want generals. we may yet hope however that the talents, which always exist among men, will shew themselves with opportunity, & that it will be found that this age also can produce able & honest defenders of their country. at what further expence however of blood & treasure is yet to be seen. perhaps this Russian mediation may cut short the history of the present war, and leave to us the laurels of the sea, while our enemies are bedecked with those of the land. this would be the reverse of what has been expected, and perhaps of what was to be wished.

I have never seen the work on Political economy of which you speak. Say, and Tracy contain the sum of that science, as far as it has been soundly traced, in my judgment. and it is a pity that Say's work should not, as well as Tracy's, be made known to our country men by a good translation. it would supplant Smith's book altogether, because shorter, clearer, and sounder.

Accept my friendly salutations and assurances of continued esteem and respect. Th: Jefferson

PoC (DLC); at foot of first page: "Col° Duane."

TJ here forwarded the manuscript treatise on political economy that Destutt de TRACY had enclosed in his letter of 15 Nov. 1811. The French newspaper *Moniteur* published Napoleon's 20 Dec. ANSWER TO HIS COUNCIL OF STATE on 25 Dec. 1812 (Friedrich C. Schlosser, *History of the Eighteenth Century and of the Nineteenth Till the Overthrow of the French Empire, with a Particular Reference to Mental Cultivation and Progress* [1852], 309). The text, of which TJ paraphrased an excerpt, was reprinted in the *Massachusetts Spy, or Worcester Gazette*, 3 Mar. 1813. Pierre Samuel Du Pont de Nemours was ONE OF THE ABLEST MEN of France who was engaged in translating

Tracy's work. Although the American navy had successfully captured THREE FRIGATES in 1812, HMS *Guerriere*, HMS *Macedonian*, and HMS *Java*, this did not fully compensate for the loss of the THREE ARMIES at Detroit, Frenchtown, and Queenston (Donald R. Hickey, *The War of 1812: A Forgotten Conflict* [1989], 84–7, 93–6). Duane had recommended a WORK OF POLITICAL ECONOMY by Charles Ganilh, *An Inquiry into the Various Systems of Political Economy; Their Advantages and Disadvantages; and The Theory Most Favourable to the Increase of National Wealth*, trans. Daniel Boileau (New York, 1812).

Promissory Note to Edmund Bacon

1813. Apr. 7.

I promise to pay to Edmund Bacon or order on or before the 1st day of August next three[1] hundred and seventy Dollars for value re-cieved. I say 370. Dollars, witness my hand this seventh day of April eighteen hundred & thirteen   TH: JEFFERSON

the above belongs to John Bacon of the County of Botetourt to whose credit the money must be Applyed when recev^d agreeable to Assignment   MARTIN DAWSON & Co

MS (Roberta B. Coscia, Memphis, Tenn., 2007); edge frayed; in TJ's hand, with postscript in Martin Dawson's hand; signed by TJ and Dawson; endorsed by Dawson: "Thomas Jefferson Esqr to Edmund Bacon} Specialty due 1st Augt 1813 $370"; notation on verso in Dawson's hand, signed by Edmund Bacon: "for value recv^d I assign to John Bacon three hundred & Twenty Seven Dollars and twelve Cents of the within to him Given under my hand Ap^l the 7th 1813"; at foot of verso in Dawson's hand: "due 1 Augt 1813.   327.12
In^t to 1 Aug 1815   39.26
                              [366.38]";
additional memorandum by TJ on verso: "Credits to be given on this bond:

	D
cash	30
a coachee [i.e., a light-weight horse carriage (*OED*)] & smith's work	150.

1822. Oct. 16. various orders assumed to wit

	D
to John Winn	40
John R. Jones	96.36
Branham & Bibb	16.62
Martin Dawson	80.
	412.98."

In his own record of this transaction, Edmund Bacon confirmed that on 7 Apr. 1813 he had assigned $327 of TJ's note to John Bacon (ViU: Edmund Bacon Memorandum Book, 1802–22). TJ was not notified until 8 Oct. 1815 that $42.88 was still due to Edmund Bacon and that the remaining $327.12 had been assigned to John Bacon (*MB*, 2:1315).

[1] Reworked from "one."

To Anthony Finley

SIR   Monticello Apr. 7. 13.

The paper now returned was by accident misplaced, & thus escaped the attention it was entitled to. I consider every thing as useful which will dignify & consecrate the great event of our independance in the minds of our fellow citizens, & impress them with the importance of maintaining it sanctimoniously. and it is equally desirable to place before their eyes the constitutions of the different states, that they may distinguish those principles which, being approved by all, are peculiarly worthy of being cherished by all. I with pleasure therefore return you the paper with my subscription, & the assurances of my respect.   TH: JEFFERSON

PoC (DLC); at foot of text: "Mr Anthony Finley"; endorsed by TJ. Enclosure not found.

Anthony Finley opened a bookshop and publishing house in Philadelphia by 1809. A sales catalog he issued in 1811 concentrated on medical, botanical, and other scientific works. By 1824 Finley was producing maps and by 1832 he specialized in cartography. Finley was an unsuccessful Democratic candidate for the Philadelphia Common Council in 1818. A founding officer of the Philadelphia Apprentices' Library, he was also a life member of both the American Sunday-School Union and the Franklin Institute. In 1826 he sat on the board of trustees of a proposed new college in Philadelphia. Finley was in business until at least 1836 (H. Glenn Brown and Maude O. Brown, *A Directory of the Book-Arts and Book Trade in Philadelphia to 1820 Including Painters and Engravers* [1950], 48; *Catalogue of Books in Medicine, Surgery, Anatomy, Physiology, Chemistry, Mineralogy, and Botany. For Sale by Anthony Finley* [Philadelphia, 1811]; J. Thomas Scharf and Thompson Westcott, *History of Philadelphia, 1609–1884* [1884], 2:1208; *The American Advertising Directory for Manufacturers and Dealers in American Goods for the Year 1832* [1832], 189; Walter W. Ristow, *American Maps and Mapmakers: Commercial Cartography in the Nineteenth Century* [1985], 268–70; Philadelphia *Franklin Gazette*, 17 Oct. 1818; Finley to TJ, 25 Jan. 1822; *The American Sunday School Magazine* 7 [1830]: 95; "Annual Report of the Franklin Institute," *Hazard's Register of Pennsylvania* 9 [1832]: 212; "College in Philadelphia," *American Journal of Education* 1 [1826]: 568; Robert Desilver, *Desilver's Philadelphia Directory and Stranger's Guide for 1835 & 36* [1835], 70; Hartford *Connecticut Courant*, 15 Aug. 1836).

From Robert Fulton

DEAR SIR   New York April 7th 1813

Much business having crowded upon me since the death of the Chancellor, I have not paid so early attention to your letter as I have wished, I hope the Dynamometer[1] answered your purpose; as I have no use for it and you may be making some further experiments you will pleas to keep it, until I have occasion for it, when I will let you

[55]

know,—Mr Quinseys soapstone Stove gives out much heat with little fuel. its durability and total conveniences or defects are not I think as yet sufficiently tested by time; he has many handsome forms and although the stone will not receive a polish[2] he has contrived to make them ornamental: his fire places I think too small for they would hardly receve a half peck of chips and therefore require frequent feeding they are good for a Library or cabinet where studious men do not require to see the fire, and as a handsome one can be had for 150$ you cannot risque much in the experiment, by ordering one, which however must not be sent until our coasters can go with safety, Like the swedish or Russian Stoves the principle of this one, is to make many circulations of the flame and Smoke to deposit the heat in a mass of Brick forming a kind of small brick kiln <u>in the room</u>, which gives the

heat out in a long time An ingenious Yanke has done this in a very good Style in Some houses in New york He cuts open the old fireplace[3] for ten or 12 feet high as from **A** to **B** thus forming a recess in the wall neatly plastered he then builds his stove of Brick[4] with an open fireplace in the recess, but detatched from the recess on the Back and Sides the fire place is about 2 feet high by 18 inches wide and sufficiently contracted to cause a draught. the flame and smoke circulates through many passages all of Brick and thus forms a mass of heated

materials in the room. there are in it passages to receive air from the outside of the room or house where it becomes heated and enters the room with its full charge of oxygen the whole is plastered and may have an ornamental front of marble as here deleneated it costs about 40 dollars, And I realy think it the best thing yet introducd into our country Should you wish to prove its good qualities I advise that you send here for the constructor who has the practical knowledge his travelling expences will cost about 40 dollars and if you approve of one such fire place you can then have many, please to command me; in this or any thing in which I can serve you—I am not Idle as to Torpedoes, but secrecy is necessary, When peace return or in 4 or 5 years from this date I Shall have a line of steam boat From Qubeck to Mexico and to St Mary's the rout is[5] up the St Laurence over Lake Champlain down the Hudson to Brunswick down the delaware to Phila, By land carriage to Pittsburgh down the ohio and mississippi[6] to Red River up it to above nachitochez the total land carriage about 500 miles the other rout to S^t mary's land carriage not more than 200 miles the most of those boats are now constructing.—

No one can feel so sinsibly as I, do the loss of the excellent Barlow for none knew him as well as I did.—

I am Sir with Sincere esteem and respect

your.   ROB^T FULTON

RC (DLC); at foot of text: "Thos Jefferson Esqr"; endorsed by TJ as received 15 Apr. 1813 and so recorded in SJL.

CHANCELLOR Robert R. Livingston died 26 Feb. 1813 (*ANB*). On 8 Mar. 1813 TJ had requested Fulton's opinion of the SOAPSTONE STOVE of Abraham Howard Quincy.

[1] Manuscript: "Dynamoeter."
[2] Manuscript: "polise."
[3] Manuscript: "fireplac."
[4] Preceding two words interlined.
[5] Preceding three words interlined.
[6] Preceding two words interlined.

To John Clarke

[DEA]R SIR   Monticello Apr. 8. 13.

[I du]ly recieved your favor of the 9th ult. on the interesting subject of ou[r] [...] trade, and the importance of defending it; a trade certainly of th[...]t value to us. a country of such extent as ours, of all the varying [...] [pro]ductions of the earth, capable of yielding in some of it's parts what[ever] [...] may want, will, at no distant period, under our rapid popula[tion] [...] internal commerce sufficient for the interchange of all [...] [pro]ductions, and needing no intercourse with any other part [...] [su]ch a commerce therefore cannot be too sedulously cultivated [...] do presume that the measures taken by Congress & the Execu[tive] [...]asing their navy, are such as they, on consultation, have [...] practicable under our circumstances; altho' I am not fully [...] [t]he extent to which they have proposed to push their naval pre[...] I think with you that whatever be our naval force it would [...]ployed on our own coast than in rambling after adventures [...] [w]hole expanse of the ocean. and I have no doubt they will be [...]oyed now that it is become unnecessary for them to go further [...] of an enemy. I believe that at present only two of our frigates [...]sent in distant seas. if Napoleon had had the attention to send [...]g squadron here before the arrival of Beauclerc's reinforcement, [...] [mi]ght, in conjunction with ours, have annihilated their force then here, [...] [b]een ready to annihilate separately the portion newly arrived. [...] passions are stronger than his head. he is great in military tac[tics] [...] but in nothing else. the British, having now full possession of the [...] [w]ill be able to keep it without danger from him. my hope however [...] [the]y will be obliged to employ so great a proportion of their navy on [...] of the atlantic, as to give him an opportunity of getting his 80. sail [...] [l]ine together and of contesting the uncontrouled dominion of the waters which they have usurped. this is the most likely motiv[...] [in]duce them to wish for a peace with us.   the anxiety you exp[ress][...] these subjects is that which we all ought to feel. for altho' ag[...] circumstances keep us remote from the active scenes, yet the [...] we feel for our younger friends who are in them, that which [...] our country at large, & that which comes home to our pur[...] do not permit us to look on what is passing as mere indiffer[ent specta]tors. I salute you with great esteem & respect.   TH: JEFF[ERSON]

PoC (DLC); edge torn away; at foot of first page: "[Mr John] Clarke."

On 19 Apr. 1813 the *Portland Gazette, and Maine Advertiser* reported from British newspapers through 10 Jan. 1813 that a SQUADRON commanded by Lord Amelius Beauclerk would immediately "proceed to the coast of America, to bombard some of the principal ports."

To John B. Colvin

SIR   Monticello Apr. 8. 13.

I thank you for the historical work you have been so kind as to send me. but to give the precise opinion on it which you ask, is not very easy. History is one of those branches of science which different persons will pursue to greater or less extent in proportion to their views and opportunities. those of higher aims will resort to the original authors that nothing known to others may be unknown to them. students to whom this branch will be a necessary, yet secondary object, will call for the larger compilers; while those whose other occupations afford little time or means to indulge their historical appetite, must be contented with the most succinct abridgments. among these different classes of readers, the scale of the Historical letters will find it's place, and will become valuable and instructive in the degree which suits them. it will also be a convenient Manual even to proficients, who often wish to consult shorter works for a refreshment of memory when occasion occurs for taking more general views. for these purposes doubtless the work you sent me will be useful, & it's cheapness as well as brevity will probably bring it into considerable demand. in wishing it success I contemplate not only your gratification, but the enlargement it may produce in the field of information among our fellow citizens. I tender you the assurance of my esteem & respect.   TH: JEFFERSON

PoC (DLC); at foot of text: "Mr J. B. Colvin"; endorsed by TJ. Printed in Colvin, *Historical Letters, Including A Brief But General View of the History of* the World, *Civil, Military, and Religious*, 2d ed. (Georgetown, 1821; Poor, *Jefferson's Library* 3 [no. 3]), v–vi.

To Robert Patterson

DEAR SIR: *Monticello, April 8, '13.*

Your favor of Mar. 15 is duly received. I think the time-piece should not be risked until our coast becomes entirely safe by an armistice, or considerably so by some remission in the vigilance of the British cruisers. In the meantime, I should be glad you could take charge of it yourself and keep it agoing. Perhaps, if Mr. Voight has prepared the apparatus for ascertaining the rod vibrating seconds, you might be willing to amuse yourself with that experiment, which will be curious at least, if not useful to be known. I write to Mr. Voight to forward me his bill, that I may direct the amount to be remitted him from Richmond.

The enquiry I am about to make will prove to you my sincere esteem and the confidence I repose in your friendship and discretion. You recollect my resignation of the office of President of the American Philosophical Society,—one which I deem the most honorable of all which have[1] been conferred upon me by my fellow-citizens. The Society were so kind as, by an unanimous reëlection, to express their pleasure that I should continue; to which also your private sollicitations were added, which had great weight with me. In addition to these, a particular friend, not resident in Philadelphia, but having intimate correspondence with it, suggested that the choice of a successor might at that time produce disagreeable scisms in the society: whereas, by giving some time, some one of the estimable characters among them might ripen itself in the general view, and render a new election easy and harmonious. I have therefore gone on receiving and acknoleging the repeated favors of the society, with a sincere consciousness, however, that I was witholding from others a place which they more merited, and in which I was useless. The last winter I had determined to make a final resignation. But an absence from home in the months of November and December, occasioned an omission until the time of election had passed by. It has been usual for the Secretary, after every election, to notify me an opportunity of repeating my acknolegment. It has also been usual for the public papers to notice the election. Both of these channels of information have failed me this year; and the propriety of a choice of a more useful president by the society, would have left no doubt in my mind that they had performed this duty by a new choice, were it not that I supposed this also would have been announced in the papers, which, however, I have not seen. In this absence of information, I have preferred asking of you rather than of any other person,—Am I in that office or not? If not, all is right; the society have done their duty, and not a member is more sensible of it than I am. I should be unworthy of the opinion that they have been so good as to entertain of me heretofore, were I to entertain a single regret but at my own failure to spare them the disagreeable task which I ought to have done myself, and really meant to do. If, on the contrary, I am continued, I wish to advise with you as a friend to myself, as well as the institution,—What is the best time of the year for me to notify my resignation? At the end of the present term? Should it be early, in order to give time to settle their minds on a successor? Or would this only give opportunity for scisms to be formed, to ripen, and to destroy the future harmony of the society? And would these effects be avoided by so late a declaration as to give no time for cabal, and to ensure their following first thoughts, as perhaps the most genuine in such a case? Be so kind as to add to the multiplied proofs of your goodness, your conscientious advice on this subject, which will be my government: and in all cases, saying nothing of this, my dear Sir, to any body, accept the assurance of my constant friendship and respect. Tʜ: Jᴇꜰꜰᴇʀꜱᴏɴ.

Printed in *Knickerbocker. or New-York Monthly Magazine* 6 (1835): 398–9.

Patterson's ꜰᴀᴠᴏʀ was dated 25 Mar. 1813, not ᴍᴀʀ. 15. TJ had written Patterson on 10 Dec. 1800 expressing his belief that "it is become my duty to desire the society to turn their views to some other person, better situated and more capable of discharging the functions of their President." Nevertheless, Patterson replied on 2 Jan. 1801 with news of TJ's ᴜɴᴀɴɪᴍᴏᴜꜱ ʀᴇëʟᴇᴄᴛɪᴏɴ (*PTJ*, 32:298, 388).

[1] Printed text: "have have."

To Benjamin Rush

Dᴇᴀʀ Sɪʀ   Monticello Apr. 8. 13.

I should not so soon have troubled you with a reply to your friendly favor of Mar. 15. but for your saying that 'if I wish to look into your work on the diseases of the mind you will send me a copy.' I read with delight every thing which comes from your pen, and the subject of this work is peculiarly interesting. the book by Bishop Porteous which you were so kind as to inclose me, was safely recieved & disposed of, as you wished, to mrs Randolph's children. they are all great readers, and when permitted by domestic exercises, recur eagerly to their books.   again & ever affectionately yours

TH: JEFFERSON

PoC (MHi); at foot of text: "Doct^r Rush"; endorsed by TJ.

To Thomas Voigt

SIR   Monticello Apr. 9. 13.

Doct^r Patterson informs me that the time piece you have been so kind as to make for me, is now ready, and advises with me as to the sending it during the present blockade of the Delaware & Chesapeake. I have written to him that I would rather it should not be risked until the coast becomes safer; and have expressed a wish that in the mean time he would take it to his house, and with the rod pendulum which I wished to be made an appendage to it, to try the experiment of the rod vibrating seconds. the object of the present letter is to ask the favor of you to send me a bill of the cost that I may direct the amount to be forwarded to you from Richmond.

Among the young men who learn with you the business of the watchmaker, I imagine some may be at a loss where to set themselves down for business. Charlottesville (3. miles from me) would be an excellent stand for one who to the trade of watchmender added that of making the seven day clocks. there is no part of the Union more at their ease and independant than this, and we have not within 50. miles a person who can do the least thing to a watch or clock. a young man with nothing but his tools, & without a shilling might get at once into full business, and would find credit for all necessaries until his business should put him at his ease. if such a subject should occur whom you would recommend for his skill & sobriety, I should take great pleasure in facilitating his establishment, and encouraging his custom. Accept the assurance of my esteem & respect.

TH: JEFFERSON

RC (VtMiM); at foot of text: "Mr Voigt." PoC (MHi); mistakenly endorsed by TJ as a letter to Henry Voigt and so recorded in SJL.

Thomas Voigt (d. 1844), maker of clocks, watches, and scientific instruments in Philadelphia, was the son of Henry Voigt, who combined this trade from 1793 until his death in 1814 with service as chief coiner of the United States Mint. The younger Voigt entered the family business as early as 1804, when he assisted his father in repairing the Rittenhouse Orrery at the College of New Jersey (later Princeton University). Voigt's Philadelphia shop also sold scales and weights to the Farmers' Bank of Virginia and the Savannah branch of the Bank of the United States. The Philadelphia city government named him to committees on the astronomical observatory in 1833 and on public clocks two years later. Voigt was in business in Philadelphia until at least 1836 (PPAmP: Henry and

Thomas Voigt Papers; Howard C. Rice Jr., *The Rittenhouse Orrery: Princeton's Eighteenth-Century Planetarium, 1767–1954* [1954], 56; New York *Columbian,* 19 Aug. 1812; John A. Paxton, *Philadelphia Directory and Register, for 1813* [1813]; Robert Desilver, *Desilver's Philadelphia Directory and Stranger's Guide for 1835 & 36* [1835], 184; Philadelphia *Hazard's Register of Pennsylvania,* 5 Oct. 1833, 6 June 1835; Silvio A. Bedini, "Thomas Jefferson, Clock Designer," APS, *Proceedings* 108 [1964]: 170, 171, 180; Philadelphia Wills and Administrations, Book P, File # A-240-1844 [Philadelphia City Archives]).

To John Devereux DeLacy

SIR   Monticello Apr. 10. 13.

Your favor of Mar. 4. is just now recieved, and I should be glad to render to mr Fulton any service in my power. of the prospect of utility from the establishment of a steam boat on the Patomac, he is a better judge than I am. James river, from Norfolk to Richmond offers[1] the only other establishment occurring to me in this state which could be profitable. but my interior situation, on an upper branch of that river, among the mountains, withdrawing me from all opportunity of seeing or consulting those immediately interested, renders me less capable of judging of the prospect such an establishment would offer, and entirely useless in promoting it. in this situation, I have thought the best service I could render mr Fulton would be to inclose the papers to some person at Richmond, & I have accordingly done so to Doct'r Wm Foushee, the most likely person to make a proper use of them. from him you can probably learn what might be expected from such an establishment. Accept the assurance of my respect.

TH: JEFFERSON

PoC (DLC); at foot of text: "M'r De Lacy"; endorsed by TJ.

John Devereux DeLacy (ca. 1781–1837), steamboat entrepreneur, was a native of Ireland and subsequently a merchant in the Bahamas. From 1801–02 he associated himself with William Augustus Bowles in attempts to organize East Florida's Indian tribes into independent states, capture the lucrative trade with

them, and eliminate Spanish power from the region. These efforts entailed much frontier travel and led to his imprisonment by the Spanish authorities, 1801–02. By 1811 DeLacy was an attorney in New York City. The following year Robert Fulton engaged him to establish steamboat lines in Virginia and the Carolinas and to defend his patent rights. In 1813 DeLacy completed a survey for an inland navigation route from Saint

Mary's in East Florida to the James River and Chesapeake Bay. Soon, however, he broke with Fulton and acted as Nicholas J. Roosevelt's counsel in an unsuccessful lawsuit against Fulton's monopoly claims. In 1821 DeLacy failed in a bid to become attorney general of Florida Territory. Seven years later he was jailed for failing to pay for a suit of clothes that he had purchased on credit (DeLacy to TJ, 3 Nov., 18 Dec. 1801 [DLC]; J. Leitch Wright Jr., *William Augustus Bowles, Director General of the Creek Nation* [1967]; Madison, *Papers, Sec. of State Ser.*, 5:520–4; Alice B. Keith, William H. Masterson, and David T. Morgan, eds., *The John Gray Blount Papers* [1952–82], 4:178–80; Cynthia Owen Philip, *Robert Fulton: A Biography* [1985]; DeLacy to James Monroe, 16 Apr. 1821 [DNA: RG 59, LAR, 1817–25]; Latrobe, *Papers*, esp. 3:390n; John H. B. Latrobe, *A Lost Chapter in the History of the Steamboat* [1871], 4–10, 42–4; New York *Herald*, 15 Apr. 1837).

For DeLacy's FAVOR OF MAR. 4., see TJ to William Foushee, 10 Apr. 1813.

[1] Word interlined in place of "is."

To William Foushee

DEAR SIR   Monticello Apr. 10. 13.

You will be sensible that the inclosed proposition on the establishment of steam boats might as well have been addressed to the man in the moon, as to an inhabitant of the mountains. yet as such a boat between Norfolk & Richmond might be interesting to both places I have thought it a duty to give the proposition a fair chance by handing it on to a place where it will be more interesting. with this view I have taken the liberty of inclosing it to you, that if you think it can be wrought into any thing useful for the city of Richmond, you may make such disposition of it as your judgment & convenience may admit. I have written to mr De Lacy that I have taken the liberty of putting it into your hands. I with pleasure avail myself of the opportunity it offers of presenting myself to your recollection, and of renewing to you assurances of my constant and great esteem & respect

                                        TH: JEFFERSON

PoC (MHi); at foot of text: "Dr Foushee"; endorsed by TJ. Enclosure: John Devereux DeLacy to TJ, 4 Mar. 1813, not found, but recorded in SJL as a "circular" received 5 Apr. 1813 from Washington.

To Thomas Lehré

DEAR SIR   Monticello Apr. 10. 13

Your favors of Mar. 9. and 23. are both safely recieved and I shall with pleasure write to the President on the subject of the last. this I do merely because it is your wish, being satisfied the President can need no excitement in your favor beyond his own knolege & approbation of the uniform line of your conduct.

We are here in a state of close blockade, tantalized indeed with propositions of armistice & mediation, the former on terms calculated merely to give time to our enemies for sending reinforcements, the latter promising little success unless[1] events should take place unfavorable to the domineering views of Great Britain.   Accept the assurances of my esteem & respect.   TH: JEFFERSON

PoC (DLC); at foot of text: "Col° Thoˢ   [1] TJ here canceled "Great Britain."
Lehré"; endorsed by TJ.

To James Madison

DEAR SIR   Monticello Apr. 10. 13.
The writer of the inclosed letter being as well known to yourself as to me, I forward it merely because he has wished me to mention his sollicitation to you. I should in like manner inclose you a letter from Dʳ Barton but that it would take you more time to decypher than you ought to give to it. the object of it is to be appointed to the Medical department of the army. his reputation is as well known to yourself as to me, and his qualifications for the office he asks are I suppose unquestionable.   I wish to communicate to you some views formerly taken of the defence of the Chesapeake, because as they respected the departments of the war & navy more immediately, I do not recollect their having then been explained to you. but I am become so averse to the writing table that I do not know whether I shall muster resolution enough. this aversion too is encouraged by the presumption that the same views will have occurred to yourself. in all cases be assured of my constant attachment & respect.   TH: JEFFERSON

RC (DLC: Madison Papers); addressed: "The President of the United States Washington"; franked; postmarked Milton, 14 Apr. PoC (DLC); endorsed by TJ. Enclosure: Thomas Lehré to TJ, 23 Mar. 1813.

From John Wayles Baker

DEAR UNCLE   Lynchburg 11ᵗʰ of april 1813
I wish to see you very much I am very well I am at school at Lynchburg to A gentleman by the name of Mr. Halcomb I like him very well he is very good to cousin and my self he and my self are going

hom[e] very soon some of my Vacations I will come and stay some time with you

Your moste obedient and affectionate nephew

JOHN WALES BAKER
Lynchburg 1813

RC (MHi); edge trimmed; endorsed by TJ as a letter dated only 1813 and received 15 May 1813 and so recorded in SJL. Enclosed in Francis Eppes to TJ, 11 Apr. 1813.

John Wayles Baker (1804–67), attorney and judge, was the son of Jerman Baker and Martha Bolling Eppes Baker. He was TJ's grandnephew through his mother, the niece of TJ's wife Martha Wayles Skelton Jefferson. As a youth Baker was often with Francis Eppes, his cousin and TJ's grandson. The two attended school together in Lynchburg under Thomas A. Holcombe and again in Charlottesville, sometimes passing weekends with TJ at Poplar Forest and Monticello. Baker moved to Lawrence County, Alabama, and about 1844 to Leon County, Florida. The Florida legislature elected him a circuit court judge for the eastern district, and he served in that capacity until at least 1852. Baker helped found a Masonic lodge in Tallahassee and served as its grand high priest, 1854–55. The 1860 census valued his estate at $8,500. Baker sometimes acted as a special representative of the governor of Florida to the Confederate government during the Civil War and the federal government thereafter (John Frederick Dorman, *Descendants of Francis Epes I of Virginia [Epes-Eppes-Epps]* [1992–], 2:397–9, 407–9; *MB*, 2:1295, 1300, 1355, 1360; DNA, RG 29, CS, Ala., Lawrence Co., 1840, Fla., Tallahassee, 1860; Tallahassee *Floridian and Journal*, 10 Aug. 1850, 18 Jan. 1851, 18 Dec. 1852; Augustus Row, *Masonic Biography and Dictionary* [1868], 355; United States War Department, *The War of the Rebellion: A Compilation of the Official Records of the Union and Confederate Armies* [1880–1901], ser. 1, vol. 49, pt. 2, p. 748; same, 53:210).

From Francis Eppes

DEAR GRAND PAPA   Lynchburg April 11 day 1813

I wish to see you very much I am very Sorry that you wont Write to me this leter will make twice I have wrote to you and if you dont answer this leter I Shant write to you any more. I have got trough my latin Gramer and I am going trough again I enclose a leter in this from My Cousin Wale Baker Give my love to all of the family

belive me to remain with the filial love your most affectionate Grand Son   FRANCIS EPPES

RC (ViU: TJP-ER); endorsed by TJ as received 15 May 1813 and so recorded in SJL. Enclosure: John Wayles Baker to TJ, 11 Apr. 1813.

To Patrick Gibson

DEAR SIR   Monticello Apr. 16. 13.

The enemy, contrary to expectations, still continuing in our waters and indicating by no movement an intention of speedy departure, with the rapid advance of the season, begin to fill me with anxiety as to the fate of my crop of flour. and I am becoming more concerned to get some price, than what that price shall be, on the principle that half a loaf is better than no bread. engagements entered into thro' the year & looking solely to the crop of the year to meet them, would occasion me great distress & mortification were that resource to fail altogether. these considerations, with the possibility that a sudden opportunity of selling might occur, which might pass by as suddenly if not seised, make me desirous of placing the sale of my flour altogether at your discretion. if such a price as 7.D. can be got any time this month at 30. 60. or even 90. days, I would not hesitate to take it, or even less if you should think it advisable. after this month the danger of the flour spoiling, altho' made of good wheat, & the approaching competition of the new crop, will render the accepting any price eligible. I therefore rest altogether on your will & judgment, without limitation or instruction, to dispose of my flour according to your own views of the prospect, only keeping in mind that an entire loss of it would be very distressing to me. this entire reference to yourself is the more necessary as within about 10. days I shall take a journey to Bedford & be absent about three weeks. with increasing[1] uneasiness on this subject, I tender you the assurance of my great esteem & respect.   TH: JEFFERSON

PoC (DLC); at foot of text: "Mr Gibson"; endorsed by TJ as a letter to Gibson & Jefferson and so recorded in SJL.

[1] Manuscript: "increaing."

To Samuel Brown

DEAR SIR   Monticello Apr. 17. 1813

Your favor of Octob. 1. came to hand with a note from mr Poindexter, on the 20th Ult. as also the Guinea grass seed, and Capsicum. they were exactly in time for sowing and were immediately sowed. they had got mixed by the way, and the capsicum seeds were difficult to find. not more than three or four could be discovered, & these rather doubtful. I dibbled them however in a pot to give them their best chance. as being the production of a more Northern climate than those we cultivate I am in hopes they will be hardier, and if so, more valuable. of the Guinea grass I know little. the gentlemen of S. Carolina have told me of it's importance to them, and I have heard it yields a good growth in the West Indies in the driest seasons. as we also are subject to long droughts, this grass may be useful to us when such occur. I wish my interior situation admitted my getting, with more facility, useful[1] articles of the growth of your region, and which would stand ours. mrs Trist has named to me several trees of use and ornament with you which would be desirable to us. but the safe transportation of the plant itself I know from experience to be desperate. should any more of the Capsicum seed fall into your hands, it will come safely by mail in a letter and will be thankfully recieved; it may ensure the success of the plant, should the three or four fail which I have planted. planting is one of my great amusements, and even of those things which can only be for posterity. for a Septuagenary has no right to count[2] on anything beyond annuals. I enjoy good health, but under increasing debility.　　　　I am happy in this opportunity of addressing you, and of acknoleging the kindness of your recollection. it gratifies me the more as it furnishes an occasion of assuring you of my constant & unchanged affections & respect, & of offering my sincere prayers for your health, happiness and prosperity.

Th: Jefferson

PoC (DLC); at foot of text: "Dr Samuel Brown"; endorsed by TJ.

Brown sent TJ CAPSICUM *annuum* var. *glabriusculum*, commonly called bird pepper (*Hortus Third*, 219). A photo-graph of this plant is reproduced elsewhere in this volume.

[1] TJ here canceled "plants."
[2] Preceding two words added in margins.

To William Cocke

Monticello April 17. 13.

I have recieved, my good old friend, your favor of Feb. 24. and rejoice to find you can still undertake distant military expeditions. it does not want much of 40. years since we were first together in the Virginia legislature. you are approaching therefore, what I have attained, the limits of the Psalmist, who says 'the days of our years are three score years and ten.' yet I hope it will be long before your 'strength'[1] shall become 'labour & sorrow.' I sincerely congratulate you that your enemies have not found it so, and that you have given the Spanish Creeks a lesson which may be useful to them as well as to us. it is a great misfortune that you were not permitted to take possession of the whole country to Florida point. a sequestration of it in our hands for wrongs recieved is a measure of rigorous justice; and with an eye to our safety, it is of absolute necessity. the use they are making of it, by the colour & character of the troops they are introducing and the certainty that it will be siesed by the British, made a thorn in our side during the war, & retained permanently by them afterwards, if the Spanish power be limited, as it will be, to Europe, forbid a moment to be lost in taking it. for this blot, left open to be hit by our adversary, we are indebted, it seems, to that Sexennial spirit of the Senate, of which you and I saw so much, which has so often defeated the wisdom and patriotism of their coordinate authorities, and is destined to produce incalculable injury and danger, if not recalled to responsibility at shorter periods. but this is for days which I am not to see. they may fall within your term, and I chearfully leave them to those whom they will more concern.

I thank you for your letter. it has revived recollections of friendship, and of joint & faithful struggles to secure & promote the freedom and prosperity of our fellow citizens. and they will be prosperous, and will be free, in despight of the parricide spirit of monarchism, masked as it is, so hypocritically, under the cloak of federalism. may you be able, when you rejoin me in the shades below, to report that 'all is yet well, and likely to continue so.' and, to lengthen the term of your testimony, as well as that of your life, health & happiness, may the period of your departure be as late as the laws of the animal structure will admit, short of the pain and imbecility which would render life a misery.

Th: Jefferson

PoC (DLC); at foot of first page: "Mr Cocke"; endorsed by TJ.

TJ's quotes from the biblical PSALMIST are in Psalms 90.10. FLORIDA POINT is near the entry to Perdido Bay, along the modern boundary between Florida and Alabama. SEXENNIAL: continuing for six years or occurring every six years (*OED*).

[1] Omitted closing quotation mark editorially supplied.

To Charles Willson Peale

Dear Sir   Monticello Apr. 17. 13.

I had long owed you a letter for your favor of Aug. 19. when I recieved, eight days ago that of Mar. 2. 1812. a slip of the pen, I suppose for 1813. and the pamphlet accompanying it strengthens the supposition. I thank you for the pamphlet. it is full of good sense & wholsome advice, and I am making all my grandchildren read it, married & unmarried: and the story of farmer Jenkins will I hope remain in their minds through life. both your letters are on the subject of your agricultural operations, and both prove the ardor with which you are pursuing them. but when I observe that you take an active part in the bodily labor of the farm, your zeal and age give me uneasiness for the result.

Your position that a small farm, well worked and well manned, will produce more than a larger one ill-tended, is undoubtedly true in a certain degree. there are extremes in this as in all other cases. the true medium may really be considered and stated as a Mathematical problem. 'Given the quantum of labor within our command, and land ad libitum offering it's spontaneous contributions; Required the proportion in which these two elements should be employed to produce a Maximum?' it is a difficult problem, varying probably in every country according to the relative value of land and labor. the spontaneous energies of the earth are a gift of nature; but they require the labor of man to direct their operation. and the question is, so to husband his labor as to turn the greatest quantity of this useful action of the earth to his benefit.   Ploughing deep, your recipe for killing weeds, is also the Recipe for almost every thing good in farming. the plough is to the farmer, what the wand is to the Sorcerer. it's effect is really like sorcery. in the county wherein I live, we have discovered a new use for it, equal in value almost to it's services before known. our country is hilly, and we have been in the habit of ploughing in strait rows, whether up and down hill, in oblique lines, or however they led; and our soil was all rapidly running into the rivers. we now plough horizontally, following the curvatures of the hills and hollows, on the dead level, however crooked the lines may be. every furrow thus acts as a reservoir to recieve and retain the waters, all of which go to the benefit of the growing plant, instead of running off into the streams. in a farm horizontally and deeply ploughed, scarcely an ounce of soil is now carried off from it. in point of beauty, nothing can exceed that of the waving lines & rows winding along the face of the hills & vallies. the horses draw much easier on the dead level, and it is in fact a conversion of hilly grounds into a plain. the improvement of our soil from this cause, the last half dozen years, strikes every one with wonder. for this improvement we are indebted to my son in law mr Randolph, the best farmer, I believe, in the United States, and who has taught us to make more than two blades of corn to grow where only one grew before. if your farm is hilly, let me beseech you to make a trial of this method. to direct the plough horizontally we take a rafter level of this form ⟋A⟍ a boy of 13. or 14. is able to work it round the hill; a still smaller one with a little trough marking the points traced by the feet of the level. the plough follows running thro' these marks. the leveller having compleated one level line thro' the field, moves with his level 30. or 40. yards up or down the hill, and runs another which is marked in like manner & traced by the plough. and having thus run what may be called guide furrows every 30. or 40. yards thro the field, the ploughman runs the furrows of the intervals parallel to these. in proportion however as the declivity of the hill varies in different parts of the line, the guide furrows will approach or recede from each other in different parts, and the parallel furrows will at length touch in one part, when far asunder in others, leaving unploughed gores between them. these gores we plough separately. they occasion short rows & turnings, which are a little inconvenient, but not materially so. I pray you to try this Recipe for hilly grounds. you will say with me 'probatum est.' and I shall have the happiness of being of some use to you, and thro' your example to your neighbors, and of adding something solid to the assurances of my great esteem & respect   TH: JEFFERSON

RC (TxU: Hanley Collection). PoC (MHi); at foot of first page: "Charles W. Peale esq."; endorsed by TJ.

In his letter to TJ of 2 Mar. 1812, Peale enclosed his pamphlet, *An Essay to promote Domestic Happiness* (Philadelphia, 1812), which contained a darkly humorous poem about the marital trials faced by FARMER JENKINS and his wife (Peale, *Papers*, 3:134–6). In 1822 the Agricultural Society of Albemarle lauded Thomas Mann RANDOLPH for "the important benefits which the Agricultural interests of our country have derived from the introduction among us of the System of Horizontal ploughing" (True, "Agricul-

tural Society," 299). TJ's statement about causing TWO BLADES OF CORN TO GROW WHERE ONLY ONE GREW BEFORE echoes Jonathan Swift's *Gulliver's Travels*: "that whoever could make two Ears of Corn, or two Blades of Grass, to grow upon a Spot of Ground where only one grew before, would deserve better of Mankind, and do more essential Service to his Country, than the whole Race of Politicians put together" (*Travels into several Remote Nations of the World . . . by Lemuel Gulliver* [London, 1726], 1:129). A RAFTER LEVEL is a type of level constructed from long spars of wood (*OED*). PROBATUM EST: "It is proved."

To James Walker

SIR   Monticello Apr. 17. 13.

I originally employed you to build my saw mill having confidence in your work & prices. when it was turned over to mr Brown, it was understood between you and myself that he was to be governed by your prices. we are now about coming to a settlement, which renders it necessary for me to ask the favor of your prices. mr Brown handed me a bill of yours, but it related only to gristmills, containing none of the articles of a sawmill. the inclosed bill contains the articles most particularly wanted. I will request the favor of you to note in that your price at the end of every article and to add such others as may be here omitted, which I shall be glad to recieve by the bearer as I expect to settle with mr Brown within two or three days. your favor herein will oblige Sir

Your humble serv^t   TH: JEFFERSON

PoC (DLC); at foot of text: "Mr James Walker"; endorsed by TJ. Enclosure not found.

Walker's reply, not found, is recorded in SJL as written and received 18 Apr. 1813 from "Moon's mill."

To John Wayles Eppes

DEAR SIR   Monticello Apr. 18. 13.

I have been in the less haste to answer your last letter, because it appeared from that as if the farther we proceeded in our negociation, the wider we got apart. in the early part of the letter you state justly as the only point of difference, the condition of providing the same quantity of open lands on the Tomahawk tract as there is on Pantops. the practicability of effecting this by hiring laborers to be employed solely in clearing having occurred to me, I was making up my mind to assent to it. but in the subsequent part of your letter, two new propositions are made which entirely change the ground of equal exchange. the 1st is that the addition of lands[1] North of Tomahawk necessary to equalize the quantity with Pantops shall be laid off so as to include the Dwelling house. now certainly from the moment of contemplating an exchange, with the idea of placing Francis's property in a mass together that of annexing to it the excellent dwelling house I have built there has been associated by me with delight. and in consequence of it I have already resumed the inside finishing, which I had not before intended. I have engaged a workman to build offices, have laid off a handsome curtilage connecting the house with the Tomahawk, have inclosed and divided it into suitable appendages to a Dwelling house, and have begun it's improvement by planting trees of use and ornament. the consideration for this was to be the gratifying him by the gift of so comfortable an establishment. but your proposition goes to take from it the character of a gift, and to make it merely a part of an equivalent for property already his. supposing the lands given in exchange to be as they are deemed, equal in quantity and value to those recieved, it is no slight proposition to throw in a house, which in it's present state is of more than half the value of the land, and if finished will be nearly of it's whole value. you say it is only 'stipulating in form what I have stated as my intention:' but the practice of the world does not prove it to be commonly thought best to make children at once independant of their good or ill conduct, by conveying to them in their infancy the whole of what is intended for them ultimately. something in reserve as an inducement to correct deportment in the object of our affections and liberalities is as salutary to the donee, as it may be necessary for the support or comfort of the donor. the difference therefore between future intention and present obligation is material for both parties. I am not willing to infer from the proposition any distrust of what my feelings towards Francis render me too conscious of being unfounded.

The 2$^\text{d}$ proposition is, that if, on an event which we both equally deprecate, but which is yet possible, the lands of Pantops should pass to his aunt, altho' this would be an act of the law, and not of mine, nor of derivation from me, I should, besides losing the land, pay 11,000. Dollars. I do not see the reasonable connection between this fact & the consequence proposed; nor why, on my losing the property and possession of the land I should have to pay it's whole value in addition to the loss.   you suggest again the original idea of purchase. but, my dear Sir, very strong reasons now present themselves which did not then exist, why both of us should be cautious of changing the form of Francis's property into that of money. if this war continues, loans will remain impracticable in Europe, as they certainly will be here. the resource of paper money will be unavoidable, and Francis's 11,000 paper Dollars might be paid with 11. silver ones. this we have seen here; we have seen it in France; we shall shortly see it in England; and as shortly perhaps here again. let us return then to our former ground of equal exchange, value for value. let us concur in placing Francis's property in mass together, which will be so much better for him than to have it in two detached parcels so distant from each other. the possibility which you had foreseen, of the possession and title being separated for a time, in case of an accident to me, had been foreseen and provided for in my will, and entirely to his advantage. I state then as my ground, an immediate exchange of title, possession to be exchanged at the determination, of T. E. Randolph's lease, the quantity of open land to be made the same as at Pantops, say 250. acres, for it is best to fix it, and farm buildings of equal value with those now at Pantops. I say, now, to guard against the future erection there of dwelling houses, or other buildings which would be useless to me. equality being the basis of this proposition, it is impossible it can injure either; and it will greatly benefit Francis by bringing his property together, and by facilitating to me the future benefits and comforts I can provide for him. for his sake, and that alone I am really anxious to have the transfer made.

Jefferson had given us reason to hope we should, ere this, have seen Francis here for the purpose of going to school. Girardin has opened a school at Milton, which however is to be removed in the fall to the other side of the river, two or three miles further from us. there is a great change in the state of Girardin's health. a visceral complaint disables him frequently from attending his school, and threatens with considerable probability a short period to his life. his pupils complain that it renders him very irritable.   besides his school, there is one kept by perhaps the best classical teacher in this state, a mr Robertson, about 8. miles from hence, between Capt Meriwether's and mr Terril's. the latter, one of the best men on earth, takes boarders, I believe. the number of pupils is small, & the master diligent and beloved by them. I do not know the terms; but these are not to concern you in either place. you can chuse between the two positions, and if you prefer the latter, I should wish to have the sanction of your decision; because Girardin, being a neighbor, I should be unwilling he should ascribe the preference to me. as soon as you have decided, I will engage a berth[2] for Francis.—since I began this letter I learn the probability[3] of your election. I sincerely congratulate you, and still more the public: and am in hopes the May meeting may render your passing this way convenient, and leaving Francis with us. ever & affectionately yours.   TH: JEFFERSON

PoC (CSmH: JF); at foot of first page: "J. W. Eppes esq."; endorsed by TJ. Enclosed in TJ to Eppes, 26 Apr. 1813.

Eppes's LAST LETTER, dated 13 Jan. 1813, is recorded in SJL as received 26 Jan. 1813 from Millbrook, but has not been found. The hypothetical EVENT

WHICH WE BOTH EQUALLY DEPRECATE would be the premature death of Francis Eppes. Martha Jefferson Randolph was Francis Eppes's AUNT.

[1] Preceding two words interlined.
[2] Manuscript: "birth."
[3] Manuscript: "probality."

From Elijah Griffiths

DEAR SIR,   Philadelᵃ April 19–1813

It is now near 4 years since I have had the satisfaction of hearing from you, I however hope, in your retirement from the busy walks of life, you have experienced much satisfaction in a retrospective view of your life, & in the present enjoyments.

We have much speculation on the subject of peace, founded on the mission of Mess. Gallatin & Bayard. This may have been a very prudent measure, to reconcile the body of the nation to sustain a tedious war, if honorable peace cannot be obtained; but I fear it will enfeble the spirit of the republican party for the present.

I think if Congress had in all cases been as spirited as the executive, we should have had less trouble from foreign & domestic foes at this time, but experience must correct these errors

This city & the neighbouring country, particularly to the north & eastward, have been for some time past, & now are considerably afflicted[1] by an epidemical disease of considerable malignity, I conceive[2] it to be a true scarlatina obliging every other febrile affliction[3] to wear its livery, agreably to the acknowledged laws of Epidemics; by this disease we have just suffered the loss of the Celebrated professor Rush who expired on the afternoon of this day, his loss will be much felt & lamented. —

Altho' Unknown personally to the President of the United States, I am about to apply to him, to be appointed treasurer of the Mint, become vacant by the death of Dr Rush

I have never before requested any office from the U.S. Government, since it has been under the management of the republican party, but this step is taken by advisement of some friends who think it correct. Should your knowledge of me have made a favorable impression, & you conceive there would be no impropriety in it, a line from you to the President in my favor, on this subject, would be gratefully acknowledged

by Dear sir your friend and very humb^e Servt

ELIJAH GRIFFITHS

RC (DLC); addressed: "Thomas Jefferson Esqr Monticello State of Virginia"; franked; postmarked Philadelphia, 20 Apr.; endorsed by TJ as received 15 May 1813 and so recorded in SJL.

Griffiths did APPLY to President James

Madison on 22 Apr. 1813 (Madison, *Papers, Pres. Ser.*, 6:228).

[1] Manuscript: "afflited."
[2] Manuscript: "concive."
[3] Manuscript: "affiction."

From John Vaughan

D SIR   Philad. 19 April 1813

Mr Joseph Allen Smith when in Italy had put into his hands in
Italy many Years ago—Astronomical observations made at Pisa by
J. S de Cadenberg in the Royal observatory

1 Vol Printed 1789—containing observations from 1778 a 1782

1 D°—1793 observations from 1782 to 1786—of this there are <u>two</u>
Copies—

By some accident, he was prevented giving them earlier—He thinks
they were to be given to the Society but as the name of Yourself
was annexed He thinks as President—I feel an uncertainty—until I
hear from you on the Subject—we have not reciev'd the Subsequent
ones—

I shall by mail Send some more Certificates of Members to be signed
by you which you will be pleased to return as soon as convenient—
I remain with respect

Your friend & ser^t   JN VAUGHAN

RC (MHi); at head of text: "Thomas Jefferson Monticello"; endorsed by TJ as
received 23 Apr. 1813 and so recorded in SJL.

To William DuVal

DEAR SIR   Monticello Apr. 20. 13.

I have occasion for the agency of a friend in the neighborhood of
Shelbyville[1] Kentucky, in a case which gives me considerable trouble
and inquietude; and I do not know that I have either a friend or acquaintance in that neighborhood. I have learnt however that you have
a son there, a practitioner of law, and I have believed that from our
acquaintance and friendship, of now half a century, I might claim
some consideration with any one so nearly connected with you. but I
have supposed it might be more readily engaged by a line of recommendation from you to your son. and this I have felt no hesitation in
asking, confident that your goodness would ensure this act of kindness. the case which calls on me to trouble your son is that of a purchase of lands adjoining me from a family of Hendersons, who
removed to the neighborhood of Shelbyville in Kentucky, the children being then mostly under age. they have honorably confirmed as
they came of age, what their mother & guardians did for their best
advantage, till now that a case occurs of refusing confirmation. it is to

obtain this on principles either of justice or compromise that I ask the interposition of your son.

I write this letter at home: but proposing to set out within a few days for Poplar Forest, I shall leave it myself at Maj[r] Flood's, to which place I shall return within about 10. days from the time of my leaving it. if, within that interval, you could forward the letter requested, addressed to me 'at Poplar Forest near Lynchburg.' I can save time by putting it directly on the road from thence to Kentucky. otherwise be so good as to lodge it at Maj[r] Flood's to await my return to that place. I am obliged to ask from you the address of your son, his Christian name not being known to me, nor exactly his residence or nearest post office. Accept the assurance of my great esteem & respect.   TH: JEFFERSON

PoC (MHi); at foot of text: "Maj[r] William Duval"; endorsed by TJ.

William DuVal (1748–1842), attorney and landowner, served as a militia captain in the Revolutionary War. He represented Louisa County and the city of Richmond in the Virginia House of Delegates in 1782 and 1804–05, respectively. DuVal was a Richmond magistrate and served as mayor, 1805–06. In the latter year he was a witness at the trials of George Wythe Swinney for the murder of his great-uncle George Wythe, TJ's mentor and DuVal's neighbor. He later wrote TJ a number of letters describing the events. Early in 1807 DuVal moved to a plantation he owned in Buckingham County and spent the rest of his life there (DNA: RG 15, RWP; Bessie Berry Grabowskii, *The DuVal Family of Virginia, 1701: Descendants of Daniel DuVal, Huguenot and Allied Families* [1931], 176, 187–93; Leonard, *General Assembly*, 146, 237; *PTJ*, 2:45, 23:404–5; Richmond *Enquirer*, 15 Aug. 1804; DuVal to TJ, 4, 8 June 1806 [DLC]; W. Edwin Hemphill, "Examinations of George Wythe Swinney for Forgery and Murder: A Documentary Essay," *WMQ*, 3d ser., 12 [1955]: 543–74; *Richmond Whig and Public Advertiser*, 11 Jan., 22 Apr. 1842).

[1] Manuscript: "Shelbyvielle."

To David Michie

SIR   Monticello Ap[l] 20[h] '13

In the disputed Case between us it was agreed that any depositions which either party wished to make use of hereafter in any arbitration or suit on the subject might be taken on due notice and should be used by Consent wishing to secure the deposition of Judge Carr before he left this neighbourhood, I applied to you by letter the last Autumn for this purpose, but was informed you Could not then Conveniently attend. Anxious to Obtain his deposition as also those of Richard Price of Milton and James L Henderson now of Louisiana,[1] and my age not permitting me to let this matter remain unsettled, I must ask the favour of your agreement as to the time, place and

mode of taking those depositions which I will gladly receive by return of the bearer, or at your earliest Convenience. Accept the assurance of my respect. Th Jefferson

Tr (ViU: TJP-LBJM); in George
Carr's hand; at foot of text: "Mr David
Michie." Enclosed in TJ's Bill of Com-
plaint in *Jefferson v. Michie*, 16 June
1813, and Michie's Plea and Answer in
Jefferson v. Michie, [by 6 Sept. 1813].

The communication from TJ to Michie
BY LETTER THE LAST AUTUMN is not
recorded in SJL and has not been found.

¹ Manuscript: "Louisanna."

From Thomas H. Palmer

Sir, Philadelphia, April 20th 1813.

I received a few weeks ago your letter containing answers to some
questions respecting the Constitution of Virginia, for which I return
you many thanks. I have taken the liberty of again addressing you, to
call your attention to the enclosed Prospectus of a new Periodical
Work to wh I intend to devote my exclusive attention. Should the
Plan meet your approbation, & should you think the work promises
to be of public utility, you will oblige me by giving it the sanction of
your name as a subscriber, & by showing the Prospectus to such gentlemen in your neighbourhood as you may think likely to patronize
the work. I intend visiting as many of the seats of government of
the different states as I can this summer for the purpose of making
arrangements to receive regularly an account of their proceedings.
The others I shall visit next summer. A line addressed, as before, to
Thos & Geo. Palmer, Phila will come to my hands, & will oblige,

Yours respectfully, Thos H. Palmer.

RC (MHi); at foot of text: "T. Jefferson, Esq."; endorsed by TJ as received 15
May 1813 and so recorded in SJL.

The ENCLOSED PROSPECTUS, not
found, was probably similar to Palmer's
"Proposals" in the Charleston, S.C., *In-
vestigator*, 30 Apr. 1813, for the publication by subscription of his serial, *The Historical Register of the United States*, 4

vols. (Washington, 1814–16; Poor, *Jefferson's Library*, 5 [no. 145]). Palmer promised that the publication would consist of
at least eight-hundred octavo pages per
half-bound, lettered morocco volume,
each of which would cost $5. On this day
he also wrote a letter asking James Madison to PATRONIZE THE WORK (Madison,
Papers, Pres. Ser., 6:221).

To Joseph Hornsby

DEAR SIR   Monticello Apr. 21. 13.

A case occurring in which your kind interposition may befriend my quiet, I take the liberty of recalling myself to your memory, and our antient acquaintance, now I believe of more than half a century. you feel the value of tranquility at our time of life, and will therefore excuse my present sollicitation. I was induced very innocently to become the purchaser of the lands of the late Bennet Henderson adjoining me. they were so cut up into little shreds of interest on the partition made by the Commissioners between the 10. children as to be rendered of little or no value to any. each had a lot of 2. acres, two of about 5. acres each, of good lands, one of 102. a^s of pine barrens, a reversionary right to an undivided piece of an acre & a half, all distant from one another; also one tenth of two thirds in a warehouse, which taking then about 1000. hhds of tob° @ 1/6 each, yielded them about 16.D. a year apiece, but from the total discontinuance of that culture here does not now take 100. hhds & will be discontinued altogether. the mother, the guardians & the children themselves thought it to their interest to sell these fragments of property, all totally unproductive except the warehouse. considering this as a transaction of general concert, adopted for the interest of the family, and relying on their honor, I became the purchaser of the shares separately, thro' the agency of mr Craven Peyton, my occupations at Washington, not then permitting my personal attention to it. all the children honorably confirmed the sales as they came of age, until now that an instance occurs of refusing to do it. this by a gentleman of your name a relation as I am told, who married one of the young ladies, and I believe lives with you. it was at the desire of the mother and their brother[1] James L. Henderson, who acted as guardian in that state, and with their own privity, confirmed afterwards by the elder brother here, their legal guardian, that mr Peyton made the purchase, for which I paid in cash £130. for each share, a sum much beyond the worth of these scattered fragments, unless they could be collected into one hand, and more than they were valued at when in mass at the division of the estate by disinterested commissioners. whether the money was to be expended in their maintenance & education, or to be revested in other property, I considered as belonging to their natural guardians to decide for them, and never doubted their own confirmation. I have the misfortune to have incurred the ill-will of Capt Wm D. Meriwether but for what cause has never been known to me. I have supposed him chiefly instrumental in changing mr Hornsby's course from the candid one pursued by the other parceners, having himself purchased the two acre lot and obtained, as he says, from mr Hornsby a power of attorney to sell all the other property. I cannot help hoping mr Hornsby will reconsider this subject, and concur with the others in doing me justice, and settle the wrong, if any has been done them with the acting guardians, as he is best situated to do. a bond and mortgage were given to Peyton for the title, of which mr Hornsby can have the benefit, if the money has not been expended for the uses of mrs Hornsby. I ask the influence of your recommendation and advice in this case and, not presuming to give you any other trouble, I have written to mr Duval a gentleman of your neighborhood, son of a very antient friend of mine, to enter into such arrangements on this subject as he and mr Hornsby shall think just and sufficient. but let me intreat that in the mean time the power to Capt Meriwether may be withdrawn, and if the matter cannot be accomodated between mr Hornsby & mr Duval, that some person here may be authorised to treat with me on the subject, with whom I can enter into conference, for capt Meriwether and myself are no longer on those terms. reposing myself on your friendly interposition in this case to save me from the inquietude of law contestations I pray you to accept the assurances of my continued esteem and respect, and my sincere prayers for the long continuance of your life and health.

Th: Jefferson

P.S. our distance will make me anxious to know certainly, and as soon as convenient, that this letter has reached your hands safely.

P.S. May 24. 1813. mr Duval's absence in Congress has induced me to send the letter and power destined for him to Governor Greenup with a request to do what had been desired of mr Duval.

PoC (ViU: TJP); at foot of first page: "Joseph Hornsby esq."; endorsed by TJ.

Joseph Hornsby (ca. 1740–1807) was a nephew of Thomas Hornsby, a Williamsburg merchant sometimes patronized by TJ. The younger Hornsby came to Albemarle County from Yarmouth, England, and married Mildred Walker, the daughter of Dr. Thomas Walker. TJ's first recorded interaction with Hornsby came in 1769, when he took his deposition. Hornsby was widowed by 1796 and relocated about 1800 to Kentucky with his son-in-law Nicholas Meriwether Lewis (George W. Frye, *Colonel Joshua Fry of Virginia and Some of His Descendants and Allied Families* [1966], 28; Merrow Egerton Sorley, *Lewis of Warner Hall: The History of a Family* (1935; repr. 1991), 382, 836; *WMQ*, 1st ser., 17 [1909]: 169; *MB*, 1:23, 82, 293, 296; *PTJ*, 28:580, 29:37, 31:142–3n; Shelby County, Ky., Will Book, 2:199–203).

John Henderson was the LEGAL GUARDIAN of the Henderson heirs. For a description of the process by which Craven PEYTON purchased the Henderson

lands, see Haggard, "Henderson Heirs,"
5–9. Joseph Hornsby's son Thomas
Hornsby MARRIED Frances Henderson.
Letters from TJ to former Kentucky governor Christopher GREENUP of 25 May
and 9 June 1813 are recorded in SJL but

have not been found. A missing letter
from Greenup to TJ of 3 Aug. is recorded
in SJL as received 20 Aug. 1813 from
Frankfort, Kentucky.

¹ Manuscript: "brothers."

From Thomas Lehré

DEAR SIR   Charleston Apr: 22ᵈ 1813
    Your favor of the 10ᵗʰ Inst. has just been handed to me, for which
be pleased to accept my sincere thanks.   I am happy to hear
that Mʳ Eppes is elected a member of the 13ᵗʰ Congress, because, he
will then have it in his power, by his great firmness and splendid
talents, to aid our Government, in vindicating our honor and
rights.   The enemies of our present administration, and the
British emmissaries among us, are continually amuseing us with the
hopes of an armistice & mediation;—as we have been so often de-
ceved by that base, and faithless nation Great Britain, I hope our
Government will be very circumspect in its conduct towards her.¹
    I remain with the highest sentiments of esteem and respect,
    Dear Sir Your very Obedᵗ & Humble Servant
                                                    THOMAS LEHRÉ

RC (DLC); at foot of text: "Tho:
Jefferson late P. of the U.S."; endorsed by
TJ as received 15 May 1813 and so
recorded in SJL.

In 1811 John Randolph of Roanoke
held his seat in the United States House
of Representatives against the challenge
of TJ's son-in-law John Wayles EPPES.

Eppes, who supported the war with
Great Britain, then countered by defeating the anti-war Randolph in an April
1813 election for the 13ᵀᴴ CONGRESS
(ANB; Washington Daily National Intelligencer, 14 Apr., 3, 12 May 1813).

¹ Lehré here canceled "and not."

From Valentín de Foronda

                                                    Coruña Abril 23 de 1813.
Foronda se ofrece à la disposicion del sublime Jefferson y le remite
unos papelítos: le tiene ya enviados otros, y no será su culpa de
que se hayan extraviado. No los remite al filosofo Madisson á pesar
de los respetos y afecto que le profesa, por que los baxo politicos
mirarian mal una accion que no tiene relacion con los negocios
Españoles

EDITORS' TRANSLATION

La Coruña April 23, 1813.

Foronda places himself at the disposal of the noble Jefferson and sends him some small scraps: he has already sent others, and he is not to blame if they have gotten lost. He does not transmit them to the philosopher Madison, despite his respect and affection for him, because low-life politicians would misconstrue an action actually unrelated to Spanish affairs

RC (DLC); dateline at foot of text; endorsed by TJ as received 8 July 1813 and so recorded in SJL. Translation by Dr. David T. Gies and Dr. Jennifer McCune. Enclosures not found.

From David Michie

SIR. Buck Island Ap^l 23^d '13

Yours of the 20^h Ins^t has been received. I am perfectly willing to have the depositions of Judge Carr & Mr Price taken at any time when the Judge may be in this neighbourhood. It will likewise give me pleasure in accomidating you in taking any others you may think necessary

Accept the tender of my respects DAVID MICHIE

Tr (ViU: TJP-LBJM); in George Carr's hand. Recorded in SJL as received 23 Apr. 1813. Enclosed in TJ's Bill of Complaint in *Jefferson v. Michie*, 16 June 1813, and Michie's Plea and Answer in *Jefferson v. Michie*, [by 6 Sept. 1813].

To Samuel Brown

DEAR SIR Monticello Apr. 24. 13.

I wrote you a few days ago in answer to your favor accompanying the seeds of the Guinea grass and Capsicum. the object of the present is to sollicit the protection of your cover for the inclosed letter to ensure it's safety as far as Natches, and then your kind aid in committing it to the proper channel of conveyance. I have been told there is a post direct from Natchez to Washita. if not, I presume there is one from N. Orleans to Washita. if you will be so good as to supply any defect in the superscription the frank will carry it to it's destination. the letter is important to me as it relates to the title of lands adjoining me which I purchased of mr Henderson to whom the letter is directed. this must apologise for my troubling you with so small a commission. it gives me too occasion of repeating to you the assurance of my constant friendship & respect. TH: JEFFERSON

PoC (DLC); at foot of text: "Doct^r Samuel Brown"; endorsed by TJ.

The INCLOSED LETTER of 21 Apr. 1813 from TJ to James L. Henderson, not found, is recorded in SJL.

To Rodolphus Dickinson

SIR   Monticello Apr. 24. 13.

Be pleased to[1] accept my thanks for your 'View of Massachusets proper.' a volume of facts is worth more than[2] whole libraries of speculations and fermentations of the brain; and those respecting Massachusets will continue to be interesting whether she continues an American state, or becomes a British province. a mind which in youth takes the useful direction of facts, promises much to[3] our real knolege in it's advancement thro' life. may you go on then as you have begun and add to those sentiments of respect and thankfulness with which I salute you.

TH: JEFFERSON

RC (ViU: TJP); addressed: "Rodolphus Dickinson esquire Greenfield Massachusets"; frank clipped; postmarked Charlottesville, 28 Apr. PoC (DLC); endorsed by TJ. Tr (MDeeP: Dickinson Family Papers); in Dickinson's hand; misdated 5 Apr. 1813.

[1] Preceding three words omitted in Tr.
[2] Preceding two words omitted in Tr.
[3] Remainder of sentence in Tr reads "the advance of our knowledge in its future course."

From Robert Patterson

SIR   Philadelphia April 24th 1813.

I have to acknowledge the receipt of your esteemed favour of the 8th. Your time-piece, agreeably to your desire, I have had set up at my own house, & shall with great pleasure make experiments on its going with the rod-pendulum.

This pendulum is at present suspended by a few inches of watch-spring attached to the upper end, as in common pendulums: But Mr Adrain, an able mathematician, in the college of Newbrunswick N. J. informs me, that he has for some time been employed in making experiments on rod-pendulums, and has the mortification to find, that his experiments do not agree with theory. His pendulums were also suspended by small pieces of watch-spring. with some the times of vibration exceeded, & with others, fell short of what the theory would give, taking into the calculation every known circumstance. Hence, I presume, the suspending spring must be abandoned, and the knife-edge substituted in its place; and with this I am persuaded (but shall test it by experiment) that theory & practice will agree.

At the meeting of the Philosophical Society for the election of officers held on the 1st of January last, you, Sir, were indeed unanimously chosen President of the Society. The election was announced in the Aurora, on the Monday following, and probably in most of the other papers of the city. But the acting secretary whose duty it was to inform you of your election, must have neglected his duty. With this circumstance, however, the society have never been acquainted

With great condescension, you are pleased to ask my conscientious advice relative to your resignation of the office of President of the Society after the expiration of the present year.—I have, Sir, most seriously & conscientiously considered the subject, in all its bearings & probable consequences; and for weighty[1] reasons, intimately connected with the prosperity of the Society, I can do no other than renew, most earnestly, my former solicitations—that you would still[2] comply with the most earnest wishes of the Society to continue you their President.

Inclosed I send you Mr Voigts bill for the time-piece, with the appendages. He does not at present know of any one he could recommend to the advantageous situation you mention; but both he & myself will bear the subject in mind; & should any suitable character be discovered, I shall not fail to acquaint you.

I have, Sir, the honour to be with the greatest respect & esteem Your obed^t Servt   R^t PATTERSON

RC (DLC); endorsed by TJ as received 15 May 1813 and so recorded in SJL.

Filed with this letter and probably enclosed by Patterson is a clipping from the Philadelphia *Aurora General Advertiser*, 4 Jan. 1813, announcing that TJ had been CHOSEN PRESIDENT in the annual election of officers of the American Philosophical Society on 1 Jan. 1813. The enclosed BILL from Thomas Voigt has not been found, but a receipt from John Lentz dated 9 Feb. 1813 records his charges to Voigt consisting of $35 for a clock case, $3 for a packing box, and 50¢ for packing the pendulum (MS in MHi). The clock did not reach Monticello until 27 Dec. 1815 (*MB*, 2:1289, 1317).

[1] Manuscript: "wiaghty."
[2] Word interlined.

To John Vaughan

Dear Sir   Monticello Apr. 24. 13.

Your favor of the 19th finds me just setting out on a journey which will occasion an absence of three weeks from home. at any time after my return from that I shall be ready to dispatch any certificates or other papers you may be pleased to send me for signature   with respect to the volumes of astronomical observations from Pisa, whether intended for myself personally or for the society, I pray you not to hesitate a moment in delivering them to the society. I shall be more gratified by their possessing them than having them my-self.   a gentleman of science in Sardinia, supposing I was form-ing a cabinet, sent me a collection of fossils, mostly I believe of differ-ent marbles; at least those on the surface of the box are such, for I did not like to unpack them, as I proposed to send them to the philosoph-ical society. they cannot go safely by land, because they would get rubbed and would destroy their labels. they must wait here therefore until the passage by sea becomes safer, when I shall have the pleasure of forwarding them for the acceptance of the society.

I am happy at all times in hearing from you. your letter gives me the presumption of your health, altho' silent on that subject and is further gratifying in furnishing me the occasion of renewing to you the assurances of my constant esteem and respect.

                                                            Th: Jefferson

RC (MHi); at foot of text: "John Vaughan esq."; endorsed by TJ.

The American Philosophical Society acknowledged receipt of the VOLUMES at its 21 May 1813 meeting, describing them as "Observationes Siderum habita Pisis in Specula Academica ab ano 1778 ad 1782 a Jos Slop de Cadenberg 4.to Pisis 1789. Idem ab anno 1782 ad 1786. Pisis 1793 From the Academy through hands J. A. Smith" (APS, Minutes [MS in PPAmP]). For the FOSSILS, see Leonar-do de Prunner to TJ, 15 Mar. 1810, and enclosure.

To John Barnes

Dear Sir   Monticello Apr. 25. 13.

I set out tomorrow for Bedford and shall be absent 3. or 4. weeks. I have between 4. and 500. barrels of flour caught at Richmond[1] by the blockade, not a barrel of it sold. my hope is that the enemy will prefer withdrawing out of the capes and cruising on the coast to catch something rather than lie where they do & catch nothing. the moment any movement of theirs gives a chance for our vessels to go out, I am assured a good sale may be made. I shall think it fortunate if the annual remittance to our friend Kosciuzko should give time for this sale, which in every preceding year has taken place before this month was out. however whenever a good opportunity or channel of remittance shall make it necessary my part of it shall be furnished at any sacrifice. Accept the assurances of my constant friendship and respect.   TH: JEFF[ERSO]N

PoC (DLC); signature faint; at foot of text: "Mʳ John Barnes"; endorsed by TJ.

[1] Preceding two words added in margins.

To John Brown

SIR   Monticello Apr. 25. 13.

On recieving from you mr Walker's bill of prices (which I now inclose) I examined your account, which I had not done before, and soon found that mr Walker's bill related only to grist mills. I therefore sent a messenger to him and asked him to state the prices of saw mill work, which he did. on comparing these with yours I found them very materially different. my original agreement for building the saw mill was with him, and when he turned it over to you, he told me you would work at his prices, and I think when you delivered me your account you said[1] you made his prices your rule of charging. I think therefore it will be better to let him take your account and extend it according to his prices. I noted to him some articles of which I wished to know the prices, and he wrote me he could not decide them without seeing them. I set out to Bedford tomorrow & shall be back in three weeks. on my return, if you consent I will get him to come here, see the work and settle the prices of every article. I am aware that his prices are by no means the lowest that even the best millwrights work at. but they are those I expected to pay, and am willing to abide by. if you will signify your consent in a line to be lodged here before my return, I will then immediately fix a day for him and yourself to meet here and will let you know it. Accept my best wishes.

                                                        TH: JEFFERSON

PoC (MHi); at foot of text: "Mʳ John Brown"; endorsed by TJ. Enclosure not found.

John Brown, millwright, worked on

TJ's sawmill. TJ recorded payments to him of $300 in July 1813 and $100 in July 1814 (*MB*, 2:1291, 1301).

[1] TJ here canceled "it was."

To Richard Fitzhugh

DEAR SIR   Monticello Apr. 25. 13.

I have unluckily got out of the Ravensworth pea, which I value so highly as to wish to recover it. I am in hopes you are able to supply me with a little. a few peas quilted into a peice of cloth, so as to lie flat, of the size and form of a letter, and inclosed in a paper cover and directed to me as a letter by mail will be sufficient to put me in seed by another year.

I inclose you the seeds of a very valuable garden vegetable which I recieved from France 2. or 3. years ago, it is called the Sprout Kale. it is sowed and transplanted as other Kale or Cabbages, and about the beginning of December it begins to furnish sprouts, and will furnish 3. crops of them thro the winter; so abundantly that a few plants will give a dish every day. it stands our winter perfectly without cover.

I am happy in this opportunity of recalling myself to your recollection and to that of mrs Fitzhugh to whom I pray you to present my affectionate respects, and accept for yourself the assurances of my friendship & best wishes.   TH: JEFFERSON

PoC (MHi); at foot of text: "Richard Fitzhugh esquire"; endorsed by TJ.

Richard Fitzhugh (1766–1821) lived on a portion of the Ravensworth tract in northern Virginia. TJ occasionally lodged with him or his brother Nicholas Fitzhugh during his trips to and from Washington. At his death Richard Fitzhugh's personal estate was valued in excess of $10,000 and included forty-eight slaves (Stella Pickett Hardy, *Colonial Families of the Southern States of America*, 2d ed. [1958; repr. 1981], 227; Nan Netherton and others, *Fairfax County, Virginia: A History* [1978], 161–3; *MB*, esp. 2:1071–2n; TJ to Fitzhugh, 10 May 1805 [MHi]; Fairfax Co. Will Book, M1:240–1, 246–7).

TJ first recorded planting the RAVENSWORTH PEA in May 1809 (Betts, *Garden Book*, 390).

To William Short

DEAR SIR   Monticello Apr. 25. 13.

Your favor of Feb. 16. remains still I believe to be acknoleged. as I did not go to the court succeeding it's reciept myself, I delivered your deed to mr Higginbotham and his mortgage to you, to himself on his way to court to have both recorded, which cannot fail to have been done; but shall be the subject of more special enquiry, mr Carter's negligence having taught me to take nothing for granted. I send you mr H's assumpsit for the rent which closes the paper transactions.

Your's of the 16th inst. just now recieved, finds me within two days of my departure for Bedford. my absence will be of about three weeks; but I will certainly make a point of being at home by the 20th of May and shall be very happy to see M. Correa here. if he comes in the stage, his rout is of course fixed; but if otherwise, the road from Washington by Fauquier court House, Culpeper C.H. and Orange C.H. at this season of the year is far the driest and least frequented & cut by waggons. lying too thro' a fertile country of substantial farmers will afford some remuneration for the labours of a journey for which I shall be so much indebted. I am sorry at the same time to lose the prospect of your visit, and that of Genl Moreau, for the season at least. mais tout ce qui est differé n'est pas perdu. Genl Moreau is one of the great objects of the attention of the world, which, expects from him, if the hand of heaven should alight on Bonaparte in this world, the reestablishment of legitimate government in France, giving to it's inhabitants as much liberty as they can bear, and in every case a government of fixed law.

Price called on me a few days ago to desire I would explain to you the delay of recieving your rents, the wheat of the tenants being caught by the blockade unsold. he assures me the rents are entirely safe. I can the more readily credit the cause of the delay, being myself caught in the same situation. I have now between 4. and 500. barrels of flour in Richmond, not a barrel of which is sold, and the fate of which depends solely on the motions of the blockading squadron. I cannot help believing they will see their own interest in withdrawing a little and cruising on the coast, in which case our vessels will go out. they will catch $\frac{1}{3}$ and send them to the markets of their W. Indies and to Quebec[1] and the remaining $\frac{2}{3}$ will get to the peninsul & feed their armies and friends there. if they remain in the Delaware and Chesapeake, their islands and armies must starve & their friends in Boston live on potatoes. this will be some consolation to us for the loss of our produce if we cannot get it to market. ever affectionately yours.

TH: JEFFERSON

RC (ViW: TJP); addressed: "William Short esquire Philadelphia"; franked; postmarked Milton, 28 Apr.; endorsed by Short as received 3 May.

Short's letter OF FEB. 16., not found, is recorded in SJL as received from Philadelphia on 26 Feb. and also abstracted in Short's epistolary record: "to enclose deed [...]" (DLC: Short Papers; in Short's hand; from a portion of his epistolary record containing entries from 24 Nov. 1812 through 8 July 1813). His letter OF THE 16TH INST., also not found, is recorded in SJL as received from Philadelphia on 21 Apr. 1813. For the DEED TO MR HIGGINBOTHAM AND HIS MORTGAGE, see TJ to Short, 10 Feb. 1813, and note. David Higginbotham's enclosed ASSUMPSIT FOR THE RENT stated that "In consideration of the immediate delivery of the lands called Indian

Camp in the county of Albemarle sold to me by William Short, (except so far as they are lawfully occupied by tenants, who are to continue until the end of their leases) and in consideration of the right transferred to me to levy on those tenants the rents they are bound to pay for the present year, I hereby assume to pay at the end of the present year, the amount of those rents to the sd Wm Short, whether the same shall have been collected by me or not. Witness my hand this 27th day of February 1813" (MS in ViU: TJP; in TJ's hand, witnessed by Carter H. Harrison, with date completed in an unidentified hand; canceled by removal of bottom corner including Higginbotham's signature; endorsed by TJ: "Higinbotham to Short } Note for rents of Indian Camp for 1813"; subjoined notation by Higginbotham: "paid"). MAIS TOUT CE QUI EST DIFFERÉ N'EST PAS PERDU: "but all that is deferred is not lost."

[1] Preceding three words interlined.

To John Wayles Eppes

DEAR SIR   Monticello Apr. 26. 13.

We are just now packing your Commode & two presses. strange as it may seem, altho' it required but 4. or 500 feet of plank to make the packing boxes, yet so difficult is that article here, that I never have been able to command that quantity beyond[1] my own constant & pressing wants till I got a saw mill of my own to work. this has enabled me now to pack them and my boat will be sent off with them within a few days to Cartersville. you once wrote me to whom to deliver them there, but I have forgotten and cannot now find the letter giving the directions. I presume however there will be no difficulty in finding store room. they will certainly be there within a fortnight from this date. I am just setting out for Bedford and believing you will get this letter and the one inclosed more quickly by lodging them at Flood's I take them with me for that purpose. with my respect to mrs Eppes & love to Francis accept the assurances of my affectionate esteem & respect.   TH:J—

PoC (MHi); at foot of text: "honble John W. Eppes"; endorsed by TJ. Enclosure: TJ to Eppes, 18 Apr. 1813.

[1] Reworked from "bef."

From the Seventy-Six Association

Charleston South Carolina. April 26. 1813.

Pursuant to a Resolution of the Seventy Six Association, we have the honor to enclose a Copy of an Oration delivered before that Society on the 4th of March last—In discharging this pleasing duty, we would not do justice to our Individual feelings, did we omit to express our good wishes for your health & happiness.

With sentiments of great respect we remain Yr Obedt servants.

JAMES JERVEY.

THO: BENNETT JUNR

CHARLES ELLIOTT

P COHEN

ROBT Y. HAYNE

Standing Committee.

RC (MoSHi: TJC-BC); in Jervey's hand, signed by Jervey, Bennett, Elliott, Cohen, and Hayne; at foot of text: "Thomas Jefferson Esqre"; endorsed by TJ as a letter from "Jervey James Etc" received 15 May 1813 and so recorded in SJL. Enclosure: Benjamin Elliott, *Oration on the Inauguration of the Federal Constitution. Delivered in Concert Hall, Charleston, March 4, 1813, by appointment of the '76 Association* (Charleston, 1813), lauding the resilience and sacrifices of the revolutionary generation; asserting that the superiority of the republican form of government derives from the sovereignty of the people; highlighting the positive effects of American freedom of the press and religion; condemning the British practice of impressment; boasting that in twenty-four years the United States Constitution "has produced a Washington, an Adams, a Jefferson, and a Madison—each of whom would have given dignity to any, the most enlightened nations, in the most enlightened age. In fifty three years the British constitution has produced—what? An Insane Idiot" (p. 24); and concluding that a secure American republic is "forming the mightiest empire that ever gemmed the globe" (p. 25).

James Jervey (1784–1845), attorney, banker, and civic leader, was educated at the College of Charleston, studied law, and was admitted to the bar in 1805. He was clerk for the United States District Court of South Carolina from about 1810 until 1839. In the latter year Jervey became president of the State Bank of South Carolina, which he had served intermit-

tently as a director since 1815, and he led the institution until his death. He was also a director of insurance companies, co-partner with his son Lewis Jervey in the firm of James Jervey & Son, and an active participant in local social and charitable organizations, including the Associated Library Society, the Protestant Episcopal Society for the Advancement of Christianity in South Carolina, and an orphanage (Alexander S. Salley Jr., "The Jervey Family of South Carolina," *South Carolina Historical and Genealogical Magazine* 7 [1906]: 36–8; Charleston *Carolina Gazette*, 11 Oct. 1805; Charleston *City Gazette & Daily Advertiser*, 28 Apr., 25 June 1810, 3, 9 Mar. 1815, 29 Oct. 1822; Charleston *Southern Patriot*, 4, 11 Apr., 2 May 1845; *Greenville Mountaineer*, 11 Apr. 1845).

Thomas Bennett (1781–1865) was a merchant, mill owner, planter, and public official. First in partnership with his namesake father and later on his own, he operated rice and lumber mills in the vicinity of Charleston. Through marriage Bennett obtained several plantations. By 1850 he owned 260 slaves, and ten years later his estimated wealth exceeded $275,000. First elected to the South Carolina House of Representatives in 1804, Bennett completed five additional House terms, 1808–17, with service as Speaker from 1814–17, and he was intendent (mayor) of Charleston, 1812–13. He was elected to the state senate in 1818 but resigned his seat two years later when he was chosen for the governorship. Bennett was a Republican who opposed the slave trade before his term as governor was disrupted by the turmoil surrounding the

[89]

alleged slave conspiracy of Denmark Vesey. Four of the accused bondsmen were members of Bennett's household. During the Nullification debate, Bennett strongly supported the Unionist position. He served a final state senate term, 1837–39 (*BDSCHR*, 4:54–6; Michael P. Johnson, "Denmark Vesey and His Co-Conspirators," *WMQ*, 3d ser., 58 [2001]: 915–76, esp. 937–8; Washington *Globe*, 5 Nov. 1832).

Charles Elliott, attorney, was called to the Charleston bar in 1810 and remained in the city until at least 1816 (John Belton O'Neall, *Biographical Sketches of the Bench and Bar of South Carolina* [1859], 2:600; Abraham Motte, *Charleston Directory and Strangers' Guide* [Charleston, 1816], 29).

Philip Cohen (ca. 1781–1866), merchant and auctioneer, was a lieutenant in the South Carolina volunteers beginning in 1809. His extensive involvement in Charleston public and philanthropic affairs included a founding membership in the Hebrew Orphan Society in 1801, a seat on the city board of health, 1819–23, and service as a commissioner of the Marine Hospital, 1826–33. Cohen was a leader of the State Rights and Free Trade Party and supported Nullification as a delegate to the state's Nullification Convention, 1832–33. His description of the civic and religious life of Jews in Charleston was published in Hannah Adams, *The History of the Jews from the Destruction of Jerusalem to the Nineteenth Century* (Boston, 1812), 2:217–20 (Barnett A. Elzas, *The Jews of South Carolina From the Earliest Times to the Present Day* [1905], 134, 143–4, 145, 189; Thomas J. Tobias, *The Hebrew Orphan Society of Charleston, S.C. Founded 1801* [1957], 4, 33; *Nelson's Charleston Directory, and Strangers Guide for the Year of Our Lord, 1801* [Charleston, 1801], 67; Philadelphia *Banner of the Constitution*, 15 Aug. 1832; *Niles' Weekly Register*, 22 Dec. 1832; Elzas, *The Old Jewish Cemeteries at Charleston, S.C.: A Transcript of the Inscriptions on Their Tombstones. 1762–1903* [1903], 61).

Robert Young Hayne (1791–1839), attorney, public official, and railroad president, was born on a South Carolina rice plantation. He was educated privately in Charleston and later studied law under Langdon Cheves. Admitted to the bar in 1812, Hayne held volunteer officer's commissions during the War of 1812. He sat in the South Carolina House of Representatives, 1814–18, with service as Speaker in the latter year, and he was attorney general of South Carolina, 1818–22. From 1822 until 1832 Hayne served in the United States Senate, where he was an outspoken opponent of protective tariffs who defended state sovereignty and the doctrine of Nullification in a series of celebrated debates with Daniel Webster in 1830. Hayne resigned his Senate seat to become governor of South Carolina in 1832, serving until 1834 and threatening to deploy militia against federal troops during the Nullification Crisis. He also sat in the state's Nullification Convention, 1832–33, and served as its president in the latter year. Hayne was mayor of Charleston, 1836–37. Hoping that rail lines would unify the interests of southern and western states, from 1837 until his death he was president of the Louisville, Cincinnati, and Charleston Railroad Company (*ANB*; *DAB*; *BDSCHR*, 4:271–4; Theodore D. Jervey, *Robert Y. Hayne and His Times* [1909; repr. 1970]; Charleston *Southern Patriot*, 28 Sept. 1839).

On this day the same committee of the Seventy-Six Association sent a copy of the enclosure to President James Madison (Madison, *Papers, Pres. Ser.*, 6:246).

From Patrick Gibson

S<small>IR</small>　　　　　　　　　　　　　Richmond 28th April 1813

I have been prevented from writing to you sooner in consequence of the dilatoriness of Mr Wm Marshall whom Mr Taylor had employed to examine the records and make out the bill of Sale for Mazzei's two lots—I have this moment obtained it from him and send it you here inclosed—it requires if I understood him right, your signature and that of Mr Randolph and I think must be certified to in your court, of this however you are best able to judge, so soon as it is returnd, the notes will be obtained—I am sorry to say that I have endeavour'd in vain to effect a sale of your flour, it is offering at 6$ but I can hear of no purchaser at that price, $5\frac{1}{2}$$ would be as much as could now be obtain'd, and as there is hardly a possibility of its being lower before I receive your answer I shall defer making a sale until then. I send you inclosed a note for your signature and also your acco^t to the 1st Ins^t. With great respect I am　　　Your ob Servt

PATRICK GIBSON

RC (ViU: TJP-ER); at head of text: "Thomas Jefferson Esqre"; endorsed by TJ as received 15 May 1813 and so recorded in SJL. Enclosures not found.

From John Barnes

DEAR SIR—　　　　　　　George Town Col^a 29th April 1813

This will be handed you, by my friend and neighbour Mr John Eliason, whom I had the Honor of introducing to you by letter the 6th Jan^y—respecting your Mills &^{c} as to a partnership—as noticed—I presume would not be agreable to either—party—but should Mr Randolph—be inclined to relinquish the business—whatever might be the condition agreed on either, with you, or Mr Randolph—from Mr Eliasons Usual manner of doing business—for his Honor, and Integrity—you may—I <u>trust</u>,—with all reasonable satisfaction—depend Upon,

I am Dear Sir, Respectfully and most sincerely—your Obed^t servant　　　　　　　　　　　　JOHN BARNES,

RC (ViU: TJP-ER); at foot of text: "Thos Jefferson Esqr Monticello"; endorsed by TJ as received 15 May 1813 and so recorded in SJL.

From John Barnes

DEAR SIR—　　　　　　　George Town Col^a 29th April 1813.

With Reference to the want of intelligence from Genl Kosciusko— I inclose you herewith Mr Geo: Williams of Baltimore his letter to me dated 29 Jany for y^r goverment as well, on Acco^t of making a further

Remittance (if advisable.) in course of the insuing Month—no Latter Acco^t has since been Recd—
  By Sir,
  your Obed^t serv^t JOHN BARNES,

I will thank you to—return me, Mr William's Lett^r in Case I sh^d have Occasion to write him, on the subject of Remitt^{ce}

RC (ViU: TJP-ER); at foot of text: "Thomas Jefferson Esqr Monticello"; endorsed by TJ as received 15 May 1813 and so recorded in SJL. Enclosure not found.

From John Mason

DEAR SIR   George Town 30 April 1813
  Mr John Eliason, Merchant of this Town, proposing to visit you on some matter of Business, has requested me to mention him to you.
  I shall take the liberty to do so with pleasure, altho' I cannot speak otherwise than generally on the Subject, having latterly been much withdrawn from mercantile business, I have had but few Transactions with Mr Eliason.
  I can however assure you Sir, that his character, and I believe very deservedly, is that of an honourable punctual Man in all his dealings, and that his credit has been well supported for the several years that he has resided here—
  with very great Regard & Respect I have the honour to be Sir Your most Ob^t Servt   J. MASON

RC (DLC); at foot of text: "Thomas Jefferson Esqre"; endorsed by TJ as received 15 May 1813 and so recorded in SJL.

To Archibald Robertson

[DE]AR SIR   Poplar Forest Apr. 30. 13.
  You had a right to expect to hear from me ere this on the su[b]ject of a paiment. but I am one among the unfortunate who have been caugh[t] by the blockade before the sale of my flour. I have between 4. & 500. barrels now in Richmond, & not a barrel sold. I have desired mr Gibson to hold up for 7.D. thro' this month, but then to sell for whatever he can get. the moment I hear from him that he has sold, you shall hear from me, and with all the effect in my power. I saw a gentleman on the road immediately from Richmond, who told me they were beginning to send off flour from Norfolk thro' the canal to be

exported from the sound; that this had occasiond flour to look up, that $6\frac{1}{2}$ D. could be got for a quantity and it was believed as this channel of exportation should get better under way, the price of flour would rise. should this prospect open on mr Gibson, he may in his prudence hold on a little longer. but I shall not consent to yield much to this expectation, but press a sale on any terms rather than risk losing the whole. Accept the assurances of my great respect & esteem.

Th: Jefferson

PoC (ViU: TJP); with errors introduced by polygraph; at foot of text: "Mr A. Robertson"; endorsed by TJ.

To Charles Clay

Dear Sir   Monticello [Poplar Forest] May.[1] 1. 13.

I think that on my recommending Tacitus to master Cyrus, you said you did not possess him, and perhaps that you had never seen him. on my return home I wrote to Philadelphia for a copy, which I now send for master Cyrus's acceptance & perusal. the solidity of his matter, his brevity, & his fondness for point & antithesis make him difficult. I would advise the use of a translation, to be read after the original in order to ensure a full understanding of it. Murphy's is preferred by those who cannot read the original, and who do not therefore know the spirit of the author. but those who do find much more of that spirit in Gordon's. his selection of Tacitus & Sallust for translation seems to have been dictated by the similar causticity of his own genius.

From the points of Tacitus I will make an humble transition to those of your asparagus bed, some of which will be acceptable, and the more so if you should come to partake of them. I salute you in all friendship & respect.   Th: Jefferson

PoC (DLC); at foot of text: "Mr Clay"; endorsed by TJ, with his additional notation: "dated Monticello instd of Pop. For." Enclosure: *C. Cornelii Taciti opera cum varietate lectionum selecta novisque emendationibus*, 4 vols. (Zweibrücken, 1779–80).

On 25 Dec. 1812 TJ wrote to the Philadelphia bookseller Nicolas G. Dufief requesting a copy of Tacitus.

[1] Reworked from "Ap."

From Charles Clay

D^R S<small>IR</small>,   May 1.—13

by boy Will I Recieved your present of Tacitus for Cyrus, your friendly attentions to the proper & useful Education of Cyrus is highly appreciated by us both, & I hope the impression will never be lessened.—I yesteday heard of your being up, & intended visiting you[1] this day with a mess of Asparagus, which grows upon us with a threating Aspect, we shall trust to your frequent Aid in keeping it within proper subjection; Billy brings you a Mess, & I purpose Coming to see how you have it dressed, with the utmost Respect I present you my

friendly Salutations   C. C<small>LAY</small>

RC (MHi); page trimmed, resulting in loss of day of receipt from TJ's endorsement. Recorded in SJL as received 1 May 1813.

[1] Word interlined.

From Archibald Robertson

D<small>EAR</small> S<small>IR</small>   Lynchburg 1st May 1813

Your favor of the 30th ult° have received & observe you are among the unfortunate holders of flour—

I have understood that some attempts are making to carry flour through the Dismal Swamp Canal, but have not heard what success the undertakers had, should they succeed no doubt many others will follow the example, in which case flour must look up, tho' it is believed the large quantity on hand in Richmond (say about 100,000 Bbles) will prevent its being much above the present price—

The arrangement you have made is perfectly satisfactory & shall rest satisfied that you will make us payment as soon as it is in your power—I am

Respectfully your mo ob S^t   A. R<small>OBERTSON</small>

RC (ViU: TJP); endorsed by TJ as received 1 May 1813 and so recorded in SJL.

From Benjamin Waterhouse

Dear Sir,   Boston 1ˢᵗ of May[1] 1813

If you will excuse my breaking in again upon your philosophical retirement, I think I may venture to promise that it shall be[2] the last time.

I little thought, when I wrote to you last, that I should have so soon to lament the loss of my revered friend & brother Dʳ Rush! By his death I feel as if one strand of the thread of my life was cut. It is a heavy, very heavy stroke to his old[3] friend Mʳ Adams. They exchanged letters about once a fortnight. Mʳ Adams was expecting a letter, when mine came to his hands containing an extract of a letter from my son (who has been under Rush the year past) with the particulars of his illness, death & last words—He told my son, not long before he expired, (for he was sensible to the last) alluding to the persecution of his father in Massachusetts[4]—"I owe my enemies nothing but forgiveness."—and not long after he added.—"They have it most[5] heartily." I hope I may be able to say so too, before I die—; but the time is not yet come; for their wrath has been cruel—

Upon the news of the death of Dʳ Rush my republican friends drew up & signed a short address to the President, recommending me to his notice, for some appointment "comporting, as they expressed it, with my years & rank in society." but without saying what, because they had heard that I had been spoken of at Washington as Physician general; but they had in view the office of[6] Treasurer of the mint, grounded on the opinion that I would gladly quit Boston for Philadelphia, & the probability of my filling some part of Dʳ R's professional stations.—It is upon this subject that I beg leave to communicate to you my feelings, views & wishes; and I have been encouraged to it by the last paragraph in your friendly letter, where you say "They (the persecuting party here) may force you to fly south of Connecticut, where no truth is feared, where science is honored, not reviled, & where you, as one of its sons, would always be received with cordiality."—These sentiments, the death of Dʳ Rush, & the Strong desire I have to get out of this La Vendee of the U. States,[7] have occasioned a strong current of thought, which I cannot resist expressing to you; not without a hope that you might express it to others.

After a seven years persecution, the leading particulars of which I am now publishing,[8] I found it expedient to dissolve all connection with Cambridge college, & take up my residence in Bosto[n] with a view of practising physic, & of giving lectures on Natural History, & continuing vaccination. To this end I took a conspicuou[s] & not inelegant house. But I soon found, that so far from relaxing, my pursuers redoubled their efforts, & encreased the oppression. No federalist <u>dare</u> employ me; and I have not vaccinated six inhabitants of Boston during the year[9] past; and, what may surprize you,[10] the college have transferred their Lectures on Natural history & botany[11] from the college to this town. And all this glaringly under the patronage of the <u>Essex</u>[12] <u>Junto</u>, so that my lectures are entirely put a stop to. These domineering people say outright "<u>We are the patrons of Science; & nothing of the sort will be patronized here, but by the Federalists.</u>"[13] Their mode of oppression often times betrays deep thought; and if they proceed as they have begun, I do not see but they will, before the year closes nearly interdict me fire & water. I do not, at present, see how I can maintain my family among them.[14] It is through "the Washington <u>benevolent</u> Society," falsely so called, that they carry on their ingenious oppressions.[15] If I could obtain the place of Treasurer of the mint, I would remove to Philadelphia without the least reluctance. of my six promising children, four are sons; the eldest a student in law with our District attorney, the 2[d] is in Physic, & just graduated at Philadelphia, where he wishes to settle, & where he is already distinguished, the 3[d] is in the counting house of our friend the opulent M[r] Gray; & the fourth just about commencing the <u>gantlet</u> through the hypocricy[16] & political nonsense of Cambridge college. All these young persons, neither of whom will ever be in the background of society,[17] are thoroughly imbued with the true principles of Jefferson, Adams,[18] & Madison. But how can they ever expect to advance in Boston,[19] unless they fall into the ranks of the enemies of the administration, as many of the Sons of Republicans are doing daily.[20] If they cannot decoy them into the <u>Washington benevolent net</u>,[21] they will be marked out & pursued as enemies to the good old cause of British superstition. You may read <u>my opinion</u> of them in the Independant chronicle of this day under the signature of "<u>a Shepherd</u>." I felt it a duty to expose this <u>new superstition</u>.

It is seven years since the <u>Essex</u>[22] <u>Junto</u> circumvallated my professorship. During this time, they made their regular approaches, & minings; but I have more than once countermined them, & several times[23] filled up their intrenchments. But this is not all.[24] I have attacked their champion <u>openly</u>, by way of repelling his <u>secret</u> attacks. I have not only called him by name, but I have cited him to the bar of the public, exposed his[25] malignant intentions.—Nay more I have draged him like <u>Cacus</u> in Virgil from the midst of his fire & smoke to light & punishment. After[26] holding this influential man, the Ahithophel of the Junto,[27] up to public view, in the firm grasp of truth & resolution, can I expect ever to be forgiven; or that they will not visit the sins of the father upon his children?

On these accounts I wish to retire from this residence of sordid merchants, & narrow minded shop keepers, & slavish lawyers, and professional rivals & political bigots, into some city where I can serve my country, finish the education of my children, & enjoy my political principles without persecution.

It has been suggested to me, by certain members of Congress, that the Government were about establishing a Surgeon general (by which I presume they meant a Physician general, as the latter includes the former) & that I was spoken of at Washingto[n] in that connection. On which I would observe that I stand ready, to obey that call, if it should ever[28] be uttered. I very well know that we suffer for want of some such arrangement, by Sea as well as by land.[29] I have been frequently consulted by the head of the medical department of the army under General Dearborne, and I believe his path to usefulness is narrowed for want of system;[30] and I have long been convinced that the late Secretary at war was not able to supply one; not for want of talents; but for want of reading.

With a general & indistinct idea that the Administration contemplated calling me into their service, in some station or other,[31] the most prominent Republican[32] characters in Cambridge, Charlestown & Boston, drew up & signed the following,

"We the undersigned having a high opinion of the abilities, learning, professional knowledge & integrity of Dr Benjamin Waterhouse,—take this method of recommending him to the notice of the President of the U. States for any office, in which the before[33] mentioned qualities are requisites; and which may comport with his years, & rank in society."—

I would here remark to you, that when this paper was brought to me, I saw with pleasure that it was the work of those gentlemen who were the most forward in displacing me from the Marine-hospital Dr Eustis, & another Physician excepted,[34] The second signer was Mr John Brazer, who was the Zealous chairman of that committee which remonstrated to you against your appointment of me to the hospital. He says to me & to others, that he acted in that business from misinformation.[35] It is also Signed by Mr Dearborne the collector; & other gentlemen of the custom house;[36] & by the Navy-agent; and by the President of the Senate, who lives at Charlestown, near the hospital, & who knows every minute circumstance of the inquisition set on foot by the Government of the University. So that after induring that calumny four years, I have lived it down; & now stand without reproach even from my bitterest political & professional enemies.—My unpardonable offence is that of exposing the jesuitical practices of the Essex Junto; expostulating with the clergy for going contrary to that injunction of scripture which forbids them "to mix linnen with woolen";—or "to plough with an Ox & an ass."—

Our republican brethren in the South, and the West, have no conception of the disagreeable situation of some of the most independent Republicans in this "La Vendee"[37] of the U.S. The publication in the N. Eng^d Palladium signed "A Friend to Peace & Commerce," may serve to shew you how near some of us are to the brink of rebellion; and the public Spectacle of yesterday under the imposing & venerable name of Washington will not lessen this apprehension. I found myself constrained to combat this New Superstition in the Chronicle.

Although I know that this peninsula is no more to the whole of the U.S. than is a nest of catterpillars on the twig of an apple-tree, compared with the whole plant yet I cannot but feel anxious for the future. Every thing here has a military aspect, & a military tendency. Even the clergy "speak daggers." Every likely, enterprizing youth is seduced, or attempted to be seduced into this Washington Society; & this society is absolutely enrolling men, & raising money. They marchd through the Streets yesterday to the number of two thousand, including between two & three hundred children of the first families, ornamented with artificial flowers & the white rose of the insurgent house of York. To crown all, that political sky-rocket Josiah Quincy, choke-full of the wild-fire of British politics, harangu'd the people from the pulpit of the old South church an hour & an half, & in the most positive manner, & with the strongest emphasis called upon the people to unite in resisting the oppression of our government. Thus situated & circumstanced, a man past the period of bearing arms, & of a literary habit, & who wishes his children to maintain their integrity, & walk agreeably to their principles, would naturally desire to withdraw from such a people.

Some of my republican brethren say, that I must not quit my post; but stand at the avenue of public opinion, resting upon the printing-press. To this I answer, I have stood there, untill I am deprived of every thing but my children & family; and until I am now living upon the last remnants of my property. I still keep up the appearance of a man in easy circumstances, but it cannot be continued much longer.

Your friendly conduct towards me has encouraged me to be thus explicit. I have sent a pretty long narrative to the President relative to the hospital <u>intrigue</u>, in which I have rather restraind than indulged resentment towards Dr Eustis, the original author of my vexations, yet I could not bring myself to write these personal & private matters to the Supreme Magistrate of the American Nation; for I deem it improper. I have nevertheless hoped that I might do it to some other very distinguished person not in a public station. Mr Adams has spontaneously, and of his own accord written to President Madison respecting my peculiar situation; but I have never seen what he wrote. Mr Gerry has done the same. So has General King, & Mr Gray. I have therefore hoped that if I wrote to Mr Jefferson, he might in like manner address a line to Mr Madison, or if he chose, send this letter. My wish being to convey facts in a proper channel. But should my ideas, for I am unlearn't in the rules & etiquette of Governments, not comport with yours, I beg you to commit this letter to the flames, and excuse my impropriety; for I know not but that I have committed one.

Should the Executive think favourably of me as the <u>Physician</u> general, it would be gratifying to know that that great & good man Dr Fothergill gave me the following certificate just before I left Europe to return to my native country.

"To all whom it may concern—
The Bearer Dr Benjamin Waterhouse of Newport in Rhode Island, having been recommended by his Friends in America to my notice— these may certify that he has steadily, & diligently pursued his studies, under the ablest Professors, & Practitioners in Physick, at Edinburgh, in London, and at Leyden, during the course of seven years; and with so much success as to gain their esteem, & approbation—   Having been likewise a part of my family, for a considerable time (about three years) I can, from my own observation, recommend him to his fellow citizens in America, as one, who by the propriety of his moral conduct, his capacity, & proficiency in his studies, is likely to become highly useful in his station as a physician, an ornament to his profession, and a credit to his country."

JOHN FOTHERGILL.

London Novr 1780—

If I have taken too great a liberty pray be so good as to excuse it; and believe me to be with a high degree of respect, esteem & gratitude your steady friend   BENJ^N WATERHOUSE

P.S. I hope the character of Mr Gallatin by "<u>Sallust</u>," in the enclosed Patriot will meet your approbation.

RC (DLC); edge trimmed and chipped; endorsed by TJ as received 15 May 1813 and so recorded in SJL. FC (MBCo: Waterhouse Papers); in Waterhouse's hand; incomplete, consisting of first four pages; only the most important of numerous textual differences from the RC are recorded below; at head of text: "Thomas Jefferson." Enclosed in TJ to James Madison, 21 May 1813, and Madison to TJ, 6 June 1813. Enclosed newspaper articles described below.

Benjamin Rush informed John Adams on 16 Mar. 1813 that Waterhouse's SON, John Fothergill Waterhouse, had "passed his examination for a degree in our University with great honor, and that he will in a few weeks be created Doctor of Medicine" (Lyman H. Butterfield, *Letters of Benjamin Rush* [1951], 2:1190). LA VENDEE (Vendée), a department in western France, was the scene of a series of peasant insurrections against the Revolutionary's government, 1793–96. Waterhouse's ELDEST son was Andrew Oliver Waterhouse, the 2ᴰ was John Fothergill Waterhouse, the 3ᴰ was Daniel Oliver Waterhouse, and the FOURTH was Benjamin Waterhouse Jr. (Philip Cash, *Dr. Benjamin Waterhouse: A Life in Medicine and Public Service [1754–1846]* [2006], 397).

Waterhouse spoke out UNDER THE SIGNATURE OF 'A SHEPHERD' against the Washington Benevolent Societies, comparing their activities to those of Jesuit societies that had been expelled from Europe; asserting that the Washington societies sought "political division, wor[l]dly honors, and a wor[l]dly despotism"; condemning members of these societies for their singleminded devotion to George Washington and declaring that the honors showered upon him ought to "be divided between *S.* and *J. Adams, Hancock, Bowdoin, Jefferson, Madison, Jay, Clinton, Gens. Lincoln, Knox,* and a great many beside"; and arguing that if Washington were alive, he would "renounce and denounce" the tendency of these societies to seek out and encourage British influence (Boston *Independent Chronicle*, 29 Apr. 1813).

The man Waterhouse regarded as the CHAMPION of his enemies was probably Theophilus Parsons. In Roman mythology CACUS was a savage, fire-breathing monster (*OCD*, 267). The LATE SECRETARY AT WAR was William Eustis. A 28 Apr. 1813 petition drawn up and signed by sixteen of the MOST PROMINENT CHARACTERS IN CAMBRIDGE, CHARLESTOWN & BOSTON was enclosed in a letter Waterhouse sent to President James Madison on 1 May 1813 (Madison, *Papers, Pres. Ser.*, 6:273). Petitions to TJ of 9 and 13 Dec. 1807, the latter signed by JOHN BRAZER, had REMONSTRATED against Waterhouse's appointment as physician to the Marine Hospital (DNA: RG 59, LAR, 1801–09). The biblical admonitions against mixing LINNEN AND WOOLEN and plowing WITH AN OX & AN ASS are found in Leviticus 19.19 and Deuteronomy 22.10, respectively.

"A FRIEND TO PEACE & COMMERCE" argued in a letter to the editor of the Boston *New-England Palladium* published 30 Apr. 1813 that seaport towns had suffered from decreased commerce as a result of the current war while other parts of the country had not yet been injured economically; that commerce had a divine origin; that if Madison could be "induced to read the good book, and pay a little more attention to the natural rights of man, and principles of the 'social compact,' we should not experience so many evils which we are now compelled to endure"; that the southern states had an ample supply of food and fuel but that the overall decrease in commerce would harm the whole nation, because "Commerce is like the circulation of the blood—if you impede its course in any part the whole body is sure to feel the ill effects"; and that in the ensuing year legislators ought to unite in oppositon to the "mismanagement of those who have gone before them."

SPEAK DAGGERS quotes from William Shakespeare, *Hamlet*, act 3, scene 2. Waterhouse SENT A PRETTY LONG NARRATIVE TO THE PRESIDENT on 29 Apr. 1813 (Madison, *Papers, Pres. Ser.*, 6:251–64). John ADAMS wrote to Madison on Waterhouse's behalf on 2 Feb. 1813 (Madison,

Papers, Pres. Ser., 5:642–3). Elbridge GERRY wrote similarly to Madison on 20 May 1809 and 15 Aug. 1812 (Madison, *Papers, Pres. Ser.*, 1:194–6, 5:158–61). No letters on this subject have been found from GENERAL KING (possibly Cyrus King, a general in the Massachusetts militia and a Federalist recently elected to the United States House of Representatives), but William GRAY sent his recommendation of Waterhouse to Madison on 6 July 1813 (Madison, *Papers, Pres. Ser.*, 6:408).

In the *Boston Patriot*, 28 Apr. 1813, "SALLUST" defended Albert Gallatin against charges leveled at him in an "illiberal paragraph" recently published in the Boston *Centinel* wherein the author had questioned Gallatin's motives for accepting the position of minister to Russia and doubted his ability to negotiate peace there.

John Fothergill (1712–80), physician, received his medical degree at the University of Edinburgh in 1736 and began a practice in London in 1740. He took a keen interest in the science of botany and created an extensive botanical garden in Upton, Essex. Fothergill was an advocate for the American colonies, working to introduce there such plants as bamboo, coffee, and tea; authoring a pamphlet calling for repeal of the Stamp Act; and cooperating with Benjamin Franklin in drafting a scheme to reconcile the colonies with Great Britain. His most famous medical treatise, *An Account of the Sore Throat* (London, 1748), was the first recognition of diphtheria in England and included a clinical description and suggested treatments (*ODNB*).

[1] Word interlined in place of "April" in FC.

[2] FC substitutes "believe it will be" for preceding ten words.

[3] FC substitutes "my venerable" for preceding two words.

[4] Preceding two words not in FC.

[5] Word not in FC.

[6] FC: "without saying what; but it was intended as successor to Dr Rush, as."

[7] FC substitutes "of my son (who has already distinguished himself) to settle down in the practice of physic in Philadelphia" for preceding thirteen words.

[8] Preceding nine words not in FC.

[9] FC: "8 months."

[10] Preceding four words not in FC.

[11] Preceding two words not in FC.

[12] Word not in FC.

[13] Sentence not in FC.

[14] Sentence not in FC.

[15] FC here adds "As the Essex Junto have all the power, & all the patronage, I do not see how I can live much longer in this 'head quarters of (Hamilton's) good principles.'"

[16] FC: "vice."

[17] Preceding eleven words not in FC.

[18] Name not in FC.

[19] FC here adds "No federalist casts a friendly eye upon them. they must starve."

[20] FC substitutes "our young gentlemen of education have already done" for preceding seven words.

[21] FC here adds "a refinement of the old Jacobin clubs."

[22] Word not in FC.

[23] FC here adds "sallied out &."

[24] FC substitutes "I have done more" for preceding four words.

[25] FC here adds "dishonest acts &."

[26] Manuscript: "after After."

[27] Preceding five words not in FC.

[28] FC substitutes "whenever it shall" for preceding four words.

[29] FC here adds "The officers & the Surgeon of the Guierrere frigate made bitter complaints when their wounded men were brought into this port."

[30] For remainder of this sentence, FC substitutes "We never yet had a good medical system in any of our camps, & yet we are now following our old customs. As I have been broken up at Cambridge, & have been prevented from doing any thing of consequence in Boston, I am more at liberty for entering upon such a task as that of Physician general, than any other medical man of my years & standing among us."

[31] Sentence to this point not in FC.

[32] Word interlined.

[33] Manuscript: "before before."

[34] Preceding six words interlined. Paragraph to this point not in FC.

³⁵ Sentence not in FC.

³⁶ Remainder of FC reads "by the District attorney, & the Marshal, & by some others concerned in my removal from the hospital. They one & all say they acted under misinformation; and they all seem eager to repair the injury. They have seen that my bitterest political & professional enemies have never once reproached me for any misconduct in the hospital because my enemies have themselves investigated it.— My."

³⁷ Omitted closing quotation mark editorially supplied.

From Louis Philippe Gallot de Lormerie

MONSIEUR   Philadᵃ 3. Avril [ca. 2 May] 1813.—

J'ai reçu derniérement la Lettre dont vous m'avés honoré; et Je metois imposé la loi de ne plus troubler du tout un repos que vous paroissés désirer, et que votre âge et dé longs, utiles, et illustres travaux vous ont Si justement mérité.

Mais l'interest que vous avés bien voulu prendre a mon retour paisible en france et la démarche que vous avés Eu la bonté de faire pour moi a cet ègard auprès de Mʳ munroë me font un devoir indispensable de vous instruire d'un nouveau Succés dans cette affaire.—Jai veillé attentivement comme vous me l'aviès conseillé, et ayant appris par les papiers publies la résignation de M crawford de sa place au sènat ce qui annonçoit Son prochain dèpart, j'ai Ecrit a Washington city a notre Ministre plenipʳᵉ (qui par ses 2 dᵉʳᵉˢ Lettres me témoigne beaucoup d'intérest) pour le prier de rapeller a M. Le secrètaire dEtat la promesse qu'il vous avoit faite en août dᵉʳ en ma faveur. ce ministre m'a répondu hier très Obligeamment sous la date du 29 dᵉʳ qu'il s'est Entretenu de ma demande avec Mʳ munroë en lui faisant part de mon Offre d'être utile a M.C. pendᵗ son passage pour le perfectionner dans notre Langue dont Je puis lui donner autant de Secors qu'il desirera. <u>M Le secrétaire d'etat a trouvé cet arrangement désirable pour tous deux</u>, et <u>n'y voit aucun Obstacle</u>. il a tèmoigne seulement le desir de le soumettre a M C. et M sérurier a la bonte de terminer sa Lettre en me disont "qu'<u>a larrivée de L'ambassadeur, qu'on <u>dit être prochaine, a washington, il <u>se fera un plaisir de me recommander lui même a ce ministre</u>"

J'ai cru vous devoir, Monsieur, a tous ègards ces détails consolans. J'ai promis toute la discrètion qu'on Exigeroit mais pour vous qui connoissés Laffaire dès le principe il ne doit point y avoir de secret.— il est vraisemblable que m crawford ne partira pas sans vous Voir ou sans communiquer avec vous par lettre s'il en est Eloigné. auriés vous la bonté de mettre la derniere main a votre beinveillant Ouvrâge, en me recommandant a lui, et alors je ne doute plus du Succés.

Jai l'honneur de vous assurer de ma trés respectueuse reconnoissance   DE LORMERIE

Ps Si le Navire qui doit transporter M. C. en france partoit de philadelphie comme le Neptune qui porte MM Gallatin & bayard a s^t pètersbourg, ce seroit une G^{de} Economie de tems, & de transport, et de bagages pour ce ministre et pour moi. les hostilités en maryland ne permettant guères de Sy Embarquer, et la route dicy a N: york etant Excessivement mauvaise par le transport continuel des marchandises de & pour cette ville.

Si nèammois il jugeoit necessaire de partir de N. york il seroit bien a dèsirer que j'en fusse informé d'avance afin d'avoir le tems dy faire transporter les malles contenant les Livres a mon usage et les Caisses destinées pour notre Museum impèrial

c'est pourquoi sans vous donner la peine de m'Ecrire veuillé avoir la bonté de Charger quelq'un exact & sur de s'informer et me faire Savoir de suite le port & l'Epoque d'Embarquement de m crawford afin que je puisse prendre mes mesures en Consequence ce seroit ajouter beaucoup a toute la reconnoissance que je vous dois

il ne seroit pas sans douté inutile d'observer a M crawford que je puis lui être utile non Se[ulem]ent pour la langue française mais aussi pour sa Santé ên mer. me[s] Etu[des et] des observations constantes en mèdeçine me rendront Secourables [...] en cas de maladies ou d'accidens. J'indiquerai si l'on veut sen rapporter a moi la composition d'une petite pharmaçie peu compliquée et Suffisante dans presque tous les Cas d'un Voyâge: Je purifierais par un procède chimique Simple l'Eau la plus corrompue et si l'on veut faire preparer les Barriques suiv^t une méthode prouvée Exçellente par l'Expérience de Longs voÿages en mer Jamais elle ne se Corrompra.

Je Connois un autre procedé chimique pour préparer du Lait tellement qu'il se peut Conserver plusieurs mois sans jamais S'aigrir même a la mer; moÿen bien prèferable a celui dEmbarquer une Vache ou chèvre parceque ces animaux peuvent périr dans un Vaisseau surtout au printems par le besoin de pâture et sa privation se fait sentir a Eux au point de les rendre malades et au moins d'altèrer la qualité de leur lait.

Enfin je Connois un moÿen Sinon de prevenir, au moins d'adoucir considérablement les Effets terribles du mal de mer et de retablir lEstomach fatigué par les Efforts qu'il occasionne et lagitation du Sistême nerveux. Je n'Exige aucuns honoraires pour tous ces Services, si ce n'est mon passâge seulem^t et celui de mes Effets.

EDITORS' TRANSLATION

SIR   Philadelphia 3. April [ca. 2 May] 1813.—
I recently received the letter with which you honored me. I had imposed on myself a rule against troubling a repose that you seem to desire and so justly deserve because of your age and your extensive, useful, and illustrious achievements.

But the interest you were so kind as to take in my peaceful return to France and the steps you had the goodness to take on my behalf with Mr. Monroe make it my indispensable duty to inform you of a recent success in this affair.—I have been alert, as you had advised me to be, and having learned through published papers of Mr. Crawford's resignation from his seat in the Senate and his impending departure, I wrote to our minister plenipotentiary in Washington City (who in his last two letters had taken a great interest in me), to ask him to remind the secretary of state of his promise to you last August to help me. This minister replied to me yesterday very obligingly with a letter dated the 29th of last month, saying that he has discussed the request I had addressed to Mr. Monroe and informed him of my offer to make myself useful to Mr. Crawford during his passage by helping him to perfect his knowledge of our language. In this I can give him as much assistance as he desires. The secretary of state found this arrangement desirable for both of us, and saw no obstacle to it. He only expressed his desire that it be submitted to Mr. Crawford and Mr. Sérurier, and he is kind enough to end his letter by telling me "that upon the Ambassador's arrival in Washington, which is said to be imminent, it will be his pleasure to recommend me to this minister himself"

I believed it to be my duty, Sir, to inform you of these details, which are comforting in every respect. I promised to be as discreet as necessary, but as you have followed this affair from the beginning, nothing must be kept secret from you.—Mr. Crawford is unlikely to leave without seeing you or communicating with you by letter if he is far away. Would you be so kind as to put the finishing touches on your friendly work, by recommending me to him? Then I will have no doubt of success.

I have the honor to assure you of my very respectful gratitude
                                                      DE LORMERIE

PS If the ship that will transport Mr. Crawford to France were to leave from Philadelphia, as will the *Neptune*, which carries Mr. Gallatin and Mr. Bayard to Saint Petersburg, it would save that minister and myself a lot of time and transportation costs for ourselves and our luggage. The hostilities in Maryland do not permit us to embark there, and the road from this place to New York is excessively bad because merchandise is constantly transported to and from that town.

However, should he deem it necessary to leave from New York, advance notice would be very desirable for me so as to give me time to have the trunks containing my books and the boxes destined for our imperial museum sent there

Therefore, without troubling to write me, please be so kind as to instruct someone accurate and trustworthy to find out and inform me immediately of the port and time of Mr. Crawford's embarkation so that I can take the appropriate measures. This would greatly increase my debt of gratitude to you

Mr. Crawford should be assured that I can be useful to him with regard not only to the French language but also concerning his health at sea. My studies and constant medical observations will enable me to help in the event of sickness or accident. I will advise him, if he decides to rely on me, on the composition of a small, uncomplicated medicine chest, which would suffice for almost any problem that might arise during a trip: by means of a simple chemical process I will purify the most tainted water, and if he is willing to have large barrels prepared according to a method proven excellent on long sea voyages, the water will never spoil.

I know of another chemical procedure that preserves milk for several months without its ever turning sour, even while at sea; this method is much preferable to taking a cow or goat on board, because these animals can perish on a ship, especially in the spring, when the absence of pasture can make them sick or, at least, alter the quality of their milk.

Finally, I know how to prevent or, at least, considerably reduce the terrible effects of seasickness and cure stomachs fatigued by the stress it causes and the agitation to the nervous system. I demand no honorarium for all these services, only my passage and the transportation of my belongings.

RC (DLC: TJ Papers, 198:35186–7); misdated by Lormerie with the date of the TJ letter to which he was replying; torn at seal; addressed: "The honourable Thomas Jefferson Esqr late president of the U.S Monticello"; franked; postmarked Philadelphia, 2 May; endorsed by TJ as received 15 May 1813 and so recorded in SJL. Translation by Dr. Genevieve Moene.

President James Madison commissioned William H. CRAWFORD as minister plenipotentiary to France on 9 Apr. 1813. The United States Senate received Crawford's nomination on 27 May and confirmed him the next day (*Annals*, 13th Cong., 2d sess., 242, 243; *JEP*, 2:346). Louis Barbé Charles SÉRURIER was the French minister to the United States. In April Madison had appointed Albert GALLATIN, James A. BAYARD, and John Quincy Adams as envoys to negotiate a peace and commercial treaty with Great Britain and a commercial treaty with Russia. On 16 June 1813 the Senate refused by a twenty-to-fourteen margin to confirm Gallatin, concluding that the treasury secretary could not accept a concurrent diplomatic appointment without risking a conflict of interest (Madison, *Papers, Pres. Ser.*, 6:491–4; *Extract from the Executive Record, Comprehending the Messages of the President of the United States in Relation to the nominations of Albert Gallatin, John Q. Adams, and James A. Bayard . . . with the proceedings of the Senate thereon* [Washington, 1813]; *JEP*, 2:355).

From Patrick Gibson

SIR   Richmond 4ᵗʰ May 1813

I wrote to you by last mail, inclosing for your signature and that of Mʳ Randolph a bill of Sale for Mazzei's two lots, which deed you will observe has been drawn by Mʳ Marshall upon the presumption that Mʳ Mazzei is a citizen of the U. States, of this fact however Mʳ Taylor will be obliged to you for information as upon that alone depends the validity of the transfer—Having been offer'd 6$ cash for flour I was induced to make a sale, in which I have included rather more than the half of yours say 195 bls: Sʳf: 23 fine 1 str: & 2 cross middlings leaving on hand 200 bls: of Sʳfine—Mʳ Randolph has paid me $805.12 on your account—with great respect

Your obᵗ Servᵗ   PATᴷ GIBSON

RC (ViU: TJP-ER); at head of text: "Thomas Jefferson Esqʳᵉ"; endorsed by TJ as received 15 May 1813 and so recorded in SJL.

Philip Mazzei became a naturalized Virginia CITIZEN in 1774 (Richard Cecil Garlick Jr., *Philip Mazzei, Friend of Jefferson: His Life and Letters* [1933], 42). sᴿF: "superfine." STR: "struck."

To Charles Clay

TH. J. TO MR. CLAY   Thursday morning, May 6, 1813.

Our spinning machine is in operation, and a piece of cloth is begun with the flying shuttle, neither goes on perfectly as yet, from the want of a little more practice; but they will give Mrs. Clay an idea of what would be their proper operation, if she can do me the favor to come and take a plantation dinner with me tomorrow. You will come of course, according to promise. Friendly salutations and assurances of respect.

Printed Tr (clipping from unidentified newspaper owned by ViCMRL, on deposit ViU: TJP); dateline beneath closing. Not recorded in SJL.

To Martha Jefferson Randolph

Poplar Forest. May 6. 13.

We arrived here, my dear Martha, well & without accident, favored on the road by the weather. the caravan also came well, except overpassing their stage the 2ᵈ day, sleeping in the woods all night, without cover, and overwhelmed by a rain, in the center of which they were, while it did not extend 5 miles in any direction from them. the spinning Jenny is at work, well while with washed cotton, but very ill when with unwashed. at least this is Maria's way of accounting for the occasional difference of it's work. the flying shuttle began a little yesterday, but owing to a variety of fixings which the loom required it exhibited very poorly. we hope to see it do better to-day. I am afraid I shall be detained here in getting Perry off before I go away. if I leave him here I shall have no confidence in his following me. still I shall not fail to be at home within a week or ten days from this date. present me affectionately to mr Randolph and our beloved children, if Ellen will permit herself to be included under that appellation, and be assured yourself of all my love and tenderness.

TH: JEFFERSON

RC (NNPM); at foot of text: "Mrs Randolph." PoC (MHi); endorsed by TJ.

From William DuVal

DEAR SIR   Richmond May 7th 1813

I received your favor of the 20th of April last in which you express a desire to obtain from the Henderson Family a conveyance for the Land you bought of them under a Contract made by their mother and Guardian; that you want some Friend in Kentucky to act for you & obtain a Title—My Son William P. DuVal lives in Bairds Town, about Forty Five Miles from Shelbyville. It would afford him Pleasure to render you any Service in his Power. I expect he will be at my House (in a Week) on his way to congress. How long he may be detained there is uncertain—He will write to you—[1]

I have a Brother by Affinity, Col° Christopher Greenup, who lives in Frankfort, about Fifteen Miles from Shelbyville, who would chearfully, I do believe, render you any Service in his Power. You may recollect him, he was in Congress about the time you were first called to represent the Nation as their Chief Magistrate. I have often heard him speak of you in Terms, which expressed his sincere Attachment for you—I was at his House in Frankfort in 1787. he then was Governour of that State, he was then your warm Friend. He was a Man of diligence & well acquainted with writing Deeds &^c—If you write to him, I think it would afford him Pleasure to serve you—Mr Hawkins who lives near Lexington has promised to call at Monticello & deliver your Letter to Mr Greenup

I have had the satisfaction of knowing you for near half an Century

The Lord has preserved you to be a blessing to your Country and the Friend of Liberty and of Virtue.

May that gracious God direct us and preserve us in our Journey Thro' Life—We know from Experience, that to love God and Man, are the two great Commandments, which afford that inward Peace, and tranquility, which The World cannot give, or take from us—

 With the Highest Respect & Esteem

I am D^r sir Yr. mo. ob^t Servt   WILLIAM DUVAL

RC (MHi); endorsed by TJ as received 18 May 1813. Mistakenly recorded in SJL as a letter of 18 May received on that date.

[1] Sentence interlined.

From Edmund Randolph

      Avon hill near Charleston Jefferson county

DEAR SIR   Virginia May 8. 1813

Immediately upon my receipt of your request to execute a deed for Mr Mazzei's property in Richmond, I announced my readiness to sign any instrument, which you might forward to me. Not having heard from you since, I suspect, that my letter has miscarried, and now therefore repeat it.

I am reached here sooner with letters by the way of Alexandria, than through any other channel of conveyance.

I am dear sir

with the highest respect Your friend & Serv.

         EDM: RANDOLPH

RC (MHi); at foot of text: "Thomas Jefferson Monticello"; endorsed by TJ as received 21 May 1813 and so recorded in SJL.

Edmund Randolph (1753–1813), attorney and public official, was the son of Virginia attorney general John Randolph (ca. 1727–1784). He studied at the College of William and Mary before reading law with his father, but the family was split during the American Revolution when his Loyalist parents moved to England. Randolph remained in Virginia with his patriot uncle Peyton Randolph. In 1775 Randolph briefly joined the Continental army as an aide to General George Washington, and the following year he became the youngest delegate to the Virginia Convention of 1776, where he helped to draft the Virginia Declaration of Rights and the new state constitution and was elected as the commonwealth's first attorney general after independence. He served in the Continental Congress in 1779 and 1781 and as governor of Virginia, 1786–88. Randolph was a delegate to the Federal Convention of 1787 in Philadelphia, where he introduced the Virginia plan for elective representation. Fearing that the executive had been made too strong, he refused to sign the final version of the new United States Constitution, but he supported the document at the Virginia Ratification Convention of 1788. Randolph served as the first

United States attorney general, 1789–94, and succeeded TJ to become the second secretary of state, 1794–95. His opposition to the Jay Treaty and the probably unfounded suspicion that he had leaked sensitive information to French minister Joseph Fauchet undermined his relationship with President Washington. Randolph accordingly submitted his resignation, published a defense of his actions, and returned to practicing law in Richmond. He published an abridgment of Virginia law in 1796, successfully defended Aaron Burr during the latter's 1807 treason trial, and in 1811 completed a history of Virginia, the surviving portions of which were first published after his death.

Randolph's final years were clouded by a massive personal debt and by declining health due to paralysis. His relationship with TJ had begun by 1774, when he took over the latter's unfinished cases after TJ retired from the law (*ANB*; *DAB*; John J. Reardon, *Edmund Randolph: A Biography* [1974]; *PTJ*, esp. 1:243–4, 26:652–3, 28:565–7; John M. Hemphill II, "Edmund Randolph Assumes Thomas Jefferson's Practice," *VMHB* 67 [1959]: 170–1; Leonard, *General Assembly*; Richmond *Enquirer*, 17 Sept. 1813).

TJ had received Randolph's earlier, undated LETTER on 26 Mar. 1813 (TJ to Patrick Gibson, 29 Mar. 1813, and note).

From Richard Fitzhugh

DEAR SIR   Ravensworth May 9th 1813

I send you agreeable to your request a few of the Ravensworth pea, and am sorry that the mode of conveyance will not admit of my sending you a larger quantity—however perhaps it will be in my power to send by M[r] Eppes, when he returns from Congress about half bushel—if you think he can convey them to you, please to write to me—I have not the pleasure of a personal acquantance with M[r] Eppes, therefore should thank you for a letter of introduction to him—my late ill health and my retirement from the world, prevented my regular inqueery at the post office, consequently your letter remained Several days before I rec[d] it—It would give me singular pleasure to see you at my House once more—if not, pray let me hear from you whenever it may be convenient for you to write—M[rs] Fitzhugh and all my family join in compliments to you, I pray you to accept of my best wishes for your health and happiness—and believe me to be your Sincere friend   RICH[D] FITZHUGH

RC (MHi); endorsed by TJ as received 21 May 1813 and so recorded in SJL.

To Robert Richardson

SIR   Poplar Forest May 10. 13.

Your letter informing me of the delivery of the iron backs at Lynchburg, was duly recieved, and they are now here. I ought sooner to have made the remittance to mr Ross as the letter desired, & I counted on surely doing. but I am one of the unfortunate whose crop of wheat not having been ground and at market in the early season, has been blockaded in Richmond, where I have now between 4. & 500. barrels of flour, & not a single one sold. I instructed my merchant there to hold it up for 7.D thro' the month of April, & then sell for whatever he could get. so that I suppose he will be able to make something of it this month. as soon as he does the paiment for the backs shall be immediately made. Accept this apology for the unavoidable delay with the tender of my best wishes & respects.

TH: JEFFERSON

PoC (MHi); at foot of text: "Mr Richardson"; endorsed by TJ.

Richardson presumably announced the DELIVERY OF THE IRON BACKS AT LYNCHBURG in an undated, missing letter recorded in SJL as received 10 Feb. 1813 from the Oxford Iron Works.

To Elizabeth Trist

DEAR MADAM   Poplar forest May 10. 13.

I brought the inclosed book to this place, the last fall, intending to forward it to you; but having a neighbor here who loves to laugh, I lent it to him to read; he lent it to another, and so it went the rounds of the neighborhood and is returned to me at my Spring visit to this place. I now forward it, and if it diverts you for an hour or two, I shall be gratified by it. I was myself amused by it's humor as much as it's object would permit me to be; for that is evidently to deride the republican branches of our government.   I left all well at Monticello, except Benjamin whose health is very precarious. Lewis is become the favorite of all. his vivacity, his intelligence, & his beauty (for the mark in his forehead is disappearing) make him a perfect pet. you will perceive from these senile details of the nursery that I am becoming old. I wish I had no other proofs. but I am weakening very sensibly. I can walk no further than my garden. I ride however, and in a carriage can come here without fatigue.

I fear however this will not long be the case. your friends mr & mrs Divers, tho' they think themselves getting crazy, are in better health than usual. I am hastening back to their first pea-dinner, but I think I shall be too late. in your Southern situation I presume you have them now. Mr Randolph has been siesed with the military fever. he expects to be called to his regiment at Blackrock this month. he will be a great loss to his family, and no man in the world a greater one to his affairs. the loss of our old friend Dr Rush you will have heard & regretted as all must who knew him. Accept the assurance of my constant & sincere friendship and respect, with a tender of my devoirs to mrs & mr Gilmer   TH: JEFFERSON

PoC (MoSHi: TJC); at foot of text: "Mrs Trist"; endorsed by TJ. Enclosure: James Kirke Paulding, *The Diverting History of John Bull and Brother Jonathan. By Hector Bull-us* (New York, 1812).

BENJAMIN and LEWIS were TJ's grandsons Benjamin F. Randolph and Meriwether Lewis Randolph. The village of BLACKROCK (Black Rock), New York, is now a part of the city of Buffalo.

From John Winn

SIR   Charlottesville May 10th 1813
    I am in want of about 3 pounds of white Lead which is not to be had in this place at present, if you have it & Can spare that quantity I will be very much Obliged to you & will either pay you for it or return it as you may wish, I am Sir
    Respectfulley Your Ob. Sert   JOHN WINN J[R]

RC (MHi); edge trimmed; addressed (one word illegible): "Thomas Jefferson esqr Monticello ⅌ M^r [Buney]"; endorsed by TJ as received 16 May 1813 and so recorded in SJL.

On 3 June 1813 TJ directed Edmund Bacon to pay $35.74 on his store account with Winn's firm, Wayt & Winn (*MB*, 2:1289).

From Charles Clay

DEAR SIR,   May 13.—13
    this Afternoon, Mr Joseph Gilmore Called on me with a letter from Col: T. M. Randolph, who write me he was Just about Setting out for Canada, in his letter to me on particular business of our own he enclosed a couple of Reciepts for Money ($1,111.78) by him paid to Messrs Gibson & Jefferson in Richmond for your use & disposial, his Reasons for sending them forward were that he did not know but you might want to make some disposition of the money immediately from Bedford where he expected you would Recieve them from me before you left this, he calculated to be certainly gone before your Return to Albemarle, as you[1] were off this Morning, I had no alternative but by the post or enclosed again by Mr Gilmore, I prefered the latter mode

[111]

as thinking it the Safest, especially as he promises to wait on you immediately on his Return at Monticello

exept Assureances of my high Respect & most friendly dispositions

C. CLAY

RC (MHi); at foot of text: "Th. Jefferson Esqre"; endorsed by TJ as received 15 May 1813 and so recorded in SJL.

The RECIEPTS have not been found.

[1] Manuscript: "your."

From William Cocke

DEAR SIR   Rutledge Grainger County 15th May 1813

Your much esteem[d] favour of the 17th of april Containing the fullest evidence that you still Recollect and appriceate my best endeavours to serve my Country has been Received with all that heart felt satisfaction which true friendship inspire. I may truly be call[d] the trenk of the times except that nothing Can ever change my Determination for a moment to be of all the service in my power to my Country: I hear with the greatest pleasure that M[r] John Randlph has lost his election and that our mutual friend M[r] Epps Succeeds him numerous as my Days are my hart still pants for Glory and two of my sons one the majour Gen[l] of East Tennessee and a nother Cap[t] of a troop of horse accompanied me to East Florida where I had the pleasure[1] to see them both in the Ranks as Volunteer Citizen soldiers and to be an eye witness that they did their duty in the hour of danger the most Romantick accounts of ancient shevalry does little surpass the Valor exhibited in the Lochway towns by my Gallant Comrades in that most dangerous & fortunate interprise they will be always dear as my children to me my Loss of M[rs] Cocke and the shamefull Surrender of Gen[l] Hull determined me to take an active part & once more to march to meet the enimys of my Country this Determination[2] I expreessed in a charge at sparta and may be seen in a paper published at Nashville Call[d] the whig I have proven my sincerity by my actions Toreys still hate me and most of the Federallists dispise me yet I still Glory in being what you know me to be and although I am Giting old I injoy Good health and a desire still to be usefull Yours most sinceerly   W[M] COCKE

RC (MHi); endorsed by TJ as received 27 May 1813 and so recorded in SJL.

In calling himself the TRENK OF THE TIMES, Cocke recalled Baron Frederic

Trenck (1726–94), a Prussian soldier and adventurer whose life included a love affair with the sister of the Prussian king Frederick II, numerous imprisonments, and ultimately execution at the behest of the French revolutionary leader Maximilien Robespierre. Trenck's autobiography was first published in German in 1787 and later translated into French and English. While he was in Paris, TJ purchased the French translation, *La vie de Frederic, Baron de Trenck*, 3 vols. (Paris, 1788; TJ's 1789 Book Catalog [MHi], 6). The LOCHWAY TOWNS were East Florida Seminole Indian settlements in the Alachua country west of the Saint

Johns River. In September 1812 a group of Georgia militia volunteers under the command of Colonel Daniel Newnan raided these villages (Stagg, *Borderlines in Borderlands*, 126–9; Henry M. Brackenridge, *History of the Late War between the United States and Great-Britain* [Baltimore, 1816], 95–6).

[1] Manuscript: "pleasue."
[2] Manuscript: "Detemination."

From Thomas Lehré

DEAR SIR   Charleston May 15th 1813

I have just been informed that the Federal Marshal of this District, has resigned his office, in consequence of which, the President, I presume, will make an early appointment of a succeessor—Permit me Sir, to solicit your friendship as early as possible upon the occasion. I remain with the highest respect

Dear Sir Your Most Obedient and Very Humble Servant.

THOMAS LEHRÉ

RC (DLC); at foot of text: "Thomas Jefferson late P. U. States Washingtn"; endorsed by TJ as received 28 May 1813 and so recorded in SJL.

Two weeks later President James Madison named Morton A. Waring to re-

place Robert E. Cochran, the FEDERAL MARSHAL for South Carolina. Lehré in turn was appointed to succeed Waring as federal commissioner of loans for the same district (*JEP*, 2:160, 161, 347, 348, 396, 401 [9, 10 Jan. 1811, 29 May, 1 June, 24, 27 July 1813]).

From Patrick Gibson

SIR   Richmond 17th May 1813—

I wrote you on the 28th of last month, inclosing a deed of Sale for Mazzeis property, and also a note for your signature to renew the one in bank due 25/28th Ins[t] and on the 4th Ins[t] I inform'd you that I had sold 221 bls: of your flour at 6$ S[r]fine—not having had the pleasure of hearing from you in reply, I am induced to believe you must have set out for Bedford, before these letters reach'd Monticello and as it is probable you may not return so as to forward the note in time for renewal, I send you one here inclosed, which I hope will be received in course—Flour dull—at 5½$ With great respect I am   Your ob[t] Serv[t]   PATRICK GIBSON

RC (MHi); at head of text: "Thomas Jefferson Esqre"; at foot of text: "Poplar Forest Bedford"; endorsed by TJ as a letter from Gibson & Jefferson received 26 May 1813 and so recorded in SJL. Enclosure not found.

From Hugh Holmes

DEAR SIR   Winch^r May 17th 1813

Since my return to this place I have procured and now enclose a reciept from One of Our manufacturers for washing merino wool

If you have determined to prepare y^r merino wool at home for the loom this reciept will be usefull—The filling ought to be spun with a $\times$ band and but slightly twisted—If however you should prefer Our management of the fabrick ab initio and will send the wool in its unwashed state by the stage addressed to me I will with much pleasure have the whole work executed for you—Or you may send me the yarn or web which will lessen the bulk weight & price of carriage and in either case I will have the work completed—a navy blue can be dyed here, but not the best blue, at least they are not in the practice of dying the best blue by reason of the increased expence which few are willing to pay—the difference of price between the best blue & any other colour is said to be 6/— per y^d—if I can render you a service sir in this business, let me repeat the assurance of my readiness to do so with pleasure—

y^r friend   H^H HOLMES

PS. Mr Divers y^r neighbour wishes to see the Reciept   H H

RC (MHi); endorsed by TJ as received 4 June 1813 and so recorded in SJL. Enclosure not found.

Hugh Holmes (1768–1825), judge and farmer, was a native of York County, Pennsylvania, who attended the College of William and Mary, studied law, and became an attorney in Winchester. He was mayor of Winchester in 1795, and he represented a district consisting of Berkeley, Frederick, Hampshire, and Hardy counties in the Senate of Virginia, 1795–99. Holmes was a presidential elector for TJ in 1800. He represented Frederick County in the House of Delegates, 1802–05, with service as Speaker, 1803–05. Resigning his seat to accept a judgeship on the General Court, he held that post until

his death. Holmes had a keen interest in agricultural improvements, wrote on the subject of stone fences in 1820, and was elected the same year to honorary membership in the Agricultural Society of Albemarle. In 1824 he chaired a citizens' committee in support of a national turnpike projected to run through Frederick County (Garland R. Quarles, *Some Worthy Lives; Mini-Biographies, Winchester and Frederick County* [1988], 127–8; ViWn: Hugh Holmes Records; Holmes to TJ, 17 Dec. 1801 [DNA: RG 59, LAR, 1801–09]; *William and Mary Provisional List*, 22; Leonard, *General Assembly*; Staunton *Political Mirror*, 3 June 1800; *JHD*, 1805 sess., 10, 11, 12 [6, 7 Dec. 1805]; Baltimore *American Farmer*, 10 Mar. 1820; Washington *Daily National*

Intelligencer, 21 Oct. 1824; True, "Agricultural Society," 288; *Richmond Enquirer*, 1 Feb. 1825; Frederick Co. Will Book, 12:346–7, 15:190–2).

✕ BAND: "cross band" is yarn with a warp or left-hand twist (Louis Harmuth, *Dictionary of Textiles* [1915], 48).

To Edmund Randolph

DEAR SIR   Monticello May 17. 13.

The sale of Mazzei's lots is at length concluded and the purchaser having deemed it necessary for me also to sign the deed as co-attorney with yourself, altho' by a separate instrument, which being special did not revoke the power given to you, I have not hesitated to do so. I now forward it for your signature, and as that must be certified by some court, I must ask the favor of you to execute it before such witnesses as will be sure to attend a court, presuming it may be inconvenient to you to attend yourself. still I must request you to have the goodness to get it back from the clerk with the proper certificate, and to re-inclose it to me, as I shall have to acknolege it before our court, which being three weeks distant I have thought it best in the mean time to send it on to you. with every wish for your health & happiness, accept the assurance of my continued esteem & respect

TH: JEFFERSON

PoC (MHi); at foot of text: "Edmund Randolph esq."; endorsed by TJ. Enclosure not found.

The PURCHASER was Thomas Taylor.

To John Vaughan

DEAR SIR   Monticello May 17. 13.

On my return from a journey after an absence of three weeks, I found here the roll of diplomas which you had forwarded: and have made it my first duty to sign them, and return them by our first mail. hoping they will get safe to hand I avail myself of the occasion of assuring you of my friendship & respect.   TH: JEFFERSON

PoC (MHi); at foot of text: "John Vaughan esq."; endorsed by TJ.

TJ returned signed American Philosophical Society membership DIPLOMAS, specimens of which include that of Nicholas Biddle, 16 Apr. 1813, cited

above at Biddle to TJ, 12 Dec. 1809, the ornithologist Alexander Wilson, 16 Apr. 1813 (MS in NjMoHP: Lloyd W. Smith Collection; printed form with blanks filled in; signed by TJ and seven other APS officers), and Rev. James P. Wilson, 15 Apr. 1814 (MS in PPAmP: APS

Archives, Manuscript Communications; printed form with blanks filled in; signed by TJ and seven other APS officers). The Biddle certificate is reproduced elsewhere in this volume.

From James P. Cocke

DEAR SIR   May 18th 1813

Untill within a few days past we have not been able to procure the chub fish, If you will send on thursday next a ceareful hand prepaired for there conveyance, I have little doubt but the nesessary supply for your pond can be made which will give pleasure to your friend & Hble sert—   J P COCKE

P.S.

Growth of the chub, at 1 year old 8 to 9 Ins long, at 2–11 to 12— 3–15 to 16—the weight not assertained but suppose the latter at 3 to $3\frac{1}{2}$ lbs—

RC (DLC); endorsed by TJ as received 21 May 1813 and so recorded in SJL.

To Patrick Gibson

DEAR SIR   Monticello. May 20. 13.

On my return from Bedford I found here your two letters of Apr. 28. & May 4. I now inclose the note for 4300.D. signed. the deed to mr Taylor I immediately executed and forwarded to mr Randolph: but as the mail is slow between this & his residence, and it is to be acknoleged by him in his court and by me in mine, this will occupy time. but it will be all done & delivered before the 1st paiment falls due. my signature was on the 17th inst. you recollect I wrote to you on the subject of a particular power of Attorney to me to sell these lots, & I thought I must have sent it to mr Jefferson, because I could not find it among my papers. a very accidental circumstance discovered to me where it had been mislaid. this being after I had sent you the statement of the title, & mr Marshal having drawn his deed according to that statement, I had to alter the date of the power of attorney to me conformably to the last one; of which finding duplicates together, I send you one to be delivered to mr Taylor. still I think it best that the deed should be executed by mr Randolph as well as myself, because his power of Attorney is on the records & mine not.

I am glad you have sold a part of my flour, altho the price be low. but better secure that than lose all. I am in hopes you will be able to sell the rest, and if for a better price, so much the better. the short price in comparison with what had been given & counted on by me will sensibly affect me in my contracts, in amount as well as time. I have generally made my contracts paiable in March & April on the presumption of a sale before that time. the present delay has occasioned some of them to press on me sorely. I am therefore obliged to avail myself of it as soon as I know you have a balance in hand. I must request you therefore to remit for me to John Barnes of Georgetown Columbia 540. Dollars: to Thomas[1] Voight watchmaker of Philadelphia 115. D 50 C and to Nicholas G. Dufief bookseller of the same place 40. Dollars: these being the most pressing calls.   I must also request of you to send me another quarter hundred of powder. but if it is possible to get it any where else, than where the two last were purchased, do so. I have the eprouvette used in our war department for proving powder. Dupont's carries that to 27. however 22. or 23. is recievable at the war office. the common store powder is from 13. down to 9. I never saw any lower than 9. the first barrel you sent me was at 9. the last at 7. it is not merely the difference in quantity which might be thought requisite to make up the difference of force: but in boring rock, even if you were to treble the size of the hole, & of course the expence of boring, yet such a quantity of powder would not all kindle, but be blown out unburnt. but this weak powder cannot force out more of the rock than barely spoils the hole bored. I had been informed that Burr's powder was even stronger than Dupont's, which was the reason of my naming that to you in a former letter. Accept the assurance of my friendship and respect   TH: JEFFERSON

PoC (DLC); at foot of first page: "Mʳ Gibson." Enclosures not found.

For Philip Mazzei's POWER OF ATTORNEY to TJ and Edmund Randolph, see enclosure to Mazzei to TJ, 15 Feb. 1811,

and note. An EPROUVETTE is an instrument used to test the strength of gunpowder (OED).

[1] Word interlined in place of "Henry."

To Thomas Voigt

DEAR SIR   Monticello May 20. 13.

On my return from a journey after an absence of 3. weeks I found here mr Patterson's letter of Apr. 24. covering your bill for the clock, amount 115. D 50 C, and I have this day desired messʳˢ Gibson & Jefferson of Richmond, my correspondents there, to remit you that sum immediately, which I hope will get safe to hand. mr Patterson writes me you will keep in mind my recommendation of Charlottesville to any young man of skill who may want a station for his business.   could a gold watch, good, and moderately ornamented for a lady, be now got in Philadelphia, for a moderate price, say from 80. to 100.D.? accept the assurance of my esteem & respect.

TH: JEFFERSON

PoC (MHi); at foot of text: "Mr Thos Voigt"; endorsed by TJ.

To John Barnes

DEAR SIR   Monticello May 21. 13.

On my return from Bedford I found here your two favors of Apr. 29. and I now return you mr Williams's letter which was inclosed in one of them. I should think it adviseable to delay the annual remittance awhile for the expected return of the vessel from Bordeaux, by which you may learn if the General approves of the channel we proposed; in the mean time, that there may be no delay on my part, I have sacrificed enough of my flour at 6.D. to have remitted to you 540.D. which by a letter of yesterday I desired mess^{rs} Gibson & Jefferson to do. 360.D. of this is for the General, and the rest to pay up my balance to you, which if I calculate rightly will be some trifle under the sum remitted you. in this case I would ask the favor of you to get mr Milligan to inclose me by mail Gardiner & Hepburn's book on gardening and to pay him for it. I owe you apologies for the tardiness of this remittance, but you know that when I do not pay my debts it is not for want of the desire to do so, and your goodness will ascribe the failure to it's true cause.

Mr Eliason's visit was during my absence. he did not come here nor see any of the family, nor have I learnt any thing more than that he was at Milton. it would have given me pleasure to have seen him. whether mr Randolph's military commission may occasion his giving up the mill I do not know. should it do so, I will make it known to mr Eliason. ever & affectionately yours   TH: JEFFERSON

PoC (DLC); at foot of text: "Mr Barnes"; endorsed by TJ. Enclosure not found.

The GENERAL was Tadeusz Kosciuszko.

To Nicolas G. Dufief

DEAR SIR   Monticello May 21. 13.
    Collecting the amount of the several books you have been so kind
as to send me, as nearly as I can from the letters accompanying them,
I conjecture it to be about 30.D. but lest I should err I have desired
my Richmond correspondents Gibson & Jefferson to remit you 40.D.
which if over the amount may stand in account for further calls of
books, and if less than the amount you must be so good as to let me
know it, and accept in the mean time the assurances of my great
esteem and respect   TH: JEFFERSON

PoC (DLC); at foot of text: "M. Dufief"; endorsed by TJ.

To James Madison

DEAR SIR   Monticello May 21. 13.
    The inclosed letter from Whit was unquestionably intended for
you. the subject, the address both of title and place prove it, and the
mistake of the name only shews the writer to be a very uninquisitive
statesman. Doct^r Waterhouse's letter too was intended for your eye;
and altho' the immediate object fails by previous appointment, yet
he seems to entertain further wishes. I inclose too the newspapers he
refers to, as some of their matter may have escaped your notice, and
the traiterous designs fostered in Massachusets and explained in
them call for attention.
    We have never seen so unpromising a crop of wheat as that now
growing. the winter killed an unusual proportion of it, and the fly is
destroying the remainder. we may estimate the latter loss at one third
at present, and fast increasing from the effect of the extraordinary
drought. with such a prospect before us, the blockade is acting severely on our past labors. it caught nearly the whole wheat of the
middle and upper country in the hands of the farmers and millers,
whose interior situation had prevented their getting it to an earlier
market. from this neighborhood very little had been sold. when we
cast our eye on the map, and see the extent of country, from New
York to N. Carolina inclusive whose produce is raised on the waters
of the Chesapeake (for Albemarle sound is, by the canal of Norfolk
become a water of the Chesapeake) and consider it's productiveness
in comparison with the rest of the Atlantic states, probably a full half,
and that all this can be shut up by two or three ships of the line, lying

at the mouth of the bay, we see that an injury so vast to ourselves and so cheap to our enemy must for ever be resorted to by them, and constantly maintained. to defend all the shores of those waters in detail, is impossible. but is there not a single point where they may be all defended by means to which the magnitude of the object gives a title? I mean at the mouth of the Chesapeak. not by ships of the line, or frigates; for I know that with our present enemy we cannot contend in that way. but would not a sufficient number of gunboats, of <u>small</u> draught, stationed in Lynhaven river, render it unsafe for ships of war either to ascend the Chesapeak, or to lie at it's mouth? I am not unaware of the effect of the ridicule cast on this instrument of defence, by those who wished for engines of offence. but resort is had to ridicule only when reason is against us. I know too the prejudices of the gentlemen of the navy and that these are very natural. no one has been more gratified than myself by the brilliant atchievements of our little navy. they have deeply wounded the pride of our enemy, and been balm to ours, humiliated on the land where our real strength was felt to lie. but divesting ourselves of the enthusiasm these brave actions have justly excited, it is impossible not to see[1] that all these vessels must be taken and added to the already overwhelming force of our enemy, that even while we keep them they contribute nothing to our defence, and that so far as we are to be defended by any thing on the water, it must be by such vessels as can assail under advantageous circumstances, and, under adverse ones, withdraw from the reach of the enemy. this, in shoaly waters, is the humble, the ridiculed, but the formidable gunboat. I acknolege that in the case which produces these reflections, the station of Lynhaven river would not be safe against land attacks on the boats: and that a retreat for them is necessary in this event. with a view to this there was a survey made by Col° Tatham, which was lodged either in the War or Navy office, shewing the depth and length of a canal which would give them a retreat from Lynhaven river into the Eastern branch of Elizabeth river. I think the distance is not over six or eight miles; perhaps not so much, thro' a country entirely flat, and little above the level of the sea. a cut of ten yards wide, and four yards deep, requiring the removal of 40. cubic yards of earth for every yard in length of the canal, at 20. cents the cubic yard, would cost about 15,000.D. a mile. but, even doubling this, to cover all errors of estimate, altho' in a country offering the cheapest kind of labor, it would be nothing compared with the extent and productions of the country it is to protect. it would, for so great a country, bear no proportion to what has been expended, and justly expended by the Union, to defend the single spot of New York.

While such a channel of retreat secures effectually the safety of the gunboats, it ensures also their aid for the defence of Norfolk, if attacked from the sea. and the Norfolk canal gives them a further passage into Albemarle sound, if necessary for their safety, or in aid of the flotilla of that Sound, or to recieve the aid of that flotilla either at Norfolk or in Lynhaven river. for such a flotilla there also, will doubtless be thought necessary, that being the only outlet now, as during the last war, for the waters of the Chesapeak. Col° Monroe, I think, is personally intimate with the face of all that country, & no one, I am certain is more able, or more disposed, than the present Secretary of the Navy, to place himself above the Navy prejudices, and do justice to the aptitude of these humble and economical vessels to the shallow waters of the South. on the bold Northern shores they would be of less account, and the larger vessels will of course be more employed there. were they stationed with us they would rather attract danger than ward it off. the only service they can render us would be to come in a body when the occasion offers, of overwhelming a weaker force of the enemy occupying our bay. to oblige them to keep their force in a body, leaving the mass of our coast open.

Altho it is probable there may not be an idea here which has not been maturely weighed by yourself, and with a much broader view of the whole field, yet I have frankly hasarded them, because possibly some of the facts or ideas may have escaped in the multiplicity of the objects engaging your notice, and because in every event they will cost you but the trouble of reading. the importance of keeping open a water which covers, wholly or considerably, five of the most productive states, containing three fifths of the population[2] of the Atlantic portion of our union, and of preserving their resources for the support of the war, as far as the state of war, and the means of the Confederacy will admit; and especially if it can be done for less than is contributed by the union for more than one single city, will justify our anxieties to have it effected. and should my views of the subject be even wrong, I am sure they will find their apology with you in the purity of the motives of personal & public regard which induce a suggestion of them. in all cases I am satisfied you are doing what is for the best as far as the means put into your hands will enable you; and this thought quiets me under every occurrence; and under every occurrence I am sincerely, affectionately & respectfully your's.

TH: JEFFERSON

RC (DLC: Madison Papers, Rives Collection); at foot of first page: "The President of the US." PoC (DLC). Enclosures: (1) Jones Whit to TJ, 27 Apr. 1813, not found, but recorded in SJL as received 15 May 1813 from Fort Norfolk. (2) Benjamin Waterhouse to TJ, 1 May 1813, and enclosures.

The SURVEY by William TATHAM was enclosed in his letter to TJ of 1 July 1807 (DLC). Governor Daniel D. Tompkins reported to the New York legislature on 31 Mar. 1813 that $569,172.18 in federal funds had been spent to DEFEND THE SINGLE SPOT OF NEW YORK (New York *Columbian*, 10 Apr. 1813).

[1] Reworked from "foresee."
[2] Preceding three words interlined.

To Samuel Pleasants

SIR   Monticello May 21. 13.

I will thank you to send me the undermentioned books, the cost of which mr Gibson will be so good as to pay you on sight of this letter. if securely wrapt up they will come safely and speedily by the stage, addressed to David Higginbotham of Milton

Accept the assurances of my esteem & respect.

TH: JEFFERSON

Gass's account of Lewis & Clarke's journey
Lee's Memoirs of the war.
Arator
the Supplement to the Virginia laws subsequent to 1807. publ^d by you
Hening's statutes at large as far as they are published, except the 1st vol. which I have.

PoC (MHi); adjacent to signature: "Mr Pleasants"; endorsed by TJ.

Since all of the UNDERMENTIONED BOOKS found their way into TJ's library, Pleasants presumably filled the order in his 25 May 1813 letter to TJ, not found, but recorded in SJL as received 28 May 1813 from Richmond.

To James P. Cocke

DEAR SIR   Monticello May 22. 13.

Your favor of Tuesday came to hand yesterday (Friday) afternoon, and expressing the expectation that you could furnish me with a supply of chub fish for my pond if I should send on <u>Thursday next</u>, now past, I send off a careful man with a cart and cask this morning. I am very thankful for this kindness having been very unsuccesful in my endeavors to get a stock for my pond. I sent a boat & a couple of hands about three weeks ago to Cartersville, where mr Harrison was so kind as to exert himself to get some. he procured 9. but they were taken with the hook & line, and 7. of them died soon. 2. only got here alive, one of them much wounded, & both having the appearance of being of the same sex; so that I had little expectation of a stock from them. Accept the assurance of my great esteem & respect.

TH: JEFFERSON

PoC (DLC); at foot of text: "James P. Cocke esq."; endorsed by TJ.

From John Eliason

Dᴿ Sᴿ   Georgetown May 22ⁿᵈ 1813
I Have taken the liberty of adresing a few lines to you on the Subject of your Mill—as I had not the Pleasure of seeing you, when at Milton—and was informed Mʳ Randolph was not at Home—
on the Recpt of this, you will be so good as to inform me whether your Mill will be for Rent—if for Rent the terms; and time you,l Rent it for if I think, it will Sute me well—will wright you my Answer on the Subject   I Remain yours
    with great Respect   JOHN ELIASON

RC (MHi); endorsed by TJ as received 26 May 1813 and so recorded in SJL.

To Elijah Griffiths

DEAR SIR   Monticello May 22. 13.
    On my return from a journey, after an absence of three weeks, I found here your favor of Apr. 19. but in the mean time had seen by the public papers that the office of Treasurer of the mint, had been given to the son of the late occupant, which of course precluded the application requested on your behalf.
    Retirement from the busy walks of life has added much to my happiness, by relieving me from great labors, anxieties, and responsibilities; sweetened indeed by the hope that they had not been unuseful, nor unapproved by my fellow citizens. to this may be added the pleasing recollection of the worth with which we have been associated by the way, and which has virtuously cooperated in the same cause. in this view your letter recalls to my mind moments which I have spent with you with great satisfaction.
    Peace is a sublime blessing to men & states. the prosperity it

promotes among these is in strong contrast with the murders & devastations of War, the burthens & oppressions it heaps on the poor, and the destruction of liberty it so often superinduces. I am not without a hope that the mediation offered & accepted may produce a peace; not indeed of full justice & retribution; but giving some assurance against future wrong. but it would be a miserable perversion of this measure were it to relax our endeavors to enforce what may not be obtained through any other motive.

The death of Dr Rush is a subject of grief to all who knew him. no better man could have left us, nor one whose continuance in life was more valued. he was my junior by several years; & indeed, like a tree standing solitary in a field, I view myself almost singly surviving the multitude of cotemporaries who formerly occupied the space around me.　　　Wishing you every good I tender you the assurance of my esteem & respect.　　　Th: Jefferson

PoC (DLC); at foot of text: "Dr Elijah Griffiths"; endorsed by TJ.

The OFFICE OF TREASURER OF THE MINT had been filled by the appointment and subsequent confirmation of James Rush, SON OF THE LATE OCCUPANT, Benjamin Rush (*JEP*, 2:347, 350 [31 May, 3 June 1813]).

To Thomas H. Palmer

Monticello May 22. 13.

Th: Jefferson presents his compliments to mr Palmer and returns the Prospectus of the Historical Register with his subscription, which he with pleasure subjoins to it, in the hope that he will have some agent in Richmond to whom the price may be annually paid. wishing him all the success which so useful a Repertory merits, he tenders him the assurance of his respect.

PoC (MHi); dateline at foot of text; endorsed by TJ. Enclosure not found.

To the Seventy-Six Association

Monticello May 22. 13.

Th: Jefferson returns his thanks to the standing committee of the Seventy six association, for the eloquent oration of mr Elliott delivered at Charleston on the 4th of March last, which they have been so kind as to send him. the subject is a great one, and the composition worthy of the subject. the zeal expressed on these anniversary occasions for our republican institutions authorises a hope that they will be long maintained; a hope peculiarly gratifying to those who, having spent a life in supporting and cherishing them, sees them delivered over to successors who know their value, and feel a holy zeal for their perpetuation. he presents to the committee the assurance of his high consideration and respect.

PoC (MoSHi: TJC-BC); dateline beneath closing; at foot of text: "Mess.rs Jervey, Bennett, Elliott, Cohen, & Hayne"; endorsed by TJ as a letter to "Jervey et al" and so recorded in SJL.

To James Walker

DEAR SIR   Monticello May 22. 13.

I recieved your former favor stating the prices of mill work, and finding that mr Brown's bill was considerably different, I proposed to him to refer the bill to you, and to ask the favor of you to come and see the work and settle the prices between us. this favor I have now to ask of you, and shall very gladly pay you for your time whatever you think proper. if you could name the day that would suit you, towards the latter part of next week, it would give me time to notify him, and would be in time for my journey to Bedford which I am to take the week following. your doing us this favor and giving me an answer by the bearer will much oblige me. accept my best wishes & respects.   TH: JEFFERSON

PoC (DLC); at foot of text: "Mr James Walker"; endorsed by TJ.   A missing letter from TJ to Walker of 8 Aug. 1814 is recorded in SJL.

From Joseph Delaplaine

SIR,   Philadelphia May 23d 1813

I have commenced the publication of a series of engraved portraits of the eminent men of our country by Mr Edwin & Leney in their best style.

Have the goodness to inform me whether there is an approved likeness of yourself, who painted by, & in whose possession it is.

I think I have understood Mr Rembrandt Peale has some time ago obtained your permission to sit for a portrait.

Hoping to hear from you on the subject,
I remain, dear sir, With great respect Your obed. ser^t
JOSEPH DELAPLAINE
Bookseller
South west Corner 7th & Chesnut streets
Philadelphia

RC (DLC); at foot of text: "Thomas Jefferson Esqre"; endorsed by TJ as received 28 May 1813 and so recorded in SJL.

From Lucy F. Smith

DEAR SIR   Richd May 23^d 1813

In consequence of the long and earnest desire of my son Walter, to enter the Navy, and the advice of his friends seconding his views, I have consented[1] to gratify him—

Presuming on the friendship which subsisted between yourself and his father, Meriwether Jones, I will take the liberty of requesting your assistance in procuring him a Midshipmans warrant—his friends are respectable and numerous, from all of whom, he has obtain'd flattering recommendations—among them are the Governor, Judge Cabell, Judge Brockenborough, and the Speaker of the H of Representatives.—

If the affection of a mother does not blind me, I think him in every respect qualified to fulfil the duties of the appointment he wishes— however, shou'd you require it, I believe his character can sustain the most minute scrutiny—Col Monroe is well acquainted with him—

I hope sir you will excuse the liberty I take in requesting such a favor—nothing but the confidence of your well wishes toward him, and your ability to render him any service, cou'd have induc'd me—I had myself intended him for different pursuits—but his inclinations leading him from his infancy to a Military life, and the scantiness of his patrimony combin'd, I am induc'd to think the station to which he aspires the most eligible—he is about 17 years of age, and has hitherto had every advantage of education—By writing to the Secretary of the Navy, and any other friend, you will confer an obligation on

Yours very respectfully   LUCY F SMITH

PS

Mr Girardin who I understand is living in your neighbourhood, can give you any information respecting my son,

RC (MoSHi: TJC); endorsed by TJ as received 28 May 1813 and so recorded in SJL.

Lucy Franklin Read Jones Smith (ca. 1773–1845) was married in 1789 to Meriwether Jones, a newspaper publisher and politician whom TJ appointed United States commissioner of loans for Virginia in 1804. After he died in 1806, she married George William Smith, whose service as governor of Virginia ended with his death in the Richmond Theatre fire of 1811 (*Lower Norfolk County Virginia Antiquary* 2 [1897]: 28–31; Richmond *Virginia Independent Chronicle*, 11 Feb. 1789; Richmond *Enquirer*, 22 Aug. 1806; John P. Kennedy, *Memoirs of the Life of William Wirt* [1849], 2:96; *Richmond Enquirer*, 18 July 1845; *Richmond Whig and Public Advertiser*, 25 July 1845). Walter F. Jones (ca. 1796–1841), the son of Lucy F. Smith, entered the United States Navy as a midshipman on 11 June 1814 and resigned 2 Nov. 1821. In 1823 he was appointed a judge advocate for the navy at Norfolk, and in 1830 he was named postmaster of that city. Jones was removed from office in 1839 after the United States government claimed that he owed the public more than $5,000 in delinquent postal accounts. The government brought suit against him the following year, but Jones died before the case was heard. After trial in the United States Circuit Court for the Eastern District of Virginia and an appeal to the Supreme Court, Jones and his sureties were cleared of wrongdoing (Callahan, *U.S. Navy*, 303; Axelson, *Virginia Postmasters*, 140; Lewis Hampton Jones, *Captain Roger Jones, of London and Virginia* [1891], 54; Walter F. Jones to James Monroe, 7 Apr. 1823, DNA: RG 45, MLRSN; Washington *Daily National Intelligencer*, 23 June 1823, 22 Apr. 1841; Benjamin C. Howard, *Reports of Cases Argued and Adjudged in the Supreme Court of the United States*, 2d ed. [1903], vol. 7 [48 *U.S. Reports*], 681–92; *Richmond Enquirer*, 4 May 1841).

The GOVERNOR was James Barbour, the SPEAKER of the United States House of Representatives was Henry Clay, and the SECRETARY OF THE NAVY was William Jones.

[1] Manuscript: "sonsented."

From Samuel Brown

DEAR SIR.   Natchez may 25th 1813—

Your letters of the 17th & 24th ult. arrived by the last mail & having just obtained a large supply of the Capsicum, it gives me great pleasure to transmit some of it, to you, in time for planting—That which I planted this spring is just coming up—the plants of last season are loaded with pods & will continue to bear both blossoms & fruit until December or january if protected from the severe frosts by a slight covering of straw. By the next mail I shall do myself the favor of sending you as much of the Capsicum as you can use until your own becomes productive A tablespoonful of the pods will communicate to Vinegar a fine aromatic flavor & that quantity is as much as would serve a northern[1] family many months. In this warm climate our relish for Capsicum is greatly increased & I am much inclined to subscribe to the opinion of Mr Bruce "that nothing is so great a preservative of health in hot climates." I have even had thoughts of hinting to the Secretary of war the propriety of substituting Capsicum for a part of the Ration of Spirits which are allowed our troops & I am very confident that the effect of this change would soon be perceptible—I am informed by those who have lately returned from S^t antonio that the Inhabitants of that part of the continent use this small indigenous Capsicum in almost every thing they eat & that they attribute to it medicinal qualities to which they acknowledge themselves indebted for the singular portion of health which they are said to enjoy In a few cases here, of disorders of the alimentary canal, I have had reason to think very highly of it but my experience has been too limited to permit me to say much of it at present—The result of future observations I shall do myself the favor to communicate to you at another time.

I was fortunate in meeting with a friend who has taken charge of your letter to Mr Henderson & will convey his answer this far on his return from Waschita. As he is very attentive to such commissions I hope to be able to forward Mr Hendersons letter in two or three weeks at the farthest. As the Mississippi floods the whole country between this place & the mouth of the wachita & as there is now no direct communication by post the voyage will be performed in a skiff & will require about 10 or 12 days.

Your kind wishes for my happiness excite in my breast emotions of the most sincere gratitude. A few months ago my Heart rec^d an incurable wound by the Death of a wife whom I most tenderly loved, who has left me three infants my oldest daughter not yet four years of age, my youngest only four months. You have _felt_ the bitterness of this species of sorrow & can judge how far it surp[asses] all others. You however enjoyed a source of consolation which is inaccessible by me—the consciousness that your life was ever useful to your country & the world. This shield cannot be penetrated by the "arrows of outrageous fortune" alas! I have it not.

The amusements of your age are such as the wise & good have always wished to enjoy—But how blest is that Country where those who have spent their youth in the dangerous toils of Planting the Tree of liberty can, in despite of the Tyrants of the earth devote the evening of their lives to the pleasing amusements of Horticulture!!! Most sincerely do I pray that you may long continue to participate in that Happiness which our country enjoys—

Your Mo Obt   SAM BROWN

I am more than ever pleased with the Guinea grass.—We have here a grass that will defy the heat of your "brown autumn." I shall send[2] it to you when the seed is ripe—   S B

RC (DLC); mutilated at seal; addressed: "Thomas Jefferson Esq. late President of the U.S. Monticello"; franked; postmarked Natchez, 25 May; endorsed by TJ as received 11 June 1813 and so recorded in SJL.

Brown's third child died not long after

the death of his WIFE, Catherine Percy Brown (*ANB*). The quote pertaining to the "slings and ARROWS OF OUTRAGEOUS FORTUNE" is from William Shakespeare, *Hamlet*, act 3, scene 1.

[1] Manuscript: "nothern."
[2] Manuscript: "sent."

From John Wayles Eppes

DEAR SIR,   Washington may 25. 1813.

I received in due time the letter forwarded from Floods—I regret that my letter contained any thing which could induce you to suppose me either unreasonable in my proposals or diffident of your attatchment to my child—Being incapable of expressing either directly or indirectly any sentiment calculated to wound your feelings I have no hesitation in solemnly disclaiming any expression not in perfect unison with the affection and respect which I have ever felt for you—The propositions contained in my letter were seperate and distinct.

1. Exchange—the quantity of land—the clearings and improvements equal—

or. 2. The House at present on the Bedford land thrown in in lieu of the clearings and improvements—This I knew would make the Bedford land more valuable than Pant-ops as it stands—but in the first place you had declared your intention of adding them hereafter and in the second place I had always considered that if Pant-ops was retained Francis had a claim to a house on it of stone instead of brick similar to the one erected in Bedford—Your letters on this subject (of which probably you have copies) place this subject out of the reach of doubt—

The other proposition viz that in the event of accident to Francis I should receive in lieu of the exchanged property the value of Pant-ops was introduced to prevent the possibility [in the event of your throwing in the house] of my deriving benefit[1] from improvement which of course it would be your choice to bestow on some one of your grand children—you may recollect that I have heretofore expressed to you my opinion on the subject of Mrs Randolphs reversionary interest— So far as it respects yourself it is merely nominal—It is in your power to make Mrs Randolph acquiese in any disposition of your property which you may think proper to make—If I had acceeded to your proposition of purchase her reversionary interest was gone—and so it ought to be as it respects me—I supposed of course the same principles would govern the exchange that would have applied to the purchase—you tell me however that it would not be your act but the act of the law—Even supposing this to be the fact I shall not consent to receive from you sheer law—I know that a mind like yours is compelled to yield me all that the relation in which we stand authorizes me to claim—I have a right to stand in relation to Pant-ops on the same footing with your other son in law—I cannot believe that my misfortunes can sever the ties by which we are bound or that either my claims on you or yours on me are hereafter to depend on mere law—Can you consider it equitable that one of your sons in law shall possess an uncontrouled authority over property conveyed for the same purposes by yourself—and the other not even a reversionary interest—Can you violate as it respects me a principle sanctioned by your own example—You yourself hold the property acquired by marriage in fee simple—So did my Father, so does colo: Skipwith—It was in my power at any time previous to my misfortune to have the fee simple in Pant-ops—This I do not require, but claim in the event of exchange that the exchanged property shall be freed from all reversionary claims on the part of yourself or family—You cannot refuse this principle having already substantially admitted it in your letter offering to purchase Pant-ops—If contrary to my expectations you were to refuse I should never cease to feel it as an act of injustice—In the relations in which I stand to you, I have scrupulously fulfilled my duties, and am not consious of any act on my part which can authorize on yours a marked distinction between myself and those who stand in the same relation to you—

If the same principles govern the exchange which would have regulated the purchase I am ready to complete it on the terms you propose viz "an immediate exchange of title possession to be exchanged at the determination of Mr Randolphs lease, the number of acres equal, the quantity of cleared land equal say 250 acres & farm buildings equal in value with those now at Pant-Ops"[2]—

In February last I received from a friend of mine information on the subject of Gerrardins school accompanied with an opinion that it would not continue long & even if it did that it was not a desirable situation for a boy as young as Francis—being better calculated for boys already advanced—In consequence of this I sent him to Lynchburg—He boards with an old school fellow of mine Seth Ward and the school at which he is placed is a very good one—The vacation takes place in August at which time Francis shall certainly come up and pass some time with you—I would have sent him up before sending him to Lynchburg but the winter was so severe that I thought it not proper for him to ride so far—I received from him a letter this morning—He is in good health. If after the vacation you consider the school of Mr Robertson in Albemarle a better situation than the one in which he is placed I shall feel pleasure in yielding on that subject my opinions to yours—

The state of parties in Congress is more favorable than we had expected—The majority in favour of the administration may be safely put down at 35—We have nothing from the army since Harrisons letter—Bad fortune blasts in the bud every expectation however reasonable—General Dearborne will probably fail to a considerable extent in his objects—a malignant fever has appeared among his Troops since the surrender of york and our last accounts state that many of his men had perished & that 400 were unfit for service—He has been compelled to send back for reinforcements & will I fear fail as to the other objects of the expedition. The Presidents message is luminous and manly & I hope we shall unite in pursuing a course calculated to destroy for ever the castles reared on the hopes of division—

Present me affectionately to the family & accept for your health & happiness every wish from yours affectionately

JNO: W: EPPES

RC (ViU: TJP-ER); brackets in original; endorsed by TJ as received 28 May 1813 and so recorded in SJL.

TJ's OTHER SON IN LAW was Thomas Mann Randolph. Eppes's MISFORTUNES included the death of his first wife, TJ's daughter Maria Jefferson Eppes. Late in April 1813 General Henry Dearborn (DEARBORNE) led a successful attack on YORK (now Toronto), the capital of Upper Canada, albeit one that incurred heavy casualties (Heidler and Heidler, *War of 1812*, 568–9). In his 25 May 1813 MESSAGE to Congress, James Madison summarized events related to a recent offer by Russian emperor Alexander I to mediate peace between the United States and Great Britain; asserted that the United States had upheld the law of nations regarding the impressment of sailors and the search and seizure of enemy ships while Great Britain continued to wage war employ-ing "a system of plunder and conflagration . . . equally forbidden by respect for national character, and by the established rules of civilized warfare"; highlighted the successes of the American navy and the capture of York as "a presage of future and greater victories"; reported on provisions to enlarge the army and appoint a new United States minister to France; and announced "the necessity of providing more adequately for the future supplies of the Treasury" by means of a "well dijested system of internal revenue," which would reduce the need for loans and improve the terms on which they could be obtained (Madison, *Papers, Pres. Ser.*, 6:339–43).

[1] Manuscript: "befit."
[2] Omitted closing quotation mark editorially supplied.

To Randolph Jefferson

DEAR BROTHER   Monticello May 25. 13

Supposing the shad season not to be quite over, and that in haul-
ing for them they catch some carp, I send the bearer with a cart and
cask to procure for me as many living carp as he can to stock my fish-
pond. I should not regard his staying a day or two extra, if it would
give a reasonable hope of furnishing a supply. he is furnished with
money to pay for the carp, for which I have always given the same
price as for shad. should he not be able to lay out the whole in carp
he may bring us 3. or 4. shad if he can get them.   I shall be
able to give you the spinning Jenny which I carried to Bedford. it is
a very fine one of 12. spindles. I am obliged to make a larger one for
that place, and the cart which carries it up shall bring the one there
to Snowden on it's return. you will have to send a person here to
learn to use it, which may take them a fortnight. but that need not
be till I return from Bedford, for which place I shall set out the day
after our court, this day fortnight, or very soon after. I will go by
Snowden if I can; but certainly will return that way, on condition
you will previously re-open the old road to the old smith's shop. you
will never find a more leisure time for your people to do that than the
present. in conversing with your son Lilburne, I found that he would
prefer employing himself in reading and improving his mind rather
than in being idle. it is late for him to begin, but he has still time
enough, to acquire such a degree of information as may make him a
very useful & respectable member of society. I formed a favorable
opinion of his understanding. if both you & he approve of it, I think
he had better come and pass some time here. I can put him on a
course of useful reading adapted to his age this would be of geography, history, agriculture, & natural philosophy: as soon as you and
he can make up your minds, he had better come without delay, as he
has not a day to lose. he can pursue his reading as well while I am
absent in Bedford, as when here.

Reflecting on the manner of managing your very valuable farm, I
thought I would suggest the following which appears to me the best,
& of which you will consider. to form your lowgrounds into two divisions, one of them to be in wheat, and the other to be half corn & half
red clover, shifting them every year. then to form your highlands into
three divisions, one to be in wheat, & the other two in red clover,
shifting them from year to year. in this way your low ground fields
would be in corn but once in 4. years, in wheat every other year, and

in clover every fourth year: and your highland in wheat once in every three years, and in clover two years in every three. they would improve wonderfully fast in this way, and increase your produce of wheat & corn every year. if it should be found that the low grounds should in this way become too rich for wheat, instead of putting them every fourth year into clover, you might put them that year into oats. your annual crop would then be half your low grounds in wheat a fourth in corn, and a fourth in oats or clover: and one third of your highland in wheat, and two thirds in clover; and so on for ever, and for ever improving. I suggest this for your consideration. present me affectionately to my sister, and be assured yourself of my constant & brotherly attachment.   Th: Jefferson

PoC (ViU: TJP-CC); at foot of first page: "Randolph Jefferson"; endorsed by TJ.

On this date TJ recorded that he had given the BEARER, "Ned's James to buy fish 2.D." (*MB*, 2:1289). James LIL-BURNE Jefferson was Randolph Jeffer-son's fifth son (*MB*, 2:1322).

From Regnault de Bécourt

chez Mr Scotti, 4e Rue N° 15 à
Très honorable Seigneur!   Philadelphie ce 26 mai, 1813.

Conformement à la lettre que Votre Seigneurie prit la peine de m'écrire en date du 6 février, de cette année-ci, je prends la liberté de lui adresser, ci-joint, un exemplaire de mon ouvrage intitulé: La Création du monde, &c, le quel vient de paraître. Si Votre Seigneurie souhaitait Se procurer quelques autres exemplaires du même ouvrage, en m'honorant d'un mot à cet égard, adressé, soit à Mr Dufief Libraire ou Soit à la suscription mise au bas de cette lettre, Elle recevrait, peu de tems àprès ce qu'Elle aurait daigné commander.

Ainsi que Votre Seigneurie aura Occasion de le remarquer, au commencement du livre, ci-inclus, je suis à la veille de publier un autre Volume ayant trait à celui susdit. Je ne saurais donc trop engager Votre très honorable Seigneurie, à faire ce qui dépendra d'Elle pour faciliter la mise Sous presse de ce nouvel ouvrage et par ce moyen la publication de mes productions; et c'est dans cet espoir,

Que j'ai l'honneur d'être avec le respect le plus profond,

de Votre très honorable Seigneurie, T. h. Seigneur, Le très hum-ble et très obéissant Serviteur.   R. de Bécourt.

house of Mr. Scotti, 4th Street Number 15,
VERY HONORABLE LORD!   Philadelphia 26 May, 1813.

Pursuant to the letter your lordship wrote me on 6 February of this year, I take the liberty of enclosing a copy of my work entitled *La Création du Monde*, &c, which just came out. If your lordship should wish to obtain a few more copies of it, send a note to that effect to either Mr. Dufief, bookseller, or to the address at the bottom of this letter. You will receive them in short order.

At the beginning of the enclosed book your lordship will also note an announcement that I am about to publish another volume related to the one mentioned above. I strongly urge your very honorable lordship to do whatever you can to facilitate the emergence of this new work, and thus the publication of my writings, and it is with this hope,

that I have the honor to be with the deepest respect,

for your very honorable lordship, most honorable lord, your very humble and very obedient servant   R. DE BÉCOURT.

RC (DLC); dateline at foot of text; endorsed by TJ as received 11 June 1813 and so recorded in SJL. Translation by Dr. Genevieve Moene. Enclosure: Bécourt, *La Création du Monde, ou Système d'Organisation Primitive Suivi De l'explication des principaux Phénomènes qui se* *sont opérés dans la Nature, depuis l'Origine de l'Univers jusqu'à nos jours* (Philadelphia, 1813; Sowerby, no. 4930).

Bécourt never published the proposed VOLUME entitled *La Raison et la Vérité*.

From Randolph Jefferson

DEAR BROTHER   may 26ᵗʰᵉ 1813.—

I received your friendly letter by the boy they cetch no shad a tall at this time so that I have sent James up to warren to try and procure some carp for you and have wrote to mr Brown a bout them if it is in his power to git any to fernish your boy with what you derected him to bring in the barril alive I have understood they cetch a number there every night in the mill race I will endeavour to fix Lilburne as soon as possible and send him a greable to your request and hope he will endeavour to improve him self by applying closely to his book I will do my best to have the rode put in better order a gainst you come a long as fare as the shop on the rode we are extreemly oblige to you in respect to the spining ginney as letting your boy come by and leaveing it with us as it was more then we could of asked of you at any rate or expected I am extreemly oblige to you for your advice as to managing my farm but am afraid it will be two great an undertakeing for me your method I highly approve of I hope mr Brown will fernish you with the carp if they cetch any you will be so good as to

tell my sister marks that we shall be extreemly happy to see her hear
and that I will retern with her if she will come over my wife Joins
with me in love to you and family.—

I am with the warmest Esteem and regard your cincearly—

RH; JEFFERSON

PS dont be in dred of the old rode I will have that put In good order
a gainst you come a long for you.—

RC (ViU: TJP-CC); endorsed by TJ
as received 26 May 1813 and so recorded
in SJL.

William BROWN kept a tavern in Warren (*MB*, 2:1327, 1367; Woods, *Albemarle*, 58, 287).

To Lancelot Minor

DEAR SIR   Monticello May 26. 13.

Your favor of Apr. 23. came here just as I had set out for Bedford,
so that I recieved it only on my return from that place, which must
apologise for the delay of the answer. that of Jan. 20. had been recieved in due time, and your order in favor of Capt Tomkins for the
survey was paid. in mine of Oct. 29. I had promised, as soon as my
wheat should be groun[d] and disposed of, that I would remit you
150.D. in order to relieve you from the most pressing of the claims of
mr Marks's creditors, to wit, Col° Callis's £21–8–8 and interest,
Kimborough's, Isaac Winston's, Yancey's & Smith's demands. I am
one of the unfortunate who had not got their crop to market when the
blockade took place. on that event, flour fell instantly to almost nothing. I desired my agent in Richmond to hold up mine for 7.D. till
May, but then to sell for whatever could be got. as soon as this is done
my promise shall be fulfilled. with respect to Col° Callis's claim of
damages for the failure of title to the 150. a^s of land sold him by mr
Marks, I must refer you to my letter of Oct. 29. where my opinion on
that claim is fully stated, and the extent to which alone an executor
could go: that is to say to refund the money actually recieved by mr
Marks for the land, with interest, which, taking a pro ratâ from the
2176. a^s sold for 1000.D. would be about 46. cents the acre, adding
thereto the interest. altho' an executor, rigorously conforming to what
the law exacts, would require proof of the nature of David Ross's
claim to the 150. acres, whether he actually recovered them by due
course of law, & if not, what was his title, and whether really a better
one than mr Marks's (of all which we are entirely uninformed) yet, as
to myself knowing Col° Callis to be incapable of saying what is not

exact, I have no hesitation in taking these facts on his word, in assuming on myself the [r]esponsibility for them, & the risk of consenting to refund to Col° Callis the mo[n]ey recieved and interest. but this, I think is as far as we can go, or ought to go, [e]ither in law or equity. mr Marks & Col° Callis bargained both with good f[a]ith. they were equally ignorant of the defect of title, and equally clear of all fraud. the error being discovered, both parties should be placed where they would have been had the truth been known at the time, & consequently no sale made. this will be done by mr Marks's refunding Col° Callis's money & interest, which is exactly what the law requires. in that case Col° Callis sustains no loss; he [onl]y misses of making a gain, which equity will not repair by throwing a loss on another party as innocent as himself. having been equally decieved, each should be contented with getting back to his former ground, without wishing to make an advantage out of his companion in error. this would be the harder on mr Marks, as he loses the land: for I presume nothing has been or can be recovered from the person whom he paid for a false title. if Col° Callis has the same view of this subject all[1] further difficulty in the settlement will be at an end.

Mrs Marks is anxious her land should be sold; and if you think this can be hastened by public advertisement, it would be well so to advertize it. and this may be by sale to the highest bidder, if you think that best; only taking care that it does not go lower than you would sell at private sale. all this we leave entirely to your better judgment, & our entire confidence in you will make us perfectly contented with any thing you do. as soon as I can hear from my merchant in Richmond that he has effected the sale of my flour, I will send you an order on him. mrs Marks prays to be remembered to mrs Minor & yourself and I tender you the assurance of my great esteem & respect.

TH: JEFFERSON

RC (NN: Thomas Jefferson Papers); torn and damaged at fold.

Minor's FAVOR OF APR. 23, not found, is recorded in SJL as received 15 May 1813 from Louisa. His letter OF JAN. 20, not found, but recorded in SJL as received 4 Feb. 1813 from Louisa, may have advised TJ of a letter from Minor to Anne Scott Marks of 20 Jan. 1813, asking her to pay William Tompkins (TOMKINS) "Six Dollars for Surveying your land in Louisa" (RC in DLC; addressed: "Mrs Ann S Marks Montechello"; with sub-

joined receipt, in Tompkins's hand and signed by him, stating that he had "Recievd Febuary the 21st 1813 of Ann Marks six dollars in full of the above order"; endorsed by TJ: "Marks Anne S. Tompkins W^{m}: reciept"). On 15 Feb. 1813 TJ recorded that he had "Pd. Reuben Grady by order of Wm. Tompkins 6.D. for surveying Mrs. Marks's land (sent by Mr. Bacon)" (MB, 2:1287; omitted closing parenthesis editorially supplied).

Missing letters from Minor to TJ of 8 Aug., 15 Oct., and 9 Nov. 1813 are recorded in SJL as having been received from Louisa on 23 Aug., 18 Oct., and 13 Nov. 1813, respectively. A letter from TJ to

Minor of 29 Oct. 1813, not found, is also recorded in SJL.

[1] Word interlined.

To John Adams

Monticello May 27. 13.

Another of our friends of 76. is gone, my dear Sir, another of the Co-signers of the independance of our country. and a better man, than Rush, could not have left us, more benevolent, more learned, of finer genius, or more honest. we too must go; and that ere long. I believe we are under half a dozen at present; I mean the signers of the Declaration. yourself, Gerry, Carroll, and myself are all I know to be living. I am the only one South of the Patomac. is Robert Treat Payne, or Floyd living? it is long since I heard of them, and yet I do not recollect to have heard of their deaths.

Moreton's deduction of the origin of our Indians from the fugitive Trojans, stated in your letter of Jan. 26. and his manner of accounting for the sprinckling of their Latin with Greek, is really amusing. Adair makes them talk Hebrew. Reinold Foster derives them from the soldiers sent by Kouli Khan to conquer Japan. Berewood from the Tartars, as well as our bears, wolves, foxes E[t]c. which he says 'must of necessity fetch their beginning from Noah's ark, which rested, after the deluge, in Asia, seeing they could not proceed by the course of nature, as the unperfect sort of living creatures do, from putrefaction.' Bernard Romans is of opinion that God created an original man & woman in this part of the globe. Doct[r] Barton thinks they are not specifically different from the Persians; but, taking afterwards a broader range, he thinks 'that in all the vast countries of America, there is but one language, nay that it may be proven, or rendered highly probable, that all the languages of the earth bear some affinity together.'[1] this reduces it to a question of definition, in which every one is free to use his own. to wit, what constitutes identity, or difference in two things? (in the common acceptation of sameness.) all languages may be called the same, as being all made up of the same primitive sounds, expressed by the letters of the different alphabets. but, in this sense, all things on earth are the same, as consisting of matter. this gives up the useful distribution into genera & species, which we form, arbitrarily indeed, for the relief of our imperfect memories. to aid the question, from whence are our Indian tribes descended? some have gone into their religion, their morals, their manners, customs, habits, and physical forms. by such helps it may be learnedly proved that our trees and plants of every kind are descended from those of Europe; because, like them they have no locomotion, they draw nourishment from the earth, they clothe themselves with leaves in spring, of which they divest themselves in autumn for the sleep of winter E^tc. our animals too must be descended from those of Europe, because our wolves eat lambs, our deer are gregarious, our ants hoard E^tc. but when, for convenience, we distribute languages, according to common understanding, into Classes originally different, as we chuse to consider them, as the Hebrew, the Greek, the Celtic, the Gothic; and these again into genera, or families, as the Icelandic, German, Swedish, Danish, English; and these last into species, or dialects, as English, Scotch, Irish, we then ascribe other meanings to the terms 'same' and 'different.' in some one of these senses, Barton, and Adair, and Foster, and Brerewood, & Moreton, may be right, every one according to his own definition of what constitutes 'identity.' Romans indeed takes a higher stand, and supposes a separate creation. on the same unscriptural ground, he had but to mount one step higher, to suppose no creation at all, but that all things have existed without beginning in time, as they now exist, and may for ever exist, producing and reproducing in a circle, without end. this would very summarily dispose of mr Morton's learning, and shew that the question of Indian origin, like many others pushed to a certain height, must recieve the same answer, 'Ignoro.'

You ask if the usage of hunting in circles has ever been known among any of our tribes of Indians? it has been practised by them all; and is to this day, by those still remote from the settlements of the whites. but their numbers not enabling them, like Genghis Kahn's 700,000. to form themselves into circles of 100. miles diameter, they make their circle by firing the leaves fallen on the ground, which gradually forcing the animals to a center, they there slaughter them with arrows, darts and other missiles. this is called firehunting, and has been practised in this state within my time by the white inhabitants. this is the most probable cause of the origin & extension of the vast prairies in the Western country, where the grass having been of extraordinary luxuriance, has made a conflagration sufficient to kill even the old, as well as the young timber.

I sincerely congratulate you on the successes of our little navy; which must be more gratifying to you than to most men, as having been the early and constant advocate of wooden walls. if I have differed with you on this ground, it was not on the principle, but the time, supposing that we cannot build or maintain a navy, which will not immediately fall into the same gulph which has swallowed, not only the minor navies, but even those of the great second rate powers of the sea. whenever these can be resuscitated, and brought so near to a balance with England that we can turn the scale, then is my epoch for aiming at a navy. in the mean time one competent to keep the Barbary states in order, is necessary; these being the only smaller powers disposed to quarrel with us. but I respect too much the weighty opinions of others to be unyielding on this point, and acquiesce with the prayer 'quod felix faustumque sit,' adding ever a sincere one for your health and happiness.   Th: Jefferson

RC (MHi: Adams Papers). PoC (DLC); at foot of first page: "John Adams esq."

Robert Treat Paine (PAYNE) and William FLOYD passed away in 1814 and 1821, respectively (DAB). James ADAIR argued that American Indians had Jewish ancestors in The History of the American Indians (London, 1775; Sowerby, no. 3997). Johann Reinhold Forster (REINOLD FOSTER) suggested that some of Kublai Khan's soldiers might have founded the empires of Mexico and Peru in Geschichte der Entdeckungen und Schiffahrten im Norden: Mit neuen Originalkarten (Frankfurt an der Oder, 1784). TJ quoted from Edward Brerewood (BEREWOOD), Enquiries Touching The Diversity of Languages, and Religions through the cheife parts of the world (Lon-

don, 1614), 97. BERNARD ROMANS wrote on the origins of man in North America in A Concise Natural History of East and West-Florida (New York, 1776; Sowerby, no. 4079). In the margin of the PoC, TJ keyed a note beside his sentence about Benjamin Smith BARTON indicating that the material on the PERSIANS came from Barton's New Views of the Origin of the Tribes and Nations of America (Philadelphia, 1797; Sowerby, no. 3998), "pa. v." Further along in the sentence, TJ added another marginal note to the PoC crediting the quoted passage to "ib. pa. 75." IGNORO: "I do not know." QUOD FELIX FAUSTUMQUE SIT: "may it bring you happiness and good fortune."

[1] Omitted closing quotation mark editorially supplied.

To Richard Fitzhugh

DEAR SIR   Monticello May 27. 13

Your favor of the 9th has been safely recieved, together with the packet of Ravensworth peas. these are now in the ground, & will abundantly supply me with seed for the next year. I will not therefore give to yourself or mr Eppes the trouble of adding to my supply.

I cannot promise myself ever taking a journey so far Northwardly again, but were it to happen, I should certainly take your friendly mansion and family in my way. I am now more happily employed than in travelling post, and am particularly engaged in those pursuits in which mrs Fitzhugh and yourself have been ever eminent; I mean in domestic manufactures. we have in our family (including my daughter's) three spinning Jennies agoing, of 24. & 40. spindles each which can spin 11. pounds of coarse cotton a day, and our looms fixed with flying shuttles, which altho' they do not perform the miracles ascribed to them, do, I think, double the effect of the common loom. we still want carding machines in our neighborhood working at such moderate prices as to relieve us from hand-carding. with this convenience, the clothing our family would be a thing really of neither trouble nor expence. even without this additional aid, the labour is a very light one.

Be so good as to present me affectionately & respectfully to mrs Fitzhugh, and to accept yourself the assurances of my constant esteem. Th: Jefferson

PoC (MHi); at foot of text: "Richard Fitzhugh esq."; endorsed by TJ.

TJ planted the PACKET OF RAVENS-WORTH PEAS on 22 May 1813 (Betts, *Garden Book*, 496).

To Madame de Staël Holstein

United States of America. May 28. 1813.

I recieved, with great pleasure, my dear Madam and friend, your letter of Nov. 10. from Stockholm[1] and am sincerely gratified by the occasion it gives me of expressing to you the sentiments of high respect and esteem which I entertain for you. it recalls to my remembrance a happy portion of my life passed in your native city, then the seat of the most amiable and polished society of the world, and of which yourself, and your venerable father were such distinguished members. but, of what scenes has it since been the theatre, & with what havoc has it overspread the earth! Robespiere met the fate, and his memory the execration he so justly merited. the rich were his victims and perished by thousands. it is by millions that Bonaparte destroys the poor, and he is eulogised and deified, by the sycophants even of science. these merit more than the meer oblivion to which they will be consigned; and the day will come when a just posterity will give to their hero the only preeminence he has earned, that of having been the greatest of the destroyers of the human race. what year of his military life has not consigned a million of human beings to death, to poverty, and wretchedness. what field in Europe may not raise a monument of the murders, the burnings, the desolations, the famines and miseries it has witnessed from him! and all this to acquire a reputation which Cartouche attained, with less injury to mankind, of being fearless of god or man.

To compleat and universalize the desolation of the globe, it has been the will of Providence to raise up at the same time a tyrant as unprincipled, and as overwhelming for the ocean. not in the poor Maniac George, but in his Government and Nation. Bonaparte will die, and his tyrannies with him. but a Nation never dies. the English Government and it's pyratical principles & practices have no fixed term of duration. Europe feels, and is writhing under the scorpion whips of Bonaparte. we are assailed by those of England. the one continent thus placed under the gripe of England, and the other of Bonaparte, each has to grapple with the enemy immediately pressing on itself. we must extinguish the fire kindled in our own house, and leave to our friends beyond the water that which is consuming theirs. it was not till England had taken 1000. of our ships, and impressed into her service more than 6000. of our citizens; till she had declared, by the proclamation of her Prince Regent that she would not repeal her aggressive orders, <u>as to us</u>, until Bonaparte should have repealed his <u>as to all nations</u>; until her minister, in formal conference with ours, declared that no proposition for protecting our seamen from being impressed, under colour of taking their own, was practicable or admissible; that the door to justice and to all amicable arrangement being closed, and negociation become both desperate and dishonorable, that we concluded that the war she had been for years waging against us might as well become a war on both sides. she takes fewer vessels from us since the declaration of war, than before, because they venture more cautiously; and we now make full reprisals where before we made none. England is, in principle, the enemy of all maritime nations, as Bonaparte is of the continental: and I place in the same line of insult to the human understanding the pretension of conquering the ocean, to establish Continental rights, as that of conquering the continent to restore Maritime rights. No, my dear Madam; the object of England is <u>the permanent dominion of the ocean</u>, and the <u>monopoly of the trade of the world</u>. to secure this, she must keep a larger fleet than her own resources will maintain. the resources of other nations then must be impressed to supply the deficiency of her own. this is sufficiently developed and evidenced by her successive strides towards the usurpation of the sea. mark them from her first war after William Pitt, the little, came into her administration. she first forbade to Neutrals all trade with her enemies in time of war, which they had not in time of peace. this deprived them of their trade from port to port of the same nation. then she forbade them to trade from the port of one nation to that of any other at war with her, altho' a right fully exercised in time of peace. next, instead of taking vessels only <u>entering</u> a blockaded port, she took them over the whole ocean if destined to that port, altho' ignorant of the blockade, & without intention to violate it. then she took them returning from that port, as if infected by previous infraction of blockade. then came her paper blockades, by which she might shut up the whole world without sending a ship to sea, except to take all those sailing on it, as they must of course be bound to some port. and these were followed by her orders of council forbidding every nation to go to the port of any other, without coming first to some port of Great Britain, there paying a tribute to her, regulated by the cargo, and taking from her a license to proceed to the port of destination; which operation the vessel was to repeat with the return cargo on it's way home. according to these orders we could not send a vessel from St Mary's to St Augustine, distant 6 hours sail, on our own coast, without crossing the Atlantic four times, twice with the outward cargo, and twice with the inward. she found this too daring and outrageous, for a single step, retracted as to certain articles of commerce, but left it in force as to others which constitute important branches of our exports. and finally, that her views may no longer rest on inference, in a recent debate, her minister has declared in open parliament, that the object of the present war is a <u>monopoly of commerce</u>. in some of these atrocities, France kept pace with her fully in speculative wrong, which her impotence only shortened in practical execution. this was called retaliation by both; each charging the other with the initiation of the outrage. as if two combatants might retaliate, on an innocent bystander, the blows they recieved from each other. to make war on both would have been ridiculous. in order therefore to single out an enemy, we offered to both that if either would revoke it's hostile decrees, & the other should refuse, we would interdict all intercourse whatever with that other; which would be war of course, as being an avowed departure from neutrality. France accepted the offer, & revoked her decrees as to us. England not only refused, but declared by a solemn proclamation of her Prince Regent that she would not revoke her orders <u>even as to us</u>, until those of France should be annulled <u>as to the whole world</u>. we thereon declared war, and with abundant additional cause. in the mean time an examination before parliament of the ruinous effects of these orders on her own manufacturers, exposing them to the nation, and to the world, their Prince issued a Palinodial proclamation, <u>suspending</u> the orders on certain conditions, but claiming to renew them at pleasure, as a matter of right. even this might have prevented the war, if done, and known here before it's declaration. but the sword being once drawn, the expence of arming incurred, and hostilities in full course, it would have been unwise to discontinue them, until effectual provision should be agreed to by England for protecting our citizens on the high seas from impressment by their naval commanders, through error voluntary or involuntary; the fact being notorious that these officers, entering our ships at sea under pretext of searching for their seamen (which they have no right to do, by the law or usage of nations, which they neither do, nor ever did, as to any other nation, but ours, and which no nation ever before pretended to do in any case) entering our ships, I say, under pretext of searching for, & taking out their seamen, they took ours, native as well as naturalised, knowing them to be ours, merely because they wanted them. it is not long since they impressed at sea two nephews of General Washington, returning from Europe, and put them, as common seamen, under the ordinary discipline of their ships of war. insomuch that no American could safely cross the ocean, or venture to pass by sea from one to another of our own ports. there are certainly other wrongs to be settled between England and us; but of a minor character, and such as a proper spirit of conciliation on both sides would not permit to continue them at war. the sword however can never again be sheathed, until the personal safety of an American on the ocean, the most important, the most vital of all the injuries we can recieve, is compleatly provided for.   as soon as we heard of her partial repeal of her orders of council, we offered instantly to suspend hostilities by an armistice, if she would suspend her impressments, and meet us in arrangements for securing our citizens against them. she refused to do it, because impracticable by any arrangement, as she pretends; but, in truth, because a body of 60. or 80,000. of the finest seamen in the world, which we possess, is too great a resource for manning her exaggerated navy, to be relinquished, as long as she can keep it open. peace is in her hand whenever she will renounce the practice of aggression on the persons of our citizens. if she thinks it worth eternal war, eternal war we must have. she alledges that the sameness of language, of manners, of appearance, render it impossible to distinguish us from her subjects. but because we speak English, and look like them, are we to be punished, are free and independent men to be submitted to their bondage? England has misrepresented to all Europe this ground of the war. she has called it a new pretension, set up since the repeal of her orders of council. she knows there has never been a moment of suspension of our reclamations against it, from General

Washington's time inclusive to the present day. and that it is distinctly stated in our declaration of war, as one of it's principal causes.—she has pretended we have entered into the war to establish the principle of 'free bottoms, free goods,' or to protect her seamen against her own right over them. we contend for neither of these.— she pretends we are partial to France; that we have observed a fraudulent and unfaithful neutrality, between her & her enemy. she knows this to be false, and that if there has been any inequality in our proceedings towards the belligerents it has been in her favor. her ministers are in possession of full proofs of this. our accepting at once, & sincerely, the mediation of the virtuous Alexander, their greatest friend, and the most aggravated enemy of Bonaparte sufficiently proves whether we have partialities on the side of her enemy. I sincerely pray that this mediation may produce a just peace. it will prove that the immortal character, which has first stopped by war the career of the destroyer of mankind, is the friend of peace, of justice & of human happiness, and the patron of unoffending and injured nations. he is too honest and impartial to countenance propositions of peace derogatory to the freedom of the seas.

Shall I apologise to you, my dear Madam, for this long political letter? but yours justifies the subject, and my feelings must plead for the unreserved expression of them; and they have been the less reserved, as being from a private citizen, retired from all connection with the government of his country, and whose ideas, expressed without communication with any one, are neither known, nor imputable to them.

The dangers of the sea are now so great, and the possibilities of interception by sea and land such that I shall subscribe no name to this letter. you will know from whom it comes by it's reference to the date of time and place of yours, as well as by it's subject in answer to that. this omission must not lessen in your view the assurance of my great esteem, of my sincere sympathies for the share which you bear in the afflictions of your country, and the deprivations to which a lawless will has subjected you. in return, you enjoy the dignified satisfaction of having met them, rather than be yoked with the abject to his car: and that, in withdrawing from oppression, you have followed the virtuous example of a father whose name will ever be dear to your country, & to mankind. with my prayers that you may be restored to it, that you may see it reestablished in that temperate portion of liberty which does not infer either anarchy or licentiousness, in that high degree of prosperity which would be the consequence of such a government, in that, in short, which the constitution of 1789 would have ensured it, if wisdom could have staid at that point the fervid but imprudent zeal of men who did not know the character of their own country men, and that you may long live in health and happiness under it, & leave to the world a well educated, and virtuous representative & descendant of your honored father, is the ardent prayer of the sincere and respectful friend who writes this letter.

RC (Maurice, duc de Broglie, Chateau de Broglie, France, 1948); torn at seal, with missing text supplied from PoC; endorsed in an unidentified hand as a letter from "Mr Jefferson New york 28 May 1813." PoC (DLC); at foot of first page: "Madame la Baronne de Staël-Holstein." Enclosed in TJ to John Graham, 29 May 1813.

Staël Holstein's NATIVE CITY was Paris, and her VENERABLE FATHER was Jacques Necker. For the 21 Apr. 1812 British PROCLAMATION OF HER PRINCE REGENT George, see *ASP, Foreign Relations*, 3:429–31. Late in August 1812 the American chargé d'affaires at London, Jonathan Russell, suggested to HER MINISTER, Lord Castlereagh, that as "an inducement to Great Britain to discontinue the practice of impressment from Ameri-

can vessels . . . a law shall be passed (to be reciprocal) to prohibit the employment of British seamen in the public or commercial service of the United States." Castlereagh expressed surprise and refused to countenance the idea, but he proposed no alternative (*ASP, Foreign Relations*, 3:589–90). The United States declared war on Great Britain on 18 June 1812, a few days prior to the PALINODIAL PROCLAMATION of 23 June that conditionally revoked the Orders in Council (*Annals*, 12th Cong., 2d sess., 1679–83; *ASP, Foreign Relations*, 3:433–4). The British navy impressed into its service John Lewis and Charles Lewis, great-NEPHEWS OF GENERAL WASHINGTON (James Monroe to Augustus J. Foster, 8 Feb. 1812 [DNA: RG 59, NFMC]).

[1] Preceding two words interlined.

From John Adams

DEAR SIR   Quincy May 29. 1813.

To leave the Pettifogger of Funivals Inn, or Cliffords Inn, his Archbishop Laud, and his Chevalier of St. Iago of Compostella Sir Christopher Gardiner, for the present; Paulo Multo[1] majora canamus.

There has been put into my hands, within a few days a gross Volume in octavo, of 544 Pages with the Title of "Memoirs of the late reverend Theophilus Lindsey. M.A." including a brief "Analysis of his works; together with Anecdotes and Letters of eminent Persons, his Friends and Correspondents: also a general View of the progress of the Unitarian doctrine in England and America. By Thomas Belsham, Minister of the Chapel in Essex Street."

Whether you have Seen this work, I know not. but this I know, the Author, and his Friends ought to have Sent you a Copy of it; and therefore I conclude they have.

With Lindsey, Disney, Price, Priestley, Jebb, Kippis &c and their

Connections, whom I could name, I was much acquainted in London from 1785 to 1788. These Characters, with Cappe, Farmer, and a multitude of others, figure in this work. The Religion, the Philosophy, the Morality, the Politicks, which these People teach, have been Objects of my anxious Attention for more than Three Score years, as I could demonstrate to you, if I could give you, a brief Sketch of my Life. But my Life has been too trifling and my Actions too insignificant for me to write or the Public to read. In my wandering romantic Life, with my incessant Res angusta Domi, and my numerous unfortunate Family, of Children and Grand Children without the honour, which you have attained of being a great grandfather, tho' I have a near prospect of it; it has been impossible for me to pursue Such Inquiries, with any thing like Learning.

what may be the Effect, of these "Memoirs" in the U.S. if they Should become public I know not; and I will add I care not; for I wish every Subject to be discussed at all Events. The human Mind is awake: Let it not Sleep. Let it however consider. Let it think, Let it pause.

This work must produce a noise in U.S. Fiat Justitia.—

The 12ᵗʰ Article in the Appendix is "Letters from Dʳ Priestley to Mʳ Lindsey: and from Thomas Jefferson Esq. President of the United States to Dʳ Priestley."² p. 525. The first Letter from you is dated March 21. 1801. at Washington. The Second April 9. 1803 at Washington. Dʳ Priestleys Letter to Mʳ Lindsey, containing remarks upon Mʳ Jeffersons Letter is dated Northumberland April 23. 1803.

I wish to know, if you have Seen this Book. I have much to Say on the Subject. And you may depend upon it, I will discuss the Subject with as much Candour, as much Friendship, as much Freedom, as Price, Priestley Lindsey, Cappe or Farmer ever displayed in their Controversies. I have not time to enlarge at present.

I will only Add have you Seen the Naval History by Mʳ Clark, published by Mathew Carey at Philadelphia? I wish I had time and Eyes and fingers to write much to you on this Subject.

I lament the death of my dear Friend of 38 years Dʳ Benjamin Rush, much the more, Since I have Seen Lindseys Memoirs.

I am, with unalterable Esteem and Affection your old Friend

JOHN ADAMS

RC (DLC); at foot of text: "The late President Jefferson"; endorsed by TJ as received 9 June 1813 and so recorded in SJL. FC (Lb in MHi: Adams Papers).

The PETTIFOGGER OF FUNIVALS INN was Thomas Morton. PAULO MULTO MAJORA CANAMUS: "let us sing a much loftier strain," from Virgil, Eclogues, 4.1

(Fairclough, *Virgil*, 1:28–9 [with "much" revised by Adams from "somewhat"; see note 1 below]). RES ANGUSTA DOMI: "cramped personal resources block your talents" (Juvenal, *Satires*, 3.165, in *Juvenal and Persius*, ed. and trans. Susanna Morton Braund, Loeb Classical Library [2004], 180–1). FIAT JUSTITIA: "Let justice be done." Priestley enclosed TJ's letter of APRIL 9. 1803 (DLC) in his own

LETTER TO MR LINDSEY of 23 Apr. 1803 (Thomas Belsham, *Memoirs of the Late Reverend Theophilus Lindsey, M.A.* [London, 1812].

[1] Word, interlined by Adams, not included in Loeb text of Virgil, *Eclogues*.
[2] Omitted closing quotation mark editorially supplied.

From Patrick Gibson

SIR   Richmond 29th May 1813

I have received your two letters of the 20th & 25th Inst the former inclosing mazzeis power of Attorney which is satisfactory to Mr Taylor the notes shall be dated from the 17th—I regret extremely not having disposed of the whole of your flour at the time I sold the last, it is next to impossible at present to force a sale at any price; it is selling from the waggons at $4\frac{1}{2}$\$ and paid for in goods—I have bespoke a keg of powder from Burr to be sent up by the first opportunity—the two last sent were from T: White, as Burr had then none on hand— The remittances you direct, have been made and I now inclose you \$150 in small notes

With great respect I am
Your obt Servt   PATRICK GIBSON

mr white is willing that the powder should be returned if you have not used it

RC (ViU: TJP-ER); at head of text: "Thomas Jefferson Esqre"; postscript in a clerk's hand; endorsed by TJ as received 1 June 1813 and so recorded (as a letter from Gibson & Jefferson) in SJL.

TJ's letter of the 25TH INST, not found, is recorded in SJL.

To John Graham

DEAR SIR   Monticello May 29. 13.

Your preceding kindnesses in forwarding my foreign letters encourage me to send you the inclosed. Madame de Stael desired it should be put under cover to our Consul at Stockholm, but I do not know who that is. this obliges me to ask the favor of you to put it under such a cover. the letter is such an one as I should be sorry should get either into French or English hands. I will ask the favor of you therefore to reserve it for one of your safest conveyances. accept always the assurances of my great esteem & respect.

Th: Jefferson

PoC (DLC); at foot of text: "John Graham esq."; endorsed by TJ. Enclosure: TJ to Madame de Staël Holstein, 28 May 1813.

The CONSUL AT STOCKHOLM was John Speyer.

From John L. Thomas

SIR   Richmond May 29. 1813

This is merely to explain to you the reasons, that has delayed the attestation of the Deed you returned—

when the succeeding Court came On after you Returned the Deed I was in south Carolinia[1]—soon after my return I was taking Very Ill which has prevented my doing any buisiness—I am now getting On the mend—& so soon as I am able your buisiness shall be attended to & the deed Returned—

Yrs respectfully   J L Thomas

RC (MHi); between dateline and salutation: "Thomas Jefferson esqr"; endorsed by TJ as received 8 June 1813 and so recorded in SJL.

[1] Thomas here canceled "and the Court."

To Joseph Delaplaine

SIR   Monticello May 30. 13.

Your favor of the 23^d is recieved, in which you enquire whether there is an approved portrait of myself, by whom painted, & in whose possession? mr Stuart has drawn two portraits of me, at different sittings, of which he prefers the last. both are in his possession. he also drew a third in water colours, a profile in the medallion stile, which is in my possession. mr Rembrandt Peale also drew a portrait in oil colours on canvas while I lived in Washington. of the merit of these I am not a judge, there being nothing to which a man is so incompetent as to judge of his own likeness. he can see himself only by reflection, and that of necessity full-faced or nearly so.

With my wishes for your success accept the tender of my esteem & respect.   Th: Jefferson

RC (LNT: George H. and Katherine M. Davis Collection); addressed: "Mr Joseph Delaplaine Philadelphia S.W. corner of 7th & Chesnut streets"; franked; postmarked Milton, 2 June; endorsed by Delaplaine. PoC (DLC); endorsed by TJ.

TJ first sat for the artist Gilbert STUART in May 1800. Stuart seems to have sent that oil painting to London for engraving, and its subsequent history is unknown. TJ sat for a second portrait in June 1805 during Stuart's residence in Washington. This work became known as the "Edgehill Portrait" because of its long association with the Randolph family home of that name. Stuart produced his MEDALLION STILE portrait (a version of which appears on the title page of each volume of this edition) from life during the same visit. REMBRANDT PEALE painted TJ's portrait at the President's House in January 1805. In 1816 Delaplaine commissioned a portrait of TJ to use in his *Repository of the Lives and Portraits of Distinguished Americans* (Philadelphia, 1817; Poor, *Jefferson's Library*, 4 [no. 139]), and he accompanied the artist Bass Otis to Monticello for the sitting (Bush, *Life Portraits*, 59–61, 68–81; Stein, *Worlds*, 139, 173).

To John Eliason

SIR   Monticello May 30. 13.

I was sorry, on my return from a journey, to find that your visit had happened in that interval. I should have been happy to have seen you, and my family would have recieved you with pleasure in my absence. perhaps, had you seen mr Randolph, you might have obtained more satisfaction on your enquiries than I can give you. as long as he chuses to keep the mill, I should prefer him to any tenant, not only from a natural wish to promote whatever he thinks his interest, but because experience has taught me not to expect from another tenant[1] the same care of the tenement which he takes, not only for it's preservation, but it's improvement and interest. whether he will keep it if called off to his military command, is not very certain. he thinks he shall do it, and trust her to an agent. I apprehend he will soon find this a losing business, in which case I should recieve his relinquishment whenever he should think his interest required it. in that case it will be to be rented, and I can notify it to you if desired. in answer to your request in your letter of the 22^d to be informed of the terms I will state in general that they will be nearly what I agreed with mr Randolph, say 55. barrels of Superfine[2] flour a quarter, payable quarterly, to retain the landlord's right of being hopper-free, as is the law & custom of this state, that is to say to have my own crop of wheat ground at any time in preference to all others, and on the usual terms, to keep the hull of the house in repair myself, but the tenant to maintain all internal repairs & deliver the running geer in as good repair as he recieves them. I maintain the body of the dam, & he jointly assists in the tightenings sometimes[3] necessary in dry seasons, & in cleaning the canal when necessary; if the dam is carried away by floods, I repair it, & the rent is suspended during the time it cannot grind, the tenant pays the taxes, the lease is not assignable but with my consent, but may be determined at the will of either party on a notice to be agreed on. this is the general outline. Accept the tender of my respects & best wishes. TH: JEFFERSON.

RC (ViCMRL, on deposit ViU: TJP); addressed: "Mr John Eliason Georgetown Col."; franked; postmarked Milton, 2 June. PoC (MHi); endorsed by TJ.

[1] Preceding three words interlined.
[2] Word interlined.
[3] Word interlined.

From Tadeusz Kosciuszko

MON CHER AMI, Paris, mai 30, 1813.

Je vous remercie pour les détails que vous me donnez sur votre patrie. Je vois que votre génie, votre prudence et votre attachement pour elle a tout préparé d'avance pour sa sureté. Les operations militaires sont faciles maintenant. La guerre juste que vous avez commencée contre l'Angleterre ne peut[1] pas effrayer, il en serait de même contre toute autre puissance qui ne voudrait point agir avec sur le pied d'égalité de nation à nation. Votre pays est riche, grand et peuplé; vos habitants sont bons, actives, et courageux. Mais ne soyez point trop ambitieux d'acquérir tout le Canada, trop de sécurité vous amollira; je serais d'opinion que votre ligne de démarcation fut de quelque point du lac Champlain ou de la rivière St. Laurent jusqu'à la mer du Sud afin que vous n'ayez rien aux autres puissances derrière vous. Je ne doute pas ques vos dispositions militaires ne soyent sagement combinées et prêtes à secourir les divers corps d'armée, d'après la connaisance générale du pays, de vos nationaux et par celle de la direction des forces de vos ennemis. Je pense aussi qu'il soit utile de se servir de beaucoup d'artillerie légère à pied et à cheval, car vos bois ne sont pas serrés et la promptitude de l'artillerie pour se porter ou il est nécessaire, décide souvent du gain de la bataille.

L'approvisionnement suffisant de l'armée est le premier besoin, vient ensuite la sévérité de la discipline, points sur lesquels personne ne disputerait pas. A l'égard de vos généraux il importe d'en faire un bon choix. L'activité, la prudence et un attachement non douteux pour leur patrie doivent être preférés à d'autres qualités et surtout exclure de cet emploi tout homme intéressé. Que vos généraux attaquent toujours les premiers vos ennemis et sur deux points, s'il est possible. Punissez sévèrement la surprise, par là vous inspirerez la confiance aux habitants et une grande circonspection aux militaires. Je suis jaloux des améliorations que vous faites dans votre propriété et par là de l'exemple² que vous donnez à vos compatriotes, tant qu'à moi je ne fais rien loin de ma patrie, vous en savez sans doute la raison, je reste dans l'inaction et ne suis d'aucun service pour l'humanité. Je vous embrasse de toute mon âme   T. Kosciuszko.

Vous me rendez un grand service en s'arrangeat³ avec Mr. Morton à qui je dois des remerciements pour la manière la plus obligeante que j'ai été traite à Paris, et par l'exactitude de son correspondant.

EDITORS' TRANSLATION

My Dear Friend,   Paris, May 30, 1813.
    I thank you for the details you have given me of your country. I see that your genius, prudence, and attachment to it have prepared everything in advance for its security. Military operations will now be easy. The just war you have launched against England cannot frighten you, any more than would such a contest against any other power unwilling to treat you as an equal. Your country is rich, large, and populous; your inhabitants are good, active, and courageous. But do not be too ambitious to acquire all of Canada; too much security will soften you. I believe that your line of demarcation should run from some point on Lake Champlain or the Saint Lawrence River to the Pacific Ocean, so as to have no other power behind you. I do not doubt that your military dispositions are wisely drawn up, with the various corps in a position to support each other and positioned in accordance with a general knowledge of the country, your citizens, and the plans of the enemy forces. I also think that it would be useful to employ numerous light foot and horse artillery, because your woods are not dense and the ability to transport artillery promptly where it is needed often decides who wins the battle.
    Provisioning the army adequately is of the highest importance, followed by strict discipline. No one would dispute this. Choosing your generals well is important. Activity, prudence, and indisputable patriotism must be preferred to other qualities, and above all else, selfish individuals must be excluded from this position. Your generals should always attack the enemy first and in two places if possible. Punish those taken by surprise severely. In this way you will inspire trust among the inhabitants and great caution within the military. I am jealous of the improvements you are making to your estate and of the example you are giving to your fellow citizens. As for me, I do nothing. Far from my homeland, you undoubtedly know why, I remain inactive and am of no use to humanity. I embrace you with all my heart
                                                          T. Kosciuszko.

    You do me a great favor by arranging things with Mr. Morton, to whom I owe thanks for the most obliging manner in which he treated me in Paris and for the punctuality of his correspondent.

Printed in Miecislaus Haiman, *Kosciuszko: Leader and Exile* (1977), 150–1; manuscript owned by ICPRCU in 1977, but apparently now missing. Dupl recorded in SJL as received 5 Nov. 1813 from Paris. Translation by Dr. Genevieve Moene. SJL records no RC; TJ may have regarded this letter as a near duplicate of Kosciuszko's missing letter of 1 Dec. 1812, for which see TJ to John Barnes, 18 Sept. 1813.

[1] Printed text: "pout."
[2] Printed text: "l'exemple."
[3] Printed text: "s'aarangeat."

To Bernard McMahon

DEAR SIR   Monticello May 30. 13.

I just now recieve information from my old friend Thouïn of the national garden of Paris that he has sent me a box of seeds of 270. kinds of trees of every sort for either use or ornament.

this box, mr Warden informs me, he sends by mr Breuil of the schooner Bellona, bound to Philadelphia. if you will be so good as to watch the arrival of this vessel, perhaps already arrived, this letter may suffice to authorise the delivery of it by Mr Breuil to you, to whom I should send it were it to come here, as being the best mode of fulfilling the intentions of the benevolent giver. if you could make up a collection of the seeds of the plants brought to us by Governor Lewis from beyond the Missisipi, it would be a just and grateful return which M. Thouïn merits at our hands. he expresses to me a great desire for the plants of the region beyond the Missisipi. if within the reasonable compass of the mail, it will come safest to me thro' that. if larger, the stage is a good conveyance if a passenger can be found who will take charge of it. such opportunities to Richmond must be almost daily with you, and if addressed to Messrs Gibson & Jefferson there it will come safely to me. Accept the assurances of my great esteem and respect.   TH: JEFFERSON

RC (Mrs. M. L. Hermanos, New York City, 1946); at foot of text: "Mr Bernard McMahon." PoC (DLC); endorsed by TJ.

To David Michie

SIR,   Monticello May 30th '13

Judge Carr being arrived in the neighbourhood of which I have notice but this moment—I have to ask the favour of you to Attend the taking his deposition in the Case between us tomorrow at 11 Oclock at Charlottesville in Garners tavern which time & place are fixed by himself,[1] as those only at which he Can attend. The shortness of my notice must appologize for that I give you. The object is, that he should state what passed at an examination of some witnesses between Peyton and Henderson at which you attended,—Should it be inconvenient to you to attend I will decline attending also, and leave to the Judge to state the transactions himself, unquestioned by either party, if in this way you Consent to the future uses of the deposition as we agreed on taking the deposition of James Lewis Your answer by the bearer will Oblige Sir

Your humble Serv[t]   TH: JEFFERSON

Tr (ViU: TJP-LBJM); in George Carr's hand; at foot of text: "M[r] David Michie." Enclosed in TJ's Bill of Complaint in *Jefferson v. Michie*, 16 June 1813, and Michie's Plea and Answer in *Jefferson v. Michie*, [by 6 Sept. 1813].

[1] Manuscript: "hmself."

From David Michie

SIR,   Buckisland May 30th 1813

The indisposition of my family will prevent my attending at Charlottesville tomorow as requested in yours of this days date.—You are I presume apprized that I have obtained from Judge Stuart a Certiorari to remove the proceedings on the forcible entry & detainer into the Superior Court of law for this district: on that, and all the points of Controversy between us, I have lately taken the advice of Counsel learned in the law. they have stated Sir, in Confirmation of my own belief, that from the law if Correctly expounded, I have nothing to fear, and have pointedly advised me against any extrajudicial proceedings, especially as the ground you meant to take has been carefully reserved.

I have the honor to be with due respect

Your Hlbe serv[t]   DAVID MICHIE

Tr (ViU: TJP-LBJM); in George Carr's hand. Recorded in SJL as received 30 May 1813. Enclosed in TJ's Bill of Complaint in *Jefferson v. Michie*, 16 June 1813, and Michie's Plea and Answer in *Jefferson v. Michie*, [by 6 Sept. 1813].

Michie obtained a writ of CERTIORARI from the Albemarle County Superior Court of Law on 13 May 1813 (Albemarle Co. Law Order Book [1809–21], 171).

To James Monroe

I thank you for the communication of the President's message which has not yet reached us thro' the public papers. it is an interesting document, always looked for with anxiety, and the late one is equally able as interesting. I hope Congress will act in conformity with it in all it's parts.   the unwarrantable ideas often expressed in the newspapers, and by persons who ought to know better, that I intermeddle in the Executive councils, and the indecent expressions sometimes of a hope that mr Madison will pursue the principles of my administration, expressions so disrespectful to his known abilities & dispositions, have rendered it improper in me to hazard suggestions to him on occasions even where ideas might occur to me, that might accidentally escape him. this reserve has been strengthened too by a consciousness that my views must be very imperfect from the want of a correct knolege of the whole ground.

I lately however hazarded to him a suggestion on the defence of the Chesapeak because altho' decided on provisionally with the Secretaries of War & the Navy formerly, yet as it was proposed only in the case of war, which did not actually arise, and not relating to his department, might not then have been communicated to him. of this fact my memory did not ascertain me. I will now hazard another suggestion to yourself, which indeed grows out of that one: it is, the policy of keeping our frigates together in a body, in some place where they can be defended against a superior naval force, and from whence nevertheless they can easily sally forth on the shortest warning. this would oblige the enemy to take stations or to cruize only in masses equal at least each of them to our whole force: and of course they could be acting only in 2. or 3. spots at a time, and the whole of our coast, except the 2. or 3. portions where they might[1] be present, would be open to exportation and importation. I think all that part of the US. over which the waters of the Chesapeake spread themselves was blockaded in the early season by a single ship. this would keep our frigates in entire safety, as they would go out only occasionally to oppress a blockading force known to be weaker than themselves, and thus make them a real protection to our whole commerce. and it seems to me that this would be a more essential service, than that of going out by ones, or by twos, in search of adventures, which contribute little to the protection of our commerce, and not at all to the defence of our coast, or the shores of our inland waters. a defence of these by militia, is most harassing to them. the applications from

Maryland, which I have seen in the papers, & those from Virginia which I suspect, merely because I see such masses of the militia call^d off from their farms must be embarrassing to the Executive, not only from a knolege of the incompetency of such a mode of defence, but from the exhausture of funds which ought to be husbanded for the effectual operations of a long war. I fear too it will render the militia discontented, perhaps clamorous for an end of the war on any terms. I am happy to see that it is entirely popular as yet, and that no symptom[2] of flinching from it appears among the people, as far as I can judge from the public papers, or from my own observation, limited to the few counties adjacent to the two branches of James river. I have such confidence that what I suggest has been already maturely discussed in the Cabinet, and that for wise & sufficient reasons the present mode of employing the frigates is the best, that I hesitate about sending this even after having written. yet, in that case it will only have given you the trouble of reading it, you will bury it in your own breast, as non-avenue, and see in it only an unnecessary zeal on my part, and a proof of the unlimited confidence of   Your's ever & affectionately   Th: Jefferson

RC (DLC: Monroe Papers); addressed: "James Monroe Secretary of State Washington. Col."; franked; postmarked Charlottesville, 2 June; endorsed by Monroe. PoC (DLC).

For the PRESIDENT'S MESSAGE, see note to John Wayles Eppes to TJ, 25 May 1813. The APPLICATIONS FROM MARYLAND included appeals from Governor Levin Winder and the state's council and legislature to President James Madison in the spring of 1813 for federal assistance in defraying the expenses incurred by Maryland for its defense against British naval forces invading the Chesapeake (Madison, *Papers, Pres. Ser.*, 6:240–1, 322–3). In a message to the state legislature dated 17 May 1813, Winder reported that military supplies were running low. In order to comply with new orders from the secretary of war to raise an additional militia force, he suggested that the legislature authorize the organization of volunteer militias with the power of electing their own officers as a way to reduce the strain of mobilizing further contingents of ordinary militia (Georgetown *Federal Republican and Commercial Gazette*, 24 May 1813). NON-AVENUE: a short form of "nul et non avenu"; not having happened, annulled (*OED*).

[1] Word interlined in place of "would."
[2] Manuscript: "sumptom." In attempting to correct this spelling error, TJ mistakenly attached the tail of the "y" to the first "m."

To William Short

Dear Sir   Monticello May 30. 13.
      I returned from Bedford on the 15th inst. and have been in the hope of having the pleasure of seeing Mr Correa here; but begin now to fear his visit to Washington might have been too early in the month

to be protracted until the time I had noted to you for my return. should this circumstance deprive me ultimately of the pleasure of seeing him it will be a subject of lasting regret. it is so rare in our country situations to meet with men of his endowments, that such a visit forms an epoch of pleasing recollection. my affairs in Bedford call for my return there about the 8th of June,[1] the mention of which is the object of this letter, lest the visit with which I had been flattered might by any accident be thrown into the period of my absence which will be of about three weeks. the months of July and August I shall pass here entire, being those of our harvest and getting out our wheat. this operation will be shortened for us this year by the ravages of the fly, which are greater than ever have been known. from these casualties which distress the farmer you are happily exempted by the form of property which you have preferred. his advantage is that while monied property is liable to the wane of depreciation from an artificial increase of it's quantity, his is kept at par at least by a rise of nominal value equivalent to every change of the[2] measure applied to it. and so it is that all things in life have their uncertainties, and life itself the greatest of all. but our schoolbooks tell us that 'levius fit patientiâ, quiequid corrigere est nefas.' Adieu, with all affection and respect.   TH: JEFFERSON

RC (ViW: TJP); addressed: "William Short esquire Philadelphia"; franked; postmarked Milton, 2 June; endorsed by Short as received 6 June 1813.

LEVIUS FIT PATIENTIÂ, QUIEQUID CORRIGERE EST NEFAS: "endurance can make lighter what no one is allowed to put right" (Horace, *Odes*, 1.24.19, in *Horace: Odes and Epodes*, trans. Niall Rudd, Loeb Classical Library [2004], 70).

[1] Preceding two words interlined in place of "instant."
[2] TJ here canceled "medium."

From Nicolas G. Dufief

MONSIEUR,   A Philad[e] ce 31. Mai. 1813
    J'ai eu l'honneur de recevoir votre lettre du 21 du Courant ainsi que la traitte de Messrs Gibson & Jefferson sur la Banque de Pennsylvania pour sa Somme de Quarante piastres. D'après le compte ci-Inclus, il vous revient une balance de dix dollars & trente-deux cents, que je tiendrai à votre disposition. Je profite de cette occasion pour vous remercier & vous prier d'agreer les assurances du profond respect, avec lequel je ne cesserai jamais d'être
    Votre très-dévoué Serviteur   N. G. DUFIEF

E D I T O R S '   T R A N S L A T I O N

Sɪʀ,   Philadelphia 31. May. 1813

I have had the honor of receiving both your letter of 21 May and the draft of Messrs. Gibson & Jefferson on the Bank of Pennsylvania for the sum of forty dollars. According to the enclosed account, a balance of ten dollars and thirty-two cents is due to you, which I will hold for you. I take advantage of this opportunity to thank you and assure you of my most profound respect, with which I will never cease to be

Your very devoted servant   N. G. Dᴜғɪᴇғ

RC (DLC); endorsed by TJ as received 4 June 1813 and so recorded in SJL. Translation by Dr. Genevieve Moene.

The balance in the enclosed account printed below is $12.32, not ᴅɪx ᴅᴏʟ-ʟᴀʀs & ᴛʀᴇɴᴛᴇ-ᴅᴇᴜx ᴄᴇɴᴛs.

E N C L O S U R E

Account for Books

Thomas Jefferson Esqr
                    To N. G. Dufief

1812		
nov. 4ᵗʰ	Simpsons Fluxions	$6.18
"	mellish's map of the Seat of war	1.00
1813		
Jany 4ᵗʰ	Tacitus	8.00
Febry 15.	Titus Livius	12.50
		$27.68
1813		
may 29.	By Cash from Messʳˢ Gibson & Jefferson	$40.00
	amt of above bill	27.68
	due Mʳ Jefferson	$12.32

MS (DLC: TJ Papers, 198:35244); in a clerk's hand; undated.

From Tobias Lear

                    Washington, may 31ˢᵗ 1813.—

Can you, my dear Sir, forgive the apparent neglect of one, who so highly respects and esteems you as I do, in not having addressed you immediately on his arrival in the U. States, after so long an absence?—Trusting in that benevolence which so strongly marks your character, I pronounce that you will; and therefore write to you as if I were already assured of[1] forgiveness.

The ten years which I have spent abroad, altho' chequered with scenes highly interesting, and to me important and mostly novel, seem to have passed but as a day.—And, upon reaching my native shore, I seem to have renewed, instead of having advanced in Age, during the period of my absence;—for I feel as if I was upon the only ground which I have trodden, that deserves the name of a free Country.—And altho' I see the strong spirit of party which now pervades our land, amounting almost to open hostility; yet I think I can perceive the American Spirit predominating, which will ultimately prevail, and raise us to be the first nation on Earth.—

I have marked the steps of our <u>truly great</u> men, so far as they have come within my view; and altho' there have appeared some shades of difference in their political opinions on certain speculative points; yet they all have aimed at the welfare, happiness and Glory of our Country; and I trust that the acts of those who have passed, joined to the intelligent and persevering conduct of those now acting, will overcome all difficulties, and open to their Successors a plainer path; shewing to the world, that altho' Freemen may bear the injuries and oppressions of other nations for a while, they will burst forth at a certain point, and display a character whose refulgence would have been longer hidden, but for these oppressions.—

I am now at Washington, settling my public accounts, which I hope to finish in a short time, after which I shall visit my relations in New England; and in the Autum I intend going to Virginia, when I promise myself one of the most pleasing occurrences, that of seeing you at Monticello.—But all this will depend on circumstances which cannot at present be faithfully calculated upon.—At any rate, whether I visit you or not, you will always be assured of my most sincere and inviolable attachment.—

As I have reason to think that you feel an interest in whatever relates to me, I will take the liberty to mention, that my Son, Benjamin Lincoln Lear (the only child I have) is now about 22 years of age.— After finishing his Collegiate Education in New England, he read about 18 months in the office of a respectable Lawyer, when I permitted him to join me at Algiers, intending, on leaving that place, to have passed through some part of Europe with him, before my return to the U. States. But, in ten days after he reached Algiers, I was obliged to quit that Regency, in the manner which you already know, and circumstances made it proper for me to proceed directly to the U. States.—I now feel anxious to place him in the way of improvement and acquirement which may hereafter make him useful to his Country, as well as enable him to provide a competency for himself; for the most he can expect from me, will be the means of coming clearly into active life.—He possesses pleasing manners, and an excellent heart, with vivacity and handsome talents.—His Education has been such as our youth receive at the Colleges in New England, which you know is not the most solid[2] or complete; but still sufficient to ground Such improvements upon, as may be lasting and useful.—It is my present intention to let him finish the Study of the law, either here, or in some other place where he can do it with advantage, and then enter upon the practice for his future support and dependence.—But while he is doing this, there are many other branches of knowledge which can be attended to, and which may be highly useful.—I will, therefore, venture to ask your advice on these points, as well as on the subject generally, of making him a useful and valuable member of Society, knowing how able you are to do this, and beleiving that it will give you pleasure to render me a service.

M[rs] Lear desire me to present you and your's with her best salutations and most sincere good wishes, in which I most cordially join.

Beleive me to be

with true respect and esteem, my dear Sir, Your obliged and attached friend   TOBIAS LEAR.—

RC (DLC); at foot of text: "The Hon[ble] Thomas Jefferson"; endorsed by TJ as received 9 June 1813 and so recorded in SJL.

Tobias Lear (1762–1816), diplomat and aide to George Washington, was born in Portsmouth, New Hampshire, and received an A.B. degree from Harvard University in 1783. He traveled in Europe and was then employed as Washington's personal secretary, 1786–93, before leaving the president's service to pursue his own business interests. Lear authored *Observations on the River Potomack, the Country Adjacent, and the City of Washington* (New York, 1793), and in 1795 he became the president of the Potomac Company, a venture dedicated to improving navigation along the Potomac River. After Washington took command of the United States Army in 1798, Lear became his military secretary with the rank of lieutenant colonel. He was in attendance when Washington died in 1799, and he received a bequest from the first president, helped to settle his estate,

and oversaw the handling of his papers. TJ appointed Lear the United States general commercial agent to Saint Domingue in 1801. The positon was fraught with difficulties due to unrest on the island, and Lear was forced to return to America the following year when the French temporarily reasserted their control there. He next accepted appointment as consul general at Algiers, an equally challenging position during the conflict with the Barbary pirates. Lear held the post until the outbreak of the War of 1812 and negotiated a number of treaties. He was serving as an accountant at the War Department when he committed suicide (*ANB; DAB;* Ray Brighton, *The Checkered Career of Tobias Lear* [1985]; Washington, *Papers, Pres. Ser.,* 1:98, and *Retirement Ser.,* 2:483–4; *PTJ,* esp. 16:554–5, 27:300, 301–2, 304–5, 33:229, 447–8; Heitman, *U.S. Army,* 1:621; *JEP,* 1:401, 404, 453, 455 [6 Jan. 1802, 11, 15 Nov. 1803]; Washington *Daily National Intelligencer,* 12 Oct. 1816).

Lear was OBLIGED TO QUIT his post as consul when Hadji Ali, dey of Algiers, expressed his displeasure with the quality of an American shipment of naval and military stores delivered in compliance with the terms of a 1795 treaty by ordering Lear and all other Americans to depart (Joseph Wheelan, *Jefferson's War:* *America's First War on Terror 1801–1805* [2003], 345–7; *Annals*, 12th Cong., 2d sess., 1222–35).

[1] Lear here canceled "your."
[2] Manuscript: "sold."

To Richard Rush

DEAR SIR   Monticello May 31. 13.

No one has taken a more sincere part than myself in the affliction which has lately befallen your family, by the loss of your inestimable and ever to be lamented father. his virtues rendered him dear to all who knew him, and his benevolence led him to do to all men every good in his power. much he was able to do, and much therefore will he be missed. my acquaintance with him began in 1776. it soon became intimate, and from that time a warm friendship has been maintained by a correspondence of unreserved confidence. in the course of this, each has deposited, in the bosom of the other, communications which were never intended to go further. in the sacred fidelity of each to the other these were known to be safe: and above all things that they would be kept from the public eye.   there may have been other letters of this character written by me to him: but two alone occur to me at present, about which I have any anxiety. these were of Apr. 21. 1803. & Jan. 16. 1811. the first of these was on the subject of religion, a subject on which I have ever been most scrupulously reserved. I have considered it as a matter between every man and his maker, in which no other, & far less the public, had a right to intermeddle. to your father alone, I committed some views on this subject in the first of the letters abovementioned, led to it by previous conversations, and a promise on my part to digest & communicate them in writing.   the letter of Jan. 16. 1811. respected a mutual friend, between whom & myself a suspension of correspondence had taken place.[1] this was restored by his kind intervention, the correspondence resumed, and a friendship revived which had been much valued on both sides. another letter of Dec. 5. 11. explains this occurrence. I very much wish that these letters should remain unseen and unknown. and, if it would be too much to ask their return, I would earnestly entreat of you so to dispose of them as that they might never be seen, if possible, but by yourself, with whom I know their contents would be safe. I have too many enemies disposed to make a lacerating use of them, not to feel anxieties inspired by a love of tranquility, now become the summum bonum of life. in your occasional visits to Philadelphia, perhaps you can lay your hand on them, which might be preferable to the drawing a marked attention to them by letter. I submit all this to your honorable & candid mind, and praying you to tender to your much esteemed mother my sincere condolances & respects, accept for yourself the assurance of my great esteem & consideration.   TH: JEFFERSON

RC (NjP: Rush Family Papers); addressed: "Richard Rush esquire Treasury office Washington. Col."; franked; postmarked Charlottesville, 9 June; endorsed by Rush on address cover, with his additional notations: "On my father's death, with tributes to him; and referring to confidential letters that had passed between them" and "Under this Letter, I became the medium of the restoration to Mr Jefferson of the letters in question"; docketed by Rush on a separate slip: "Received at Washington soon after the death of my Father." PoC (DLC); endorsed by TJ. Tr (PU: William Pepper Papers); entirely in Rush's hand.

The MUTUAL FRIEND was John Adams.

[1] Rush here placed a ⚹ symbol keyed to a note he wrote in the left margin of RC and at foot of page in Tr: "The elder Adams is here meant," adding to the Tr that it was a "(Note by Richd Rush)."

To Lucy F. Smith

MADAM   Monticello May 31. 13.
Your favor of May 13. is duly recieved, requesting my application to the government for a midshipman's warrant for mr Walter Jones, son of the late Meriwether Jones. could I permit myself in any case to make such an application, I should surely do it in favor of the son of mr Jones, for whose character I had a just respect, and whose labors in support of the sound principles of our government were great & meritorious. when I first retired from the government in 1809, sollicitations from my friends, to aid them in their applications for office, drew from me an unwary compliance, until they so multiplied that, however indulgently they were attended to, they became embarrassing to the government, and afflicting to myself, as keeping me ever before them in the attitude of a Suppliant solliciting favors. an occasion, long wished for, of putting an end to these unceasing importunities, offering itself on the change of that part of the administration to which they were chiefly addressed, I availed myself of it by a determination to stop at that point, and relieve the government & myself from this source of uneasiness to both. to this I have stedfastly adhered, and I find it's rigid observance too necessary for my own satisfaction, & to preserve the friendship of the administration, to

permit myself ever more to depart from it. I should regret this necessity the more in the present case, but for the friendship of Col° Monroe towards the late mr Jones, whose zeal and situation cannot fail to render all auxiliary application unnecessary. with every wish that your desires may recieve the gratification of which I do not doubt, I beg leave to tender you the assurance of my great esteem & respect.

TH: JEFFERSON

PoC (MoSHi: TJC); at foot of text: "Mrs Smith"; endorsed by TJ.

Smith's earlier FAVOR was actually dated 23 May 1813.

Account with Reuben Perry for Work on Main House at Poplar Forest

[ca. May 1813]

Mr Thomas Jefferson

In account with R. Perry

To 330 feet Double Jambs & face grounds @ 1/	£16.10.
44 feet Single grounds @ 4d	.14.8
9 Chimney grounds @ 4/6	2. 0.6
156 feet base & Surbase grounds @ 6d	3.18.0
76 feet grounds for Cornice @1 6d	1.18
81 feet grounds for Cornce @2 9d	3. 0.9
165 feet 4I base & Surbase @ 6d	4. 2.6
188 feet grounds for Cornce @3 6d	4.14
2 Cuddy & 2 trap doors @ 2/3	. 9.
12 Double work pannels @ 4/3	2.11.
12 window Sill puting in @ 1/6	.18.
132 feet 8I Cornce grounds @4 6d	3. 6.0
120 feet base & Surbase @ 6d	3. 0.
20 Curtain board @ 3d	. 5.
4 feet ground @ 3d	. 1.
	£47. 8.5
⅓ for Board	15.16.2
	£63. 4.7

MS (ViW: TC-JP); written in Perry's hand on one side of a single sheet, with penciled question and check marks in left margin in an unidentified and possibly later hand; undated, but compiled after TJ indicated that this work was not yet complete in a 6 May 1813 letter to Martha Jefferson Randolph and before TJ listed this debt in a 10 Dec. 1813 account with Perry; endorsed on verso by Perry as "Bill Mr Jeffersons Work" and by TJ as "Perry Reuben. acct work at Pop. For.";

attached at some point to a separate sheet containing Account with Reuben Perry, [ca. 28 Nov. 1811].

SURBASE: a border or molding just above the lower paneling of a wainscoted room; a chair rail (*OED*).

Perry's letter to TJ of 4 Mar. 1813, received six days later from Lynchburg, and

TJ's reply of 26 Mar. 1813 are both recorded in SJL, but neither has been found.

[1] Perry here canceled "9^d."
[2] Perry here canceled "1/."
[3] Perry here canceled "9^d."
[4] Perry here canceled "9^d."

From John Martin Baker

SIR,   Mahon—Island of Minorca June 1st 1813—

I have had the Honor to address you frequently from the Island of Majorca, where in June 1810 I had the Satisfaction to remit you, per the American Schooner Hellen of Salem Cap William Brown, to the particular care of the Collector of that port, One Box containing an Extensive Petrel collection, natural productions of the Island of Sardinia—one q^r Cask albaflor wine, one Sack soft shelled almonds— &^{c}—all which I hope have been Safely received, and that I may be So fortunate, as that they were to Your entire Satisfaction.—   I now take the liberty Sir, to inform You that after seeing in Safety embarked to the last man of American destitute Seamen, which were at majorca; on towards the United states; I have embarked with my family for this Island, So as to judge and if possible decide upon what step I could with Safety take towards once more to regain the United states, and get away from our present particularly unpleasant Situation, Environés by . . . . —!: (all which I beg leave to submit to Your feeling Judgment and Benevolent consideration.) indeed sir, having unfortunately been disappointed in every just expectation, Since my again resuming my Consular Balearic Station, where in view of my former Sacrifices in my official Character, during my Serving there upwards of four Years, (of which Sir, I had the Honor to make you informed.) I never would have returned: to leave my Home and Families Birth right Assylum: Had not the founded expectation of a Squadron of the United states, to come into the mediterranean, (meditatedly fixed upon on my last leaving the United States.) to rendez-vous, or provision at port-Mahon: (with the Honorable Paul Hamilton, Secretary of the Navy's promise to me at Washington, to appoint me Navy agent, and that my Commission, I would receive per the first United States vessel coming to minorca.) were the motives which actuated and urged me for advancement in Service, and

Support of an Amiable wife, and four Infant Children, to exercise every practicable Effort to arrive in time in this quarter, where, Since verified, after a passage of Storms and disagreeable events: I have experienced but disappointment in that expectation; and for the first ten months after my arrival at my Station, was, without the arriving of one American Vessel within the district of my Consulate: notwithstanding I have the pleasing Satisfaction to console me under the heavy pressure of the present times, (in my peculiar station, where no American trading vessel can with Safety venture during our present war's.) that I have used every practicable Effort in my power to do my duty, as nationally useful and interesting, as the Extent of my public powers could permit me: in which I have protected, assisted, preserved and returned to their Country, and distressed families and friends, many valuably useful, then destitute—American Seamen: Several of whom delivered up to me by British Admirals and Commanders, after persevering applications &ᶜ.— I have at the port of Palma, (Island of Majorca) obtained for our flag, (the preeminenc[e] enjoyed by the British nation.) the right, "that no trading vessel bearing the flag of the United states, may be Searched, until the expiration of eight clear working days, counting from the day of delivering the manifest." And during Ten Years, and three months, that I have the Honor to be a Consul of the United states of America, I have never had a provoked or disputed controversy with the authorities of the Departments of my Consulate: and every complaint of whatsoever reasonable nature from a Citizen, made through me, immediately redressed to their fullest Satisfaction; And for my Zeal, Justice and attention, to our Public rights, and individual interests: I appeal to every Citizen of the United states, that has arrived within the District of my Consulate, Since the date, I have had the Honor to Serve the United States of America.—

I beg leave sir, to add, that Since the commencement of Hostile acts, By the Regency of Algiers, I have done all in my power to alleviate and releive our unfortunate fellow Citizens in Suffering Captivity at said place, which I trust will be approved of by the President, and Secretary of State; I now avail of this occasion to ask the favor of your interceding in my behalf with the President, and secretary of State: (in the event of Consul General Lear's retiring.) to be appointed as Consul at Algiers, or if that vacancy, by possibility may have been already filled up, I beg leave to Solicit any other affrican Consulate vacant: or in preference, the Consulate of Lisbon: being just informed of the death of the late United States Consul George Jefferson Esquire; I further beg leave to offer myself in any Agency with the Regency of Algiers, knowing the Lengua-franca, and customs of that quarter, I hope it would be in my power to become useful, and confide with hope, that my Zeal, and general conduct, during my Service in a consular capacity &ᶜ—for upwards of Ten Years:— unfortunately now in this Eloigné from friends, quarter, with a large infant family, and awaiting every day under the blessing of Divine Providence to be encreased: will aid my pleading and claim feeling; And I pray the Supreme Ruler, will influence and accelerate the acting of your Benevolent good wishes, and friendly kind offers towards myself and Family: acknowledging with Gratitude your Beneficence Mʳˢ Baker, Children and myself pray for your Long Life and Happiness And with Sincere reliance on Divine Providence, with hopes to hear Soon from you, I have the Honor to be

with the Highest Respect
Sir Your Faithful Obedient Humble Servant—

JOHN MARTIN BAKER

RC (MHi); edge clipped; ellipsis in original; at foot of text: "To The Most Honorable Thomas Jefferson &c &c &c Monti-cello Virginia"; endorsed by TJ as received 14 Jan. 1814 and so recorded in SJL.

Baker informed TJ that he would for-ward the BOX on 14 May 1810. The EXTENSIVE PETREL COLLECTION was a box of mineral specimens from Sardinia (Leonardo de Prunner to TJ, 15 Mar. 1810, and enclosure). ENVIRONÉS (environnés): "surrounded." ELOIGNÉ: "distant."

From Thomas Clark

SIR,   Philadelphia, June 1st. 1813.

The Publisher of the Sketches of the Naval History of the United States, having determined on printing a second edition of that work, I take the liberty to request of you, if convenient, a detailed account of the Naval Engagements and Expeditions, by vessels of the United States, in which you have been personally concerned, or the accounts of which you have received from persons of veracity, who have been in them; likewise of any gallant exploit of American Naval Officers or Seamen.

Any other information on the Naval affairs and Commerce of the United States, or biographical memoirs of distinguished Naval Commanders, you may be pleased to communicate, will be thankfully received and acknowledged by,

Your most obedient humble servant,   THOMAS CLARK.

Please direct your communication to the Publisher, Mr. M. Carey.

RC (DLC); consisting entirely of a printed circular; endorsed by TJ as received 9 June 1813 and so recorded in SJL.

Thomas Clark (1787–1860), a native of Lancaster, Pennsylvania, attended Saint Mary's College in Baltimore before entering the United States Army as a third lieutenant of artillery in 1813. He reached the rank of captain and served with the topographical engineers before his honorable discharge in 1815 (James Grant Wilson and John Fiske, *Appletons' Cyclopædia of American Biography* [1887–89], 1:631; Heitman, *U.S. Army*, 1:305; *JEP*, 2:358, 380 [18 June, 1 July 1813]; Clark to James Madison, 24 Jan. 1814 [DLC: Madison Papers]; Clark to James Monroe, 31 Oct., 29 Nov. 1814 [DNA: RG 107, LRSW]; Philadelphia *Public Ledger*, 26 Apr. 1860).

From John Barnes

DEAR SIR—   George Town, 3ᵈ June 1813.

Your favᵣ 21ˢᵗ Ultᵒ as well that of Messʳˢ Gibson & Jefferson, of the 29ᵗʰ—Covering $540: are duly recd. and the Amoᵗ placed—as you directed—as more particularly Appears, from the inclosed statemᵗ of your a/c—which, I have Ventured—(being on so near a Scale) to Balance—   with Referance to the intended Remittance to the good Genˡ—I yesterday—again wrote Mʳ George Williams—Baltimore—who I still hope—has recd Correct advices—from Mʳ Morton—Bourdeau and that his Mʳ Mortons Bill of ex—has been duly paid—but that, the Genˡˢ letters of Acknowledgemᵗ (if any were Writtⁿ) has most probably—miscarried—

Mʳ Eliason should have proceeded on to Monticello—notwithstandᵍ your Absense—and waited on Mʳ Randolp, but not having any letter to him—he returned without seeing either. it is I think— most probable—Mʳ Rˢ other engagemᵗˢ will induce him to give up, that difficult & troublesome charge—where his almost daily Attendance is Necessary. of all Men—in the Circle of my knowledge I do really—think, Mʳ Eliason—is the most suitable person—Mʳ R— could engage with—for that particular purpose

I am Dear Sir
most Respectfully—your Obedᵗ Servant,   JOHN BARNES.

RC (ViU: TJP-ER); at foot of text: "Thomas Jefferson Esqʳ Monticello"; endorsed by TJ as received 9 June 1813 and so recorded in SJL.

The GOOD GENˡ was Tadeusz Kosciuszko.

Account with John Barnes

Thomas Jefferson Esqr In. a/c—with John Barnes.

1809				
July & Aug^t	To Amo^t of Acco^t rendered		141.07—	
1812	since when viz—			
March 24th	To sundry Acct^s paid	206.14.		
	deduct Remit^{ce} by G & J	200—	6.14.	
June 27th	To your man Davy		2.50.	
1813.			149.71—	

May 31st with Reference to Int. on the
former Bal^e of Acc^t rendered
in July & Aug 1809 $141—to the   } 29.29.
present time say 3½ yrs. I say
with G & H. Book on Gardening   } 1 —. $180.—

May 31st By part of Remittance recd from
Messrs Gibson & Jefferson—for
$540. $360—of which is passed
to a/c of Genl Kosciusko—for Int.   } $180—.
due the 1st April last
I have Ventured to close the above a/c
(if not correct be pleased to make
it satisfactory so)[1]

E:E—George Town Co^a 31st May 1813—   JOHN BARNES.

MS (ViU: TJP-ER); entirely in Barnes's hand.

For the SUNDRY ACCT^s Barnes paid in 1812, see Barnes to TJ, 27 Mar. 1812. The BOOK ON GARDENING was John Gardiner and David Hepburn, *The American Gardener, containing ample di-rections for working a Kitchen Garden, Every Month in the Year* (Washington, 1804; Sowerby, no. 809; Poor, *Jefferson's Library*, 6 [no. 274]). E:E: "errors excepted."

[1] Omitted closing parenthesis editorially supplied.

From Mathew Carey

SIR,   Philad^a June 3. 1813

I have taken the liberty to transmit You by mail, & request your acceptance of, a copy of "Sketches of the Naval History of the U. States," which, due allowance being made for the haste in which it was prepared, will I hope be found not uninteresting.

Respectfully, Your ob^t h^{ble} serv^t MATHEW CAREY

RC (MHi); dateline at foot of text; at head of text: "Hon Thomas Jefferson, Esqr"; endorsed by TJ as received 9 June 1813 and so recorded in SJL. Enclosure:

Thomas Clark, *Sketches of the Naval History of the United States from the commencement of the Revolutionary War to* *the present time* (Philadelphia, 1813; for a later ed., see Sowerby, no. 531).

From John Barnes

DEAR SIR— George Town 4th June 1813

On mature reflection I have thought, your paying for those four years passed 8 per C[t] Int—on Gen[l] K—$4,500 (transferred to your a/c with him)[1]—without being Allowed—on that Acco[t] the Amo[t] of an extra premium[2] and expences the Gen[l] must have been at, in the purchase of some Other Public stock, that would immediately produce the like Interest, for Instance, the Bank of Col[a] a Virginia Bank and many Others are from 5—to 10 & even 15 per C[t]—the ten shares—you may Recollect I sold of the Gen[ls] Penn[a] Bank Stock—produced him 23 per C[t] advance while his present Stock there now produces him 10 per C[t] Annually—from all these Circumstances—in strict Justice, to either party—I must presume to say you ought to be Allowed at least the Amo[t] of one years Int vz $360—in lieu thereof—nor will the Good Gen[ls] Annual remittance to be made be less than a 1000 dollars—as heretofore—you will be pleased to Reconsider these circumstances—and advise the Result

To Dear Sir—
your very Obedient JOHN BARNES,

RC (ViU: TJP-ER); dateline beneath signature; at foot of text: "Thomas Jefferson Esq[r] Monticello"; endorsed by TJ as received 9 June 1813 and so recorded in SJL.

GEN[L] K: Tadeusz Kosciuszko.

[1] Omitted closing parenthesis editorially supplied.
[2] Manuscript: "premiun."

From Patrick Gibson

SIR Richmond 5th June 1813

M[r] Taylor informs me that being about to leave town and expecting to be absent when his notes will fall due, he would prefer taking them up now provided a liberal discount were allowed and requested that I would propose it to you—his offer is $6250 in money—I am induced to mention it to you under an impression that it might be to the interest of M[r] Mazzei to take advantage of the present low rate of exchange, which a prospect of peace would immediately raise so as to occasion to him a difference of much more moment—A report is in circulation that an order of Council has been issued permitting vessels loaded & loading having licences to sail—this I hope will tend to bring a few purchasers forward, I have offer'd yours at 5$—A part of Burr's powder mill has blown up and four lives lost—With great respect Yours   PATRICK GIBSON

RC (MHi); at head of text: "Thomas Jefferson Esqre"; endorsed by TJ as received 8 June 1813 and so recorded in SJL.

From James Madison

DEAR SIR   Washington June 6. 1813

I rec^d your favor of   and now return the letter of Doc^r Waterhouse, with the Newspapers sent with it. He appears to be a man of Ability & learning, and to have been rendered interesting to[1] several distinguished friends to the Administration by the persecutions he has suffered from its Enemies. Like many others however I see at present no reward for him, but in his own virtues. The Treasury of the Mint, was allotted by the general sentiment to Dr J. Rush. And Doc^r Tilton has long since been had in view for the superintendence of the Medical Department of the Army.

Your suggestions for protecting the trade of the Chesapeak by Gun boats at the S. End of it, with a safe retreat provided for them, have been taken into consideration, with all the respect due to the importance as well as the motives of them. The present Sec^y of the Navy, is not unfriendly to Gun boats; and in general, the call for them by the Inhabitants of the Coast, proves a diffusive sense of their Utility. It seems agreed at the same time, that being too slow in sailing, and too heavy for rowing, they are limited in their use to particular situations, and rarely for other than defensive co-operations. That an adequate number of them, in Lynhaven bay, with a safety of retreat would be useful, can not be doubtful; but if the Enemy chuse to bring such a force as they have applied & with appearances of an intended increase, the number of Gun boats necessary to controul them would be very great; and their effect pretty much restricted to guarding the interior navigation of the Bay. Cruisers on the outside of the Capes beyond the range of the Gun boats, would Still blockade the external Commerce.

Commodore Barney has suggested a species of Row Galley which he considers as better fitted for protecting the interior trade of the

Bay, than the Gun boat, or rather as an essential auxiliary to the Gunboats. His plan is to allow them twenty oars & Muskets[2] on each side, to be planked up for protection of the oarsmen agst small arms in the Enemies launches; & to have one long & heavy Gun; their construction to fit them for speed & for shallow water, & their length & form to be such that at the end of the war, they might be easily raised on & become ordinary[3] Coasters. Twenty of these, costing 50 or 60, thousand dollars, he thinks would put an end to the depredations of the smaller vessels, which have been the greatest; and might even attack large ones in the night, or under special circumstances. I have not yet ascertained the opinion of the Se^y of the Navy, who adds to a sound judgment, a great deal of practical knowledge on such subjects.

You have in the newspapers all the latest news both foreign & domestic.

Be assured of my constant & sincerest affection

JAMES MADISON

RC (DLC: Madison Papers); at foot of text: "Mr Jefferson"; endorsed by TJ as received 9 June 1813 and so recorded in SJL. Enclosure: Benjamin Waterhouse to TJ, 1 May 1813, and enclosures.

TJ's FAVOR was dated 21 May 1813. Joshua BARNEY drafted a plan for the defense of the Chesapeake Bay region that won approval from the Maryland Senate but was defeated in the House of Delegates on 28 May 1813 (*Votes and Proceedings of the General Assembly of the State of Maryland* [Annapolis, 1813], 19–21; William S. Dudley, Michael J. Crawford, and others, eds., *The Naval War of 1812: A Documentary History* [1985–2002], 2:373–6). On 5 July 1813 Congress approved the expenditure of $250,000 by the president to build "barges for the defence of the ports and harbours of the United States" (*U.S. Statutes at Large*, 3:3).

[1] Manuscript: "to to."
[2] Preceding two words interlined.
[3] Word interlined.

From John Taggart

MOST RESPECT^D SIR,   Philadelphia June 6th 1813.

With diffidence I take the liberty of addressing you again on a subject the most essential to my happiness, as it respects my son in whose behalf I wrote you on the 20th of Novr last, when he applied for a Midshipmans warrant in the United-States Navy, as he cannot content himself in any other employment,—He has since that time been applying himself to that part of education most suitable for that station, you had the goodness to write me on the 25th Dec^r & 8th of Jany with Mr Hamiltons letter to you enclosed, which I showed to Mr Jones before he left here for Washington, and according to your permission I forwarded your letter to him the 25th Jany last, I have not heard from him since,—I have thought that perhaps he might be affronted by my writing to you on this Subject, but as I am not a judge of this, may I beg the favor of you to Judge for me in this case, and a line from you to him for to let you know if he has done any thing for my Son, I fear Dear Sir I am encroaching too far on your goodness. I shall not write to Mr Jones until I have the pleasure of hearing from you,—. With sentiments of the highest

Respect I Remain Y^r Ob^t Servt JOHN TAGGART

RC (MHi); in a clerk's hand, signed by Taggart; between dateline and salutation: "The Honorable Thos Jefferson"; endorsed by TJ as received 11 June 1813 and so recorded in SJL.

YOUR LETTER: TJ to Taggart, 8 Jan. 1813.

From James Monroe

DEAR SIR   washington June 7. 1813.

During the last session of Congress the current business pressed so heavily on me, and after its adjournment, the preparation of instructions for our ministers employed under the mediation of Russia, and in other duties connected with it, kept me so constantly engaged[1] that[2] I have scarcely had a moment of respite since I left you. I seize one to communicate some[3] details, which it may be satisfactory to you to know. As I make the communication in confidence, it will be without reserve.

when we were together last summer,[4] we conferr'd on the then state of the dep^{ts} of war & navy, and agreed, that whatever might be the merit of the gentlemen in them, which was admitted in certain respects,[5] a change in both was indispensable. I mentiond that I had intimated to the President, before we left washington, my willingness to take the former, if he thought that the public interest would be advanc'd by it. It seemed to be your opinion that it would. on returning here, such was the pressure of public opinion, supported by all our friends in Congress, that a change in the dep^t of war was soon decided on, & even solicited by m^r Eustis himself. In conversation with the President I repeated what I had said before, and intimated that I would either take that dep^t, or a military station, as might be thought most adviseable.[6] On the surrender of Hull, I had offer'd to proceed to the state of ohio, and to[7] take the command in that quarter,[8] with a volunteer commission, to which he willingly assented. In

[171]

consequence, I had, with his approbation,[9] sent off the cannon &ca from this place, and made every other[10] arrangment, for the prosecution of the campaign against upper Canada,[11] and was on the point of setting out when it was thought best[12] to decline it. The President was particularly inducd to adopt this latter counsel, by the appointment conferr'd on General Harrison, by the gov^r of Kentuckey, and his apparent popularity in the western country.[13] I do not recollect that I mention'd this to you before.[14] To the offer which I now repeated, the President replied, that he did not wish me to leave my present station, which tho' inactive at the time, might not long continue so, for an inferior one, to hold it while I remaind in service.[15] The state of public[16] affairs led again to a general view of the whole subject. our military operations had been unsuccessful,[17] one army had been surrenderd, under circumstances which impeached the integrity of the commander;[18] and to the north in the whole extent of that country, so important & delicately circumstanc'd, as it was, the managment had been most wretched. The command at the important post of Niagara had been sufferd to fall into state hands, and to be perverted to local & selfish purposes.[19] Van Ranslear, a weak incompetent man with high pretentions, took it. It was late in the year, before General Dearborn left Boston,[20] and repaird to albany. He had given no impulse to the recruiting business in the Eastern States by passing thro' them, and making appeals to the patriotism of the people, and when he took the command at albany, it was in a manner to discourage all hope of active operations during the favorable season. The commander[21] ought to lead every important mov'ment. If intended to assail montreal, that being the grand attack, his station was there If a smaller blow only could be given, the feint against montreal, should have been committed to another, while he commanded in person where real service was to be performed. It was soon seen that nothing would be done against lower Canada; Genl D. doubtless saw it on his first arrival at albany, if he did not anticipate it before he left Boston. niagara was the object, next, in importance,[22] and had he taken the command there, he might and probably would, by superceding little people[23] & conducting our military operations, have prevented the riotous & contentious scene exhibited there, saved the country and the gov^t from the disgraceful defeat of Van Ranslaer, & the more disgraceful[24] & gaschonading discomfiture[25] of Smyth.[26]

The experience[27] of the campaign had excited a doubt with many, if not with all,[28] whether our military operations would prosper under General Dearborn; he was known to have merit as a patriot, a republican, and that in many other respects he was a safe man,[29] but he was advanc'd in years, infirm, and had given no proof of activity or military talent during the year. He did not animate, or aid, in any way, the republican party to the Eastward, while by his[30] conduct as a partizan, he excited, &[31] invigorated the opposition to the government. Being at war, every thing would depend on success, and if he was not likely to succeed, a substitute ought to be provided.[32] If he could not sustain his ground, those next in rank would push him aside,[33] and as the army would be encreased, and, if the war continued,[34] become strong, attention ought to be paid, with a view to the liberties of the country, to the character of the person to be plac'd in the chief command. I stated that if it was thought necessary[35] to remove me from my present station, on the idea that I had some military experience, and a change in the command of the troops was resolved on, I would prefer it, to the dep^t of war, in the persuasion that I might be more useful. In the dep^t of war a man might form a plan of a campaign, & write judicious letters on military operations,[36] but still these were nothing but essays. Every thing would depend on the execution. I thought that with the army I should have better controul over operations & events, and might even aid, so far as I could give aid at all,[37] to the person in the dep^t of war. I offer'd to repair instantly to the northern army, to use my best efforts to form it, to promote the recruiting business, in the Eastern States, to conciliate the people to the views of the government, and unite them, so far as it might be possible, in the war.[38] The President was of opinion that if I quitted my present station I ought to take the command of the army.[39] It being necessary to place some one immediately in the dep^t of war, to supply the vacancy made by m^r Eustiss retreat, the President requested me to take it pro tempore, leaving the ultimate decision on the other question open to further consideration. I did so, and immediately set to work, on the important duties of the office. I send you a copy of a report which I made to the military committies of congress, which laid the foundation of some changes in the military establishment, with which you are acquainted. It was intended merely as a skeleton.[40] It was soon found to be improper, at a period of so much danger & urgency, to keep that dep^t[41] in the hands of a temporary occupant.[42] It ought to be filled by the person, who would have to form the plan of the campaign in every quarter, & be responsible for it.[43] It being indispensible to fill it with a permanent character, and the question remaining undecided, relative to the command of the army, most persons thinking a change[44] urgent, and the opinion of the President in regard to me being the same, General Armstrong, was put in the dep^t of war. Had it been decided to continue the command of the army under Gen[l] Dearborne, and the question been with me, would I take the dep[t] of war, the President & other friends wishing it, I would not have hesitated a moment in complying. But it never assumed that form. To secure the command of all important stations, along the coast & elsewhere,[45] to men of talents & experience, who should be in the service of the U States, I had recommended[46] a considerable augmentation of general officers, which was approved by General Armstrong & adopted by Congress. on the day that the nomination of these officers was made to the senate, the President sent for me, & stated that the Secretary at war, had plac'd me, in his list of major Generals, at their head, and wished to know whether I would accept the appointment, intimating that he did not think that I ought to do it, nor did he wish me to leave my present station. I asked where I was to serve. He supposed it would be with the northern army, under General Dearborn. I replied that if I left my present office for such a command, it would be inferr'd that I had a passion for military life, which I had not: that in such a station, I could be of no service in any view to the general cause, or to military operations, even perhaps with the army in which I might serve:[47] that, with a view to the public interest, the commander ought to receive all the support which the gov[t] could give him: by accepting the station proposed, I might take from Gen[l] Dearborne, without aiding the cause, by any thing that I might add. I stated however that the grade made no difficulty with me, a desire to be useful being my only object, and that if the command was given me,[48] even with a lower grade, than that suggested,[49] admitting the possibility, I would accept it. The difficulty related to General Dearborn, who could not well be removed to an inactive station. I observd that if it was intended to[50] continue him in the command, he would have my best support, as he already had had, as no one respected or esteemd him more than I did.[51] To a strong desire to make you acquainted with the real state of things in regard to this question, I have felt an additional motive growing out of the conversation between us, above alluded to, to communicate to you, the causes of certain events which may have[52] excited your surprise.[53] It is proper to add that, had I been transferr'd to the army, m[r] Gallatin claimed & would have succeeded to the vacancy in this department.

The campaign has commencd tolerably well and with a good prospect of success,[54] tho' the mov'ment has been rather slow,[55] which may give time for reinforcments from Europe.[56] An opinion begins to circulate here,[57] that a person of more vigorous mind should be on the frontier with the northern army, to direct its movments, & that the secretary of war is that person. This idea is founded on a doubt of the competency[58] of those now there. The effect would be to make the Secretary at war commander in chief of the army, in the character of[59] secretary at war. While here, orders emanate from the President, in which case, the President, the secretary at war, and commander of the troops, are checks on each other; but in the other case, the powers of all three would be united in the Secretary, much to the disadvantage of the President, who by the distance[60] could have nothing to do in the business. Besides, if the secretary takes the command of the northern army, who would supply his place in the dep^t of war, and direct the operations of the army against detroit & upper canada, of that on the mississippi, and of the extensive & burthensome[61] operations along the coast, and of the supplies in munitions of war & provisions necessary to each, forming separately an important duty, but in the whole a very complicated & arduous one, requiring also daily attention.[62] Troops have been collecting for sometime at Bermuda, destind against some part of our country. Should they be brought to bear against this city, or new orleans,[63] & the Secretary be absent, what the effect? These objections have weight, yet a new, & serious[64] discomfiture, might shake the administration to the foundation, and endanger the republican party & even the cause. so nicely balancd are the dangers,[65] attending either course, in the present state of things, admitting that the Secretary might be able to supply any deficiency in those with the northern army,[66] that it is difficult to say which scale preponderates. my reflections on the subject are known to the President, but I take no part in the question.

The mediation of Russia offers some prospect of accomodation with G Britain, but no certainty of it. It is not known that she has accepted the overture. The Russian minister was informd[67] that the President accepted it because he wished peace on honorable conditions, and was willing to avail himself of every fair opportunity to promote[68] it: that he did not ask whether G Britain had accepted the mediation, because it was sufficient that the Emperor had offerd it; and that the President sought by the manner of accepting it, to evince his high respect for the character of the Emperor. It became a question whether authority should be given to m^r[69] adams alone to manage the negotiation, or eclat be attachd to the mission, by adding two Envoys to it, to be sent from this country. The latter course was preferr'd, & Mr Gallatin being desirous, of acting in it, he was employed. Before I knew this latter fact, I had thought that it would be well, to engage in the service, some distinguished popular man, from that portion of our country, the western, which had given such support, and suffer'd so much by the war, to secure[70] the confidence of its people in the negotiation, & reconcile them to any result of it.[71] But on finding that Mr Gallatin, for whom I have always entertaind a very high respect & esteem,[72] desird the appointment, and that the President was willing to confer it on him, I readily acquiesc'd, tho' not without serious[73] apprehension of the consequences—m^r King has begun his new career by an attack on the measure, objecting to m^r Gallatins absence at this time, to the union of two such important offices in the same person &ca. The nomination is still depending before the senate. It will I doubt not terminate favorably, but still it has encreased our difficulties.

I had written the above some days since, when I had the pleasure to receive your letter of the 30th ult°. To the very interesting observations it communicates I will pay attention at an early day. I am forc'd to close this, to avail myself of this days mail for its conveyance. I am dear Sir with great respect

very sincerely your friend   JA^s MONROE

Be so good as to return me the enclosed paper, it being the only copy which I have

RC (DLC); endorsed by TJ as received 9 June 1813 and so recorded in SJL. 2d Dft (DLC: Monroe Papers, 19:3432–5); lacks closing, signature, and postscript; endorsed by Monroe on last page as a letter of "June 7. 1813" to "Mr Jefferson." 1st Dft (DLC: Monroe Papers, 19:3436–7); undated; incomplete. Enclosure: Monroe's "Explanatory Observations" to the military committees of the United States Congress, [ca. 23 Dec. 1812], stating that in order to succeed in the war, the northeast coast should be divided into seven military districts as follows: Boston, including Massachusetts and New Hampshire; Newport, including Connecticut and Rhode Island; New York City, including New Jersey and the state of New York; Philadelphia, including Delaware and Pennsylvania; Norfolk, including Maryland and Virginia; Charleston, including North Carolina and South Carolina; and Georgia; that each district should be garrisoned with regular-army artillery and infantry contingents under the command of a brigadier general to whom an engineer should be attached; that local militia and volunteers should be called into action as needed; that this organization is economical and practical; that stationing forces on the coast may discourage enemy attacks; that special provision should be made for Savannah and East Florida, whether the latter is in Spanish or American hands; and that if East Florida remains under Spanish control, the British will use it "for annoying us in every mode which may be made instrumental to that end"; laying out further defensive plans for New Orleans and Natchitoches, Detroit and the western frontier, and for the border with Lower Canada; calling for 20,000 additional regular army soldiers and a 10,000-man reserve in order to "demolish the British force from Niagara to Quebec"; suggesting that, while volunteer acts can be used to increase troop levels, "these Acts must be radically altered to enable the President to raise the force"; proposing that the president be given sole power to appoint all officers under the rank of colonel and that the recruiting bounty be increased to $40; and concluding that the additional forces should be raised for the period of one year and would so strengthen the military already in place that the British would have no hope of retaining Canada or continuing the war for long (MS in DLC: Monroe Papers, 19:3282–9; printed in Stanislaus Murray Hamilton, *The Writings of James Monroe* [1901], 5:227–35).

The GENTLEMEN previously in charge of the war and navy departments were William Eustis and Paul Hamilton, respectively. Following Monroe's interim service as secretary of war, John Armstrong assumed that post, and William Jones became the new secretary of the navy. The GOVᴿ OF KENTUCKEY was Charles Scott. The proposed AUGMENTATION OF GENERAL OFFICERS was approved on 29 Jan. 1813 (*U.S. Statutes at Large*, 2:794–6). Rufus KING began his NEW CAREER representing New York in the United States Senate after his election in 1812 (*ANB*).

[1] 2d Dft: "laboriously employed."
[2] Remainder of paragraph in 1st Dft reads "I was forc'd to discontinue almost altogether private correspondence. In general, the proceedings are so public that there is little to add to what the gazettes give. except of a private confidential nature, such as the following." Monroe also added a related note in the left margin of the first page: "Knowing your devotion to free govᵗ & desire to know the whole truth I shall communicate it without reserve."
[3] 2d Dft here adds "interesting."
[4] Preceding two words not in 2d Dft.
[5] Reworked in 2d Dft from "in many respects."
[6] 2d Dft: "as he might preferr."
[7] Preceding seven words interlined in 2d Dft in place of "there with all haste, &."
[8] Preceding three words interlined in 2d Dft.
[9] Preceding three words interlined in 2d Dft.
[10] 2d Dft here adds "necessary."
[11] Preceding nine words interlined in 2d Dft.
[12] In 2d Dft "adviseable" is interlined in place of "best."
[13] 2d Dft here adds "I was satisfied either to go or stay, <*being compelled to offer my service only, by the danger to the republican party & cause*> as he might think most adviseable."
[14] Preceding five sentences not in 1st Dft.
[15] 1st Dft here adds "I was willing to take it with its consequences, & should the country soon be blessed with peace, to withdraw, if I had nothing interesting to do in the depᵗ of war." 2d Dft here adds and then deletes "He knew, that I had no wish to leave present office, being acquainted with its duties, with my family, & every other inducment to <*remain*>. I stated however that I was willing to take the depᵗ of war with its consequences <*to withdraw should our country be blessed with peace, and*> to hold it during the war, & to retire afterwards shold there be nothing of importance to <*perform in that dept*> attend to."
[16] Word interlined in 2d Dft in place of "our."
[17] Remainder of sentence in 1st Dft reads: "In the nº W. they had been miserably managed, if not betrayd; to the north, the management was wretched, there no treason but nothing else could be said in their favor."
[18] 2d Dft: "surrender'd, if not betrayd."
[19] Clause not in 1st Dft. Preceding six words rendered in 2d Dft as "abused for local purposes."
[20] 1st Dft here describes Dearborn as "having tarried long at Boston."
[21] In 2d Dft Monroe here canceled "in that quarter."
[22] Preceding two words not in 2d Dft.
[23] 1st Dft: "competitors."
[24] Monroe here interlined "gaschonade &" in 2d Dft.
[25] 1st Dft substitutes "abortion" for preceding three words.
[26] 1st Dft here adds "& the admⁿ from the imputation of incompetency in the general managment of the campaign in that quarter."
[27] Both Dfts: "experiment."
[28] 1st Dft here adds "military men." The word "military" is canceled in 2d Dft.
[29] Preceding two clauses not in 1st Dft.
[30] 2d Dft here adds "unsuccessful."
[31] Preceding two words not in 2d Dft.

[32] 1st Dft here adds "with as much delicacy to his feelings, as was due to a man of real merit."

[33] Clause in 1st Dft rendered as "without a timely provision, those next in rank admitted to be more competent would succeed."

[34] Clause interlined in 2d Dft, rendered as "if the war went on."

[35] 2d Dft: "expedient."

[36] Preceding three words not in either Dft.

[37] Clause interlined in 2d Dft, rendered as "if I co^d give aid any where."

[38] Sentence not in 1st Dft.

[39] In 2d Dft Monroe here canceled "I should not have brought myself to speak on the subject, under other circumstances <*than those above stated,*> and particularly that of the frequent expression of a wish by our friends here that such an arrangment might take place, w^h was communicated <*as he informed me, to him, as well as to me*> to the P. as well as to me, & the necessity I was under to say something in reply."

[40] Variation of preceding sentence interlined in 2d Dft.

[41] Preceding two words rendered in 2d Dft as "a dep^t so important as that of war."

[42] Manuscript: "occcupant."

[43] Preceding three sentences rendered in 1st Dft as "After a while it became necessary to fill the office."

[44] Monroe here canceled "equally" in 2d Dft.

[45] Preceding five words not in either Dft.

[46] 1st Dft here adds "while in the dept of war."

[47] Remainder of sentence not in 1st Dft. Monroe composed and then canceled remainder of sentence in 2d Dft, p. 5, left margin.

[48] Remainder of sentence rendered in 1st Dft as "& gen^l D. placd so that I might be somewhere else, I wo^d take it."

[49] Preceding three words not in 2d Dft.

[50] Monroe here canceled "rem."

[51] Sentence not in 1st Dft.

[52] Both Dfts here include "otherwise."

[53] 1st Dft ends here.

[54] 2d Dft interlines a slight variant of preceding seven words.

[55] In 2d Dft Monroe here canceled "indicating a want of energy, proceeding I fear, from."

[56] Preceding two words interlined in 2d Dft.

[57] Preceding two words interlined in 2d Dft in place of "gain ground."

[58] Preceding four words rendered in 2d Dft as "belief of the incompetency."

[59] Preceding four words rendered in 2d Dft as "by virtue of his power as."

[60] 2d Dft interlines a slight variant of preceding three words.

[61] Preceding three words interlined in 2d Dft in place of "expensive, & complicated important."

[62] Preceding four words not in 2d Dft.

[63] Preceding three words interlined in 2d Dft.

[64] Preceding two words interlined in 2d Dft.

[65] Word interlined in 2d Dft in place of "evils."

[66] Preceding two clauses not in 2d Dft.

[67] Preceding five words rendered in 2d Dft as "I told the Russian minister."

[68] Preceding two words rendered in 2d Dft as "of <*attaining*> promoting."

[69] Monroe here canceled "G" in 2d Dft.

[70] Word interlined in 2d Dft in place of "draw."

[71] In 2d Dft Monroe here canceled "I anticipated several inconveniences resulting from M^r G's appointment, among w^h were his absence from his post at this time; w^h I feard would injure him; the depriving the gov^t of the aid to be derivd from the appointment of another person as already noted, <*with others which will occur*> & the combining two offices in one person, but he desiring it, & the Pr. willing to conferr it, I acquies'd, & have given to it all the support in my power. m^r K. began his new career by an attack on it."

[72] 2d Dft interlines a slightly different version of this clause.

[73] 2d Dft: "without <*fearful*> painful."

From John L. E. W. Shecut

MOST EXCELLENT SIR Charleston June 8th 1813.

A few Literary and Scientific Citizens of Charleston, having it in contemplation to form a Society to be called the "Antiquarian Society of charleston" Having for their objects primarily, the collection and preservation of articles and things of antiquity, rare useful & curious and Secondarily the promotion and encouragement of the arts and Sciences generally, including Natural and Moral Philosophy. Have in the proposed Rules for the organization of the said Society Resolved

"Rule 5. Sec[t] 4. The Society shall Petition the Legislature of this State to grant them an act of Incorporation, as also the Congress of the United States to extend to them the fostering aid of Government, and shall also Solicit the Patronage of the President of the united States, and of his Excellency Thomas Jefferson Esq[r]."—

In Conformity with the foregoing Rule I avail myself of the honour of Soliciting of your Excellency in behalf of the Contemplated Society, your Excellencys Patronage and Sanction, together with your influence with the Scientific and literary characters of the united States towards the furtherance of their views, which I trust will be deemed laudable and worthy of encouragemt by y[r] Excellency

Be pleased most Excellent Sir to accept the assurances of my[1] great esteem and regard for your character and Person, as our late much lov'd chief magistrate as a Philosopher, and in your private character as the most amiable friend and worthy Citizen.

In behalf of the Gentlemen forming the antiquarian Society of charleston. I remain very respectfully

Your Excellencys most Obed[t] Sev[t]   J L E W SHECUT M.D.

RC (DLC); at head of text: "His Excellency Thomas Jefferson Esq[r]"; endorsed by TJ as received 25 June 1813 and so recorded in SJL.

John Linnaeus Edward Whitridge Shecut (1770–1836), botanist, physician, and author, was born in Beaufort, South Carolina, but moved permanently to Charleston during his childhood. He studied medicine under David Ramsay and may also have had some training in Philadelphia. Shecut eventually established an extensive medical practice, sold drugs, and experimented with electrical therapy. He took a keen interest in botany and promoted a simplification of the Lin-

naean system of classification. Only one of a projected two volumes of his *Flora Carolinæensis; or, a Historical, Medical, and Economical Display of the Vegetable Kingdom; According to the Linnæan, or Sexual System of Botany* (Charleston, 1806; Sowerby, no. 1076) was published. In 1808 Shecut founded the South Carolina Homespun Company, an early cotton mill, but he later sold it at a loss. He argued that yellow fever was caused in part by a lack of electricity in the atmosphere and rejected bleeding and mercury as cures in *An Essay on the Prevailing, or Yellow-Fever, of 1817* (Charleston, 1817; Poor, *Jefferson's Library*, 5 [no. 199]). Some of his medical research also appeared in *Shecut's Medical and Philosophical Essays* (Charleston, 1819), which he issued after failing in an effort to secure a federal appointment to assist his publication efforts. Shecut also wrote two novels that were published posthumously. TJ corresponded occasionally with him on medical matters (*ANB*; *DAB*; Shecut to TJ, 4 Mar. 1807 [DLC]; Shecut to James Madison, [1814] [DNA: RG 59, LAR, 1809–17]; *Charleston Courier*, 2 June 1836).

On this day Shecut sent President James Madison a similar request for "Patronage & Sanction" of the new organization (Madison, *Papers, Pres. Ser.,* 6:378–9).

[1] Manuscript: "my my."

From John Adams

DEAR SIR   Quincy June 10. 1813.

In your Letter to Dr Priestley of March 21. 1801, you ask "What an Effort, of Bigotry in politics and religion have We gone through! The barbarians really flattered themselves, they should be able to bring back the times of Vandalism, when ignorance put every thing into the hands of power and priestcraft. All Advances in Science were proscribed as innovations; they pretended to praise and encourage education, but it was to be the education of our ancestors; We were to look backwards, not forwards, for improvement; <u>the President himself</u> declaring, in one of his Answers to addresses, that We were never to expect to go beyond them in real Science." I Shall [stop] here. Other parts of this Letter, may hereafter be considered if I can keep the Book long enough: but only four Copies have arrived in Boston, and they have Spread terror, as yet, however in secret.

"The President himself declaring, that We[1] were never to expect to go beyond them in real Science." This Sentence Shall be the theme of the present Letter.

I would ask, what President is meant? I remember no Such Sentiment in any of Washingtons Answers to addresses. I, myself, must have been mean'd. Now I have no recollection of any Such Sentiment ever issued from my Pen, or my tongue, or of any Such thought in my heart for, at least Sixty years of my past life. I Should be obliged to you, for the Words of any Answer of mine, that you have thus misunderstood. A man of 77 or 78 cannot commonly be expected to recollect promptly every passage of his past life, or every trifle he has written. Much less can it be expected of me, to recollect every Expression of every Answer to an Address, when for Six months together, I was compelled to answer Addresses of all Sorts from all quarters of the Union. My private Secretary has declared that he has

copied fifteen Answers from me in one morning. The greatest Affliction, distress, confusion of my Administration arose from the necessity of receiving and Answering these Addresses. Richard Cromwells
Trunk, did not contain So many of the Lives and Fortunes of the
English Nati[on,] as mine of those in the United States, For the
hon[our] of my Country I wish these Addresses and Answe[rs were]
annihilated. For my own Character and repu[tation, I] wish every
Word of every Address and every Answer were published.

The Sentiment, that you have attributed to me in your letter to D^r
Priestley I totally disclaim and demand in the French Sense of the
Word demand[2] of you the proof. It is totally incongruous to every
principle of my mind and every Sentiment of my heart for Threescore
years at least.

you may expect, many more expostulations from one who has loved
and esteemed you for Eight and thirty years   JOHN ADAMS

When this Letter was ready to go, I rec^d your favour of May 27th
came to hand, I can only thank you for it, at present

RC (DLC); torn at seal, with missing
text supplied from FC; at foot of text:
"Thomas Jefferson Esqr late President of
U.S."; endorsed by TJ as received 23
June 1813 and so recorded in SJL. FC
(Lb in MHi: Adams Papers); with post-
script and one revision in Adams's hand.

After the English monarchy was restored in 1660, the revolutionary leader
Richard Cromwell, son of Oliver Cromwell, reputedly kept a TRUNK filled with
faithless pledges of the LIVES AND FOR-
TUNES of his fellow countrymen (James

Hardie, *The New Universal Biographical
Dictionary and American Remembrancer
of Departed Merit* [New York, 1801],
2:171). In English the word DEMAND implies authority and insistence, but in
French it is more often used to communicate a request, desire or wish.

[1] Redundant opening quotation mark
at beginning of this word editorially omitted.
[2] Adams interlined the preceding eight
words in RC and added them (save the
last word) to FC.

To Eli Alexander

SIR   Monticello June 10. 13.

Mr Bacon had to buy 60. barrels of corn for me, and he understood
that you had agreed at court to deliver that quantity. but a note which
he sent you for a waggon load this morning being returned to him
without any other answer, seemed to imply a negative of the bargain.
my people at Lego having been without bread yesterday, & to be so
to-day[1] till we could buy it, I was obliged to send off immediately to
try to get 30. barrels offered him at court but refused because he

thought you had agreed to furnish us. if we get that, I shall still want 30. barrels, & before sending to look for it I have thought it best to ask a more explicit answer.

if it does not suit you to furnish the other 30. barrels, I do not propose to require it, whether you had agreed to do so or not. if you furnish them I should expect to have it delivered either this week or the next according to your convenience. understanding always that the corn shall have sustained no damage by being exposed to the weather till now. be so good as to let me know by the bearer & accept my best wishes.   TH: JEFFERSON

PoC (MHi); at foot of text: "M^r   ¹ Word interlined.
Alexander"; endorsed by TJ.

From Chapman Johnson

DEAR SIR,   Staunton 10th June 1813.

I have to acknowledge your's of the 4th, received this morning, and to promise you my attention, to the case of David Michie against yourself, depending in the Albemarle circuit Court,—

I was apprised of the application for a certiorari, during the sitting of the last court, and on the authority of your former letter, would have contested the propriety of granting it, if the application had been made the subject of discussion in Court—But it was not—Mr Michie made a personal application to the judge, and when informed by him, that he was disposed to hear counsel, Mr M. informed the judge that he had no counsel—This circumstance was mentioned to me, by Mr Stuart; He said that he felt some doubt upon one point, and in order that an argument might be had, he thought it best to grant the <u>certiorari</u>. The point I think was this—The warrant is for— forcible <u>entry</u> <u>and</u> <u>detainer</u>—The verdict of the jury finds only the forcible <u>detainer</u>. For myself I can only say, that I have not examined the subject sufficiently to perceive the cause for doubt here—The judge entertaining it however, is sufficient to prevent me from saying that the law on this subject is perfectly plain.

I thought it would be satisfactory to you to make this statement of the ground, on which I believe the cause has been removed into the circuit court—

Very respectfully Y^r Ob^t Se^t   C. JOHNSON

RC (MHi); endorsed by TJ as received   TJ's missing letter to Johnson OF THE
22 June 1813 and so recorded in SJL.   4TH is recorded in SJL.

[182]

From John Adams

Quincy June 11. 1813

I rec^d yesterday your favour of may 27th. I lament with you the loss of Rush. I know of no Character living or dead, who has done more real good in America. Robert Treat Paine Still lives, at 83 or 84, alert drol and witty though deaf.[1] Floyd I believe, yet remains, Paine must be very great; Philosopher and Christian; to live under the Afflictions of his Family. Sons and Daughters with Genius and qualities and Connections and prospects the most pleasing, have been Signally unfortunate. A Son, whose name was altered, from Thomas to Robert Treat has left a Volume of Prose and Verse, which will attract the attention of Posterity to his Father, more than his Signature of Independence. It is the History of a Poet, in Genius Eccentricity, Irregularity Misfortune and Misery, equal to most in Johnsons Lives.

To your ignoro, I add non curo. I Should as soon Suppose that the Prodigal Son, in a frolic with one of his Girls made a trip to America in one of Mother Careys Eggshels, and left the fruits of their Amours here: as believe any of the grave hypotheses, and Solemn reasonings of Philosophers or Divines upon the Subject of the peopling of America. If my Faith in Moses or Noah depended on any of these Speculations, I would[2] give it up,

I Sincerely thank you for your congratulations on the Successes of our Navy. I wish to write you more, than my paralyttic Fingers will justify or tollerate upon[3] this Subject. I believe, but am not certain, that you was present in Congress, on the 5th of October 1775, when it appears by the Journal, the first foundation of an American Navy was laid. I wish to know, whether you recollect the opposition that was made to the appointment of that Committee, to their report, and to the Adoption [of][4] the Resolution. Do you retain any recollection of the Speeches of Edward Rutledge Robert Treat Paine, or any other Member, on that occasion? It is, to be Sure a question of idle curiosity, but the curiosity is very Strong.

I have another Curiosity, more ardent Still. I have ever believed that you were the Author of the Essay towards a Navy when you was Secretary of State. I have reason to suspect that Hamilton was averse to that Measure. That you were always for a Navy to compell the Barbary Powers to peace, I distinctly remember in many of our personal Conversations in Europe: and I have carefully preserved very Strong Letters from you full of arguments for Such a Navy. If I am mistaken in ascribing to you the measures taken in Washingtons Administration, looking towards a Navy, I wish you to correct my Error.

Till that is done I Shall Sincerely believe myself orthodox. The Mail approaches, and I must cease

with Assurances of respect and Esteem   JOHN ADAMS

P.S. We must have a Navy now to command The Lakes, if it costs Us 100 Ships of the Line; whatever becomes of the Ocean   J. A.

RC (DLC); at foot of text: "President Jefferson"; endorsed by TJ as received 23 June 1813 and so recorded in SJL. FC (Lb in MHi: Adams Papers).

The eldest son and namesake of ROBERT TREAT PAINE died in 1798. Three years later a Massachusetts statute ALTERED the name of the dead man's brother from Thomas to Robert Treat Paine (Sarah Cushing Paine, comp., and Charles Henry Pope, ed., *Paine Ancestry: The Family of Robert Treat Paine, Signer of the Declaration of Independence, Including Maternal Lines* [1912], 41, 51). *The Works, in Verse and Prose, of the Late Robert Treat Paine, Jun., Esq. With Notes. to which are prefixed, Sketches of his Life, Character and Writings* was published in Boston in 1812. IGNORO: "I do not know." NON CURO: "I do not care." The parable of THE PRODIGAL SON is in the New Testament book of Luke, chapter 15. MOTHER CAREYS chicken is another name for the storm petrel, a seabird associated in nautical lore with a sea-spirit named for the Virgin Mary (*OED*). TJ returned to Philadelphia on 30 Sept. 1775 after a visit to Monticello. He was thus very likely in attendance in the Continental CONGRESS, ON THE 5TH OF OCTOBER 1775, when its JOURNAL recorded the ap-

pointment of a "Committee of three" to "prepare a plan for intercepting two vessels, which are on their way to Canada, loaded with arms and powder" (*PTJ*, 1:247n; *MB*, 1:406; Worthington C. Ford and others, eds., *Journals of the Continental Congress, 1774–1789* [1904–37], 3:277). Early in 1813 Adams recalled that the committee had consisted of himself, Silas Deane, and John Langdon (Adams to Langdon, 24 Jan. 1813 [Lb in MHi: Adams Papers]). Adams's notes on further debates regarding naval preparations held on 7 Oct. 1775 indicate that during the contentious discussion, a group of delegates including Paine and John Rutledge were "lightly skirmishing" (Paul H. Smith and others, eds., *Letters of Delegates to Congress, 1774–1789* [1976–2000], 2:131). As SECRETARY OF STATE, TJ privately supported the use of naval power to protect American shipping interests from the Barbary pirates, having already expressed similar ideas to Adams on 11 July 1786 (*PTJ*, 10:123–5).

[1] Preceding two words interlined.
[2] Manuscript: "woul." FC: "should."
[3] Manuscript: "up." FC: "upon."
[4] Omitted word supplied from FC.

From Elbridge Gerry

Washington 11th June 1813.

Here I am, my dear Sir, by the partiality of my friends, & discomfiture of my political enemies; again in the vortex of national politicks. My line of duty is plain & easy, & I shall endeavour to adhere to it. But I must confess, that I am much disappointed in a very pleasing anticipation, an interveiw at the seat of government with my ancient & highly respected friend of Monticello; for I am informed by our mutual friends, that he has never been at Washington during the session of Congress, since he has been indulged in his expressed wish to retire from his exalted Station; that of the Supreme magistracy of [1] the U States.

I had the honor of receiving your very friendly & cordial letter of the 11ᵗʰ of June 1812, whilst in my sick chamber, & of answering it on the 15ᵗʰ of august following; but whether you recᵈ the answer or not,[2] I am not informed. If not, I shall be much mortified by the impressions of incivility & disingenuity, which such an apparent neglect must have produced in your mind; & will send a copy of my answer. I seldom take copies of such correspondence, unless with my friends of the highest estimation.

The efforts to supplant our mutual friend Mʳ Madison have been happily defeated. His re-election[3] was a matter, in my mind, of vast importance. If the British administration could have effected his overthrow; it would have prostrated at their feet, the Government of the U States. To have substituted General Washington, had he been alive, Yourself, or any other Citizen, under existing circumstances for Mʳ Madison, would not have altered the case; the impression at home & abroad would have been the same, that the british administration had an irresistible influence in this nation, & the sovereign controul of our politicks. accept dear Sir, the cordial wishes for the happiness of yourself & amiable family, of your sincere, respectful & affectionate friend—   E Gerry

RC (DLC); at foot of text: "President Jefferson"; endorsed by TJ as received 17 June 1813 and so recorded in SJL. Tr (MHi: Russell W. Knight Collection); in Gerry's hand and endorsed by him.

On 10 Feb. 1813 the United States Senate certified the RE-ELECTION of James Madison as president and the election of Gerry as vice president (*JS*, 5:256).

[1] Manuscript: "of of."
[2] Preceding two words interlined.
[3] Prefix interlined.

To Patrick Gibson

DEAR SIR   Monticello June 12. 13.

Yours of May 29. with 150.D. inclosed was duly recieved as is that also of June 5. I should not be for recieving the paiment of the monies for mr Mazzei before they are due on any other discount than of legal interest, say ½ per cent per month. I inclose you a letter I have recieved from mr Edmund Randolph, by which you will see that he executed our joint deed to mr Taylor on the 22ᵈ of May, five days after my signature, but as his execution of it must be certified by his court, and mine by the court of Albemarle there will be some delay before mr Taylor can recieve it; a delay the more uncertain as mr Randolph states that he was too unwell at that time to go to court.

The keg of Burr's powder is recieved. it's force by the eprouvette is 16. I had informed you that that of White was 7. & 9. the common store powder never exceeds 13. as far as I have seen. Mr Burr's is the best I have ever bought in this state. but Dupont's of Wilmington goes to 27. I am afraid I shall still have to call for more; however not, as I hope, till the unfortunate accident to Burr's works will have been repaired.   Accept the assurances of my friendly respect

TH: JEFFERSON

PoC (CSmH: JF); at foot of text: "Mr Gibson"; endorsed by TJ as a letter to Gibson & Jefferson and so recorded in SJL. Enclosure: Edmund Randolph to TJ, 22 May 1813, not found, but recorded in SJL as received 4 June 1813 from Avonhill.

From Richard Rush

DEAR AND RESPECTED SIR,   Washington June the 12th. 1813.

I received, yesterday, your favor of the 31. of last month, and beg leave to return my warm thanks for your kind and obliging sympathy on the melancholy occasion of the death of my father. Few men, I believe, who have lived ever acted up more faithfully to what he took to be the line of rectitude and duty in all the actions of his laborious life; but in whatever lights he may have appeared to the world, his family best knew his virtues and worth. To them his loss is indeed great. Constant and strong in his friendships, to you, sir, he ever cherished an unalterable attachment. Much of the pride and much of the pleasure of his life was derived from the intercourse which it was his lot, personally and by letter, to have maintained with you. Your illustrious services, and the many other titles to his great esteem for you, was the frequent subject of his fireside conversations, and now that he is gone the impressions they left upon his family must be but the more strong.

I appreciate all you have said of the confidential letters that passed between you, and it will be a duty to which I shall most scrupulously pay attention to fulfil your wishes upon this subject. The two letters which you have particularly designated I will ask permission to enclose to you together with any others that may seem to be of a similar complexion.

But, as the afflicting event of my father's death summoned me to

Philadelphia whence I have but lately returned, and as it is probable I may not find it practicable to go there again for sometime—perhaps a twelvemonth—I have had thoughts of writing in the meanwhile to my mother in order that your wishes may, through me as the channel of communication, be complied with at an earlier day. Not being on the spot I am not at present the depositary of my father's manuscripts. Their custody now is chiefly with Dr James Rush, the brother next in age to me, to whose discretion and honor all things may be confided; yet it is possible, though not probable, that in the work of looking through voluminous papers some accident or inadvertence (no caution being previously hinted) might exhibit a private letter to some eye from which it had as well be hidden. I know how promptly[1] and sacredly any request I might make either of him or my mother to enclose the letters in question to me would be attended to, and in this doubtful state I will wait until it may be my pleasure to receive at your hands another line.

With fervent wishes for the unalloyed happiness and tranquility of your declining and venerable years, I beg, sir, to offer to you the assurances of my highest and most respectful attachment.

RICHARD RUSH.

RC (DLC); at foot of text: "Ths: Jefferson Esq."; endorsed by TJ as received 16 June 1813 and so recorded in SJL.

[1] Manuscript: "promply."

From Samuel Brown

DEAR SIR.   Natchez June 13th 1813

I hope that the small package of Capsicum, which I sent you, a few weeks ago, has arrived in safety—You may even a month hence be very certain of obtaining Plants which, with a little care, can be preserved through the Winter & which will yeild fruit before the last of May—I now send you as much as you will be able to use until that time—The Spaniards generally use it in fine Powder & seldom eat any thing without it—The Americans who have learned to use it make a Pickle of the green Pods with Salt & Vinegar which they use with Lettuce, Rice Fish Beefstake and almost every other dish. a single Table spoonful will communicate to as much Vinegar as I can use in six months, as strong a taste of capsicum as I find agreeable & I find this taste growing so fast that it will soon become as essential to my health as salt itself—Many of my friends to whom I have recommended it, here ascribe to it Medicinal qualities for which I am not prepared to vouch I do believe however that in cases of debility of the stomach & alimentary canal it may be employed with great advantage—A Spanish officer with whom I conversed yesterday on the subject says that in Cuba it is called Achi & that the wealthy Inhabitants not only season almost every dish with it but place a cup of it beside every plate that each guest may use it ad libitum—I have not yet been able to learn with certainty its 'habitat.' It is abundant at S^t antonio & some distance North of that Post. I shall continue my enquiries & communicate the result—

This morning I rec^d from St Antonio a small package of seeds— The gentleman who procured them for[1] me has given me but a very imperfect account of them—

The Red Bean called Friholio has been often described to me by the Inhabitants of Texas; & the Indians who inhabit the sources [of the][2] Red River seldom travel without it as it is their only means of Intoxication. They pulverize it between two stones mix it with warm water & drink it throug a cane until it produces violent vomiting & a most <u>frantic</u> kind of intoxication accompanied with an unstable disposition to violent bodily exercise The dose is often renewed[3] & the debauch continued for three or four days: Mr Davenport of Nacagdoches & a half Indian who lived several years with me often described these scenes But I never could procure the Bean before this day & have made no experements of my own—They are an article of commerce (as opium is in the east.) among all the tribes west of Nacagdoches.—I suspect the plant which produces them is a species of the Erythryna—The Erythryna corolladendron grows abundantly here & is a[4] most beautiful Plant—I send you some of the seeds. I have often Planted them but they did not vegetate. I have somewhere read an acc^t of a method of exposing such seeds to the action of the gastric juice of Turkeys in order to fit them [for][5] vegetation—But of this I have only an indistinct recollection.—

The round Black nut is said to be used at St Antonio as a Poison for animals & insects & this is all the information that accompanies them—

The Gallavanec Peas are the growth of St Antonio & much esteemed—They are sometimes cultivated in Louisiana—

It is much to be regretted that no man of much knowledge of Botany or natural History has been permitted to visit the Country surrounding the Gulf of Mexico—I do not look for much from such men as compose the army of Patriots who are now marching towards Santa

Fe. Their object must be rapine & Plunder—The French have cured us of that excess of credulity which accompanied their apostolical missions in the great cause of Liberty. If the people of New [Spain]⁶ really wish for a better Govᵗ some change may be effected by their own exertions—I am doubtful of effect of external cooperation—especially as no man of more than ordinary talents has yet joined the army at Sᵗ antonio unless Toledo has lately superceded Kemper & Barnardo It is said here that Colᵒ Burr has been solicited to take the command—I know Adair has refused it & has gone to Kʸ to offer his services against the British & Indians. It does not appear, from any information that I have been able to obtain that these Invaders of the Royalists have any communication with the interior or can form any correct judgment of the dispositions [of]⁷ the great mass of the people—on which success must ultimately depend—a number of young men have gone on to share the fortunes of these Reformers & it is mortifying to see many Yankees among them who ought to fly to the standard of their Country when her calls are so loud & her dangers so pressing—

The difficulty of supporting an invading army may for some time protect our sea Coast from the British—We certainly are not as strong as the money which Govᵗ has expended for our defence should have made us. It is said that the most horrid frauds have practised & by agents in whom the administration has confided. I was told yesterday that a ship which cost an officer of Govᵗ only $500 had been bought for the Public by him or his friend for $8000. My informant is an officer in whom the administration always has & always ought to confide. Had he not assured me [he]⁸ would be apprised of this nefarious transaction, I should have been tempted [to] put the Secʸ of the Navy on his guard—I wish our Patriots had a little more common honesty—& our Rulers a little more suspicion—

The state of Louisiana & this Territory have sustained a loss of perhaps a million of Dollars by the present inundation of the Mississippi. It is not possible to conjecture what may be the consequence of a continuance of the rise for a few days more on the City of N Orleans & the Sugar land on the Coast—Some of the Levés are broken & the Inhabitants every where greatly alarm The whole county of Concordia (opposite to this place) is completely under water & the Inhabitants quitting their plantations never to return

I have not yet recᵈ a letter from Mr Henderson but have learned that at the time your letter should have reached him he was very ill of a fever which no doubt has prevented him from attending business—

I ought to apologize for this long & desultory letter—but this would still add to its length—

Most respectfully & most sincerely Yours   SAM BROWN

RC (DLC); hole in manuscript; endorsed by TJ as received 1 July 1813 and so recorded in SJL.

Garavance (GALLAVANEC PEAS), *Cicer arietinum*, are commonly known as garbanzo beans or chickpeas (Betts, *Garden Book*, 527). José Álvarez de TOLEDO y Dubois along with Samuel KEMPER and José BARNARDO (Bernardo) Maximiliano Gutiérrez de Lara participated in an 1812–13 expedition into Texas intended to free that region from Spanish rule. General John ADAIR had declined to lead

the campaign due to his animosity toward Toledo. When Gutiérrez's leadership faltered, Toledo assumed that role. Spanish royalist forces eventually prevailed (Stagg, *Borderlines in Borderlands*).

[1] Manuscript: "from."
[2] Omitted words editorially supplied.
[3] Manuscript: "renewned."
[4] Manuscript: "a a."
[5] Omitted word editorially supplied.
[6] Omitted word editorially supplied.
[7] Omitted word editorially supplied.
[8] Omitted word editorially supplied.

From Louis Philippe Gallot de Lormerie

Devant New york a bord du Brig Argus, State vessel—
MONSIEUR   13th Juin. 1813—

L'intérest que vous aves pris Si genereusement a mon Passage me fait un devoir presque indispensable de Vous informer que par un heureux Concours de Circonstançes Je suis Enfin parvenu a m'Embarquer Effectivement avec Lagrement de M.C. a bord du Brig de LEtat Sus mentionné ou Je suis maintenant nous n'attendons qu'un Vent favorable pour mettre a la voile tandis que LEscadre-Ennemie est occupée a N. London—

J'Espére que nous aurons un heureux voÿage—quoiqu'il en puisse Etre daignés agreer finalement Les assurances de ma gratitude et du sincére Respect—avec lequel Jaÿ L'honneur d'Etre tout a vous

DE LORMERIE

EDITORS' TRANSLATION

off New York on board the Brig *Argus*, State vessel—
SIR   13th June. 1813—

The interest you have so generously taken in my passage makes it my almost indispensable duty to inform you that by a happy combination of circumstances I finally managed to embark, with the agreement of M.C., on board the state brig mentioned above, and I am there now. We await only a favorable wind to set sail while the enemy squadron is occupied at New London—

I hope for a successful trip—whatever it may be, please be assured of my gratitude and the sincere respect—with which I have the honor to be yours   DE LORMERIE

RC (DLC); at foot of text: "Th^s 18 June 1813 and so recorded in SJL.
Jefferson Esqre Late presid. of the us.   Translation by Dr. Genevieve Moene.
Monticello"; endorsed by TJ as received

M.C.: William H. Crawford.

From John Adams

DEAR SIR   Quincy June 14. 1813

In your Letter to Dr Priestley of march 21. 1801, you "tender him, the protection of those laws which were made for the wise and good, like him; and disclaim the legitimacy of that Libel on legislation, which, under the form of a Law, was for Sometime placed among them." This Law, I presume was, the Alien Law, as it was called.

As your name is Subscribed to that law, as Vice President, and mine as President, I know not why you are not as responsible for it as I am. Neither of Us were concerned in the formation of it. We were then at War with France: French Spies then swarmed in our Cities and in the Country. Some of them were, intollerably, turbulent, impudent and Seditious. To check these was the design of this law. Was there ever a Government, which had not Authority to defend itself against Spies in its own Bosom? Spies of an Ennemy at War? This Law was never executed by me, in any Instance.

But what is the conduct of our Government now? Aliens are ordered to report their names and obtain Certificates once a month: and an industrious Scotchman, at this moment industriously labouring in my Garden is obliged to walk once a month to Boston, eight miles at least, to renew his Certificate from the Marshall. And a fat organist is ordered into the Country. &c &c. &c. All this is right. Every Government has by the Law of Nations a right to make prisoners of War, of every Subject of an Enemy. But a War with England differs not from a War with France. The Law of Nations is the same in both.

I cannot write Volumes in a Single Sheet: but these Letters of yours require Volumes from me.

"The mighty Wave of public opinion, which has rolled over"! This is, in your Style, and Sometimes in mine, with less precision, and less delicacy. Oh! Mr Jefferson! What a wave of public opinion has rolled over the Universe? By the Universe here, I mean our Globe. I can yet Say there is nothing new Under the Sun, in my Sense. The Reformation rolled a Wave of public opinion over the Globe, as wonderful as this; A War of thirty years, was necessary to compose this wave. The Wars of Charlemaigne rolled a Wave. The Crusades rolled a Wave, more mountainous than the French Revolution. Only one hundred years ago, a Wave was rolled; when Austria England and Holland in Alliance, contended against France, for the dominion or rather the Alliance of Spain.

Had "The Clock run down," I am not So Sanguine, as you, that the Consequence would have been as you presume. I was determined in all Events to retire. You and Mr Madison are indebted to Bayard, for an Evasion of the Contest. Had the Voters for Burr, addressed the Nation, I am not Sure that your Convention would have decided in your Favour. But what Reflections does this Suggest? What Pretensions had Aaron Burr to be President or Vice President?

What "a Wave" has rolled over Christendom for 1500 years? What a Wave has rolled over France for 1500 years Supporting in Power and Glory the Dinasty of Bourbon? What a Wave Supported the House of Austria? What a Wave has Supported the Dinasty of Mahomet. for 1200 years? What a Wave Supported the House of Hercules, for So many Ages in more remote Antiquity? These waves are not to be Slighted. They are less resistable than those in the Gulph Stream in an hurricane. What a Wave has the French Revolution Spread? And what a Wave is our Navy of five Frigates raising?

If I can keep this book, "Memoirs of Lindsey" I Shall have more to Say. Meantime I remain your Friend   JOHN ADAMS.

RC (DLC); addressed: "Thomas Jefferson Esquire late President of U. S. Montecello Virginia"; franked; postmarked Quincy, 14 June; endorsed by TJ as received 23 June 1813 and so recorded in SJL. FC (Lb in MHi: Adams Papers).

Adams here conflates two of the Alien and Sedition Acts of 1798. TJ regarded the Alien Friends Act, which authorized the president to deport any alien he deemed dangerous, as a LIBEL ON LEGISLATION. While TJ and Adams both signed this statute, TJ was arguably NOT AS RESPONSIBLE for a law he simply certified as president of the Senate as Adams was for approving a measure on which he could have exercised a presidential veto. The act expired in 1800, but not before

Adams signed arrest warrants that were NEVER EXECUTED only because those who were named in them evaded capture. The Alien Enemies Act provided for the control of aliens from nations with whom the United States was at war. It was not used in 1798 because war was never formally declared on France, but it remained in force and was implemented against British nationals during the War of 1812 (U.S. Statutes at Large, 1:570–2, 577–8; James Morton Smith, Freedom's Fetters: The Alien and Sedition Laws and American Civil Liberties [1956]). THE MIGHTY WAVE OF PUBLIC OPINION, WHICH HAS ROLLED OVER quotes from TJ to Joseph Priestley, 21 Mar. 1801 (PTJ, 33:394). THERE IS NOTHING NEW UNDER THE SUN comes from the Bible, Ecclesiastes

1.9. THE CLOCK RUN DOWN paraphrases another passage from TJ to Priestley, 21 Mar. 1801 (*PTJ*, 33:394). In the contested election of 1800, James Ashton BAYARD, a Federalist and sole member of the United States House of Representatives from Delaware, entered a blank ballot on the decisive vote that helped TJ to defeat AARON BURR for the presidency (*ANB*).

To John Adams

DEAR SIR   Monticello June 15. 13.

I wrote you a letter on the 27th of May, which probably would reach you about the 3d inst. and on the 9th I recieved yours of the 29th of May. of Lindsay's Memoirs I had never before heard, & scarcely indeed of himself. it could not therefore but be unexpected that two letters of mine should have any thing to do with his life. the name of his editor was new to me, & certainly presents itself, for the first time, under unfavorable circumstances. religion, I suppose, is the scope of his book: and that a writer on that subject should usher himself to the world in the very act of the grossest abuse of confidence, by publishing private letters which passed between two friends, with no views to their ever being made public, is an instance of inconsistency, as well as of infidelity of which I would rather be the victim than the author. by your kind quotation of the dates of my two letters I have been enabled to turn to them. they had compleatly evanished from my memory. the last is on the subject of religion, and by it's publication will gratify the priesthood with new occasion of repeating their Comminations against me. they wish it to be believed that he can have no religion who advocates it's freedom. this was not the doctrine of Priestley, and I honored him for the example of liberality he set to his order.

the first letter is political. it recalls to our recollection the gloomy transactions of the times, the doctrines they witnessed, and the sensibilities they excited. it was a confidential communication of reflections on these from one friend to another, deposited in his bosom, and never meant to trouble the public mind. whether the character of the times is justly portrayed or not, posterity will decide. but on one feature of them they can never decide, the sensations excited in free yet firm minds, by the terrorism of the day. none can concieve who did not witness them, and they were felt by one party only. this letter exhibits their side of the medal. the Federalists no doubt have presented the other, in their private correspondences, as well as open action. if these correspondencies should ever be laid open to the public eye, they will probably be found not models of comity towards their adversaries. the readers of my letter should be cautioned not to confine it's view to this country alone. England & it's alarmists were equally under consideration. still less must they consider it as looking personally towards you. you happen indeed to be quoted because you happened to express, more pithily than had been done by themselves, one of the mottos of the party. this was in your answer to the address of the young men of Philadelphia. [see Selection of patriotic addresses. pa. 198.] one of the questions you know on which our parties took different sides, was on the improvability of the human mind, in science, in ethics, in government E^{t}c. those who advocated reformation of institutions, pari passu, with the progress of science, maintained that no definite limits could be assigned to that progress. the enemies of reform, on the other hand, denied improvement, & advocated steady adherence to the principles, practices & institutions of our fathers, which they represented as the consummation of wisdom, & akmé of excellence, beyond which the human mind could never advance. altho' in the passage of your answer alluded to, you expressly disclaim the wish to influence the freedom of enquiry, you predict that that will produce nothing more worthy of transmission to posterity, than the principles, institutions, & systems of education recieved from their ancestors. I do not consider this as your deliberate opinion. you possess, yourself, too much science, not to see how much is still ahead of you, unexplained & unexplored. your own consciousness must place you as far before our ancestors, as in the rear of our posterity. I consider it as an expression lent to the prejudices of your friends; and altho' I happened to cite it from you, the whole letter shews I had them only in view. in truth, my dear Sir, we were far from considering you as the author of all the measures we blamed. they were placed under the protection of your name, but we were satisfied they wanted much of your approbation. we ascribed them to their real authors, the Pickerings, the Wolcotts, the Tracys, the Sedgwicks, et id genus omne, with whom we supposed you in a state of Duresse. I well remember a conversation with you, in the morning of the day on which you nominated to the Senate a substitute for Pickering, in which you expressed a just impatience under 'the legacy of Secretaries which Genl Washington had left you' and whom you seemed therefore to consider as under public protection. many other incidents shewed how differently you would have acted with less impassioned advisers; & subsequent events have proved that your minds were not together.   you would do me great injustice therefore by taking to yourself what was intended for men who were then your secret, as they are now your open enemies.   should you write on the subject, as you propose, I am sure we shall see you place yourself farther from them than from us.   As to myself, I shall take no part in any discussions. I leave others to judge of what I have done, and to give me exactly that place which they shall think I have occupied. Marshall has written libels on one side; others, I suppose, will be written on the other side; and the world will sift both, and separate the truth as well as they can. I should see with reluctance the passions of that day rekindled in this, while so many of the actors are living, & all are too near the scene not to participate in sympathies with them. about facts, you and I cannot differ; because truth is our mutual guide. and if any opinions you may express should be different from mine, I shall recieve them with the liberality and indulgence which I ask for my own, and still cherish with warmth the sentiments of affectionate respect of which I can with so much truth tender you the assurance.   TH: JEFFERSON

RC (MHi: Adams Papers); edge trimmed, with missing text supplied from PoC; brackets in original; endorsed by Adams; docketed by Charles Francis Adams. PoC (DLC); at foot of first page: "John Adams, late Pr. US."

Theophilus Lindsey's EDITOR was Thomas Belsham. EVANISHED: "disappeared from view" (*OED*). In his 7 May 1798 ANSWER TO THE ADDRESS OF THE YOUNG MEN OF PHILADELPHIA, Adams remarked that "Without wishing to damp the ardor of curiosity, or influence the freedom of inquiry, I will hazard a prediction that after the most industrious and impartial researches, the longest liver of you all, will find no principles, institu-

tions, or systems of education, more fit, in general, to be transmitted to your posterity, than those you have received from your ancestors" (*A Selection of the Patriotic Addresses, to the President of the United States. Together with The President's Answers. Presented In the year One Thousand Seven Hundred and Ninety-Eight, and the Twenty-Second of the Independence of America* [Boston, 1798; Sowerby, no. 3525], 198). ET ID GENUS OMNE: "and everyone of that type." In the last year of his presidency, Adams replaced Secretary of State Timothy PICKERING with John Marshall (Adams to Pickering, 10 May 1800 [MHi: Pickering Papers]; *JEP*, 1:353, 354 [12, 13 May 1800]).

To Bernard McMahon

DEAR SIR   Monticello June 15. 13

I have just recieved some Capsicum of the province of Techas, where it is indigenous as far Eastwardly as the Sabine river. it's roots are perennial there, and it is believed it will stand our frosts with a little covering. it grows in great abundance there and the inhabitants are in the habit of using it as a seasoning for every thing as freely as salt, and ascribe much of their health to it. the other kinds cultivated with us, coming from still warmer climates are difficult of cultivation. my expectation is that this being indigenous so much nearer our latitudes, may be easier raised. of what I recieved I send you a part. altho' probably too late for the season, I have sowed a few seeds in a pot, and reserve others for the spring. they will be more likely however to be preserved in your hands. Accept the assurance of my esteem & respect   TH: JEFFERSON

P.S. I hope you have recieved the box of seed

PoC (DLC); endorsed by TJ.

TJ was enquiring about the BOX OF

SEED that André Thoüin reported having sent care of David Bailie Warden in his letter of 15 Mar. 1813.

Bill of Complaint in
Jefferson v. Michie

To the worshipful the County Court of Albemarle Setting in Chancery, the bill of Complaint of Thomas Jefferson humbly sheweth — that Bennett Henderson late of the County of Albemarle being in his lifetime seized and possessed in fee simple of a tract of Land in the same County lying on the South side of the Rivanna river and around the town of Milton died intestate leaving a widow Elizabeth Henderson and eleven children one of whom also dying soon after intestate an assignment of dower to the widow and partition among the surviving Children took place, under the Authority of this Court; which assignment and partition were made by first laying off the said Land into larger Sections one of which Containing about fifteen acres adjacent to the river & touching or nearly touching the Northern Corner of the said town of Milton was assigned to the widow as part of her dower, and the other larger sections were Subdivided each into ten parts: one of which parts in each of the said Sections was allotted to each child, and particularly the section between the town of Milton & the river Containing twenty acres, was subdivided into ten lotts distinguished by numbers from 1 to 10 whereof N° 1 was the lowest on the river and the others extended upwards in Numerical order; the 8^h 9th & 10th bordering on the dower section, of which the 8^h was allotted to Ch^s Henderson the 9^h to James L Henderson & the 10^h to Jno Henderson three of the Coparceners that the said Charles Henderson having sold the said lott N° 8 to James L Henderson, the said James L sold the same with his own lott N° 9 and his other portions of said land to Craven Peyton of the said County of Albemarle who sold the same to your Orator, that your Orator then residing out of the state, Authorised the said Craven Peyton to purchase for your Orator such other portions of the said Lands of said Bennett Henderson as should be offered for sale at reasonable prices; in persuance of which authority he purchased nearly the whole of the s^d Lands and particularly the widows right of dower in the section of fifteen acres before mentioned as well as other of her[1] rights for the Consideration of two hundred & fifty pounds, as also most of the reversionary rights therein for other valuable Considerations. that the said John Henderson holding rightfully the said lott N° 10 with some other portion of the said lands of the said Bennett, setting up also some pretended title to the lotts N° 8 & 9 and to the passing a Canal through the said dower lands to his lot N° 10 which he Called a mill Seat and thence a tail race along the lines of the dower lands & N° 9 & 8 and being involved in Considerable debts to James Lewis then of the same County of Albemarle, but now of the state of Tennessee to Matthew Henderson then of Albemarle but now of the state of Kentucky and to Sundry others, did, for the purpose of paying the said debts Convey to the said James Lewis and Matthew Henderson as joint and Several trustees by deed of bargain & Sale bearing date the 9^h Of October 1806 and duly recorded in this worshipful Court, all his estate right and title in law and equity to the said Lands adjacent to the town of Milton Specifying particularly his said mill seat with all the rights & priviledges thereto Annexed his rights & interests in the dower lands and houses held for life by the said Elizabeth Henderson widow of the said Bennett adjoining the said town and then in the occupency of Tho Eston Randolph and other property, not now necessary to be noted, in trust, to make sale of the same and to apply the proceeds to the payment of the debts due to themselves or for which they were responsible in the first place, and then to the payment of his other debts generally, of some of which the deed only Contains a schedule. that they accordingly proceeded both publickly and privately to endeavour to make sale of the said lands; And the said Craven acting for your Orator thinking the occasion favourable for purchasing the said lott N° 10 the reversionary rights of the said John in the dower lands, and whatever remaining interests he might have in other sections of said lands, and at the same time of quieting the rights purchased in the lots N° 8 & 9 and the dower lands by buying in the pretensions of the said John however groundless, offered for the same $750 which being more than any other person offered either publickly or privately the said James Lewis closed the sale by a deed of bargain and Sale bearing date the 8^h day of November 1808

Conveying all the said Lands and the rights of the said John therein to the said Craven in fee simple, giving a special warranty only, against himself and those Claiming under him, but not undertaking any responsibility for the title of the said John therein; which sum of $750 he accordingly received from the said Craven for the purposes of the said trust who received possession for your Orator, and afterwards to wit on the   day of August 1809 Conveyed the premises to him by deed of bargain & Sale in fee Simple.

But now, so it is, may it please your worships that a Certain David Michie of the County of Albemarle Combining and Confederating with the said John Henderson and others to your Orator unknown, to injure your Orator herein by Clandestine and fraudulent[2] bargains and deeds on false Considerations never actually paid, without due authentication and Concealed from public knowledge pretending a right to said lots and lands, forcibly entered into the same and ousted your Orator and the same detained until by process of forcible entry and detainer, sued out by your Orator according to law, restitution of possession was made to him on the inquest of a Jury found on the 30[h] day of July 1812 and a warrant founded thereon, and persevering in his fraudulent and unlawful purposes, the said David threatens at times that he will bring suits against your Orator to recover the premises, or some part thereof, yet delaying to bring such suits while your Orators witnesses are living and accessible, places him in danger of having his rights Called into question when these witnesses shall be dead or removed beyond the reach or knowledge of your Orator; that Richard Price of the same County of Albemarle would be a Material witness for your Orator to prove the Nullity of the Claims of the said John Henderson to open a Canal thro' the said dower lands, on which the pretensions of the said David are understood to be founded and also a fraudulent Concealment by the said David of his Claims to the premises, which said Richard Price is now aged and infirm, and your Orator therefore in danger of losing the benefit of his testimony in the event of a future suit; that the said Elizabeth Henderson and James L Henderson are also material witnesses for your Orator to prove in like manner the Nullity of said Claims of the said John Henderson & Consequently of his pretended Conveyance of them to the said David; which said Elizabeth and James L Henderson reside now out of the limits of this Commonwealth, the said Elizabeth in the state of Kentucky[3] and the said James as your Orator is informed and believes in the Washita in the state of Louisianna; and that the said Elizabeth is morover aged and infirm; that the said James Lewis is also a material witness to prove a fraudulent Concealment of Claim on the part of the said David, and is now resident without this Commonwealth and within the state of Tennessee; that Dabney Carr & Benjamin Brown are also material witnesses to prove a fraudulent Concealment of Claim on the part of the said David, that they live out of the jurisdiction of this Court in distant parts of the state, and being subject to the Ordinary Casualties of human life, your Orator is runing the risk of losing the benefit of their testimony: that the said Craven Peyton having been the agent of your Orator in these transactions from begining to end is a material witness to almost every part of them, and the sole one existing of some material parts, whose testimony therefore, if lost by the accident of death Could not be Supplied by that of any other person, that your Orator in Consideration hereof, proposed and had prepared a bill of Complaint against the said David to be addressed to this worshipful Court Sitting in Chancery praying their authority to take de bene esse and to perpetuate on their records the testimony of the said Richard Price, Elizabeth Henderson, James L Henderson James Lewis Dabney Carr Benjamin Brown & Craven Peyton when he was diverted therefrom by the said David, agreeing with your Orator that any depositions thought material by either party might be taken by Consent, on due Notice being given to the other of the time and place of examination, and might be used with the same effect in any Subsequent difference or litigation as if they had been taken in perpetual memorial of the testimony by a bill in Chancery for that purpose and a decree thereon; That in persuance of this agreement, and on due notice by your Orator to the said David he met your Orator at the house of John Watson Esq[r] in Milton, a justice of the peace on the 1st day of July 1812 and took in the presence, and under the authority of the said John Watson the deposition on oath of the said James Lewis who happened at that time to be within this Commonwealth, which original deposition authenticated by the said John Watson is hereto Annexed, one of the same tenor verbatim & equally original having been delivered to the said David by the said Jno Watson That your Orator desireous of taking the depositions of the said Dabney Carr, Richard Price and James L Henderson requested the said David by letter dated the 20 April 1813 (a Copy of which is hereto annexed) to agree on a time, place and mode of taking those depositions to which he Consented by his answer of the 23[d] of the same month (hereto also annexed) proposing therein that the depositions of the said Dabney Carr and Richard Price should be taken at any time when the said Dabney Carr might be in this neighbourhood, and the said Dabney being known to be in this neighbourhood on the 30[h] of May 1813

Your Orator addressed to the said David the letter of that date (of which a Copy is annexed) and received his answer of the same day (hereto also annexed) declining all further extrajudicial proceedings and Consequently all further Compliance with his agreement aforesaid; which several letters and Answers your Orator prays may be Considered as exhibits in this Cause, and in proof of the direct support which the said testimony will give to the rights of your Orator and to the nullification of the Claims of the said David he refers to the deposition of the said James Lewis taken as aforesaid by agreement, and to those of the said Richard Price and James L Henderson regularly taken in a former Controversy in the high Court of Chancery and under authority of that Court, between the said John Henderson under whom the Def^t Claims and the said Craven Peyton agent for your Orator, wherein those very rights were in question of which depositions your orator lost the benefit on that trial either by failure of the Commissioners appointed by the Court to return them until after the decree or by some other Circumstance preventing their being known to the Court or to your Orators Counsel at the date of the decree.

In tender Consideration whereof and for as much as your Orator is without remedy in the premises save only by the aid of this Court, Setting in Chancery; To the end therefore that the said deposition of the said James Lewis taken by Consent as aforesaid may be established according to agreement as if taken de bene esse by authority of this Court, and that your Orator may further secure the benefit of the testimony of the said Richard Price, Elizabeth Henderson, James L Henderson Dabney Carr Benjamin Brown and Craven Peyton. — May it please your Worships to grant to your Orator a writ of Sub^a to be directed to the said David Michie, requireing him to Shew Cause if any he hath why the said deposition of the said James Lewis should not be established according to agreement as if taken by authority of a decree of this Court, and why Authority should not be granted for taking the depositions of the s^d Richd Price Elizabeth Henderson, James L Henderson Dabney Carr Benjn Brown & Craven Peyton relative to the premises & for preserving the same together with the said^4 deposition of the said James Lewis, in the records of this Court, in perpetuam reimemoriam and de bene esse, to be used hereafter according to the equitable and established rules of law & equity and granting to your Orator such aid in the premises as is agreeable to equity and good Conscience and your Orator as in duty bound shall ever pray &^{c}

TH JEFFERSON
June 16^h 1813

[200]

Tr (ViU: TJP-LBJM); in George Carr's hand. Enclosures: (1) Deposition by James Lewis, with Queries Posed by Thomas Jefferson and David Michie, 1 July 1812. (2) TJ to Michie, 20 Apr., 30 May 1813. (3) Michie to TJ, 23 Apr., 30 May 1813.

Craven Peyton and his wife formally deeded the Henderson lands to TJ on 22 AUGUST 1809 (Craven and Jane Peyton's Conveyance of the Henderson Lands, [22 Aug. 1809]; TJ's Declaration to Craven Peyton, 22 Aug. 1809). DE BENE ESSE: "in anticipation of a future need" (*Black's Law Dictionary*).

The depositions of James L. Henderson and Richard Price TAKEN IN A FORMER CONTROVERSY (*Peyton v. Henderson*) were dated 15 Apr. and 17 May 1805, respectively. Henderson maintained that, although his brother John Henderson had received verbal permission in 1800 from his mother, Elizabeth Henderson, to run a canal through her dower lands, he had not begun such a project prior to her sale of the property to Craven Peyton in 1802, and so she considered the earlier agreement to be void; stated that the sale to Peyton had been made without reserve and that "Not the most distant hint" had been given of John's supposed right to construct a millrace there; declared that in 1803 John had "after much persuasion" received written permission from his mother to build the canal, with the stipulation that the agreement not inter-

fere with her contract with Peyton; revealed that he had acted as an unofficial guardian of his younger siblings; and avowed that all of the abovementioned "infant legatees" had ratified the sales made by him on their behalf after coming of age (Tr in ViU: TJP-LBJM; in George Carr's hand; attested by Garland Carr and Dabney Minor). Price testified that in 1804 he had seen an agreement between John Henderson and his mother granting the former the right to run a millrace through her dower lands; suggested that John might have added an important interlineation "in the most obligatory part" after his mother had signed it; accused him of being dishonest and lacking character; admitted that he (and many others) had been involved in disputes with John in the past, but claimed that he bore "no Animosity against the Deft whatever"; and inferred from the presence of Kemp Catlett's signature as a witness on the document that Price had seen an original rather than a copy (Tr in ViU: TJP-LBJM; in George Carr's hand; attested by John Watson and Martin Dawson).

IN PERPETUAM REIMEMORIAM: "perpetual remembrance"; usually referring to a deposition taken to preserve one's testimony (*Black's Law Dictionary*).

[1] Word interlined in place of "their."
[2] Manuscript: "fraudilent."
[3] Manuscript: "Kemtucky."
[4] Manuscript: "sad."

From James Monroe

DEAR SIR   washington June 16th 1813

At the commencment of the war I was decidedly of your opinion, that the best disposition which could be made of our little navy, would be to keep it in a body in a safe port, from which it might sally only, on some important occasion, to render essential service. Its safety, in itself, appeard to be an important object, as while safe, it formed a check on the enemy in all its operations along our coast, and increased proportionally its expence, in the force to be kept up, as well to annoy our commerce, as to protect its own. The reasoning against it, in which all our naval officers have agreed, is, that if stationd together, in a port, new york for example, the British would immediately block it up there, by a force rather superior, & then harrass our coast & commerce without restraint, & with any force however small: in that case, a single frigate might, by cruising along the coast and plundering & menacing occasionally, at different points, keep great bodies of our militia in motion: that while our frigates are at sea, the expectation that they may be together, will compell the British to keep in a body, wherever they institute a blockade, or cruize, a force, equal at least to our whole force: that being the best sailors, they hasarded little by cruizing separately, or together occasionally, as they might bring on an action or avoid one, whenever they thought fit: that in that manner they would annoy the enemy's commerce wherever they went, excite alarm in the W Indies & elsewhere, and even give protection to our own trade, by drawing at times the enemy's squadron off from our own coast: that by cruizing, our commanders would become more skilful, have an opportunity to acquire glory, and if successful, keep alive the public spirit. The reasoning in favor of each plan is so nearly equal, that it is hard to say, which is best. I have no doubt at some future day, that a fortification will be erected on the bank in the middle of the bay, and be connected in the manner you propose with a naval force in Lynhaven bay, for the protection of norfolk, and all the country dependant on the chessapeake. In time of war it will be difficult to accomplish so extensive an object.

The nomination of ministers, for Russia is still before the Senate. Mr Giles, & Genl Smith uniting with Mr King, & others, against Mr Gallatin have so far succeeded in preventing its confirmation. They appointed a committee, the object of which was, to communicate with the President, on the subject, & give him to understand that if he would supply his place in the Treasury, they would confirm the nomination to Russia. The President, had before answer'd a call of the senate, that the appointment to Russia, did not vacate the commiss^n in the dep^t of the Treasury[1] & that the secretary of the navy, did the business in Mr Gs absence. To the chairman, who asked & obtaind a personal interview, he communicated his objections, to a conference with the committee, on the ground, that the resolution under which they were appointed, did not authorise it, even could any advantage result from it, which however was improbable, as neither party would be apt to change its opinion, and on the principle of compromise that nothing could be done, or ought to be done. various resolutions tending to embarrass the nomination, divide the republican party in the Senate, & perpetuate that division, by irritating its members towards each other, have been introducd & are still depending. Among these is one, intended to express the sense of the house, against the compatability of the two offices. The delay has done harm & doubtless was intended to have that effect. The result is yet uncertain.

with great respect & esteem your friend & servant

JA[s] MONROE

The President is indisposed, with a bilious attack, apparently slight.

RC (DLC); endorsed by TJ as received 18 June 1813 and so recorded in SJL.

[1] Remainder of sentence interlined.

To Jeremiah A. Goodman

DEAR SIR   Monticello June 17. 13.

The unexpected difficulty of getting water to my saw mill and threshing machine has made it impossible for me to leave those works a day; and the harvest is now so near as not to leave me time for a visit to Poplar forest. I must therefore put it off till the harvest is over. as soon after that as I shall suppose you may have brushed over your tobacco, I will go; because I imagine you will be as well at leisure[1] to spare your hands a week at that time as at any other. I wish to have the work ready for Chisolm in case he gets released from military duty in time to do it.   I have not yet sold my flour. even five dollars cannot now be got for it. when I come up I shall bring a spinning machine of 24. spindles which is now finished. the one now at the Forest I have given to my brother. Accept my best wishes

TH: JEFFERSON

PoC (DLC); at foot of text: "M[r] Goodman."

SJL records missing letters from Goodman to TJ of 7 and 11 Apr., received from Poplar Forest on 15 and 14 Apr., respectively, of 20 and 23 May, both received 2 June, of 24 July, received 28 July, and of 31 July, received from Poplar Forest on 4 Aug. 1813.

[1] Preceding two words interlined in place of "able."

To Richard Rush

DEAR SIR   Monticello June 17. 13.

Your favor of the 12th came to hand yesterday and I thank you for the kind attention you are so good as to pay to the subject of my letters.[1] my entire confidence in the family will render satisfactory to me your addressing any member of it you think proper on the subject of those letters. an occurrence since my letter to you has justified my anxiety to prevent their getting into unfriendly hands. on the 9th of Apr. 1803. having recieved from Dr Priestley his 'Jesus & Socrates[2] compared' & returning my thanks to him for the work, I mentioned to him my promise of a letter to Dr Rush on a similar subject, but on a broader scale, and gave him the outlines of my views of the subject, which I pressed him to undertake, being so much better qualified for it. it was on this occasion he wrote his 'Heathen Philosophy compared with revelation.' Twelve days after this letter to him, the subject being in my mind I wrote the one to Dr Rush. the letter to Dr Priestley it seems he communicated to his friend Dr Lindsay in England, who dying, a mr Belsham has published memoirs of him, & in them my letters to Dr Priestley. of this mr Adams gave me the first notice in a letter recieved on the 9th inst. these will probably soon find their way into the newspapers, and the whole kennel of priests will open upon me. my letter to Dr Rush, written more in detail than that to Dr Priestley[3] would much enlarge the field of their declamations, and that it should not get into their hands cannot but be a subject of some anxiety. tranquility is now my object, and that my mind may not be harrowed up by the renewal of contentions, which while I was young I met with the zeal of youth. I pray you to accept the assurance of my great esteem & respect.　　　　　　　TH: JEFFERSON

PoC (DLC); at foot of text: "Richard Rush esq."; endorsed by TJ.

[1] Preceding five words interlined in place of "it."

[2] Superfluous closing quotation mark editorially omitted.

[3] Manuscript: "Priestly."

To William Short

DEAR SIR　　　　　　　　　　　　　　Monticello June 18. 13.

Yours of the 2^d is recieved, and a copy of Higgenbotham's mortgage is now inclosed. the journey to Bedford which I proposed in my last, my engagements here have obliged me to postpone till after harvest which is now approaching; it is the most unpromising one I have seen. we have been some days in expectation of seeing M. Correa. if he is on the road, he has had some days of our very hottest weather. my thermometer has been for two days at 92. & 92½ the last being the maximum ever seen here. altho' we usually have the hottest day of the year in June, yet it is soon interrupted by cooler weather. in July the heat, tho' not so great, is more continuous & steady.

On the duration of the war I think there is uncertainty. ever since the rupture of the treaty of Amiens, the object of Gr. Britain has visibly been the permanent conquest of the ocean, and levying a tribute on every vessel she permits to sail on it, as the Barbary powers do on the Mediterranean which they call their sea. she must be conscious she cannot from her own resources maintain the exaggerated fleet she now has, and which is necessary to maintain her conquest: she must therefore levy the deficiency by duties of transit, on other nations. if she should[1] get another ministry with sense enough to abandon this senseless scheme, the war with us ought to be short: because there is no material[2] cause now existing, but impressment: and there our only difference is how to establish a mode of discrimination between our citizens which she does not claim, and hers which it is neither our wish or interest ever to employ. the seamen which our navigation raises had better be of our own. if this be all she aims at, it may be settled at Saint-Petersbg. my principle has ever been that war should not suspend either exports or imports. if the pyracies of France & England however are to be adopted as the law of nations, or should become their practice it will oblige us to manufacture at home all the material comforts.

this may furnish a reason to check imports until necessary manufactures are established among us. this offers the advantage too of placing the consumer of our produce near the producer. but I should disapprove of the prohibition of exports even to the enemy themselves, except indeed refreshments and water to their cruisers on our coast, in order to oblige them to intermit their cruises to go elsewhere for these supplies. the idea of starving them as to bread is a very idle one. it is dictated by passion, not by reason. if the war is lengthened we shall take Canada, which will relieve us from Indians, and Halifax[3] which will put an end to their occupation of the American seas, because every vessel must then go to England to repair every accident. to retain these would become objects of first importance to us, and of great importance to Europe, as the means of curtailing the British marine. but at present being merely in posse, they should not be an impediment to peace. we have a great and a just claim of indemnifications against them for the thousand ships they have taken pyratically, and 6000. seamen impressed. whether we can on this score succesfully insist on curtailing their American possessions by the meridian of lake Huron, so as to cut them off from the Indians bordering on us, would be matter for conversation and experiment at the treaty of pacification.—I sometimes allow my mind to wander thus into the political field; but rarely, & with reluctance. it is my desire as well as my duty to leave to the vigour of younger minds to settle concerns which are no longer mine, but must long be theirs. affectionately Adieu.   TH: JEFFERSON

RC (ViW: TJP); endorsed by Short as received 26 June 1813. PoC (DLC); at foot of first page: "Mr Short."

at TJ to Short, 10 Feb. 1813. IN POSSE: potentially, but not currently in existence (*Black's Law Dictionary*).

Short's letter OF THE 2^D, recorded in SJL as received 9 June 1813 from Philadelphia, has not been found. For the COPY OF HIGGENBOTHAM'S MORTGAGE enclosed here, see second enclosure noted

[1] TJ here canceled "ever."

[2] TJ here canceled "point."

[3] TJ here interlined and canceled "whe," but he left it undeleted in PoC.

To Mathew Carey

SIR   Monticello June 19. 13.

I thank you for the copy of mr Clarke's Sketches of the naval history of the US. which you have been so kind as to send me. it is a convenient Repertory of the cases of that class, and has brought to my recollection a number of individual cases of the Revolutionary war which had escaped me. I recieved also one of mr Clarke's circulars asking supplementory communications for a 2^d edition. but these things are so much out of the reach of my inland situation, that I am the least able of all men to contribute any thing to his desire. I will indulge myself therefore in two or three observations, of which you will make the use you may think they merit. 1. Bushnel's turtle is mentioned slightly. would the description of the machine be too much for the scale of the work? it may be found very minutely given in the American Philos. transactions. it was excellently contrived, and might perhaps by improvement be brought into real use. I do not know the difference between this & mr Fulton's submarine boat. but an effectual machine of that kind is not beyond the laws of nature, and whatever is within these is not to be despaired of. it would be to the US. the consummation of their safety.   2. the account of the loss of the Philadelphia does not give a fair impression of the transaction. the proofs may be seen among the records of the Navy office. after this loss, Capt Bainbridge had a character to redeem. he has done it most honorably, and no one is more gratified by it than myself. but still the transaction ought to be correctly stated.   3. but why omit all mention of the scandalous campaigns of Commodore Morris? a two years command of an effective squadron, with discretionary instructions wasted in sailing from port to port of the Mediterranean and a single half day before the port of the enemy against which he was sent. all this can be seen in the proceedings of the court on which he was dismissed. and it is due to the honorable truths with which the book abounds to publish those which are not so. a fair & honest narration of the bad is a voucher for the truth of what is good. in this way the old Congress set an example to the world, for which the world amply repaid them by giving unlimited credit to whatever was stamped with the name of Charles Thomson. it is known that this was never put to an untruth but once, & that where Congress was misled by the credulity of their general. (Sullivan) the first misfortune of the revolutionary war induced a motion to suppress or garble the account of it. it was rejected with indignation. the whole truth was given in all it's details, and there never was another attempt in that body to disguise it. these observations are meant for the good of the work, & for the honor of those whom it means to honor.   Accept the assurance of my esteem & respect.

TH: JEFFERSON

RC (PHi: Conarroe Papers); at foot of first page: "Mʳ Matthew Cary"; endorsed by Carey as received 3 July and answered 13 July. PoC (DLC).

The submarine popularly known as David Bushnell's TURTLE is described in APS, *Transactions* 4 (1799): 303–12.

William BAINBRIDGE commanded the USS *Philadelphia* in 1803 when it surrendered after running aground off Tripoli (*ANB*). The ineffectual Richard Valentine MORRIS was ordered in the same year to relinquish his command of a naval squadron deployed against the Barbary pirates (*DAB*).

To Elbridge Gerry

DEAR SIR   Monticello June 19. 13.
Yours of the 11ᵗʰ is just recieved, and I repeat the sincere pleasure it has given me to see you once more come forward on the stage of the nation. I have ever thought the post you now occupy the most agreeable one the nation can give, & very far preferable to that which it's highest favor confers. and I have hoped that, within three days journey of one another, it would afford some occasion of interview. not indeed at Washington: for I am too old, and too much engaged to propose such a journey of mere indulgence to my moral feelings at the expence of my physical ones. but the chance I looked to was that of some short & occasional adjournment of Congress, during the interval of which at a loss how otherwise to fill it, you might think a

tour thro some parts of this state not merely supervacaneous. were this to happen, I had hoped that an acquaintance of half a century & a fellow laborer in good works might be an object in the tour. in no part of it could you be recieved with more pleasure, or retained with greater cordiality. let me then believe this possible, & in the mean time assure you of the unceasing sentiments of friendship & respect of

Yours most affectionately and respectfully   TH: JEFFERSON

RC (NNPM); addressed: "Elbridge Gerry Vice President of the US. at Washington"; franked; postmarked Milton, 24 June; with FC of Gerry to TJ, 6 July 1813, on verso of address cover; endorsed by Gerry: "Virginia Monticello President Jefferson 19th June & copy of my answer 6 July 1813." PoC (DLC); endorsed by TJ.

SUPERVACANEOUS: "superfluous; redundant" (*OED*).

To Tobias Lear

DEAR SIR   Monticello June 19. 13.

Your letter of May 31. is but recently recieved. I had learnt with pleasure your safe arrival in the US. since it had pleased the potent Dey to break with us, to his disadvantage, to ours, & whether to yours or not you can best judge. mrs Lear at least must be glad to be once more among friends. I suppose we can do little with the Dey till we have peace with England. but then I would, at any expence, hunt him from the ocean. a navy equal to that object we should ever keep. I sincerely congratulate you on the possession of a son whose talents & dispositions may promise unspeakable comforts to mrs Lear and yourself. as you intend him for the bar, I know no state in the Union now superior to Maryland in that science. in the hours of relaxation from this laborious study, (which ought to be at least half the hours of study) he will be able to enlarge the general field of information with the auxiliary sciences of history, ethics, politics, and to cultivate the imagination, and chasten style & taste by Poetry, and it's kindred arts of Oratory & Rhetoric. I presume he has at College laid a decent foundation of Mathematics, Natural philosophy, & perhaps of Nat[l] history.

I shall be much gratified if the tour you contemplate, should give us the pleasure of seeing you here. it is well to see all places, and to fix at last on what you have seen to be the best. in agriculture commerce, manufactures, this state has some advantages, which may merit to be weighed with those offered by other situations. but whatever you adopt for your future course will have all my prayers for it's prosperity, as I tender you sincerely those for the health & happiness of mrs Lear & yourself, with the assurances of my constant & affectionate esteem & respect.   TH: JEFFERSON

PoC (DLC); at foot of text: "Col° Lear"; endorsed by TJ.

To James Monroe

DEAR SIR   Monticello June 19. 13.

Your favors of the 7th & 16th are recieved, & I now return you the Memoir inclosed in the former. I am much gratified by it's communication because, as the plan appeared in the newspapers soon after the new Secretary at War came into office, we had given him the credit of it. every line of it is replete with wisdom; and we might lament that our tardy enlistments prevented it's execution, were we not to reflect that these proceeded from the happiness of our people at home. it is more a subject of joy that we have so few of the desperate characters which compose modern regular armies. but it proves more forcibly the necessity of obliging every citizen to be a souldier. this was the case with the Greeks & Romans and must be that of every free state. where there is no oppression there will be no pauper hirelings. we must train & classify the whole of our male citizens, and make military instruction a regular part of collegiate education. we can never be safe till this is done.

I have been persuaded ab initio that what we are to do in Canada, must be done quickly: because our enemy, with a little time, can empty pickpockets upon us faster than we can enlist honest men to oppose them. if we fail in this acquisition, Hull is the cause of it. Pike in his situation would have swept their posts to Montreal, because his army would have grown as it went along. I fear the reinforcements arrived at Quebec will be at Montreal before Genl Dearborne, & if so the game is up. if the marching of the militia into an enemy's country be once ceded as unconstitutional (which I hope it never will be) then will their force, as now strengthened, bid us permanent defiance. could we acquire that country, we might perhaps insist succesfully at St Petersbg on retaining all[1] Westward of the Meridian of L. Huron, or of Ontario, or of Montreal, according to the pulse of the place, as an indemnification of the past, & security for the future. to cut them off from the Indians, even West of the Huron would be a great future security.

Your kind answer of the 16th entirely satisfies my doubts as to the employment of the navy, if kept within striking distance of our coast; & shews how erroneous views are apt to be with those who have not all in view. yet as I know from experience that profitable suggestions sometimes come from lookers on, they may be usefully tolerated, provided they do not pretend to the right of an answer. they would cost very dear indeed were they to occupy the time of a high officer in writing when he should be acting. I intended no such trouble to you, my dear Sir: and were[2] you to suppose I expected it, I must cease to offer a thought on our public affairs. altho' my entire confidence in their direction prevents my reflecting on them but accidentally, yet sometimes facts, & sometimes ideas occur, which I hazard as worth the trouble of reading but not of answering. of this kind was my suggestion of the facts which I recollected as to the defence of the Chesapeake, and of what had been contemplated at the time between the Secretaries of War & the navy & my self.[3] if our views were sound, the object might be effected in one year, even of war, and at an expence which is nothing compared to the population & productions it would cover.   We are here laboring under the most extreme drought ever remembered at this season. we have had but one rain to lay the dust in two months. that was a good one, but was three weeks ago. corn is but a few inches high & dying. oats will not yield their seed. of wheat the hard winter & fly leave us about $\frac{2}{3}$ of an ordinary crop. so that, in the lotteries of human life you see that even farming is but gambling. we have had three days of excessive heat. the thermometer on the 16th was at 92. on the 17th 92$\frac{1}{2}$ & yesterday at 93. it had never before exceeded 92$\frac{1}{2}$ at this place; at least within the periods of my observation. ever & affectionately yours

Th: Jefferson

RC (DLC: Monroe Papers). PoC (DLC); at foot of first page: "Col° Monroe." Enclosure: enclosure to Monroe to TJ, 7 June 1813.

The NEW SECRETARY AT WAR was John Armstrong. Concerning the EXTREME DROUGHT, TJ wrote that from late in April to late in May 1813, "no rain fell" (MHi: Weather Memorandum Book).

[1] TJ here canceled "beyond."
[2] TJ here canceled "I to."
[3] Preceding three words interlined.

To John Taggart

DEAR SIR   Monticello June 19. 13.

Your favor of the 6th is duly recieved. considering that you had communicated to mr Jones my letter to mr Hamilton & mr Hamilton's answer and after that had sent him my letter to you, I think (since you are pleased to refer it to my judgment) it would be better to avoid importuning him. I know the practice to be to put these applications on a file, and when a vacancy happens to take up the file & give a preference, among approved candidates, according to turn of application. and this without having before given a word of explanation to the applicants which, for obvious reasons can never be done. I have the greater satisfaction in looking forward to the effect of the application already made because it would not be in my power to repeat it. when I retired from the government in 1809. sollicitations from my friends to aid them in their applications for office drew from me an unwary compliance, until these were so multiplied that, however indulgently they were recieved by the government, they became embarrassing to them, & afflicting to myself, as keeping me ever before them as a suppliant, solliciting favors. respect to them as well as to my self had suggested the necessity of my putting an end to these unceasing importunities, & the change in the two departments of war & the Navy, to which they were mostly addressed, offered me the occasion: and from that date I decided to cease all farther interposition. it was a circumstance of satisfaction to me that, the case of your son occurring before the change, enabled me, by the application which had preceded, to manifest my desire to do what would gratify you: and I repeat my confident hope that what was done will have the desired effect in maturity of time, according to the rules of the government. Accept the assurance of my best wishes for this result, & of my respect and esteem for yourself.   TH: JEFFERSON

PoC (CtY: Franklin Collection); at foot of text: "Mr Taggert"; endorsed by TJ.

From John Barnes

DEAR SIR,   George Town 20th June 1813

since I had the pleasure of Answering your fav^r of the 4th Ins^t Mr Geo Williams of Balt^o has favrd me with answer to my 2^d letter to him—on the expected advices from G K—or Messrs Russell & Morton, paym^t of your last years Remittance—the rate of present

Ex—and withal—if it was possible for the parties Concern'ed to fall upon <u>to effect</u>, some mode of Remittance & paym^{ts} otherwise then by Bill of Ex—And thereby avoid the Risque of Capture to and from Bourdeau—trouble, and disquietude &c^a—.

it strikes my idea!—it is possible—at least[1] it might be attempted—By your addressing a letter to Mess^r R & M—to pass thro the hands of Mr G. W. (unsealed) for his perusal[2]—and goverm^t purporting—to lodge in his GW^{s}[3] hands, $500, every 6 M^{os} for the Sole purpose and—on Acco^t of Mess^r R & M—engaging to pay to that Amo^t (on Messrs R & M—receiving advise thereof)[4]—to the Order of G. K—at Paris, and for Messrs R & M to debit the Acco^t of Mr G. W. who has already recd & made Use of said $500—in Balti^o but whether or not—one or both of these Gent^n may not object, to this proposition—is, the question—as merch^{ts} they may each expect a Commiss^n from 2$\frac{1}{2}$ a 5 ⅌Ct—would be equal to the pres^t Ex: say 10 ⅌C^t above par—this rise of ex—above par is a convincing proof to me, that the Commerce produce, and Manufactures in France is at this present time— in a florishing State—

while the rest of Europe—are labouring Under the greatest distresses & dificulties—for the want of these most essensial advantages—

The survivers of Bonaparts Armies—who suffered so much by that <u>Deadly frost</u>, in Russia—are determined—and most probably—will—They say—"If the Russian Froze us last Winter we shall smoke some of them this summer"—he will at least force them back—into their Famaged—Desolate distressed Country—while—the Lawless—division of Poland—by Russia Prusia and Austria—is now to be Avenged.—

with great Esteem I am always—Dear Sir, your most Obed^t—

JOHN BARNES,

PS. I inclose you—M^r G W^s letters—for your better Goverm^t—.

RC (ViU: TJP-ER); addressed: "Thomas Jefferson, Esquire, Monticello Virginia"; franked; postmarked Georgetown, 21 June; endorsed by TJ as received 23 June 1813 and so recorded in SJL. Enclosures not found.

The FAV^R OF THE 4TH INS^T was actually a letter from Barnes to TJ. G K: General Tadeusz Kosciuszko. The DIVISION OF POLAND by Russia, Prussia, and Austria occurred between 1772 and 1795.

[1] Preceding two words interlined.
[2] Manuscript: "persual."
[3] Initials added in margin.
[4] Omitted closing parenthesis editorially supplied.

To Regnault de Bécourt

S<small>IR</small>   Monticello June 20. 13.

I thank you for the work you have sent me, & which I have no doubt I shall peruse with equal pleasure & instruction. I percieve by a glance of the eye over it that it brings into question both moral & physical doctrines of long & general standing. but we ought never to fear truth, nor hesitate to follow wherever she leads. I shall be glad to be a subscriber for a couple of copies of the volume you are about to publish, when printed. I shall have occasion ere long to make a remittance to M. Dufief for some other books I propose to ask of him, and will include in that the price of the volume sent & of the two now subscribed for. I tender you the assurances of esteem & respect.

T<small>H</small>: J<small>EFFERSON</small>

PoC (DLC); at foot of text: "M. de Becourt"; endorsed by TJ.

To Joseph Hunter

S<small>IR</small>   Monticello June 20. 13.

Having two clocks out of order which I would wish to have put to rights, and understanding from you that you would come to do it if you could get a horse, I send one by the bearer. he goes on to Scott's ferry on other business and will leave the horse with you, if you can come. if you cannot, he will take it on with him and return from Scott's ferry. you shall in like manner be furnished with a horse to return on. in hopes you can make this convenient, I tender you my best wishes.   T<small>H</small>: J<small>EFFERSON</small>

PoC (MHi); at foot of text: "Mr Hunter"; endorsed by TJ.

From Joseph Hunter

S<small>IR</small>   Warren June 20th 1813

I have rec'd yours of the morning and have to informe you that it was & is my intention to wate on you in A few days if I can arrainge my business at home in A manner to justify it. I have sent the beast back by the barer as I have within[1] A few days past got a[2] horse at my command. [In] ten or twelve days without some unforeseen accident [I sh]all be with you. I am Your much Obliged Humb[l] Serv[t]

J<small>OSEPH</small> H<small>UNTER</small>

RC (MHi); mutilated at seal; addressed: "Tho⁸ Jefferson Esqr Monticello"; endorsed by TJ as received 21 June 1813 and so recorded in SJL.

Hunter did WATE ON TJ, who paid him $18 on 18 July for "repairing clock" and $5 on 1 Aug. 1813 for "repairing the large clock" (*MB*, 2:1290, 1291).

[1] Manuscript: "wthin."
[2] Manuscript: "at."

To Randolph Jefferson

DEAR BROTHER   Monticello June 20. 13.

The unexpected difficulties of bringing water to my saw mill & threshing machine, & the necessity of doing it before harvest, have obliged me to put off my visit to Bedford till after harvest. the spinning Jenny for Bedford is now ready but will not be sent until I go. while it is here it offers a good opportunity for your spinner to learn upon it. after it is gone there will be no idle machine for a learner to practise on. I send the bearer therefore to inform you of this, that you may not lose the opportunity of getting the person taught whom you intend to employ in that way. I should think she had better come immediately, as it will require a month or more to become perfect in roving and spinning. by the time she is taught, the machine will go off to Bedford, & the cart which carries it will return by Snowden & leave the 12. spindle machine there, on which she may go to work immediately. this will be early in August. I do not know whether I can call on you as I go. I will if I can, but certainly will as I return. is your road cleared out?

My sister desired that when I should send her seeds of any kind I would give her directions how to plant & cultivate them. knowing that there was an excellent gardening book published at Washington, I wrote for one for her, which I now inclose. she will there see what is to be done with every kind of plant every month in the year. I have written an index at the end that she may find any particular article more readily: and not to embarras her with such an immense number of articles which are not wanting in common gardens, I have added a paper with a list of those I tend in my garden, & the times when I plant them. the season being over for planting every thing but the Gerkin, I send her a few seeds of them. she will not find the term Gerkin in the book. it is that by which we distinguish the very small pickling cucumber. affectionate salutations to you both.

TH: JEFFERSON

PoC (ViU: TJP-CC); endorsed by TJ. Enclosure: John Gardiner and David Hepburn, *The American Gardener, containing ample directions for working a*

Kitchen Garden, Every Month in the Year (Washington, 1804; Sowerby, no. 809; Poor, *Jefferson's Library*, 6 [no. 274]). Other enclosures not found.

The BEARER was James Gillette. MY SISTER: Mitchie Pryor Jefferson, Randolph Jefferson's wife.

From Randolph Jefferson

DEAR BROTHER.   Snowden June 21: 1813

I Received your letter by James and also the book which you sent: my wife is extreemly oblige to you for your present and is very much pleased with it the girl we will send in the course of a week we have not a woman except a girl of twelve or fourteen years old but what has children we expected the reason of your not coming on was on account of the weather being so worm but shall look for you certainly on your retern from bedford my wife is very much indesposed at present we shall certainly expect my sister marks over this summer Lilbourn has goind the volunteers but expect he will be over by the midle of July I wrote very pressingly to capt Brown by your boy in respect to the carp for you but found it was all in vane from what James tells me he got non if you should not conclude to come this way going up I would be extreemly oblige to you to mark out the ram to your overseer and I will send up this fall for him as soon as the weather gits cool so that he can be brought with safety. my wife goins me in love and respect to all the family.

I am Dr brother your most affectionately.— RH; JEFFERSON

RC (ViU: TJP-CC); endorsed by TJ as received 21 June 1813 and so recorded in SJL.

JAMES Gillette was TJ's slave, and the GIRL was Randolph Jefferson's slave Fanny. LILBOURN: Randolph Jefferson's son James Lilburne Jefferson.

From Chapman Johnson

DEAR SIR,   Staunton. 21. June 1813.

The last saturdays mail, brought me Your favor of the 16th covering a statement of the proceedings on the writ of forcible entry and detainer, in the case between yourself and David Michie—

Yours of the 4. had been previously received and answered;—

My answer, which I suppose you have [here?] received, gives you the ground on which I suppose that the[1] certiorari was awarded. I believe that the judge was fully satisfied that the justices did right in negating the traverse that was offered—I suppose there can be doubt of that point—What was offered as a traverse is nothing—Nothing is affirmed by it,—nothing denied—

with great respect Your Very Obt Sv^t   C. JOHNSON

RC (MHi); one word illegible; endorsed by TJ as received 24 June 1813 and so recorded in SJL.

TJ's FAVOR OF THE 16TH, not found, is recorded in SJL. His STATEMENT OF THE PROCEEDINGS ON THE WRIT OF

FORCIBLE ENTRY AND DETAINER is also missing. The JUDGE was Archibald Stuart and the JUSTICES were John Watson and David Jackson Lewis.

[1] Johnson here canceled "supersedeas."

To James Madison

DEAR SIR   Monticello June 21. 13.

your favor of the 6th has been recieved, and I will beg leave to add a few supplementory observations on the subject of my former letter. I am not a judge of the best forms which may be given to the gunboat; and indeed I suppose they should be of various forms suited to the varied circumstances to which they would be applied. among these no doubt Commodore Barney's would find their place. while the largest & more expensive are fitted for moving from one seaport to another coast-wise, to aid in a particular emergency, those of smaller draught & expence suit shallower waters; and of these shallow & cheap forms must be those for Lynhaven river. Commodore Preble in his lifetime undertook to build such in the best manner for two or three thousand Dollars. Col° Monroe, to whose knolege of the face of the country I had referred, approves, in a letter to me of such a plan of defence as was suggested, adding to it a fort on the Middle grounds; but thinks the work too great to be executed during a war. such a fort certainly could not be built during a war, in the face of an enemy. it's practicability at any time has been doubted, and altho' a good auxiliary, is not a necessary member of this scheme of defence. but the canal of retreat is really a small work, of a few months execution; the laborers would be protected by the military guard on the spot, and many of these would assist in the execution, for fatigue rations & pay. the exact magnitude of the work I would not affirm; nor do I think we should trust for it to Tatham's survey: still less would I call in a Latrobe, who would immediately contemplate a canal of Languedoc. I would sooner trust such a man as Thomas Moore to take the level, measure the distances, and estimate the expence. and if the plan were well matured the ensuing winter, & laborers engaged at the proper season, it might be executed in time to mitigate the blockade of the next summer. on recurring to an actual survey of that part of the country, made in the beginning of the Revolutionary war under the orders of the Govr & Council, by mr Andrews I think, a copy of which I took with great care, instead of the half dozen miles I had conjectured in my former letter, the canal would seem to be of not half that length. I send you a copy of that part of the map, which may be useful to you on other occasions, & is more to be depended on for minutiae, probably, than any other existing. I have marked on that the conjectured rout of the canal, to wit, from the bridge on Linhaven river to Kemp's landing on the Eastern branch. the exact draught of water into Linhaven river you have in the Navy office. I think it is over 4. feet.

When we consider the population & productions of the Chesapeak country, extending from the Genissee to the Saura towns and Albemarle sound, it's safety & commerce seem entitled even to greater efforts, if greater could secure them. that a defence at the entrance of the bay can be made, mainly effective, that it will cost less in money, harrass the militia less, place the inhabitants on it's interior waters freer from alarm and depredation, & render provisions and water more difficult to the enemy, is so possible as to render thoro' enquiry certainly expedient. some of the larger gunboats, or vessels better uniting swiftness with force, would also be necessary to scour the interior, & cut off any pickaroons which might venture up the bay or rivers. the loss on James river alone this year is estimated at 200,000. barrels of flour, now on hand, for which the half price is not to be expected. this then is a million of Dollars levied on a single water of the Chesapeake, & to be levied every year during the war. if a concentration of it's defence at the entrance of the Chesapeak should be found inadequate, then we must of necessity submit to the expences of detailed defence, to the harrasment of the militia, the burnings of towns & houses, depredations of farms, and the hard trial of the spirit of the middle states, the most zealous supporters of the war, and therefore the peculiar objects of the vindictive efforts of the enemy. those North of the Hudson need nothing, because treated by the enemy as neutrals. all their war is concentrated on the Delaware & Chesapeak; and these therefore stand in principal need of the shield of the Union. the Delaware can be defended more easily. but I should not think 100. gunboats (costing less than one frigate) an overproportioned allotment to the Chesapeak country, against the overproportioned hostilities pointed at it.

I am too sensible of the partial & defective state of my information to be over-confident, or pertinacious in the opinion I have formed. a thoro' examination of the ground will settle it. we may suggest, perhaps it is a duty to do it. but you alone are qualified for decision by the whole view which you can command: and so confident am I, in the intentions as well as wisdom of the government, that I shall always be satisfied that what is not done, either cannot, or ought not to be done. while I trust that no difficulties will dishearten us, I am anxious to lessen the trial as much as possible. heaven preserve you under yours, & help you thro' all it's perplexities and perversities.

TH: JEFFERSON

PoC (DLC); at foot of first page: "President Madison." Enclosure not found.

PICKAROONS: knaves, brigands, or small pirate ships (*OED*).

From Benjamin Romaine

MOST RESPECTED SIR,   New York 23rd June 1813.

As I have taken the liberty of using several of your Sentiments, in composing the enclosed Address,—the further freedom has been assumed of transmiting a Copy to you.

Sir,—I also am one of the remaining survivers of our revolutionary war—was five years in the service (from the age of Sixteen to its close) in the New Jersey militia. During that time, was twice wounded, and once a prisoner.

In our flourishing Society of Tammany, we are about altering all our Indian forms, and changing the paraphernalia. The times call for such alteration. The tenor of the Address will show the spirit of the institution amongst us.—you will, perhaps, recollect my name in an address to you, on the subject of honorary membership.

With the highest consideration and respect I have the honor to be your Obedient Servt   BJN ROMAINE

RC (DLC); addressed: "Thomas Jefferson, Montecello Virginia"; franked; postmarked New York, 26 June; endorsed by TJ as received 30 June 1813 and so recorded in SJL. Enclosure: Romaine, *Tammany Society, No. 1, Twenty Fourth Anniversary Address . . . 12th May, 1813* (New York, 1813), declaring that the Tammany Society had been named for a "renowned native chief" who had been a friend to early settlers and who "embraced their religion, and principles of civilization" (p. 3); that the society was founded before "party distinction had obtained a characteristic existence; and has never failed to oppose faction, and irregular personal aggrandizement at the expence of the peace and happiness of the people" (p. 4); that despite opposition it will continue to promote liberty and virtue; that the United States is "the only free representative commonwealth" in the world; that no American should believe that external enemies or internal factions are capable of destroying the "sacred charter of *Union*" (p. 5); that "every lover of his country" should support the current war (p. 8); that New York mayor DeWitt Clinton has revived a dangerous factional spirit of "Anti-federalism" (pp. 9–14); that freedom of speech and the press must be maintained, citing TJ as an authority; and that "*genuine federalism*" can now be described as "UNION OF THE STATES;—FREE TRADE AND SAILOR'S RIGHTS" (p. 16).

Benjamin Romaine (1762–1844), politician and author, served as a sergeant in the Revolutionary War and operated a school in New York City from 1790 to about 1798, numbering Washington Irving among his students. In 1798 he became city collector. He was removed from office in 1806 for involvement in a fraudulent land acquisition, but he escaped prosecution and served as a city assessor in 1809 and 1810. Romaine was prominent in the Tammany Society of New York and held the office of grand sachem in 1809 and 1813. In this role he headed an effort to build a tomb for American seamen who died on British prison ships in New York's Wallabout Bay during the Revolution. Romaine was deputy quartermaster general with the rank of major in the United States Army, 1814–15. His several pamphlets included *Observations, Reasons and Facts, Disproving Importation, and also, all Specific Personal Contagion in Yellow Fever, from any Local Ori-* gin, except that which arises from the common changes of the Atmosphere (New York, 1823) and *State Sovereignty, and a Certain Dissolution of the Union* (1832), in which he opposed John C. Calhoun's position on Nullification (DNA: RG 15, RWP; William Cullen Bryant, *A Discourse on the Life, Character and Genius of Washington Irving* [1860], 11; *New-York Directory and Register* [New York, 1790], 85; *Longworth's New-York Directory* [1798]; *Minutes of the Common Council of the City of New York, 1784–1831* [1917–30], esp. 2:472, 4:302, 319, 5:561, 6:383; Gustavus Myers, *The History of Tammany Hall* [1917], 22, 23, 25, 33, 34, 61; *JEP*, 2:475, 501 [17, 28 Feb. 1814]; Heitman, *U.S. Army*, 1:844; *Cleveland Herald*, 8 Feb. 1844).

Concerned lest it appear to be indifferent to the wartime suffering of settlers on the American frontier, in 1813 the Tammany Society of New York abandoned its practice of wearing INDIAN garb and markings during its annual parades. Romaine supported the change, which led some members to resign (Myers, *Tammany Hall*, 34). In 1808 he had signed a letter in which the society expressed support for TJ's administration and the Embargo (Romaine, William Mooney and Jonas Humbert to TJ, [11 Jan. 1808] [DLC]). Shortly thereafter a Tammany committee extended TJ HONORARY MEMBERSHIP (Samuel Cowdrey, Mooney, and Judah Hammond to TJ, 25 Jan. 1808 [DLC]).

To Nicolas G. Dufief

[24 June 1813]

Th: Jefferson asks the favor of M. Dufief to send him the books noted below, always bearing in mind the Weekly mission in small parcels for the ease of the mail: and also to note to him the prices that he may make his remittances at convenient intervals.

Tull's horsehoeing husbandry, an old book in 8vo
Young's Experiments in Agriculture. (I think it is in 3. vols. 8vo)
Memoirs of Theophilus Lindsay by Belsham. a new work in 2. v. 8vo
    just publ^d

The Lounger's Common place book. the latest[1] edition to be had. 8vo
Dufief's Dict. Fr. & Eng. 3. vols.
the latest Philadelphia Directory.

PoC (DLC: TJ Papers, 198:35286);
undated; endorsed by TJ as a letter of 24
June 1813 and so recorded in SJL.

The COMMON PLACE BOOK was Jeremiah Whitaker Newman, *The Lounger's
Common-Place Book, or, Alphabetical*

*Arrangement of Miscellaneous Anecdotes;
a Biographic, Political, Literary, and
Satirical Compilation, in Prose and Verse,*
2 vols. (London, 1792–93), and later eds.

[1] Reworked from "last."

To John Wayles Eppes

DEAR SIR   Monticello June 24. 13.
    This letter will be of Politics only. for altho' I do not often permit
myself to[1] think on that subject, it sometimes obtrudes itself and suggests ideas which I am tempted to pursue. some of these relating to
the business of finance, I will hazard to you, as being at the head of
that committee, but intended for yourself individually, or such as you
trust, but certainly not for a mixt Committee.[2]
    It is a wise rule, and should be fundamental in a government dis-
posed to cherish it's credit, and at the same time to restrain the use of
it within the limits of it's faculties, 'never to borrow a dollar without
laying a tax in the same instant for paying the interest annually, and
the principal within a given term: and to consider that tax as pledged
to the creditors on the public faith.' on such a pledge as this, sacredly
observed, a government may always command on a <u>reasonable inter-
est</u>, all the lendable money of their citizens, while the necessity of
an equivalent tax is a salutary warning to them & their constituents
against oppressions, bankruptcy, & it's inevitable consequence Revolution. but the term of redemption must be moderate, and at any rate
within the limits of their rightful powers. but what limits, it will be
asked, does time prescribe to their powers? what is to hinder them
from creating a perpetual debt? the laws of nature, I answer. the
earth belongs to the living, not to the dead. the will & the power of
man expires with his life, by Nature's law. some societies give it an artificial continuance, for the encouragement of industry, some refuse
it, as our aboriginal neighbors, whom we call barbarians. the generations of men may be considered as bodies, or corporations. each generation has the usufruct of the earth during the period of it's
continuance. when it ceases to exist, the usufruct passes on to the succeeding generation, free and unincumbered, and so on successively

from one generation to another for ever. we may consider each generation as a distinct nation with a right, by the will of it's majority, to bind themselves, but none to bind the succeeding generation, more than the inhabitants of another country. or the case may be likened to the ordinary one of a tenant for life, who may hypothecate the land for his debts during the continuance of his usufruct; but at his death the reversioner (who is also for life only) recieves it exonerated from all burthen. the period of a generation, or the term of it's life is determined by the laws of mortality, which, varying a little only in different climates, offer a general average, to be found by observation.[3] I turn, for instance, to Buffon's tables of 23,994. deaths, and the ages at which they happened, and I find that of the numbers of all ages living at one moment, half will be dead in 24. years, 8. months. but (leaving out minors, who have not the power of self government) of the adults (of 21. years of age) living at one moment, a majority of whom act for the society, one half will be dead in 18. Y 8. M. at 19. years then from the date of a contract, the majority of the contractors is dead, and their contract with them.　　　let this general theory be applied to a particular case. suppose the annual births of the state of N. york to be 23,994. the whole number of it's inhabitants, according to Buffon, will be 617,703. of all ages. of these there would constantly be 269,286. minors. and 348,417. adults, of which last 174,209. will be a majority. suppose that majority, on the 1st day of the year 1794. had borrowed a sum of money equal to the feesimple value of the state, and to have consumed it in eating, drinking & making merry in their day; or, if you please, in quarreling & fighting with their unoffending neighbors. within 18. Y 8 M one half of the[4] adult citizens were dead. till then, being the majority, they might rightfully levy the interest of their debt annually on themselves & their fellow revellers, or fellow champions. but at that period, say at this moment, a new majority is come into place, in their own right, and not under the rights, the conditions, or laws of their predecessors. are they bound to acknolege the debt, to consider the preceding generation as having had a right to eat up the whole soil of their country in the course of a life, to alienate it from them (for it would be an alienation to the creditors) and would they think themselves either legally or morally bound to give up their country, and emigrate to another for subsistence? every one will say No: that[5] the soil is the gift of God to the living, as much as it had been to the deceased generation: and that the laws of Nature impose no obligation on them to pay this debt. and altho', like some other natural rights, this has not yet entered into any Declaration of rights, it is no less a law, and ought to be acted on by honest governments. it is at the same time a salutary curb on the spirit of war and indebtment which, since the modern theory of the perpetuation of debt, has drenched the earth with blood, and crushed it's inhabitants under burthens ever accumulating. had this principle been declared in the British bill of rights, England would have been placed under the happy disability of waging eternal war, and of contracting her thousand millions of public debt.   in seeking then for an ultimate term for the redemption of our debts, let us rally to this principle, and provide for their paiment within the term of 19. years, at the farthest.   our government has not, as yet, begun to act on the rule of loans & taxation going hand in hand. had any loan taken place in my time, I should have strongly urged a redeeming tax. for the loan which has been made since the last session of Congress, we should now set the example of appropriating some particular tax, sufficient to pay the interest annually and the principal within a fixed term, less than 19. years. and I hope yourself and your committee will render the immortal service of introducing this practice. not that it is expected that Congress should formally declare such a principle. they wisely enough avoid deciding on abstract questions. but they may be induced to keep themselves within it's limits.

I am sorry to see our loans begin at so exorbitant an interest. and yet, even at that, you will soon be at the bottom of the loan-bag. we are an Agricultural nation. such an one employs it's sparings in the purchase or improvement of land or stocks. the lendable money among them is chiefly that of orphans & wards in the hands of executors & guardians, & which the farmer lays by till he has enough for the purchase in view. in such a nation there is one, and one only, resource for loans, sufficient to carry them thro' the expence of a war: and that will always be sufficient, and in the power of an honest government, punctual in the preservation of it's faith. the fund I mean is, the mass of circulating coin.[6] every one knows that, altho' not literally, it is nearly true that every paper dollar emitted banishes a silver one from the circulation. a nation therefore making it's purchases and paiments with bills fitted for circulation thrusts an equal sum of coin out of circulation. this is equivalent to borrowing that sum, and yet the vendor recieving paiment in a medium as effectual as[7] coin for his purchases or paiments, has no claim to interest. and so the nation may continue to issue it's bills as far as their wants require, and the limits of the circulation will admit.[8] those limits are understood to extend with us[9] at present to 200. millions of Dollars, a greater sum than would be necessary for any war.[10] but this, the only resource

which the government could command with certainty the states have
unfortunately fooled away, nay corruptly alienated to swindlers and
shavers under the cover of private banks. say too, as an additional
evil that the disposable funds of individuals, to this great amount,
have thus been withdrawn from improvement, and useful enterprize,
and employed in the useless, usurious, and demoralizing practices of
bank directors & their accomplices.[11]   in the war of 55. our
state availed itself of this fund by issuing a paper money bottomed on
a specific tax for it's redemption, and, to ensure it's credit, bearing an
interest of 5. percent. within a very short time not a bill of this emission was to be found in circulation. it was locked up in the chests
of executors, guardians, widows, farmers E'c. we then issued bills,
bottomed on a redeeming tax, but bearing no interest. these were
readily recieved, & never depreciated a[12] single farthing. in the revolutionary war the old Congress and the states issued bills without interest, and without tax. they occupied the channels of circulation very
freely, till those channels were overflowed by an excess beyond all
the calls of circulation.[13]   but altho we have so improvidently
suffered the field of circulating medium to be filched from us by private individuals, yet I think we may recover it in part, and even in the
whole if the states will cooperate with us.[14] if treasury bills are emitted on a tax appropriated for their redemption in 15 years and (to
ensure preference in the first moments of competition) bearing an interest of 6. per cent. there is no one who would not take them in preference to the bank paper now afloat, on a principle of patriotism as
well as interest: and they would be withdrawn from circulation into
private hoards to a considerable amount. their credit once established, others might be emitted, bottomed also on a tax, but not bearing interest: and if ever their credit faultered, open public loans,
on which these bills alone should be recieved as specie. these, operat-
ing as a sinking fund, would reduce the quantity in circulation, so as
to maintain that in an equilibrium with specie.[15]   it is not easy
to estimate the obstacles which, in the beginning, we should encounter in ousting the banks from their possession of the circulation:
but a steady & judicious alternation of emissions & loans, would
reduce them in time.   but while this is going on, another
measure should be pressed to recover ultimately our right to the
circulation. the states should be applied to to transfer the right of
issuing circulating paper to Congress exclusively, in perpetuum, if
possible, but during the war at least, with a saving of charter rights.
I believe that every state West & South of Connecticut river, except
Delaware, would immediately do it: and the others would follow in

time. Congress would of course begin by obliging unchartered banks to wind up their affairs within a short time, and the others as their charters expired, forbidding the subsequent[16] circulation of their paper. this they would supply with their own, bottomed, every emission, on an adequate tax, & bearing, or not bearing interest as the state of the public pulse should indicate. even in the non-complying states, these bills would make their way, and supplant the unfunded paper of their banks, by their solidity, by the universality of their currency, and by their receivability for customs, and taxes. it would be in their power too to curtail those banks to the amount of their actual specie, by gathering up their paper, and running it constantly on them. the national paper might thus take place even in the non-complying states. in this way I am not without a hope that this great, this sole resource for loans in an agricultural country, might yet be recovered for the use of the nation during war: and, if obtained in perpetuum, it would always be sufficient to carry us thro' any war; provided that in the interval between war & war, all the outstanding paper should be called in, coin be permitted to flow in again and to hold the field of circulation until another war should require it's yielding place again to the National medium.[17]

But it will be asked, are we to have no banks? are merchants & others to be deprived of the resource of short accomodations found so convenient? I answer, let us have banks: but let them be such as are alone to be found in any country on earth; except Gr. Britain. there is not a bank of discount on the continent of Europe, (at least there was not one when I was there) which offers any thing but cash in exchange for discounted bills. no one has a[18] right to the trade of a money lender but he who has the money to lend. let those then among us, who have a monied capital, & who prefer employing it in loans rather than otherwise, set up banks, and give cash, or national bills for the notes they discount. perhaps, to encourage them, a larger interest than is legal in other cases might be allowed them, on the condition of their lending for short periods only. it is from Gr. Britain we copy the idea of giving paper in exchange for discounted bills: and while we have derived from that country some good principles of government & legislation; we unfortunately run into the most servile imitation of all her practices, ruinous as they prove to her,[19] and with the gulph yawning before us into which those very practices are precipitating her. the unlimited emission of bank paper has banished all her specie, and is now, by a depreciation acknoleged by her own statesmen, hurrying[20] her rapidly to bankruptcy, as it did France, as it did us, and will do us again, and every country permitting paper to be circulated, other than that by public authority, rigorously limited to the just measure for circulation. private fortunes, in the present state of our circulation are at the mercy of those self-created money lenders, and are prostrated by the floods of nominal money with which their[21] avarice deluges us. he who lent his money to the public[22] or to an individual, before the institution of the United-States-bank, 20 years ago, when wheat was well sold at a dollar the bushel, and recieves now his nominal sum when it sells at two dollars[23] is cheated of half his fortune: and by whom? by the banks which since that have thrown into circulation 10. Dollars of their nominal money where was one at that time.[24]

Reflect, if you please, on these[25] ideas, and use them or not as they appear to merit. they comfort me in the belief that they point out a resource ample enough, without overwhelming war taxes, for the expence of the war, and possibly still recoverable, and that they hold up to all future time a resource within ourselves, ever at the command of government, & competent to any wars into which we may be forced. nor is it a slight object to equalize taxes thro' peace and war.

I was in Bedford a fortnight in the month of May, and did not know that Francis and his cousin Baker were within 10. miles of me at Lynchburg. I learnt it by letters from themselves after I had returned home. I shall go there early in August and hope their master will permit them to pass their Saturdays & Sundays with me. ever affectionately Yours   TH: JEFFERSON

RC (ViU: TJP); upper left corner of second page torn away, with word supplied from PoC; at foot of first page: "John W. Eppes esq." PoC (DLC: TJ Papers, 198:35287, 197:35157–9). Tr (ViU: TJP-Ca, TB [Thurlow-Berkeley] no. 1299); consisting of extracts in Joseph C. Cabell's hand of this letter and of TJ to Eppes, 11 Sept., 6 Nov. 1813; misdated 24 June 1814; at head of text: "Extracts from M[r] Jefferson's letters on Finance— addressed to M[r] John W. Eppes, Chairman of the Committee of ways & means in the House of Representatives"; endorsed by Cabell. Enclosed in TJ to James Monroe, 28 Sept. 1813, 3 Aug. 1814, Monroe to TJ, 1 Oct. 1813, 26 Apr. 1815, TJ to Cabell, 17 Jan. 1814, and Cabell to TJ, 6 Mar. 1814.

Eppes had recently been appointed chair of the Ways and Means COMMITTEE of the United States House of Representatives (JHR, 9:10 [26 May 1813]). On 6 Sept. 1789 TJ wrote James Madison from Paris on the notion that THE EARTH BELONGS TO THE LIVING, NOT THE DEAD (PTJ, 15:384–99). TABLES of mortality probability prepared by Nicolas François Dupré de Saint-Maur appeared in George Louis Leclerc, comte de Buffon, Histoire Naturelle, Générale et Particulière (Paris, 1749; for another ed., see Sowerby, no. 1024), 2:590–9. On 8 Feb. 1813 Congress authorized contracting a sixteen-million-dollar LOAN, stipulating that lenders would receive "a six per cent. stock, the interest payable quarter yearly, redeemable at the pleasure of the United States, at any time after the end of the year 1825, at the rate of eighty-eight per cent. or 100 dollars in stock for eighty-eight in money" and that for each hundred dollars invested, they would collect "one hundred dollars in the same species of six per cent. stock, and an annuity for thirteen years, from the first day of January, 1813, of one dollar and fifty cents, payable quarter yearly" (*U.S. Statutes at Large*, 2:798–9; *ASP, Finance*, 2:646–7). IN PERPETUUM: "forever."

¹ TJ here canceled "enter that field."

² Tr begins here.

³ Tr ends here and summarizes the next section as follows: "Mr Jefferson states 19 years to be the period within which the majority of the adults of a generation will die. He says if the majority of a generation should incur a debt equal to the fee simple value of the whole of the soil of the country they inhabit, no one would say the succeeding generation ought to pay the debt."

⁴ TJ here canceled "state."

⁵ Tr resumes here.

⁶ Tr ends here.

⁷ Preceding three words interlined in place of "equivalent to."

⁸ Tr resumes here.

⁹ Preceding two words interlined.

¹⁰ Tr ends here.

¹¹ Tr resumes here.

¹² Manuscript: "a a."

¹³ Tr ends here.

¹⁴ Tr resumes here.

¹⁵ Tr ends here.

¹⁶ TJ here canceled "alienat."

¹⁷ Tr resumes here.

¹⁸ TJ here interlined "natural" on PoC. That word also appears in Tr.

¹⁹ Remainder of sentence not in Tr.

²⁰ Word overwritten as "carrying" in PoC, with the latter word also appearing in Tr.

²¹ RC: "there." Word overwritten as "their" in PoC, with the latter word also appearing in Tr.

²² Tr: "Gov^t."

²³ Preceding six words interlined.

²⁴ Tr ends here.

²⁵ TJ here canceled "things."

To James Monroe

TH: JEFFERSON TO COL° MONROE.   Monticello June. 24. 13.

Not doubting that you have in your office Centuplicates at least of the last Census, and of the reports of the patents for new inventions which are made I believe annually from the patent office, you will gratify me much by having a copy inclosed to me. affectionately Adieu.

PoC (MHi); dateline at foot of text; endorsed by TJ.

The CENSUS sought by TJ was *Aggregate amount of each description of Persons* *within the United States of America, and the Territories thereof, agreeably to actual enumeration made according to law, in the year 1810* (Washington, 1811; Poor, *Jefferson's Library*, 11 [no. 686]).

From John Adams

DEAR SIR   Quincy June 25. 1813

your favour of the 15th came to me yesterday, and it is a pleasure to discover that We are only 9 days apart.

Be not Surprised or alarmed. Lindsays Memoirs will do no harm to you or me. you have right and reason to feel and to resent the breach of Confidence. I have had enough of the same kind of Treachery and Perfidy practiced upon me, to know how to Sympathize with you. I will agree with you, in unquallified censure of Such Abuses. They are the worst Species of Tyrany over private Judgment and free Enquiry. They Suppress the free communication of Soul to Soul.

There are critical moments, when Faction, whether in Church or State, will Stick at nothing. Confidence of Friendship the most Sacred, is but a cobweb tie. How few! Oh how few are the exceptions! I could name many Cases of the rule: but will mention but one. Do you remember Tenche Coxe?

you must have misunderstood me, when you understood that I "proposed to write[1] on the Subject," if you meant, to the Public. I have written enough and too much. I have no thought, in this correspondence, but to Satisfy you and[2] myself. If our[3] Letters Should be Shewn to a friend or two, in confidence; and if that confidence Should be betrayed: your Letters will do you no dishonour. As to mine I care not a farthing, My Reputation has been So much the Sport of the public, for fifty years, and will be with Posterity, that I hold it, a bubble, a Gossameur, that idles in the wanton Summers Air.   Now for your Letter

During the three years, that I resided in England, I was Somewhat acquainted, with Lindsay, Disnay, Farmer[4] Price, Priestley, Kippis, Jebb, Vaughans, Bridgen, Brand Hollis &c &c &c. even D[r] Towers was not personally unknown to me, A Belsham was once introduced to me, probably the Author of Lindsays Memoirs. I had much conversation with him. Whether he is a Brother of Belsham the Historian, I know not, Lindsay was a Singular Character, unless Jebb was his parrallel, Unitarianism and Biblical Criticism were the great Characteristicks of them all. All were learned, Scientific, and moral, Lindsay was an heroic Christian[5] Philosopher. All, professed Friendship for America, and these were almost all, who pretended to any Such Thing.

I wish you could live a year in Boston, hear their Divines; read their publications, especially the Repository. you would See how Spiritual Tyranny, and ecclesiastical Domination are beginning in our Country: at least Struggling for birth.

Now, for your political Letter. — No. I have not done, with Spiritual Pride, in high places and in low. I would trust these liberal Christians in London and in Boston, with Power, just as Soon, as I would, Calvin or Cardinal Lorrain; just as Soon as I would the Quakers of Pensylvania; just as Soon as I would Methodists or Moravians; just as Soon as I would Rochefoucault and Condorcet; just as Soon as I would the Œconomists[6] of France; just as Soon as I would Bolingbroke and Voltaire, Hume and Gibbon; nay just as Soon, as I would Robespierre or Brissot. I can go no higher, unless I add The League and the Fronde in France, or Charles the first and Archbishop Laud in England and Ireland.

Let me Say, however, by the Way, that I fully believe, that Priestley is only guilty of an indiscretion, very pardonable, in this thing. Lindsay is perfectly innocent. Belsham has done the wrong. I cannot but contrast his Conduct, with that of Disney, who found among the Papers of Brand Hollis, Letters from me and my Wife, which We had both forgotten. He wrote to Us and asked leave to publish them. Neither of Us recollected a Word of them for We had no Copies. We both left to his discretion to publish what he pleased and he has done it. I expected much more nonsense and extravagance in mine than appears, for I wrote to Hollis without reserve.

Checks and Ballances, Jefferson, however you and your Party may have ridiculed them, are our only Security, for the progress of Mind, as well as the Security of Body.—Every Species of these Christians would persecute Deists, as Soon as either Sect would persecute another, if it had unchecked and unballanced Power. Nay, the Deists would persecute Christians, and Atheists would persecute Deists, with as unrelenting Cruelty, as any Christians would persecute them or one another. Know thyself, human Nature!

I am not Sure, that I am yet ready to return to Politicks.

Upon the whole, I think this is enough for one Letter. Politicks Shall be adjourned to a future day. not a very distant one, however.

JOHN ADAMS

RC (DLC); at foot of text: "President Jefferson"; endorsed by TJ as received 8 July 1813 and so recorded in SJL. FC (Lb in MHi: Adams Papers).

Robert Burns alluded to the fragile COBWEB TIE of good fellowship in an 8 June 1789 letter to Robert Ainslie (Robert H. Cromek, *Reliques of Robert Burns; Consisting Chiefly of Original Letters, Poems, and Critical Observations on Scottish Songs* (Philadelphia, 1809), 61. GOSSAMEUR, THAT IDLES IN THE WANTON SUMMERS AIR quotes from William Shakespeare, *Romeo and Juliet*, act 2, scene 6. The Catholic (or Holy) LEAGUE of the sixteenth century attempted to eliminate French Protestants, while the FRONDE was the French civil war of the mid-seventeenth century. In 1799 and 1800 Tench COXE published private letters and conversations with Adams in an effort to prove that the president was a monarchist (Jacob E. Cooke, *Tench Coxe and the Early Republic* [1978], 357–60, 378–85). Adams became acquainted with the VAUGHANS, Benjamin and William, during his residence in London (J. C. D. Clark, *The Language of Liberty, 1660–1832: Political Discourse and Social Dynamics in the Anglo-American World* [1994], 329). Having ASKED LEAVE from John Adams and Abigail Smith Adams, John Disney published some of their letters in his *Memoirs of Thomas Brand-Hollis* (London, 1808), 30–40.

¹ Extraneous closing quotation mark editorially omitted.
² Preceding two words not in FC.

³ FC: "your."
⁴ Word interlined.
⁵ Manuscript: "Christion." FC: "Christian."
⁶ Manuscript: "Œconomits." FC: "œconomists."

From John Strode

Allum Spring Mills Near Fredbg 25 June '13

My faithfull, and indeed I ought to Add, Worthy frd, Mʳ William G. Arms, in Calling to See me affords me, Illustrious Sir, the Opportunity, Your goodness had Once confer'd on me to exercise, of Addressing You. In the Chain of Creation, I am not insensible how very elevated Your Situation is from mine, which is lost from the great Ocean of Universal good like a drop from the Bucket, altho' dame fortune has made me as poor as Diogenus, Yet in her despite, I am as proud . . Altho' I am not a disciple of Zeno, I Cannot boast of Stoic Philosophy, Yet I am bearing the frowns of fate with that Resignation as becomes the dignity of human nature . . at present I only wish for some employment, to aquire an honest existence, I could bring into my Countries Service abillities and Zeal; many ways, to Serve essential purposes . . I am a Soldier bred . . . an Artizan, an Accountant, in these Respects consciencously & proudly I am not inferiour. my moral principles, truth or honor have suffer'd no taint, Reflection has not any thing to Reproach me with! I can not descend to ask, or indeed Recieve Letters of Commendation to Our beloved President, if I could, it would be to Suffer me at this Age, to enter the Ranks as a Common Soldier. and if I met with preferment, let it be the Reward of military Skill or hardy deeds of enthuastic bravery . . pardon as often You have, my most Worthy Sir, the trouble of reading this presumtious scrawle, which I well know, a momentarry Reflection might prevent . . . I am not troubling You for a Word in my favour—even if I invited Such a Boon—I wᵈ Rather be pushᵈ Lower (if possible) in the gradation of human infelicity, than Rank among & increase the Number of insignificant Applicants for favour—Thro' every Vicisitude, devotedly & truly—I Revere and admire thro every Stage Your exalted, and unparrllelld Character   with all due Regard

JOHN STRODE

RC (MHi); ellipses in original; addressed: "Thomas Jefferson esquire" by "Mr Arms"; endorsed by TJ as received 2 July 1813 and so recorded in SJL.

Strode's financial difficulties included longstanding debts to James Madison, to whom he had mortgaged a piece of land in 1810. He wrote to the president later in 1813 seeking a public position (Strode to Madison, 13 June 1808, and to Augustine Davis, 11 June 1808 [both in DLC: Madison Papers]; Madison, *Papers, Pres. Ser.*, 2:223–4, 407, 6:507–8).

Diogenes (DIOGENUS) "the Cynic" was known for his proud rejection of convention and a pursuit of a minimalist lifestyle that included begging or scavenging for his basic needs. ZENO of Citium founded Stoicism (*OCD*, 473–4, 1634).

From Frank Carr

MY DEAR SIR,   Charlottesville June 26th 1813
Enclosed is a specimen of the Sulphuret of Antimony, which was found in this neighbourhood—It's appearance, and the chemical tests to which I have exposed it shew it to be very pure—As we have not been able to discover the place from which this has been obtained, it's value cannot be ascertained—
With great respect
I am &c   FRANK CARR

RC (ViU: TJP-CC); addressed: "Thomas Jefferson Esqʳ Monticello"; endorsed by TJ as received 27 June 1813, but recorded in SJL as received the day it was written; with attached scrap, containing portions of another letter in an unidentified hand, and TJ's docket: "the specimen sent to mr Correa at Philadelphia," a reference to TJ to José Corrêa da Serra, 27 Dec. 1814.

Frank Carr (1784–1854), physician and newspaper editor, owned the Red Hills estate in Albemarle County. He provided medical services at Monticello on several occasions. During the War of 1812 Carr was a surgeon for the county militia. He served as a county magistrate in 1816 and as sheriff in 1839. Beginning late in the 1820s, Carr was the co-owner and editor of the Charlottesville *Virginia Advocate*, and he printed the first edition of *TJR* in 1829. He was also an early member of the Agricultural Society of

Albemarle and held the office of assistant secretary in 1820. Carr ran schools on more than one occasion, including one attended by Hore Browse Trist and Nicholas P. Trist. In addition, he served as trustee and secretary of the board for the Albemarle Academy and as proctor of the University of Virginia (*VMHB* 3 [1896]: 209; Lay, *Architecture*, 128, 129; *MB*, 2:1276, 1289, 1334; Woods, *Albemarle*, 96, 377, 379; *Richmond Enquirer*, 10 Oct. 1829, 29 Nov. 1831; Elizabeth Copeland Norfleet, "Newspapers in Charlottesville and Albemarle County," *MACH* 50 [1992]: 71; True, "Agricultural Society," 269, 291; Bruce, *University*, 1:121, 124, 126, 2:351, 3:198; Elizabeth Trist to Catharine Wistar Bache, 12 Sept. 1817 [PPAmP: Bache Papers]; Hore Browse Trist to Nicholas P. Trist, 13 May [Apr.] 1819 [DLC: Nicholas P. Trist Papers]; *Richmond Whig & Public Advertiser*, 11 July 1854).
SULPHURET: sulphide (*OED*).

From John Hopkins

SIR   Philadelphia June 26. 1813

I have taken the liberty to request your Excellency, amongst other Patriots of the American Revolution, to patronize a work, which is intended to be a faithful narrative; of those interesting events.

It is presumed, that your Ex is acquainted, with many facts, & circumstances of that period; in which you bore, so splendid,[1] & honourable a part; & which it would be important to know, & if it would not trespass too much upon your valuable time, to communicate them to me; I should deem it an especial favor. The work has already received 6.000 Sub[s], & it would particularly gratify me to add your Ex name, to the list. May the ruler of the universe, spare you here, to see a happy termination, to our just struggle; with the enemy of the human race, is the sincere wish of Your ob[t] serv[t]

JOHN HOPKINS

RC (DLC); at foot of text: "His Ex, Thomas Jefferson"; endorsed by TJ as received 2 July 1813 and so recorded in SJL.

Hopkins hoped that TJ would PA-TRONIZE Paul Allen's proposed work, *A History of the American Revolution; comprehending All the Principal Events both* *in the Field and in the Cabinet*, 2 vols. (Baltimore, 1819). Although Allen was the author of record, John Neal and Tobias Watkins wrote much of the text. Subscribers reputedly pledged $75,000 for the publication (*ANB*, "Paul Allen").

[1] Manuscript: "spendid."

To John Adams

Monticello June 27. 13.

Ἴδαν ἐς πολύδενδρον ἀνὴρ ὑλητόμος ἐλθών,

Παπταίνει, παρέοντος ἄδην, ποθεν ἄρξεται ἔργου·

Τί πρᾶτον καταλεξῶ; ἐπεὶ πάρα μυρία εἰπῆν.

and I too, my dear Sir, like the wood-cutter of Ida, should doubt where to begin, were I to enter the forest of opinions, discussions, & contentions which have occurred in our day. I should exclaim[1] with Theocritus Τί πρᾶτον καταλεξῶ; ἐπεὶ πάρα μυρία ειπῆν. but I shall not do it. the summum bonum with me is now truly Epicurean, ease of body and tranquility of mind; and to these I wish to consign my remaining days. men have differed in opinion, and been divided into parties by these opinions, from the first origin of societies; and in all governments where they have been permitted freely to think and to speak. the same political parties which now agitate the US. have

{ 231 }

existed thro' all time. whether the power of the people, or that of the ἄριϛτοι should prevail, were questions which kept the states of Greece and Rome in eternal convulsions;[2] as they now schismatize every people whose minds and mouths are not shut up by the gag of a despot. and in fact the terms of whig and tory belong to natural, as well as to civil history. they denote the temper and constitution of mind of different individuals. to come to our own country, and to the times when you and I became first acquainted. we well[3] remember the violent parties which agitated[4] the old Congress, and their bitter contests. there you & I were together, and the Jays, and the Dickinsons, and other anti-independants were arrayed against us. they cherished the monarchy of England; and we the rights of our countrymen. when our present government was in the mew, passing from Confederation to[5] Union, how bitter was the schism between the[6] Feds and Antis. here you and I were together again. for altho' for a moment,[7] separated by the Atlantic from the scene of action, I favored the opinion that nine states should confirm the constitution, in order to secure it, and the others hold off, until certain amendments, deemed favorable to freedom, should be made,[8] I rallied in the first instant to the wiser proposition of Massachusets, that all should confirm, and then all instruct their delegates to urge those amendments. the amendments were made, and all were reconciled to the government. but as soon as it was put into motion, the line of division was again drawn; we broke into two parties, each wishing to give a different direction to the government; the one to strengthen the most[9] popular branch, the other the more permanent branches, and to extend their permanence.[10] here you & I separated for the first time: and as we had been longer than most others[11] on the public theatre, and our names therefore were more familiar to our countrymen, the party which considered you as thinking with them, placed your name at their head; the other, for the same reason, selected mine. but neither decency nor inclination permitted us to become the advocates of ourselves, or to take part personally in the violent contests which followed.[12] we suffered ourselves, as you so well expressed it, to be the passive subjects of public discussion. and these discussions[,] whether relating to men, measures, or opinions,[13] were conducted by the parties with an animosity, a bitterness, and an indecency,[14] which had never been exceeded. all the resources of reason, and of[15] wrath, were exhausted by each party in support of it's own, and to prostrate[16] the adversary opinions. one was upbraided with recieving the Antifederalists, the other the old tories & refugees into their boso[m.] of this acrimony[17] the public papers of the day exhibit ample testi-

mony in the debates of Congress, of state legislatures; of stump-
orators, in addresses, answers, and newspaper essays. and to these
without question may be added, the private correspondences of individuals; and the less guarded in these, becaus[e] not meant for the
public eye, not restrained by the respect due to that; but poured forth
from the overflowings of the heart into the bosom of a friend, as a
momentary easement of our feelings. in this way, and in answers to
addresses,[18] you & I could indulge ourselves. we have probably done
it, sometime[s] with warmth, often with prejudice, but always, as we
believed, adhering to[19] truth[.] I have not examined my letters of
that day. I have no stomach to revive the memory of it's feelings. but
one of these letters, it seems, has got before the public, by accident
and infidelity, by the death of one friend to whom it was written, and
of his friend to whom it was communicated, and by the malice and
treachery[20] of a third person, of whom I had never before heard,
merely to make mischief, and in the same Satanic[21] spirit, in which
the same enemy had intercepted and published, in 1776, your letter
animadverting on Dickinson's character. how it happened that I
quoted you in my letter to Dr Priestly, and for whom, and not for
yourself, the strictures were meant, has been explained to you in my
letter of the 15th which had been committed to the post[22] 8. days
before I received yours of the 10th 11th and 14th that gave you the reference which these asked to the particular answer alluded to in the
letter to Priestley.   the renewal of these old discussions, my
friend, would be equally useless and irksome. to the volumes then
written on these subjects, human ingenuity can add nothing new:
and the rather, as lapse of time has obliterated many[23] of the facts.
and shall you & I, my dear Sir,[24] like Priam of old, gird on the 'arma,
diu desueta, trementibus aevo humeris'? shall we, at our age, become
the Athletae of party, and exhibit ourselves, as gladiators, in the
Arena of the newspapers?[25] nothing in the universe could induce me
to it. my mind has been long fixed to bow to the judgment of the
world, who will judge me by my acts, and[26] will never take counsel
from me as to what that judgment shall be. if your objects and opinions have been misunderstood, if the measures and principles of
others have been wrongfully imputed to you, as I believe they have
been, that you should leave an explanation of them, would be an
act of justice to yourself. I will add that it has been hoped[27] you
would leave such explanations as would place every saddle on it's
right horse, and replace on the shoulders of others the burthens they
shifted on yours.

But all this, my friend, is offered, merely for your consideration and judgment; without presuming to anticipate what you alone are qualified to decide for yourself. I mean to express my own purpose only, and the reflections which have led to it.   to me then it appears that there have been differences of opinion, and party differences, from the first establishment of governments, to the present day; and on the same question which now divides our own country: that these will continue thro' all future time: that every one takes his side in favor of the many, or of the few, according to his constitution, and the circumstances in which he is placed: that opinions, which are equally honest on both sides, should no[t] affect personal esteem, or social intercourse: that as <u>we</u> judge between the Claudii and the Gracchi, the Wentworths and the Hampdens of past ages, so, of those among us whose names may happen to be remembered for awhile, the next generations will judge, favorably or unfavorably, according to the comple[x]ion of individual minds, and the side they shall themselves have taken: that nothing new can be added by you or me to what has been said by others, & will be said in every age, in support of the conflicting opinions on governmen[t:] and that wisdom & duty dictate an humble resignation to the verdict of ou[r] future peers. in doing this myself, I shall certainly not suffer moot question[s] to affect the sentiments of sincere friendship & respect, consecrated to you by so long a course of time, and of which I now repeat sincere assurances[.]   Th: Jefferson

RC (MHi: Adams Papers); edge trimmed, with missing text supplied from Dft; endorsed by Adams; docketed by Charles Francis Adams. Dft (DLC: TJ Papers, 198:35291–2); undated and unsigned.

Ἴδαν ἐς πολύδενδρον . . . πάρα μυρία ἐιπῆν: "Now when the feller goes up to thick woody Ida / he looks about him where to begin in all that plenty; / and so I, where now shall I take up my tale," from Theocritus, *Idylls*, 17.9–11 (*The Greek Bucolic Poets*, Loeb Classical Library, trans. John M. Edmonds [1912; repr. 1977], 211; for editions of Theocritus owned by TJ, see Sowerby, nos. 4378–81). ἄριϛτοι: "best men; nobles." IN THE MEW: "undergoing transformation" (*OED*). TJ's letter to Joseph Priestley GOT BEFORE THE PUBLIC after the latter COMMUNICATED it to Theophilus Lindsey. Thomas Belsham was the THIRD PERSON responsible for its publi-

cation (Adams to TJ, 29 May 1813; TJ to Richard Rush, 17 June 1813). Adams's letter of 24 July 1775 to James Warren, which alluded to John Dickinson as a "piddling Genius" who had "given a silly Cast to our whole Doings," was INTERCEPTED AND PUBLISHED in the *Massachusetts Gazette and the Boston Weekly News-Letter* on 17 Aug. 1775 (Robert J. Taylor, Richard Alan Ryerson, C. James Taylor, and others, eds., *Papers of John Adams* [1977–], 3:89–90). ARMA . . . HUMERIS: "arms, long unused, on shoulders trembling with age" paraphrases Virgil, *Aeneid*, 2.509–10 (Fairclough, *Virgil*, 1:350–1). ATHLETAE: "wrestlers; athletes."

¹ Dft: "say."
² Remainder of sentence interlined in Dft.
³ Word interlined in Dft.
⁴ Preceding two words interlined in Dft in place of "in."

[5] In Dft TJ here canceled "the present."

[6] Preceding three words interlined in Dft in place of "division into."

[7] Reworked in Dft from "for a moment indeed, and."

[8] In Dft TJ here canceled "but."

[9] Word interlined in Dft.

[10] Reworked in Dft from "to make them still more permanent."

[11] Preceding three words interlined in Dft.

[12] Word interlined in Dft in place of "arose."

[13] Reworked in Dft from "men or measures."

[14] Preceding two words interlined in Dft in place of "a scurrility."

[15] Preceding two words interlined in Dft in place of "as well as of."

[16] Word interlined in Dft in place of "repel."

[17] Preceding sentence and sentence to this point interlined in Dft in place of "and of this."

[18] Preceding five words interlined in Dft in place of "and this way only."

[19] Preceding five words interlined in Dft in place of "with."

[20] Word interlined in Dft in place of "Satanism."

[21] Word interlined in Dft.

[22] Preceding four words interlined in Dft in place of "sent off."

[23] Word interlined in Dft in place of "abundance."

[24] Word interlined in Dft in place of "friend."

[25] Word interlined in Dft in place of "press."

[26] Preceding seven words interlined in Dft.

[27] Word interlined in Dft in place of "expected."

From Richard Rush

DEAR SIR   Washington June 27. 1813.

Immediately after the receipt of your favor of the 17th instant I wrote to Philadelphia, and have received from my mother an answer which I beg leave to lay before you, in her own words, as far as relates to the subject of our correspondence.

"Both James and I have made search for the letters for Mr Jefferson; the first he names (that of April 21. 1803) is not to be found; those I enclose must I imagine be the others refered to, though the dates are not such as he has mentioned. I think it probable that the one on religion was destroyed by your father, perhaps at Mr Jefferson's request at the time though he may have forgotten it. I well remember the interest it excited in your father and that he was very careful of it while he was reading and considering it. If however he should have put it in some more secret place than where we found the others and we find it at any time to come, it shall immediately be sent to you. I know that he burned a great many letters not three months ago; I have also heard him say that he had confidential letters that he should never wish to be exposed; therefore I think the one alluded to has been put beyond the power of chance, by being destroyed. One from Mr Jefferson was received and read to him by me only two days before his death, and it was the last he ever heard read".

I here send the two my mother enclosed, and cannot help joining her in the supposition that the one principally[1] wished has been destroyed. I know how scrupulous he was upon these subjects, how often he used to enjoin, even in his own family, the sacredness of these kind of private communications. He too, sir, in his turn, though in a degree far less indeed than you, had suffered from the clamor of enemies and the falsehoods of the press.

The pamphlet containing an account of the proceedings of the government against the intrusion of Mr Livingston on the beach adjacent to New orleans, which you were kind enough to send to my father, he sent to me; and I must be allowed this occasion, though so late, to say with how much pleasure and conviction I read it. Indeed, its truth is not to be resisted, and besides its conclusiveness as a legal argument to the point in issue, I have had it bound up for my library as an erudite and elementary disquisition upon an important title in the law, the more especially valuable as the civil law is so little studied and its books so rare among us.

It gives me great pleasure to be able to say that the President is much better today, and that his health, so precious to the country at a moment like this, is likely to be soon restored.

That yours, sir, may long continue, with every blessing yet left for you, is most ardently my wish. History, when it comes to do its office, will not fail to say how many you have earned.

RICHARD RUSH.

Monday the 28. The President continues to mend.   R. R.

RC (MHi); between signature and postscript: "Ths: Jefferson Esq."; endorsed by TJ as received 30 June 1813 and so recorded in SJL. Enclosures: (1) John Adams to TJ, 1 Jan. 1812. (2) TJ to Adams, 21 Jan. 1812. (3) TJ to Benjamin Rush, 21 Jan. 1812.

[1] Manuscript: "pricipally."

From John Adams

DEAR SIR   Quincy June 28th 1813

It is very true, that "the denunciations of the Priesthood are fulminated against every Advocate for a compleat Freedom of Religion."[1] Comminations, I believe, would be plenteously pronounced, by even the most liberal of them, against Atheism, Deism; against every Man who disbelieved or doubted the Resurrection of Jesus or the Miracles of the New Testament. Priestley himself would denounce[2] the man who Should deny The Apocalyps, or the Prophecies of Daniel.

Priestley and Lindsay both have denounced as Idolaters and Blasphemers, all the Trinitarians and even the Arrians. Poor weak Man, when will thy Perfection arrive![3] Perfectibility I Shall not deny: for a greater Character than Priestley or Godwin has Said "Be ye perfect &c."[4] For my part, I cannot deal damnation round the land on all I judge the Foes of God or Man, But I did not intend to Say a Word on this Subject, in this Letter. As much of it as you please hereafter: but let me now return to Politicks.

With Some difficulty, I have hunted up, or down, "the Address of the young men of the City of Philadelphia, the District of Southwark, and the Northern Liberties:"[5] and the Answer.

The Addressers Say "Actuated by the same principles on which our forefathers atchieved their independence, the recent Attempts of a foreign Power to derogate from the dignity and rights of our country, awaken our liveliest Sensibility, and our Strongest indignation." Huzza my brave Boys! Could Thomas Jefferson or John Adams, hear these Words, with insensibility, and without Emotion? These Boys afterwards add "We regard our Liberty and Independence, as the richest portion given Us by our Ancestors." And, who were these Ancestors? Among them were Thomas Jefferson and John Adams. And I very cooly believe that no two Men among those Ancestors did more towards it than those two. Could either, hear this like Statues? If, one hundred years hence, your Letters and mine Should See the light I hope the Reader, will hunt up this Address and read it all: and remember that We were then engaged or on the point of engaging in a War with France. I Shall not repeat the Answer, till We come to the paragraph, upon which you criticised[6] to D[r] Priestley: though every Word of it is true, and I now rejoice to See it recorded; and though I had wholly forgotten it.

The Paragraph is "Science and Morals are the great Pillars on which this Country has been raised to its present population, Oppulence and prosperity, and these alone, can advance, Support and preserve it." "Without wishing to damp the Ardor of curiosity, or influence the freedom of inquiry, I will hazard a prediction, that after the most industrious and impartial Researches, the longest liver of you all, will find no Principles, Institutions, or Systems of Education, more fit, in general to be transmitted to your Posterity, than those you have received from your[7] Ancestors."

Now, compare the paragraph in the Answer, with the paragraph in the Address, as both are quoted above: and See if We can find the Extent and the limits of the meaning of both.

Who composed that Army of fine young Fellows that was then

before my Eyes? There were among them, Roman Catholicks English Episcopalians, Scotch and American Presbyterians, Methodists, Moravians, Anababtists, German Lutherans, German Calvinists Universalists, Arians, Priestleyans, Socinians, Independents, Congregationalists, Horse Protestants and House Protestants, Deists and Atheists; and "Protestans qui ne croyent rien." Very few however of Several of these Species. Never the less all Educated in the <u>general Principles</u> of Christianity: and the general Principles of English and American Liberty.

Could my Answer, be understood, by any candid Reader or Hearer, to recommend, to all the others, the general Principles, Institutions or Systems of Education of the Roman Catholicks? or those of the Quakers? or those of the Presbyterians? or those of the Menonists?[8] or those of the Methodists? or those of the Moravians? or those of the Universalists? or those of the Philosophers? No.

The <u>general Principles</u>, on which the Fathers Atchieved Independence, were the only Principles in which, that beautiful Assembly of young Gentlemen[9] could Unite, and these Principles only could be intended by them in their Address, or by me in my Answer. And what were these <u>general Principles</u>? I answer, the general Principles of Christianity,[10] in which all those Sects were United: And the <u>general Principles</u> of English and American Liberty, in which all those young Men United, and which had United all Parties in America, in Majorities Sufficient to assert and maintain her Independence.

Now I will avow, that I then believed, and now believe, that those general Principles of Christianity, are as eternal and immutable, as the Existence and Attributes of God: and that those Principles of Liberty, are as unalterable as human Nature and our terrestrial, mundane System. I could therefore Safely Say, consistently with all my then and present Information, that I believed they would never make Discoveries in contradiction to these <u>general Principles</u>. In favour of these <u>general Principles</u> in Phylosophy, Religion and Government, I could fill Sheets of quotations from Frederick of Prussia, from Hume, Gibbon, Bolingbroke, Reausseau and Voltaire; as well as Newton[11] and Locke: not to mention thousands of Divines and Philosophers of inferiour Fame.

I might have flattered myself that my Sentiments were Sufficiently[12] known to have protected me against Suspicions of narrow thoughts contracted Sentiments, biggotted, enthusiastic or Superstitious Principles civil political philosophical, or ecclesiastical. The first Sentence of the Preface to my Defence of the Constitutions, Vol. 1, printed in 1787 is in these Words "The Arts and Sciences, in general, during the three or four last centuries, have had a regular course of <u>progressive</u> improvement. The Inventions in Mechanic Arts, the discoveries in natural Philosophy, navigation and commerce, and the Advancement of civilization and humanity, have occasioned Changes in the condition of the World and the human Character, which would have astonished[13] the most refined Nations of Antiquity."[14] &c I will quote no farther: but request you to read again that whole page, and then Say whether the Writer of it, could be Suspected of recommending to youth, "to look backward, instead of forward" for instruction and Improvement.

This Letter is already too long. In my next I Shall consider "The Terrorism of the day."[15] Mean time, I am as

ever; your Friend   JOHN ADAMS

RC (DLC); dateline added in a different ink; at foot of text: "President Jefferson"; endorsed by TJ as received 8 July 1813 and so recorded in SJL. FC (Lb in MHi: Adams Papers).

The GREATER CHARACTER was Jesus, who exhorted his followers: "Be ye therefore perfect, even as your Father which is in heaven is perfect" (Matthew, 5.48). PROTESTANS QUI NE CROYENT RIEN: "Protestants who have faith in nothing."

[1] Omitted closing quotation mark editorially supplied. Adams is paraphrasing from TJ's letter to him of 15 June 1813.
[2] RC: "denounc." FC: "denounce."
[3] FC here adds "Thy."

[4] Sentence interlined. Omitted closing quotation mark editorially supplied.
[5] Omitted closing quotation mark editorially supplied.
[6] RC: "crticised." FC: "criticised."
[7] RC: "you." FC: "your."
[8] Preceding five words not in FC.
[9] FC: "men."
[10] RC: "Chistianity." FC: "Christianity."
[11] RC: "Neuton." FC: "Newton."
[12] RC: "Suffiently." FC: "sufficiently."
[13] RC: "astonighed." FC: "astonished."
[14] RC: "Antiqty." FC: "Antiquity."
[15] Omitted closing quotation mark editorially supplied. Adams is quoting from TJ's letter to him of 15 June 1813.

To John Barnes

DEAR SIR   [M]onticello June 28. 13.

I should like much the proposition in your's of the 20th to pay our remittances to G. Williams in Baltimore, and for Russel and Morton, on advice of that paiment, to pay the same to G[l] Kosciuzko. but neither of them could be entitled to a commission; because it would be as if we bought G.W's bill on R. & M. in which case neither drawer or drawee would be entitled to a commission. the only difference to them[1] would be their paying on recieving <u>advice</u> of a paiment here, instead of <u>a bill of exchange</u>: and the difference to us would be the transmission of that <u>advice</u>, instead of transmitting their <u>bill</u>.   but should we not avoid acting through them any more until we learn the fate of the former remittance thro' them? to be more than a year without their having informed their correspondent here what they have done, is not like the practice of punctual merchants. I knew nothing of them but from mr Isaac Coles, who knew them well at Bourdeaux, where they had all the exterior appearances & trappings of good credit. but you know this might change in a moment without it's being known to him. Morton promised to send me some wine immediately for which I was to make paiment to mr Williams; but I have heard nothing from him. this silence may bear a favorable, or an unfavorable construction; and I think until it is explained, we had better look out for some other channel of remittance. could it not be done through the opportunity of mr Crawford's going as minister to France? you being on the spot are the best judge of that, or what other means may be best. ever affectionately your's   TH: JEFFERSON

I return mr Williams's letter

PoC (DLC); dateline faint; adjacent to signature: "Mr Barnes"; endorsed by TJ. Enclosure not found.

[1] Preceding two words interlined.

From John Graham

DEAR SIR   Washington 28th June 1813.

I had the Honor some time since to receive a Letter from you, covering one for the Baroness de Staël-Holstein[1] which you wished me to forward[2] to Stockholm—at the time I received it I had hoped that I should be able to send it by mr Russell in a few days—and therefore delayed acknowledging the receipt of the Letter until I could have the pleasure of telling you that I had found so good a conveyance for it—I am now quite mortified that I took this course, for mr Russell is yet here—and my silence may induce you to suppose that I have not been attentive to your commands—

The facts stated will, however, I hope plead my apology and I beg leave to enquire whether if, mr Russell does not go—(& the course taken by the Senate on his nomination seems to make it probable) it will be satisfactory to you, that we should put your Letter under cover to mr Speyer the american agent at Stockholm, and ask the favor of the Russian minister to forward it with his Despatches—?

I have the pleasure to inform you that the President is considered much better today than he has been for some days past.   with Sentiments of the Highest
    Respect & Regard
    I am Dear Sir your mo Obt Ser^t   JOHN GRA[HAM]

RC (DLC); edge frayed; endorsed by TJ as received 2 July 1813 and so recorded in SJL.

The RUSSIAN MINISTER plenipoten-

tiary to the United States was André Daschkoff.

[1] Manuscript: "Holsein."
[2] Manuscript: "forwarded."

From James Monroe

DEAR SIR   washington June 28th 1813.

From the date of my last letter to you the President has been ill of a bilious fever; of that kind called the remittent. It has perhaps never left him, even for an hour, and occasionally the simptoms have been unfavorable. This is I think the 15th day. Elzey of this place, & Shoaff of Annapolis, with Dr Tucker, attend him. They think he will recover. The first mention'd, I have just seen, who reports that he had a good night, & is in a state to take the bark,[1] which indeed he has done on his best day, for nearly a week. I shall see him before I seal this, & note any change, should there be any, from the above statement.[2]

The federalists aided by the malcontents have done, and are doing, all the mischief that they can. The nominations to Russia,[3] & Sweden, [the latter made on an intimation, that the crown prince would contribute his good offices to promote peace on fair conditions] they have embarrassed, to the utmost of their power. The active partizans are King, Giles, and [as respects the first nomination] s smith. Leib German & Gilman, are habitually in that interest,[4] active, but useful to their party by their votes only. The two members from Louisiana, Gailliard, Stone, Anderson, & Bledsoe, are added to that corps, on those questions. They have carried a vote 20. to 14. that the appointment of Mr Gallatin to the Russian mission, is incompatable, with his station in the treasury, & appointed a committee, to communicate the resolution to the President. They have appointed another committee to confer with him on the nomination to Sweden. The object is to usurp the Executive power in the hands of a faction in the Senate. To this, several mention'd, are not parties, particularly the four last.

A committee of the Senate ought to confer with a committee of the President, that is, a head of a dep^t, and not with the ch: majestrate, for in the latter case a committee of that house is equal to the Executive. To break the measure, & relieve the President from the pressure, at a time when so little able to bear it, indeed[5] when no pressure whatever should be made on him, I wrote the committee on the nomination to sweden, that I was instructed by him to meet them, to give all the information they might desire, of the Executive.[6] They declind the interview. I had intended to pursue the same course respecting the other nomination, had I succeeded in this. Failing, I have declined it. The result is withheld from the President. These men have begun, to make calculations, & plans, founded on the presum'd deaths of the President & Vice President, & it has been suggested to me that Giles, is thought of to take the place of President of the senate, as soon as the Vice President with draws.

Genl Dearborne is dangerously ill, & Genl Lewis,[7] doing little. Hampton has gone on, to that quarter, but I fear on an inactive command. Genl Wilkinson is expected soon, but I do not know what station will be assignd him. The idea of a com^r in ch: is in circulation, proceeding from the war dep^t, as I have reason to believe. If so, it will probably, take a more decisive form, when things are prepard for it. A security for his the Secry's[8] advancment to that station, is I presume the preparation desird.

Your friend   JAS MONROE

I have seen the President & found him in the state represented by Dr Elzey.

RC (DLC); brackets in original; endorsed by TJ as received 30 June 1813 and so recorded in SJL.

The CROWN PRINCE of Sweden was Napoleon's former marshal Jean Baptiste Jules Bernadotte. The senators FROM LOUISIANA were James Brown and Eligius Fromentin. After President James Madison nominated Jonathan Russell as minister plenipotentiary to Sweden, the Senate declared that it was "inexpedient" to fill this position (*JEP*, 2:347, 384 [31 May, 9 July 1813]). The Senate COMMITTEE ON THE NOMINATION TO SWEDEN appointed on 14 June 1813 consisted of William Hill Wells, William B. Giles, and Rufus King (*Annals*, 13th Cong., 1st sess., 95). COM^R IN CH: "commander in chief," with Monroe suggesting that Secretary of War John Armstrong was angling for the post.

[1] Monroe here canceled "today."
[2] Manuscript: "statment."
[3] Manuscript: "Russian."
[4] Manuscript: "interst."
[5] Manuscript: "inded."
[6] Monroe here canceled "on the subject."
[7] TJ recopied this word above the line for clarity.
[8] Preceding two words interlined.

From Robert Fulton

DEAR SIR   New York June 29th 1813

As You take a lively interest in every discovery which may be of use to america I[1] will communicate one I have made, and on which I have[2] finished Some very satisfactory experiments, that promise important[3] aid, in enabling us to enforce a respect for our commerce, if not a perfect[4] liberty of the seas; [My researches on torpedoes led me to reflections on firing guns under water, and it is about a month Since I commencd a suit of experiments—][5]

Experiment First

A Gun 2 feet long one inch diameter was loaded with a lead ball and one ounce of powder; I put a tin tube to the touchole made it water tight and let it under water three feet, Before it I placed a yellow pine plank 4 Inches thick 18 inches from the muzzle on firing the ball went through the 18 inches of water, and the plank.

Fig 1

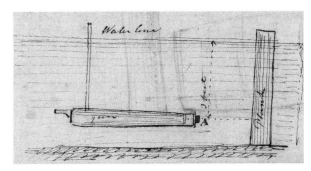

When the gun is loaded as usual, a tompkin or plug is put in the muzzle to keep the water out of the barrel as at A,

In this experiment the gun being immerced with the pressure of three feet of water on all its parts. that circumstance might be assigned as a reason for its not bursting; It then became necessary to try the effect with the muzzle in water and the britch in air

Second experiment

I procured a common wine pipe and inserted the gun, loaded as before, into one end near the bottom, the muzzle in the wine pipe 6 inches, the Britch out 18 inches the pipe was then filled with water to the bunghole, having a head of water of 2 feet 3 inches above the gun, and a body of water[6] three feet long through which the bullet had to pass, I then placed the opposite end of the pipe against a yellow pine post, in such manner that if the ball went through the water and pipe it should enter the post, I fired the ball passed through the three feet of water, the end of the pipe and 7 Inches into the post, the cask was blown to pieces the gun not injured.—

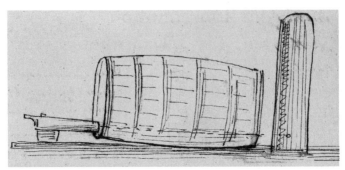

Figure 2

Third Experiment

I obtained a cannon, a 4 pounder for which I cast a lead ball that weighed 6 pounds two ounces the Charge $1\frac{1}{2}$ pounds of powder I placed it under water 4 feet fired at a target distant 12 feet the ball passed[7] through the 12 feet of water, and a yellow pine log 15 inches thick the gun not injured.

Fourth experiment

I Put an air box round the same cannon, except one foot of the muzzle, so that the muzzle might be in water the Britch in air then let it under water 4 feet and fired as before through 12 feet of water and 15 inches of yellow pine gun not injured;

Figure 3

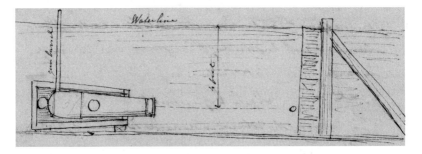

Fifth Experiment

I ordered a frame to be made of two pine logs each 13 inches Square 45 feet long, on one end of which I placed a Columbiad carrying a ball 9 inches diameter 100 pounds weight on the other end I erected a target 6 feet square three feet thick of seasoned sound oak. braced and bolted very Strong thus

figure 4[h]

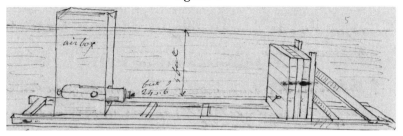

The Columbiad except two feet of the muzle was in an air box, the muzle 24 feet 6 inches from the target, the Charge of powder 10 pounds, when fired the ball entered only 9 inches; That is its diameter into the oak; the columbiad <u>not Injured</u>; this experiment proved the range of 24 feet 6 inches through the water to be too great. —

Sixth Experiment

I took away the columbiad and Box and put a 24 pounder in its place loaded with 9 pounds of powder, the muzle 22 feet from the target on firing it entered the target only its diameter that is about 6 Inches; Without mathematical experience the conclusion would have been that the 24 pounder having a quantity of powder equal to near[8] one half the weight of the ball, and the Ball $5\frac{1}{2}$ inches diameter presenting little more than one third the resistance to the water and Wood that was presentd by the 9 Inch Ball, it should have intered further into the target[9] <u>it did not</u>, momentum was wanting.

Seventh Experiment;

I loaded the Columbiad with 12 pounds of powder and placed the muzle 6 feet from the target the muzle of the gun 2 feet under water the place where the ball struck the target 5 feet under water, in this case the ball went through the target 3 feet thick, and where is not known, the target[10] was torn to pieces; In this experiment I fortunately proved[11] beyond a doubt, that columbiads can drive balls of one hundred pounds weight through 6 feet of Water and the side of a first[12] rate man of war[13]

On examining doctor Huttons experiments, and theory of projectiles <u>in air</u>, and comparing the density of air with water, the theory is that the columbiad fired, might have been 10 feet from the target, the Ball would then have struck with a velocity of 650 feet a second; and have passed through 3 feet of oak; had the columbiad been 16 feet long and made of a strength to fire with 20 pounds of Powder, the range might have been 15 feet through water. But I will take the medium distance of 10 feet,—And then the[14] first undeniable principle is that one Vessel can range alongside of another within ten or 6 or even 5 feet, where giving the Broadside of only two 9 inch balls through the side of the enemy 8 feet below her water line[15] the water would rush in with a velocity of 16 feet in a second and Sink her[16] in 20 or 30 minutes;[17] but from what I have seen in this Sluggish kind of Shot I believe if they were put in about 5 feet from each other, they would destroy timbers between the two points of shock and[18] open a Space of many square feet as thus

figure 5

To put this discovery of submarine firing into practice against the enemy I have invented a mode for placing my Columbiads in Ships; from 4 to 8 feet below the waterline as in the following drawing

Figure 6

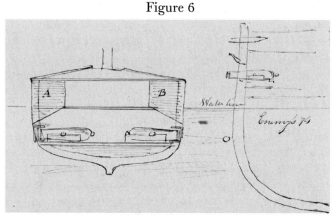

My guns are to be cast with two rims round the muzzle thus

The space a, b to be moulded with hemp and covered with thick leather the gun then forms a piston like that of a steam engines,[19] or[20] the piston of a forcing pump, the gun So prepared there is a Brass cylinder with a strong head cast and boared and bolted in the side of the vessel When as in figure 8[th21] the gun is run into this cylinder it fits it exactly as the piston does a pump, than if the Caliber of the gun be 9 Inches diameter[22] there must[23] be a hole through the bottom of the cylinder of 11 inches as at c to let the bullet pass which

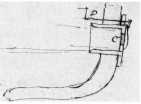

figure 8

hole is covered with a strong sliding valve the Axis of which comes inside of the vessel as at D, when the gun is run into the cylinder and ready to be fired the valve openes, On firing the gun recoils shuts the Valve and Stops out the water, thus my guns can be loaded and fired under the water line with near the same ease they are now worked above the water line[24] my present Idea is to have 4 Columbiads on each Side of a vessel and two in her Bow So that whether She runs on Bow or Side to the enemy the Bullets must pass through her as in

figure 9

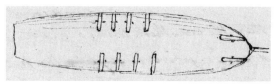

you will observe in these sketches that not using guns above the waterline I have no port holes and the sides above the water may be 7 or 8 feet thick of pine logs which renders them not only bullet proof; but the Vessel so Buoyant that She cannot be sunk in this manner my men who worke the guns are out of danger under the waterline and those who steer or work the sails are guarded by walls of wood as A B figure 6th, For harbour defence and perhaps finally for sea service I have combined a Steam engine with this kind of vessel to bring her up to the enemy in a calm or light Breezes; In harbours I would not use masts or rigging, there would be nothing to Shoot away, nor to hold by in case of attempts at boardage, and in such case as my deck would not be wanted for fighting or any other purpose while in action I could make it inclined to 25 degrees, and Slush it So that[25] Boarders could not keep[26] their feet but must slide into the water they not having a pin or rope to hold by, The steam engine would give a Vessel of this description the means of playing round the Enemy, to take choice of position on her Bow or quarter and with little or no risque sink every thing which came into our waters,

For sea Service[27] we must depend more on numbers of which the calculations are[28] in favour of my plan,—

A 74 will cost 600,000 dollars and then the 74 of an enemy is equal to her in power, the enemy also have such fleets as will enable them to bring two to one; therefore the chances are against us, For 600,000 dollars I can build 7 Vessels; were they to attack a 74 she could not dismast the whole of them, some one must get within the range of 8 or 10 feet of her where[29] one fire from any one of them would certainly destroy her This changes the chances [to][30] Seven to one[31] In our favour and Against the enemy for the same capital expended—

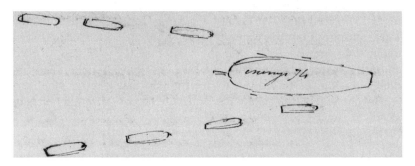

This represents the 7 vessels bearing down on an Enemy here it is obvious that She cannot bring her guns to bear on more than one or two of them, if She lies too to fight they must surround her, But if she sails better than any of them and[32] runs away our object is gained for them She can be driven off the ocean into port. As columbiads of 9 inch caliber are tremendious engines for close quarters I could have

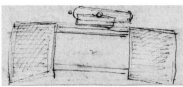

two on pivots and Circular carriages within my wooden walls as thus which being loaded with semi Shot and chains 20 feet long would at 200 yards distance while bearing down, cut her rigging and disable her before coming to close action;—

We are now engaged in a war for principles important to our independence and interest as an active and great commercial nation, and if we fail generations to come must contend for it until they suceed; at all events millions must be expended, which if[33] as successful as our present hope; will fall far short of the liberty of the[34] seas, In expectation[35] to discover in the consealed magazines of science some[36] certain mode for destroying military navies, and thereby establishing a perfect liberty of the seas I have laboured at intervals with much ardor for 13 years, I now submit to your reflections whether I have found it, My present impression—and commodore Decatur is that I have this is also the opinion of many friends for you will consider that if those Vessels can destroy such as now exist they cannot be used against each other without both parties going to the bottom and such war cannot be made as duels would never be fought if both parties were obliged to Sit on a cask of powder and ignite it with quick match.[37]

2 millions of dollars would build 20 Such Vessels 60 men to each would be sufficient total 1200 men. Such a fleet would clear our coast, and the probability is it would be the most powerful fleet in the world;—one however should be built by government to establish principles in the public mind which are[38] already proved in private[39]—On the whole of this subject after you have maturely reflected It will give me great pleasure to have your opinion—and if it coinsides with mine, your influence at washington may be necessary to carry it into effect, I Sincerely hope this new art may give many pleasing hours to Your evening of life, as this wish is from the heart it is better than the usual unmeaning[40] compliments with which letters are concluded—   ROBᵀ FULTON

Dft (PPAmP: Thomas Jefferson Papers); bracket in original; at head of text: "Thomas Jefferson Esqʳ"; with two later attestations at foot of text: "This document is, I am confident, genuine. R. H. Thurston" and "The foregoing document is in the handwriting of Robert Fulton—with which I am well acquainted. Geo: H. Moore Librarian &ᶜᵃ New York: October 19. 1874"; notation by Fulton on separate sheet: "In 1663 the Marquois of Worcester discovered the power of Steam"; with docket on that sheet in an unidentified hand: "Copy of a Letter to Mʳ Jefferson on Submarine Guns. This Paper is in the handwriting of that Great Benefactor of his Country Robert Fulton Esq." Tr (NHi: LeBoeuf Collection); in Fulton's hand and signed by him; at foot of page: "To Thomas Jefferson June 29 1813"; extract consisting of a copy of figure six. Recorded in SJL as a letter of 29 June received 10 July 1813 from New York. Enclosed in TJ to James Madison, 13 July 1813.

The BRITCH (breech) of a firearm is the part located at the rear of the barrel, while a COLUMBIAD is a type of heavy cast-iron cannon or howitzer once used by the United States Army (*OED*). DOCTOR Charles Hutton, a professor of mathematics at Great Britain's Royal Military Academy, was the author of *The Force of Fired Gun-Powder, and the Initial Velocities of Cannon Balls, determined by Experiments; From which is also deduced The Relation of the Initial Velocity to the Weight of the Shot and the Quantity of Powder* (London, 1778).

[1] Reworked from "As every advance in the arts which may be of use to america will give you pleasure, I."
[2] Fulton here canceled "just."
[3] Word interlined in place of "much."
[4] Word interlined in place of "complete."
[5] Omitted closing bracket editorially supplied.
[6] Preceding four words interlined.
[7] Manuscript: "passeed."
[8] Word interlined, with an illegible word interlined and canceled above it.

⁹ Preceding three words interlined in place of "than the latter."

¹⁰ Word interlined in place of "whole thing."

¹¹ Preceding six words interlined in place of "here then it is proved."

¹² Manuscript: "frst."

¹³ Preceding six words interlined in place of "any vessel of War."

¹⁴ Manuscript: "The the."

¹⁵ Word interlined in place of "line, it will drive in her side at least two holes nine inches diameter each into which the."

¹⁶ Reworked from "and she must Sink."

¹⁷ Manuscript: "minuets."

¹⁸ Preceding nine words interlined in place of "drive in the space between them and."

¹⁹ Reworked from "those of our steam engines." In making this revision, Fulton neglected to cancel the "s" in "engines."

²⁰ Fulton here canceled "say like."

²¹ Preceding four words interlined.

²² Word interlined.

²³ Word interlined in place of "is to."

²⁴ Preceding thirteen words interlined.

²⁵ Preceding two words interlined in place of "well."

²⁶ Draft here consists of two versions of the remainder of this and the whole of the following two paragraphs. Fulton heavily reworked the initial version, then canceled it and copied it with minor variations onto a separate sheet. This latter formulation is used here.

²⁷ Initial version used "operations" instead of this word.

²⁸ In initial version Fulton here canceled "all."

²⁹ Manuscript: "were."

³⁰ Omitted word editorially supplied.

³¹ Reworked in initial version from "here the chances are 100 to 1 against" to "Consequently the chances are changed 7 to one."

³² Manuscript: "an."

³³ Fulton here canceled "even."

³⁴ Manuscript: "they."

³⁵ Word interlined in place of "hope."

³⁶ Fulton here canceled "new."

³⁷ Preceding two words interlined in place of "a red hot Iron."

³⁸ Preceding six words interlined.

³⁹ Preceding two words interlined.

⁴⁰ Word interlined.

From Thomas Lehré

DEAR SIR   Charleston June 29ᵗʰ 1813

Yesterday was celebrated here with great enthusiasm and Joy, as the anniversary of the 28ᵗʰ June 1776, when the British Fleat under Sir Peter Parker, was beat off[1] by Fort Moultrie.—

Enclosed is a paper which contains the Toasts that were drank upon the occasion, by which you will find that you[2] have not been forgotten by your Republican friends.

I am truly sorry at the loss of the Chesapeake, and also have many fears concerning our army on the Lakes.   From information lately recᵈ from Washington, I am induced to think, the President will have a very arduous time of it. If ever there was a time for Americans to rally round & support the Chief Magistrate, & Government of their Country, now is that time. The President has received more applause in this State, for his appointment of Mʳ D. R. Williams as a

Brig^r General of the army of the United States, than[3] any appointment he has made since he has been in office

I remain with the highest consideration

Dear Sir Your Obedient & very Humble Servant

THOMAS LEHRÉ

RC (DLC); at foot of text: "Thomas Jefferson late President of the U. States. Monticello"; endorsed by TJ as received 21 July 1813 and so recorded in SJL.

On 28 June 1776 British admiral SIR PETER PARKER launched an attack on Fort Sullivan in Charleston Harbor. The invasion was successfully repulsed by Colonel William MOULTRIE, in whose honor the fort was renamed later that year (*ANB*). Lehré ENCLOSED a copy of the thirty-five TOASTS printed in the 5 July 1813 Charleston *City Gazette and Commercial Daily Advertiser*, which were offered at the 28 June 1813 celebration of the Palmetto Society. The fifth toast hon-

ored "*Thomas Jefferson*—The Statesman and the Philosopher, the great champion of Republicanism, and the scourge of Aristocracy." The first American frigate lost in the War of 1812 was the CHESAPEAKE, defeated by the British frigate *Shannon* on 1 June 1813 (Heidler and Heidler, *War of 1812*, 98–9). President James Madison had recently appointed former South Carolina congressman David Rogerson WILLIAMS a brigadier general (*JEP*, 2:352, 354 [10, 14 June 1813]; *ANB*).

[1] Manuscript: "of."
[2] Manuscript: "will find will you."
[3] Manuscript: "that."

To John L. E. W. Shecut

SIR   Monticello June 29. 13.

I am very sensible of the honor done me by the Antiquarian Society of Charleston, in the Rule for the organisation of their society which you have been so good as to communicate, and I pray you to do me the favor of presenting to them my thanks. age and my inland and retired situation make it scarcely probable that I shall be able to render them any services. but should any occasion occur wherein I can be useful to them, I shall recieve their commands with pleasure, & execute them with fidelity. while the promotion of the arts and sciences is interesting to every nation, and at all times, it becomes peculiarly so to ours, at this time, when the total demoralisation of the governments of Europe has rendered it safest, by cherishing internal resources, to lessen the occasions of intercourse with them.   the works of our aboriginal inhabitants have been so perishable that much of them must have disappeared already. the antiquarian researches therefore of the Society cannot be too soon, or too assiduously directed to the collecting & preserving what still remain.

Permit me to place here my particular thankfulness for the kind sentiments of personal regard which you have been pleased to express.

I have been in the constant hope of seeing the 2^d vol. of your excellent botanical work. it's alphabetical form & popular style, it's attention to the properties & uses of plants, as well as to their descriptions, are well calculated to encourage and instruct our citizens in botanical enquiries.—I avail myself of this occasion of inclosing you a little of the fruit of a Capsicum I have just recieved from the province of Texas, where it is indigenous and perennial, and is used as freely as salt by the inhabitants. it is new to me. it differs from your Capsicum minimum, in being perennial and probably hardier; perhaps too in it's size which would claim the term of minutissimum. this stimulant being found salutary in a visceral complaint known on the seacoast, the introduction of a hardier variety may be of value. accept the assurance of my great respect and consideration.

Th: Jefferson

PoC (DLC); at foot of text: "Doct^r John L. E. W. Shecut."

Shecut's EXCELLENT BOTANICAL WORK was his *Flora Carolinæensis; or, a Historical, Medical, and Economical Display of the Vegetable Kingdom; According to the Linnæan, or Sexual System of Botany* (Charleston, 1806; Sowerby, no. 1076). He never published a second volume. CAPSICUM MINIMUM is another name for *Capsicum frutescens,* commonly called tabasco.

From Caspar Wistar

My Dear Sir   Philadelphia June 29th 1813

After a long interval I have great pleasure in writing to you on the present occasion. The Bearer, Correa da Serra, has a wish to See you, & all your friends here are desirous that he Should do So. He leaves this to morrow, for that purpose, & I am now to State to you my Reasons for wishing him to make the visit. He is a Gentleman of excellent understanding, greatly improved by education—He has passed many years, at different periods of his life, in Italy—Eight or nine in England, and nearly as many in France—in England he appears to have been on the most intimate footing with Sir Jos: Banks & his associates—& in France with the Gentlemen of the National Institute. He has improved So well these golden opportunities, that I believe we never have had in America any person who knew So much of the actual State of Science in Europe—My letters describe him as a most amiable man; & so he has appeared to be, during his residence of near a year & half with us.

This is warm eulogium, but my voucher Carries it—
I make a transition to a very different Subject—You have had great reason to be Surprized at finding no account of your, mammoth bones &ᶜ &ᶜ; yet published—I believe I have mentioned to you that I have long been engaged in Composing[1] a System of Anatomy.—This work has required infinitely more time than I expected, & has occasioned me to part from every thing in which I was engaged, that would admit of delay—In two or three months it will be finished, & then I take up the Subject, & believe it will appear that there are among them[2] two very interesting non descript heads—which must have belonged to Animals much larger than the Deer.

I take great interest in the subject last mentioned, but what follows is more interesting to the Heart—

Jefferson Randolph did not remain here long enough to receive complete & permanent impressions of any of the Subjects taught at this place—whether he is to travel in Europe, or to be fixed in America, it would be useful to have more exact and precise ideas—If you will Send him another winter, I will do every thing in my power to fix him in a proper family for the french, & to promote his progress in Such Studies as you think will be best for him—Your great kindness to me for more than twenty years, inspires me with a Sincere desire to promote your happiness by every means in my power, & this seems to be one of the best opportunities I can expect to have—

Mʳ Correa will tell you all the news I therefore only Say further, that
    I am with undiminished gratitude and respect
    Your much obliged friend   CASPAR WISTAR

RC (DLC); dateline adjacent to signature; at foot of text: "His Excellency Thoˢ Jefferson"; endorsed by TJ as received 31 July 1813 and recorded in SJL as delivered on that date by "Mʳ Correa de Serra."

[1] Word interlined.
[2] Preceding two words interlined.

From John Adams

DEAR SIR   Quincy June 30ᵗʰ 1813

Before I proceed to the order of the day, which is the terrorism of a former day: I beg leave to correct an Idea, that Some readers may infer from an expression in one of your Letters. No Sentiment or expression in any of my Answers to Addresses were obtruded or insinuated by any Person about me. Every one of them was written with my own hand. I alone am responsable for all the Mistakes and Errors in them. To have called Council to deliberate upon Such a Mass of   would have taken all the time; and the Business of the State must have been[1] Suspended. It is true, I was Sufficiently plagued by P[s] and T[s] and S[s]. These however, were but Puppets danced upon the Wires of two Jugglers behind the Scene: and these Jugglers were Hamilton and Washington. How you Stare at the name of Washington! But to return, for the present to

"The Sensations excited, in free yet firm Minds by the Terrorism of the day." you Say, none "can conceive them who did not witness them; and they were felt by one party only."[2]

Upon this Subject I despair of making myself understood by Posterity, by the present Age, and even by you. To collect and arrange the documents illustrative of it, would require as many Lives as those of a Cat. you never felt the Terrorism of Chaises Rebellion in Massachusetts. I believe you never felt the Terrorism of Gallatins Insurrection in Pensilvania: you certainly never reallized the Terrorism of Fries's, most outragious Riot and Rescue, as I call it, Treason, Rebellion as the World and great Judges and two Juries[3] pronounced it.

you certainly never felt the Terrorism, excited by Genet, in 1793. when ten thousand People in the Streets of Philadelphia, day after day, threatened to drag Washington out of his House, and effect a Revolution in the Government, or compell it to declare War in favour of the French Revolution, and against England. The coolest and the firmest Minds, even among the Quakers in Philadelphia, have given their opinions to me, that nothing but the yellow Fever, which removed D[r] Hutchinson and Jonathan Dickenson Sargent from this World, could have Saved the United States from a total[4] Revolution of Government. I have no doubt you was fast asleep, in philosophical Tranquility, when ten thousand People, and perhaps many more, were parading the Streets of Philadelphia, on the Evening of my Fast Day. When even Governor Mifflin himself, thought it his Duty to order a Patrol of Horse And Foot to preserve the peace, when Markett Street was as full as Men could Stand by one another, and even before my Door; when Some of my Domesticks in Phrenzy, determined to Sacrifice their Lives in my defence; when all were ready to make a desperate Salley among the multitude, and others were with difficulty and danger dragged back by the others; when I myself judged it prudent and necessary to order Chests of Arms from the War Office to be brought through bye Lanes and back Doors: determined to defend my House at[5] the Expence of my Life, and the Lives of the few, very few Domesticks and Friends within it. what think you of Terrorism, M[r] Jefferson? Shall I investigate the Causes, the

Motives, the Incentives to these Terrorisms? Shall I remind you of Phillip Freneau, of Loyd! of Ned Church? of Peter Markoe of Andrew Brown? of Duane? of Callender? of Tom Paine? of Greenleaf, of Cheetham, of Tennison at New york? of Benjamin Austin at Boston? But above all; Shall I request you, to collect the circular Letters from Members of Congress in the middle and Southern States to their Constituents? I would give all I am worth for a compleat Collection of all those circular Letters. Please to recollect Edward Livingstones motions and Speeches and those of his Associates in the case of Jonathan Robbins.

The real terrors of both Parties have allways been, and now are; The fear that they shall loose the Elections and consequently the Loaves and Fishes; and that their Antagonists will obtain them. Both parties have excited artificial Terrors and if I were summoned as a Witness to Say upon Oath, which Party had excited, machiavillialy, the most terror, and which had really felt the most, I could not[6] give a more Sincere Answer, than in the vulgar Style "Put Them in a bagg and Shake[7] them, and then See which comes out first."[8]

where is the Terrorism, now, my Friend? There is now more real Terrorism in New England than there ever was in Virginia. The Terror of a civil War, a La Vendee, a division of the States &c &c. &c. How shall We conjure down this damnable Rivalry between Virginia, and Massachusetts? Virginia had recourse to Pensilvania, and New york, Massachusetts has now recourse to New york. They have almost got New Jersey and Maryland, and they are aiming at Pennsilvania. And all this in the midst of a War with England, when all Europe is in flames.

I will give you a hint or two more, on the Subject of Terrorism. When John Randolph in the House and Stephens Thompson Mason in the Senate were treating me, with the Utmost contempt, when Ned Livingston was threatening me with Impeachment for the murder of Jonathan Robbins the native of Danvers in Connecticutt. When I had certain Information, that the daily Language in an Insurance office in Boston, was, even from the Mouth of Charles Jarvis "We must go to Philadelphia, and dragg that[9] John Adams from his Chair."

I thank[10] God that Terror, never yet Seized on my mind. But I have had more excitements to it, from 1761 to this day than any other Man. Name the other if you can. I have been disgraced and degraded and I have a right to complain. But as I always expected it, I have always Submitted to it; perhaps often with too much tameness.

The amount of all the Speeches of John Randolph in the House for two or three years is, that himself and myself, are the only two honest and consistent Men in the United States. Himself eternally in opposition to Government, and myself as constantly in favour of it. He is now in Correspondence with his Friend Quincy, What will come of it, let Virginia and Massachusetts Judge. In my next, you may find Something, upon "Correspondencies"[11] whigg and Tory; Federal and democratic; Virginian and Novanglian; English and French; Jacobinic and despotic. &c

Mean time, I am as ever your Friend.   JOHN ADAMS

RC (DLC); at foot of text: "President Jefferson"; mistakenly endorsed by TJ as received 14 June 1813 but correctly recorded in SJL as received 14 July 1813. FC (Lb in MHi: Adams Papers).

P[s] AND T[s] AND S[s]: such men as Timothy Pickering, Uriah Tracy, and Theodore Sedgwick. CHAISES REBELLION: during Shays's Rebellion (1786–87), citizens in western MASSACHUSETTS rose up against high taxes and poor economic conditions. By GALLATINS INSURRECTION Adams means the Whiskey Rebellion, a 1794 protest against federal excise taxes on liquor led primarily by farmers in western Pennsylvania. United States senator Albert Gallatin represented this constituency and was blamed for the unrest by Federalists, even though he was instrumental in restoring the rule of law in the region (ANB). During John FRIES's Rebellion of 1799, eastern Pennsylvania farmers opposed a direct federal property tax. As president, Adams called in federal troops and state militia to quell the disturbance, but when Fries and two associates were convicted of treason and sentenced to hang, Adams overruled his cabinet and pardoned them (Paul Douglas Newman, Fries's Rebellion: The Enduring Struggle for the American Revolution [2004]). For more on THE TERRORISM, EXCITED BY GENET, IN 1793, see PTJ, vols. 26–7. TENNISON: David Denniston. NOVANGLIAN: "New Englander" (OED).

[1] Preceding three words interlined.
[2] Omitted opening quotation mark supplied from FC. Adams is quoting from TJ's letter to him of 15 June 1813.
[3] Preceding three words interlined.
[4] FC: "fatal."
[5] RC: "att." FC: "at."
[6] Word interlined.
[7] RC: "Skake." FC: "shake."
[8] Omitted closing quotation mark editorially supplied.
[9] Extraneous opening quotation mark editorially omitted.
[10] RC: "thak." FC: "thank."
[11] Omitted opening quotation mark editorially supplied.

From James Monroe

DEAR SIR   30 June 1813.

The President's health is rather improved since my last to you. He had a bad night, but his fever is slighter than it has been at any time since his indisposition. The phisicians think him convalescent—

in haste—respectfully & sincerely yrs.   JA[s] MONROE

RC (MHi); dateline at foot of text; endorsed by TJ as received 2 July 1813 from Washington and so recorded in SJL.

Account with Reuben Perry for Work on Barn at Monticello

A Bill of work done for Thoˢ Jefferson Esqr

Sq. feet.	In			$ .Cts
127.57.	6 Framing		@ 6/–	127.57½
19.60.	Sheeting & shingling		@ 10/6	34.30
16.62.	Sheeting Shed		@ 1/6	4.15
20.86.	4 planking		@ 3/–	10.43
53	Shingling hips say per foot		@ 1/6	13.25
7.85.	10 flooring		@ 6/–	7.85½
3.75	flooring loft		@ 6/–	3.75
	making & hanging 5 Dble doors		@ 12	10.00
78	Barge board		@ 2ᵈ	1.56
				$212.87

A Bill of Scantling

					Feet In		$ .Cts
8 Sills	16 feet long	10 by 12 In	469. 4	@ 6/–	4.69
6 do	26 do	10 – 12	572.	@ 6/–	5.72
2 plates	37 do	10 – 4	86. 4	@ 6/–	.86
1 do	24 do	9 – 4	26.	@ 6/–	.26
1 hip Joist	24 do	9 – 4	26.	@ 6/–	.26
30 Joist	16 do	10 – wide	400.	@ 6/–	4.00
55 sleepers	14 do	12 – do	770	@ 6/–	7.70
15 do	12 do	12 –	180.	@ 6/–	1.80
8 Sidepost	7 do	10 –	46. 8	@ 6/–	.46½
62 Rafters	16 do	3 – 5	661. 4	@ 6/–	6.61
6 plank	27 do	15 wide	202. 6	@ 6/–	2.02½
					34.39
		Amᵗ brought down			212.87
					247.26
		add ⅓ for board			82.42
					$329.68

1ˢᵗ July 1813—

MS (ViW: TC-JP); in Perry's hand; notation by Perry on verso: "Bill Mr Jefferson's Work"; endorsed by TJ: "Perry Reuben."

sq.: a square is an area of one-hundred square feet, a standard by which carpenters measure their work (*OED*). The numbers in the three leftmost columns in the upper table are thus expressed in squares, square feet, and square inches.

[257]

From Thomas Voigt

Dear Sir   Philaᵈ July 1ˢᵗ 1813

I Recᵈ your favour of the 20ᵗʰ on the 27ᵗʰ and would have answered it sooner but I thought it best to delay it untill Such times as
I Should hear of a Watch to answer the disscription which you mentioned in your Letter, In Concequence of the War, watches have
taken a Verry Considerable Rise; and I find that I Can get no Good
ones of that disscription, such as I Could Recommend, for less than a
$100—or a 110 Dollars,—

Should I be so fortunate as to hear of a young man of good Carac-
ter in my Line of Buisiness that would wish to Settle himself in your
part of the Cuntry, I will Imediately Let you Know—

I do acknowledge to have Received on the 26ᵗʰ of May, from Messʳˢ
Gibson & Jefferson a Draft on the Bank of Pennsylvania for
$115:50—which is in full for the Clock & Case

I am verry respectfully your Obᵗ Servᵗ   Thoˢ Voigt

RC (MHi); dateline at foot of text; at head of text: "Thoˢ Jefferson; Esqʳ"; endorsed
by TJ without date of receipt. Recorded in SJL as received 8 July 1813.

From John Adams

Dear Sir   Quincy [ca. 3–5] July 1813

Correspondences! The Letters of Bernard and Hutchinson, and
Oliver and Paxton &c were detected and exposed before The Revolu-
tion. There are I doubt not, thousands of Letters, now in being, but
Still concealed, from[1] their Party to their Friends, which will, one day
See the light. I have wondered for more than thirty years that So few
have appeared: and have constantly expected that a Tory History of
the Rise and progress of the Revolution would appear. And wished it.
I would give more for it than for Marshall, Gordon Ramsay and all
the rest. Private Letters of all Parties will be found analogous to the
Newspapers Pamphlets[2] and Historians of the Times. Gordon's and
Marshall's Histories were written to make money: and fashioned and
finished; to sell high in the London Market. I Should expect to find
more Truth in a History written by Hutchinson, Oliver or Sewell.
And I doubt not, Such Histories will one day appear. Marshall's is a
Mausolœum, 100 feet Square at the base, and 200 feet high. It will
be as durable, as the monuments of the Washington benevolent
Societies. your Character in History may be easily foreseen. your

Administration, will be quoted by Philosophers, as a model, of profound Wisdom; by Politicians, as weak, Superficial and Short Sighted. Mine, like Popes Woman will have no Character at all. The impious Idolatry to Washington, destroyed all Character. His Legacy of Ministers, was not the worst part of the Tradgedy. Though by his own express confession to me, and by Pickerings confession to the World, in his Letters to Sullivan: two of them, at least were fastened upon him by Necessity, because he could get no other. The Truth is, Hamiltons Influence over him was So well known, that no Man fit for the Office of State or War would accept either. He was driven to the Necessity, of appointing Such as would accept. And this necessity was, in my opinion the real Cause, of his retirement from Office. for you may depend upon it, that retirement was not voluntary.

My Friend! you and I have passed our Lives, in Serious Times. I know not whether We have ever Seen any moments more Serious than the present. The Northern States are now retaliating, upon the Southern States, their conduct from 1797 to 1800. It is a mortification to me, to See how Servile Mimicks they are. Their Newspapers, Pamphlets, hand Bills, and their Legislative Proceedings, are copied from the Examples Sett them, especially by Virginia and Kentucky. I know not which Party has the most unblushing Front, the most lying Tongue, or the most impudent and insolent not to Say the most Seditious and rebellious Pen.

If you desire explanations on any of the Points in this Letter you Shall have them. This Correspondence I hope will be concealed as long as Hutchinsons and Olivers. But I Should have no personal objection to the Publication of it in the national Intelligencer. I am, and Shall be for Life

your Friend   JOHN ADAMS

RC (DLC: TJ Papers, 198:35349); partially dated; at foot of text: "President Jefferson"; endorsed by TJ as a letter of July 1813 received 14 July 1813 and so recorded in SJL. FC (Lb in MHi: Adams Papers); partially dated; situated between letters of 5 and 3 July 1813.

Of woman, Alexander Pope wrote that "Nothing so true as what you once let fall, *Most Women have no Characters at all*" (*Of the Characters of Women: An Epistle to a Lady* [London, 1735]). In a letter to James sullivan dated 22 Apr. 1808, Timothy Pickering recalled that late in 1794 George Washington had appointed him secretary of war after the resignation of Henry Knox, and that in 1795, following the resignation of Edmund Randolph, "he tendered to me the office of Secretary of State. At the same time he frankly told me the names of several gentlemen whom he had invited to accept, but who had declined the office" (*Interesting Correspondence between His Excellency Governour Sullivan and Col. Pickering* [Boston, 1808], 30).

[1] Superfluous opening parenthesis in front of this word editorially omitted.
[2] RC: "Pamphets." FC: "pamphlets."

From Englehart Cruse

Dear Sir   Saint mareys July 3ᵗʰ 1813
    hearing of the Repeated Barbarrities Committed by the Ship of
the Enemy on ower Defenceless towns, I felt sorely for the same,
and tried My tallent whether I might not discover Some plan by
which we might not Counteract those Savage Cruelteys, I Acordingly
Invented the Inclosed plan; a faint drauft of which with a specification, I take the Libberty to transmit and Submit, to your Judgement,[1] your pattriotism I make no doupt will Contanence the same,[2]
and hand it over to the propper Authorrities, Shold you Aprove of
it, wich Shold it be the Means of disarming the Brttish thunder
as It regards ower Seaports, I shall think myself Suffitiently Rewarded,   I shold not have given you the trouble of it had I
Been Aquainted with the Pressident of the united states[3] or Aney
other tried friend of ower Cuntry, and you probaly have forgot me, as
fortune has placed me in this Remote Corner of the union where I
still spend my tallents in the steam Buissness with Considderable
sucsess of Late years,[4] but you will no doupt Recolect me by Repeating the Lasts Clause of an[5] Introduterry Letter given me to you by
Doctor James Mᶜhenrey, which was . . . his Cientific Acquirements
are not Maney, but his Natturrel tallents are verrey Considderable, I
rite this to you that you may see what ower soil produses without the
help of Culture . . .[6] your gennerrossity will I hope pardon My freedom, as also Exquse My scollership as it Regards my Riting, as I
found it not safe to make my Sending you this known, Least it wold
not find its way to you, and if you will Condecend to Let me know by
a Line whether you have received this you will Confer a Lasting
obligation on your[7] Sincere friend & humble Servant
                                            Englehart Cruse

NB you was Secratary of state in filadelphia and I Lived in Baltimore
at the time I handed you the Letter of Introduction   E. C

RC (DLC); ellipses in original; endorsed by TJ as received 21 July 1813 and
so recorded in SJL. Dupl (DLC); dated
10 July 1813; text of substantially the
same import, with significant variations
recorded below; lacking postscript; endorsed by TJ as received 28 July 1813
and so recorded in SJL; enclosed in
George M. Troup to TJ, 24 July 1813.

Englehart Cruse, mechanic and mill-
wright, concentrated his efforts as an inventor on improving steam technology.
He defended the originality of his ideas
in a pamphlet entitled *The Projector Detected or, Some Strictures, On the Plan of
Mr. James Rumsey's Steam Boat* (Baltimore, 1788). The following year Cruse
applied to Congress for a patent for his
perpetual cylinder, and he put his idea to
work in a steam gristmill in Baltimore at
about the same time. In 1791 he secured

a patent, although James B. Pleasants claimed to have originated the concept. Cruse was in Georgia by 1796 and later moved to Charleston, South Carolina, where he patented a cotton gin in 1816 (*JHR*, 1:35 [14 May 1789]; *List of Patents*, 6, 170; *PTJ*, 16:xlii–xliii, 412–3, 17:320, 27:803–4; Washington, *Papers, Pres. Ser.*, 5:384–6; John W. McGrain, "Englehart Cruse and Baltimore's First Steam Mill," *Maryland Historical Magazine* 71 [1976]: 65–79; *Columbian Museum & Savannah Advertiser*, 30 Sept. 1796; *The Directory and Stranger's Guide, for the City of Charleston . . . for the Year 1822* [Charleston, 1822], 34; *Directory and Stranger's Guide, for the City of Charleston . . . for the Year of Our Lord 1825* [Charleston, 1824], 39). JAMES McHenry introduced Cruse in a letter dated 18 Apr. 1791 (*PTJ*, 16:413n).

[1] RC: "Judement." Dupl: "Judgement."

[2] Remainder of sentence in Dupl reads "I have no doupt but you will recommend it to the notice of the Pressident of the united states, or other propper Authorrityes, as it is I trust for the good of our Cuntrey, the Inclosed plan Avoids all that danger and uncertainty of Simmeler plans that have Been proposed, as it is attended with no danger in Laying it, and in my opinion Cannot fail to produce the Effect for which it is Intended."

[3] RC: "stats." Dupl: "states."

[4] Dupl here adds "I fain wold have offered my <*perssonable*> perssonal sirvisses to that native Countrey of mine, in Executing the within apperratus, but my funds or rather the want of them prevent me."

[5] Manuscript: "and."

[6] Dupl here adds "{If you received my letter wich I rote the last mail in which I Inclosed also the same plan of an apperratus for Blowing up Enemys ships,} you will no doupt wonder at this Repatition, but sir I have reason to doupt of its finding its way to you, since it was put in the post office, I therefore thought it nessary to send the same plan to you again under Cover of M[r] troups name."

[7] RC: "you." Dupl: "your."

Englehart Cruse's Drawing and Explanation of an Apparatus for Blowing Up Ships

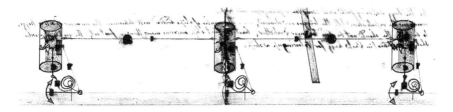

Explanation of the above drawing of an apperratus for Blowing up Enemys Ships, when attempting to Enter our harbours with an hostile Intention, to wit, **AAA.** keggs of powder too thirds full, with a weight at one side to keep that side down, so that the Emty part of the keggs lies uppermost, which keggs must be made water tight. **B.B** a Rope that holds them together, **c.c.c.** gun locks, placed within the keggs above the gunpowder fastened to the side of a Crosspiece[1] for that purpose, **D.D.D.** Brass or Copper Rods which Enter through the heads of the keggs, Corked tight, so as to be waterproof, the inner end fastened to the triggers by a Sink, **E.E.E.** the above metioned weight to keep the keggs Ballasted, **F.F.F.** Ropes fastened to the keggs underside; the Lower end to the Anchors or Aney other weight that will not Easily dragg, which Ropes or Cords are only to be of strenght suffitient to hold the kegg stationary a Lietle underwater, but to Brake by the ships Running against the Rope that Conects the keggs, **H.H.H.** Ropes fastened to the outer end of the Brass Rods, sufitiently long to lie in a Coil at the Bottom of the Channel, the lower end fastened to the Rings of the Anchors, **I.I.I.–K.K.** Small Bouys with a hole through them so that they[2] may slide on the Couppeling rope, and keep the same from sinking, **L.** the vessels stern, Running against the Rope. **B.B.** snapping the Ropes **F.F.F.** and driving the Rope **B.B.** with its keggs ahead, by which the Ropes **HHH** become taut[3] and draw the triggers of the locks, by means of the Brass rods and if the locks are good will Cause an Explotion,   Note the keggs must be no more distance apart then about 150 feet so that if the Channel is wide a greater number will be required, for If [they] are too far apart they[4] will swing behind the Ship Insted under it this apperatus may be kep Redy and nead not be Laid till the Enemy is in sight or Immediatly Expected, and if not wanted may be taken up again, by untying the ropes from the Brass rods, a gard bote ought be kep at the place, to warn freindly vessels, till the apperratus is out of the way,

NB the kegg not being full will Bouy the Copling rope and together with the Bouys on the Rope itself will not let it slide downwards on the vessels stern till the triggers are drawn, —the number of ships dredded will determine the number of sets of keggs, to be Laid, they[5] should not be Laid too near Each other, least the first ship overruns more then the first set, the qantity of powder Shold be suffitient in Each kegg for Blowing up a ship,

MS (DLC: TJ Papers, 198:35306–7); entirely in Cruse's hand; mutilated; undated. Also enclosed in TJ to Cruse, 23 July 1813, and George M. Troup to TJ, 24 July 1813.

[1] Manuscript: "Crosspice."
[2] Manuscript: "the."
[3] Manuscript: "taught."
[4] Manuscript: "the."
[5] Manuscript: "the."

From John Barnes

DEAR SIR   George Town 6th July 1813—

Your favr 28th Ulto I recd yesterday—The more I contemplate on the proposed plan of Remitting to Paris—viz Messr G. W. & R & M—the more my doubts and dificulties encreases—

permit me, to prefer another, I think more favorable off—   Suppose Genl K—could engage his Banker at Paris, to Negociate for him—his—the Genls Bills of Exchange on me—a 20 a 30 days after sight—for $500—every 6 Mos—The Banker to pay the Genl in Franks—at the then Currt rate of Ex—if this mode could

[be][1] Acceded to, it would be the most safe & satisfactory to all parties—and in order to forward its execution—(if approved of)—it would be proper for you to propose this plan—in a letter—a duplicate & triblicate to the Gen[l] these I could hand—in person & converse with M[r] G. W. on the subject, and forward them by way of Bourdeau—and in the course of a few months The General might be relieved—as well his friends here, from the very great uncertainty of his Remittances getting safe to his hands—

Most Respectfully & truly—

I am Dear Sir—Your Obedient servant   JOHN BARNES,

PS. The gen[ls] 6 M[os] dividend is due, I may as well receive[2] it—as to let it lay in Bank—with your Approbation—

RC (ViU: TJP-ER); at foot of text: "Thomas Jefferson Esq[r] Monticello"; endorsed by TJ as received 20 July 1813 and so recorded in SJL.

G. W.: George Williams. R & M: Russell & Morton. GEN[L] K: Tadeusz Kosciuszko.

[1] Omitted word editorially supplied.
[2] Manuscript: "rceive."

From Elbridge Gerry

DEAR SIR   Washington 6 July 1813

Your very friendly letter of the 19th of June has given me great pleasure. The preference you express for the office holden by me, to the first office of Government, is correspondent with your veiw of the same subject, when you was elected to the former place. The latter you then justly considered as a "station of splendid misery." My opinion on both these points is perfectly coincident with your own.

Permit me to enclose a duplicate of my letter of the 15th of august last, in which was fully expressed my intention, in case of the election which has since taken effect, to pay my respects to you, at Monticello. But in addition to that, I had hoped for & expected the previous pleasure of meeting you here, in the bosom of your political family; & regret that any circumstances exist to defeat those veiws. My motive for sending the duplicate is, an apprehension existing at the date of the letter, that the activity of electioneering partizans would endanger its passage, & subject me to an apparent negligence; & the confirmation of that apprehension, by the silence of your last letter on the subject. The duplicate is in the hand writing of my eldest son, who graduates at Cambridge in august next, & is now here from a journey to Marietta for his health, which has been impaired by his academical studies. Present me in the most friendly terms to your amiable family, & be ever assured dear sir of the most aff & respectful Sentiments of your unfeigned friend   signed E GERY

PS. My son desires me to present "his best respects to the venerable President Jefferson."

FC (NNPM); in Gerry's hand; on address cover of RC of TJ to Gerry, 19 June 1813; at head of text: "Copy of the answer"; at foot of text: "His Excell^y Mr Jefferson" and "turn over"; endorsed by Gerry. Recorded in SJL as received 14 July 1813. Enclosure: Gerry to TJ, 15 Aug. 1812.

On 13 May 1797 TJ wrote Gerry that while the role of vice president was "honorable and easy," the presidency was a SPLENDID MISERY (*PTJ*, 29:362). Gerry's ELDEST SON and namesake was soon to graduate from Harvard University in CAMBRIDGE, Massachusetts.

From Elizabeth Trist

DEAR SIR   Bird wood Henry C^ty July 7th — 13

I shou'd have made my acknowledgements ere now for your kind favor accompanying The History of John <u>Bull</u> and Brother Jonathan, but I was on a visit to Mrs Tucker in Pittsylvania when it arrived, and just as I got home Mr Burwells carriage came to take me to Franklin, tho prevented from setting off for three days in consiquence of two days heavy rain swelling the water courses your letter cast a gloom over my mind and until that was dissipated I cou'd not derive amusement from it — tho Peachey was excessively diverted with it, I took it with me to Franklin and read it in company with Mrs Burwell it excited a hearty laugh which was of servise to both of us, the absence of Mr Burwell and the delicate state of her health had depress'd her exceedingly but I had the satisfaction to see her daily improve in health and Spirits and for about three weeks I never saw her look so well but the extreme heat of the weather which continued without intermission for ten days or a fortnight occasion'd her to relapse and the condition of my neice had a claim to my attention which I cou'd not be reconciled to withhold and was therefore under the necessity of leaving my truly amiable friend (whoes attention to me is that of an affectionate daughter) before the return of her husband I am apprehensive that Congress will spin out the session to a longer period than was expected for it appears as if they consumed a great deal of time on trifling matters The little excursions I have made has been of advantage to[1] my health which had undergone a change for the worse in course of a few months, perhaps occasiond by want of exercise that consideration induced me to accept the kindness of my friends to whom I feel and ever shall every sentiment of gratitude but I am really becoming too much attach'd to the quiet and ease of my own cabin to relinquish it for any other situation Mr Tucker has a handsome establishment and the grounds about it handsomely improved incommonly so for this part of the world he possesses great taste he has one of the most amiable and sweetly disposed women I know for a wife and a lovely family of children wood Ridge the name of their seat is Thirty miles from here and about Seven miles from the sorrow Towns where he has an estate that he got by his first wife Miss Farley I had an opportunity of returning some visits on Leather wood where in the circumference of three miles there is a charming society of Ladies Mrs Fountain a daughter of Patrick Henry is Mrs Edmund Randolph over gain in her manners and person she is an exact resemblance of her[2] daughter Mrs Dandridge is an elegant woman beside several others who wou'd not disgrace any drawing Room and their kind and flattering attentions to me, I shall never forget; I have no cause to subscribe to the general received opinion that age and poverty are repellants against the kindness and friendly dispositon of the world, I have not found it so but in very few instances, and have every reason to be thankful Considering my hard fortune for many comforts and tho it has pleased God to afflict me He has given me strength to bear it, at present there is great mourning in our Neighbourhood in consiquence of a volunteer Company of Militia being orderd to the low part of the state which at this season creates more terror than the Guns of our enemies coud effect poor fellows many of them will leave distress'd families, whoes only support was derived from their labour poor Dear Patsy I feel for her, tho I can not but admire the Sentiment that has animated the soul of her brave husband and induced him to embrace the perilous life of a soldier yet I cannot but think a man with so large a family might have been excused and given place to one of less importance, but I have become as great an enthusiest in the cause as I was in our revolutionary war and had I been a man I shou'd have buckled on my armour long since and have done my part to revenge the Cruelties that has been perpetrated on my brave but unfortunate Country men but nothing is left me, but to weep over the fallen and to pray for the success of our arms The loss of the Chesapeake has grieved my heart but it has occasion'd no mortification as the crew fought like Heroes, but the loss of so many brave fellows is a severe stroke I tremble for the fate of the rest of our Frigates and also for that of Norfolk for the enemy appear to meditate

somthing serious against this State by the great force they have assembled in the Bay if they effect a landing the next Diabolical act of
theirs will be to arm the Slaves, for there is nothing that is base and
cruel that they will not have recourse to, for our destruction but I
dont fear with dejection "evil is uncertain in the same degree as good
whatever is a float in the stream of time may when it is very near us
be driven a way by an accidental blast which shall happen to cross the
general course of the current our enemies may become weak or we
grow Strong before our encounter,"[3] but what gives me pain is the
melancholy picture you have drawn of your self The sudden debility
that has taken place in your system is not produced by age two years
wou'd not have made so great a change had you been as careful of
your self as you ought to have been your exploits upon that Canal
have effected what wou'd have taken a Dozen years to bring about
Good Heaven! how strange it is "that we do not estimate any thing
to the worth whilst it [is][4] in our possession"[5] I cou'd not but admire
when I last saw you the little change that time had made in you, like
an ever green your appearence was always the same, and now you are
experiencing the imbecility that has long visited me but I hope that
your spirits will not be diminish'd and that your life will measure out
a length of years if only on Mrs Randolphs account, my own happiness depends on the preservation of my friends altho I may never
see them again therefore am not altogether disinterested in wishing
for their safety.[6] I dont know what shou'd make us wish for long life
particularly under circumstances like my own that can render little
Servise to any one, tis a melancholy reflection that the effect of long
life is to mourn for those we have loved and lost, yes I have heard and
regretted the Death of Docter Rush he was one of the best men in
the world and many will have cause to mourn his loss, it was some alleviation of my sorrow for his death to hear from you so favorable a
report of the health of my friends at Farmington for I had many
painful apprehensions for the safty of Mrs Divers from the accounts
we received from Albemarle your details of the nursery wou'd have
afforded me great pleasure but for the account you give of my favorites want of health I always thought Lewis a lovly Boy My Grand
Sons are all my fondest wishes cou'd make them Nicholas is at the
college in Orleans and his tutors speak of him in the highest terms for
his application and amiable deportment Their Mother writes me that
their Ideas of honor and Religion are of the purest kind that she
never had seen any minds so strongly impress'd with Reverence for
the Great author of our existance The character of the youngest is
strongly markd with detirmination his remarks are extremely judi-

cious tho deliverd with the simplicity of a child but she regrets his want of softness and polish which his Brother possesses in an eminent degree, from their letters which I receive every month I shou'd suppose they possess'd more than common capacities for their age They read a great deel but what delights me most is the high respect and affection they appear to have for each other and the Republican sentiments they have adopted, but they have frequent attacks of Ill health which makes me fear that I shall never have the happiness of seeing them again, even if my own life is prolong'd to that period when I might look for so great a blessing I have obtruded on you a very long epistle but it is my habit when I address a friend I dont know when to stop, M^r and Mrs Gilmer are pleased with your kind remembrance of them and beg me to present their best wishes for your health, and the same to Mrs Randolph and family, assure her that my faithful and affectionate attachment to her will never change, even if all Remembrance of me is obliterated from her mind I shall now conclude in the words of L. Bolingbroke to Swift Adieu my old and worthy friend may the Physical evils of life fall as easily upon you as ever they did on any man who lived to be old, and may the moral evils which Surround us make as little impression as they ought to make on one who has such superior sense to estimate things by and so much virtue to wrap him self up in

God bless and preserve you is the[7] fervent wish of your obliged friend   E. TRIST

PS our Gardens have been unusually backward this season and what with Storms of hail and the want of Seasonable Rains many parts of this Country are suffering

RC (MHi); endorsed by TJ as received 28 July 1813 and so recorded in SJL.

Trist's NEICE Mary House Gilmer was the wife of Peachy R. Gilmer. SORROW TOWNS: Saura Towns. PATSY: Martha Jefferson Randolph. EVIL IS UNCERTAIN ... BEFORE OUR ENCOUNTER: Samuel Johnson, *The Rambler* (London, 1752), 1:254. LEWIS: TJ's grandson Meriwether Lewis Randolph. Trist's GRAND SONS were Nicholas Philip Trist and Hore Browse Trist, the older and younger sons of Mary Brown Trist Jones. Lord BOLINGBROKE directed his closing words to Jonathan SWIFT in a letter dated 5 Oct. 1729 (*Dean Swift's Literary Correspondence, For Twenty-four Years; from 1714 to 1738* [London, 1741], 100).

[1] Manuscript: "to to."
[2] Manuscript: "her her."
[3] Omitted closing quotation mark editorially supplied.
[4] Omitted word editorially supplied.
[5] Omitted closing quotation mark editorially supplied.
[6] Manuscript: "fafety."
[7] Manuscript: "the the."

From Dabney Carr

The inclosed Deed was this moment delivered to me by mr Randolph, with a request, that I would forward it to you: I do so without loss of time, as I know that you are anxious to receive it, & to close the business to which it relates. you will see that it has been reacknowledged by mr R. & ordered to be certified from this County—this was done at the last County Court—It is very well that this has not been delayed longer; for mr R is so low, that it seems to me impossible for him to last much longer—yet he is still carried about.

yrs truly   D Cᴀʀʀ

my Court is sitting, & the business pressing heavily upon, which must be my apology for this hasty note   DC

RC (ViU: TJP-CC); endorsed by TJ as received 20 July 1813 and so recorded in SJL.

The ɪɴᴄʟᴏꜱᴇᴅ ᴅᴇᴇᴅ, not found, was for the sale of Philip Mazzei's Richmond property. Edmund Randolph did not ʟᴀꜱᴛ ᴍᴜᴄʜ ʟᴏɴɢᴇʀ, dying on 12 Sept. 1813 (*DAB*).

From John Devereux DeLacy

The importance of the object contemplated induces me without apology to solicit your patronage for the inclosed which will shew you also, sir, what the result of my labors and researches have been since I last [had]¹ the honor of addressing you—

With the greatest Respect I have the honor to subscribe myself sir Your most obedient Servᵗ   Jᴏʜɴ Dᴇᴠˣ DᴇLᴀᴄʏ

P.S. Be so good sir as to direct to me to the general post office in washington, I am anxious to get some order made in the business during the present Session of Congress—

RC (DLC); dateline adjacent to signature; addressed: "Thomas Jefferson Esqʳ Monticello Virginia"; franked; postmarked Charleston, S.C., 10 July, and Charlottesville, 21 July; endorsed by TJ as received 21 July 1813 and so recorded in SJL.

DeLacy summarized his ʟᴀʙᴏʀꜱ ᴀɴᴅ ʀᴇꜱᴇᴀʀᴄʜᴇꜱ in an untitled broadside published in South Carolina in July 1813 (copy at PPAmP) and probably enclosed above, which described his work as an agent for Robert R. Livingston and Robert Fulton in exploring the "the sounds and waters of the River Potomack, and Chesapeak Bay"; reported three obstructions "to an Inland communication between St. Mary's at East Florida, and the waters of the James River and Chesapeak Bay"; calculated the total distance of those obstructions at $5\frac{7}{8}$ miles; and concluded that $3,500 per mile would be "fully sufficient for cutting and completing it to the breadth and depth that is requisite, and that the whole of the clearings I have spoken of, will cost but a trifle in addition." DeLacy enclosed a petition on the same subject, not found, which TJ returned without his signature on 23 July 1813.

¹ Omitted word editorially supplied.

From Peter Derieux

MONSIEUR   Richmond ce 8. July 1813.

Comme ma mauvaise Situation depuis bien des années, m'oblige d'errer continuellement Ça et la, afin de pouvoir obtenir les moyens d'exister et de faire Exister ma famille, je me Suis trouvé contraint de quitter la Caroline, pour chercher de l'emploi ailleurs. dans cette Vue je viens d'arriver a Richmond ou javois esperé pouvoir obtenir de vos bontes La faveur de faire usage de la maison de M^r mazzei, mais japprends quelle a eté vendue, et que tout espoir de bonheur est desormais evanoui pour nous, malgré toutte la raison que nous avions de croire que mr mazzei ayant par contrat de mariage constitué ma femme Son heritiere univeselle des Biens quil laisseroit a Son Décés, et que celui la etant desormais le Seul qu'il avoit ici, il nous lauroit abandonné en equivalent de ses promesses. jusqualors nous avions quelquespoir que notre Situation pourroit changer avec le tems et que nous pourrions un jour vivre a labri du Besoin mais dieu Seul Sait Le Sort qui nous attend;

Cependant Monsieur, notre destinée Est encore dans vos mains et Si vous le voulliés vous pouriés encore nous Sauver de la situation deplorable qui nous menace, en devenant notre pere et notre Bienfaiteur auprès de mr mazzei, qui Jose bien lesperer ne Se refuseroit pas a vous laisser prelever une petitte Somme Sur Lobjet qui lui revient, et dont Sachant que vous voudriés bien avoir la Bonté de le garder En vos mains pour En faire le placement de la maniere que vous croiriés la plus permanente et La plus profitable, que dans cette persuasion nous osons esperer quil ne Se refuseroit pas a votre consideration de nous procurer ce moyen dexister dans notre Vieux age¹ et qui pourroit nous fixer et prevenir Les Changements forcés de residence que nous sommes Si Souvent obligés de Subir dans La vie errante que nous menons avec Les 3. Enfants qui nous restent encore.

Jai laisse ma femme a Petersbg, tenant une petitte Ecolle qui est insuffisante pour nous faire vivre, et je Suis Venu ici accepter une place de Clerc quon ma offert à LEagle Tavern, mais mon age et quelques infirmités que jai me font craindre que je ne pourrai pas resister aux grandes fatigues que cette occupation exige presque nuit et jour. mais touttes mes recherches nont pu me procurer celle que jaurois desiré dans un genre plus tranquil, et plus analogue a mon age et a mon inclination

Nous serons reconnoissants Monsieur daucune des manieres dont vous voudries bien ameliorer notre Situation, Soit par votre influence auprès de Mr Mazzei, ou en nous faisant la grace de nous donner pendant ma vie et celle de ma femme quelques acres de Terre en Bedford où peut etre nous pouvions obtenir que quelques uns de nos Enfants Viennent nous joindre pour nous aider a la Cultiver et ma femme pouvant peut etre dans une Situation qui Seroit permanente, obtenir quelques Ecoliers, nous nous trouverions tous rassemblés et a même de nous Entrâider Les uns les autres dans une age ou la Viellesse et les infirmites, Laissent bien peu de pouvoir pour Soi même. Jose Espere Monsieur que votre reponse fera renaitre l'espoir dans notre ame et que la doulleur dont elle est remplie se dissipera. jai pris La Liberté de vous Citer Bedford, comme une county ou nous desirerions nous fixer dabord parceque nous aurions L'honneur dy etre plus près de vous et quon nous a dit que les habitants en etant generalement a laise ma femme pourroit y avoir une Ecol[e] qui jointé aux autres exertions du re[ste] de la famille pourroit nous procur[er] plus aisement les necessaires de la vie Si nous pouvions Emprunter quelques Bestiaux pour les commencements de notre Etablissement

Vieuillés Je vous en Supplie, Monsieur Excuser mon importunite et la precipitation avec laquelle je Suis forcé de vous ecrire ayant desja commencé a agir dans La nouveau Et desagreable Employ que jai eté force d'accepter pour pouvoir faire Subsister ma famille a Peterb^g jusquaceque nous ayons pu obtenir Les moyens de nous rejoindre et de nous mieux placer.

Jai L'honneur detre avec Le plus grand respect
Votre obs S^r   PETER DERIEUX

EDITORS' TRANSLATION

SIR   Richmond 8 July 1813.
    As my unfortunate situation has obliged me for many years to wander continuously from place to place in order to support my family, I was compelled to leave Carolina to seek employment elsewhere. In consequence, I recently arrived in Richmond, where I had hoped to obtain from you the favor of using Mr. Mazzei's house. I find, however, that it has been sold, and that all hope of happiness has now vanished for us, despite all our reasons to believe

that Mr. Mazzei would leave it to us as he had promised, because of the marriage contract that made my wife the heir to all the goods he was to leave on his death and because this was his last possession here. Until then we had hoped someday to be able to live free from need, but God only knows what fate awaits us now;

However, Sir, our destiny remains in your hands. If you wished, you could still save us from the deplorable situation that threatens us by becoming our father and benefactor concerning Mr. Mazzei who, I dare hope, would not refuse to place in your hands a small part of that which belongs to him. Knowing that you would be so kind as to keep and invest it in the most permanent and profitable manner, we venture to hope that under these circumstances he would not refuse your procuring us the means of subsistence in our old age and that which would allow us to settle down and forestall the forced changes of residence that we have so often suffered in the wandering life we have led with the three children still living with us.

I have left my wife in Petersburg, where she manages a small school that cannot support us, and come here to accept a clerkship at the Eagle Tavern. But I fear that due to my age and infirmities I will be unable to withstand the great stress of working almost day and night. Despite all my efforts I have not gotten the occupation I wanted, one more tranquil and according better with my age and inclination

We would be grateful, Sir, for anything you would be willing to do to improve our situation, either through your influence with Mr. Mazzei or by being so kind as to give us during my life and that of my wife a few acres of land in Bedford, where we could perhaps get some of our children to join us and help us to cultivate it. In a permanent situation my wife could perhaps enroll a few pupils; we would all be gathered together; and we would be able to help each other when old age and infirmity make it difficult to take care of oneself. I dare hope, Sir, that your reply will revive our hopes and dissipate the pain that fills our hearts. I took the liberty of mentioning Bedford as a county where we would like to settle, because we would be honored to be close to you and because we have been told that the inhabitants are generally well off. My wife could thus open a school there which, added to the exertions of the rest of the family, would more easily procure us the necessities of life, if we could borrow some livestock to start our establishment

I beg you, Sir, to excuse my importunity and the great hurry with which I am forced to write you, having already begun to work at the new and unpleasant job I was forced to accept in order to support my family in Petersburg until we can obtain the means to be reunited and become better situated.

I have the honor to be with the greatest respect
Your obedient servant   PETER DERIEUX

RC (DLC); mutilated at seal; addressed: "The Honble Ths Jefferson Monticello Near Charlotteville albemarle Virginia"; stamped; postmarked Richmond, 10 July, and Charlottesville, 17 July; endorsed by TJ as received 20 July 1813 and so recorded in SJL. Tr (DLC); ex- tract in TJ's hand in TJ to Patrick Gibson, 30 July 1813, consisting of a translation of part of the second paragraph. Translation by Dr. Genevieve Moene.

[1] Translated extract by TJ begins at "notre destinée" and ends here.

From Robert Fulton

SIR   New york July 8th 1813

on the fourth inst, I sent you a letter containing drawings details and observations on my experiments on firing cannon under water, and the consequence of such a mode of conducting maritime war, on the preceding pages is an exact copy of Commodore Decaturs opinion in favor of this discovery, which from so experienced an officer must have weight with those who are not familiar with nautical affairs

The object now is to give a fair experiment to this discovery By building a Vessel and fitting her in the best manner to secure success and for which Congress should appropriate 100,000 dollars. In which good work I hope for the friendly aid of your influence on your friends in both houses, Since my last letter to you I have composed the steam engine to work in the ship In such manner that it is within the wooden walls principally below the water line and out of danger of shot from the enemy. I have this day sent a copy of the commodores opinion to Mr Madison you will have the goodness to send the letter to him, with such opinion of the plan as you think it merits

I am Sir respectfully your most obedient   ROB^T FULTON

RC (DLC); addressed: "Thomas Jefferson Esqre Monticello Virgina"; franked; postmarked New York, 7 July; endorsed by TJ as received 14 July 1813 and so recorded in SJL.

No letter from Fulton to TJ of THE FOURTH INST has been found, and none is recorded in SJL. Fulton's letter to TJ of 29 June matches his description above. Fulton wrote to President James Madison THIS DAY, enclosing Stephen Decatur's opinion and stating that "I have succeeded in some very interesting experiments on firing cannon under water of which I intended sending you the drawings and details, but as I wished also to communicate them to Mr Jefferson and fearing that your indisposition would not at the time permit you to Study them with attention, I Sent them first to him, he will forward them to you" (Madison, *Papers, Pres. Ser.,* 6:409–11). TJ did indeed SEND Fulton's earlier letter to the president (TJ to Madison, 13 July 1813).

ENCLOSURE

Stephen Decatur's Opinion of Robert Fulton's Experiments with Underwater Artillery

New york May 6th 1813.

I Stephen Decatur having examined the model of a Machine, invented by Robert Fulton, for cutting cables under water; and a piece of 15 inches Cable, which was cut by him 12 feet below the Surface; which effect was produced, by firing a Sharp piece of iron, from a gun $2\frac{1}{2}$ feet long, one inch caliber, with

2 ounces of powder, which powder was ignited Said 12 feet under water, with a water proof lock invented by Said Fulton, and the experiment made at the Navy yard near New york, in the year 1810, in the presence of Commodore Chauncey and many other Gentlemen; which demonstrated the practicability of firing a gun under water with Sufficient force to cut cables.

Having also examined a yellow pine plank, four inches thick, through[1] which, the Said Fulton did on the 27th day of April, fire a lead ball one inch diameter, the gun and plank being 3 feet 6 inches under water, and the plank one foot from the muzle of the gun.

And having heared his account of a third experiment, in which he inserted a loaded gun, of the before mentionned length and caliber, into one end of a water hogshead, near the bottom, and filled the hogshead with water, leaving out the bung; the Gun was fired, the bullet passed through three feet of water, the opposite end of the hogshead, and Six inches into a post of white pine. These experiments presenting a flattering hope of farther success, and the Said Fulton now preparing to try, to what distance a 6 pound Shot and balls of greater diameter, can be fired under water to useful effect, either with the gun totally immersed in water, or its muzle in water and breech in air. as though the muzle passed through the Side of a Ship 6 or more feet below the water line, and the breech inside, and he having Shewn me the Drawing[2] of a piece of mechanism, by which a loaded cannon, can have the muzle passed through the Side of a Ship, at any depth below the water line, and there fired, will recoil into the Ship without letting in any inconvenient quantity of water, and can be loaded and fired as often as need may[3] require.

I have deliberately considered these experiments, and give it as my opinion, that Should Said Fultons future essays prove, as he hopes they will, that 36 or 42 pound Shot, or columbiads of 50 or 100 lb., can be fired from 15 to 20 or 50 feet, through water, and from 3 to 10 feet under the Surface, with Such force as to pass through the Side of a Ship of the line, no vessel can be Saved after a broad Side well directed of only four or Six Such guns; For as the bullets would pass through her from 6 to 10 or more feet below the water line, where the pressure is great, the water would rush in with a rapidity, that could not be cleared by the pumps and She would Sink in a few minutes. The practice then Should be, to run along Side as near as possible, fire one broad Side and retire. the act would be that of a few minutes, and the risque to the assailants little compared to the present mode of combat. Thus, thick Sided Ships of 3 or 4 hundred tons, with 4 or 6 guns on a Side, from 3 to 9 feet under water, could destroy vessels of '100 guns, as they are now constructed. And I perfectly agree with Mr Fulton, that Should his experiments prove, that the above mentionned weight of metal can be fired as he contemplates, and as I have much reason to believe, this new mode of Maritime warfare must[4] anihilate the present System, by rendering Small vessels equal to large ones, for both must Sink if attacked in a like manner. Hence I feel it a duty which I owe to my country, to Solicit the Governement, to prosecute of these experiments and the practice of them to their utmost extent.[5]

Signed STEPHEN DECATUR

Tr (DLC).

Stephen Decatur (1779–1820), United

States naval officer, was born on the Eastern Shore of Maryland but soon moved with his family to its Philadelphia home.

His father, of the same name, commanded a privateer during the Revolutionary War and became a United States naval captain in 1798. The younger Decatur attended the University of the State of Pennsylvania and then joined the Philadelphia shipping firm of Gurney & Smith. He was commissioned a midshipman in the United States Navy in 1798 and served during the undeclared sea war with France, 1798–1800. Promoted to lieutenant in 1799 and captain in 1804, Decatur won wide acclaim for daring and largely successful exploits during the expeditions against the Barbary pirates and the War of 1812. He was appointed to the three-man Board of Navy Commissioners in 1815. Thereafter Decatur and his wife lived in Washington and participated fully in its social life. He was fatally wounded in a duel with fellow naval officer James Barron, the culmination of years of hostility beginning when Decatur sat on Barron's 1808 court-martial (*ANB*; *DAB*; Callahan, *U.S. Navy*, 155; *JEP*, 1:334, 336, 472, 474, 3:4, 7 [8, 15 Jan. 1800, 12, 20 Nov. 1804, 15, 20 Dec. 1815]; Washington *Daily National Intelligencer*, 23 Mar. 1820).

¹ Manuscript: "throug."
² Manuscript: "Draving."
³ Manuscript: "my."
⁴ Manuscript: "most."
⁵ Manuscript: "extend."

From William Short

DEAR SIR   Philad: July 8—13

I hastily noted to you the reciept of your favor of the 18th ulto inclosing the mortgage of Higginbotham. I sent at the same time the first volume of the Bareith memoirs—I now send the second volume—& with it my sincere thanks for the perusal of the <u>bavardage</u> of this Princess, which has amused me much. I explained to you formerly how she came to be dressed up here in a new covering.

Correa had fixed the day of his departure—but he allowed it to pass by on account of the excessive heat of that day—He is not the less firmly resolved to visit Monticello—& he is every day expecting to set out—He means now to go via Washington, but not to stop there—He has consulted, as he tells me, with Mr Coles, the Prests secretary who is here—As he goes by the stage, he will be obliged to take the route of Fredericksbergh—The harvest I suppose will last during the month of July.—You may count with absolute certainty on Correa— He tells me no consideration could induce him to leave America without seeing you.

I am not surprized that you seldom allow your mind to wander, as you say, into the political field—a well cultivated wheat field is a much more pleasing object. As to myself, living as I do, in the midst of those who feel & suffer too much from passing events, to be able to abstract themselves from them, I am obliged to hear a great deal of political conversation—no one engages in it so little as I do, but yet I am unavoidably forced sometimes to speak instead of listening, or turning a deaf ear. I prefer however every other subject.—On Politics as a mere speculative subject, the interlocutors[1] so seldom understand each other, that I am always surprized they are not disgusted themselves, to be thus wasting words—as well might they take up the old scholastic disputes, & _ergoter_ on them—but on the war, which is a practical & intelligible question, it is different—This is one which every man can understand, when passion is kept down—& on this, my opinion is fixed & settled—& I have no hesitation in giving it—The events hitherto have confirmed me but too much in it—& I fear that succeeding events will go on increasing & exagerating my conviction.—That we have had a _right_ to go to war with both England & France from the first year of their hostilities, is what cannot be questioned by any man, I should suppose, of common sense & common candor—but surely Statesmen, whom we put over us to take care of our interests & our happiness are bound to have intelligence enough to be able to judge of the _expediency_ as well as the _right_. Now if any of our Rulers who have declared this war, did really think it expedient, at the time & in the manner, we have a right to say they had more need of guardians themselves, than capacity to act as such (for this war will go immediately contrary to their own views & shew their real folly)—and if they did not think it expedient for their country, & still declared it, then they must be left to their own consciences, which the succeeding & increasing execration of their countrymen, will, I do not doubt, furnish with whips & stings. and this execration will not be confined to their party enemies—in time it will be equally strong, if not more so, with their present friends & flatterers—those who are now toasting them & comparing them with heroes, sages &c.—& who will probably be so much ashamed of this vain & bombastical idolatry, that they will think it necesary to overwhelm the idols with reproach & infamy, to shew how perfectly they are detached from them.

I am always mortified when I see the public persisting in their idea, that you still direct the President—my conviction has ever been that you abstained altogether from interfering—& I have never failed to give this as my full conviction, founded on my knowlege of you—& pretending to no positive information—But they have been so long accustomed to consider Mr Madison, as a mere appendage to you, that nothing which another could say, has any weight in changing that opinion. This is of that class of popular prejudices, which the people in their sovereignty will never give up—and I think it one of the many misfortunes of public life in this country—that this sovereign people not only act the tyrant in fixing on their servants opinions which are often the contrary of those they avow, but also make them responsible often for the follies of others, follies which perhaps they actually abhor.

On the subject of the conquest of Canada; to judge from what I saw from Black Rock to Newark, the space of 33. miles, I should have said that the whole population would have joined our arms—They were all, with very few exceptions, settlers from America, & generally worthless men who had no principle, & left our side on account of some vice—Hull has probably destroyed the confidence of such people—but still there can be no doubt that the U.S. could conquer the whole of Canada (except Quebec) even if the whole of the population were hostile to them. As to Quebec, I can have no opinion of my own, in opposition to that of the first military genius that has been ever on our territory—On speaking with him on this subject—he said most positively, that if the place was properly fortified & properly defended, there would be a physical imposibility in taking it from a power that commanded the sea—For said he, when the river is frozen the earth is too hard for the seige.—& when the river is open, supplies can be brought.

On the duration of the war there must, as you say, be uncertainty. nothing within my knowlege gives me any hope of its present termination—Unfortunately the English, though they have many strong reasons for wishing its end, have many also for desiring its continuance under present circumstances, & also strong passions enlisted against us.—There is no doubt that the war bears much harder on our government than it does on theirs—& if they can believe that the thermometer of our suffering is 100. & theirs only 50. they will be disposed to suffer a little longer I fear, for the pleasure of seeing the torture of our administration—& with the hope of seeing the next Congress prepared for different measures.—They have a Parliament for near seven years, & who seem "up to the hub" men—our Parliament changes every two years—& if the people become wearied & disgusted with the war, they will certainly send men averse to it also.

The ways & means in the mean time will probably act as a stimulus in this way—And if such men go to the next Congress, as probably will go, (the war, disgrace, taxes &c. &. continuing) there is great probability that Mr Madison will be impeached for his agency in it, & if impeached, under such a stimulus & such a charge, we can very well judge how, & with what calmness & impartiality he would be tried:—Let us hope that such a series of events will not be exhibited, & pray that peace may come & relieve us all.

I have been for some days indisposed with a bilious attack shewing signs of inflamation & dysentery—The Doctor aided by the Apothecary & the Bleeder, has restored me, & I purpose leaving this City for the Northward in a few days.   Whenever you will do me the favor to let me hear from you, be pleased to direct to Philad:—m^r Taylor takes up my letters in my absence & forwards them—In all places & under all circumstances, believe me most affectionately yours   W: SHORT

RC (MHi); addressed: "Thomas Jefferson Monticello"; endorsed by TJ as received 14 July 1813 and so recorded in SJL. Enclosure: *Mémoires de Frédérique Sophie Wilhelmine de Prusse, Margrave de Bareith, Soeur de Frédéric-le-Grand; Ecrits de sa main* (Paris, 1811; Sowerby, no. 271), vol. 2.

Short's missing 26 June 1813 acknowledgment of TJ's letter of THE 18ᵀᴴ UL^TO is recorded in SJL as received 30 June 1813. SJL also records missing letters from Short to TJ of 12 June, received 18 June from Philadelphia, and of 24 July, received 30 July 1813 from New York. BAVARDAGE: "babbling; prattling." ERGOTER: "to cavil or wrangle." By THE FIRST MILITARY GENIUS THAT HAS BEEN EVER ON OUR TERRITORY, Short probably meant Jean Victor Marie Moreau. UP TO THE HUB: "in to the hilt, as far as possible."

¹ Manuscript: "inlertocutors."

From John Adams

Quincy July 9 1813

Lord! Lord! What can I do, with So much Greek? When I was of your Age, young Man, i.e. 7 or 8 or 9 years ago I felt, a kind of pang of Affection, for one of the flames of my youth, and again paid my Addresses to Isocrates and Dionissius Hallicarnassensis &c &c &c I collected all my Lexicons and Grammers and Sat down to περι ενθεςεως¹ ονοματων &c. In this Way I amused myself for sometime: but I found, that if I looked a word to day, in less than a Week I had to look it again. It was to little better purpose, than writing Letters on a pail of Water.

Whenever I Sett down to write to you, I am precisely in the Situation of the Wood Cutter on mount Ida: I cannot See wood for Trees. So many Subjects crowd upon me that I know not, with which to begin. But I will begin, at random with Belsham; who is, as I have no doubt, a Man of merit. He had no malice against you, nor any thought of doing mischief: nor has he done any, though he has been imprudent. The Truth is the Dissenters of all Denominations in England and especially the Unitarians, are cowed, as We used to Say at Colledge. They are ridiculed, insulted, persecuted. They can Scarcely hold their heads above water. They catch at Straws and Shadows to avoid drowning. Priestley Sent your Letter to Linsay, and Belsham printed it from the same motive, i.e, to derive Some countenance from the Name of Jefferson. Nor has it done harm here. Priestley Says to Linsay "you See he is almost one of Us, and He hopes will Soon be altogether Such as We are."[2] Even in our New England I have heard a high Federal Divine Say, your Letters had increased his respect for you.

"The same political parties which now agitate U.S. have existed through all time."[3] Precisely. And this is precisely the complaint in the preface to the first volume of my defence. While all other Sciences have advanced, that of Government is at a Stand; little better understood; little better practiced now than 3 or 4 thousand years ago. What is the Reason? I say Parties and Factions will not Suffer, or permit Improvements to be made. As Soon as one Man hints at an improvement his Rival opposes it. No sooner has one Party discovered or invented an Amelioration of the condition of Man or the order of Society, than the opposite Party, belies it, misconstrues it, misrepresents it, ridicules it, insults it, and persecutes it. Records are destroyed. Histories are annihilated or interpolated, or prohibited Sometimes by Popes, Sometimes by Emperors, Sometimes by Aristocratical and Sometimes by democratical[4] Assemblies and Sometimes by Mobs.

Aristotle wrote the History and description of Eighteen hundred Republicks, which existed before his time. Cicero wrote two Volumes of discourses[5] on Government, which, perhaps were worth all the rest of his works. The works of Livy and Tacitus &c that are lost, would be more interesting than all that remain. Fifty Gospells have been destroyed, and where are St. Lukes World of Books that had been written?

If you ask my Opinion, who has committed all the havoc? I will answer you candidly; Ecclesiastical and Imperial Despotism has done it, to conceal their Frauds.

Why are the Histories of all Nations, more ancient than the Christian[6] Æra, lost? Who destroyed the Alexandrian Library? I believe that Christian Priests, Jewish Rabbis Grecian Sages and Roman Emperors had as great a hand in it as Turks and Mahomitans.

Democrats, Rebells and Jacobins, when they possessed a momentary Power, have Shewn a disposition, both to destroy and to forge Records, as vandalical, as Priests and Despots. Such has been and Such is the World We live in,

I recollect, near 30 years ago to have said carlesly to you, that I wished I could find time and means to write Something upon Aristocracy. you Seized upon the Idea, and encouraged me to do it, with all that friendly warmth that is natural and habitual to you. I soon began, and have been writing upon that Subject ever Since. I have been So unfortunate as never to be able to make myself understood. your "ἄριϛτοi" are the most difficult Animals to manage, of any thing in the whole Theory and practice of Government. They will not Suffer themselves to be governed. They not only exert all their own Subtilty Industry and courage, but they employ the Commonalty, to knock to pieces every Plan and Model that the most honest Architects in Legislation can invent to keep them within bounds. Both Patricians and Plebeians are as furious as the Work men in England to demolish labour-saving Machinery.

But who are these "ἄριϛτοi"? Who shall judge? Who Shall Select these choice Spirits from the rest of the Congregation? Themselves? We must first find out and determine, who themselves are. Shall the congregation choose? Ask Xenophon. perhaps hereafter I may quote you Greek. Too much in a hurry at present, english must Suffice. Xenophon Says that the ecclesia, always chooses the worst Men they can find, because none others will do their dirty work. This wicked Motive is worse than Birth or Wealth. Here I want to quote Greek again. But the day before I received your Letter of June 27. I gave the Book to George Washington Adams going to the Accademy at Hingham. The Title is Ηθικη Ποιεσισ. a Collection of Moral Sentences from all the most ancient[7] greek Poets. in one of the oldest of them I read in greek that I cannot repeat, a couplet the Sense of which was

"Nobility in Men is worth as much as it is in Horses Asses or Rams: but the meanest blooded Puppy, in the World, if he gets a little money, is as good a man as the best of them." yet Birth and Wealth together have prevailed over Virtue and Talents in all ages. The Many, will acknowledge no other "αριϛτοi." your Experience of this Truth will not much differ from that of your old Friend

JOHN ADAMS

RC (DLC); at foot of text: "President Jefferson"; endorsed by TJ as received 21 July 1813 and so recorded in SJL. FC (Lb in MHi: Adams Papers).

Dionysius of Halicarnassus was the author of περι ενθεϛεως ονοματων ("On Literary Composition") (Dionysius of Halicarnassus, *The Critical Essays*, trans. Stephen Usher, Loeb Classical Library [1985], 2:14–243). LINSAY: Theophilus Lindsay. ἄριϛτοi: "best men; nobles." XENOPHON was once thought to be the author of an extant ancient treatise on the Athenian constitution, but it is now believed to be the work of an anonymous author sometimes called the "Old Oligarch" (Xenophon, *Scripta Minora*, trans. Edgar Cardew Marchant, and Pseudo-Xenophon, *Constitution of the Athenians*, trans. Glen Warren Bowersock, Loeb Classical Library [1925; repr. 1968]).

In the last paragraph of the letter above, Adams translates freely from the Greek writer Theognis. The COLLECTION OF MORAL SENTENCES from which he drew was Brunck, *Gnomici Poetæ Græci*, 8. In addition to the original Greek, Brunck's edition contained translations into Latin by Hugo Grotius and James Duport, into French by Jean Pierre Bougainville, and into Italian by Girolamo Pompei. For direct quotations and other translations Adams sent TJ after retrieving this book, see Adams to TJ, [ca. 14] Aug., 2, [22] Sept., [ca. 4 Oct.] 1813.

[1] RC: "ενθεεως." TJ corrected the spelling of the RC as indicated and also rewrote the word in the margin for clarity. FC: "ενθεϛεως."

[2] Omitted closing quotation mark editorially supplied.

[3] Adams is here quoting from TJ's letter to him of 27 June 1813.

[4] RC: "democratial." FC: "democratical."

[5] RC: "discoures." FC: "discourses."

[6] RC: "Chrtian." FC: "Christian."

[7] RC: "ancien." FC: "ancient."

From Nicolas G. Dufief

MONSIEUR   A Philadelphia ce 10 de Juillet. 1813

Il m'a été impossible de trouver à Philadelphie Tull's horse hoeing husbandry, The memoirs of Theophilus Lindsay, & the Lounger's common place book. Je puis vous procurer Les ouvrages Suivans d'Young

"The Farmer's tour through the East of England, containing the minutes of above five hundred original experiments &ca 4 vol 8vo London

Young's Northern tour containing the register of many Curious and useful experiments in Agriculture, 4 vol, 8vo London

The Farmer's calendar 8th edition London

Six weeks tour through the Southern counties of England and Wales London (Second hand) 8vo

Young's France, 2 vol 8vo Dublin"[1]

Je vous envoye par la poste le dernier directory de Philad^e prix 1.25. Un vol du dictionnaire Le Suivra à la poste prochaine. vos ordres Seront toujours fidèlement exécutés

Agreez les assurances du profond respect avec lequel Je Suis votre très-dévoué Serviteur   N. G. DUFIEF

EDITORS' TRANSLATION

SIR   Philadelphia 10 July. 1813

I could not find Tull's horse hoeing husbandry, The memoirs of Theophilus Lindsay, & the Lounger's common place book in Philadelphia. I can get you the following works by Young

"The Farmer's tour through the East of England, containing the minutes of above five hundred original experiments &ca 4 vol 8ᵛᵒ London

Young's Northern tour containing the register of many Curious and useful experiments in Agriculture, 4 vol, 8ᵛᵒ London

The Farmer's calendar 8ᵗʰ edition London

Six weeks tour through the Southern counties of England and Wales London (Second hand) 8ᵛᵒ

Young's France, 2 vol 8ᵛᵒ Dublin"

I send you by post the most recent Philadelphia directory, price 1.25. A volume of the dictionary will follow it by the next post. Your orders will always be faithfully executed

  With profound respect I am
  your very devoted servant   N. G. DUFIEF

RC (DLC); endorsed by TJ as received 20 July 1813 and so recorded in SJL. Translation by Dr. Genevieve Moene.

Dufief had access to the following OUVRAGES by Arthur Young: *The Farmer's Tour through the East of England*, 4 vols. (London, 1771); *A Six Months Tour through the North of England*, 4 vols. (London, 1770); *The Farmer's Calendar: containing the Business Necessary to be Performed on Various Kinds of Farms during Every Month of the Year*, 8th ed.

(London, 1809); *A Six Weeks Tour, through the Southern Counties of England and Wales* (London, 1768); and *Travels during the Years 1787, 1788 and 1789, Undertaken more particularly with a View of ascertaining the Cultivation, Wealth, Resources, and National Prosperity, of the Kingdom of France*, 2 vols. (Dublin, 1793; Sowerby, no. 744).

¹ Omitted closing quotation mark editorially supplied.

To John Graham

DEAR SIR   Monticello July 11. 13.

Your favor of the 28ᵗʰ was recieved on the 2ᵈ instant, and the busy season of the harvest in which we are still engaged, leaving me only this day (Sunday) to answer it, must apologise for the delay. I have had too many proofs of your kind attention to my foreign letters to doubt it in the case of Madᵉ de Staehl. the channel which you suggest, of sending it under cover to mr Speyer thro' the Russian Minister appears to me liable to less risk than thro' mr Russell, who will be liable to be taken by the English. it is the more proper it should go through mr Speyer because he forwarded the letter from Madᵉ de Staehl to which mine is an answer. I presume the British would not violate the Russian minister's packet, and if the Russian Post office should open it, no harm can ensue. We are all anxious to hear of the President's recovery. every one is sensible that the safety of the nation depends on his life Accept the assurances of my great esteem & respect.

                                              TH: JEFFERSON

P.S. the Secretary of State was so kind as to send me from the Superfluous stores of the Dep^t of State,
reports of the patents for inventions from 1790—to 1804.
1812—to 1813
would it be possible to spare a copy of those from 1805—to 1811.

PoC (DLC); at foot of text: "Mr John Graham"; endorsed by TJ.

André Daschkoff was the RUSSIAN MINISTER plenipotentiary to the United States. From SECRETARY OF STATE James Monroe, TJ had received two REPORTS OF THE PATENTS: *Letter from the Secretary of State Accompanied with a List of the Names of Persons who have Invented any New and Useful Art, Machine, Manufacture or Composition of Matter, or any Improvement Thereon, and to whom Patents have Issued for the Same, from the Office of the Department of State* (Washington, 1805; reprinted in *List of Patents,* 4–48) and *Letter from the Secretary of State, Transmitting a List of the Names of Persons to whom Patents have been Issued for any New or Useful Art, Machine, Manufacture or Composition of Matter, or any Improvement thereon, from January 1, 1812, to January 1, 1813* (Washington, 1813; reprinted in *List of Patents,* 107–30; Poor, *Jefferson's Library,* 6 [no. 224]).

From Randolph Jefferson

DEAR BROTHER   July 11 1813
I have sent the girl by Squire and hope she will answer to learn and should of sent her before but we have bin so very busy a bout my wheat that I could not spare a hand out of the field to bring her & would be very much oblige to you to put her under one of the grone hands to keep her in good order I suppose we may send for her in three or four weaks I would be glad you would let us know whether you Can come by we are all well heare my wife Joins me in love to the family
I am Dr brother your most affectionately . . . —

RH JEFFERSON

RC (ViU: TJP-CC); ellipsis in original; endorsed by TJ as received 11 July 1813 from Snowden and so recorded in SJL.

The GIRL was Randolph Jefferson's slave Fanny.

To Benjamin Romaine

SIR   Monticello July 11. 13.
Your favor of June 23. was duly recieved, & in that the Oration you were so kind as to forward me. the sentiments it expresses are worthy

of a souldier of 1776. and of a society uniformly distinguished by it's zeal for the republican principles of our constitution. so long as sentiments like these prevail, we need not fear the opposition either of the old, or the new school of tories, who array themselves against us, either from their inveterate love of monarchy, or the wish to yoke us again to the British car. Accept the assurance of my great respect

TH: JEFFERSON

RC (ViU: TJP); at foot of text: "Dr Benj. Romayne." PoC (DLC); endorsed by TJ.

To Richard Rush

DEAR SIR   Monticello July 11. 13.

I have duly recieved your favor of June 27. and in that mine of Jan. 21 1812. I pray you to present my high respects to mrs Rush your mother, and my thanks for the trouble she has been so kind as to take in searching for the two letters specified in my former one, as well as to your brother.

I have no doubt that those two letters were of the number of those which mrs Rush mentions to have been burnt by Doct^r Rush. it is an additional proof of his great delicacy in a confidence of that nature. but even if they still exist I am perfectly satisfied of their safety in his family.

We are all anxious to hear of the President's entire recovery. the welfare & even the safety of so many millions depend on his life. Accept the assurances of my great respect & esteem

TH: JEFFERSON

PoC (MHi); at foot of text: "Richard Rush esq."; endorsed by TJ.

From John Adams

DEAR SIR   Quincy July 12. 1813

I forgot in my last to remark, a very trifling Inaccuracy in yours of June 27th. The Letter intercepted in Hichbournes Trunk which was reported to glance at Mr Dickenson, was not in 1776. It was in the month of June 1775. Had it been June 1776, the English would not have printed it. The Nation had then too maturely reflected, on the necessity of Independence, and was too ripe and too hot for a Proclamation of it. Neither Mr Dickenson, nor any of his Friends would have dared to express the Smallest resentment of it, out of their own gloomy circles. The Penns the Allens the Chews and the Willings, in other Words the Proprietary Gentlemen of Pensilvania, I mean those of them who had not ran away to the English, would have been Silent. The Quakers instead of producing my Letters and reading and recording them in their General Meeting, and holding me up to the detestation of their whole Society as the most odious of Men aiming, or at least having in contemplation the Possibility of Independence in any case whatsoever: would have concealed and dissimulated their hypocritical cant. The Pembertons, (even Israel,) the Drinkers, the Shoemakers and all the rest would have been Silent. The Spirit would not have moved one of them, to open his Lips.

In June 1776, my Friends would not have put on, long faces, and lamented my imprudence. None of them would have wondered, as Some of them did in 1775, that a Man of Forty years of Age, and of considerable Experience in business, and in life Should have been guilty of Such an Indiscretion. Others would not have Said "it was a premature declaration of Independence,"[1] and Joseph Reed Soon afterwards private Secretary of General Washington, and after that Governor of Pennsilvania, would not have Said to me, as he did, "I look upon the Interception and publication of that Letter, as an Act of the Providence of God, to excite the Attention of the people to their real Situation, and to Shew them, what they must come to."

you Say, "it has been hoped, I would leave such explanations as would place every Saddle on its right Horse, and replace on the Shoulders of[2] others, the burthens they Shifted on yours."

Hoped! by whom? They know not what they hope? I have already "replaced on the Shoulders of"[3] Franklin, burthens he Shifted on mine. Shall I "replace on the Shoulders of"[4] Washington the burthens that a bastard Bratt of a Scotch Pedlar, placed on his Shoulders, and he Shifted on mine?

How many Gauntletts, am I destined to run? How many Martyrdoms must I Suffer?

Be they more or less, I have enjoyed a happy Life, and I would not exchange Life, Character or Fortune with any of them.

There are few Men now living if any[5] who know more of me than you do. Yet you know but little of the Life I have led; the hazards I have run, or the "light Afflictions for a moment" I have endured.

I will conclude this grave Solemn Letter, with a merry Story: but as true as it is diverting.

In my youth I was acquainted, with one of our New England

Nobility, Representative, Counsellor, Colonel, Judge, John Chandler of Worcester, of whom I could tell you, twenty, humerous and instructive Anecdotes. He was a good, tho a rapid and free Character. He had great Influence in our Legislature, Upon Some occasion there was a complaint against him As a Justice of the Peace, in the County of Worcester. He arrived in Boston[6] and the Counsell Sent for him, and interrogated him and threatened him. When he came down from the Counsell Chamber, one of his Brother Representatives asked him, "what can the matter be?" "God damn them" Said Chandler, "they talk of uncreating their Creator."

If you do not understand this, and wish an explanation you Shall have it.

Not to Say too much at once. JOHN ADAMS

RC (DLC); at foot of text: "President Jefferson"; endorsed by TJ as received 21 July 1813 and so recorded in SJL. FC (Lb in MHi: Adams Papers).

For Adams's INTERCEPTED letter of 24 July 1775 (not THE MONTH OF JUNE), see note to TJ to Adams, 27 June 1813. Over a three-year period beginning in 1809, Adams published a series of newspaper essays justifying his career and attempting to correct the public record on Benjamin FRANKLIN, among others (*Boston Patriot*, esp. 15 May 1811). BASTARD BRATT OF A SCOTCH PEDLAR: Alexander

Hamilton. LIGHT AFFLICTIONS: Adams is quoting the Bible, 2 Corinthians 4.17, "For our light affliction, which is but for a moment, worketh for us a far more exceeding and eternal weight of glory."

[1] Omitted closing quotation mark editorially supplied.
[2] Manuscript: "of of."
[3] Omitted closing quotation mark editorially supplied.
[4] Omitted closing quotation mark editorially supplied.
[5] Preceding two words interlined.
[6] Preceding two words interlined.

To Randolph Jefferson

DEAR BROTHER Monticello July 12. 13.

Your's is recieved by Squire, and the girl begins this morning the first necessary branch, which is roving, or spinning into candlewick to prepare it for the spinning Jenny.[1] this will take her some days, more or less, according to her aptness, and then she will commence on the Jenny. as she appears rather young, it will probably take her a month or 6. weeks to learn well enough to be relied on for carrying it on herself where she can have no further instruction. however I will by any opportunity which occurs let you know her progress and when you may send for her. it will be near a month before I shall be able to set out for Bedford, and uncertain whether I can go by Snowden or not; but if I do not, I will certainly return by there, and the machine will go to you at the same time; about which time I imagine it will be best that your girle should meet it there, continuing to spin here till then, that she may be more perfect. with affectionate salutations to my sister and yourself accept my Adieux. TH: JEFFERSON

PoC (ViU: TJP-CC); at foot of text: "Randolph Jefferson esq."; endorsed by TJ.

Fanny was the GIRL. MY SISTER: Mitchie Pryor Jefferson.

[1] Word interlined.

From John Adams

DEAR SIR   Quincy July 13th 1813

Let me allude, to one circumstance more, in one of your Letters to me, before I touch upon the Subject of Religion in your Letters to Priestley.

The first time, that you and I differed in Opinion on any material Question; was after your arrival from Europe; and that point was the french Revolution.

you was well persuaded in your own mind that the Nation would Succeed in establishing a free Republican Goverment: I was as well persuaded, in mine, that a project of Such a Government, over five and twenty millions people, when four and twenty millions and five hundred thousands of them could neither write nor read: was as unnatural irrational and impracticable; as it would be over the Elephants Lions Tigers Panthers Wolves and Bears in the Royal Menagerie, at Versailles. Napoleon has lately invented a Word, which perfectly expresses my opinion at that time and ever Since. He calls the Project Ideology. And John Randolph, tho he was 14 years ago, as wild an Enthusiast for Equality and Fraternity, as any of them;[1] appears to be now[2] a regenerated Proselite to Napoleons opinion and mine, that it was all madness.

The Greeks in their allegorical Style Said that the two Ladies Αριστοκρατια and δημοκρατια,[3] always in a quarrel, disturbed every neigbourhood with their brawls. It is a fine Observation of yours that "Whig and Torey belong to Natural History."[4] Inequalities of Mind and Body are So established by God Almighty in his constitution of Human Nature that no Art or policy can ever plain them down to a Level. I have never read Reasoning more[5] absurd, Sophistry more gross, in proof of the Athanasian Creed, or Transubstantiation, than the subtle labours of Helvetius and Rousseau to demonstrate the natural Equality of Mankind. Jus cuique; the golden rule; do as you would be done by; is all the Equality that can be Supported or defended by reason, or reconciled to common Sense.

It is very true, as you justly observe, I can Say nothing new on this or any other Subject of Government. But when LaFayette harrangued you and me, and John Quincy Adams, through a whole evening in your Hotel in the Cul de Sac, at Paris; and develloped the plans then in operation to reform France: though I was as silent as you was, I then thought I could Say Something new to him: In plain Truth I was astonished at the Grossness of his Ignorance of Goverment and History, as I had been for years before at that of Turgot, Rochefaucault, Condorcet and Franklin. This gross Ideology of them all, first Suggested to me the thought and the inclination which I afterwards hinted to you[6] in London, of writing Something upon Aristocracy. I was restrained for years, by many fearful considerations. Who and what was I,?[7] A Man of no name or consideration in Europe. The manual Exercise of writing was painful and distressing to me, almost like a blow, on[8] the elbow or the knee; my Style was habitually negligent, unstudied, unpolished; I should make Enemies of all the French Patriots, the Dutch Patriots, the English Republicans, Dissenters, Reformers, call them what you will; and what came nearer home to my bosom than all the rest, I knew, I Should give offence to many, if not all of my best Friends in America, and very probably destroy all the little Popularity I ever had, in a Country where Popularity had more omnipotence than the British Parliament assumed. where Should I get the necessary Books? What Printer or Bookseller would undertake to print Such hazardous Writings?

But when the French Assembly of Notables met, and I Saw that Turgots "Government in one Centre and that Center the Nation" a Sentence as misterious or as contradictory as the Athanasian Creed, was about to take place; and when I Saw that Shaises Rebellion was breaking out in Massachusetts, and when I Saw that even my obscure Name was often quoted in France as an Advocate for Simple Democracy; when I Saw that the Sympathies in America had caught the French flame: I was determined to wash my own hands as clean as I could of all this foulness. I had then Strong forebodings that I was Sacrificing all the honours and Emoluments of this Life; and So it has happened: but not in so great a degree as I apprehended.

In Truth my "defence of the Constitutions"[9] and "Discourses on Davila," laid the foundation of that immense Unpopularity,[10] which fell like the Tower of Siloam upon me. your Steady defence of democratical Principles, and your invariable favourable opinion of the french Revolution laid the foundation of your unbounded Popularity.

Sic transit Gloria Mundi.

Now, I will forfeit my Life, if you can find one Sentence in my Defence of the Constitutions, or the Discourses on Davila, which by a fair construction, can favour the introduction of hereditary Monarchy or Aristocracy into America.

They were all written to Support and Strengthen the Constitutions of the United States.

The woodcutter on Ida, though he was puzzled to find a Tree to chop, at first, I presume knew how to leave off, when he was weary; But I never know when to cease, when I begin to write to you

JOHN ADAMS

RC (DLC); at foot of text: "President Jefferson"; endorsed by TJ as received 23 July 1813 and so recorded in SJL. FC (Lb in MHi: Adams Papers).

Αριστοκρατια AND δημοκρατια: "aristocracy and democracy." JUS CUIQUE: "justice for everyone." In a 1778 letter to Richard Price, Anne Robert Jacques Turgot contrasted his vision for GOVERNMENT IN ONE CENTRE with the division of powers finding favor in American constitutions. Adams disagreed emphatically with Turgot (Gustav Schelle, *Œuvres de Turgot et Documents Le Concernant* [1972], 5:532–40; Zoltán Haraszti, *John Adams & the Prophets of Progress* [1952; repr. 1964], 139–54). The collapse of the

TOWER OF SILOAM is mentioned in the Bible, Luke 13.4.

[1] Preceding four words interlined.

[2] Word interlined.

[3] RC and FC: "Αριϛτοϲρατια and δημοϲατια."

[4] Adams is here quoting from TJ's letter to him of 27 June 1813.

[5] FC: "so."

[6] Preceding three words not in FC.

[7] FC here adds "Why."

[8] RC: "on on."

[9] Omitted closing quotation mark editorially supplied.

[10] RC: "Unpopulaty." FC: "unpopularity."

To James Barbour

DEAR SIR   Monticello July 13. 13.

I think you cannot be unacquainted with old mr Strode of the county adjoining to yours, with his former fortunes, and the misfortunes perhaps by which he has lost them. his qualifications for business too are generally known. he is now in indigence, and want. how this happens while his son is otherwise I know not. I have recieved a letter from him, by which I find he wishes for some employment which would give him bread in return for industry. I have no doubt that his talents and integrity might be made serviceable to the public in some place. the army, particularly the Commisary & Q. M's departments, the foundery, the Armoury the Penitentiary[1] might certainly make him useful. I have known him[2] long, and am firmly persuaded that any emploiment analogous to his talents would be fulfilled with skill & fidelity, and I have thought I should render a public service in giving you an opportunity of engaging him in some business for the public. I do this on my own motion only his letter authorising no such application; but rendering it presumable he would undertake any service, primary or secondary which would subsist him. excuse me for a suggestion which I make merely because you may find some occasion of using it for the good of the public as well as of a worthy individual, and be assured of my great esteem & respect   TH: JEFFERSON

RC (Vi: RG 3, Governor's Office, Letters Received); addressed: "His Excellency Governor Barbour Richmond"; franked; postmarked Milton, 17 July; endorsed by Barbour. PoC (DLC); endorsed by TJ.

SJL records a missing letter of 4 June 1813 from TJ to Barbour's brother Philip Pendleton Barbour.

[1] Preceding two words interlined.
[2] Word interlined.

From Mathew Carey

SIR,   Philad[a] July 13. 1813
   Your favour of the 19th ult. (which I rec[d] only the 3[d] inst.) was handed to M[r] Clarke, who detained it several days; which prevented its being answered in due course.
   For the various valuable suggestions it contains for the improvement of the Naval History, accept my sincere acknowledgments. M[r] Clarke promise[s] to pay due attention to them. Should any thing further occur on the subject, have the goodness to communicate it, which shall be regarded as an additional favour conferred upon
      your ob[t] h[ble] serv[t]   MATHEW CAREY

RC (MHi); edge trimmed; dateline at foot of text; at head of text: "His Excellency Thomas Jefferson, Esq[r]"; endorsed by TJ as received 22 July 1813 and so recorded in SJL.

To James Madison

DEAR SIR   Monticello July 13. 13.
   I was so unlucky as to write you a long letter of business, when, as I learned soon afterwards, you were too ill to be troubled with any

matter of business. my comfort has been in the confidence that care would of course be taken not to disturb you with letters. my hope in writing the present is of a pleasanter kind, the flattering one that you are entirely recovered. if the prayers of millions have been of avail, they have been poured forth with the deepest anxiety. the inclosed letter from mr Fulton will inform you why a similar one did not go to you direct, and that this is forwarded by express desire. mr Fulton's ingenuity is inexhaustible, and his disinterested devotion of it to his country very laudable. if his present device depended on me I should try it, on the judgment of an officer so well skilled as Decatur. it is one of those experiments which neither the personal interest nor the faculties of a private individual can ever bring into use, while it is highly interesting to the nation. intersected as we are by many and deep waters, and unable to meet the enemy on them with an equal force, our only hope is in the discovery of the means which ingenuity may[1] devise whereby the weak may defend themselves against the strong. this is done at land by fortifications, and, not being against any law of nature, we may hope that something equivalent may be discovered for the water.

You know the present situation of our friend Strode, entirely penniless. how he comes to be left to subsist himself by his labours in subordinate emploiments, while his son is at his ease, I am not informed; nor whether they have had any difference. yet the fact is that he is in indigence, and anxious to get his living by any services he can render. you know his qualifications. the public iron works, the Armoury, the Army or some of the sedentary offices at Washington may perhaps offer some employment analogous to his talents. his wish is to earn a livelihood; and altho' in his letter to me he does not propose to sollicit any thing, yet the expressions of his situation shew that some decent emploiment could not fail to be very acceptable.

We are at the close of the poorest harvest I have ever seen. I shall not carry into my barn more than one third of an ordinary crop. but one rain to wet the ground since April. a remarkeable drying wind with great heats the first days of the harvest dryed up the stem of the wheat so that it fell before the scythe instead of being cut. I have seen harvests lost by wet, but never before saw one lost by dry weather. I have suffered more by the drought than my neighbors. most of them will make half a crop; some two thirds. much of the evil had been prepared by the winter and the fly. it is not too late yet for the corn to recover should there come rains shortly. it never was seen so low before at this date. our gardens are totally burnt up: and the river so low that you may almost jump over it in some places. Wishing a speedy and perfect reestablishment of your health I pray you to accept the assurance of my constant & affectionate esteem & respect

Th: Jefferson

RC (DLC: Madison Papers, Rives Collection). PoC (DLC); at foot of first page: "President Madison"; endorsed by TJ. Enclosure: Robert Fulton to TJ, 29 June 1813.

[1] TJ here canceled "furnish."

From Rembrandt Peale

DEAR SIR   Philadᵃ July 13. 1813,

In a Box of Books which general Armstrong presented to the Pennsylvania Academy of Fine-Arts there were packed up several articles belonging to himself which he requested me to take charge of, It was a long time after I had them before I remarked a small package for you, containing 3 Stones which you were desirous of possessing, accompanied with a letter from the gentleman who purchased them for you. The small piece which he mentions having cemented, I found again loose—but no other damage. Dʳ marks & afterwards a near neighbour of yours promised to take charge of them but they failed giving me notice of their departure, and I now remit them by Mʳ Correa for whom they have been long waiting.

Having purchased the museum in Baltimore, I mean to form a handsome establishment in that City, the general plan of which will differ from my fathers museum, it being my intention to render it more properly a museum of Arts & Sciences, and, without neglecting any branch of Natural History to bestow my chief attention to the formation of a Picture Gallery & Depository of the course and products of manufactures—

I still hope some fortunate leisure will enable me to pay a Visit to Monticello. In the meanwhile believe me Sir

Your friend Respectfully.   REMBRANDT PEALE

RC (MHi); endorsed by TJ as received 1 Aug. 1813 and so recorded (as delivered "by Mʳ Correa de Serra") in SJL. Enclosure: Claude Antoine Prieur Duvernois to TJ, 5 Sept. 1810.

In 1813 Peale PURCHASED the collection formerly exhibited by James Savage as the Baltimore New Museum and, later, by Caleb Boyle as the Baltimore Permanent Museum (Peale, *Papers*, 3:170n, 344).

Peale's undated "Prospectus of a Museum of Arts and Sciences, to be established in Baltimore," a copy of which came into TJ's possession at some point, laments that, "except in the capital cities of Europe, the inquisitive mind labours under the want" of instruction; suggests that institutions displaying "Natural and

Artificial objects" scientifically are exceeded in importance only by public libraries; states that museums provide "a School of universal Knowledge" and "the means of rational Amusement, even to the most idle"; and proposes, with the aid of liberal patrons, to form such a repository, containing "Pictures, Statues, Birds, Beasts, Fishes, Insects, Shells, Plants, Minerals, Philosophical, Mechanical, Agricultural and Commercial objects of demonstration" (printed circular in DLC: TJ Papers, 228:40745–6; addressed in an unidentified hand: "Edward Johnson Esq.").

To John Strode

DEAR SIR   Monticello July 13. 1813.

I duly recieved your favor of June 25th. I had before heard of the unfortunate turn of your affairs, but did not know your losses had been so entire as to leave you wholly dependant on your personal industry and at this age. it is a consolation that you have always possessed the resources of talent, industry, & integrity, and that at your age you have still health to use them efficiently in any business. I have seen the day when, if offered, they would have been gladly engaged in something for the public good; and knowing that the Executives of the Union & of the State have equal anxieties to have the public trusts ably and faithfully discharged, I have taken the liberty, in my own name, & without your authority, to indicate to them, when they shall be at a loss for a faithful agent, (as I have often been) where they may seek one whose qualifications they both personally know. I sincerely wish such an occasion may occur for your comfortable situation as well as for the public benefit; being ever with particular esteem & respect

Your friend & serv^t   TH: JEFFERSON

PoC (MHi); at foot of text: "John Strode esq."; endorsed by TJ.

TJ wrote this day on Strode's behalf to President James Madison and Governor James Barbour, the EXECUTIVES OF THE UNION & OF THE STATE.

To Samuel Brown

DEAR SIR   Monticello July 14. 13.

Your favors of May 25. and June 13. have been duly recieved as also the 1st supply of Capsicum, and the 2d of the same article with other seeds. I shall set great store by the Capsicum if it is hardy enough for our climate the species we have heretofore tried, being too tender. the Galavanic too will be particularly attended to, as it appears very different from what we cultivate by that name. I have so many grand children & others who might be endangered by the poison plant, that I think the risk[1] over balances the curiosity of trying it. the most elegant thing of that kind known is a preparation of the Jamestown weed, Datura-Stramonium, invented by the French in the time of Robespierre. every man of firmness carried it constantly in his pocket to anticipate the Guillotine.[2] it brings on the sleep of death as quietly as fatigue does the ordinary sleep, without the least struggle or motion. Condorcet, who had recourse to it was found lifeless on his bed, a few minutes after his land lady had left him there, and even the slipper which she had observed half suspended on his foot, was not shaken off. it seems far preferable to the venesection of the Romans, the Hemlock of the Greeks, and the Opium of the Turks. I have never been able to learn what the preparation is, other than a strong concentration of it's lethiferous principle. could such a medicament be restrained to self-administration, it ought not to be kept secret. there are ills in life, as desperate as intolerable, to which it would be the rational relief: e.g. the inveterate cancer. as a relief from tyranny indeed, for which the Romans recurred to it in the times of the emperors, it has been a wonder to me that they did not consider a poignard in the breast of the tyrant as a better remedy.

I am sorry to learn that a banditti from our country, are taking part in the domestic contests of the country adjoining you: and the more so as from the known laxity of execution in our laws they cannot be punished, altho the law has provided punishment. it will give a wrongful hue to the rightful act of taking possession of Mobile and will be imputed to the national authority as Miranda's enterprize was, because not punished by it. I fear too that the Spaniards are too heavily oppressed by ignorance & superstition for self-government, and whether a change from foreign to domestic despotism will be to their advantage remains to be seen.

We have been unfortunate in our first military essays by land. our men are good, but our generals unqualified. every failure we have incurred has been the fault of the general, the men evincing courage in every instance. at sea we have rescued our character; but the chief fruit of our victories there is to prove to those who have fleets that the English are not invincible at sea, as Alexander has proved that Bonaparte is not invincible by land. how much to be lamented that the world cannot unite and destroy these two land and sea-monsters! the one drenching the earth with human gore, the other ravaging the ocean with lawless piracies and plunder. Bonaparte will die, and the nations of Europe will recover their independance with, I hope, better governments. but the English government never dies, because their king is no part of it. he is a mere formality, and the real government in the aristocracy of the country, for their house of commons is of that class. their aim is to claim the dominion of the ocean by conquest, and to make every vessel navigating it pay a tribute to the support of the fleet necessary to maintain that dominion, to which their own resources are inadequate. I see no means of terminating their maritime dominion & tyranny but in their own bankruptcy which I hope is approaching. but I turn from these painful contemplations to the more pleasing one of my constant friendship & respect for you.

Th: Jefferson

PoC (DLC); at foot of first page: "Doct^r Saml Brown."

GALAVANIC: garavance; garbanzo or chickpea (Betts, *Garden Book*, 527). LETHIFEROUS: deadly (*OED*). POIGNARD: "poniard." For the operations of the BANDITTI of the American Southwest and the seizure of Mobile by forces under the command of General James

Wilkinson, see Stagg, *Borderlines in Borderlands*, 131, 134–68. For Francisco de Miranda's 1806 ENTERPRIZE against Spanish control of Venezuela, see TJ to Valentín de Foronda, 4 Oct. 1809, and note.

[1] TJ here interlined and canceled "of it outdist."

[2] TJ here canceled "it extinguishes."

To Patrick Gibson

Dear Sir   Monticello July 14. 13.

Mr Edmund Randolph's indisposition has probably prevented as yet his attendance at his court to acknolege and forward the deed for mr Mazzei's lot. the first court of Albemarle after he shall have forwarded it to me, it shall be dispatched. I presume that the deed having been actually executed, as before advised, the delay of the formality of acknolegement will occasion no hesitation in mr Taylor as to the first paiment to be made on the 17th instant.

The present difficulties of the sea, of intercourse and exchange between nations would prevent my attempting to hazard a remittance to Italy, but under the special directions of mr Mazzei, were it certain he would wish to have his money there rather than here. but I think he will prefer it's remaining here at our interest of 6. percent which is so much more than it would yield him there. it is not long since he consulted me on the best mode of transferring his whole property hither, under contemplation of reestablishing[1] his family here.

I shall immediately write to him and take his directions on the subject. in the mean time it may be as well employed for your relief from responsibility by taking up my note at the bank, which has remained there so much longer than my expectations. it will spare me too the renewals so frequently recurring, and only transfer my paiments of interest from the bank to mr Mazzei. the surplus beyond the amount of the note will be a seasonable aid to the deficiencies occasioned by the short sales of my flour. engagements made on confidence of the usual proceeds from that fund, press on me disagreeably; insomuch that I should be obliged to apply mr Taylor's <u>first</u> paiment to these, and reserve the two last only for taking up the note. I will thank you therefore for information the moment of the 1st paiment that I may at once relieve the distress of several persons who have been waiting with me, to their own inconvenience, until my flour could be sold. I defer till then also the notification of the transaction to mr Mazzei. Accept the assurance of my great esteem & respect.

TH: JEFFERSON

PoC (DLC); at foot of first page: "Mr Gibson." Recorded in SJL as a letter to Gibson & Jefferson.

Philip Mazzei advised TJ of his inter-

est in REESTABLISHING HIS FAMILY in Albemarle County in his letter of 15 Feb. 1811.

¹ Prefix interlined.

From Patrick Gibson

SIR   Richmond 14th July 1813

I am sorry to inform you that it has not yet been in my power to sell your flour I do not know what price could be obtain'd for it were it put up to the highest bidder but it has been and is offering at $4 without a purchaser; be pleased to say whether I shall dispose of it at such a price as I can obtain or wait some favorable change m^r Taylor has lodged $6,000 in my hands on account of the purchase of mazzei's property, the discount on which will be deducted from the balance that may still be due—he desired I would inform you that a Frenchman who married m^r mazzei's daughter had called upon him for the purpose of giving him due notice, that he should claim from him the property in question by virtue of a marriage contract, provided it should hereafter appear that Mr Mazzei was dead at the date of the deed, and requests you will retain the money in your hands until this fact shall be ascertained—With great respect I am

Yours &c   PATRICK GIBSON

RC (MHi); at head of text: "Mr Thomas Jefferson"; endorsed by TJ as received 16 July 1813 and so recorded in SJL.

Peter Derieux was the FRENCHMAN WHO MARRIED MR MAZZEI'S stepdaughter Maria Margherita Martin Derieux.

From John Adams, with Postscript by Abigail Adams

Quincy July 15th 1813

Never mind it, my dear Sir, if I write four Letters to your one: your one is worth more than my four.

It is true that I can Say and have Said nothing new on the Subject of Government. yet I did Say in my Defence and in my Discourses on Davila, though in an uncouth Style, what was new to Lock, to Harrington, to Milton, to Hume[1] to Montesquieu to Reauseau, to Turgot, Condorcet, to Rochefaucault, to Price to Franklin and to yourself; and at that time to almost all Europe and America. I can prove all this by indisputable Authorities and documents. Writings on Government had been not only neglected, but discountenanced and discouraged, throughout all Europe, from the Restoration of Charles the Second in England, till the french Revolution commenced. The English Commonwealth, the Fate of Charles 1st and the military despotism of Cromwell had Sickened Mankind with disquisitions on Government to Such a degree, that there was Scarcely a Man in Europe who had looked into the Subject. David Hume had made himself, So fashionable[2] with the Aid of the Court and Clergy, Atheist as they call'd him,[3] and by his elegant Lies against the Republicans and gaudy daubings of the Courtiers, that he had nearly laughed into contempt Rapin Sydney and even Lock. It was ridiculous and even criminal in almost all Europe to Speak of Constitutions, or Writers upon the Principles or the Fabricks of them.

In this State of Things my poor, unprotected, unpatronised Books appeared; and met with a Fate, not quite So cruel as I had anticipated. They were At last however[4] overborne by Misrepresentations and will perish in obscurity, though they have been translated into German as well as french. The three Emperors of Europe, the Prince Regents, and all the ruling Powers would no more countenance[5] or tolerate Such Writings, than the Pope, the Emperor of Haiti, Ben. Austin or Tom Paine.

The Nations of Europe, appeared to me, when I was among them, from the begining of 1778, to 1785 i.e to the commencement of the Troubles in France, to be advancing by Slow but Sure Steps towards an Amelioration of the condition of Man, in Religion and Government, in Liberty, Equality, Fraternity Knowledge Civilization and Humanity. The French Revolution I dreaded; because I was Sure it would, not only arrest the progress of Improvement, but give it a retrograde course, for at least a Century, if not many Centuries. The French Patriots appeared to me, like young Schollars from a Colledge, or Sailors flushed with recent pay or prize Money, mounted on wild Horses, lashing and Spurring, till they would kill the Horses and break their own Necks.

Let me now ask you, very Seriously my Friend, Where are now in 1813, the Perfection and perfectability of human Nature? Where is now, the progress of the human Mind? Where is the Amelioration of Society? Where the Augmentations of human Comforts? Where the diminutions of human Pains and Miseries? I know not whether the last day of D^r young can exhibit; to a Mind unstaid by Phylosophy and Religion, for I hold there can be no Philosophy without Religion; more terrors than the present State of the World.

When? Where? and how? is the present Chaos to be arranged into order?

There is not, there cannot be, a greater Abuse of Words than to call the Writings of Calender, Paine, Austin and Lowell or the Speeches of Ned. Livingston and John Randolph, Public Discussions. The Ravings and Rantings of Bedlam, merit the Character as well; and yet Joel Barlow was about to record Tom Paine as the great Author of the American Revolution! If he was; I desire that my name may be blotted out forever, from its Records.

You and I, ought not to die, before We have explained ourselves to each other.

I Shall come to the Subject of Religion, by and by.　　　your Friend　　　　　　　　　　　　　　　　　JOHN ADAMS.

I have been looking for some time for a space in[6] my good Husbands Letters to add the regards,[7] of an old Friend, which are Still cherished and perserved through all the changes and vissitudes which have taken place since we first became acquainted, and will I trust remain as long as　　　　　　　　　　　　A ADAMS.

RC (DLC); at foot of text: "President Jefferson"; endorsed by TJ as a letter from John Adams received 28 July 1813 and so recorded in SJL. FC (Lb in MHi: Adams Papers); lacks Abigail Adams postscript.

Abigail Smith Adams (1744–1818), noted letter writer and first lady of the United States, 1797–1801, was born in Weymouth, Massachusetts, to William Smith, a Congregationalist minister, and Elizabeth Quincy Smith. Both the custom of the day and her own delicate health restricted her education to her parents' and grandparents' homes. Nonetheless, with the aid of educated relatives and a well-stocked library she became well versed in literature and history. In 1759 she met John Adams. After a long-distance epistolary courtship, the couple married in 1764. Four of their five children survived to adulthood, including future United States president John Quincy Adams. During her husband's long absences as he attended to public duties, Adams adroitly managed a household and farm on her own, even during the tumultuous years of the American Revolution. She joined her husband in Paris in 1784 and subsequently traveled with him to London, New York, Philadelphia, and Washington before they retired to Quincy in 1801. Adams's extensive correspondence with her family and such others as Mercy Otis Warren and TJ attest to her political acumen and keen interest in the success of the American republic while also providing valuable and revealing details about daily life (*ANB*; *DAB*; Phyllis Lee Levin, *Abigail Adams: A Biography* [1987]; Edith Belle Gelles, *Portia: The World of Abigail Adams* [1992]; Margaret A. Hogan and C. James Taylor, eds., *My Dearest Friend: Letters of Abigail and John Adams* [2007]; Lyman H. Butterfield, Richard Alan Ryerson, C. James Taylor, and others, eds., *Adams Family Correspondence*, 8 vols. [1963–]; *PTJ*, 8:178–80; Peter Whitney, *A Sermon Delivered on the Lord's Day Succeeding the Interment of Madam Abigail Adams . . . November 1, 1818 . . . With an Appendix, Containing an Extract of a Letter, From President Jefferson, to President Adams, and Four Obituary Notices* [Boston, 1819]).

Edward YOUNG was the author of *Last Day. A Poem In Three Books* (Philadelphia, 1786). John LOWELL (1769–1840) was a Boston political writer closely associated with Timothy Pickering (*DAB*).

[1] Preceding two words interlined.
[2] Preceding two words interlined.
[3] Preceding five words interlined.
[4] RC: "hower." FC: "however."
[5] RC: "countenanc." FC: "countenance."
[6] Manuscript: "in in."
[7] Manuscript: "regades."

From John Adams

DEAR SIR   Quincy July 16. 1813

your Letters to Priestley, have encreased my Grief if that were possible, for the loss of Rush. Had he lived, I would have Stimulated him to insist on your promise to him to write him on the Subject of Religion. your Plan, I admire.

In your Letter to Priestley of March 21. 1801, dated at Washington you call "The Christian Philosophy, the most Sublime and benevolent, but the most perverted System that ever Shone on Man." That it is the most Sublime and benevolent, I agree, But whether it has been more perverted than that of Moses, of Confucius, of Zoroaster, of Sanchoniathan of Numa, of Mahomet of the Druids, of the Hindoos &c &c &c I cannot as yet determine;

because I am not sufficiently acquainted with those Systems or the History of their Effects to form a decisive opinion of the result of the Comparison.

In your Letter dated Washington April 9. 1803, you Say "In consequence of Some conversations with Dr Rush in the years 1798–99, I had promised Some day to write him a Letter giving him my View of the Christian System. I have reflected often on[1] it Since, and even Sketched the outlines in my own mind. I Should first take a general View of the moral doctrines of the most remarkable of the ancient Philosophers, of whose Ethicks We have Sufficient information to make an estimate; Say of Pythagoras, Epicurus, Epictetus Socrates, Cicero, Seneca, Antoninus. I Should do justice to the branches of Morality they have treated well, but point out the importance of those in which they are deficient. I Should then take a view of the Deism and Ethicks of the Jews, and Shew in what a degraded State they were, and the necessity they presented of a reformation. I Should proceed to a view of the Life, Character,[2] and doctrines of Jesus, who, Sensible of the incorrectness of their Ideas of the Deity, and of morality, endeavoured to bring them to the Principles of a pure Deism, and juster Notions of the Attributes of God; to reform their moral doctrines to the Standard of reason, justice and Philanthropy and to inculcate the belief of a future State. This View would purposely omit the question of his Divinity, and even of his Inspiration. To do him Justice, it would be necessary to remark the disadvantages his doctrines have to encounter, not having been committed to Writing by himself, but by the most unlettered of Men, by memory, long after they had heard them from him, when much was forgotten, much misunderstood, and presented in very paradoxical Shapes. yet Such are the fragments remaining, as to Show a master workman, and that his System of Morality was the most benevolent and Sublime, probably that has been ever taught, and more perfect than those of any of the ancient Philosophers. His Character and Doctrines, have received Still greater injury from those who pretend to be his Special Disciples, and who have disfigured and Sophisticated his Actions and precepts from views of personal interest, So as to induce the unthinking part of Mankind, to throw off the whole System in disgust, and to pass Sentence, as an Impostor, on the most innocent, the most benevolent, the most eloquent and Sublime Character, that ever has been exhibited to Man. This is the outline."!

"Sancte Socrate! ora pro nobis."! Erasmus.

Priestley in his Letter to Lindssey inclosing a Copy of your letter to him Says "He is generally considered as an Unbeliever: if So, however, he cannot be far from us, and I hope in the way to be not only almost, but altogether what We are. He now attends publick worship very regularly, and his moral Conduct was never impeached."

Now, I See not, but you are as good a Christian as Priestley and Lindsey. Piety and Morality were the End and Object of the Christian System according to them, and according to you. They believed in the Resurrection of Jesus, in his Miracles, and in his inspiration: but what inspiration? Not all that is recorded in the New Testament, nor the old. They have not yet told Us, how much they believe, nor how much, they doubt[3] or disbelieve. They have not told Us, how much Allegory how much Parable, they find, nor how they explain them all, in the old Testament or the new.

John Quincy Adams, has written for years, to his two Sons, Boys of 10 and 12, a Series of Letters, in which he pursues a plan more extensive than yours, but agreeing in most of the essential points. I wish these Letters could be preserved in the Bosoms of his Boys: but Women and Priests will get them: and I expect, if he makes a peace he will be obliged to retire like, a Jay to Study Prophecies to the End of his Life.

I have more to Say, upon this Subject of Religion.

JOHN ADAMS.

RC (DLC); at foot of text: "President Jefferson"; endorsed by TJ as received 28 July 1813 and so recorded in SJL. FC (Lb in MHi: Adams Papers); dated 17 July 1813.

SANCTE SOCRATE! ORA PRO NOBIS: "Saint Socrates! Pray for us" comes from Desiderius ERASMUS, "The Religious Treat" (Nathan Bailey, trans., *All the Familiar Colloquies of Desiderius Erasmus, of Rotterdam, Concerning Men, Manners, and Things, translated into English* [London, 1725], 119). The letters on religion from JOHN QUINCY ADAMS to his youthful sons are printed in Charles Francis Adams, ed., *Letters of Mrs. Adams, the Wife of John Adams*, 4th ed. (1848), 427–72, with the originals in MHi: Adams Papers.

[1] FC substitutes preceding two words for "upon."
[2] RC: "Charater." FC: "Character."
[3] Preceding five words not in FC.

From John Strode

Allum Spring Mills 17 July '13

Altho' I am well aware, that if every one to whom your beneficence have been extended, was to trespass on your Attention with equal professions of gratitude, it would have a Severe effect on your private Repose. Yet, good and benevolent Sir, notwithstanding that conviction, full at my Heart, I cannot for my life, Refrain from Acknowledgeing, the benignity of your inestimable favour of the 13th, this moment Rec[d]. Your condescending notice has inspired me with hopes of two important objects; One, is the prospect of being further usefull to my beloved country; the other is not less laudible, to gain Something by industry to discharge a few Small balances, yet unpaid. If Such be the will of propitious Heaven; bound as I now must be, under the Strongest of Additional obligations; Zealously and ardently devoted, no opportunity shall be lost, or in the least neglected, to perform the duties of Any Station, however humble, with which I may be honord. with every Sentiment of due Regard.

   I am worthy Sir

Your ever obliged hble Serv[t]   JOHN STRODE

The Governor of V[a] has often Spoke in terms of great kindness to me, good & kind as He is, how could I Shew his Letter to a personage, equally, or perhaps better, acquainted with me. I never tho[t] of Such a thing untill this morning. if I can muster presumption enough, I will go to the City.

RC (MHi); beneath postscript: "Thomas Jefferson esquire"; endorsed by TJ as received 21 July 1813 and so recorded in SJL.

James Barbour was the incumbent GOVERNOR OF V[A].

From John Adams

DEAR SIR   Quincy July 18th 1813

I have more to Say, on Religion. For more than Sixty years I have been attentive to this great Subject. Controversies, between Calvinists and Arminians, Trinitarians and Unitarians, Deists and Christians, Atheists and both, have attracted my Attention, whenever the Singular Life, I have lead would admit, to all these questions. The History of this little Village of Quincy, if it were worth recording would explain to you, how this happened. I think, I can now Say I have read away Bigotry, if not Enthusiasm.

what does Priestly mean, by an Unbeliever? when he applies it to you? How much, did he "unbelieve," himself?[1] Gibbon had him right, when he denominated his Creed, "Scanty." We are to understand, no doubt, that he believed The Resurrection of Jesus Some of his Miracles. His Inspiration, but in what degree? He did not believe in the Inspiration of the Writings that contain his History. yet he believed in the Apocalyptic Beast, and he believed as much as he pleased in the Writings of Daniel and John. This great, excellent[2] and extraordinary Man, whom I Sincerely loved esteemed and respected, was really a Phenomenon; a Comet in the System,[3] like Voltaire Bolingbroke and Hume. Had Bolingbroke or Voltaire taken him in hand, what would they have made of him and his Creed?

I do not believe you have read much of Priestleys "Corruptions of Christianity." His History of early opinions of Jesus Christ. His Predestination, his No Soul System or his Controversy with Horseley.

I have been a diligent Student for many years in Books whose Titles you have never Seen. In Priestleys and Lindsay writings; in Farmer, Cappe, in Tuckers or Edwards Searches, Light of Nature pursued; in Edwards and Hopkins. and lately in Ezra Styles Ely; his reverend and learned Panegyrists and his elegant and Spirited opponents. I am not wholly uninformed of the Controversies in Germany and the learned Researches of Universities and Professors; in which the Sanctity of the Bible and the Inspiration of its Authors are taken for granted or waived; or admitted, or not denied. I have also read Condorcets Progress of the human mind.

Now, what is all this to you? No more, than if I Should tell you that I read D[r] Clark and D[r] Waterland and Emlyn, and Lelands View or Review of the Deistical Writers more than fifty[4] years ago; which is a litteral Truth.

I blame you not for reading Euclid and Newton, Thucidides and Theocritus: for I believe you will find as much entertainment and Instruction in them as I have found, in my Theological and Ecclesiastical Instructors: or even as I have found in a profound Investigation of the Life Writings and Doctrines of Erastus, whose Disciples were Milton, Harrington, Selden, St. John, the Chief Justice, Father of Bolingbroke, and others the choicest Spirits of their Age: or in Le Harpes History of the Philosophy of the 18th Century, or in Van der Kemps vast Map of the Causes of the Revolutionary Spirit, in the Same & preceding[5] Centuries. These Things are to me, at present, the Marbles and Nine Pins of old Age: I will not Say the Beads and Prayer Books.

I agree with you, as far as you go. Most cordially and I think solidly. How much farther I go, how much more I believe than you, I may explain in a future Letter.

Thus much I will Say at present, I have found So many difficulties, that I am not astonished at your Stopping where you are. And So far from Sentencing you to Perdition, I hope Soon to meet you in another Country.   JOHN ADAMS

RC (DLC); at foot of text: "President Jefferson"; endorsed by TJ as received 28 July 1813 and so recorded in SJL. FC (Lb in MHi: Adams Papers).

TJ owned Joseph Priestley, *An History of the Corruptions of Christianity*, 2 vols. (London, 1793; Sowerby, no. 1526) and *An History of Early Opinions Concerning Jesus Christ, Compiled from Original Writers; Proving that the Christian Church was at First Unitarian*, 4 vols. (London, 1786; Sowerby, no. 1527). Priestley's NO SOUL SYSTEM was *Disquisitions Relating to Matter and Spirit. To Which is Added, The History of the Philosophical Doctrine concerning the Origin of the Soul, and the Nature of Matter* (London, 1777). His CONTROVERSY WITH HORSELEY was documented in *Letters to Dr. Horsley, in Answer to His Animadversions on the History of the Corruptions of Christianity. with Additional Evidence that the Primitive Christian Church was Unitarian* (Birmingham, 1783). LIGHT OF NATURE PURSUED: under the pseudonym of Edward Search, the English philosopher Abraham Tucker prepared *Light of Nature Pursued*, 3 vols. in 9 (London, 1768–77). The Congregationalist minister and philosopher Jonathan EDWARDS was the mentor and tutor of the theologian and reformer Samuel HOPKINS (*ANB*). In his library Adams had a copy of CONDORCETS *Outlines of an Historical view of the Progress of the Human Mind: being a posthumous work of the late M. De Condorcet* (London, 1795; for French editions owned by TJ, see Sowerby, no. 1247; Poor, *Jefferson's Library*, 13 [no. 829]). John Leland's VIEW OR REVIEW was *A View Of the Principal Deistical Writers that have Appeared in England in the last and present Century; with Observations upon them* (London, 1754). Oliver St. John, the CHIEF JUSTICE of England, 1648–60, was the great-grandfather, not the FATHER, of Henry St. John, viscount Bolingbroke (*ODNB*). A HISTORY OF THE PHILOSOPHY OF THE 18TH CENTURY was included in Jean François de La Harpe, *Lycée, ou Cours de Littérature Ancienne et Moderne*, 16 vols. (Paris, 1799–1805). Francis Adrian Van der Kemp enclosed a manuscript copy of his outline of a MAP OF THE CAUSES OF THE REVOLUTIONARY SPIRIT, not found, to Adams on 2 Dec. 1811, and he added a supplement on 20 May 1812 (MHi: Adams Papers). For texts of the synopsis and addendum that went to TJ, see Van der Kemp to TJ, 18 Feb. 1812, enclosure, and 14 Apr. 1812.

[1] Superfluous closing quotation mark editorially omitted.
[2] Word canceled in FC.
[3] RC: "Systom." FC: "system."
[4] FC: "58."
[5] RC: "preeceeding." FC: "preceding."

Agreement with William Ballard

William Ballard engages himself to serve Thomas Jefferson as an overseer at his place called Tufton during the year[1] ensuing, to commence the 1st day of December next[2] and faithfully to do his duty in that capacity: and the sd Thomas Jefferson agrees to find him six hundred weight of pork, corn bread sufficient for himself & family, and a barrel of flour, and moreover to allow him sixty five pounds as wages for the year, paiable on the sale of the crop of wheat or flour which shall be made by him. Witness their hands this 18th day of July 1813.

TH: JEFFERSON
WILLIAM BALLARD

MS (MHi); in TJ's hand, signed by TJ and Ballard; endorsed by TJ: "Ballard William"; with MS of Account with William Ballard, 20 Oct. 1815, subjoined.

William Ballard (ca. 1788–1874) served as overseer at Tufton for two years, 1813–15. He later farmed in Albemarle County (Account with Ballard, 20 Oct.

1815; *MB*, 2:1312; Woods, *Albemarle*, 140; DNA: RG 29, CS, Albemarle Co., 1850–70; Albemarle Co. Will Book, 29:3–5, 36; *Petersburg Index and Appeal*, 11 Feb. 1874).

[1] Blank in MS filled in by TJ with preceding two words in a different ink.
[2] Blank in MS filled in by TJ with preceding six words in a different ink.

From John G. Gamble

SIR. Richmond July 20th 1813

My apology for giving you the trouble of reading this letter, is, that I have purchased of Mr David Higgenbotham the lott conveyed to him by you.

In your deed of conveyance the lott is said to be bounded "on the North Western side, by the Common laid off as a road from Shockoe Warehouse to the[1] Wharf. The South Western side bounded by a Common towards the River." Both of these Commons, are claimed as individual property; but the claim upon that on the South Western side may be easily set aside.

The fact of the North Western side of the lott,[2] being, or not being, upon a Common, will make an incalculable difference in its value. The Common upon that side is claimed by Colo Jno Mayo, under a deed executed in 1781 by Colo Byrd to James Lyle. I understand that your purchase from the late Colo Byrd, was in 1774, but have not been able to find, in any of the offices kept in this City, a record of the deed to you, from Col° Byrd or his Trustee. If that deed shall prove to be of date prior to 1781, my right of Common will be established.

If it is within your recollection, I will esteem it a singular favor, that you inform me of the date of your deed, & where I will find it recorded.

Very respectfully Your Mo. Ob Servt   JOHN G GAMBLE

RC (MHi); between dateline and salutation: "Thos Jefferson Esq^e"; endorsed by TJ as received 27 July 1813 and so recorded in SJL.

John Grattan Gamble (1779–1852), merchant, banker, and planter, accompanied John Marshall on a diplomatic mission to Paris in 1797. He studied science at the College of New Jersey (later Princeton University) and was awarded an honorary certificate in 1801 and an honorary A.M. degree there three years later. In 1805 he entered into a mercantile partnership with his brother Robert Gamble in Richmond. John G. Gamble became a prominent businessman and civic leader, and he was one of four men who acted as bail bondsmen for Aaron Burr during the latter's 1807 treason trial. Gamble was also a superintendent of the new Farmers' Bank of Virginia in 1812 and was elected a director of that institution in 1816. He was first lieutenant of the Richmond Light Infantry Blues when the unit was mustered for active duty in 1814, and he acted as a commissioner for various turnpikes. Gamble relocated by 1827 to Tallahassee in Florida Territory, where

he owned a plantation, served as postmaster for Jefferson County, and became the president of the Union Bank (FTaSA: Gamble Family Notes; Richmond *Enquirer*, 10 May 1805; Faculty Minutes, College of New Jersey, 29 Sept. 1801, 26 Sept. 1804 [NjP]; *Reports of the Trials of Colonel Aaron Burr* [Philadelphia, 1808], 106; *Acts of Assembly* [1811–12 sess.], 7, 51–2; [1817–18 sess.], 132; "Richmond Light Infantry Blues of Richmond, Virginia," *Huddy & Duval's U.S. Military Magazine* 3 [1841]: 28; Norfolk *American Beacon and Commercial Diary*, 8 Jan. 1816; *Terr. Papers*, 23:982, 25:109–10; Washington *Daily National Intelligencer*, 25 Oct. 1852).

TJ's DEED OF CONVEYANCE to David Higginbotham is printed above at the end of November 1811. Charles Carter of Shirley (1732–1806) was the surviving TRUSTEE of the estate of William Byrd (1728–77) on 9 Nov. 1777, the date on which, according to TJ's records, the deed for the lot in Richmond was executed (*MB*, 1:453–4).

¹ Gamble here canceled "River."
² Preceding three words interlined.

To Patrick Gibson

DEAR SIR   Monticello July 20. 13.

My last was of the 14th. your's of the same date was received two days after. the Frenchman who laid in the claim with mr Taylor, must have been mr Peter Derieux who married the daughter of mr Mazzei's wife, long since dead. they live in N. Carolina, and were many years¹ my near neighbors, and intimate in my family. during that intimacy, Derieux never pretended any claim on Mazzei, and I was too intimate with the affairs of both not to have known of such a claim if it existed. the so-called marriage-settlement I know gives him none. I shall write to him, and I am certain he will retract to me the levity he has been guilty of. mr Taylor having paid the greatest part of the money, I will within a few days decide on it's application in the whole. from a rough view already taken I am afraid I may have to leave 1500.D. still unpaid of my note in the bank; but I am not yet certain. in the mean time I must ask the favor of you to forward me by post 700.D. of which 400.D. may be in bills of 100.D. each and the rest in bills of from 20. down to 5.D. as also to remit to the bank of Fredericksburg 76. D 60 c paiable to Nathaniel H. Hooe, and 30.D. to the bank of Winchester paiable to judge Hugh Holmes. I drew on you yesterday for 80.D. in favor of David Higgenbotham. with respect to my flour on hand, my wish is to sell it for any thing rather than let it spoil on my hands. I would therefore have it sold for 4.D. the price you mention as going, unless you have a near prospect of a favorable change in the market. of this we cannot judge here, and therefore I must leave it to yourself. be so good as to let me know the exact amount of the sale to mr Taylor, and of the discount which the prompt paiment will deduct, that I may be exact in my statement to Mazzei. will you do me the favor to send me 10.℔ of chocolate by the mail stage?

Your's with esteem & respect   TH: JEFFERSON

P.S. I recieved yesterday the deed acknoleged in court by mr Randolph. our court will be Monday sennight, when I will acknolege & forward it. I omitted to say that by a letter of the 1ˢᵗ of Apr. last from our Consul at Paris he informed me he had forwarded one from Mazzei by a preceding vessel, which has probably been taken, as I have not recieved it. it proves however he was then living; & there is no particular reason for doubting his continuance in life, & his accustomed health

PoC (DLC); postscript written perpendicularly along left margin; adjacent to signature: "Mʳ Gibson"; endorsed by TJ as a letter to Gibson & Jefferson and so recorded in SJL.

Philip Mazzei's first WIFE was Marie Hautefeuille "Petronille" Martin Mazzei. On this date TJ recorded his request that Gibson & Jefferson make payments to NATHANIEL H. HOOE "for negro hire in full" and to JUDGE HUGH HOLMES "to be employed in getting our cloth manufactured." His payment of 80.D. to David Higginbotham included "50.D. for   Sharp for a pr. of oxen" (MB, 2:1290). The CONSUL AT PARIS was David Bailie Warden.

¹ Preceding two words interlined in place of "long."

To John Barnes

DEAR SIR   Monticello July 21. 13.

Your favor of the 6th was exactly two weeks getting to this place instead of the two days in which it ought to have come. I recieved it yesterday. I have not yet lost my hope in mr Morton, and that he may yet be the most convenient channel of supplying Genl Kosciuzko; because if he continues firm, he could give the General cash there always for a draught on you. we will therefore yet wait awhile to hear from him, or of him. I inclose you the order requested for the half years dividend on the bank of Pensylvania. ever affectionately yours

TH: JEFFERSON

PoC (DLC); at foot of text: "Mr John Barnes"; endorsed by TJ. Enclosure not found.

From William A. Burwell

SIR   July 21st 1813

I wrote Mrs Burwell to send my horses to meet me at Monticello, under an expectation I should reach your house on thursday—the unexpected delay of the Tax bills compels me to remain longer, may I beg the favor of you to detain my Servant until I can leave this place, which I propose doing in a Hack—we have been much commotion for a week past—the whole City is under arms & on militia duty at the forts & elsewhere—they are preparing forts at Navy y'd & Greenleafs point;

I can not believe the British will attempt this City. but if they do, they will be Severely handled—there are 4 or 5000 troops well armed—accept my best

wishes for your happiness   W. A BURWELL

RC (DLC); endorsed by TJ as received 23 July 1813 from Washington and so recorded in SJL.

Clothing and Bedding Distribution List for Poplar Forest Slaves

[after 21 July 1813]

Poplar Forest. Grown persons		plains	home-spun	shirting
Hall.		√ 3	√ $2\frac{1}{2}$	√ 7.
Hanah.		√ 3	√ 3	√ 7
Sally (Hanah's)	98	√ 2	√ 1	6[1]
Lucinda		√ 2	√ 3	√ 7
Maria (Nanny's)		2	√ 5	6[2]
Nisy.	99	√ 2	√ $2\frac{1}{4}$	$5\frac{1}{3}$[3]
Nace		√ 3	√ $2\frac{1}{2}$	√ 7
Phill Hubard		√ 3	√ 3	√ 7
Abby.		√ 2	√ 3	7[4]
Will		√ 3	√ 3	√ 7
Manuel	94	√ 3	√ $2\frac{1}{2}$	√ $7\frac{2}{3}$
Amy.	97	√ 2	√ $2\frac{3}{4}$	√ $6\frac{1}{3}$
Edy		√ 2	√ 3	√ 7
Gawen.		√ 3	√ $2\frac{1}{2}$	√ 7
Sal. (Will's)		√ 2	√ 3	√ 7
Milly	97	√ 2	√ $2\frac{3}{4}$	√ 6
Sandy. 13.				
Dick		√ 3	√ $2\frac{1}{2}$	√ 7
Dinah		√ 2	√ 3	√ 7
Hanah (Dinah's)		√ 2	√ 3	√ 7
Aggy		√ 2	√ 3	7[8]
Evans		√ 3	√ $2\frac{1}{2}$	√ 7
Bess.		√ 2	√ 3	7
Ambrose		√ $2\frac{1}{4}$	√ 2	$5\frac{1}{3}$
Betty		√ 2	√ 3	√ 7
Hercules		√ 3	√ $2\frac{1}{2}$	7
Jesse.		√ 3	√ $2\frac{1}{2}$	7
		$63\frac{1}{4}$	$71\frac{3}{4}$	$174\frac{2}{3}$[10]

	Children	woolen homesp.	shirtg
Hanah's	Jamy. 05	√ $2\frac{3}{4}$	√ $3\frac{1}{3}$
	Phil. 08	√ 2	√ $2\frac{1}{3}$
	Edmund. 09.	√ $1\frac{3}{4}$	√ 2
	George Welsh. 12	√ 1	√ 1
		$7\frac{1}{2}$	$8\frac{2}{3}$
Lucinda's	Melinda. 09	$1\frac{3}{4}$	√ 2.
	Rebecca. 12.	1	√ 1
		$2\frac{3}{4}$	3
	Nancy. Edy's. 12.	1	√ 1
Sal's	Betty 01.	√ $3\frac{3}{4}$	√ $4\frac{2}{3}$[5]
	Abby. 04.	3	√ $3\frac{2}{3}$
	Edy. 06.	$2\frac{1}{2}$	√ 3.
	Martin. 09.	$1\frac{3}{4}$	2
	Moses. 11.	$1\frac{1}{4}$	$1\frac{1}{3}$
	Mary Anne. 12.	1	1
		$13\frac{1}{4}$	$15\frac{2}{3}$
Dinah's	Lucy. 99.[6]	√ $4\frac{1}{4}$	√ $5\frac{1}{3}$[7]
	Jamy. 02.	√ $3\frac{1}{2}$	√ $4\frac{2}{3}$
	Briley. 05.	$2\frac{3}{4}$	√ $3\frac{1}{3}$
		$10\frac{1}{2}$	$13\frac{1}{3}$
	Sally. Aggy's. 12.	1	√ 1
Bess.	Prince. 04.	3	√ $3\frac{2}{3}$
	Joe. 06.	$2\frac{1}{2}$	√ 3
	Shepherd. 09	$1\frac{3}{4}$	√ 2
		$7\frac{1}{4}$	$8\frac{2}{3}$
		$43\frac{1}{4}$	$51\frac{1}{3}$[9]

Blankets

√ Jamy, Phill } Hanah's
√ Nisy
√ Nace
√ Will
√ Abby
√ Sal. Will's

√ Edy
Martin } Sall's
√ Amy Will's
√ Aggy
Sally }
√ Evans.
√ Hanah Dinah's
√ Ambrose
Prince. } Bess's

Beds.
Sall. Will's
Milly
Hanah. Dinah's[11]

Bear Creek. Grown persons	plains	home-spun	shirt[g]
Jame Hubbard.	√ 3.	√ 3.	√ 7.
Cate.	√ 3	√ 3	√ 7.
Armistead.	√ 3.	3.	√ 7.
Cate. Rachael's 97.	√ 2	√ 3	√ 7
Maria. Cate's	√ $2\frac{1}{2}$	√ 3.	7.
Sally. Cate's.	√ 2.	√ 3.	√ 7.
Reuben.	√ 3.	$2\frac{1}{2}$	√ 7.
Austin	√ 3.	$2\frac{1}{2}$	√ 7.
Flora.	√ 2	√ 3	√ 7.
Fanny.	√ 2.	√ 3.	√ 7.
Caesar.	√ 3.	√ $2\frac{1}{2}$	7.
Cate. Suck's.	√ 2	√ 3.	7.
Daniel.	√ 3.	$2\frac{1}{2}$	7.
Stephen	√ 3.	$2\frac{1}{2}$	√ 7.
Cate. Betty's	√ 2	√ 3.	7.
Mary. Betty's	√ 2.	√ 3.	7.
Nanny.	√ 2	√ 3	7.
	$42\frac{1}{2}$	$48\frac{1}{2}$	119

	Children	woolen homespun	shirt[g]
Maria's.	Johnny. 04.	√ 3	√ $3\frac{2}{3}$
	Isaac. 09.[12]	$1\frac{3}{4}$	√ 2
		$4\frac{3}{4}$	$5\frac{2}{3}$
Sally's	Billy. 08.	2.	√ $2\frac{1}{3}$
	Anderson. 10.	$1\frac{1}{2}$	√ $1\frac{2}{3}$
	Henry. 12.	1.	1.
		$4\frac{1}{2}$	5.
Flora's	Gawen. 04.	√ 3	√ $3\frac{2}{3}$
	Aleck. 06.	$2\frac{1}{2}$	3.
	Billy. 08.	2	$2\frac{1}{3}$
	Boston. 11.	$1\frac{1}{4}$	$1\frac{1}{3}$
		$8\frac{3}{4}$	$10\frac{1}{3}$
Fanny's	Rachael. 07.	√ $2\frac{1}{4}$	$2\frac{2}{3}$
	Rhody. 11.	$1\frac{1}{4}$	$1\frac{1}{3}$
	Zacharias. 13.		
		$3\frac{1}{2}$	4.
Cate's	Davy. 06.	$2\frac{1}{2}$	√ 3.
	John. 11.	$1\frac{1}{4}$	√ 1.$\frac{1}{3}$
		3.$\frac{3}{4}$	4.$\frac{1}{3}$
Nanny's	Phill. 01.	√ $3\frac{3}{4}$	√ $4\frac{2}{3}$
	Milly. 06.	√ $2\frac{1}{2}$	√ 3.
	George Denis. 08.	2.	√ $2\frac{1}{3}$
	Janetta. 12.	1	√ 1.
		$9\frac{1}{4}$	11
		$34\frac{1}{2}$	$40\frac{1}{3}$[13]

Blankets
√ Sally. Cate's
    Billy
√   Anderson   ⎫
    Henry.   ⎬
√ Gawen. ⎫
   Aleck   ⎬ Flora's
   Rachael   ⎫
√ Rhody   ⎬ Fanny's
   Zacharias ⎭
√ Caesar
√ George Dennis ⎫
√ Janetta   ⎬ Nanny's

Beds
  Maria. Cate's
  Flora.
  Nanny.

Wanting for cloathing all the people.

	homespun wollens	shirting
for the grown people 105¾ yds plains.	120. yds	294.[14] yds
for the young ones	78. yds	92.
	198.	386.[15]

MS (PPAmP: Thomas Jefferson Papers); in TJ's hand, with check marks possibly in two different hands and other revisions in an unidentified hand; written on one sheet folded to form four pages; undated, but composed after the 21 July 1813 birth of Sandy (Betts, *Farm Book*, pt. 1, 131).

[1] An unidentified hand here inserted "3½."
[2] An unidentified hand here inserted "3½."
[3] An unidentified hand here inserted "3½."
[4] An unidentified hand here inserted "3½."
[5] An unidentified hand here inserted "2."
[6] Reworked from "Sandy Milly's."
[7] An unidentified hand here inserted "2½."
[8] An unidentified hand here inserted "3½."
[9] First page of manuscript ends here.
[10] Correct figure is 175⅔.
[11] Second page of manuscript ends here.
[12] TJ here canceled an entry for "Dolly. 12.," who was to receive one yard each of woolen homespun and shirting.
[13] Third page of manuscript ends here.
[14] Correct figure is 295.
[15] Correct figure is 387.

From John Wayles Eppes

DEAR SIR,   Washington July 21st 1813.

Your letter of the 24th of June has been received and read with great pleasure—If the war continues and with it the present rate of expenditure nothing but a rigid adherence to principles such as you state can secure us against the evils of a permanent debt—The duration of the Taxes reported to the present Session of Congress has been limited to the war and one year after its conclusion in consequence of the principle having been settled by a vote of the House of Representatives at the last Session—At the next meeting of Congress a new loan must be authorized and we will then endeavour to incorporate with it a new Tax sufficient to meet the interest and to discharge the principal within 15 years—

I am extremely happy to find that this subject has been deemed worthy of your attention—The idea that you may be induced to devote a small portion of your time to developing the resources of our country inspires me with something like confidence & hope—we have already imposed a land Tax to the amount of 3000.000. of dollars. when we consider the large portion of land in the Southern and Western country which must be classed as unproductive capital, perhaps nothing more can be expected from this fund—The other Taxes on Stills Bank notes & negotiable paper, on sugar refined on sales at auction on retailers and on carriages are estimated at 2,750000. including the expences of collection—During the next year we must resort either to a loan or to notes of the description you mention to the amount of at least 22.000:000 of dollars—What shall be the Tax to meet the interest on this new loan and reimburse the principal in 15. years—

The continuance of the Land Tax after the war will be impracticable—Indeed the mode of apportioning every direct Tax within the U.S. according to population without any regard to the ability to pay, appears to interpose an insurmountable barrier to the extension of this species of Tax to any amount corresponding with the wants of the community—Considered merely as an engine to force on a Government oeconomy, the system of direct Taxation is unquestionably the best—In every other point of view it is unquestionably the worst— The ability to pay appears to be the plain and obvious basis of every just system of Taxation—Under our constitution every direct Tax must be apportioned to population without regard to improvement in agriculture commerce or manufactures—Under this rule entirely arbitrary a given population inhabiting an uncultivated Forrest (where all the surplus capital and labour is necessary for improvement) must pay according to numbers the same Tax with portions of country where almost every acre is productive capital and agriculture commerce and manufactures have arrived at their highest state of improvement. The State of Ohio for instance just rising into political existence must pay the same Tax with the State of N. Jersey—Since I have been placed in a situation where it was my duty to think of ways and means I have entertained strong doubts as to some of the principles of political œconomy which I had heretofore considered as sound—Direct Taxes for example I had considered as in principle the best—The rule of apportionment however under the constitution renders them so extremely unequal that I am strongly inclined to acknowledge my error and to view the system of indirect Taxation as the only practicable one without oppression to the people—

In the event of issuing Treasury notes bottomed on a Tax in the way you propose, in what mode would you put them into circulation—To sell them in market would subject us to loss as so large a sum could not be put at once into market but at a discount—To issue them as a medium of commerce or in fact as money to meet the demands on the Gov^t until it was asscertained how far the public might repose confidence in them would probably be attended with difficulty & bring into operation the prejudices which are still strong against any thing like paper money—on what do you ground the opinion that so large an amount as 200.000.000 may be put into circulation—

I know you are not fond of long letters and I fear I shall tire you—My apology must be the strong desire I feel to obtain information—without experience and having on the subject of political œconomy read only a few of the most common books any thing on this subject which your time will permit will be received as a token of your friendship and employed solely for the benefit of our Country—The outline of a system adequate to meet the exigencies of the country during the continuance of the war is a subject worthy of your attention—Between the present time and the next meeting of Congress ample time will be afforded—By executing such a task you will add one more essential benefit to the long list of important services already registered in the hearts of your countrymen—

The British are still progressing up the river—Their force amounts to 20 vessels of every description—The force on board probably the same that was near Norfolk—viz 2,700—Fort Warburton is well supplied with cannon and men & the militia of the surrounding country together with about 800 regular Troops which were here on their march to the Lakes are at different points on the river ready to oppose them—The alarm has subsided—many doubt whether they will attempt to come up—should such however be the case the preparations to meet them are considered as sufficient not only to secure us from injury but to punish their rashness—

The Senate yesterday rejected the Nomination of Mʳ Gallatin as minister to Russia—a majority of that body may be considered hostile to the administration—Nothing however need be said of their political feelings when they reject Mʳ Gallatin & confirm Bayard and Addams—The first one of the most bitter foes of the party and the last a thoroughgoing Federalist—

With Sincere regard I am yours   JNO: W: EPPES

RC (DLC); addressed: "Th. Jefferson Esqʳ"; endorsed by TJ as received 23 July 1813 and so recorded in SJL.

During the second session of the Twelfth Congress, the United States HOUSE OF REPRESENTATIVES resolved that wartime duties and taxes "shall con-
tinue until one year after the conclusion of peace with such foreign nation, and no longer" (*JHR*, 8:206, 230 [26 Feb., 4 Mar. 1812]). A LAND tax and the OTHER TAXES listed by Eppes became law during the first session of the Thirteenth Congress (*U.S. Statutes at Large*, 3:22–34, 35–8, 40–1, 42–4, 44–7, 72–3, 77–81).

To Robert Fulton

DEAR SIR   Monticello July 21. 13.

Immediately on the reciept of your favor of July 8. I forwarded it to the President, and had no hesitation in expressing my own wish that it should be tried. in fact as we cannot meet the British with an equality of Physical force, we must supply it by other devices, in which I know no body equal to yourself, and so likely to point out to us a mode of salvation. accordingly I hope this honor is reserved for you, and that either by subaqueous guns, torpedoes, or diving boats you will accomplish it by the aid of government. the New York Evening post has given us a Quiz on this subject, hoping, I presume, to draw a flimsy veil of jest over his habitual lies, and wishing us to suppose all those were but jests. I confess I have more hopes of the mode of destruction by the submarine boat, than any other. no law of nature opposes it, and in that case nothing is to be despaired of by human invention, nor particularly by yours. Accept the just tribute of an American citizen, & of a friend in the assurances of my great esteem & respect.   TH: JEFFERSON

RC (CtY: Franklin Collection); addressed: "Robert Fulton esquire New York"; franked; postmarked Milton, 22 July. PoC (DLC); endorsed by TJ.

On 13 July 1813 TJ had FORWARDED Fulton's letter of 29 June, not that of 8 July, to PRESIDENT James Madison. An article entitled "*Bushnell the Second*" in the NEW YORK EVENING POST, 9 July 1813, reported on an unnamed Norwich resident who, reminiscent of Revolutionary War inventor David Bushnell, had invented "a diving boat, which by means of paddles he can propel under water at the rate of three miles an hour, & ascend & descend at pleasure." The new inventor allegedly failed in three successive attempts to sink HMS *Ramillies* but alarmed its captain enough that he moved the vessel away from New London.

To Hugh Holmes

DEAR SIR   Monticello July 21. 13.

Availing myself of your kind offer, I forwarded to Staunton by the stage 39.℔ unwashed Merino wool which I hope has reached you safely. the cloth when made I would wish to have dyed of the darkest blue colour they can give it, which I think you said was what they called a navy blue. I yesterday wrote to Gibson & Jefferson to forward to the bank of Winchester, subject to your call, 30. Dollars which as well as I could judge from your information, would cover the expences of manufacture. with many apologies for giving you all this trouble, and thanks for your[1] undertaking it, be pleased to accept the assurance of my great esteem & respect.   TH: JEFFERSON

PoC (MHi); at foot of text: "The honble Hugh Holmes"; endorsed by TJ.

[1] Word interlined.

To Nathaniel H. Hooe

SIR   Monticello July. 21. 13.

I am one of the unfortunate upon whom the blockade came before I had sold a barrel of my flour. I am now offering it for 4.D. at Richmond, which will be $2\frac{1}{2}$ D. after paying for grinding, for the barrel and transportation. it is not yet sold. I was waiting either for it's sale or for the maturity of another resource, due the 17th inst. to have the remittance made to you, when I recieved your favor of the 6th and recieving information that the paiment I expected on the 17th was made in Richmond, I desired Gibson & Jefferson, by yesterday's post, to remit to the Fredsbg bank 76. D 60. C Subject to your call, being the amount of Tom's hire and interest. I presume it will be in the bank by the time you recieve this letter; and with this apology for the delay, I pray you to accept the assurance of my esteem and respect

Th: Jefferson

PoC (MHi); at foot of text: "Nathan[l] H. Hooe esq."; endorsed by TJ. Hooe's letter OF THE 6TH, not found, is recorded in SJL as received 10 July 1813 from "Forest hill."

From Thomas Hornsby

Dear Sir   July 21th 1813

your letter of aprile 21th inclosed by one from Col Greenup came to hand yesterday, my Father to whom it was addressed has departed this life many years Since my brother who bears his name opened it upon findeing its contents concerned me alone handed it to me my Father allways expressed the highest esteem and respect for you. and nothing shall be wanting in his Son to render you all the justice in his power I finde you have been mutch desceived the property was not soald to Mr Peyton by the Guardian of the children in Kentucky Charles Henderson was their Guardian here neither was it soald by the approbation of themselves or mother they knew nothing of it at the time it was transacted nor for some time after neither was the proceeds of the sale ever received by them or [invested] to their use. Frances Henderson now my wife soald her interest in the warehouse some time in March [1805 an]d the deed which conveys it to Peyton bearing date [Feby] 25 of the same year in the letter to Mr Meriwather wherein was incloased the power of attorney was mentioned this matter I relinquished all right to the warehouse I am sorry to finde that a difference has taken place between yourself and Mr Meriwather your Suspicion of his haveing changed my course from the candid one persued by the rest of the party is certainly unmerited by him. those who have confirmed the sale made by James Henderson have received full payment (Isham Henderson received 150£ for his share). James Henderson,s intention was I suppose as each one of the legatees became of age to perchase their sheare and have the deed ratefyed by them. Some Short time previous to my marrying his sister James Henderson passed through this county on his way to Washhita in Louesiana where he now resides, requested his mother to tell me as soon as we were married that he wished to perchase the property in Virginia and was obliedged to have it which Mrs Henderson did Some few months after. I wrote to him mentioning the circumstances offering him the land for sale and requesting an immediate answer. he never answered my letter, his situation when he left this country was mutch embarrased as to mony matters and from all the circumstances which I have been able to collect do not believe he is now in a situation to perchase. The same poast which conveys this to you will likewise convey one to Mr Meriwather—requesting him to suspend acting on the power of attorney untill you can have time to concider the matter fully, if any arrangment can be made which will be satisfactory between us it shal be entierly withdrawn, I have written to Col Greenup—giving him all the information which I possess requesting him to mention a time and place for an interview what I have mentioned respecting the sale made by James Henderson [was] without the consent or knowledge of Mrs Henderson or her daughters and the proceeds not being appropriated to their use and that he never was their Guardian is <u>positive matter, of, fact,</u> and if you wish it such depositions and other papers as go to prove it shal be sant on to you. how and by whom a misrepresentation has been made to you I can not conceive unless by Peyton. Rest assured sir that I feel not the smallest disposi[tion] to disturb your tranquility. and I think when the [ma]tter is fully examined you will do me the justice to attach no blame to my conduct in the business I can not quit the subject without one remarke more Some of your expresions towards my conduct are harsh and certainly unmerited by me I never have quit the path of candure & honor in this, affare and I impute them to the rong information which you have received and the author I leave with you to detect.

With the highest Esteem & Respect I remain yours &cc

THOMAS HORNSBY

RC (ViU: TJP); ink stained and mutilated at folds; addressed: "Mr Thomas Jefferson—Albermarle County Sharlotsvill Virginia"; stamped; postmarked Shelbyville, 22 July, and Charlottesville, 5 Aug.; endorsed by TJ as received 6 Aug. 1813 and so recorded in SJL. Enclosed in TJ to Craven Peyton, 8 Aug. 1813.

Thomas Walker Hornsby (b. 1779) moved with his family to Kentucky in about 1800. In 1805 he married Frances Henderson, the daughter of Bennett Henderson and Elizabeth Lewis Henderson. He lived in Shelby County until at least 1830 (*WMQ*, 1st ser., 17 [1909]: 169; Merrow Egerton Sorley, *Lewis of Warner Hall: The History of a Family* (1935; repr. 1991), 382; *PTJ*, 31:142n; *Kentucky Marriage Records* [1983], 743; TJ to Craven Peyton, 12 May 1811; DNA: RG 29, CS, Ky., Shelby Co., 1830).

From Thomas Lehré

DEAR SIR   Charleston July 21ˢᵗ 1813

Permit me to introduce to your acquaintance, Mʳ Joseph Bellinger of Barnwell District in this State.—He is a Gentleman of great respectability—he has been a member of the House of Representatives in our State Legislature, for many Years, and is now one of our State Senators, for the above District.

In 1808, he had the honor of being one of our Republican Electors of President & Vice President, of the United States. He is well known throughout this State, to be a firm and undeviating Republican, and one of the Warmest friends, that you, Mʳ Madison, and the Present Administration ever had. It has been greatly owing to his firmness, and exertions in, and out of our State, Legislature, that the Republican party here, has been enabled to triumph over their political opponents in the manner they have done. Any civilities shewn him, will be duly appreciated by him. when you can find time to write, I shall be glad to hear from you

I remain with the highest Consideration Dear Sir Your Obedᵗ Humble Servᵗ   THOMAS LEHRÉ

RC (DLC); at foot of text: "Thomas Jefferson late President of the United States Monticello Virginia"; endorsed by TJ as received 16 Sept. 1813 and so recorded in SJL.

Joseph Bellinger (ca. 1773–1830), planter and public official, represented Saint Luke Parish in the South Carolina House of Representatives, 1802–05. After moving to his Aeolian Lawn planta-tion, he represented the Barnwell District in the House, 1806–09, and in the state senate, 1810–13. Bellinger served one term as a Republican in the United States House of Representatives, 1817–19. In 1824 he owned more than 8,500 acres of land and 122 slaves. From 1826–30 Bellinger was a director of the Bank of the State of South Carolina (*BDSCHR*, 4:53–4; *Charleston Observer*, 23 Jan. 1830).

From John Adams

DEAR SIR   Quincy. July 22. 1813

Dʳ Priestley, in a letter to Mʳ Lindsey Northumberland Nov. 4. 1803 Says

"As you were pleased with my comparison of Socrates and Jesus, I have begun to carry the same comparison to all the heathen Moralists, and I have all the books that I want for the purpose, except Simplicius and Arrian on Epictetus, and them I hope to get from a Library in Philadelphia: lest however I should fail there, I wish you or Mr Belsham would procure and Send them from London. While I am capable of any thing I cannot be idle, and I do not know that I can do any thing better. This too is an Under taking that Mr Jefferson recommends to me."

In another Letter dated Northumberland Jan. 16. 1804 Dr Priestley Says to Mr Lindsey "I have now finished and transcribed for the Press, my comparison of the Grecian Philosophers, with those of Revelation, and with more ease and more to my own Satisfaction, than I expected. They who liked my pamphlet entitled "Socrates and Jesus compared," will not, I flatter myself dislike this work. It has the Same Object and completes the Scheme. It has increased my own Sense of the unspeakable value of Revelation, and must, I think, that of every person, who will give due attention to the Subject." I have now given you all that relates to yourself in Priestleys Letters.

This was possibly and not improbably, the last Letter this great, this learned, indefatigable, most excellent and extraordinary Man, ever wrote: for on the fourth of February 1804, he was released from his labours and Sufferings. Peace, Rest, Joy and Glory to his Soul! For I believe he had one; and one of the greatest.

I regret; oh how, I lament, that he did not live, to publish this Work! It must exist in Manuscript. Cooper must know Something of it. Can you learn from him where it is, and get it printed? I hope you will Still perform your promise to Dr Rush.

If Priestley had lived, I Should certainly have corresponded with him. His Friend Cooper, who unfortunately for him and me, and you, had as fatal an influence over him as Hamilton had over Washington; and whose rash hot head led Priestley into all his Misfortunes and most[1] his Errors in Conduct[2] could not have prevented explanations between Priestley and me.

I Should propose to him a thousand, a million Questions. And no M[an] was more capable or better disposed to answer them candidly than Dr Priestley. Scarcely any thing that has happened to me, in my curious Life has made a deeper Impression upon me, than that Such a learned ingenious Scientific and talented Madcap as Cooper, could have had influence enough to make Priestley my Enemy.

I will not yet, communicate to you, more than a Specimen, of the Questions I would have asked Priestley.

One is, learned and Scientific Sir! you have written largely about matter and Spirit, and have concluded, there is no human Soul. Will you please to inform me, what matter is? and what Spirit is? Unless We know the meaning of Words, We cannot reason in, or about

Words. I Shall never Send you all my Questions that I would put to Priestley; because they are innumerable: but I may hereafter Send you two or three. I am in perfect

Charity your old Friend   JOHN ADAMS

RC (DLC); mutilated at seal, with text supplied from FC; at foot of text: "President Jefferson"; endorsed by TJ as received 4 Aug. 1813 and so recorded in SJL. FC (Lb in MHi: Adams Papers).

The work on the HEATHEN MORALISTS, Priestley, *Heathen Philosophy*, had,

in fact, already been published (Northumberland, Pa., 1804; Sowerby, no. 1528). Priestley died on 6 Feb. 1804, not THE FOURTH (*ANB*; *ODNB*).

[1] In FC "of" is here interlined.
[2] Preceding seventeen words interlined.

To Englehart Cruse

SIR   Monticello July 23. 13.

I recieved duly your favor of the 3^d and in it the Description of your apparatus for blowing up ships, which I have considered and now reinclose. my inland situation has made me the least of all men a judge of any thing nautical. mr Fulton communicated to me the plan of his floating torpedo, which appeared to me plausible. I should think the same of yours, could I permit myself to form a judgment in a case wherein I am so ignorant. not meddling at all now in the affairs of the government I return you the paper because it would go better from yourself; and because too it is possible you may wish to obtain a patent for the invention, in which case it must go from yourself in the ordinary form. with my thanks for it's communication accept the assurance of my respects.   TH: JEFFERSON

PoC (DLC); at foot of text: "Mr Englehart Cruse"; endorsed by TJ. Enclosure: enclosure to Cruse to TJ, 3 July 1813.

To John Devereux DeLacy

SIR   Monticello July 23. 13.

I have duly recieved your favor of the 8th and entirely concur in opinion with you as to the ease & importance of the inland navigation from St Mary's to James river, and will certainly give it whatever aid may be in my power. as this may be best done by way of letters to those on whom the measure would rest, I return you the blank petition. I go out so little & see so few people that I could do nothing with the petition, altho' it is one which every man in the state would readily sign.

I am now myself pressing on the government to station from 50. to 100. gunboats in Lynhaven river, as a sufficient defence for the Chesapeak bay & all it's waters. I am satisfied that were such a force there, no vessel of war would ever pass a night in the Chesapeak. but a previous operation absolutely necessary would be to open a Canal from the head of Lynhaven river into the East river, to give a safe retreat to the gunboats if attacked from the shore of the river, and to enable them to go to the defence of Norfolk if attacked. as a military work the government has power to do it; altho' for the mere purposes of navigation they have not the power. there is a proposition now before Congress for an amendment to the Constitution to give them that power. Accept the assurance of my respect.

Th: Jefferson

RC (NNGL, on deposit NHi); mutilated at folds, with missing text supplied from PoC; at foot of text: "Mr John Dev. De Lacy." PoC (DLC); endorsed by TJ. Enclosure not found.

On 10 July 1813 Virginia representative John G. Jackson placed a resolution BEFORE CONGRESS FOR AN AMEND- MENT TO THE CONSTITUTION that would grant Congress the "power to make canals in any State, with the consent of the State within which the same shall be made." Jackson successfully moved on 24 Jan. 1815 to postpone "indefinitely" consideration of that and other constitutional amendments he had proposed (*JHR*, 9:87, 685).

To Peter Derieux

Dear Sir   Monticello [J]u[ly] 23. 13.

I have duly recieved yours of the 8th and am really concerned for the difficult circumstances of your family. I should undoubtedly be willing to represent the same to mr Mazzei in informing him of the sale of his lot in Richmond, and to interest him in your relief. but I am informed from mr Taylor that you notified him not to let the money go out of his hands, as in the event of mr Mazzei's death before the sale you claimed the money under a marriage settlement. in the 1st place by a letter from our Consul at Paris of Apr. 1. I know he was living & in his usual good health. in the next place I know the settlement alluded to authorises no such claim. and altho' your letter of the 8th implies sufficiently an acknolegement of this, I could not avoid stating to mr Mazzei this adversary measure, unless it be expressly withdrawn; which there is still time to do by post before I

write to mr Mazzei. I defer writing to him until I shall have acknoleged the deed in our court on Monday sennight. Accept my best
wishes for your well-being with the assurances of my esteem.

TH: JEFFERSON

PoC (DLC); dateline faint; at foot of text: "Mr P. Derieux"; endorsed by TJ as a letter of 23 July 1813 and so recorded in SJL.

David Bailie Warden was the American CONSUL AT PARIS.

From Patrick Gibson

SIR   Richmond 24th July 1813

In compliance with your favor of the 20th I have remitted to M^r
Hooe and Judge Holmes the sums mention'd and now send you inclosed $700 in such notes as you directed, the chocolate will be sent
by the mail stage—Your dft in favor of David Higginbotham is
paid—I shall send you a statement of the sale to Mr Taylor so soon as
the survey is made—Mr T. informs me that Mr Derieux is now living
at the Eagle Tavern in this place, the paper shown to him by Mr Derieux he says is in French, which he does not understand but according to M^r D$^{'s}$ interpretation of it, it gives him a title to all the landed[1]
property in this Country which Mr Mazzei may be in possession of at
his death—I shall do all in my power to dispose of your flour

With great respect
Your ob^t Servt

PATRICK GIBSON

RC (ViU: TJP-ER); between dateline and salutation: "Thomas Jefferson Esqre"; endorsed by TJ as a letter from

Gibson & Jefferson received 27 July 1813 and so recorded in SJL.

[1] Word interlined.

From George M. Troup

DEAR SIR   Washington 24th July 1813

I enclose at the request of a person unknown to me a letter for
you—the author declares it to contain nothing but the disclosure of a
project which he has formed for the destruction of the enemie's Fleet
& upon this declaration alone I make myself the medium of its conveyance. I hope Dear sir you enjoy your usual health & spirits

with great respect your friend & sev^t GEO M TROUP

RC (MHi); endorsed by TJ as received 28 July 1813 and so recorded in SJL. Enclosure: Englehart Cruse to TJ, 3 July 1813, and enclosure.

George Michael Troup (1780–1856), planter and public official, was born in a section of Georgia that later became Alabama. He studied under private tutors in Savannah; attended Erasmus Hall in Flatbush, New York; graduated from the College of New Jersey (later Princeton University) in 1797; read law; and began practicing in 1799 in Savannah. Troup represented Chatham County as a Republican in the Georgia House of Representatives for three terms beginning in 1801. After moving to Bryan County in the same state, he sat in the United States House of Representatives, 1807–15, with service as chair of the Committee on Military Affairs during the War of 1812.

Troup was generally a supporter of TJ and James Madison. He served as a United States senator, 1816–18, and after two unsuccessful gubernatorial races, he won that office in 1823 and again in 1825. As governor, Troup promoted internal improvements and successfully orchestrated the removal of Cherokee and Creek Indians from their native lands. He served again in the United States Senate in 1829–33, where he supported Nullification, and he remained a vocal supporter of states' rights thereafter (*ANB*; *DAB*; Edward J. Harden, *The Life of George M. Troup* [1859]; Porter L. Fortune, "George M. Troup: Leading State Rights Advocate" [Ph.D. diss., University of North Carolina, 1949]; Troup to TJ, 15 Dec. 1807 [DNA: RG 59, LAR, 1801–09]; Madison, *Papers, Pres. Ser.*; Savannah *Daily Morning News*, 7, 14 May 1856).

From Henry M. Brackenridge

SIR   Baton Rouge July 25th 1813

From a knowledge that research into the history of the primitive inhabitants of America, is one of your favorite amusements, I take the liberty of making this communication. my attention to the subject, was first awakened on reading when a boy, the observations contained in the "Notes on Virginia" and it has become, with me, a favorite theme of speculation. I often visited the mound,[1] and other remains of Indian Antiquity in the neighbourhood of Pittsburgh, my native town, attracted by a pleasing interest of which I scarcely[2] knew the cause, and afterwards read, and heard with delight, whatever related to these monuments of the first, or rather earlier, inhabitants of my native country. Since the year 1810. (without previously intending it) I have visited almost every thing of this kind, worthy of note on the Ohio and mississippi, and from examination and reflection, something like hypothesis, has taken the place of the vague wanderings of fancy. The following is a sketch of the result of those observations.

Throughout what is denominated by Volney, the valey of the mississippi, there exist the traces of a population far beyond what this extensive and fertile portion of the Continent, is supposed to have possessed: greater perhaps, than could be supported of the present white inhabitants, even with the careful agriculture practised in the most populous parts of Europe. The reason of this, is to be found in the peculiar manners of the inhabitants by whom it was formerly occupied; like those of mexico their agriculture had for its only object their own sustenance; no surpluss was demanded for commerce with foreign nations, and no part of the soil susceptible of culture, was devoted to pasturage; yet, extensive forests filled with wild animals would still remain. The aggregate population of the country might be less, but that of particular districts much greater. We must in this way, account for the astonishing population of the vale of mexico when first known to the Spaniards: perhaps equal to any district of the Same extent[3] of china.[4] (See Humbolt page 127 vol: 2) The astonishing[5] population of Owhyhee, and Otaheita, must be accounted for in the same way. There are certainly many districts[6] on the ohio and mississippi equally favourable to a numerous population: when I contemplate the beauty and fertility of those spots, I could scarcely beleive it possible, that they should never have supported a numerous population; such a fact would form an exception to what has usually occured, in every other part of the Globe;[7]

In The valley of the mississippi, there are discovered the traces of two distinct races of people, or periods of population, one much more ancient than the other. The traces of the last are much more[8] numerous, but mark a population less advanced in civilization; in fact they belong to the same race as existed in the country when the French and English effected their settlements on this part of the Continent: but Since the intercourse of these people with the whites and the astonishing[9] dimunition in numbers, many of their customs have fallen into disuse—it is not more than a hundred and twenty years, since the character of the population, which left the traces of the second period, underwent a change. The appearances of fortifications of which so much has been Said, and which have been attributed to a colony of Welch, are nothing more than the traces of pallisadoed towns or villages. The first travellers mention this custom of surrounding their towns with pallisades; the earth was thrown up a few feet and pickets placed on the top: I have Seen old volumes in which they are represented in the engravings[10] The Arikara and Mandan villages are still fortified in this way. The traces of these are astonishingly[11] numerous in the Western country: I should not exagerate if I were to say <u>five thousand</u> might be found. Some of them enclose more than an hundred acres. From some cause or other (and we know that there [are][12] enough which might suffice to effect it) the population had been astonishingly[13] diminished immediately before we became acquainted with them; and yet Charlevoix mentions a town of the mascutin tribe (at present incorporated with the kickapoos) containing a thousand families. the barrows, or general resceptacles of the dead, such as examined by yourself, may be classed with the pallisadoed towns, though they are much more numerous; they are in fact, to be found in almost every cornfield in the Western country. The tumuli or mounds are often met with, where there is no appearance of pallisadoed villages or fortifications, or of barrows.

The first and more ancient period, is marked by those extraordinary tumuli or mounds. I have reason to beleive that their antiquity is verry great. The oldest Indians have no tradition as to their Authors, or the purposes for which they were originally intended; yet they were unconsciously formerly[14] in the habit of using them for one of the purposes for which they were at first designed to wit as places of defence. The old chief Du Coin, told mr Rice Jones that the mounds in the American Bottom had been fortified by the Kaskaskias in their wars with the Iroquois.[15] An old work by Lafitau a jesuit, which I met with at New Orleans, contains a curious plate in which one of these mounds fortified by pallisades on the top and large beams extending to the bottom, is assaulted by enemies. These tumuli as well as the fortifications, are to be found at the junction of all the considerable rivers, in the most eligible positions for towns, and in the most extensive bodies of fertile land. Their number exceeds perhaps three thousand; the smallest not less than twenty feet in height, and one hundred in diameter at the base. Their great number, and the astonishing size of some of them, may be regarded as furnishing with other circumstances evidence of their antiquity: I have been Sometimes induced to think that at the period when those mounds were constructed, there existed on the mississippi, a population as numerous as that which once animated the borders of the nile or of the Euphrates, or of mexico and Peru.

The most numerous, as well as the most considerable of these remains, are found precisely in the part of the country where the traces of numerous population might be looked for, to wit, from the mouth of the Ohio (on the East Side of the mississippi) to the Illinois river, and on the west Side from the S[t] Francis to the missouri: I am perfectly Satisfied that cities Similar to those of Ancient Mexico, of several hundred thousand souls have existed in this part of the country. Nearly opposite S[t] Louis there are the traces of two such cities, in the distance of five miles, on the bank of the cohokia, which crosses the American bottom at this place.[16] There are not less than one hundred mounds, in two different groups; one of the mounds falls little short of the Egyptian pyramid Mycerius.[17] when I examined it in 1811, I was astonished[18] that this stupendious monument of Antiquity Should have been unnoticed by any traveller: I afterwards published an account in the newspapers at St Louis, detailing its dimensions describing its form, position &^{a}, but this, which I thought might almost be considered a discovery, attracted no notice: and yet I stated it to be eight hundred paces in circumference (the exact Size of the pyramid of Asychis.) and one hundred feet in height. The mounds at Grave creek and Marietta are of the Second or third class. The mounds at St Louis, at new Madrid, and at the commencement of Black river, are all larger than those of Marietta. The following is an enumeration of the most considerable mounds on the mississippi and on the Ohio; the greater part I examined myself with such attention as the short time I had to spare would permit.

1. At Great[19] creek, below Wheeling
2. At Pittsburgh
3. At Marietta
4. Cincinati
5. New Madrid—one of them 350 feet diameter at the base
6. Bois [Brule][20] bottom, 15 miles, below St Genevieve
7. At St Genevieve
8. mouth of the marameck
9. St Louis—one with two Stages another with three
10. mouth of the missouri
11. on the cohokia river—in two groups—
12. twenty miles below—two groups also, but the mound of a smaller size—on the back of a lake formerly the bed of the river.
13. near Washington (M.T.) 146 feet in height
14 At Baton Rouge and on the bayou [Manchac][21] one of the mounds near the lake is chiefly composed of shells. the inhabitants have taken away great quantities for the purpose of making lime—
15. The mound on Black river—of two stages,—with a group around it—

At each of these places there are groupes of mounds; and at each there probably once existed a city. On the other considerable rivers which are tributary to the Ohio and mississippi, in Kentucky Tennessee, State of Ohio, Indiana Territory &^{a} they are equally numerous. But the principal city and center of population was between the ohio, mississippi, missouri, and Illinois, I have been informed that in the plains between the Arkansa and St Francis they are numerous and some verry large—They resemble the Teocalli,[22] in these important features. 1—in their positions the cardinal points are observed with considerable accuracy. 2—The larger mounds have several stages, 3—in every group there are two mounds much larger than the others—4 The Smaller mounds are placed around Symetrically. A closer examination would show a resemblance in other particulars. It is doubted by Humboldt whether advantage had not been taken of some natural rise, in the formation of the pyramid[23] of cholula; with respect to the mound of Cohokia there can be no doubt for it stands in the midst of Alluvium, and there is no natural hill nearer than two miles. (See the account of the Teocalli[24] of New Spain by Humboldt pages 16.—41.—44.—123.—170. &[a] vol 2[25])

Such are the appearances of Antiquity in the western country, which I consider as furnishing proof of an ancient and numerous population. The resemblance to those of New Spain would render probable the existence of the Same arts and customs; perhaps an intercource. The distance from the large mound on red river to the nearest in New Spain, is not so great but that they might be considered as existing[26] in the same country.—

From the description of the adoratorios, as they are called,[27] it appears highly probable that the mounds on the mississippi were destined for the same purposes. Solis tells us, that every considerable place, had a number of them, upon which a kind of tower was erected, and which gave rise to the beleif of those who first visited the coast of new Spain that they had seen cities with numerous steeples, (D[r28] Robertson who is disposed to lessen every thing American, and to treat with contempt unworthy of a philosopher, all their arts and advancement in civilization, attributes this to the imaginations of the Spaniards, inflamed with the spirit of Quixottic adventure) from which circumstance they bestowed upon it the name of their native country. The four great cities to which the general name of Mexico was given, contained two thousand of these adoratorios or teocalli; at the first glance this vast population, equal perhaps to London or Paris, appeared to be crowned with inumerable towers and steeples. Architecture was perhaps too much in its infancy to enable them to build to any great height, a mound was therefore raised, and a building erected on the top. It was in this way the temple of Belus, at Babylon was erected, and the Egyptian pyramids of the Second class which are Solid and probably the most ancient. Besides being places of adoration, the Teocali also Served as fortresses; they were usually the last places, to which the inhabitants of the cities conquered by Cortes, resorted after having been driven from every other quarter.

They were enabled from the position, form, and the tower on the top, to defend themselves in these places[29] to great advantage. Placed from the bottom to the top of the mount, by gradations above each other, they appear'd (as Solis in his animated Style expresses it) to constitute "a living hill"; and at first, judging only from the experience of their own wars, they fancied themselves impregnable.[30]

From the oldest book extant, the bible, we see exemplified in numerous instances, the natural predilection for resorting to high places; for the purpose of worship; this prevailed amongst all nations, and probably the first edifice dedicated to the Deity was an elevation of earth, the next step was the placing a temple on it, and finally churches & mosques were built with steeples. This has prevailed in all countries: it may be considered the dictate of Nature. The most ancient temples of the Greeks: were erected on artificial, or natural elevations of earth; at the present day, almost every part of Europe and Asia, exhibit these remains of tumuli, the rudest, though perhaps the most lasting of human works. (See appendix to Volney's view of America, Clarks travels in Russia &[a]) The mausoleum, generally holds the next place to the temple; and what is remarkable, all nations in their wars have made the last stand in the edifices consecrated to their Gods, and near the tombs of their Ancestors. The <u>Adoratorio</u> of New Spain, like all works of the kind answered the three purposes, of the temple, the fortress and the mausoleum. Can we entertain a doubt but that this was also the case with those of the mississippi?

The antiquity of these mounds, is certainly verry great; this is not infered from the growth of trees, which prove an antiquity of a few centuries, but from this Simple reflection; a people capable of works requiring So much labour, must be numerous, and if numerous Somewhat advanced in the Arts; we might therefore look for works of Stone or brick the traces of which would remain at least eight or ten centuries. The great mound of Cohokia, is evidently constructed with as much regularity as any of the Teocalli of new Spain, and was doubtless cased[31] with brick or stone, and crowned with buildings, but of these no traces remain. Near the mound at S[t] Louis, there are a few decaying Stones, but which may have been casually brought there. The pyramid of Papantla, in the Northern part of the Intendency of Vera Cruz unknown to the first conquerers, and discovered a few years ago, was still partly cased[32] with brick. we might be justified[33] in considering the mounds of the mississippi more ancient than the Teocalli: a fact worthy of notice, although the stages are still plain in Some of them, the gradations or steps have disappeared, in the course of time the rains having washed them off. The peices of obsidian or flint, are found in great quantities near them, as is the case with the Teocalli: Some might be Startled if I should say that the mound of Cohokia is as ancient as those of Egypt. The Mexicans possessed but imperfect traditions of the construction of their Teocalli: their traditions, attribute them to the Toultecs or to the Olmecs— who probably migrated from the mississippi.—

who will pretend to speak with certainty as to the Antiquity of America—The races of men who have flourished and disappeared— of the thousand revolutions which like other parts of the Globe it has undergone? The philosophers of Europe with a narrowness and Selfishness of mind have endeavoured to depreciate every thing which relates to it. They have called it the New world, as though its formation was posterior to the rest of the habitable globe. A few[34] facts suffice to repel this idea: the antiquity of her mountains, the remains of Volcanoes, the alluvial tracts, the wearing away of Cataracts &[a], and the number of primitive languages, greater perhaps than in all the rest of the world besides. The use of letters, and the discovery of the mariners compass, the invention of gunpowder & of printing, have produced incalculable changes in the Old world. I question much whether before those periods, comparitively recent, there existed [or could exist][35] any natiares more civilized than the mexicans, or Peruvians. In morals, the Greeks and Romans in their most enlightened days were not Superior to the mexicans. We are told that these people Sacrifised human beings[36] to their Gods! did not the Romans Sacrifise their unfortunate prisoners to their depraved and wicked pleasures, compelling them to kill each other. What was the sacrifice of Ephigenia, to obtain a favourable Wind? an act of less barbarity than the sacrifises by the mexicans of their prisoners on the altar of their Gods? The Peruvians were exempt from these crimes— perhaps the mildest and most innocent people that ever lived, and in the arts as much advanced as were the ancient Persians or Egyptians, not only in the arts but even in the Sciences. Was ever any work of the old world superior to the two roads from Quito to Cusco?

Pardon me, Sir, for troubling you with this long, and perhaps tiresome letter, dictated[37] probably by the vanity of personally communicating my crude theories to one who holds so distinguished a place in that temple of Science which is of no country and of no age—[38]

with Sentiments of the highest respect I am, Sir Your most obedient Humble Servant   H: M: BRACKENRIDGE

I am mistaken as to the pyramid of Papantla being cased[39] with bricks: The Teocalli of   & that of Chilula, are partly composed of Brick, but that of papantla differs in this respect—

See the curious account of the <u>Casas Grandees</u> on the Rio Gila Intendency of Senora & the mitle in the Intendency of Oaxaca— (Humboldt)

Tr (PPAmP: Benjamin Smith Barton Papers, Series II, Indian materials); in an unidentifed hand, with one word added, probably by Barton. Recorded in SJL as received 15 Sept. 1813. Enclosed in TJ to Caspar Wistar, 19 Sept. 1813. Printed in APS, *Transactions*, new ser., 1 (1818): 151–9, under the heading "On the Population and Tumuli of the Aborigines of North America. In a Letter from H. H. Brackenridge, Esq. to Thomas Jefferson.—Read Oct. 1, 1813," and in *Speeches on the Jew Bill, in the House of Delegates of Maryland by H. M. Brackenridge, Col. W. G. D. Worthington, and John S. Tyson, Esquire* (1829), 192–205; both printed texts lack postscript.

Henry Marie Brackenridge (1786–1871), author, attorney, and judge, was a native of Pittsburgh and the son of the author Hugh Henry Brackenridge. He read law and was admitted to the Pennsylvania bar in 1806. Brackenridge began his legal career in western Pennsylvania before moving his practice in 1810 to what would soon become known as the Missouri Territory, where he studied natural history, geography, and Native American antiquities. Late in 1811 he traveled to New Orleans to verse himself in Spanish law. Following the War of 1812, Brackenridge moved to Baltimore, where he continued to practice law and advocated American recognition of the rebelling Spanish colonies in Central and South America. After service as secretary of an 1817 diplomatic mission to study political conditions in Latin America, he represented Baltimore County for two terms in the Maryland House of Delegates, 1818–20, where he supported the abolition of Jewish civil disabilities. A fortuitous meeting with Andrew Jackson in 1821 induced Brackenridge to join the Florida governor's staff as a private secretary and interpreter. President James Monroe appointed him judge of the West Florida District in June 1822, and he continued in that capacity until May 1832, when Jackson replaced him. Brackenridge won a special election as a Whig to fill a vacant Pennsylvania seat in the United States House of Representatives, but he failed to secure his party's renomination and served only for the 1840–41 session. His publications included *Views of Louisiana; together with a journal of a voyage up the Missouri River, in 1811* (Pittsburgh, 1814); *History of the Late War, between the United States and Great-Britain* (Baltimore, 1816); *South America: A Letter on the Present State of that Country to James Monroe* (Washington, 1817); *Voyage to South America, performed by order of the American government, in the years 1817 and 1818*, 2 vols. (Baltimore, 1819); *A Eulogy, on the Lives and Characters of John Adams & Thomas Jefferson* (1826); *Recollections of Persons and Places in the West* (1834); and *History of the Western Insurrection in Western Pennsylvania, commonly called the Whiskey Insurrection. 1794* (1859). Brackenridge died in Pittsburgh and was buried on his large estate near that city (*DAB*; William F. Keller, *The Nation's Advocate: Henry Marie Brackenridge and Young America* [1956]; Papenfuse, *Maryland Public Officials*, 1:389; *Speeches on the Jew Bill*, 59–100; Jackson, *Papers*, 5:34, 6:214, 215n; *Terr. Papers*, 22:451, 24:704; *JEP*, 3:298, 303, 314, 329 [29 Apr., 4 May, 23 Dec. 1822, 31 Jan. 1823]; *Pittsburgh Daily Gazette*, 19 Jan. 1871).

OWHYHEE: Hawaii. OTAHEITA: Tahiti. The AMERICAN BOTTOM is a floodplain of the Mississippi River in Southern Illinois. RUSSIA, Tartary, and Turkey were included in the first part of Edward Daniel Clarke's *Travels in Various Countries of Europe, Asia, and Africa* (Philadelphia, 1811). EPHIGENIA (Iphigenia) was the daughter of Agamemnon and Clytemnestra whom Artemis demanded as a sacrifice in return for a fair wind to send the Greeks to Troy (*OCD*, 765–6).

[1] Tr: "mounds." *Transactions* and *Speeches*: "mound."

[2] Tr: "sarcely." *Transactions* and *Speeches*: "scarcely."

[3] Remainder of sentence omitted in *Speeches*.

[4] *Transactions*: "climate."

[5] *Speeches*: "prodigious."

[6] Tr: "distincts." *Transactions* and *Speeches*: "districts."

[7] Preceding paragraph and next three paragraphs numbered "I." through "IV." in *Transactions* and *Speeches*.

[8] *Transactions* and *Speeches*: "are the most."

[9] *Speeches*: "their very great."

[10] *Transactions* and *Speeches* use an asterisk to key a note to this point, which reads "These are to be seen in many old volumes in the present library of Congress, which contains the most valuable collection of Books on America to be found in any part of the world."

[11] *Speeches*: "exceedingly."

[12] Word, omitted from Tr, supplied from printed texts.

[13] *Speeches*: "greatly."

[14] *Transactions*: "yet they were formerly." *Speeches*: "yet they were formerly, I might almost say instinctively."

[15] Word inserted in blank space, probably by Barton.

[16] *Transactions* and *Speeches* use an asterisk to key a note to this point, which reads "See the Chapter on the Antiquities of the Valley of the Mississippi, in the "Views of Louisiana," by the author of this Memoir, p. 181. Pittsburg edition, 1814."

[17] Tr: "mycerenus." *Transactions* and *Speeches*: "Mycerius."

[18] *Speeches*: "surprised."

[19] Tr: "Grave." *Transactions* and *Speeches*: "Great."

[20] Blank left in Tr, with word supplied from *Speeches*. *Transactions*: "Bois Brulie."

[21] Blank left in Tr, with word supplied from printed texts.

[22] Tr: "Holali." *Transactions* and *Speeches*: "Teocalli."

[23] Tr: "pyramids." *Transactions* and *Speeches*: "pyramid."

[24] Tr: "Teoculi." *Transactions* and *Speeches*: "Teocalli."

[25] To this note *Transactions* and *Speeches* add "New York edition, 1811."

[26] *Speeches*: "living."

[27] Unmatched closing parenthesis in Tr editorially altered to a comma.

[28] *Transactions*: "Mr."

[29] *Transactions* and *Speeches*: "situations."

[30] *Transactions* and *Speeches*: "unassailable."

[31] Tr and *Transactions*: "chased." *Speeches*: "cased."

[32] Tr: "chased." *Transactions* and *Speeches*: "cased."

[33] *Transactions* and *Speeches*: "warranted."

[34] Tr: "Only few." *Transactions* and *Speeches*: "A few."

[35] Preceding three words added from *Transactions* and *Speeches*.

[36] Tr: "being." *Transactions* and *Speeches*: "beings."

[37] Tr: "distated." *Transactions* and *Speeches*: "dictated."

[38] *Transactions* and *Speeches*: "which belongs to every age and every country."

[39] Tr: "chased."

From Robert Fulton

Sir   New york July 25th 1813

On the 4th inst I had the honor to write you inclosing an account of my experiments on submarine firing, have the goodness to inform me if received it and have sent it to M[r] Madison,

With veneration for your virtues   Rob[t] Fulton

RC (MHi); at foot of text: "Thomas Jefferson Esqr"; endorsed by TJ as received 28 July 1813 and so recorded in SJL.

Fulton's ACCOUNT OF MY EXPERIMENTS is printed above at 29 June 1813.

To Jeremiah A. Goodman

DEAR SIR   Monticello July 26. 13.

Hercules arrived here on the 22^{d} having been discharged from Buckingham jail on the 20th where he had been confined as a runaway. the folly he has committed certainly justifies further punishment, and he goes in expectation of recieving it, for I have assured him that I leave it to yourself altogether and made him sensible that he deserves & ought to recieve it. I believe however[1] it is his first folly in this way, and considering his imprisonment as a punishment in part, I refer it to yourself whether[2] it may not be passed over for[3] this time, only letting him recieve the pardon as from yourself alone, and not by my interference, for this is what I would have none of them to suppose.

The time of my coming up is still unfixed, as I cannot leave home till I see the water brought to my mill, and the getting out of my wheat commenced. this part of the country has never seen so melancholy a prospect since the year 1755. we had not had the ground moistened but once since April when the harvest came on. the winter & fly had greatly thinned it, & the stalks being dried like stubble it fell down before the scythe. the neighborhood will not get half a common crop into the barn; myself not one third. our corn is as unpromising. mine generally from a foot to 4. feet high. we have had a small rain but no change can now make half a crop. I hope it has been better with you. the wheat should be got out immediately, and we must have the flour in Richmond by November, to take the chance of the winter exportation, when the enemy cannot lie closely in or before the bay. Accept my best wishes.   TH: JEFFERSON

RC (MoSW); at foot of text: "Mr Goodman." PoC (DLC); endorsed by TJ.

[1] Word interlined.
[2] TJ here canceled "he."
[3] Word interlined in place of "at."

To George Hay

Monticello July 26. 13.

Th: Jefferson presents his friendly respects to mr Hay and incloses him an order on Gibson & Jefferson for 50.D. for his services in the suit of Scott against him. he hopes it will be forced on at the first calling that he may be rid of the obligation which the purchaser required of him. he salutes mr Hay with friendship & respect.

PoC (DLC); dateline at foot of text; endorsed by TJ. Enclosure not found.

The OBLIGATION required by Samuel J. Harrison, the PURCHASER of TJ's Ivy Creek property, entitled him to a cash payment or a portion of TJ's Poplar For-est tract if Samuel Scott's claim to the former tract was sustained (Harrison to TJ, 13 Mar., 27 Apr. 1812; TJ to Harrison, 2 Apr. 1812; Mortgage of Campbell County Land to Samuel J. Harrison, 18 May 1812).

From Peter Derieux

MONSIEUR   Richmond 27th July 1813.

J'ai recu la lettre que vous m'avés fait L'honneur de m'ecrire le 23. courant, mais trop tard pour y repondre par Le même courier.   Je Suis très reconnaissant Monsieur de linteret que vous voulés bien temoigner au malheur qui vient d'arriver a ma famille par le Depart precipité d'une partie des habitants de Petersburg, qui en consequence de Lalarme generale apres laffaire de Hampton, nous fit perdre touttes les Ecolieres qui Composoient notre academie.

Aussitot la reception de votre lettre je fus voir Mr Gibson au Sujet de Son contenu, il me parut Satisfait de ce que je lui dis, et doit vous ecrire en consequence par ce même courier.

Quoique les informations que j'ai fait pour M'assurer de l'existance de Mr Mazzei, ne Soient que bien naturelles, j'espere, Monsieur que vous voudrés bien les lui laisser ignorer, afin de ne pas lindisposer en lui donnant lieu de croire que j'aurois pu envisager Sa mort, comme un Evenement qui pouvoit me relever et ma famille de lindigence et Lobscurité ou nous sommes reduits.

Veuillés je vous en Supplie, Monsieur nous accorder la continuation de vos bontés et etre persuadé que mes Sentiments de reconnaissance egaleront toujours ceux du plus profond Respect avec lequel j'ai L'honneur d'etre

Monsieur

Votre tres humble et très obeis^t Serviteur   PETER DERIEUX

EDITORS' TRANSLATION

SIR   Richmond 27ᵗʰ July 1813.

I received your letter of the 23d of this month but got it too late to reply by the same post.   I am very grateful, Sir, for your kind interest in the misfortune that recently struck my family due to the hasty departure of a portion of Petersburg's inhabitants and the consequent removal of all the schoolgirls from our academy, which resulted from the panic arising out of the attack on Hampton.

As soon as I received your letter I went to see Mr. Gibson about its contents. He seemed satisfied by what I told him and is, as a result, going to write you by this same post.

Although my desire to learn whether Mr. Mazzei was still alive is quite natural, I hope, Sir, that you will not reveal my inquiries to him, so as not to upset him by letting him believe that I could have considered his death as an event that might have pulled me and my family out of the indigence and obscurity into which we have fallen.

I beseech you, Sir, to continue granting us your kindness and to believe that my feelings of gratitude will always be equal to the profound respect with which I have the honor to be

Sir

Your very humble and very obedient servant   PETER DERIEUX

RC (DLC); dateline at foot of text; endorsed by TJ as received 4 Aug. 1813 and so recorded in SJL. Translation by Dr. Genevieve Moene.

A British force 2,400 strong landed three miles from HAMPTON on 25 June and, after a brief fight with the state militia, captured the town. It reembarked the following day after having removed all the guns, ammunition, and foodstuffs it could find (Richmond *Enquirer*, 29 June 1813).

From John Tayloe

SIR   July–27ᵗʰ 1813

I trust you will excuse the liberty I take—in having the honor to enclose you the within letter—as it contains money I was fearfull it might miscarry—is the cause why I trouble you—

very respectfully I am sir Your obedᵗ Servt—   JOHN TAYLOE

RC (MHi); dateline beneath signature; addressed: "Thomas Jefferson Esqʳ Monticello—near Milton—Vᵃⁿ"; franked; postmarked 28 July; endorsed by TJ as received 30 July 1813 and so recorded in SJL. Enclosure not found.

John Tayloe (1771–1828), public official and iron manufacturer, was born at Mount Airy plantation in Richmond County and schooled in England at Eton College, 1788–89, and at Saint John's College, Cambridge University, before returning to the United States in 1792. He represented Richmond County in the Virginia House of Delegates in 1793 and served in the Senate of Virginia for four sessions between 1798 and 1802. Tayloe owned land in several counties in Virginia, in Maryland, and in Washington,

D.C., where he hired the architect William Thornton to design a home that became known as the Octagon and cost him just over $28,000. During the War of 1812 Tayloe commanded cavalry troops in Washington. He bred and raced horses for contests in and near that city, allegedly selling one for $3,500 in 1803. Tayloe was reputedly the wealthiest man in Virginia during his lifetime, and he left sizable bequests to his children (John Venn and John A. Venn, *Alumni Cantabrigienses: A Biographical List of All Known Students, Graduates and Holders of Office at the University of Cambridge, from the Earliest Times to* *1900* [1922–54], pt. 2, 6:119; Leonard, *General Assembly*; *MB*, 2:1235; Charles M. Harris and Daniel Preston, eds., *Papers of William Thornton* [1995–], 1:492, 576–8, 584–8; Orlando Ridout, *Building the Octagon* [1989]; Madison, *Papers, Pres. Ser.*, 4:240–1; Wilhelmus Bogart Bryan, *A History of the National Capital: From its Foundation through the Period of the Adoption of the Organic Act* [1914–16], 1:304, 609; Wesley E. Pippenger, comp., *District of Columbia Probate Records: Will Books 1 through 6 1801–1852 and Estate Files 1801–1852* [1996; repr. 2003], 143–4; *Richmond Enquirer*, 7 Mar. 1828).

From Patrick Gibson

SIR   Richmond 29th July 1813

Mr Derieux called upon me a few days ago not a little alarmed by the letter he had just received from you, and in consequence of the late intelligence you have received relative to Mr Mazzei he relinquishes all the claim, over the property in question, which he would have consider'd himself entitled to, had Mr M: been dead previous to the sale—he appears to be extremely uneasy at the threat you hold out to him of informing Mr M: of the step he had taken, as altho' his expectations from that quarter are not very sanguine, he is in hopes thro' your intercession, that Mr M: (whose situation he understands to be opulent) may be induced to grant him some assistance, he showed me, in defence of his conduct, what he stated to be an extract from the marriage settlement, which from this specimen must be a singular paper—Article 10th constitutes in one line Mrs D: sole heiress to all the property he might leave at his death without <u>any reserve</u>, and in the next retains the right of disposing of the whole by will—what benefit was meant to be conveyed by this deed, is not easy to determine—certain it is that poor Derieux has been flattering himself with the hope of acquiring something under it for the benefit of a numerous family, and it is not surprising that he should have felt a serious disappointment on hearing of the sale of that property which he had some reason to suppose would revert to his children—he has eleven who are at present entirely dependant for their support on the little pittance he obtains as bar-keeper at the Eagle-tavern until the late alarm occasion'd by the entrance of the enemy into our waters

M^{rs} D: had been keeping a school in Petersburg and by her industry obtaind a decent support for her family, this she is now deprived of by the absence of many of those whose children were entrusted to her care—If Mr Mazzei has the means of assisting them it would be an act of humanity to inform him of his daughter's situation a small part of the proceeds of this sale would be of infinite service to them— Inclosed I hand you a statement of this sale n^t proceeds $6342:21 subject to your order—I have at length succeeded in effecting a sale of your flour to Manuel Judah, and with difficulty altho at 4$ on 60^d/ credit, as most of it was very oily—this acco^t of Sales is also inclosed the N. Proceeds $2124.92 will when received appear at your credit— with great respect I am
    Your ob^t Servt PATRICK GIBSON

RC (MHi); addressed: "Thomas Jefferson Esqr monticello"; franked; postmarked Richmond, 31 July; endorsed by TJ as received 3 Aug. 1813 and so recorded in SJL. Enclosures not found.

From Hugh Holmes

DEAR SIR   Winch^r July 29th 1813
    I delayed the acknowledgement of the receipt of the wool for the purpose of ascertaining the time when you might expect the[1] Cloth— I am still without this information, but not without apprehensions that much of our patience will be required on the part of the manufacturer—soon after the arrival of the wool the Foreman of the Factory being a militia draft and called upon to march deserted and is supposed to have gone back to new England <u>where he will be protected from such inconvenient calls</u>. Another however is expected shortly to supply his place—I am assured by m^r Baldwin (the manufacturer) that he will loose no time in completing the fabric and that he will be Able to dye the <u>best</u> blue—it will cost more but I have directed it to be done
    I assure you my dear Sir that it gives me pleasure to serve you in this business and in proportion shall I feel mortified if in point of time or the perfection of the cloth I should be disappointed by the manufacturer—with sentiments of the sincerest esteem & regard I am
    Dr Sir
    your friend & Servt H^H HOLMES

PS the $30 shall be appropriated but it was unnecessary so long to have anticipated their use   H H

RC (MHi); endorsed by TJ as received   [1] Manuscript: "the the."
4 Aug. 1813 and so recorded in SJL.

From James Barbour

DEAR SIR   Richmond July 30th 1813

A transient visit to Orange prevented me from receiving, and by consequence of answering, the letter, you addressed me (under date the 15th instant) till this time.

The misfortunes which have overwhelmed M[r] Strode are to me a Source of deep regret; to contribute to their alleviation would be highly gratifying—more especially when in So doing I could give you a proof of my anxiety to comply with your requests. I have taken the earliest opportunity of presenting the Subject to the Council and should a vacancy occur in any of our Public institutions, which can be Supplied by M[r] Strode it is not improbable, but, we shall be able to make for him Some provision.

Accept assurances of my very high respect.   JS BARBOUR

RC (DLC); endorsed by TJ as received   TJ's letter to Barbour was dated 13
3 Aug. 1813 and so recorded in SJL.   July 1813, not THE 15TH INSTANT.

To Joseph Darmsdatt

DEAR SIR   Monticello July 30. 1813.

I am really very thankful to you for the patience with which you have waited for the paiment I should have made you. I am one of the unfortunate on whom the blockade came before I had sold a barrel of my flour. I am now authorising mr Gibson to sell it for 4.D. which after the expence of barrel grinding & transporting, neats me $2\frac{1}{2}$ D. a barrel or 47. cents a bushel for my wheat. in the mean time I am enabled from another resource now to direct paiment to be made you by mr Gibson as well of the former sum due, as for the half dozen barrels of herrings you sent here lately, and half a dozen barrels to Bedford to be sent now, if they were not sent when those to this place were forwarded. they are to be addressed as usual to the care of Mess[rs] Brown & Robertson Lynchburg. Accept the assurance of my great esteem & respect.   TH: JEFFERSON

P.S. I write accordingly to mr Gibson by this post.

PoC (MHi); at foot of text: "Mr Joseph Darmsdatt"; endorsed by TJ.

NEATS: to make a net gain (*OED*).

To Patrick Gibson

DEAR SIR   Monticello July 30. 13.

Your favor of the 24th is recieved and the 700.D. therein inclosed. I have a letter from Derieux of the 8th a paragraph of which will shew you that he is conscious of having no legal claim on mr Mazzei it is in these words. 'our destiny, Sir, is in your hands. and if you will, you can yet save us from the deplorable situation which threatens us, by becoming our father & benefactor [advocate] with mr Mazzei who, I dare hope, would not refuse to let you withold some little sum of what is coming to him; and knowing that you would have the goodness[1] to keep it in your hands and dispose of it in the most permanent and profitable manner for us, we dare hope he would not refuse at your request to procure us this means of existing in our old age.' but to put the matter out of question, I have required from him an express renunciation which I am sure he will give. the reason of his proposing that I should dispose of the money for him, is that I had formerly been the means of procuring him considerable sums of money from his relations in France, which he immediately fooled away. he has respectable relations in France, particularly an aunt with whom I was well acquainted, ruined I believe by the revolution & now probably dead.

My engagements having been delayed to this late[2] season of the year, altho' mostly entered into for March & April, I am impatient to satisfy them. on the 26th therefore I drew on you in fav^r George Hay for 50.D. on the 27th for 39.28 in favor of James Kinsolving for taxes, and on the 28th in fav^r of Wayt & Winn for 43.50 & of Martin Dawson for 95.43 and I shall now immediately draw in favor of Wm Wirt 50.D. David Ross 64.55 Lancelot Minor 150.D. and Messrs Leitch of Charlottesville[3] a thousand Dollars. I must moreover request you to pay to mr Darmsdatt his account of the last year, and what he has furnished me this year, including $\frac{1}{2}$ doz. barrels of herrings ordered to Bedford; and to remit to Thomas Voigt of Philadelphia, watchmaker, 130.D.[4] which I have notified him would be done. my note in bank I would wish to be reduced to 1500.D. at the first renewal. whether I can take it up entirely or further from present funds depends on some claims on me not yet ascertained. accept the assurance of my constant esteem & respect   TH: JEFFERSON

P.S. since writing the above I have desired Voigt to draw on you, not exceeding 130.D. the precise sum not being known.

PoC (DLC); brackets in original; at foot of first page: "Mr Gibson"; endorsed by TJ.

Peter Derieux's AUNT was Marie Françoise Plumard de Bellanger. TJ noted on 27 July that his payment to JAMES KINSOLVING included $2.74 for "ticket. clk. Chanc. Richmd. Gilliam v. Wayles's exrs."; $2.45 to "Th:J. ads. Scott"; $19.16 to "clk. Ct. Appeals Peyton v. Henderson"; and $14.93 to "Mrs. Molly Lewis's order on me." On 28 July he wrote that the payments to WAYT & WINN and MARTIN DAWSON were both for "merchandize." On 1 Aug. he indicat-

ed that the payment to LANCELOT MINOR was "to pay debts of Hastings Marks." On 2 Aug. TJ recorded that the $1,000 to Samuel & James LEITCH included $618.40 for the "principal of my note to Jas. Dinsmore assd. them"; $159 for "interest from 1809. Apr. 7. to 1813. July 31."; and the $222.60 "balance to be credited in my acct. with them" (*MB*, 2:1290–1).

[1] Manuscript: "good-" (at the end of a line).
[2] Word interlined.
[3] Manuscript: "Charlottesvill."
[4] Reworked from "120.D."

To Thomas Voigt

SIR   Monticello July 30. 13.

Your favor of the 1st inst. is recieved, and I will now ask the favor of you to procure for me such a gold watch as I described in my letter of May 20. that is to say, excellent in it's quality, but only moderately ornamented, just enough to make it fit for a lady. on a similar occasion of such a watch from your father in 1808.[1] mr Short procured for me a chain of Paris gold (in[2] several strands of very minute links), price 18.D. and a chrystal seal, not set, but in a solid peice of the form in the margin price 2.D. I should be glad to recieve such now with the watch. mr Short, if in Philadelphia, will more particularly advise you as to the chain and seal.   Next as to the mode of sending it, opportunities by a person coming are too rare to be waited for: but I think it may come safely by the mail if properly packed, first in a tin box well lined with cotton, and something within[3] the top to guard the chrystal particularly, and keep it from ever jarring against the top of the box: the tin box to be put between 2. pieces of paste board of the size of an ordinary letter, well stuffed also with cotton, and put under an ordinary paper cover addressed to me. if you could besides this get a trusty passenger to take it on to Fredericksbg, and there put it into the post office with directions to send it by the mail <u>stage</u>, not the <u>horse</u> mail it would be more safe: tho' I believe it might be safely committed at once to the mail at Philadelphia. I desire, by this post, Gibson and Jefferson of

Richmond to pay your draught on them to the amount of 130.D. or on your application to remit you the money. let me hear from you, if you please when you forward the watch. Accept my respects.

TH: JEFFERSON

RC (PPAmP: Thomas Jefferson Papers); addressed: "Mʳ Thomas Voigt Watchmaker 44. N. 7ᵗʰ street Philadelphia"; frank and part of postmark clipped; postmarked Milton, [. . .] Aug. PoC (MHi); endorsed by TJ.

Late in 1807 TJ asked Henry Voigt (YOUR FATHER) to help him procure a gold watch for his granddaugher. The timepiece was likely a gift for Ann C. Randolph (Bankhead), who would celebrate her seventeenth birthday in January 1808. The elder Voigt procured the watch at a cost of $85 from Chaudron & Company, the firm from which William

Short also purchased the CHAIN OF PARIS GOLD and CHRYSTAL SEAL (*MB*, 2:1218; TJ to Henry Voigt, 3 Dec. 1807, receipt from Chaudron & Company, 18 Dec. 1807, and Voigt to TJ, 19 Dec. 1807 [all MHi]; Short to TJ, 28 Apr. 1808, and TJ to Short, 5 May 1808 [both DLC]). The watch now being ordered was for TJ's granddaughter Ellen W. Randolph (Coolidge), who would turn seventeen years old in October 1813 (*MB*, 2:1291).

¹ TJ here canceled "I had procured."
² Word interlined in place of "to wit."
³ Word interlined in place of "on."

From Tunis Wortman

SIR New York July 30. 1813.

With diffidence I have undertaken the task to establish and conduct a new press in this city, under the title of Standard of Union.

A copy of its prospectus is inclosed for your perusal.

Not venturing to make any promise in regard to the talent of the paper, I shall only answer for the integrity of its principles, and its unshaken devotion to that great cause, which from my youth upwards, I have always believed inseparable from the happiness of our country.

Personally a stranger to you, nothing but a firm conviction that you continue to approve and wish success to those sentiments which have governed the tenor of your life, could justify my writing.

I disdain flattery, but why should I withhold the expression of honest and sincere esteem? For years I have been in the habit of revering your virtues. I wish you much felicity in the shade of retirement and in the evening of your days.

I venture to request your name as a subscriber to the paper; and, should you approve the undertaking, a line expressive of your good opinion would be doubly gratifying and encouraging.

With every sentiment of sincere respect. Yours.

T WORTMAN
5 Frankfort Street

RC (CSmH: JF-BA); at foot of text: "Thomas Jefferson Esquire"; endorsed by TJ as received 11 Aug. 1813 and so recorded in SJL. Enclosure: Wortman, *Prospectus Of a New Paper, to be entitled The Standard of Union* (New York, July 1813), lamenting that, although the present war is just and necessary, the government and Constitution are under threat from a domestic faction; calling on faithful citizens to "rally around the ark of our liberties—the Standard of our Constitution"; lauding a free and independent press; asserting that the proposed newspaper is experimental and will be devoted to the rights and best interest of the people, the public good, and truth; promising not to defame private characters; seeking the patronage of the Republican party; and indicating that the paper will be similar in size and organization to the Washington *National Intelligencer*, be published twice a week, on Tuesdays and Fridays, and cost five dollars annually. The other enclosure, a subscription list, has not been found.

Tunis Wortman (d. 1822), attorney, author, and politician, enlisted in the New York militia in 1794 and served as a lieutenant until 1797. He was the first secretary of the New York Democratic Society and a member of the Tammany Society of New York. Wortman wrote *A Treatise Concerning Political Enquiry, and the Liberty of the Press* (New York, 1800), a clas-

sic libertarian response to the Sedition Act, and on the occasion of TJ's presidential inauguration in 1801, he delivered *An Address to the Republican Citizens of New-York* (New York, 1801). He worked as a New York City clerk from 1801 until he was replaced in 1807 following a political upheaval. He regained this position in 1808 but was briefly jailed the following year. The official charge was debt, but Wortman's incarceration probably grew out of further internal political machinations. He also operated a law practice, acted as a notary, became a master in chancery in 1817, and was appointed a ward justice in 1818 (*Military Minutes of the Council of Appointment of the State of New York, 1783–1821* [1901–02], 1:278, 295, 368; *Minutes of the Common Council of the City of New York, 1784–1831* [1917–30], esp. 1:22, 4:375; New York *American Citizen and General Advertiser*, 17 July 1801; New York *Public Advertiser*, 6 May 1807; Washington *Monitor*, 11 May 1809; New York *National Advocate*, 1 Sept. 1817; *New-York Daily Advertiser*, 27 Apr. 1818; Robert W. T. Martin, *The Free and Open Press: The Founding of American Democratic Press Liberty, 1640–1800* [2001], 157–9, 161–2; *New York Evening Post*, 30 Sept. 1822).

The New York *Standard of Union* was published from 5 Oct. 1813 until May of the following year (Brigham, *American Newspapers*, 1:694).

From Edward Hansford and John L. Clarke

MOST HONORABLE SIR,   Portsmouth Vᵃ July 31ˢᵗ 1813.

We the subscribers most earnestly solicit, that your honor will give us your opinion, on the following extraordinary Phenomenon Viz:

At   hour on the night of the 25ᵗʰ instant, we saw in the South a Ball of fire full as large as the sun at Maridian which was frequently obscured within the space of ten minutes by a smoke emitted from its own body, but ultimately retained its briliancy, and form[1] during that period, but with apparent agitation. It then assumed the form of a Turtle which also appeared to be much agitated and as frequently obscured by a similar smoke. It descended obliquely to the West, and raised again perpendicular to its original hight which was on or about 75 degrees. It then assumed the shape of a human skeleton which was frequently obscured by a like smoke and as frequently descended and ascended—It then assumed the form of a Scotch Highlander arrayed for battle and extremely agitated, and ultimately passed to the West and disappeared[2] in its own smoke. we are honorable

Sir with Sentiments of very high respect & esteem Your most Obedient very humble Serv[ts]

EDWARD HANSFORD, Keeper of
the Washington Tavern in
the Town of Portsmouth Virginia—
JOHN L. CLARKE, of Baltimore

RC (DLC); in an unidentified hand, signed by Hansford and Clarke; at head of text: "Thomas Jefferson M.A."; addressed: "Thomas Jefferson Esq[r] Monticello Virginia"; franked; postmarked Portsmouth, 1 Aug., and Charlottesville, 26 Aug.; endorsed by TJ as received 14 Sept. 1813 and so recorded in SJL.

Edward Hansford, tavern keeper, carpenter, and joiner, was harbormaster for the Norfolk and Portsmouth district by 1805 (Norfolk Co. Deed Book, 27:48–9; *JHD*, 1805 sess. [19 Dec. 1805], 36; DNA: RG 29, CS, Portsmouth, Norfolk Co., 1810).

John L. Clarke (ca. 1777–1816), a native of Newport, Rhode Island, had recently been discharged as a master or midshipman in the United States Navy. He was a sea captain residing in Baltimore at the time of his death (Callahan, *U.S. Navy*, 116; *The United States Kalendar, and Army and Navy Register, for 1813* [New York, 1813], 44; *The Baltimore Directory and Register for the Year 1816* [Baltimore, 1816], 42; *Newport Mercury*, 3 Feb. 1816).

[1] Manuscript: "from."
[2] Reworked from "disappointed."

To Samuel & James Leitch

July 31. 13.

25.℔ brown sugar

TH:J.

RC (ViU: TJP); dateline beneath signature; at foot of text: "Mess[rs] Leitch." Not recorded in SJL.

From Ferdinand R. Hassler

MOST HONORED SIR! London. August 1st 1813.

With the present I have the honor to forward You two Boocks which M[r] Warden, Consul general of the Un: St: at Paris charged me to deliver to You, & I hoped to have the honor to present to You myself; but as my mission here is not so near at its end as I expected at that time, the Instruments being not yet near finished as I expected, I take the Liberty to forward them to You to avoid longuer delay.

I have the honor to be with perfect respect and esteem
Most honored Sir
Your mos obed[t] h[ble] Serv[t] F: R: HASSLER

I join the Rapport of the Vaccine Institution here.

RC (DLC); endorsed by TJ, in part and incorrectly, as a letter from the "Swedish consul in London" received 10 Oct. 1813, and recorded in SJL with this date of receipt but without this identification.

Ferdinand Rudolph Hassler (1770–1843), geodesist and first superintendent of the United States Coast Survey, was born in Aarau, Switzerland, and studied mathematics and scientific surveying in Switzerland, France, and Germany. Political instability in Europe limited his employment opportunities there, and he immigrated to the United States in 1805 as part of an effort to establish a Swiss enclave in South Carolina. When the plan proved abortive, Hassler settled in Philadelphia. He was elected to the American Philosophical Society in 1807, the same year that he was hired as a professor of mathematics at the United States Military Academy at West Point and chosen to head a government survey to chart the Atlantic coast. He left West Point in 1809 and taught for the next two years at Union College in Schenectady, New York. In 1811 Secretary of the Treasury Albert Gallatin sent Hassler to Europe to gather equipment for the coastal survey, which had not yet begun work, but he was detained there by the outbreak of the War of 1812 and did not return until

1815. The following year he was formally appointed superintendent of the United States Coast Survey. Highly able but tactless and politically unskilled, Hassler introduced new scientific instruments and precise techniques in America but was forced out of the survey in 1818 by a law restricting its work to naval and military officers. He spent much of the next twelve years farming in New York state and writing mathematics textbooks. Hassler unsuccessfully sought a teaching position at the University of Virginia on several occasions and taught briefly in Richmond at Burke's Seminary late in the 1820s. In 1830 Andrew Jackson appointed him superintendent of the Bureau of Weights and Measures. Hassler returned to head the Coast Survey in 1832 and held that post until his death (*ANB*; *DAB*; *DSB*; Florian Cajori, *The Chequered Career of Ferdinand Rudolph Hassler, First Superintendent of the United States Coast Survey* [1929]; Robert Patterson to TJ, 3 Mar. 1806 [DLC]; APS, Minutes, 17 Apr. 1807 [MS in PPAmP]; Hassler to TJ, 14 June 1824; TJ to Hassler, 22 June 1824; Baltimore *Niles' National Register*, 25 Nov. 1843).

David Bailie Warden CHARGED Hassler with delivering to TJ a work by François Emmanuel, vicomte de Toulongeon, the *Histoire De France, depuis La Révolution De 1789; Écrite d'après les mémoires et manuscrits contemporains, recueillis dans les dépôts civils et militaires* (Paris, 1801–03; Sowerby, no. 240), after his first effort to convey it to TJ failed (Warden to TJ, 1 Apr. 1813). The other book he sent via Hassler has not been identified. Neither has the RAPPORT of the London VACCINE INSTITUTION, which was founded in 1806 and merged with the Jennerian Society after the establishment of a national vaccine board in 1813 (*DNB*, 20:533).

Account with David Higginbotham

1812			Mr Thomas Jefferson		a/c with David Higginbotham						
						$	Ct	$	Ct	$	Ct
Aug^t	3		To 2^{lb} Powder ℔ note	83		1:66					
"	"		Cash paid stage driver for bringing up tin			25					
"	6	"	8^{lb} 15 oz loaf sugar ℔ note	34		2 97					
"	"	"	140^{lb} bar Iron $11.67, 2 × Cut saw files	41		12 8					
"	"	"	1 sack salt $10 1^{lb} powder	83		10 83	$27	79			
"	7	"	1 pain Glass 8 x 10 for bunkers hill ℔ D H			17					
"	"	"	2 Bunches lines. ℔ note	42.		84					
"	"	"	2 Loaves sugar 18^{lb}	34		6.					
"	17	"	200^{lb} spinning Cotton	25.		50	57	01			
"	25	"	42^{lb} sugar $7 2^{lb} Tea $5,50 17$\frac{1}{2}$^{lb} Loaf sugar $5 84						18	34	$103	14
Sep^t	11	"	6 yds linen Cambrick sent you by (Jeff R)						32	50		
"	18	"	17$\frac{1}{2}$^{lb} Loaf sugar ℔ note	34		5 95					
"	"	"	62^{lb} bro Sugar "	21		13. 2					
"	"	"	1^{lb} fig blue 1,50 1 oz nutmeg 1,50			3.					
"	"	"	6^{lb} Sugar for Mrs MClure ℔ note			1 26					
"	21	"	1 quire paper ℔ Bacon			34	23	57			
"	26	"	41^{lb} Bacon for m^r Stark ℔ note						6	83	$62	90
"	28	"	1 Curry comb 50 1 horse brush 75 ℔ note			1,25					
"	"	"	2^{lb} Glover salts	42		84					
"	"	"	2^{lb} tea $6 13$\frac{1}{4}$^{lb} Loaf sugar $4 51			10 51	12	60			

Oct	3	"	1 sack salt		9			
"	5	"	6 pair weavers Brushes					
			sent by Ja^s	4/9	4 75			
"	"	"	547^{lb} Bar Iron ℔ note	6^d	45 38			
"	"	"	6 Plough Plates 96	8^d	10 67	69 80		
"	10	"	68^{lb} bar Iron ℔ note	6^d	5 67			
"	"	"	2 Loaves Sugar wt					
			14^{lb} 10 oz	2/	4 88	10 55		
"	12	"	1 sack salt 9 2^{lb} Tea 6			15		
"	18	"	1 Bar Blisterd steel 23$\frac{1}{2}$^{lb}			3 99	111 94	
			Amount Car^d forward				$277 98	
Oct	20	"	17 Pains 8 by 10 window Glass		2 83			
"	"	"	1 Cowskin whip 25		25			
"	"	"	$\frac{1}{2}$ yd Linen		63			
"	"	"	1 doz wine Glasses	21	2 52	6 23		
"	28	"	3$\frac{1}{2}$ yds Drab Cloth ℔ note		10 50			
"	"	"	1$\frac{1}{2}$ yds via cloth	50	63			
"	"	"	1 Slip Co^{ld} Thread					
			12 1 doz buttons	42	54			
"	"	"	1 oz nuns thread		34			
"	"	"	48$\frac{1}{2}$^{lb} bar Iron 4—4 43$\frac{3}{4}$^{lb}					
			Cheese 7—30		11 34			
"	"	"	7 yds via Cloth	50	3 50			
"	"	"	1$\frac{1}{2}$^{lb} tea 4 50 3 awl Blades 4		4 54	31 39	37 62	
nov "	2	"	3$\frac{1}{2}$^{lb} Putty ℔ note	1/3		74		
"	10	"	3 sets steel knitting pins	1/		50		
"	13	"	1 Double bolted pad lock			75		
"	16	"	9$\frac{3}{4}$ Ger steel ℔ note of Bacon		4— 4			
"	"	"	41$\frac{1}{2}$^{lb} Iron	6^d	3 47	7 51	9 50	
"	25	"	1$\frac{1}{2}$ Bushels salt ℔ note of					
			newby	15/		3 75		
"	"	"	1 Pad lock ℔ Bacon			34		
De^b "	2	"	1 Gallon whiskey ℔ do			75		
"	11	"	519 yds Planes ℔ note	5/3	420.63			
"	"	"	500 yds best Ticklenburg	43	215			
"	"	"	36 Large Dutch Blankets	21/	126			
"	"	"	15 " " "	19/6	48.75			
"	"	"	40 Wool Hats	7/6	50	$860 38	865 22	
"	16	"	2 sacks salt ℔ note of Bacon		18.			
"	"	"	31^{lb} bar Iron "	6^d	2 58	20 58		
"	19	"	2 Pair angolo hoes ℔ self		3,50			
		"	80 yds Ticklenburg		34,40			

		"	4 Bottles Mustard	1/9	1,17				
		"	1^{lb} salt Petre 6/9 1 hair broom[1] 3/9		1,76	40	83	61	41
			Amount Card forward					$1,251	73[2]
Dec^b	19	"	81 yds rolls ℔ reqt & Bacon	2/	27				
"	"	"	100 W C needles		1				
"	"	"	3 Bed cord ℔ note	4/6	2 25	30	25		
"	22	"	6^{lb} Sugar		1.25				
"	"	"	100 W C needles		1				
"	"	"	4^{lb} Co^{ld} Thread		8				
"	"	"	10^{lb} ozbs Thread		12 50				
"	"	"	3½ yds hemp rolls		1 83	24.	58		
"	26	"	25 yds blue cloth ℔ note		31 25				
"	"	"	30 yds Ticklingburg	43	12 90				
"	"	"	6 yds white flanel	4/6	4 50				
"	"	"	6 yds humhams	1/9	1 75				
"	"	"	Cash sent you		10				
"	28	"	243^{lb} Bar Iron ℔ note	6^d	20 25	80.	65		
"	31	"	2 large Phiols Castor oil ℔ note	4/6		1	50	136	98
1813									
Jany	1	"	3 Hanks silk	"	8^d		34		
"	"	"	3¼ Ga^{ls} rum	"	15/	8,12			
"	"	"	4 pair wool cards	"	7/	4 67	12,	79	
"	5	"	13^{lb} sole Leather ℔ m^r Bacon	2/		4,	34		
"	6	"	4½ yds Blue cloth ℔ note	18/	13 50				
"	"	"	28½^{lb} Blisterd Steel	1/6	7 12	20	62		
"	7	"	2^{lb} Tea ℔ note	18/	6				
"	"	"	1^{lb} Pepper 4/6 1^{lb} salt Petre	6/9	1 87	7	87	45	96
"	12	"	4 yds blue Coating ℔ note	24/	16				
			3½ yds bro Do	21/	12 42				
			18 Large Plated Buttons	4/6	1 12				
			1½ yds yellow flanel	6/	1 50				
			6 hanks silk	8^d	67				
			1¾ yds bro holland	3/9	1 20				
			1 oz Cold Thread		12				
			4 yds silk ferret		50				
			10 yds Ticklingburg		4 30				
			3¾^{lb} sole leather ℔ Bacon		1.25				
			1 sack salt ℔ note		9				
			1 " " ℔ Burnley		9				
			paid Mrs MClure ℔ note		6			63	8
								1497	75

Jany	14	"	1 Pair angolo Hose ℔ note	1 75			
"	"	"	10^{lb} 4^d Cut nails	3			
"	"	"	3½ Gallons whiskey	3 50			
"	"	"	1 Pint Do	12	8 37		
"	15	"	paid stage driver for Bringing up boots		25		
"	21	"	3 sack bags ℔ m^r Bacon	3			
"	"	"	1 Do "	68			
"	"	"	6 yds napt Cotton	3 75			
"	"	"	3 yds ferret	38			
"	"	"	1 Sack salt	9	16 81		
"	22	"	8^{lb} German steel[3] ℔ note		2	27 43	
"	25	"	1^{lb} salt Petre ℔ note	1 12			
"	"	"	2 yds Brown holland 3/9	1 25	2 37		
"	"	"	6¾^{lb} sole leather	2 25			
"	"	"	21^{lb} bro Sugar 1/3	4 37			
"	"	"	11½^{lb} Coffee	3 83	10 45		
Feby	2	"	29^{lb} 3 oz loaf sugar ℔ note 2/	9 72			
"	"	"	2^{lb} Imperial Tea	6	15 72		
"	10	"	10½^{lb} sole Leather ℔ m^r Bacon	3 50			
"	"	"	1 half Inch auger 30 1¾ Do 50	80			
"	"	"	1 Cowhide whip 25 1. Reem letter paper 33/	5 75			
"	"	"	2 hand saw files 1/6 20½^{lb} Iron 1,70	1 95	12 00		
"	15	"	2 yds Ticklingburg ℔ Burnley		86	41 40	
"	18	"	26^{lb} Bro Sugar ℔ note	5 42			
"	"	"	25^{lb} Coffee	8 34			
"	"	"	2 Loaves white sugar 15¼^{lb} @ 2/	5 8			
"	"	"	2^{lb} Imperial Tea 18/	6	24 84		
"	20	"	1 stock lock & key ℔ self	2 50			
"		"	2 Gallons[4] Molases ℔ note	2	4 50		
Mar	1	"	6^{lb} bro sugar for M^r MClure ℔ note	1 25			
"	"	"	290½^{lb} bar Iron 6^d	24 20			
"	"	"	1 smiths fine Polishing file	83	26 28	55 62	
			Am^t Card forward				1622 20
Mar	4	"	4 bars Iron 201^{lb} ℔ note @ 6		16 75		
"	16	"	6 Spades ℔ m^r Bacon		9		
"	25	"	14½ quarts whiskey ℔ note		3 63		
"	30	"	1 Curry Comb ℔ J Randolph	1. 25			
"	"	"	4^{lb} 4^d Cut nails ℔ m^r Johnson	8			
"		"	1 quire Paper ℔ Bacon	34	1 67		

			Description								
April	3	"	15^{lb} Coffee	2/	5						
"	"	"	3 Loaves white Sugar 20^{lb} 3 oz		7 54						
"	"	"	1^{lb} 14 oz Tea	18/	5 68						
"	"	"	3¼ Gallons old spirits	15/	8 13						
"	"	"	Cash paid Cochran for 30^{lb} bro sugar		6 25						
"	"	"	30^{lb} Spinning Cotton ℔ note		7 50						
"	"	"	3¾^{lb} sole Leather		1 25	41	35		72	40
"	7	"	1 Inch auger ℔ note	4/	67					
"	"	"	1¾ Inch Do "		50					
"	"	"	3 Smith files	3/9	1 89	3	6			
"	13	"	1 sack salt ℔ m^r Bacon			9				
"	15	"	1 Cowhide whip ℔ self		25					
"	"	"	75 yds Ger ozbs	43	32 25					
"	"	"	2 Loaves white sugar 14^{lb} 1 oz		5 86					
"	"	"	Cash paid cochren for ¾^{lb} Tea		2 25	40	61			
"	20	"	15^{lb} Coffee ℔ note		5					
"	"	"	20^{lb} 2 oz loaf sugar		8 39					
"	"	"	114^{lb} tin Iron		9 75					
"	"	"	Cash paid Cochran for 30^{lb} bro sugar		6 25					
"	"	"	1 Pair sheep shears ℔ m^r Randolph		68	30	7			
"	24	"	1 Sack salt ℔ note		9					
"	"	"	1 sack do ℔ m^r Ham		9					
"	"	"	2 yds Irish Linen ℔ Miss E Randolph		3 50	21	50		104	24
"	29	"	1½^{lb} 6^d nails to repair Cot				21			
May	7	"	125^{lb} bar Iron ℔ Joe		10 42					
"	"	"	6 Plough Plates 90^{lb}	@ 8^d	10	20	42			
"	12	"	1 Curry comb ℔ m^r Burnley				42		21	5
			Am^t Card forward						1819	89
May	19	"	2 ✕ cut saw files ℔ self		50					
"	"	"	1 smiths file half round		63	1	13			
"	"	"	48^{lb} Bar Iron ℔ note		4					
"	"	"	1 Curry Comb		42	4	42			
"	29	"	paid M^{rs} MClure ℔ note		4					
"	"	"	3½ Gallons whiskey ℔ D^o		3 50	7	50			
June	5	"	2^{lb} Glover salts				68			
"	8	"	2 sets white bone knives & forks ℔ note			8			21	73
"	9	"	2 smiths Large files ℔ self	3/9	1 25					

[347]

"	"	" 1 Dᵒ Polishing Dᵒ	5/	83					
"	"	" 2 ✕ Cut saw files	1/6	50					
"	"	" 2 handsaw Dᵒ	9ᵈ	25					
"	"	" 1 Pen knife 50 1 Cider cock 17		67					
"	"	" 6 yds Cotton shirting	4/6	4 30					
"	"	" 22 nutmegs ℔ note		2 64					
"	"	" 1ˡᵇ alspice 63 1ˡᵇ Pepper 75		1 38	12	2⁵		
"	10	" 1 silk hat Cover ℔ self		1				
"	"	" 50ˡᵇ bro sugar ℔ note		12 50				
"	"	" 2ˡᵇ Tea $7 ½ doz bottles mustard $2		9				
"	"	" 4 Loaves white sugar 26ˡᵇ 13ᵒᶻ		11 18	33.	68		
"	15	" 7½ˡᵇ Sole Leather ℔ mʳ Bacon		2 50				
"	"	" 1 sack salt ℔ note		9				
"	"	" 4 bed Cords ℔ Do	4/6	3	14	50		60	20
"	23	" 117ˡᵇ thin tin Iron ℔ note	@ 7	11 38				
"	"	" 2 smith files half round		1 25	12	63		
July	1	" 56ˡᵇ Bro Sugar ℔ note		14				
"	"	" 4 Loaves white sugar 27½ˡᵇ		11 37				
"	"	" 2ˡᵇ Gunpowder Tea		7				
"	"	" 1 Sack salt		9	41	37		
"	16	" 13¼ˡᵇ Putty ℔ note		3 65				
"		" 2 Pad locks		83	4	48		58	48
		Amount Carᵈ forward						$1960	30
July	21	" 2ˡᵇ Gun Powder Tea ℔ note		7				
"	"	" 28ˡᵇ 5 oz loaf sugar		11 81	18	81		
"	24	" 4 Printed Pocket handkf for Mrs Marks		2 50				
"	"	" 2 Painted Mugs		1				
"	"	" 1 Pewter Bason		83	4	33		
"	27	" 4¼ˡᵇ Blisterd steel ℔ Bacons note			1	6		24	20
								$1984	50
1812		Cr							
Oct	17.	By David Higginbotham for fire wood one year at B. Hill ending 1ˢᵗ oct 12			11.	00.		
Feby.	6	By ditto for rent of House at B. Hill from 1ˢᵗ Feby 1812 to 1ˢᵗ Feby 1813.			60	00		
"	16	By Cash recᵈ 30th Janʸ 1813. ℔ barg. out of a $50. note to replace mony lent			10			81
		Balˡ due D H 1ˢᵗ Augᵗ 1813						$1903	50⁶

[348]

MS (MHi); in Higginbotham's hand; repeated intermediate sums at head of pp. 2–7 omitted; endorsed by TJ: "Higginbotham David. accᵗ to Aug. 1. 1813"; with MS of TJ's Notes on Account with David Higginbotham, [3 Feb. 1814], on verso of last page.

JEFF R: Thomas Jefferson Randolph. FIG BLUE: soluble blue coloring (*OED*). Glauber's salts (GLOVER SALTS) are a colorless, crystalline form of sodium sulphate used medicinally and in dyeing. COᴸᴰ THREAD: colored thread. NUNS THREAD: a fine, white thread (*OED*). Angola hose (ANGOLO HOES): stockings made of angora wool (*OED*). OZBS (osnaburgs): a coarse linen or cotton cloth

(*OED*). HUMHAMS (humhums): a coarse Indian cotton cloth (*OED*). JOE: Joseph Fossett (TJ's slave). TJ borrowed $50 from Higginbotham in January 1812 and a further $10 on 26 Dec. 1812. On 31 Jan. 1813 he recorded the repayment of the MONY LENT in December (*MB*, 2:1272, 1273, 1285, 1286).

[1] Manuscript: "broon."
[2] Manuscript: "$12,51 73."
[3] Manuscript: "stell."
[4] Manuscript: "Gollons."
[5] Correct figure should be $11.82.
[6] Because of Higginbotham's error when he totaled his 9 June 1813 entries, the total owed by TJ should have been $1,903.30.

To Robert Richardson

SIR   Monticello. Aug. 1. 13.

Your favor of July 2. came to hand a few days ago and I am thankful to yourself as well as to mr Ross for the indulgence therein expressed as to the paiment for the castings which I should have made before. I counted on making it from the resource of my flour which I have usually sold in March. but the blockade has prevented & still prevents the sale. in the mean time another resource occurring has enabled me to inclose to mr Ross an order for the amount, being 66. D 50 C the amount of the bill and 6. months interest. should I have occasion for any other castings, I shall avail myself of the circumstance proffered by you of your furnace getting into blast.

Accept the assurance of my esteem & respect.

TH: JEFFERSON

PoC (MHi); at foot of text: "Mʳ Robert Richardson"; endorsed by TJ.

Richardson's FAVOR OF JULY 2, record-ed in SJL as received 8 July 1813 from the Oxford Iron Works, has not been found.

To David Ross

DEAR SIR   Monticello Aug. 1. 13.

In February last I had some castings from your Oxford-works amounting to 64. D 55 C for which mr Richardson desired me to make paiment to you. this I promised to do as soon as my flour could be got to market & sold; but before that took place, the blockade shut us up, and my flour is still unsold. in the mean time another resource occurs which enables me to inclose you an order on Gibson and Jefferson, which I now do for 66. D 50 C interest included. mr Richardson, by a letter of the present month, and by your instruction as he informed me, had desired me to make the paiment at my own convenience only, for which indulgence be pleased to accept my thanks. I learn with pleasure that you continue in good health, which at your age and mine is a peculiar favor of heaven. Accept my prayers for it's long continuance to you with the tender of my great respect & esteem.

TH: JEFFERSON

PoC (MHi); at foot of text: "David Ross esq."; endorsed by TJ. Enclosure not found.

David Ross (ca. 1737–1817), merchant and agent, land investor, and ironworks proprietor, emigrated from Scotland in the 1750s. By the beginning of the American Revolution he had established himself as a tobacco merchant and shipowner on a plantation at Point of Fork in Fluvanna County. In 1780 TJ appointed Ross a commercial agent responsible for procuring military supplies for the state. During his tenure in this position he countered criticism and accusations of Loyalism by drawing on his own financial resources to fulfill demands for goods. Ross resigned as commercial agent in 1782 so that he could represent Fluvanna County in two successive sessions of the House of Delegates. After the Revolutionary War ended he concerned himself primarily with the operation of the Oxford Iron Works, located on the James River near Lynchburg. TJ reported in his *Notes on the State of Virginia* that this facility produced about 150 tons of bar iron per year. By the end of the 1780s his widely distributed accumulation of land and slaves made Ross one of the wealthiest men in Virginia. However, he was often overextended and beset by foreign and domestic creditors. For a decade beginning in 1793, a consortium of his creditors controlled much of his property, including the ironworks and many of his slaves. Ross eventually took charge of his own affairs again, but ill health, increasing competition in the iron market, and other factors thwarted his hopes of further expansion. While he was governor, TJ communicated frequently with Ross, and he conducted personal business with him sporadically thereafter. Although their relationship was generally congenial, in 1802 a dispute over the sum that TJ owed on his account to Ross had to be settled by arbitrators (Charles B. Dew, "David Ross and the Oxford Iron Works: A Study of Industrial Slavery in the Early Nineteenth-Century South," *WMQ*, 3d ser., 31 [1974]: 189–224; ViHi: David Ross Letterbook; *PTJ*, 4:226–8, 8:358; Leonard, *General Assembly*, 145, 149; Henry R. McIlwaine and others, eds., *Journals of the Council of the State of Virginia* [1931–82], 3:537; *Notes*, ed. Peden, 27, 28, 29; *MB*; Henrico Co. Will Book, 5:185–6; *Richmond Enquirer*, 6 May 1817).

To William Wirt

Monticello. Aug. 1. 13.

Th: Jefferson presents his friendly respects to mr Wirt, and incloses him an order on Gibson & Jefferson for 50.D. for the kindness of his services in the suit of Scott against him. he is anxious it should be forced on at the first calling that he may be rid of the obligation which the purchaser required of him. he salutes mr Wirt with friendship & respect.

PoC (MHi); dateline at foot of text; endorsed by TJ. Enclosure not found.

Account with the Mutual Assurance Society

[ca. 2 Aug. 1813]

Thomas Jefferson Esq.

<u>0</u>   To Mutual A. Society D^r
<u>389</u>

For Quota due 1811	12.84	
Interest	1.73	
" Quota due 1812	12.84	
Interest	" 96	
" Quota due 1813	12.84	
Commission	2.06	$^{s}43.27

Thos Jefferson esq^r for Henderson's Legatees

<u>0.</u>   To Mutual A. Society D^{r1}
<u>335</u>

[Notation by TJ:] this is for the millhouse which I never bought. see Brown's letter Aug. 12. 12.				South Milton[2]
	Quota for 1809	$18 . 50		
	Interest	4 . 72		
	Quota for 1810	18 . 50		
	Interest	3 – 61		
	Quota for 1811	18 – 50		
	Interest	2 – 50		
	Quota for 1812	18 – 50		
	Interest	1 – 38		
	Quota for 1813	18 – 50		
	Commission	5 – 24	$^{s}109–95	

MS (MHi); in Benjamin Brown's hand except for TJ's marginal notation; date conjectured from information in TJ's Account with the Mutual Assurance Society, [ca. 7 Aug. 1813]; endorsed by Brown: "Tho. Jefferson." Tr (MHi); entirely in TJ's hand; lacking marginal notation; subjoined to PoC of TJ to Clifton Garland, 7 Aug. 1813.

[1] In Tr TJ replaced this heading with "The part of the acc^t for the mill is as follows."

[2] Preceding two words not in Tr.

From Horatio G. Spafford

HON^D & ESTEEMED FRIEND—   Albany, (NY.,) 8 Mo. 2, 1813.

My Gazetteer of the State of New York being nearly out of press, I seize an occasion which my ardent wishes afford, to present my respects, & enquire how I can forward thee a copy, without too great expense.

Pardon me, my venerable friend, should the truth seem like folly; for, on this occasion, I can hardly refrain from tears.

Addressing one of the venerable Fathers of our Republic, & one whom I had ardently hoped to see; that Father far advanced in the vale of years, & my prospect reduced[1] to a faintest hope—my hand trembles as if extended for a parting blessing:—& I can only say how sincerely I desire that boon. I am a boy of the Revolution—& still more & more is my wonder & admiration excited, when I Survey the difficulties & atchievements of that period, with the aids that my pursuits procure: for I am now writing a History of this State, which embraces that period. If I mourn[2] the memory of these worthies, generally, who conducted the Bark of State in such times, why may I not indulge the desire of my heart to see as <u>many as may be</u>, of the few who still survive? I pray thee to let me recieve from thee an occasional remembrance, & none of the Sons of our glorious Republic shall retain more lasting & grateful affection. Devoted to the records of remembrance in the past & present history of our country, I should feel all the value & importance of thy good-will.

Of thy former Letter, I have made a due use in preparing for a second edition of my Geography.

With sentiments of the highest esteem, I remain thy friend,

HORATIO G. SPAFFORD.

RC (MHi); at foot of text: "Thomas Jefferson, Esq."; endorsed by TJ as received 11 Aug. 1813 and so recorded in SJL.

In his FORMER LETTER, dated 14 May 1809, TJ suggested some revisions for the proposed SECOND EDITION of Spafford's *General Geography, and Rudiments of Useful Knowledge* (Hudson, N.Y., 1809; Sowerby, no. 3828).

At some point Spafford also sent TJ a broadside dated 15 Apr. 1813, in which he provides an update on his new work on the state of NEW YORK, reporting that the printing is nearing completion; that the volume is now larger and more expensive than he had originally predicted, necessitating a price increase to $2.50; that the work will be printed in octavo on high-quality paper using brevier type and will be approximately 360 pages in length; that he has circulated nearly 2,500 letters in search of material for the work; that the initials of correspondents who provided assistance will be placed at the end of the pertinent entries; and that, having invested $7,000 and two years of his own time in the publication, he is unable to reward his correspondents with complimentary copies (printed circular in DLC: TJ Papers, 198:35199).

[1] Manuscript: "rduced."
[2] Manuscript: "morn."

From Isaac McPherson

RESPECTED FRIEND   Baltimore August 3d 1813

In the year 1790 or thereabout I presented to thee letters of recommendation from George Mason, Ralph Wormley, & Henry Lee Esq[re] on business. From thy attention to me at that time, I take the liberty of now addressing thee without restraint on a subject that I am in no way interested in, more than as far as respects the good of my country at large, and if I am correctly informed thou hast it in thy power to be useful.

Some years ago Congress passed a Law giving Oliver Evans an exclusive right of vending machinery used in mills, Commonly called his machinery, for 14 years.

After his patent right had expired[1] and going back to all who had erected mills, between the expiration of the old patent and the new law, he has met with considerable opposition when suits were instituded, by persons being summoned that were supposed to be the real inventors of the machinery, but he appears to have a particular talent in procuring testimony so pointed, (altho not always credited,) that the court and Jury must be for him.

In a suit lately decided in this city, a miller that did not manufacture perhaps more than 5 or 600 Barrells of flour yearly was fined 1850 dollars with costs of suit.

The Judges have said since that decision, and with a great deal of truth, that every opportunity was given to the defendant to prove that O. Evans was not the real inventor. That is saying, that had it been proven to their satisfaction, that he was not the inventor, they would have directed the jury to find for the defendant.

I am told that thou hast in thy possession a Book of an old date that has the plates of the screw and elevator at work in a mill, for the same purpose as he has them. If this should be the case, he may have seen that book or some other which he took his works from.

I shall be much obliged to have a reply from thee on the subject. I am with real regard Thy Friend   Isaac McPherson

RC (DLC); in a clerk's hand, signed by McPherson; at head of text in clerk's hand: "Thomas Jefferson Esq^e"; endorsed by TJ as received 6 Aug. 1813 and so recorded in SJL.

Isaac McPherson (1759–1827), miller and manufacturer, was a merchant in Alexandria by 1792. He married Andrew Ellicott's daughter in 1796, operated the Occoquan Mills in Prince William County by 1798, and moved by 1803 to Baltimore, where he manufactured millstones (*PTJ*, 23:120–1; Charles W. Evans, *Biographical and Historical Accounts of the Fox, Ellicott, and Evans Families* [1882], 80; *Federal Gazette & Baltimore Daily Advertiser*, 24 Jan. 1798, 29 Jan. 1801; Baltimore *Republican; or, Anti-Democrat*, 14 Jan. 1803; G. Terry Sharrer, "The Merchant-Millers: Baltimore's Flour Milling Industry, 1783–1860," *Agricultural History* 56 [1982]: 144; *Baltimore Patriot & Mercantile Advertiser*, 24 Mar. 1826, 23 Jan. 1828, 29 Apr. 1829; R. J. Matchett, *Matchett's Baltimore Directory for 1827* [1827], 183; Records of Deceased Members of Baltimore Monthly

Meeting [ca. 1658–ca. 1895], 67 [PSC-Hi]).

TJ received letters from George Mason and Henry Lee introducing McPherson in April 1792, not 1790 (*PTJ*, 23:120–1). On 21 Jan. 1808 Congress passed "An Act for the relief of Oliver Evans," which gave him "for a term not exceeding fourteen years, the full and exclusive right and liberty of making, constructing, using, and vending to be used, his invention, discovery and improvements in the art of manufacturing flour and meal" (*U.S. Statutes at Large*, 6:70–1; *List of Patents*, 62). His old patent, which had expired after fourteen years, was dated 18 Dec. 1790 (*List of Patents*, 4). Early in December 1812 the United States Circuit Court for the Maryland District awarded $1,850 in damages to Oliver Evans in his patent infringement lawsuit against Samuel Robinson, a Montgomery County miller (*Baltimore Patriot*, 14 Jan. 1813).

[1] Thus in manuscript, but the intent may have been to combine the preceding two sentences thus, "for 14 years after his patent right had expired."

From John Wilson

Respected Sir,   Washington City aug 3^d 1813

we learn that in Europe, however obscure an author may be, he freely addresses the highest literary adepts; and altho' he may not possess any previous knowledge of the gentlemen, he runs no risk of incurring the imputation of obtruding.—That an indulgence so cheerfully granted in Europe, could meet in our Country with the slightest damp, is what my pen would blush to intimate.

Various considerations have urged me to try my hand at M.S.S., in hopes to acquire that countenance which (often) cannot be sustained without an unwilling dependence on old friends. Friends whose efforts, after all, I have persuaded myself, are not like anything from self which may chance to meet the public approbation; that chance I venture to commit myself to. Vain adventure, Mr Morse, methinks I hear you exclaim of a virginian—an obscure man beset with a thousand cares. Well, well, I shall not quarrel with him about that. Mr Eppes has afforded me the opportunity of what I have so ardently desired, and I am very happy of having one of my M.S.S. submitted to you.

Your opinion will be esteemed a favor as a recommendation, in which I hope you will unite with[1] me to establish a correct rule for certain plurals; and until that is done, to batter down the prejudices of education, if the °rule shall have been learnt which is undoubtedly not correct.

Very respectfully I am Sir Your M° Obed^t Servt

JN° WILSON.

°decried in my M.S.

RC (CSmH: JF-BA); endorsed by TJ as received 14 Aug. 1813 and so recorded in SJL.

John Wilson was a native of Norfolk and the namesake son of a former member of the Virginia House of Burgesses and House of Delegates. He invested what little capital he had in an ill-fated mercantile firm in his hometown before moving by January 1803 to the District of Columbia, where he kept his own shoe shop in Washington City and also briefly managed another man's shoe store in Alexandria. Owing in part to his earlier experience as an engrosser for the Virginia legislature, Wilson obtained a clerkship in the War Department's accounting office in about 1804 and held it for more than a decade (Leonard, *General Assembly*; Wilson to TJ, 27 Aug. 1803 [DNA: RG 59, LAR, 1801–09]; *Washington*

Federalist, 28 May 1804; Wilson to TJ, Nov. 1814; *ASP, Miscellaneous*, 2:310).

Enclosed separately in a missing letter of 31 July 1813 from John Wayles Eppes to TJ, recorded in SJL as received 4 Aug. 1813 from Washington, Wilson SUBMITTED the MS, not found, for his work, *A Volume for all Libraries . . . Being a System of Philological Entertainments, Comprising Altogether an Extensive Ground Work for Immense Improvements in the English Language* (Washington, 1814; Sowerby, no. 4888), in which he aggressively attacked the RULE that "If the singular ends in y, or ey, preceded by a consonant, the plural shall end in ies" (p. 15; see also Wilson to TJ, 3 June 1814). Wilson also sent the MS to James Madison at about the same time (Madison, *Papers, Pres. Ser*, 6:490–1).

[1] Manuscript: "with with."

From Elbridge Gerry

DEAR SIR,   Washington 4th August 1813

My eldest Son will have the honor of presenting this. He is on a visit to his friends & relations at Pittsylvania, & it would have been impossible for him to have passed near to Monticello, without[1] manifesting that reverence & respect which he has always entertained for the friend & father of his Country. In presenting him[2] to yourself & family, I am favored with an opportunity of repeating assurances of my high esteem & respect for yourself, & of requesting you to renew the sincere wishes for the welfare of your family, of your affectionate friend   E. GERRY

RC (MHi); at foot of text: "President Jefferson"; endorsed by TJ as received 11 Aug. 1813 and so recorded in SJL.

Gerry's ELDEST SON was Elbridge Gerry (1793–1867). The younger Gerry graduated from Harvard University in 1813 and went on to study law with his brother-in-law James T. Austin. He was appointed surveyor and inspector of the revenue for the port of Boston by James Monroe in 1817 and reappointed to the same post by John Quincy Adams in 1826, but Andrew Jackson let his term expire in 1830. Gerry then served as a representative to the Massachusetts General Court, 1831–35 (*Harvard University Quinquennial Catalogue of the Officers and Graduates, 1636–1925* [1925], 190; DNA: RG 59, LAR, 1809–17 and 1817–25; William T. Davis, *Bench and Bar of the Commonwealth of Massachusetts* [1895], 1:255; *JEP*, 3:96, 98, 262, 270, 462, 470 [12, 15 Dec. 1817, 7, 23 Jan. 1822, 26 Dec. 1825, 3 Jan. 1826]; *JS*, 19:390; New York *Evening Post*, 21 May 1867).

The younger Gerry's FRIENDS & RELATIONS in Pittsylvania County were the family of his recently deceased uncle, Isaac Coles, including the latter's widow, Catharine Thompson Coles (*DVB*).

[1] Reworked from "with."
[2] Reworked from "himself."

From Patrick Gibson

SIR   Richmond 4th August 1813—

I have received your favor of the 30th Ult° and shall attend to the several drafts therein mention'd Your note in bank fell due on the 30th and was paid, as you supposed it probable that your demands would exceed the amount in hand I have had Judah's note discounted so that you may consider the whole as received—I have not yet been able to recover the money from Philpots for the 4 Hhds Tob° sold him in March '12, altho suit has long since been brought upon his note by Wm Hay Jr—

    With great respect I am
    Your obt Servt   PATRICK GIBSON

RC (ViU: TJP-ER); between dateline and salutation: "Thomas Jefferson Esqre"; endorsed by TJ as received 6 Aug. 1813 and so recorded in SJL.

To Paul Allen

Monticello Aug. 5. 13.

Not being able to go myself in quest of the information respecting Govr Lewis which was desired in your letter of May 25. I have been obliged to wait the leisure of those who could do it for me. I could forward you within a few days a statement of what I have collected, but more time would improve it, if the impression of the work will not be delayed. I will ask the favor of you therefore to name the latest time which the progress of the other part will admit, by which time you shall not fail to recieve it. my matter may fill perhaps 20. 8vo pages, and as these may be paged independantly of the body of the work, I suppose it may be the last sheet printed.

Of General Clarke I shall be able to give you nothing. he was indeed born within 2. miles of Charlottesville,[1] & 4. of the place of my birth in the county of Albemarle, but he was so much my junior, that before I could know him, his father removed to another part of the country. Accept the assurance of my great respect.

T<small>H</small>: J<small>EFFERSON</small>

RC (MH); at foot of text: "Mr Paul Allen." PoC (DLC); endorsed by TJ.

Paul Allen (1775–1826), poet and editor, was born in Providence, Rhode Island, and graduated from Rhode Island College (later Brown University) in 1793. He published a number of orations and several volumes of poetry, including *Original Poems, Serious and Entertaining* (Salem, Mass., 1801). Allen also edited Biddle, *Lewis and Clark Expedition*, an important labor for which he rarely receives credit. In 1814 he moved from Philadelphia to Baltimore, where he edited several newspapers, including the *Baltimore Telegraph and Commercial Advertiser*, 1814–16, the *Federal Republican and Baltimore Telegraph*, 1816–18, the *Journal of the Times*, 1818–19, and the *Morning Chronicle*, 1819–24. Although Allen is credited with writing *A History of the American Revolution* (Baltimore, 1819), the vast majority of this work seems to have been prepared by others. During his final years he managed the Baltimore *Saturday Evening Herald* (*ANB*; *DAB*; *Historical Catalogue of Brown University, 1764–1904* [1905], 79; Lester J. Cappon, "Who Is the Author of *History of the Expedition under the Command of Captains Lewis and Clark* [1814]?," *WMQ*, 3d ser., 19 [1962]: 257–68; Brigham, *American Newspapers*, 2:1369; *Baltimore Patriot & Mercantile Advertiser*, 21 Aug. 1826).

Allen's letter of M<small>AY</small> 25, not found, is recorded in SJL as received 2 June 1813 from Philadelphia.

[1] Manuscript: "Charlottesvill."

From Charles L. Lewis

DEAR SIR   Livingston, K.K 5 August 1813

myself & daughters being in reduced circomstances have been constrained to ask of several of our friends in Virginia if conveniant the friendly assistance of a few dollars I take the liberty to ask the same of you I can ashure you my dear Sir nothing short of rail want would or could induce me to make such an application to my relations and friends my Friend m^r Woods will be the barer of this letter should you be inclin'd to assist us he will be a safe hand to send by I hope you will excuse me for asking this favour. want alone is the rail cause my daughters Joins me in Love &
respect   CHA^S L. LEWIS

RC (Margaret Taylor and Olivia Taylor, on deposit ViU: TJP); with TJ's penciled note adjacent to signature: "Salem. post town Kent^y"; endorsed by TJ as received 16 Sept. 1813 from Salem, Ky., and so recorded in SJL.

Lewis's DAUGHTERS were TJ's nieces Martha C. Lewis (Monroe), Lucy B. Lewis (Griffin), and Ann M. Lewis. Rev. William "Baptist Billy" WOODS (d.

1819), a longtime friend of the Lewis family, represented Albemarle County in the Virginia House of Delegates, 1799–1800, moved about 1810 to Livingston County, Kentucky, and later served as a justice of the peace there (Woods, *Albemarle*, 354, 390; Boynton Merrill Jr., *Jefferson's Nephews: A Frontier Tragedy* [1976], 297–8, 319, 420; Leonard, *General Assembly*, 215).

From John Rhea

DEAR SIR   Washington 5th August 1813

With my sincere wishes <u>for</u> Your felicity please to accept the inclosed[1] copy of a circular
with sincere Esteem Your ob^t s^t   JOHN RHEA

RC (MHi); at foot of text: "Thomas Jefferson Esqr Late President U States"; endorsed by TJ as received 11 Aug. 1813 and so recorded in SJL. Enclosure: Rhea to his constituents, Washington, D.C., 28 July 1813, suggesting that the present war between the United States and Great Britain originated from causes similar to those that sparked the American Revolution; asserting that Britain has actively defied the terms of two treaties with the United States by plundering its commerce, forcibly impressing its seamen, and inciting Indian tribes to break

treaties and perpetrate acts of war; demonstrating that the expenditures required to execute the war have strained the treasury and caused the government to take out loans; asserting that the national financial situation now requires internal duties and taxes in order to avoid an increased debt; summarizing the acts of the recent congressional session, including authorization of internal duties and a direct tax to be apportioned among the states based on population; and noting that the internal duties will cease one year after a treaty ends the war (printed circular in DLC: Madison Collection, Rare Book and Special Collections Division; reprinted in Noble E. Cunningham Jr., ed., *Circular Letters of Congressmen to Their Constituents, 1789–1829* [1978], 2:840–4).

This day Rhea also sent the enclosure to President James Madison (Madison, *Papers, Pres. Ser.*, 6:501).

[1] Manuscript: "incosed."

From Isaac A. Coles

DEAR SIR,   Fredericksburg Aug. 6ʰ 1813.

This will be handed you by mʳ Gerry, the Son of your old Acquaintance & friend the Vice President—

Being on a visit to his relations in Pittsylvania, & being desirous of taking Monticello in his route, I cannot resist the desire of introducing him to your acquaintance and civility—

I have been for some weeks in daily expectation of an order to go on to Fort George—it has now been so long delayed that I almost dispair of active employment this fall

with the sincerest and most respectful attachmᵗ,

I am Dʳ Sir yʳ frnᵈ & Servᵗ   I. A. COLES

RC (DLC); at foot of text: "Thomas Jefferson"; endorsed by TJ as received 11 Aug. 1813 and so recorded in SJL.

To Josef Yznardy

MY EXCELLENT AND VENERATED

FRIEND   Monticello August 6. 13.

I am living retired in the mountains of Virginia, & so far removed from any seaport, that I never hear of a vessel sailing to Cadiz until she is gone. this is the true & sole reason why so many of your kind letters to me remain unacknoleged. M. Correa de Serra, of Lisbon, having done me the favor of a visit, and being to sail for the peninsul within a few weeks, furnishes me at length the opportunity of conveying a letter, of which I gladly avail myself, to recall myself to your recollection, and to assure you that I retain a lively sense of your kindness & friendship, of which I had so many proofs while you were in the US. as well as since your return to Spain. in the distresses of that country, & of Cadiz particularly, I have had just feelings for the sufferings of the inhabitants generally, but especially for yourself. to be forced from your own comfortable[1] habitation, & exposed to the brutalities & oppressions of the military, at your time of life, is truly afflicting. I hope you have had health & spirits to bear up under them, and that blessed peace will at length relieve you & your country from suffering. I enjoy good health myself, & am living amidst a croud of grand children, & great grand children, as happily as the debilities of age will permit. I here cherish the recollection of the friendships I have contracted in my journey thro' life, & think with particular pleasure on that which I have borne to yourself and shall continue to bear thro' life. Accept the assurance of this, with my prayers for your health, happiness & life through long years yet to come

Th: Jefferson

PoC (CSmH: JF-BA); at foot of text: "Don Joseph Yznardi"; endorsed by TJ.

José Corrêa da Serra had arrived to visit Monticello around 31 July 1813,

bearing letters from TJ's correspondents in Paris and Philadelphia (SJL, 31 July, 1 Aug. 1813).

[1] TJ here canceled "house."

Account with the Mutual Assurance Society

[ca. 7 Aug. 1813]

Thomas Jefferson in account with the Mutual assurance company.

		D C		D C
1811. Apr. 1. To quota on Monticello houses		12.84	int. to Sep. 1. 1813	1.73
1812.		12.84		.96
1813.		12.84		.00
		38.52		2.69
To quota on Henderson's warehouses at Milton to wit. A. Scale house valued at	400.D.		int.	
B. Transfer house	250.			
C. Warehouse 11.2 × 30	360			
1809. Apr. 1.	1110	*6.69		1.77
1810.		6.69		1.37
1811.		6.69		.97
1812		6.69		.57

1813.

	6.69		.17
	33.45		4.85
	38.52		
	2.69		
	4.85[1]		
	79.51		
To[2] commission on	79.51		
	4.		
	83.51		

D   D c   D   D C

* as settled by mr Brown. to wit as 1510 : 9.11 :: 1110 : 6.69[3]

Note. Brown mistook in adding the values of A.B.C. which amount to 1010, & not 1110. this reduces the insurance to 6.09 & not 6.69. besides I think I withdrew these houses from insurance, & this I suppose is the reason why the account presented to me Aug. 2. 13 by mr Rhodes agent of the company contained no charge for these houses. The charge for the mill house,[4] stated in that acc^t at 109.95 I have nothing to do with, because I never owned the mill house; it was excepted out of all my deeds from the family. besides the mill house was sold by them to   who pulled it down & carried it away I believe in 1808.

my true account with them therefore with interest to Sep. 1. 13. is 38.52 + 2.69 + 2.06 = 43.27 D

MS (MHi); entirely in TJ's hand; date conjectured from TJ's 7 Aug. 1813 recapitulation of this account in *MB*, 2:1292, and his related letter to Clifton Garland, 7 Aug. 1813; endorsed by TJ: "Fire insurance. Acc^t 1811–13." PoC (MHi); with final section added separately and lacking concluding note.

Benjamin Brown MISTOOK the value of the three commercial buildings in question in his Mutual Assurance Society Account for Insuring Milton Warehouses, [ca. 1 Sept. 1811]. The society's version of its account with TJ, printed above at 2 Aug. 1813, was evidently delivered by Garland, not MR RHODES.

[1] Remainder added separately to both texts after removal from polygraph.

[2] Word not in PoC.

[3] PoC ends here.

[4] Word interlined.

To Clifton Garland

SIR   Monticello Aug. 7. 13.

I have examined the account of the Mutual insurance co. which you put into my hands. so much of it as respects the houses at Monticello is right: but the account for the mill house which[1] was the property of the Hendersons, I have nothing to do with, having never purchased nor owned it. it was excepted out of all my deeds. but indeed that account lies against nobody; for on their being obliged to pull down their dam, by a decree in Chancery, the mill became useless, as no water could ever more be brought to it. they therefore sold the house to some person who pulled it down & carried away the materials. the soil then reverted to me. this happened I believe in 1808. but I am not quite sure of this date, as the demolition did not concern me. the part of the account which is right, I copy below, amounting to 43. D 27 c and inclose you an order on Gibson & Jefferson in Richmond for that sum, with the assurance of my respects

TH: JEFFERSON

PoC (MHi); adjacent to signature: "Mr Garland Agent for the M. A. co."; endorsed by TJ, with his additional notation: "1811–13"; with subjoined Tr of TJ's Account with Mutual Assurance Society, [ca. 2 Aug. 1813].

Clifton Garland (d. 1814), merchant and attorney, was a resident of Warren in southern Albemarle County. He was a tobacco inspector there in the 1790s, a partner in the firm of Walker & Garland, a justice of the peace in 1806, the longtime master of Warren's Masonic lodge, and a captain in the Albemarle County militia. Garland's law practice encompassed Albemarle, Amherst, Buckingham, Fluvanna, and Nelson counties when he became the Albemarle agent of the Mutual Assurance Society in the spring of 1813. He ran unsuccessfully in the same year for the Virginia House of Delegates. A lifelong bachelor, Garland owned five slaves in 1810 (Woods, *Albemarle*, 58–9, 200, 373, 377, 400; *JHD* [1791–92 sess.], 64;

Va. Reports, 11 [1 Hening & Munford], 423; Freemasons, Grand Lodge of Virginia, *Proceedings of a Grand Annual Communication* [1801]: 48; [1811]: 31; [1814]: 25; DNA: RG 29, CS, Albemarle Co., 1810; Garland to Samuel Greenhow, 28 Apr. 1813 [Vi: Mutual Assurance Society, Incoming Correspondence]; Albemarle Co. Will Book, 5:346–7, 7:47–8).

The Mutual Assurance Society continued trying to collect the insurance on the Henderson MILL HOUSE from TJ until the summer of 1817 (James Rawlings to TJ, 9 July, 25 Aug. 1817; TJ to Rawlings, 31 July 1817). For the 1799 DECREE IN CHANCERY forcing the Hendersons to pull down their milldam, see *PTJ*, 31:208, and Haggard, "Henderson Heirs," 4–5. Although the enclosed ORDER has not been found, TJ recorded the transaction in *MB*, 2:1292.

[1] Preceding four words interlined in place of "what."

From John Graham

DEAR SIR   Washington 7th augt 1813

after some difficulty I have at last found the Report from the Patent office which you want and have now the pleasure to send you a Copy of it. The President continues to gain strength His recovery will I hope be more rapid when he gets to the Mountains—I understand his Departure is fixed for Monday—

we hear but little now of the Enemy—Their vessels are moving about in the Bay in such a manner as almost to justify the belief that their only object was to excite alarm and to plunder defenceless Places Perhaps they are waiting for reenforcements from the west Indies, before they strike a blow meaning to make it a terrible one—The delay is at least so far favorable to us that we are every day gaining confidence in our ability to resist them—

with Sentiments of the Highest Respect & Esteem

I have the Honor to be, Sir Your Most Hble Sert

JOHN GRAHAM

RC (DLC); at foot of text: "Thomas Jefferson Esqr"; endorsed by TJ as received 11 Aug. 1813 and so recorded in SJL. Enclosure: *Letter from the Secretary of State, transmitting a List of the Names of Patentees, their Places of Residence, and the Nature of their Inventions or Improvements, agreeably to a Resolution of the House of Representatives of the United States of The Seventh Ultimo* (Washington, 1811; Poor, *Jefferson's Library*, 6 [no. 224]; reprinted in *List of Patents*, 49–103).

On 3 Sept. 1813 the Washington *Federal Republican, and Commercial Gazette* reported that British naval vessels (the ENEMY) had been "sailing up and down the Bay, without any determinate object," and that the frigate *Success* had recently arrived "from England via the West Indies, full of troops."

From Randolph Jefferson

DEAR BROTHER   august 8^{the} [7] 1813

I have sent Squire over to see whether I could borrow fort'y dollers of you as I am compelled to have as much at Court. if it is possible to borrow as much of you which shall certainly be replaced a gane in three weaks which will be a bout the time I shall dispose of my crop of wheat and will take extreemly kind of you if it is in your power to help me at this time which I shall feel my self under many obligations to you for the loan of be pleased to discharge Squire as soon as possible and would be glad to heare how Fanny comes on my wife goins me in love to you & family.—

I am your affectionately yours.—   RH JEFFERSON

RC (ViU: TJP-CC); evidently misdated; endorsed by TJ as a letter of 8 Aug. 1813 received 7 Aug. 1813 and so recorded in SJL.

From Thomas Newton

D^R S<small>IR</small>   Richmond Augt 7. 1813

Mr Rich^d E Lee of Norfolk a friend of mine, is on a visit to that part of the State in which you reside—

He feels desirous of calling on you before he leaves it—as he is not personally acquainted with you permit me to make you acquainted with him. Mr Lee is a firm republican—you will find him intelligent and devoted to the interest & honor of our Common Country—I remain with great

    respect & esteem yr Obt Servt   T<small>HO</small> N<small>EWTON</small>

RC (MoSHi: TJC-BC); endorsed by TJ as received 13 Oct. 1813 and so recorded in SJL.

Richard Evers Lee (ca. 1754–1814) represented Norfolk County and Norfolk Borough in the Virginia House of Delegates in 1790 and 1803–04, respectively, served as a borough alderman for many years, and was Norfolk's mayor, 1807–08. During the last eight years of his life, he was president of the Branch Bank of Virginia in Norfolk (National Society of the Daughters of the American Revolution, *DAR Patriot Index* [2003], 2:1624; *WMQ*, 2d ser., 17 [1937]: 525–6; Leonard, *General Assembly*, 180, 232; *New-York Gazette & General Advertiser*, 1 July 1807; Sowerby, no. 3239; Norfolk City Will Book, 3:149; Washington *Daily National Intelligencer*, 22 June 1814).

From David Ross

D<small>EAR</small> S<small>IR</small>   Richmond 7 August 1813—

I received last evening your polite and friendly letter of the 1st instant—covering your order upon Messrs Gibson & Jefferson, for 66$–50 Cents—this includes interest for the short time the payment was suspended, which was occaisioned by the[1] interuption to our Commerce, & I hope you'll excuse me from receiving it, the Am^t of the bill $64-\frac{56}{100}$ $ is quite sufficient—

Your having long enjoyd steady good health, has been to me very pleasing information—I have lately learned to appreciate that blessing; more than ever, without which, we can have but very little relish for life—I have been infirm for two years.

Our memories are wonderfully tenacious of early impressions, while recent transactions in old age, frequently fleets and passes away like a dream—Looking back to days of Yore, and recollecting innocent & trivial incidents in youth, I am induced to believe there is little difference between your age & mine; Surely, we cannot reasonably Complain of decaying vigour, when we reflect Since we were in action +[2] how many fabricks[3] bound by wood & Iron have mould-

ered away & long forgotten—I pray you to receive my ardent
wishes for your happiness, and to accept of my sincere esteem and
Regard   Most Respectfully   DAVID ROSS

RC (MHi); endorsed by TJ as received
11 Aug. 1813 and so recorded in SJL. FC
(ViHi: Ross Letterbook).

¹ In FC "anticipation" is here canceled.

² Preceding five words interlined in RC
and FC, with the "+" absent from the latter.
³ Ross here canceled "strong."

From Joseph Dougherty

SIR   Washington City Aug[t] 8th—13
   In consequence of the packets being prevented from playing between[1] this and Philad[a], I am deprived of the means of doing any
thing in the porter line.
   S. H Smith being lately appointed Commissioner of the revenue,
will have the disposing of a variety of offices, Such as, assessors,
stamper &c. Collectors will be appointed by the President.
   A line from you to the President and m[r] Smith, would be the
means of procuring one of these places for me.
   Sorry am I sir to give you any farther[2] trouble. I was doing well,
and happy in my occupation. and I can assure you sir, that it is real
necessity that causes me to ask your intercession, because I know that
it is a delicate undertaking, but I confess sir, that I can approach you
with a confidence that I cannot others
   I hope that you and your family enjoy good health
   I am sir your Humble Serv[t]   JO[s] DOUGHERTY

RC (DLC); at foot of text: "M[r] Tho[s]
Jefferson"; endorsed by TJ as received 10
Aug. 1813, but recorded in SJL as re-
ceived the following day.

Dougherty had run a business that bot-
tled ale and PORTER in Washington since
1810 (Dougherty to TJ, 6 Dec. 1810).
President James Madison appointed

Samuel H. SMITH commissioner of the
revenue on 29 July 1813, and the Senate
confirmed him two days later (Madison,
Papers, Pres. Ser., 6:484–5, 486; *JEP*,
2:416, 435).

¹ Manuscript: "betwen."
² Manuscript: "farthe."

To David Higginbotham

TH:J. TO MR HIGGENBOTHEM   Aug. 8. 13.
M[r] Gamble writes to me to know if I have any evidence that there is
a Common on the N.W. side of the lot I sold you in Richm[d] & which

he says he has bought. I had no information of that but from James Buchanan, and I presume I gave you his letters & plat Col° Byrd's letter, & the rough copy of Carter's deed to me.

did you give these to mr Gamble? if not, be so good as to send them to me, & I will forward them to him retaining copies.

RC (ViU: TJP); dateline at foot of text; addressed: "Mr Higgenbotham." Not recorded in SJL.

A missing letter of 8 Aug. 1813 from Higginbotham to TJ is recorded in SJL as received the same day.

To Randolph Jefferson

DEAR BROTHER   Monticello Aug. 8. 13.

Your letter of yesterday found me unprovided with the sum you desired; but I have been able to borrow it among our merchants who are not much better off than others, all business being at a stand. we are experiencing the most calamitous year known since 1755. the ground has been wet but once since the 14th of April. my wheat yielded but a third of an ordinary crop, about treble the seed. of 230. acres of corn, about 15. acres may make 2. or 3. barrels to the acre; and about 215. acres will not produce a single ear; not half of it will tossil, a great deal not 2. feet high. we usually make about 7. or 800. barrels; we shall certainly not make above 30. I shall be obliged to drive all my stock to Bedford to be wintered, and to buy 400. barrels of corn for bread for my people.

Your girl comes on tolerably well. she was some time learning to rove, for without good roving there cannot be good spinning. she has been sometime spinning, and by the time of my return from Bedford, when the machine will be carried to you, she will be able to spin by herself. the time of my going is yet unfixed: it may be within a week, or not within 2. or 3. weeks. my route is equally uncertain; but if I do not go by Snowden I will certainly return by it. present my respects to my sister. ever affectionately yours   TH: JEFFERSON

P.S. do not think of selling your wheat till the winter drives off the blockading ships when it will bring a good price.

PoC (ViU: TJP-CC); postscript added in a different ink; at foot of text: "Randolph Jefferson esq."; endorsed by TJ.

TOSSIL: "tassel." The GIRL was Randolph Jefferson's slave Fanny. MY SIS-

TER: Randolph Jefferson's wife, Mitchie Pryor Jefferson.

On this date TJ recorded that he had "Inclosed to my brother 40.D. of which he asks a loan" (*MB*, 2:1292).

To Craven Peyton

DEAR SIR   Monticello Aug. 8. 13.

I inclose you a letter I have just recieved from mr Hornsby in answer to one I had written his father, for I did not know of his death. it puts his claim on the land on an entire new footing, denying that the mother, or daughters ever knew of the sale, or recieved a farthing of the money. if I were stronger I would ride down to see you. as it is I can only request if your business should bring you to Milton or near this place that you would be so good as to call on me; for I must be active in getting this matter settled while Capt Meriwether's powers are suspended, and the rather as mr[1] Hornsby appears to be a reasonable man. Accept my best wishes   TH: JEFFERSON

[...] to return the letter

PoC (MHi); lower left corner torn away; endorsed by TJ. Enclosure: Thomas Hornsby to TJ, 21 July 1813.

The MOTHER was Elizabeth Lewis Henderson, while her three youngest DAUGHTERS were Frances Henderson Hornsby, Lucy Henderson, and Nancy C. Henderson.

A missing letter of 8 Aug. 1813 from Peyton to TJ is recorded in SJL as received the same day.

[1] TJ here canceled "Hender."

From John Adams

                                        Quincy Aug. 9. 13.

I believe I told you in my last, that I had given you all in Lindseys Memoirs, that interested you. But I was mistaken. In Priestleys Letter to Lindsey Decr 19. 1803, I find this Paragraph

"With the Work I am now composing I go on much faster and better than I expected; so that in two or three months, if my health continue as it now is, I hope to have it ready for the Press; though I Shall hardly proceed to print it, till We have dispatched the Notes. It is upon the Same plan with that of 'Socrates[1] and Jesus compared,' considering all the more distinguished of the Grecian Sects of Philosophy, till the establishment of Christianity in the Roman Empire. If you liked that Pamphlet, I flatter myself you will like this. I hope it is calculated to Show, in a peculiarly Striking Light, the great Advantage of Revelation, and that it will make an impression on candid Unbelievers, if they will read. But I find few that will trouble themselves to read any thing, on the Subject; which considering the great magnitude and interesting nature of the Subject, is a proof of a very improper State of mind unworthy of a rational Being."

I Send you this extract for several reasons. 1ˢᵗ because you Sett him upon this work. 2ᵈˡʸ because I wish you to endeavour to bring it to light and get it printed. 3ˡʸ Because I wish it may Stimulate you, to pursue your own plan which you promised to Dʳ Rush. I have not Seen any Work which expressly compares the Morality of the old Testament with that of the New in all their Branches: nor either with that of the ancient Philosophers.[2] Comparisons with the Chinese, the East[3] Indians, the Affricans, the West Indians &c would be more difficult; with more ancient Nations, impossible. The Documents are destroyed.   JOHN ADAMS

RC (DLC); at foot of text: "President Jefferson"; endorsed by TJ as received 20 Aug. 1813 and so recorded in SJL. FC (Lb in MHi: Adams Papers).

The work being composed in December 1803 had already been PRINTED as Priestley, *Heathen Philosophy*.

[1] Omitted opening quotation mark editorially supplied.
[2] RC: "Philosopers." FC: "Philosophers."
[3] Word interlined.

From Regnault de Bécourt

MONSEIGNEUR,   chez Mʳ Dufief, à Philadelphie ce 9 août, 1813.

Une maladie très grâve dont j'étais accablé depuis six mois, et laquelle vient de me quitter presque subitement, est cause que la lettre que Votre Excellence eût la bonté de m'écrire à la date, du 20 Juin dernier, est, jusqu'à ce jour, restée sans réponse.

A vue de la dite lettre Mʳ Dufief a payé à mon Imprimeur, deux gourdes pour prix de l'exemplaire du livre intitulé: la Création du monde &c, que Votre Excellence eût la Complaisance de recevoir. Quant à l'impression du livre supplémentaire que je me proposais de mettre sous presse pour étendre tout ce qui a rapport à la partie physique, astronomique, &c, &c, si faiblement esquissée dans ma création du monde &c, il paraît qu'elle n'aura point lieu: car tous mes efforts pour réunir assez de Souscripteurs pour assurer une somme de 2, ou 300 gourdes pour les frais d'impression, ont été infructueux. Cependant la multitude de choses singulières, neuves, piquantes, extraordinaires; la foule de découvertes que je me disposais à y traiter, pourraient jeter un grand Jour sur l'obscurité plus que ténébreuses à travers laquelle se manipulent presque toutes les sciences ou opérations réputées telles. Mais il est à croire, Monseigneur, d'après la nullité des encouragemens, pour ces sortes d'objets, en Amérique, que la publication de mes matières n'aura point lieu, dans ces contrées-ci. Dans tous les Cas, Monseigneur, quelque soit le pays où je les mette sous presse, Votre Excellence peut Compter que les premiers exemplaires lui seront adressès avec autant d'exactitude que si je résidais dans cette partie du globe qu'on appelle le <u>nouveau monde</u>; et c'est dans ces dispositions,

Que j'ai l'honneur d'être avec autant de vénération que de respect,

de Votre Excellence, Monseigneur, Le très humble et très obéissant Serviteur　　　　　　　　　　　　　　　　R. DE BÉCOURT

EDITORS' TRANSLATION

MY LORD,　　　　　　house of Mr. Dufief, Philadelphia 9 August, 1813.

Due to a very grave illness, which overwhelmed me for six months and then left me almost suddenly, the letter that Your Excellency kindly wrote on 20 June has remained unanswered until today.

On sight of the abovementioned letter, Mr. Dufief paid my printer two dollars for the copy of the book entitled *La Création du Monde* &c, which Your Excellency was kind enough to accept. The supplementary book that I planned to have published in order to extend the parts relating to the physical, astronomical, &c, &c, so superficially sketched in my *La Création du Monde* &c, apparently will not be printed, because all of my efforts to obtain enough subscribers to underwrite printing costs of 200 or <u>300 dollars</u> proved fruitless. The multitude of peculiar, new, puzzling, and extraordinary things and the numerous discoveries that I planned to discuss in it, however, could enlighten the more than murky darkness in which almost all of the sciences or so-called operations are conducted. But it is believed, my Lord, that because of the total failure to encourage these sorts of things in America, my writings will not be published here. In any event, my Lord, wherever I have them printed, Your Excellency can count on receiving the first copies, with as much punctuality as if I resided in that part of the globe called the <u>New World</u>; and it is with this in mind

that I have the honor to be with as much veneration as respect,

for Your Excellency, my Lord, the very humble and very obedient servant
　　　　　　　　　　　　　　　　　　　　　　R. DE BÉCOURT

RC (DLC); dateline at foot of text; endorsed by TJ as received 14 Aug. 1813 and so recorded in SJL. Translation by Dr. Genevieve Moene.

From Harry Innes

DEAR SIR,　　　　　　　　State of Kentucky August 9ᵗʰ 1813

Since your return from Europe I have heard it repeatedly stated that you had imported the <u>genuine</u> Shepherds dog & occasionally distributed them among your friends. Such an acquisition to this State will be of immense importance, as the people are turning their attention to the raising of Sheep & are rapidly progressing in the merino breeds.

If my information is correct & you still possess that species of Dog to spare, will it be possible to obtain a male & female either puppies or others. Should it be convenient to comply with my request, I can next Spring procure a conveyance for them thro' the attention of my friend Judge Todd who will spend this winter in Washington & has promised to send a special messenger to Monticello if you can make it convenient to spare two of your stock.

The request of two dogs may appear avaricious—but it is to secure the breed to our country for a common good as the remoteness of our situation from the Seaboard renders the obtaining such animals difficult & uncertain.

We have no certain intelligence from F^t Meigs at the rapids of the Miami of Lake Erie, but no fears are entertained for its safety, but there[1] are of Genl Harrison should he attempt to raise the seige without having a decidedly superior force to the enemy—his troops are raw & undisciplined—& has a horrible Swamp of 20 or 30 miles to pass which at this time is from 9 to 18 inches deep with water & mud.

Governer Shelby is endeavouring to raise a Corps of Volunteers to reinforce Genl Harrison, instead of drafted[2] militia, for the purpose of invading upper Canada, so soon as[3] Com. Perry gets the asscendency on L.E. The Governor will command in person & I have no doubt of his inducing by his example the best sons of our State to accompany him & that the—real—Hero of Kingsmountain will add another wreathe of Laurel to his brow in the eve of life if an opportunity presents itself I shall be pleased by your answer as soon as convenient & shall be happy to hear of your enjoying good health & tranquil hours in the decline of your life

With sentiments of great respect & sincere friendship I am dear sir your mo. ob. serv^t HARRY INNES

Direct your answer to Frankfort—via Washington H.I.

RC (MHi); endorsed by TJ as received 14 Sept. 1813 and so recorded in SJL.

Harry Innes (1753–1816), federal judge, was a native of Caroline County who moved to Bedford County and became an attorney prior to the Revolutionary War. During that conflict he administered gunpowder mills and lead mines for the Virginia Committee of Safety and served as an escheator, a commissioner settling claims to unpatented lands, and a tax collector. The state legislature appointed Innes a judge of the Kentucky

District's supreme court in 1782 and attorney general over that portion of western Virginia two years later. In the spring of 1785 he moved to what later became the state of Kentucky and lived there for the rest of his life. Although Innes opposed the ratification of the United States Constitution, he accepted President George Washington's appointment as a federal judge for the Kentucky District in 1789 and remained on the bench until his death. A firm Republican and an early proponent of Kentucky statehood, in the mid-1790s he communicated his strong belief that the Mississippi River had to be opened to navigation to both TJ and the Spanish governor at Natchez. Innes's secret contacts with the latter, coupled with his friendship with James Wilkinson, led to allegations that he had supported a Spanish plot to seduce Kentucky from the Union. Congress conducted an investigation in 1808, but Innes kept his judgeship. TJ maintained a cordial, albeit sporadic, correspondence with him for more than thirty years. In 1790 Innes sent TJ an old Indian sculpture, and nine years later he forwarded information regarding the 1774 murder of the Mingo Indian Logan's family that TJ incorporated into

later editions of his *Notes on the State of Virginia* (*DAB*; *PTJ*; *JHD* [1785–86 sess.], 51; Merrill Jensen, John P. Kaminski, and others, eds., *The Documentary History of the Ratification of the Constitution* [1976–], 8:221–3, 385–7; *JEP*, 1:29, 32 [24, 26 Sept. 1789]; Arthur Preston Whitaker, "Harry Innes and the Spanish Intrigue: 1794–1795," *Mississippi Valley Historical Review* 15 [1928]: 236–48; *Notes*, ed. Peden, 231–2, 237, 241–2; Clay, *Papers*, 1:319–20; *ASP, Miscellaneous*, 1:922–34; Lexington, Ky., *Western Monitor*, 27 Sept. 1816; Washington *Daily National Intelligencer*, 9 Oct. 1816).

The British and their Indian allies made two unsuccessful attempts to capture FORT MEIGS (in present-day Perrysburg, Ohio) during the spring and summer of 1813 (Stagg, *Madison's War*, 326). The MIAMI OF LAKE ERIE is the Maumee River. Isaac Shelby helped to organize and conduct the campaign which ended in an American victory at the Battle of KINGSMOUNTAIN in western North Carolina, 7 Oct. 1780 (*ANB*).

[1] Manuscript: "these."
[2] Word interlined.
[3] Manuscript: "a."

To John G. Gamble

SIR   Monticello Aug. 10. 13.

When I conveyed to mr Higginbotham the lot which is the subject of your letter of July 20. I delivered to him all the documents I possessed relative to it. among these were two statements by James Buchanan describing the shape, position & boundaries of the lot. this was the only evidence I possessed of these circumstances; but James Buchanan was considered then as the oracle of the place as to it's lots. it was on information from him that I purchased, and no other evidence of what I bought, except the deed from mr Carter. the rough draught of this which I retained, I also gave to mr Higginbotham. you will observe by inspection of it, that it had been prepared as a fair one, for execution. but containing a general warranty mr Carter objected to it. the erasures & alterations visible on it, were then made, it was fairly copied, executed & acknoleged by him in Henrico court, where, if it is not now to be found it must have been among the papers destroyed by the British when in possession of Richmond. I am sorry it is not in my power to give you any other information on this subject, and tender you the assurance of my esteem & respect.

TH: JEFFERSON

PoC (MHi); at foot of text: "Mr John G. Gamble"; endorsed by TJ.

In his papers TJ retained a copy of an extract he had made of Charles Carter of Shirley's 1777 DEED for the lot in Richmond, including the specification that the property line on the northwest was bounded "on the Common laid off as a road from Shockoe warehouse to the wharf and is 39 yards long." The extract also contains a plat giving the length of each side of the tract, the names of two neighbors, and the lot's proximity to the James River (PrC of Tr in CSmH: JF; in TJ's hand; undated, but filed at 27 Dec. 1773; see also *MB*, 1:453–4). A GENERAL WARRANTY guarantees a property against the claims of all other persons (*Black's Law Dictionary*).

To Craven Peyton

DEAR SIR   Monticello Aug. 10. 13.

The sum I owe you is between five hundred and forty or fifty Dollars. I have this day written to mr Gibson that I shall draw on him for it the next month, and I will take care that it be paid there by the day you name, the 17th of December. Accept my respects

TH: JEFFERSON

RC (ViHi); addressed: "Craven Peyton esq. Monteagle." Not recorded in SJL.

TJ's letter to Gibson of THIS DAY is recorded in SJL but has not been found. SJL records a missing letter from Peyton to TJ of 15 Aug. 1813 as received the following day.

From Alexander H. Stevens

SIR,   Washington 10 August 1813.

I have the honor here with to forward you Two or three publications which I brought with me from Paris. They were placed in my hands by Mr Warden in Jany last Since which time I have been making the best of my way to this Capital. Hoping they may safely reach Monticello & find you in health & happiness I am with the greatest respect Your very obedient &

humble Servant   ALEXR H. STEVENS

RC (MHi); dateline beneath signature; at foot of text: "To, Thos. Jefferson Esq"; endorsed by TJ as received 20 Aug. 1813 and so recorded in SJL. Enclosures: (1) *Code d'Instruction criminelle. Édition originale et seule officielle*, 2 vols. (Paris,

1810; Sowerby, no. 2219). (2) *Code de Commerce, collationné sur les Registres du Conseil d'État, par M. Raynal, Chef du Bureau des Procès-Verbaux* (Paris, 1807; Sowerby, no. 2220).

Alexander Hodgdon Stevens (1789–1869), physician, was a native of New York City who received a B.A. from Yale College in 1807 and an M.D. from the University of Pennsylvania in 1811. After a visit to Europe, during which he honed his medical skills in England and France and was detained by British warships both going and coming, he returned to the United States. Stevens had a long association with the New York Hospital, and he was professor of surgery at Queen's College (later Rutgers University), 1815–26. He held similar faculty positions at the College of Physicians and Surgeons (later merged with Columbia University), 1826–44; served as one of its trustees, 1820–26 and 1843–55; and was its president, 1843–55. Stevens eventually developed an interest in agriculture, and he was the second president of the American Medical Association, 1848–49 (*DAB*; Samuel W. Francis, *Biographical Sketches of Distinguished Living New York Surgeons* [1866], 133–8; Hartford *Connecticut Courant*, 23 Sept. 1807; Milton Halsey Thomas, *Columbia University Officers and Alumni 1754–1857* [1936], 227–8; *New York Times*, 2 Apr. 1869).

To John Hopkins

SIR   Monticello Aug. 11. 13.

I subscribe with pleasure to the work of mr Allen's which you propose to print: but as to assisting with materials, it is really not in my power. my life has been too busy a one to collect materials, or even to retain notes of what has been passing. those who act are generally too much occupied to write what is doing: lookers on, alone, have leisure for that. were I to resort to my memory, it would offer but a confused mass, difficult to be digested, and too indistinctly retained to be relied on. if there be any body who possesses materials either written, or on memory, I should suppose it to be Charles Thomson, who is in your neighborhood. he must have retained many anecdotes at least.
Accept the tender of my respects.   TH: JEFFERSON

PoC (DLC); at foot of text: "Mr John Hopkins"; endorsed by TJ.

To Rembrandt Peale

DEAR SIR   Monticello Aug. 11. 13.

I duly recieved by mr Correa your favor of July 13. and with it the peices of agate & Madrepore sent me thro' Genl Armstrong & to your care. the transaction stated in the letter accompanying them had so entirely escaped my memory, that the name being subscribed in illegible characters, I am not able to ascertain from whom it comes.

I am not however the less obliged to one who recollects to do a kind office when I had forgotten the having requested it. I sincerely wish you success in the establishment of your museum. these things kindle a thirst for knolege, and often draw to useful objects those who would otherwise employ themselves frivolously. should any circumstance ever lead you within striking distance of Monticello I should be very happy to recieve you. Accept the assurance of my great esteem & respect.   TH: JEFFERSON

PoC (photocopy in Vi: Personal Papers Collection); at foot of text: "Mr Rembrandt Peale"; endorsed by TJ.

To Samuel Pleasants

SIR   Monticello Aug. 11. 13.
    I will trouble you to send me by stage the following books:
Junius, the new edition with fac similes.
Franklin's works. Duane's edition.
Pike's journey thro' Mexico & Techas.
The Book. [concerning the Princess of Wales.]¹
when I wrote for what had come out of Hening's statutes, I mentioned that I had only his 1ˢᵗ vol. you sent me the 3ᵈ alone. I must now ask for the 2ᵈ. the stage office requires to have it's memory jogged at times, or it forgets to forward these things. present your bill always to mr Gibson for paiment, who knows that I am in the habit of getting books from you from time to time. Accept the assurance of my esteem and respect.   TH: JEFFERSON

PoC (MHi); bracket in original; at foot of text: "Mr Samuel Pleasants"; endorsed by TJ.

The NEW EDITION was *Junius: including Letters by the same Writer, Under Other Signatures (now first collected)*, ed. Henry S. Woodfall, 2 vols. (Philadelphia and New York, 1813; Sowerby, no. 2742). Zebulon Montgomery Pike's JOURNEY THRO' MEXICO & TECHAS (Texas) formed the third part of his *Account of Expeditions to the Sources of the Mississippi* (Philadelphia, 1810; Sowerby, no. 4169; Poor, *Jefferson's Library*, 7 [no. 371]). The PRINCESS OF WALES, Caroline Amelia Elizabeth, the estranged

wife of the prince regent, had been investigated in 1806 at the behest of King George III amidst rumors that she had borne or would soon bear a child out of wedlock (*ODNB*, 10:208). The related title was *"The Book!" or, The Proceedings and Correspondence upon the subject of the Inquiry into the Conduct of Her Royal Highness The Princess of Wales, under a commission appointed by The King, in the Year 1806*, 1st American ed. (New York and Boston, 1813; Sowerby, no. 410; Poor, *Jefferson's Library*, 4 [no. 111]).

¹ Omitted closing bracket editorially supplied.

From Richard Rush

DEAR SIR. Washington August 12. 1813.

Since I had the pleasure to receive your letter of the 11th of last month, the two written to my father, mentioned in your favor to me of the 31. of May, have come to light. As was thought possible, they had been put away even with more care than the rest, and on that account were not found as soon as the rest. I lose no time in enclosing them to you, happy in accompanying them with the assurance that they have been exposed to no eyes but our own.

Lest it should not in any other way reach you, I also beg permission to send you a newspaper containing an address from Mr Ingersoll, of the house of representatives, to his constituents. It looks, moreover, so long, and the print is so small, that perhaps it requires a voucher, beforehand, in every case, before it would be taken up to be read. It treats of the foreign influence to which our government is said to have been subject for many years past, and altho, a common topick, I will take the liberty to say that it is here handled in no common way. If ever you look back for a moment upon these things from the loop holes of your retreat, I have ventured to think that this piece of Mr Ingersoll's will strike you as doing great justice to some portions of our publick history; and it is under the hope that it may possibly serve you as amusement for an hour, I have taken the liberty to send it. The redundance of a mind still young, you will observe in it.

I hope, sir, you keep your health in all things. often have I heard my father express a wish, that you might find leisure and feel the desire, even now in your retirement, still to look to your country; that in addition to all you have already done and written for it, you would yet favor it with something more, some work upon its past history, or peculiar interests, to be made the medium of the further treasures of your knowledge, and the still riper reflections of your wisdom. But I forbear to say more, asking pardon for thus much of encroachment, and begging permission to offer you the assurances of my great devotion and respect. RICHARD RUSH.

RC (MHi); at foot of text: "Ths: Jefferson Esq."; endorsed by TJ as received 18 Aug. 1813 and so recorded in SJL. Enclosures: (1) TJ to Benjamin Rush, 21 Apr. 1803. (2) TJ's "Syllabus of an Estimate of the doctrines of Jesus, compared with those of others," [ca. 21 Apr. 1803] (nos. 1–2 in DLC: TJ Papers, 131:22617–8, and elsewhere; published in *EG*, 331–6). (3) TJ to Benjamin Rush, 23 Apr. 1803 (DLC). (4) TJ to Benjamin Rush, 16 Jan. 1811.

The enclosed ADDRESS of Charles Jared Ingersoll to his Pennsylvania constituents, dated Washington, D.C., 27

July 1813, asks whether "a perverse French influence over the constituted authorities of the U. States" exists; admits that many viewed France positively because of its assistance to the American side during the Revolutionary War and the liberal ideas it espoused during the early days of the French Revolution, but stresses that the United States had even stronger linguistic, literary, legal, social, and commercial ties to Great Britain; argues that the contentious relationship between the United States and Britain grew, in large part, out of the attitudes expressed and policies pursued by the latter: the widespread contempt for American manners, accomplishments, and political principles, the illegal retention of the frontier posts, the seizure of American ships and impressment of its mariners on the high seas and, since the outbreak of war, the atrocities committed by the British army and its Indian auxiliaries; emphasizes that America's independence from French influence is best demonstrated by the removal at American insistence of the French minister plenipotentiary Edmond Charles Genet in 1793, TJ's reluctance to push for war at the time of the *Chesapeake* affair, the fact that the Embargo and Non-Intercourse acts were directed equally against both France and Great Britain, and longstanding American antipathy toward the despotic, expansionistic political system of Napoleon Bonaparte; and hails the conflict with Britain as moral, justified, and necessary if the United States is ever to be respected by that power as an equal member of the family of nations (Washington *Daily National Intelligencer*, 30, 31 July 1813, and elsewhere).

From John L. E. W. Shecut

ESTEEMED & HIGHLY
RESPECTED SIR   Charleston S° Carolina August 12ʰ 1813.

Your truly acceptable and very satisfactory answer to my Communication respecting the Establishment of an Antiquarian Society in Charleston, has been duly received, and is gratefully acknowledged, and I shou'd have done myself the Honor of an earlier acknowledgement of its receipt, but that a regular meeting of the contemplated Society was soon to take place, when I promis'd myself the additional pleasure of writing to you Officially.—This meeting took place yesterday, and to my extreme mortification and disappointment, a total change was effected by an overwhelming Majority, The innovations are of such a nature as to mark them in my estimation as having originated from Political division, and the Purely intended Scientifical Society of Antiquarians, has Commenced, in a change disagreeable to my feelings and very different from, the original outlines which I had the Honor of submitting to my Fellow Citizens, as the Constitution of the Antiquarian Society.—

Permit me to trespass still farther on your goodness, while I point out what I conceive to be not only innovations, but rather an insult to my feelings—They are these, The Constitution of the propos'd Society of Antiquarians, had expressly provided in their fifth Rule. "The Society shall solicit the Patronage of the President of the United

States and of his Exellency Thomas Jefferson Esqr"—also, Resolv'd "that this Society shall be known and distinguish'd by the name & Title of the Antiquarian Society of Charleston[1] The objects of which are primarily the collection and preservation of articles and things, Rare, ancient, curious and useful & secondarily, the promotion and encouragement of the Arts, Sciences & Literature generally."—

At the Meeting held yesterday, The Officers were Selected from those Characters who are known to be oppos'd to Republicans, they have adopted a new name and Title to the Society, calling it the Literary and Philosophical Society of South Carolina, they have destroyed the fifth Rule entirely, and have substituted in its stead a Resolution that a Committee shall address, The president of the US. and your Excellency informing then, that the Society had enlarged its views, and had altered its name & Character; and that you were to be nominated Honorary members thereof.—Mortified at the ungenerous desertion of a few, whom I conceived friendly, and overpowered by a majority. The Responsibility of having called your attention & of having Solicited your Acceptance of the Patronage of the Antiquarian Society, Seems likely to devolve upon myself. I am aware, the goodness of your Excellencys heart will readily excuse me for the zeal which I have suffered to expose me to such an unmerited[2] and unlook'd for disappointment, While I renew to you afresh the motives which have actuated me, were the exalted opinion of your Character as a Citizen, and your talents as a Philosopher—In the mean time I pray you to Continue your Patronage to the <u>Antiquarian Society</u> of Charleston. Which Society tho very few in number now, are disirous of continuing, agreeably to their original design, and notwithstanding they have been overwhelmed by a majority in the opposition, have concluded the Continuance of the Same—

I expect the Corresponding Secretary of the Literary and Philosophical Society will also agreeably to his instructions Notify your Excellency of their having nominated you an Honorary member, in whatever light you may be pleased to receive this mark of their attention, I must entreat you to have the goodness to consider that it has originated from the circumstances before alluded to. and that you will, (if you accept the latter) still Continue the "<u>Patron of the Antiquarian Society of Charleston</u>"

The fruit of the <u>Capsicum minutissimum</u>, you were so obliging as to enclose me, has afforded me much satisfaction, and I take leave to inform you, that in the autumn of last year, I successfully administered, pills prepared of the <u>Capsicum Annuum</u> in <u>Meleno</u> or Black vomit, and that it has in nineteen cases of twenty six effectually stopp'd that truly alarming symptom and the patients recovered— This practice has met opposition, and they wish to deprive me of the Honor of the discovery of its application in that disease—an author in England was produced, who mentions it as having been the practice of the West India Physicans as early as 1801.—The publication of the first volume of the Flora, has Cost me $2000.—I have lost $1800 by it.—I regret the improbability of its completion and am gratefully indebted for your high opinion of it.—

I pray you my dear and Esteemed Sir to pardon this very lengthy communication, it may serve to divert your attention in your retirement. it may also Serve to shew you, that by being decidedly Republican, I have committed an unpardonable Sin, but above all I hope it will especially serve to assure you of the very high esteem in which I have ever held you, and request to be considered among your sincere friends and admirers—

Yours with great Respect   J L E W SHECUT

RC (DLC); at foot of text: "His Excellency Thomas Jefferson Esqʳ"; endorsed by TJ as received 23 Aug. 1813 and so recorded in SJL.

After petitioning the South Carolina General Assembly, the association formerly known as the Antiquarian Society of Charleston was incorporated as the LITERARY AND PHILOSOPHICAL SOCIETY OF SOUTH CAROLINA in 1814 (Shecut, *Shecut's Medical and Philosophical Essays* [Charleston, 1819], 48–9; undated petition for incorporation [ScCoAH: South Carolina General Assembly Petitions]). The CORRESPONDING SECRETARY was John Sen Trescot. William Wright, a British physician in the West Indies, reported on the use of capsicum pills for the treatment of melaena, also known as BLACK VOMIT, and yellow fever (*OED*; A. Philips Wilson, *A Treatise on Febrile Diseases*, 2d ed. [Winchester, 1803], 1:706–7).

[1] Superfluous closing quotation mark here editorially omitted.
[2] Manuscript: "umerited."

From Francis Smith

SIR   Louisa 12ᵗʰ Augˢᵗ 1813

I have Applyeᵈ to Mʳ L. Minor for the Ballance due me from Mʳ H. Markes estate being Ten Dollers 65 Cents—my Overlooker tells me he refereᵈ us to you.—I will take it as a favour to Send me the above ballance by the Bearer Peter—Mʳˢ Markes Can informe you Respecting the Debᵗ—to whome I send my respects

and am Sir your Most Obᵗ   FRANCIS SMITH

I will Give Mʳ Minor a recpᵗ

RC (MHi); dateline at foot of text; addressed: "Mʳ Thoˢ Jefferson.—Albermarle. By Peter"; endorsed by TJ as received 16 Aug. 1813 and so recorded in SJL.

To Isaac McPherson

Sir   Monticello August 13. 13.

Your letter of Aug. 3. asking information on the subject of mr Oliver Evans's exclusive right to the use of what he calls his Elevators, Conveyers, and Hopper-boys, has been duly recieved. my wish to see new inventions encouraged, and old ones brought again into useful notice, has made me regret the circumstances which have followed the expiration of his first patent. I did not expect the retrospection which has been given to the reviving law. for altho' the 2$^\text{d}$ Proviso seemed not so clear as it ought to have been, yet it appeared susceptible of a just construction; and the retrospective one being contrary to natural right, it was understood to be a rule of law that where the words of a statute admit of two constructions, the one just and the other unjust, the former is to be given them. the 1$^\text{st}$ Proviso takes care of those who had lawfully used Evans's improvements under the 1$^\text{st}$ patent; the 2$^\text{d}$ was meant for those who had lawfully erected and used them after that patent expired, declaring they 'should not be liable to damages therefor.' these words may indeed be restrained to uses already past; but as there is parity of reason for those to come, there should be parity of law. every man should be protected in his lawful acts, and be certain that no ex post facto law shall punish or endamage him for them. but he is endamaged, if forbidden to use a machine lawfully erected, at considerable expence, unless he will pay a new and unexpected price for it. the proviso says that he who erected and used lawfully shall not be liable to pay damages. but if the Proviso had been omitted, would not the law, construed by natural equity, have said the same thing. in truth both Provisos are useless. and shall useless provisos inserted pro majori cautelâ only,[1] authorise inferences against justice? the sentiment that ex post facto laws are against natural right is so strong in the United States, that few, if any, of the State constitutions have failed to proscribe them. the federal constitution indeed interdicts them in criminal cases only; but they are equally unjust in civil as in criminal cases and the omission of a caution which would have been right, does not justify the doing what is wrong. nor ought it to be presumed that the legislature meant to use a phrase in an unjustifiable sense, if by any rules of construction, it can be even strained to what is just. the law books abound with similar instances of the care the judges take of the public integrity. laws moreover abridging the natural rights of the citizen, should be restrained by rigorous constructions within their narrowest limits.

Your letter however points to a much broader question, Whether what have recieved from mr Evans the new and the proper name of Elevators are of his invention. because, if they are not, his patent gives him no right to obstruct others in the use of what they possessed before.   I assume it as a Lemma that it is the invention of the machine itself which is to give a patent right, and not the application of it to any particular purpose of which it is susceptible. if one person invents a knife convenient for pointing our pens, another cannot have a patent right for the same knife to point our pencils. a Compass was invented for navigating the sea; another could not have a patent right for using it to survey land. a machine for threshing <u>wheat</u> has been invented in Scotland. a 2^d person cannot get a patent right for the same machine to thresh <u>oats</u>, a 3^d <u>rye</u>, a 4th <u>peas</u>, a 5th <u>clover</u> E^{t}c. a string of buckets is invented & used for raising water, ore E^{t}c can a 2^d have a patent right to the same machine for raising wheat, a 3^d oats, a 4th rye, a 5th peas E^{t}c?   the question then whether such a string of buckets was invented first by Oliver[2] Evans, is a meer question of fact in Mathematical history.   now turning to such books only as I happen to possess, I find abundant proof that this simple machinery has been in use from time immemorial. Doct^r Shaw, who visited Egypt & the Barbary coast in the years 1727. 8. 9. in the margin of his map of Egypt, gives us the figure of what he calls a Persian wheel, which is a string of round cups or buckets, hanging on a pully, over which they revolve, bringing up water from a well, and delivering it into a trough above. he found this used at Cairo, in a well 264.f. deep, which the inhabitants believe to have been a work of the patriarch Joseph. Shaw's travels. 341. Oxford edition of 1738. in folio. and the Universal history I. 416. speaking of the manner of watering the higher lands in Egypt, says 'formerly they made use of Archimedes's screw, thence named the Egyptian pump; but they now generally use wheels (wallowers) which carry a rope or chain of earthen pots, holding about 7. or 8. quarts apiece, and draw the water from the canals. there are besides a vast number of wells in Egypt, from which the water is drawn in the same manner to water the gardens & fruit trees; so that it is no exaggeration to say, that there are in Egypt above 200,000. oxen daily employed in this labour.' Shaw's name of Persian wheel has been since given more particularly to a wheel with buckets, either fixed, or suspended on pins, at it's periphery. Mortimer's husbandry I. 18. Duhamel III. 11. Ferguson's Mechanics plate XIII. but his figure, and the verbal description of the Universal history prove that the string of buckets is meant under that name. his figure differs from Evans's construction in the circumstances of the buckets being round, and strung thro' their bottom on a chain. but it is the principle, to wit a string of buckets, which constitutes the invention, not the form of the buckets, round, square, or hexagon; nor the manner of attaching them, nor the material of the connecting band, whether chain, rope, or leather. Vitruvius L. X. c. 9. describes this machinery as a Windlas, on which is a chain descending to the water, with vessels of copper attached to it; the windlas being turned, the chain moving on it will raise the vessels which, in passing over the windlas, will empty the water they have brought up into a reservoir. and Perrault, in his edition of Vitruvius. Paris 1684. fol. Plates 61. 62. gives us three forms of these water elevators, in one of which the buckets are square, as mr Evans's are. Bossut Histoire des Mathematiques I. 86. says 'the drum wheel, the wheel with buckets & the Chapelets, are hydraulic machines which come to us from the antients. but we are ignorant of the time when they began to be put into use.' the Chapelets are the revolving band of buckets which Shaw calls the Persian wheel, the moderns a Chainpump, and mr Evans Elevators.   the next of my books in which I find these Elevators is Wolf's Cours de Mathematiques I. 370. & Pl. 1. Paris 1747. 8vo. here are two forms. in one of them the buckets are square, attached to two chains, passing over a cylinder or wallower at top, & under another at bottom, by which they are made to revolve. it is a nearly exact representation of Evans's elevators. but a more exact one is to be seen in Desagulier's Experim^l Philosophy II. Plate. 34. in the Encyclopedie de Diderot et D'alembert 8vo edn of Lausanne, 1$^{'st}$ vol. of Plates, in the 4. subscribed Hydraulique. Noria, is one where round earthen pots are tied by their collars, between two endless ropes suspended on a revolving lanthern or wallower. this is said to have been used for raising ore out of a mine. in a book which I do not possess, 'L'architecture Hidraulique de Belidor, the II^d vol. of which is said [De la Lande's continuation of Montucla's Histoire des Mathematiques III. 711.] to contain a detail of all the pumps, antient and modern, hydraulic machines, fountains, wells E^{t}c. I have no doubt this Persian wheel, chain-pump, Chapelets, Elevators, by whichever name you chuse to call it, will be found in various forms.   the last book I have to quote for it is Prony's Architecture Hydraulique I. Avertissement vii. and §. 648. 649. 650. in the latter of which passages he observes that the 1st idea which occurs for raising water is to lift it in a bucket by hand. when the water lies too deep to be reached by hand, the bucket is suspended by a chain, and let down over a pulley or windlass. if it be desired to raise a continued stream of water, the simplest means which offers itself to the mind is to attach to an endless chain or cord a number of pots or buckets, so disposed that, the chain being suspended on a lanthern or wallower above, and plunged in water below, the buckets may descend and ascend alternately, filling themselves at bottom, and emptying at a certain height above, so as to give a constant stream.   some years before the date of mr Evans's patent, a mr Martin of Caroline county in this state, constructed a drill-plough, in which he used the band of buckets for elevating the grain from the box into the funnel, which let them down into the furrow. he had bands with different sets of buckets adapted to the size of peas, of turnep seed Eᵗc. I have used this machine for sowing Benni seed, also, and propose to have a band of buckets for drilling Indian corn, and another for wheat. is it possible that in doing this I shall infringe mr Evans's patent? that I can be debarred of any use to which I might have applied my drill, when I bought it, by a patent issued after I bought it?

These verbal descriptions, applying so exactly to mr Evans's elevators, and the drawings exhibited to the eye; flash conviction both on reason and the senses, that there is nothing new in these elevators but their being strung together on a strap of leather. if this strap of leather be an invention, entitling the inventor to a patent right, it can only extend to the strap, and the use of the string of buckets must remain free to be connected by chains, ropes, a strap of hempen girthing, or any other substance, except leather. but indeed mr Martin had before used the strap of leather.

The Screw of Archimedes is as antient, at least, as the age of that Mathematician, who died more than 2000. years ago. Diodorus Siculus speaks of it L. I. pa. 21. and L. V. pa. 217. of Stevens's edition of 1559. folio. and Vitruvius X. 11. the cutting of it's spiral worm into sections for conveying flour or grain, seems to have been an invention of mr Evans, & to be a fair subject of a patent right. but it cannot take away from others the use of Archimedes's screw, with it's perpetual spiral, for any purposes of which it is susceptible.

The Hopper-boy is an useful machine; &, as far as I know, original.[3]

It has been pretended by some (and in England especially) that inventors have a natural and exclusive right to their inventions; & not merely for their own lives, but inheritable to their heirs. but while it is a moot question whether the origin of any kind of property is derived from nature at all, it would be singular to admit a natural, and even an hereditary right to inventions. it is agreed by those who have seriously considered the subject, that no individual has, of natural right, a separate property in an acre of land, for instance. by an universal law indeed, whatever, whether fixed or moveable, belongs to all men equally and in common, is the property, for the moment, of him who occupies it; but when he relinquishes the occupation the property goes with it. stable ownership is the gift of social law, and is given late in the progress of society. it would be curious then if an idea, the fugitive fermentation of an individual brain, could, of natural right, be claimed in exclusive and stable property. if nature has made any one thing less susceptible, than all others, of exclusive property, it is the action of the thinking power called an Idea; which an individual may exclusively possess as long as he keeps it to himself; but the moment it is divulged, it forces itself into the possession of every one, and the reciever cannot dispossess himself of it. it's peculiar character too is that no one possesses the less, because every other possesses the whole of it. he who recieves an idea from me, recieves instruction himself, without lessening mine; as he who lights his taper at mine, recieves light without darkening me. that ideas should freely spread from one to another over the globe, for the moral and mutual instruction of man, and improvement of his condition, seems to have been peculiarly and benvolently designed by nature, when she made them, like fire, expansible over all space, without lessening their density in any point; and like the air in which we breathe, move, and have our physical being, incapable of confinement, or exclusive appropriation. inventions then cannot in nature be a subject of property. society may give an exclusive right to the profits arising from them as an encouragement to men to pursue ideas which may produce utility. but this may, or may not be done, according to the will and convenience of the society, without claim or complaint from any body. accordingly it is a fact, as far as I am informed, that England was, until we copied her, the only country on earth which ever by a general law, gave a legal right to the exclusive use of an idea. in some other countries, it is sometimes done, in a great case, and by a special & personal[4] act. but generally speaking, other nations have thought that these monopolies produce more embarrasment than advantage to society. and it may be observed that the nations which refuse monopolies of invention, are as fruitful as England in new and useful devices.

Considering the exclusive right to invention as given not of natural right, but for the benefit of society, I know well the difficulty of drawing a line between the things which are worth to the public the embarrasment of an exclusive patent, and those which are not. as a member of the Patent-board for several years, while the law authorised a board to grant or refuse patents, I saw with what slow progress a system of general rules could be matured. some however were established by that board. one of these was, that a machine, of which we were possessed, might be applied by every man to any use of which it is susceptible, and that this right ought not to be taken from him, and given to a monopolist, because he first perhaps had occasion so to apply it. thus a Screw for crushing plaister might be employed for crushing corn-cobs. and a Chain-pump for raising water might be used for raising wheat: this being merely a change of application. Another rule was that a change of material should not give[5] title to a patent. as the making a ploughshare of cast rather than of wrought iron; a Comb of iron, instead of horn, or of ivory. or the connecting buckets by a band of leather, rather than of hemp or iron. a third was that a mere change of form should give[6] no right to a patent. as a high quartered shoe, instead of a low one. a round hat, instead of a three square. or a square bucket instead of a round one. but for this rule, all the changes of fashion in dress would have been under the tax of patentees.   these were among the rules which the uniform decisions of the board had already established; and under each of them mr Evans's patent would have been refused. 1. because it was a mere change of application of the chain pump, from raising water to raise wheat. 2. because the using a leathern, instead of a hempen band, was a mere change of material: and 3^{ly} square buckets instead of round are only a change of form; and the antient forms too appear to have been indifferently square or round. but there were still abundance of cases which could not be brought under rule, until they should have presented themselves under all their aspects; and these investigations occupying more time of the members of the board than they could spare from higher duties, the whole was turned over to the judiciary, to be matured into a system, under which everyone might know when his[7] actions were safe and lawful. instead of refusing a patent in the first instance, as the board was authorised to do, the patent now issues of course, subject to be declared void on such principles as should be established by the courts of law. this business however is but little analogous to their course of reading, since we might in vain turn over all the lubberly volumes of the law to find a single ray which would lighten the path of the Mechanic or Mathematician. it is more within the information of a board of Academical professors, and a previous refusal of patent would better guard our citizens against harrassment by lawsuits. but England had given it to her judges, and the usual predominancy of her examples carried it to ours.

It happened that I had myself a mill built, in the interval between mr Evans's 1ˢᵗ and 2ᵈ patents. I was living in Washington, and left the construction of the mill entirely to the mill wright. I did not even know he had erected elevators, conveyers, and hopper-boys, until I learnt it by an application from mr Evans's agent for the patent price. altho' I had no idea he had a right to it by law (for no judicial decision had then been given) yet I did not hesitate to remit to mr Evans the old and moderate patent price, which was what he then asked, from a wish to encourage even the useful revival of antient inventions. but I then expressed my opinion of the law in a letter either to mr Evans, or to his agent.[8]

I have thus, Sir, at your request, given you the facts & ideas which occur to me on this subject. I have done it without reserve, altho' I have not the pleasure of knowing you personally. in thus frankly committing myself to you, I trust you will feel it as a point of honor & candor, to make no use of my letter which might bring disquietude on myself.[9] and particularly I should be unwilling to be brought into any difference with mr Evans whom however I believe too reasonable to take offence at an honest difference of opinion. I esteem him much, and sincerely wish him wealth & honor. I deem him a valuable citizen, of uncommon ingenuity & usefulness. and had I not esteemed still more the establishment of sound principles, I should now have been silent. if any of the matter I have offered can promote that object, I have no objection to it's being so used. if it offers nothing new, it will of course not be used at all. I have gone with some minuteness into the Mathematical history of the Elevator, because it belongs to a branch of science, in which, as I have before observed, it is not incumbent on lawyers to be learned; and it is possible therefore that some of the proofs I have quoted may have escaped on their former arguments. on the law of the[10] subject I should not have touched, because more familiar to those who have already discussed it; but I wished to state my own view of it merely in justification of myself; my name and approbation being subscribed to the act. with these explanations accept the assurance of my respect.   Th: Jefferson

PoC (DLC); brackets in original; at foot of first page: "Mʳ Isaac MPherson." Printed in *Memorial to Congress on Evans' Patent,* 7–16.

HOPPER-BOYS are rakes that push meal over an opening in the floor of a mill (*OED*). ENDAMAGE: to damage, injure, or discredit (*OED*). PRO MAJORI CAUTELÂ: as a precaution; to give additional security (*Black's Law Dictionary*).

The United States CONSTITUTION prohibits the passage of ex post facto laws by either the federal government or the states (Article 1, sections 9–10). L.: liber ("book"). Vitruvius discusses the use of a windlass to raise water in book 10, chapter 4 of his work on architecture, not X. C. 9 (*Vitruvius on Architecture,* trans. Frank Granger, Loeb Classical Library [1962], 2:302–5). NORIA: "chain-pump." STEVENS'S EDITION: Henri Estienne's edition of the works of Diodorus Siculus (Sowerby, no. 37). Vitruvius actually describes Archimedes's screw in book 10, chapter 6, not x. 11 (*Vitruvius on Architecture*, 2:307–11). From its establishment by the Patent Act of 10 Apr. 1790 until its abolition early in 1793, TJ served on the PATENT-BOARD, a body consisting of the secretary of state, the secretary of war, and the attorney general (*PTJ*, 22:361–2n, 25:398–9, 27:853–4; *U.S. Statutes at Large*, 1:109–12). The MILL WRIGHT who assisted in the construction and outfitting of TJ's Shadwell Mills was James Walker (*MB*, esp. 2:1162; Betts, *Farm Book*, 342, 353). For the application for the patent price by EVANS'S AGENT, John Moody, and TJ's response giving his OPINION OF THE LAW in question, see Moody to TJ, 20 Oct. 1808 (MHi), and TJ to Evans, 6 Dec. 1808 (DLC). TJ's NAME AND APPROBATION became attached to the "Act for the relief of Oliver Evans" when he signed it into law on 21 Jan. 1808 (*U.S. Statutes at Large*, 6:70–1).

[1] Preceding five words interlined.

[2] Manuscript: "Oliliver."

[3] *Memorial to Congress* here keys a footnote stating that "The enlightened author was not apprised of the depositions contained in No. III. where the evidences are so conclusive against Mr. Evans on the subject of the Hopper-boy. EDITOR."

[4] Reworked from: "permanent."

[5] Preceding three words interlined in place of "is not a."

[6] Preceding two words added in place of "gave."

[7] Reworked from "their."

[8] Preceding eight words interlined.

[9] *Memorial to Congress* here keys a footnote stating that "It is proper to observe, that though the author did not at the time of writing this letter, contemplate its publication, yet his permission has been obtained. EDITOR." The reference is to TJ to McPherson, 18 Sept. 1813.

[10] TJ here canceled "case."

From John Adams

Quincy [ca. 14] August 1813

Κριοὺς μὲν [καὶ][1] ὄνους διζήμεθα, Κύρνε, καὶ ἵππους
  εὐγενέας· καί τις βούλεται ἐξ ἀγαθῶν
κτήσασθαι. γῆμαι δὲ κακὴν κακοῦ οὐ μελεδαίνει
  ἐςθλὸς ἀνήρ, ἤν οἱ χρήματα πολλὰ διδῶ.

Behold my translation

"My Friend Curnis, When We want to purchace, Horses, Asses or Rams, We inquire for the Wellborn. And every one wishes to procure, from the good Breeds. A good Man, does not care to marry a Shrew, the Daughter of a Shrew; unless They give him, a great deal of Money with her."

What think you, of my translation? compare it with that of Grotius, and tell me, which, is nearest to the original in letter and in Spirit. Grotius renders it

> Nobilitas asinis et equis Simul, arietibus que
> Dat pretium: nec de Semine degeneri
> Admissura placet. Sed pravæ e Sanguine pravo,
> Si dos Sit, præsto est optima conditio.

[386]

Bird Pepper

Jefferson's Flour Mill

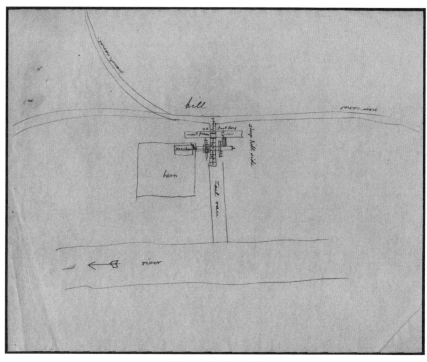

Jefferson's Sawmill

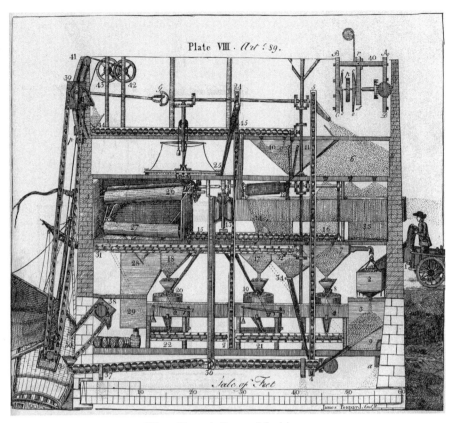

Oliver Evans's Patent Machinery

Robert Fulton

American Philosophical Society Membership Diploma

Jefferson's Greek Handwriting

John Adams's Greek Handwriting

The House of John and Abigail Adams

Dear Brother   August the 8: 1813

I have sent Squire over to
see whether I could borrow forty doll
ers of you as I am compelled to have
as much at Court if it is possible
to borrow as much of you which shall
certainly be replaced again in three
weeks which will be about the time
I shall dispose of my crop of Wheat and
will take extreemly kind of you if it
is in your power to help me at this time
which I shall feel my self under many obl
igations to you for the loan of be pleased to
discharge Squire as soon as possible and would
be glad to heare how Franny comes on my wife
Goins me in love to you & family.
                    I am your affectionately
                    yours.
                    Rh: Jefferson

Letter from Jefferson's Brother Randolph

This flower of Greek Poetry, is extracted, from the
ΘΕΟΓΝΙΔΟΣ ΜΕΓΑΡΕΩΣ ΠΑΡΑΙΝΕΣΕΙΣ.

Theognis lived five hundred and forty four years before Jesus Christ. Has Science or Morals, or Philosophy or Criticism or Christianity, advanced or improved, or enlightened Mankind upon this Subject, and Shewn them, that the Idea of the "Well born" is a prejudice, a Phantasm, a Point no point, a Cape Fly away, a dream?[2]

I Say it is the ordonance of God Almighty, in the Constitution of human nature, and wrought into the Fabrick of the Universe. Philosophers and Politicians, may nibble and quibble, but they never will get rid of it. Their only resource is, to controul it. Wealth is another Monster to be Subdued. Hercules could not Subdue both or either. To Subdue them by regular approaches by a regular Seige and Strong fortifications was my Object in writing on Aristocracy, as I proposed to you in Grovenor Square.[3]

If you deny any one of these Positions, I will prove them to demonstration by Examples drawn from your own Virginia, and from every other State in the Union, and[4] from the History of every Nation civilized and Savage, from all We know of the time of the[5] Creation of the World.

Whence is the derivation of the Words Generous, Generously, Generosity &c? Johnson Says "Generous. a. Generosus Latin, Not of mean Birth; of good extraction. Noble of mind. magnanimous. open of Heart Liberal, munificent. Strong, vigorous."[6] and he might have added, Couragious heroic, patriotic.

Littleton happens to be at hand. Generosus. Nobilis, ex præclaro genere ortus: qui a genere non deflectit. γεναῖος, ἐυγενής. Born of a noble Race, a Gentleman born. See his Examples.

What is the origin of the Word Gentleman?

It would be a curious critical Speculation for a learned Idler to pursue this Idea, through all Languages

We may call this Sentiment a prejudice, because We can give what names We please, to Such things as We please; but in my opinion it is a part of the Natural History of Man: and Politicians and Philosophers may as well project to make The Animal live without Bones or Blood, as Society can pretend to establish, a free Government without Attention to it.

Quincy August 16. 1813. I can proceed no farther, with this Letter, as I intended.

your Friend, my only Daughter, expired, yesterday morning in the Arms of Her Husband her Son, her Daughter, her Father and

Mother, her Husbands two[7] Sisters and two of her Nieces, in the 49th year of her Age, 46 of which She was the healthiest and firmest of Us all: Since which, She has been a monument to Suffering and to Patience.   JOHN ADAMS

RC (DLC: TJ Papers, 199:35381–2); partially dated, with day conjectured from death of Abigail Adams Smith early on 15 Aug. 1813; at foot of text: "President Jefferson"; endorsed by TJ as a letter of 16 Aug. 1813 received 14 Sept. 1813 but recorded in SJL as a letter of Aug. 1813 received 14 Sept. 1813. FC (Lb in MHi: Adams Papers); partially dated; partly in Adams's hand.

ΘΕΟΓΝΙΔΟΣ ΜΕΓΑΡΕΩΣ ΠΑΡΑΙΝΕΣΕΙΣ: "The Advice of Theognis of Megara." For the work from which Adams copied the quotation in question in Greek and Latin, see note to Adams to TJ, 9 July 1813. A modern edition translates the extract thus: "We seek out rams and asses and horses that are purebred, Cyrnus, and everyone wishes that they mount (females) of good stock; but a noble man does not mind marrying the base daughter of a base father if the latter gives him a lot of money" (Gerber, *Greek Elegiac Poetry*, 200–1 [lines 183–6]). TJ and Adams discussed aristocracy at the latter's GROVENOR SQUARE (Grosvenor Square) residence in London in March or April of 1786, a year prior to the publication of Adams's *A Defence of the Constitu-*

tions of Government of the United States of America (London, 1787–88; Sowerby, no. 3004; Poor, *Jefferson's Library*, 11 [no. 650]) (McCullough, *Adams*, 354–61; *PTJ*, 11:118). Adams is quoting from the first volume of Samuel JOHNSON, *A Dictionary of the English Language* (London, 1755; Sowerby, no. 4874). The work by Adam LITTLETON was his *Linguæ Latinæ Liber Dictionarius Quadripartitus. A Latine Dictionary, In Four Parts* (London, 1678; Sowerby, no. 4796). Adams's ONLY DAUGHTER was Abigail Adams Smith. Of her three surviving children, John Adams Smith and Caroline Amelia Smith waited on her during her final illness (Edith Belle Gelles, *Portia: The World of Abigail Adams* [1992], esp. 150).

[1] Word, which is omitted from both RC and FC, editorially supplied.
[2] FC to this point in Adams's hand.
[3] Sentence interlined.
[4] RC: "and and."
[5] Preceding three words interlined.
[6] Omitted closing quotation mark editorially supplied.
[7] Word interlined.

From William C. C. Claiborne

DEAR SIR,   New Orleans August 14th 1813.

In the suit brought by Edward Livingston Against Le Breton D'orgenoy late marshal of the District of Orleans, The Honorable mr Hall, Judge of the District of Louisiana, has decided, the dispossessing of mr Livingston of the Batture, by order of the late President to be illegal, & he directs the Plaintiff to be reinstated in his possession.—The Public Sentiment on this occasion is evidently wounded, & the Public feeling greatly excited.—The enclosures, A, & B. are Copies of two Arretis of the City Council, and the paper marked C, of a Short address, which I made to the council.—Considering the

Batture as a Part of the Bed of the mississippi and included within the Port of New Orleans, I Shall have recourse to our State Courts, to enjoin m^r Livingston against exercising any act of ownership over the Same, or in any manner obstructing the navigation of the <u>mississippi</u>, which is declared to be <u>a great high way</u>, the free use of which, as well to the Inhabitants of this State, as of the other States, is one of the conditions on which Louisiana was admitted into the Union. How far I Shall be enabled to Succeed, is impossible to Say;—m^r Livingston has found means, either to neutralise, or to make active partizans of most of the Lawyers in this State;—The people however are fortunate, in receiving the Support of the Attorney General, (m^r F. X. martin), & of mess^{rs} moreau Lislet & Fielding Turner, three distinguished Lawyers, & I entertain Strong Hopes, that we may yet be enabled, to maintain the Rights of the Public.—

The Creek nation of Indians have commenced Hostilities, & the Frontiers of the mississippi Territory are much exposed; We Shall Soon however have in that quarter, a respectable force, & I trust our Troops Will be ordered to march immediately into the Nation, as the Surest means of Punishing & puting down these faithless people.— In a letter I received from my Brother, General Claiborne of the mississippi Territory dated Fort Stoddert 3^d of August 1813, he says—"I arrived at this Post on the 30th ultimo, & found the country in great confusion and alarm. The Creeks are making every preparation to attack us, and on my part, I have and Shall make every arrangement for the protection of our frontier. General Flournoy promised, in case of a rupture, to reinforce me, with the 7th Regiment; Should he do this, & will authorise me, I Shall march into the Nation, & Shall enter it with Sanguine hopes of Success.—The Indians <u>are unquestionably Supplied with arms & amunition by the Governor of Pensacola.</u>— a party on their return from that place with ammunition &c, were attacked by a party of militia under Colonel Callier, & must have been defeated, but for the improper[1] conduct of Some of the militia officers. Colonel Callier behaved bravely; he is missing, & is Supposed to have been Killed on the retreat."—

Louisiana has hitherto been fortunately exempt from the immediate Horrors of the war;—But I am not without apprehensions, that in the course of the insuing winter, we Shall be Called upon to repel an invasion; & to meet an event of the Kind, I Shall make all the preparations which my powers, and the <u>Resources</u> of the State (<u>feeble at best</u>) will admit.

I have the honor to be Sir, with the greatest respect Your faithful friend WILLIAM C. C. CLAIBORNE

RC (DLC); in a clerk's hand, with closing and signature by Claiborne; at foot of text in Claiborne's hand: "m^r Thos Jefferson Monticello"; endorsed by TJ as received 15 Sept. 1813 and so recorded in SJL.

ARRETIS: "decrees." The 8 Apr. 1812 act admitting Louisiana into the UNION stipulated that "the river Mississippi, and the navigable rivers and waters leading into the same, and into the gulf of Mexico, shall be common highways, and for ever free" (*U.S. Statutes at Large*, 2:703). Colonel James Caller (CALLIER) actually survived the 27 July 1813 encounter with a party of Creek Indians, passing away more than six years later (New York *Columbian*, 15 Sept. 1813; Saint Stephens, Ala., *Halcyon, and Tombeckbe Public Advertiser*, 1 Dec. 1819).

[1] Word interlined by Claiborne.

ENCLOSURES

I

Decree of the New Orleans City Council

Le conseil de Ville informé que l'honorable Dominique A. Hall, Juge de la Cour de district des Etats-Unis Séante en cette ville, vient de rendre Mardi dernier trois du présent mois d'Août, un jugement par lequel il déclare illégal l'acte de dépossession exercé par M^r Le Breton Dorgenoy Ex maréchal agissant en vertu des ordres du Président des Etats-Unis alors en fonctions, contre le sieur Edouard Livingston, dans l'affaire de la Batture en face du faubourg s^{te} Marie.

Considérant que cette batture fait partie du Port de la N^{lle} Orléans: qu'elle ne peut pas plus devenir la propriété d'un individu, en Vertu daucun Jugement quelconque, que le sol des rues et places publiques.

Considérant que cette propriété est surtout nécessaire à l'existence de la Cité de la N^{lle} Orléans, à cause de la terre sablonneuse quelle fournit au public pour batir ainsi que pour remblayer les levées, les rues et les cours qui sont constamment dégradées par les pluies qui entrainent ces mêmes remblais vers la Cypriere, en raison de l'inclination du sol; au point que l'on peut évaluer à cent mille charretées la quantité de terre sáblonneuse qui est extraite tous les ans et cette batture, pour les besoins du public.

Considérant que depuis l'origine et la fondation de cette colonie, les habitans de cette ville ont joui imperturbablement du droit dextraire cette terre pour leurs besoins et pour ceux de leur administration municipale.

Considérant que cet une violation manifeste du droit public et du droit civil que davoir essayé de faire dune chose de cette nature la propriété de Mr Livingston.

Considérant enfin que tous les citoyens de l'état sont intéressés, comme ceux de la ville, a ne point voir cette propriété sortir de la possession et jouissance du Public, Arrête qu'en sa qualité de representant immédiat d'une des grandes portions de la population de l'Etat de la Louisiane il se regarde comme étant le défenseur et le Gardien naturel du Port de la N^{lle} Orléans; qu'en conséquence il place sous sa propre sauve-garde, sous celle des Citoyens, et sous celle de son Excellence Wm C. C. Claiborne, Gouverneur de cet état, la Batture du faubourg S^{te} marie, ainsi que, toutes les Parties du Port, des Rues et des places publiques de cette ville;

Arrête de plus que, séance tenante, communication sera donnée à son Excellence le Gouverneur du présent Arrête, avec invitation de se rendre à l'assemblée du Conseil pour y coopérer comme Chef de l'Etat, par ladhésion qu'il est prié de donner aux dispositions qu'il renferme.

Délibération du Conseil de ville en Séance du 7 Aout 1813.

(Signé) MISSONET, Recorder.

Approuvé les dits Jour et an

(signé) N. GIROD Maire

EDITORS' TRANSLATION

The city council has been informed that last Tuesday, the third day of this month of August, the honorable Dominick A. Hall, judge of the United States district court sitting in this city, handed down a decision in which he declares illegal the act of dispossession enforced by Mr. Le Breton D'orgenoy, ex-marshal, acting under the orders of the president of the United States then in office, against Mr. Edward Livingston, in the case of the batture in front of the Faubourg Sainte Marie.

Considering that this batture is part of the port of New Orleans: that it can no more become the property of an individual, by virtue of any ordinary decision, than can the soil of the streets and public squares.

Considering that this property is most necessary to the existence of the city of New Orleans because it furnishes sandy soil to the public, for construction as well as for filling levees, streets, and avenues, which are constantly damaged by rain and washed toward the cypress swamp, because of the inclination of the land; the need being so great that an estimated one-hundred-thousand cartloads of sandy soil are extracted annually from this batture to meet the needs of the public.

Considering that since the origin and foundation of this colony, the inhabitants and municipal administration of this city have enjoyed the uninterrupted right to extract this soil to meet their needs.

Considering that the attempt to make something of this nature the property of Mr. Livingston obviously violates public and civil law.

Finally, considering that all the citizens of the state, as well as those of the city, have an interest in preventing this property from leaving the possession and enjoyment of the public, the council declares, in its capacity as local representative of one of the most populated portions of the state of Louisiana, that it considers itself to be the defender and natural guardian of the port of New Orleans; consequently, it places under its own protection, under that of the citizenry, and under that of his excellency William C. C. Claiborne, governor of this state, the batture of the Faubourg Sainte Marie, as well as the remainder of the port, the streets, and the public places in this city;

It is ordered moreover that this decision be communicated to his excellency the governor forthwith and that he be invited to attend the council's meeting so that he can be asked to cooperate with it as chief of state and provide his assistance to its arrangements.

Proceedings of the City Council at its 7 August 1813 session.

(Signed) MISSONET, Recorder.

Approved on the said day and year

(Signed) N. GIROD Mayor

[391]

Tr (DLC); at head of text: "Conseil de Ville de la N^{elle} Orléans" ("New Orleans City Council") and "Copie" ("Copy"); notation in right margin of verso: "A"; at foot of text: "Pour copie conforme" ("Certified copy"). Translation by Dr. Genevieve Moene.

Pierre François Missonnet (ca. 1750–1833), attorney, city council president/recorder, and a justice of the peace of Orleans Parish for several years, maintained a legal practice in New Orleans until at least 1823 (1833 Orleans Parish Death Index, 3:220 [L-Ar]; note to TJ to James Monroe, 26 May 1812; Claiborne, *Letter Books*, 4:385; *Whitney's New-Orleans Directory, and Louisiana & Mississippi Almanac for the year 1811* [New Orleans, 1810], 38; John Adems Paxton, *The New-Orleans Directory and Register* [New Orleans, 1823]).

Nicolas Girod (1747–1840), businessman and local politician, emigrated late in the 1770s from France to Louisiana, where he became a commission merchant and landowner. He served as the first popularly elected mayor of New Orleans, 1812–15, during which time he staunchly supported General Andrew Jackson's successful effort to repel the British force threatening the city. Girod was also a director of the Louisiana Bank, a city alderman, 1824–25, and a warden at Saint Louis Cathedral. He evidently intended to leave $160,000 to local charities, but as a result of posthumous litigation this sum was substantially reduced (Glenn R. Conrad, ed., *Dictionary of Louisiana Biography* [1988], 1:346; New York *Public Advertiser*, 13 Feb. 1807; Jackson, *Papers*, vol. 3; New York *National Advocate*, 7 Mar. 1815; gravestone inscription at Saint Louis Cemetery no. 2, New Orleans; New Orleans *Bee*, 2 Sept. 1840; *Michoud et al. v. Girod et al.* [1846] [4 Howard], *U.S. Reports*, 45:503–66).

II

Decree of the New Orleans City Council

Le Conseil de Ville informé, d'après la déclaration de Son Président, que M. Le Breton Dorgenoy, malgré l'offre que lui a faite le Conseil de Se porter caution du résultat de l'appel qu'il a été invité de faire devant La Cour Suprême des Etats-Unis, a refusé de faire cet appel;

Considérant que l'action intentée contre cet exmaréchal par M. Livingston n'est point une action qui lui Soit personnelle, et qu'elle ne lui est relative que comme Agent du Président des Etats Unis, et par conséquent du public;

Considérant que Suivant le bon Sens, l'équité et les Lois de tous les pays, le refus que fait un mandataire d'exécuter ou de donner Suite à la volonté de Son mandant n'enlève point à ce dernier le droit d'agir pour la défense de Ses intérêts;

Considérant que le Corps Municipal de cette ville et le Gouverneur de cet Etat, chacun en ce qui les concerne, sont les conservateurs et les défenseurs naturels des propriétés publiques, en l'absence de l'autorité exécutive, ou d'après le refus de Son mandataire:

arrête que le Corps municipal de cette ville le considère comme compétent pour porter devant la Cour Suprême des Etats Unis, appel du Jugement de première instance rendu le trois du présent mois par l'honorable Dominique A. Hall en faveur de M. Edouard Livingston, et qu'en conséquence M. Moreau Lislet, avocat de la Corporation, devra de Suite introduire le dit appel devant la Cour Suprême des Etats Unis, au nom de la Corporation municipale de la N^{elle} orléans; en expliquant dans Sa pétition à ce Sujét que cet appel est ainsi introduit sur le refus qu'a fait l'exmaréchal M Le Breton Dorgenoy de l'introduire, et que le Maire, en Sa qualité, fournira tous cautionnemens voulus par la Loi en pareil cas.

arrête aussi que Son Excellence Wm C. C. Claiborne Gouverneur de cet Etat, sera prié de concourir avec le Conseil de Ville pour former également un appel dans cette affaire, en Sa qualité de premier Magistrat de l'Etat de la Louisiane.

arrête aussi que dans le cas où l'avocat de la Corporation eprouverait un refus dans la notification, a qui de droit, de l'appel recoit, il devra faire constater ce refus par deux Notaires de cette ville; et il remettra à la Corporation expédition de l'acte qu'ils dresseront à cet égard.

arrête en outre que la présente délibération Sera transmise immédiatement à l'approbation du Maire qui en enverra copie officielle à son Excellence le Gouverneur et à l'avocat de la Corporation.

Délibération du Conseil de ville, en Sa Séance du 9 août 1813.

(signé) MISSONNET, Recorder.

approuvé le dit Jour et an

(signé) N. GIROD, Maire.

EDITORS' TRANSLATION

The city council has been informed by a declaration from its president that Mr. Le Breton D'orgenoy, despite the council's offer to stand surety for the result of the appeal he was invited to make to the United States Supreme Court, has refused to make this appeal;

Considering that the action is not brought against this former marshal by Mr. Livingston personally, but only as it relates to him in his capacity as an agent of the president of the United States and consequently of the public;

Considering that according to common sense, equity, and the laws of every country, the refusal of a proxy to execute or follow the directives of the person who gave him his mandate does not take away from that person the right to act in defense of his own interests;

Considering the municipal body of this city and the governor of this state, with regard to that which concerns them, as the conservers and natural defenders of public properties in the absence of executive authority or in consequence of a proxy's refusal to act:

It is ordered that, as this city's municipal body considers itself competent to come before the United States Supreme Court, it appeal the decision of the lower court rendered on the third of the current month by the honorable Dominick A. Hall in favor of Mr. Edward Livingston. In consequence, Mr. Moreau Lislet, attorney for the corporation, will immediately bring the said appeal before the United States Supreme Court in the name of the municipal corporation of New Orleans, explaining in his petition that it is introduced in its name due to the refusal of the ex-marshal Mr. Le Breton D'orgenoy to do so, and that the mayor, in his official capacity, will supply all the sureties required by law in such a case.

It is ordered, in addition, that his excellency William C. C. Claiborne, governor of this state, be asked to cooperate with the city council and also to file his own appeal in this case in his capacity as first magistrate of the state of Louisiana.

It is also ordered that, if the attorney for the corporation meets with a refusal on the part of the court to take up this appeal, he must have this refusal verified by two notaries of this city and remit to the corporation a copy of the document they will draw up on the subject.

It is ordered moreover that the current proceedings be immediately submitted to the approbation of the mayor, who will send official copies to his excellency the governor and to the corporation attorney.

Proceedings of the City Council at its 9 August 1813 session.

(Signed) Missonnet, Recorder.

Approved on the said day and year

(Signed) N. Girod, Mayor.

Tr (DLC); at head of text: "Conseil de Ville de la N^elle orléans" ("New Orleans City Council") and "Copie" ("Copy"); with signed attestation by Girod: "Pour copie conforme" ("Certified copy"); notation in right margin of verso: "B." Translation by Dr. Genevieve Moene.

III
William C. C. Claiborne's Address to the New Orleans City Council

Mᴿ Recorder, & Gentlemen of the Council,

Had my health permited, I should have availed myself of the Honor of your Invitation, and been present at the sessions of the council on saturday last. . . . The question as to the right of property to the batture in front of the suburb[1] Sᵗᵉ mary is of very general concern. . . . that the Public right should be maintained[2] against the claims of Individuals, is not only interesting to the city but to the state, and the whole western Country;—to this end therefore, any <u>measure which the laws authorise</u>, will[3] meet my best wishes, and zealous Co-operation. . . . a decision of the honorable the district court of Louisiana, in the suit brought by Mʳ Livingston against mʳ Dorgenoy late marshal of the district, Declares the removal of Mʳ Livingston from the Batture by order of Mʳ Jefferson late President of the united States, illegal and directs the Plaintiff to be restored to his possession. I am sorry the defendant has declined appealing from this decision to the supreme Court of the united States, The High[4] standing of the officer whose authority is denied; the importance of the stake,[5] and of the principles involved, make it desirable (for the satisfaction of all parties)[6] that the case should have been carried before the highest Judicial Tribunal of this Nation. . . . I beleive however, there is no way of obtaining an appeal but thro' the agency of mʳ Dorgenoy, and that the arrêté of the council which proposes an appeal in the name of the city Council & the Governor of the state will be in operative.[7] Neither the one nor the other are parties to the suit, and it is understood to be an established Rule, that a party can alone take an appeal.—The operation of the Rule, in the present case, is unfortunate, since mʳ Dorgenoy has in fact been only, <u>an</u>

Agent, and his personal <u>interest</u> much less, than <u>that</u> of the public, involved in the issue. The title of m^r Livingston is not embraced by the decision of the Honorable the district Court. This title however has long been the subject of private & Public discussion. my opinions formed at an early period of this discussion were (as my duty enjoined) fully and freely expressed in my official Correspondance with the General Government, whilst I acted as Governor of the late Territory of Orleans.—From what I have seen, the Batture can only be considered a shoal of the mississippi, a part of the port of new Orleans, covered with water from four to five and six months in every year, and is the spot, where Boats and Barges Coming from the Upper Country can lie and land with greatest convenience & safety. From what I have heard, there exists no doubt in my mind,[8] but the Batture at low-water, has from the foundation of the city (with the extent, it had from time to time) been used as a Public Landing and common, where Boats were loaded and unloaded and where the Inhabitants of New Orleans obtained Earth for building and for raising the streets and Court yards; and that the French and Spanish Governors of Louisiana had invariably prevented the exercise of Individual ownership over the same, and removed all intruders. Should the batture be reclaimed, from my own observation on the mississippi, and the information of much older settlers than myself I verily beleive it would change the Current of the River in front of the City, to the Great injury of the Port of new-Orleans, and the lower suburbs and Plantations.—Such have been, and such are still my impressions; Perhaps they are erroneous; Contrary sentiments are intertained by others, and it is Contended that the Batture is alluvion land susceptible of private ownership & the property of Mr Livingston. The laws must ultimatly decide, and to maintain the Public Right, we must alone resort to the means, which these Permit.

Considering the Batture as a part of the Bed of the mississippy, it is an object of enquiry What measures ought or can be taken by the state authorities, to prevent obstructions on that <u>Great High way</u>, the free use of which as well to the Inhabitants[9] of this state, as of all the other states, is made one of the conditions upon which Louisiana was admitted into the American Union.—the subject has been submitted to the Consideration of the attorney General, the constitutional adviser of the executive, and the result of his enquiries, shall be communicated to you.—as far as the laws and the Principles of the Government authorise my immediate Agency, or give me a Controul over public functioneries, whose province it may be to enterfere, you may be assured of a Prompt and faithful discharge of duty.—But if upon examination the powers of the state authorities, should on the Present Occasion, be found incompetent, we must speedily & respectfully solicit the further enterference & support of the General Government. <u>More we cannot do</u>,—to proceed further than the laws justify would furnish an example of evil tendency, & injure the best of causes.—

New Orleans, aug^t 9th 1813.

Tr (DLC); in a clerk's hand, with corrections and emendations by Claiborne, only the most important of which are noted below; ellipses in original; at head of text in clerk's hand: "Batture in front of the Suburg [Suburb] Ste Mary. The city Council of New Orleans, having solicited the Governor to assist at their deliberations on the subject of the batture he attended at the city Hall on the 9th of August 1813. and addressed the council as follows"; on verso of last page: "C."

The city council's RECORDER was Pierre François Missonnet. ARRÊTÉ: "decree." Louisiana's ATTORNEY GENERAL was François Xavier Martin.

1 Manuscript: "suburg."
2 Reworked by Claiborne from "entertained."

3 Here is canceled "not."
4 Reworked by Claiborne from "slight."
5 Manuscript: "state." A transcription based on a different text renders this word as "Stake" (Claiborne, *Letter Books*, 6:254).
6 Here is canceled "I should."
7 Reworked by Claiborne from "operation."
8 Preceding seven words interlined by Claiborne in place of "exerts on my mind."
9 Manuscript: "Inhabitans."

From Patrick Gibson

SIR   Richmond 14th Augt 1813

I have received your favor of the 10th and agreeably to your request send you inclosed one hundred dollars in small notes, together with a promisary note of $1500. for your signature—the date you will be pleased to leave blank—Your several drafts shall be duly attended to—

The deed for Mr Taylor shall be given to him on his return from the Springs—With great respect I am

Your obt Servt   PATRICK GIBSON

RC (ViU: TJP-ER); at head of text: "Thomas Jefferson Esqre"; endorsed by TJ as a letter from Gibson & Jefferson received 17 Aug. 1813 and so recorded in SJL. Enclosure not found.

SJL records a missing letter from TJ to Gibson of 18 Aug. 1813, which evidently covered a signed "note for 1500.D. to Patr. Gibson for the bank, date blank" (*MB*, 2:1292).

To Joseph Dougherty

DEAR JOSEPH   Monticello Aug. 15. 13.

Agreeably to the request in your letter of the 8th I have this day written to mr Saml H. Smith, recommending you to his recollection in the disposal of any suitable office which may be in his gift. when such an one occurs, you will of course bring yourself to his notice. I am sorry your porter business has failed you from the circumstances of the times; as a dependance on one's own exertions is so much more agreeable than to be at the will of others. however some of the berths1 about the public offices are a good enough mainstay, where they give time for some other calling in aid of them. the Merino fever is so entirely spent, that our country people will not even accept of them; preferring those breeds giving most wool to what gives the finest. wishing you success in your application for employment, or whatever else you engage in I subscribe with the assurance of my constant attachment and good will.   TH: JEFFERSON

PoC (DLC); at foot of text: "M^r   ¹ Manuscript: "births."
Joseph Dougherty"; endorsed by TJ.

To James Madison

DEAR SIR   Monticello Aug. 15. 13.
I congratulate you on your release from the corvée of a session of Congress, and on the pleasure of revisiting your own fields & friends: and I hope your fields have been more fortunate than ours which have been wet but once since the 14th of April, and present an aspect never seen since the year 1755. when we lost so many people by famine. but the present drought is only partial; that was general. there are now districts of country that have suffered little.—I am obliged to set out for Bedford on Wednesday or Thursday next, to be absent 3. or 4. weeks. on my return I shall have the pleasure of seeing you at Montpelier, by which time I hope a perfect reestablishment of your health and relief from influenza will render the visit you promise us for mrs Madison and yourself as recreating to you as welcome to us. the paper you were so kind as to inclose me presents me the first copy I have seen of the Assesment law. in the appointment of Collector we shall feel little interest; but that of principal Assessor will be awfully important, as he alone is to decide the quantum of tax each man is to pay in 4. counties. if indeed he is to be governed by the state valuations pro ratâ, he will need to be only a good Arithmetician; otherwise he should be just, capable, clear of party and personal biasses beyond all suspicion. I suppose he would best be taken from either Nelson or Albemarle, the two central counties. I am too little acquainted to know whether there now lives in either such a man as Col° Nicholas Lewis was. I will endeavor to get the best men of our county to consult and enquire and give their opinions, presuming it may be in time to send their recommendation to you. present me with all affection to mrs Madison in which mrs Randolph joins me, and accept for yourself assurances of my constant attachment & respect.
                                        TH: JEFFERSON

RC (DLC: Madison Papers, Rives Collection); at foot of text: "The President of the US." PoC (DLC); endorsed by TJ.

TJ actually departed for Poplar Forest not on WEDNESDAY OR THURSDAY NEXT (18–19 Aug. 1813), but on the 24th (*MB*, 2:1292). Madison enclosed a copy of the 22 July 1813 ASSESMENT LAW, "An Act for the assessment and collection of direct

taxes and internal duties," in a missing letter of 14 Aug. 1813 that is recorded in SJL as received the same day from Montpellier. Albemarle and Nelson were the TWO CENTRAL COUNTIES of Virginia's nineteenth collection district, which also included Amherst and Fluvanna counties (*U.S. Statutes at Large*, 3:22–34, esp. 24).

To Peter Minor

DEAR SIR   Monticello Aug. 15. 13.

I recieved yesterday the inclosed act for the assesment of Congressional taxes. I see by that that a Collector and principal assessor are to be appointed for our district (Nelson, Amherst, Albemarle & Fluvanna). the former officer is of little concern to those who mean to pay punctually; but the principal assessor is all important; because the sum to be paid by our district being fixed by law, he is to divide it among the taxables of the district according to his estimate of their property. it is highly interesting to us then that a just & capable character, free from party or personal bias be named. if indeed he is to be governed by the state assesment, pro ratâ, this rule for his government would secure us all. this will depend on the instructions from the Secretary of the Treasury.[1] if these leave him at large, our only reliance will be on his character. I propose to consult with as many persons as I can, acquainted in the district, to fix on the person whom we shall recommend to the President. may I be permitted to undertake your acceptance of it? the whole duties will be to be performed at your own house except the 25. days hearing appeals, prescribed in the 14th section. besides some smaller perquisites in other sections, the 30th fixes the principal emoluments, which are indeed not a great object, but perhaps not entirely inadequate for services to be done at one's home & ease. will you think of this, and return me the act with your answer before Tuesday night, as on Wednesday I set out to Bedford, and at Warren and on my road there I shall have an opportunity of consulting with some whose opinions will be of weight. accept assurances of my friendship and respect.   TH: JEFFERSON

PoC (MoSHi: TJC-BC); at foot of text: "Peter Minor esq."; endorsed by TJ. Tr (ViHi: Minor Family Papers); in the hand of John Barbee Minor (b. 1852).

The SUM TO BE PAID by Albemarle County was set at $9,497.50 in "An Act to lay and collect a direct tax within the United States" of 2 Aug. 1813 (*U.S.*

Statutes at Large, 3:60). The enclosed copy of "An Act for the assessment and collection of direct taxes and internal duties," 22 July 1813, authorized the following EMOLUMENTS for each principal assessor: "two dollars for every day employed in hearing appeals and making out lists . . . and four dollars for every hundred taxable persons contained in the tax list as delivered by him to the collector" (*U.S. Statutes at Large*, 3:22–34, esp. 34).

¹ Preceding three words interlined.

To Samuel H. Smith

DEAR SIR   Monticello Aug. 15. 13.

Altho' sollicitation for appointment is generally an irksome office, it is rendered the less so in the present instance by the occasion it furnishes of addressing you after so long an interval. first then as to the direct object. Joseph Dougherty, who lived with me 8. years in Washington rather as a riding agent than as the head of my stable, informs me you are appointed Commissioner of the revenue, and wishes to get some berth¹ under you. I can say with truth that he is intelligent, industrious, sober, and I think entirely honest. in this be so good as to consider me merely a witness, leaving to yourself to decide the occasion when such qualifications may be useful to you. the next matter of business is to pray your forgiveness of my remissness as a subscriber to the National intelligencer. I am in long arrearage, and pray you, either by yourself or mr Gale, for I do not know to which of you I am in default, to send me a note of the amount I am in arrear, which shall be instantly remitted. matters of business being thus disposed of, I congratulate you on the appointment which Dougherty has announced to me. yet I doubt if the change from your rural retirement will add to your happiness, and I doubt still more for mrs Smith, who I think would have preferred Arcadia to Athens. should your new office give leisure for a visit from her and yourself at any time, it would be a great gratification to us. mrs Smith would find I have made no progress in the improvement of my grounds, all my spare labor having been in constant demand for the improvements of my farms; mills, canals, roads E^{t}c having given me constant occupation. to these are added our establishments for spinning & weaving, which occupy time, labor & persons. present me affectionately to mrs Smith & be assured of my great esteem & respect

TH: JEFFERSON

RC (ViU: TJP); at foot of text: "Mr Samuel H. Smith." PoC (DLC); endorsed by TJ.

¹ Manuscript: "birth."

To Horatio G. Spafford

Sir   Monticello Aug. 15. 13.

Your favor of the 2ᵈ inst. is duly recieved and I thank you for the mark of attention it expresses in proposing to send me a copy of your new Gazetteer. it will come safely to me under cover by the ordinary mail. but I owe abundant additional thanks for the kind expressions of respect which the letter conveys to me. at the end of a career thro' a long course of public troubles, if my countrymen are satisfied that my endeavors to serve them have been zealous & pure, I stand fully rewarded. 40. years elapsed since the commencement of those troubles have strowed the field with the dead of those who were old enough to be actors in them. but we have reason to be satisfied with the spirit we see manifested to maintain for our posterity the rights of self government acquired for them at the expence of so many struggles and sacrifices. and I do hope that this our beloved country will long exhibit to mankind an example for their imitation, of a government pursuing no object but the best interests of the society which institutes & maintains it. I should have been happy in the visit you proposed to Monticello, as I shall be should any future circumstance give me that pleasure; and I tender you the assurance of my esteem & respect   Th: Jefferson

RC (PWW); lacks address cover. RC (NjMoHP: Lloyd W. Smith Collection); address cover only; addressed: "Mʳ Horatio G. Spafford Albany," with the last word canceled and "Ballston Springs" added in another hand; franked; postmarked Milton, 18 Aug.; with endorsement by Spafford evidently indicating that this letter was a response to his own letter of 2 Aug., that it was received 26 Aug., and that Spafford sent the "book" on 28 Aug. PoC (DLC); left edge torn away; endorsed by TJ.

To Tunis Wortman

Sir   Monticello Aug. 15. 13.

I return your subscription paper with my name willingly placed on it. I have said <u>for one year</u>, and inclose the price, because I find myself happier in other branches of reading, than of newspapers. I read 2. or 3. a week of the old ones still, but engage for no new ones; and have done it in your case, because I am confident it will be conducted in a good spirit, and I wish it therefore to be set agoing. I have no doubt it will afterwards stand firmly on it's own merits. a great object will be to redeem the character of our newspapers for falsehood, now so abandoned to it, that no one can believe, even probable things, at all the more for their being affirmed in a newspaper. it is much better to publish late truths than early falsehoods. were I the publisher of a paper, instead of the usual division into Foreign, Domestic E^{t}c I think I should distribute every thing under the following heads—1. True. 2. Probable. 3. wanting confirmation. 4. lies, and be careful in subsequent papers to correct all errors in preceding ones. at present it is disreputable to state a fact on newspaper authority; and the newspapers of our country by their abandoned spirit of falsehood, have more effectually destroyed the utility of the press than all the shackles devised by Bonaparte. hoping that this evil may[1] cure itself, by a wholesome application of the public countenance & patronage,[2] and that you will have the merit of being instrumental to the restoration of value[3] to this source of public information, I tender you my best wishes for success & the assurance of my esteem & respect

TH: JEFFERSON

PoC (CSmH: JF-BA); at foot of text: "Mr Tunis Wortman"; endorsed by TJ.

TJ enclosed $5 along with the SUB-SCRIPTION PAPER, not found, for the New York *Standard of Union*, requesting that he be dropped from the subscription list at the end of the first year (*MB*, 2:1292).

[1] Word interlined in place of "will."
[2] Word interlined in place of "protection."
[3] Manuscript: "valu."

From Peter Minor

DEAR SIR   Ridgeway Augt 16th 1813

I return you the Act which you so obligingly enclosed to me yesterday,[1] with my thanks for your friendly & polite consideration of me as a person qualified to fill the office of a principal assessor. Such an office would interfere but little with my present avocations. I therefore agree to accept the appointment if confered on me, with the hope that your self & other intelligent Friends will aid me with your counsel in any difficulties that may occur in discharging the office, the duties of which, from a mere perusal of the Law I confess I do not fully comprehend—   Accept assurances of my sincere friendship & respect   P. MINOR

RC (MHi); at foot of text: "Mr Jefferson"; endorsed by TJ as received 16 Aug. 1813 and so recorded in SJL. FC (ViU: TJP); entirely in Minor's hand. Enclosure: enclosure to TJ to Minor, 15 Aug. 1813.

[1] In FC "agreeably to your request, together" is substituted for preceding eight words.

To John Waldo

Sir   Monticello Aug. 16.[1] 13.

Your favor of Mar. 27. came during my absence on a journey of some length. it covered your 'Rudiments of English grammar,' for which I pray you to accept my thanks. this acknolegement of it has been delayed until I could have time to give the work such a perusal as the avocations to which I am subject would permit. in the rare & short intervals which these have allowed me, I have gone over, with pleasure, a considerable part, altho' not the whole of it. but I am entirely unqualified to give that critical opinion of it, which you do me the favor to ask. mine has been a life of business; of that kind which appeals to a man's conscience, as well as his industry, not to let it suffer; and the few moments allowed me from labor, have been devoted to more attractive studies; that of Grammar having never been a favorite with me. the scanty foundation laid in it at school, has carried me thro' a life of much hasty writing, more indebted for style to reading and memory, than to rules of grammar.   I have been pleased to see that in all cases you appeal to Usage, as the arbiter of language; & justly consider that as giving law to Grammar, & not Grammer to Usage. I concur entirely with you, in opposition to the Purists, who[2] would destroy all strength & beauty of style, by subjecting it to a rigorous compliance with their rules. fill up all the Ellipses and Syllepses of Tacitus, Sallust, Livy E{t}c and the elegance & force of their sententious brevity are extinguished. 'deorum injurias, diis curae.'[3]—'alieni appetens, sui profusus; ardens in cupiditatibus; satis loquentiae, sapientiae parum.'—'Annibal peto pacem.'—'per diem Sol non <u>uret</u> te neque luna per noctem.' wire-draw these expressions, by filling up the whole syntax and sense, & they become dull paraphrases on rich sentiments. we may say then truly with Quinctilian 'aliud est Grammaticé, aliud Latiné loqui.' I am no friend therefore to what is called <u>Purism</u>; but a zealous one to the <u>Neology</u> which has introduced these two words without the authority of any dictionary. I consider the one as destroying the nerve & beauty of language, while the other improves both, and adds to it's copiousness. I have been not a little disappointed and made suspicious of my own judgment, on seeing the Edinburg Reviewers, the ablest critics of the age, set their faces against the introduction of new words into the English language. they are particularly apprehensive that the writers of the United States will adulterate it. certainly so great and growing a population, spread over such an extent of country, with such a variety of climates, of productions, of arts, must enlarge their language, to make it answer it's purpose of expressing all ideas, the new as well as the old. the new circumstances under which we are placed call for new words, new phrases and for the transfer of old words to new objects. an American dialect will therefore be formed; so will a West-Indian, and Asiatic, as a Scotch and an Irish are already formed. but whether will these adulterate, or enrich the English language? has the beautiful poetry of Burns, or his Scottish dialect, disfigured it? did the Athenians consider the Doric, the Ionian, the Aeolic & other dialects as disfiguring, or as beautifying their language? did they fastidiously disavow Herodotus, Pindar, Theocritus, Sappho, Alcaeus as Grecian writers? on the contrary, they were sensible that the variety of dialects, still infinitely varied by poetical license constituted the riches of their language, and made the Grecian Homer the first of poets, as he must ever remain, until a language, equally ductile & copious shall again be spoken.

Every language has a set of terminations, which make a part of it's peculiar idiom. every root among the Greeks was permitted to vary it's termination, so as to express it's radical idea in the form of any one of the parts of speech; to wit, as a noun, an adjective, a verb, participle or adverb. and each of these parts of speech again, by still varying the termination, could vary the shade of idea existing in the mind. I will explain myself by an example. a Greek root could assume any one of these terminations.

subst.	αληθ-εια -ιοτης	ευθυ-νη -ωρια	ωθ-ιϛμος -ηϛις. -ωϛης	ψυχ-ωϛις -αριον
Adject.	αληθ-ης -ινος -ευτικος	ευθυ-ς -ωρος		
Verbs.	αληθ-ευω -ιζω.	ευθυ-νω -ωρειν	ωθ-εω	
particip.	αληθευ-ων -ως. -ας. -ομενος -εις			
adv.	αληθ-ες -ως -ινως	ευθυ ευθυ- ωρον		

it was not then the number of Grecian roots (for some other languages may have as many) which made it the most copious of the antient languages; but the infinite diversification which each of these admitted. let the same license be allowed in English the roots of which, native & adopted, are perhaps more numerous, and it's idiomatic terminations more various than of the Greek, and see what the language would become. it's idiomatic terminations are

subst.   Gener-ation-ator-osity-ousness-alship-alissimo. degener-acy. King-dom-ling. Joy-ance. Enjoy-er-ment. Herb-age-alist. Sanct-uary-imony-itude. Royal-ism. Lamb-kin. Child-hood. Bishop-ric. Proced-ure. horseman-ship. worthi-ness.

adject.   Gener-ant-ative-ic-ical-able-ous-al.-Joy-ful-less-some. Herb-y-aceous-escent-ulent. child-ish. Wheat-en

verb   Gener-ate-alise.

part.   Gener-ating-ated.

adv.   General-ly.

I do not pretend that this is a compleat list of all the terminations of the two languages. it is as much so as a hasty recollection suggests; and the omissions are as likely to be to the disadvantage of the one as the other. if it be a full, or equally fair, enumeration, the English are the double of the Greek terminations.

But there is still another source of copiousness more abundant than that of termination. it is the composition of the root, & of every member of it's family 1. with prepositions, & 2. with other words. the prepositions used in the composition of Greek words are αμφι, ανα, αντι, απο, δια, εκ, εν, επι, κατα, παρα, περι, προ, προς, ϛυν, ὑπερ, ὑπο. now multiply each termination of a family, into every preposition, & how prolific does it make each root! but the English language, besides it's own prepositions, about 20. in number, which it compounds with English roots, uses those of the Greek for adopted Greek roots, and of the Latin for Latin roots.[4] the English prepositions, with examples of their use are a, as in a-long, a-board, a-thirst, a-clock. be, as in be-lie. mis, as in mishap; these being inseparable. the separable, with examples, are above-cited, after-thought, gain-say, before-hand, fore-thought, behind-hand, by-law, for-give, fro-ward, in-born, on-set, over-go, out-go, thorough-go, under-take, up-lift, with-stand. now let us see what copiousness this would produce, were it allowed to compound every root & it's family, with every preposition, where both sense & sound would be in it's favor. try it on an English root, the verb 'to place' [Anglo-Saxon+Plæce] for instance, and the Greek and Latin roots of kindred meaning, adopted in English, to wit θεϛις, and locatio, with their respective prepositions.

+ Johnson derives 'Place' from the French 'Place' an open square in a town. but it's Northern parentage is visible in it's synonim Platz, Teutonic, and Plattse, Belgic, both of which signify locus, and the Anglo-Saxon Plæce platea, vicus.

mis-place	amphithesis	a-location	interlocation
after-place	anathesis	ablocation	introlocation
gain-place	antithesis	abslocation	juxtalocation
fore-place	apothesis	allocation	oblocation
hind-place	diathesis	antelocation	perlocation
by-place	ekthesis	circumlocation	postlocation
for-place	enthesis	cislocation	prelocation
fro-place	epithesis	collocation	preterlocation
in-place.	catathesis	contralocation	prolocation
on-place	parathesis	delocation	retrolocation
over-place	perithesis	di-location	relocation
out place	prothesis	dislocation	selocation
thoro'-place	prosthesis	elocation	sublocation
under-place	synthesis	exlocation	superlocation
up-place	hyperthesis	extralocation	translocation
with-place	hypothesis.	illocation.	ultralocation

Some of these compounds would be new; but all present distinct meanings, and the synonimes of the three languages offer a choice of sounds to express the same meaning. add to this that, in some instances, usage has authorised the compounding an English root with a Latin preposition; as in deplace, displace, replace. this example may suffice to shew what the language would become in strength, beauty, variety, and every circumstance which gives perfection to language, were it permitted freely to draw from all it's legitimate sources.

The 2ᵈ source of composition is of one family of roots with another. the Greek avails itself of this most abundantly, & beautifully. the English once did it freely, while in it's Anglo-Saxon form. e.g. boc-cɲæɼꞇ, book-craft, learning. eoɲꝹ-ȝemeꞇ, earth-mate, geometry. ɼꞇɲɲȝenꝺe-ꝺɲenc, stirring-drink, a cathartic. ɲihꞇ-ȝeleaɼ-ɼull, right-belief-ful, orthodox. but it has lost by desuetude much of this branch of composition, which it is desirable[5] however to resume.

If we wish to be assured from experiment of the effect of a judicious spirit of Neology, look at the French language. even before the revolution, it was deemed much more copious than the English; at a time too when they had an Academy, which endeavored to arrest the progress of their language, by fixing it to a Dictionary, out of which no word was ever to be sought, used, or tolerated. the institution of Parliamentary assemblies in 1789. for which their language had no apposite terms or phrases, as having never before needed them, first obliged them to adopt the Parliamentary vocabulary of England; & other new circumstances called for corresponding new words; until, by the number of these adopted, & by the analogies for adoption which they have legitimated, I think we may say with truth that a Dictionnaire Neologique of these would be half as large as the Dictionary of the Academy; & that, at this time, it is the language in which every shade of idea, distinctly percieved by the mind, may be more exactly expressed, than in any language at this day spoken by man. yet I have no hesitation in saying that the English language is founded on a broader base, native and adopted, and capable, with the like freedom of employing it's materials, of becoming superior to that in copiousness & euphony. not indeed by holding fast to Johnson's dictionary:[6] but by encouraging and welcoming new compositions of it's elements. learn from Lye & Benson what the language would now have been if restrained to their Vocabularies. it's enlargement must be the consequence to a certain degree, of it's transplantation from the Latitude of London into every climate of the globe; and the greater the degree, the more precious will it become, as the organ for the developement of the human mind.

These are my visions on the improvement of the English language, by a free use of it's faculties. to realise them would require a course of time. the example of good writers, the approbation of men of letters, the judgment of sound critics, and of none more than of the Edinburg Reviewers, would give it a beginning, & once begun, it's progress might be as rapid as it has been in France, where we see what a period of only 20. years has effected. under the auspices of British science and example it might commence with hope. but the dread of innovation there, and especially of any example set by France, has, I fear, palsied the spirit of improvement. here, where all is new, no innovation is feared which offers good. but we have no distinct class of literati in our country. every man is engaged in some industrious pursuit; and science is but a secondary occupation, always subordinate to the main business of his life. few therefore, of those who are qualified, have leisure to write. in time it will be otherwise. in the mean while necessity obliges us to neologise. and should the language of England continue stationary, we shall probably enlarge our employment of it, until it's new character may separate it in name, as well as in power, from the mother tongue.

Altho' the copiousness of a language may not in strictness make a part of it's grammar, yet it cannot be deemed foreign to a general course of lectures on it's structure & character. and the subject having been presented to my mind by the occasion of your letter, I have indulged myself in it's speculation, and hazarded to you what has occurred, with the assurance of my great respect.

TH: JEFFERSON

RC (CtY: Franklin Collection); brackets in original; at foot of first page: "Mr Waldo." Dft (DLC).

DEORUM INJURIAS, DIIS CURAE: "the gods must look to their own wrongs" (Tacitus, *Annals*, 1.73, in *Tacitus*, trans. Clifford H. Moore and John Jackson, Loeb Classical Library [1925–37; repr. 1969], 3:368–9). ALIENI APPETENS . . . SAPIENTIAE PARUM: "Covetous of others' possessions, he was prodigal of his own; he was violent in his passions. He possessed a certain amount of eloquence, but little discretion" (Sallust, *The War with Catiline*, book 5, in *Sallust*, trans. John C. Rolfe, Loeb Classical Library [1921; repr. 1995], 8–9). ANNIBAL PETO PACEM: "I, Hannibal, am suing for peace" (Livy, *From the Founding of the City*, 30.30, in *Livy*, trans. Frank Gardner Moore, Loeb Classical Library [1949], 8:480–1). PER DIEM . . . PER NOCTEM: "The sun shall not smite thee by day, nor the moon by night" (Psalms 121.6). ALIUD EST GRAMMATICÉ, ALIUD LATINÉ LOQUI: "it is one thing to speak Latin and another to speak grammar" (Quintilian, *The Institutio Oratoria*, 1.6.27, in *The Institutio Oratoria of Quintilian*, trans.

Harold E. Butler, Loeb Classical Library [1921–22; repr. 1969], 1:122–3). TJ characterized the Académie Française as attempting to ARREST THE PROGRESS OF THEIR LANGUAGE. He owned works on Anglo-Saxon vocabulary edited by Edward LYE and Thomas BENSON (Sowerby, nos. 4862–3).

[1] Reworked in both RC and Dft from "12."

[2] In Dft TJ here canceled "by dint of regularity."

[3] In Dft TJ interlined a second quotation from Tacitus: "auferre, trucidare, rapere, falsis nominibus, imperium appellant" ("To plunder, butcher, steal, these things they misname empire") (Tacitus, *Agricola*, 30, in *Tacitus*, trans. Maurice Hutton and others, Loeb Classical Library [1914–25; rev. ed. 1970; repr. 1980], 1:80–1).

[4] In Dft TJ here canceled "making in all about 70."

[5] Preceding two words interlined in Dft in place of "ought."

[6] In Dft TJ here added "not by raising a hue and cry against every word he has not licensed."

From Augustus B. Woodward

SIR,   George-Town, August 16th 1813.

It would have been a great satisfaction to me to have had the pleasure of rendering you a visit at a more early period than the present.

As I contemplate a resignation of the station I have held in the Western country, and settling in New-york, I propose to myself the happiness of seeing you previous to my return to the latter place.

At this time, and in this place, I may consider the greater part of the journey already accomplished, I have leisure, Mr Randolph informs me you are at home, and in health, and have even expressed an expectation of my calling.

At a future period to execute the same purpose might be to incur a journey of three times the extent, at a real want of time, and attended with incertitude.

These, in union with a number of other considerations, have

impressed it on me as a duty by no means to fail in availing myself of the present favorable opportunity of paying you my respects.

I anticipate the honor of communicating to you the outlines of a scientific undertaking which has occupied the greater part of my attention during life, and with respect to which the period of action may now be considered as having arrived, or at least as closely approaching.

What was done in France, between the years 1782 and 1787, in relation to the science of chemistry, you are of course fully aware of.

To do that for all human knowledge which was then done for one subject of it in particular might concisely designate the object contemplated.

The essential improvements then imparted to a particular science consist in the exact arrangement and classification, and the correct nomenclature.

To effect the same object in every science would require the concurrent exertion of all the men of learning of a nation, and of different nations; but the principles of a clear and distinct arrangement and classification of human knowledge, generally, must, from necessity, and in the nature of things, derive their origin from a single mind.

My attention was first devoted to this subject in the year 1788. At that time I was entirely unacquainted with what had been effected in France, in relation to the science of chemistry. My mind was however fully occupied with the other grand example of arrangement and classification, which has distinguished our age, presented in the Linnæan system. I did not complete my classification and nomenclature until 1795. Since that period I have frequently revised them, but have made no alterations.

I have collected, in the research, almost every arrangement which has ever been attempted of human knowledge; both those of antiquity, and those of modern times.

Among them is not omitted your own. I take it from the distribution of your library.

The principle of this arrangement is the same with that of D'Alembert, as displayed in the grand encyclopedia. That is, in its turn, derived from Lord Verulam. This is indeed the original of all the systems at present received.

It is only necessary for me, at the present time, to say that the principle of the system which I have formed is original; and bears no resemblance to any other.

You will thus, Sir, be enabled on its being explained to you, to make an immediate comparison; and at once to determine whether a real scientific advancement has been made.

It will be the most certain criterion of a good and accurate system that subjects allied by nature are not separated by artificial arrangement; and that objects distinct and unassociated in nature are not assembled into the same branch or department, by the operation of some fanciful principle.

The Linnæan system is marked with defects in this respect.

In the botanical department they are not absent.

In the zoölogical they are very conspicuous.

The general feelings of mankind revolt, at once, against any classification which shall bring together objects so diversified, as the horse, the bat, the ape, the whale, and man. Reason imperiously requires that the inhabitants of the water, the earth, and the air, so widely separated in nature, should also be separated in science.

So, in the system of Lord Verulam, matters very distinct and unassociated in nature are brought together by the accidental acceptation of a single word. Fossils and minerals, political events, religion, are comprehended in the same branch of human knowledge, and this is named history; taking its ramifications into natural, civil, and ecclesiastical. What license of the imagination shall consociate matters so diverse, as the sensitive plant, the formica leo, the republic of Carthage, the Roman Pontificate, the tenets of Luther and of Calvin?

In the system which I have devised the kindred sciences are found together. Objects remote in nature are not, by any fanciful principle, assembled. The ramifications are distinct, and well defined. Not only do the cognate sciences stand together, but their order and precedence are equally clear. No room is left for a suggestion that that which is subsequent ought to be anterior; or to claim any other position than that which it occupies.

As to the comprehension of certain portions of human knowledge within a single science, or their distribution into a number of distinct sciences, room must necessarily be left for the exercise of the judgment; and so, in the nomenclature, some indulgence of the imagination may be allowed, even after leading postulata have been admitted.

Thus, admitting that the radix of every term ought to be selected, as far as practicable, from the Greek language; admitting that the terms designating specific sciences should possess a uniformity of termination; admitting that the terms indicating genera, possessing also uniformity among themselves, should be distinguished by a difference of termination from the names of specific sciences; even constantly exacting, in order to avoid cumbrous terms, a specific[1] dissyllabic radix; yet, in new terms, which habit has not familiarized, one taste will relish that which displeases another, and one ear will consider that as soft and melodious which another regards as harsh and dissonant.

The principal value which I attach to the system is derived from its precision.

The eventual number of the specific sciences may be enlarged or contracted, as information may accumulate, or as their relative importance may change; the nomenclature may be amended, or simply altered, as taste may fluctuate; but the relationship and concatenation of the several[2] sciences, as comprehending all the subjects of human knowledge, will be insusceptible of any, the slightest, variation.

From the original trunk to the remotest ramifications the divisions are characterized by an immutable exactitude. The mind, in its progress, is filled with satisfaction and certainty. It perceives, even to the degree of mathematical conviction, not only that a division is correct and good, but that it is exclusively so; and can admit no doubt and encounter no competition.

Aware that on a subject of such magnitude as the arrangement of all human knowledge it would not be proper to ask attention to what was immature, undigested, juvenile, stamped with imperfections; I have looked forward to an advance in life before the actual developement of so important a task.

I have also seriously examined whether France, England, or America, ought to be selected as the theatre on which to propound a measure of so much interest as an exact classification and correct nomenclature of all human science.

Attachment to my own country has governed my determination.

If the exertion should, in every respect, be abortive, it is better that it should receive its termination at the place of its origin.

If, on the contrary, what is proposed should eventually meet with the support and adoption of the literary world, an event which could only be expected at a period beyond the existence of its author, it might not be entirely uninteresting to my country that its origin should be susceptible of definite recognition.

It is by no means essential to the reception and prosperity of any scientific undertaking, of which the basis and principles are solid, that it should emanate from Europe.

In science the world is literally a republic. The mind, intuitively, rejects control; and will, universally, assert its freedom. Truth and reason, virtue and impartiality, are the pillars which sustain scientific decisions. Science acknowledges no tyrant, and accredits no party.

The rule of the Roman poet,

"<u>nonumque prematur in annum</u>," prescribed merely in relation to productions of the imagination, will, in a work aspiring to mathematical exactness, have been more than doubled.

The arrangement and classification of all human knowledge is essentially associated with its future advance and improvement.

The idea of an American National Institute is, therefore, intimately connected with that of a classification and nomenclature[3] of the sciences, proceeding from America.

Accept, Sir, my warmest esteem and respect.

A. B. WOODWARD.

RC (DLC); at foot of text: "The Honorable Thomas Jefferson, Monticello"; endorsed by TJ as received 23 Aug. 1813 and so recorded in SJL.

Woodward ultimately decided against resigning his federal judgeship in the WESTERN COUNTRY. The important work on the SCIENCE OF CHEMISTRY was Louis Bernard Guyton de Morveau and others, *Méthode de Nomenclature Chimique* (Paris, 1787). By 1783 TJ was arranging most of the books in his LI-BRARY by subject, along the lines laid down by Jean Le Rond d'Alembert and Francis Bacon (LORD VERULAM) (Douglas L. Wilson, *Jefferson's Books* [1996], 34–43). The larvae of the FORMICA LEO (*Myrmeleon formicarius*), or ant lion, dig conical pits to trap ants and other insects. POSTULATA: "demands; requirements; desiderata" (*OED*). NONUMQUE PRE-MATUR IN ANNUM: before publishing a work, "keep it back till the ninth year," from Horace, *Ars Poetica*, 388 (Fairclough, *Horace: Satires, Epistles, and Ars Poetica*, 482–3).

Woodward eventually published his meditations on the classification of knowledge as *A System of Universal Science* (Philadelphia, 1816; Poor, *Jefferson's Library*, 14 [no. 930]).

[1] Word interlined.
[2] Word interlined in place of "various."
[3] Preceding two words interlined.

To George Divers

DEAR SIR   Monticello Aug. 17. 13.

I have just recieved a copy of the Congressional assesment law, and find that it highly concerns our interest and attention. two officers for our district (of Amherst, Nelson, Albemarle & Fluvanna) are to be appointed by the President, 1. a Collector, and 2. a Principal assessor. the first is of no concern to those of us who mean to pay punctually: but the 2^d is all important. the quota of our county or district (I know not which) is fixed by Congress in another law not come to hand, and this quota is to be partitioned among the taxable persons by the Assessor according to his estimate of our property. you are sensible how a bad man may indulge his partialities and prejudices in the execution of such a power. we ought immediately then to look out for & recommend to the President some man, just, capable, and without party or personal bias. I presume he should be taken from Albemarle or Nelson the two central counties. my acquaintance is not general enough to make the selection; and I wish therefore that those of more knolege of the characters among us, would give their opinions, which I will undertake to forward to the President. as far as my acquaintance goes among those who would accept such an office, I should prefer Peter Minor. but there may be others preferable unknown to me. be so good as to give me your opinion of the fittest person, & by the bearer if you can, as I set out on Saturday for Bedford. ever affect^ly yours   TH: JEFFERSON

PoC (MHi); at foot of text: "George Divers esq."; endorsed by TJ.

From George Divers

D^R SIR   Farmington aug: 17. 1813
your favor of this days date I have receiv'd by your servant, I had intended & still intend to be at monticello tomorrow, in any event I will see you before you leave home, in the meantime I will think of a person most proper to fill the office of a principal [a]ssessor for the district to which we belong, at present I cannot think of [a]¹ man within the district that I would prefer to Peter Minor, but I fear he will not accept it. I hope you will Come up & dine with us before you go to Bedford. with sincere affection
I am yr. fr^d   GEO: DIVERS

RC (MHi); edge chipped; endorsed by   ¹ Omitted word editorially supplied.
TJ as received 17 Aug. 1813 and so
recorded in SJL.

From Samuel Pleasants

RESPECTED SIR,   Richmond Aug. 17, 1813.
Agreeably to your request, I send you by the stage-driver, the Books ordered in your esteemed favor of the 11th inst. I regret that my young man (in my absence) when making up the last package, omit-

ted the 2nd vol. of the Statutes at Large—it is now forwarded. I hope in the course of the ensuing fall to publish the 4th vol. of this work, which shall be forwarded without delay.   With the greatest respect, I am yr. ob^t SAM^L PLEASANTS

[*on verso of address leaf:*]

Woodfall's Junius	$5.00
The Book,	1.12$\frac{1}{2}$
Pike's Expedition	3.50
Franklin's works, vols. 2, 3, 4, 5—	
the 1st vol. cont^g his <u>Life</u>, not yet published,	10.00
	19.62\frac{1}{2}$

RC (MHi); addressed: "Thomas Jefferson Esquire Monticello"; franked; postmarked Richmond, 18 Aug.; endorsed by TJ as received 20 Aug. 1813 and so recorded in SJL.

To Francis Smith

SIR   Monticello Aug. 17. 13.

Your favor of the 12th is recieved. I inclosed to mr Minor about a fortnight ago, an order on Richmond for a sum of money for the paiment of some particular debts due from mr Marks's estate, of which he had sent me a list. yours of ten dollars was one of these, and I have no doubt as soon as he has had time to draw the money from thence, you will recieve your debt. accept the assurance of my respects.

                                  TH: JEFFERSON

PoC (MHi); at foot of text: "Mr Francis Smith"; endorsed by TJ.

SJL records a missing letter from TJ to Minor of 31 July 1813 that probably covered this order.

To John Wilson

SIR   Monticello Aug. 17. 13.

Your letter of the 3^d has been duly recieved. that of mr Eppes had before come to hand, covering your MS. on the reformation of the orthography of the plurals of nouns ending in y, and ey, and on orthoepy. a change has been long desired in English orthography, such as might render it an easy and true index of the pronuntiation of words. the want of conformity between the combinations of letters, and the sounds they should represent increases to foreigners the difficulty of acquiring the language, occasions great loss of time to children in learning to read, and renders correct spelling rare but in those who read much. in England a variety of plans & propositions have been made for the reformation of their orthography. passing over these two of our countrymen, Dr Franklin and Doct^r Thornton have also engaged in the enterprize; the former proposing an addition of two or three new characters only, the latter a reformation of the whole alphabet nearly. but these attempts in England, as well as here, have been without effect. about the middle of the last century an attempt was made to banish the letter <u>d</u>, from the words bridge, judge, hedge, knowledge, E^t others of that termination, & to write them as we write age, cage, sacrilege privilege; but with little success. the attempt also was made, which you mention in your 2^d part to drop the letter <u>u</u> in words of Latin derivation ending in <u>our</u>, and to write honor, candor, rigor E^tc instead of honour, candour rigour. but the <u>u</u> having been picked up in the passage of these words from the Latin, thro' the French, to us, is still preserved by those who consider it as a memorial of our title to the words. other partial attempts have been made by individual writers, but with as little success. pluralising nouns in y, & ey by adding <u>s</u> only, as you propose would certainly simplify the spelling, and be analogous to the general idiom of the language. it would be a step gained in the progress of general reformation, if it could prevail.[1] but my opinion being requested, I must give it candidly, that, judging of the future by the past, I expect no better fortune to this than similar preceding propositions have experienced. it is very difficult to persuade the great body of mankind to give up what they have once learned, & are now masters of, for something to be learnt anew. time alone insensibly[2] wears down old habits, and produces small changes at long intervals; and to this process we must all accomodate ourselves, and be content to follow those who will not follow us. our Anglo-Saxon ancestors had 20. ways of spelling the word 'many.' ten centuries have dropped all of them and substituted that which we now use.   I now return your MS. without being able, with the gentlemen whose letters are cited to encourage hope as to it's effect. I am bound however to acknolege that this is a subject to which I have not paid much attention; and that[3] my doubts therefore[4] should weigh nothing against their more favorable expectations.[5] that these may be fulfilled, and mine prove unfounded, I sincerely wish, because I am a friend[6] to the reformation generally of whatever can be made better; and because it could not[7] fail of gratifying you to be instrumental in this work. Accept the assurance of my respects.   TH: JEFFERSON

PoC (DLC); at foot of first page: "Mr John Wilson." Extracts printed in Wilson, *A Volume for all Libraries . . . Being a System of Philological Entertainments, Comprising Altogether an Extensive Ground Work for Immense Improvements in the English Language* (Washington, 1814; Sowerby, no. 4888), xiv. Enclosure: MS, not found, of Wilson, *Volume for all Libraries.*

For earlier attempts by TJ's COUNTRYMEN to render the English language more phonetic, see Benjamin Franklin's 1768 experiments with a new alphabet (Leonard W. Labaree and others, eds., *The Papers of Benjamin Franklin* [1959–], 15:173–8), which would have been known to TJ from a 1779 edition of Franklin's works (Sowerby, no. 3053); [Joseph Gaston Chambers], "Elements of Orthography; or an Attempt to form a Complete System of Letters," *Universal Asylum, and Columbian Magazine* 2 (1791): 33–8, 113–7, 175–8, 225–8 (Sowerby, no. 4902); and William Thornton, *Cadmus: or, a Treatise on the Elements of Written Language* (Philadelphia, 1793; Sowerby, no. 1126).

E^T: "and."

Wilson called for dropping THE LETTER u from words ending in "our" and simplifying the PLURALISING of nouns ending in "y" and "ey" in *Volume for all Libraries*, 87–8 and 15–66, respectively. He quoted encouraging letters from such GENTLEMEN as Joel Barlow, Alexander Scott, and James Monroe on pp. xiii–xiv of the same work.

[1] Preceding two sentences quoted in *Volume for all Libraries*, with the second "general" omitted.

[2] Word interlined.

[3] Text from this point to "whatever can be made better" quoted in *Volume for all Libraries*.

[4] Word omitted in *Volume for all Libraries*.

[5] Preceding four words rendered in *Volume for all Libraries* as "the favorable expectations of the gentlemen whose letters are cited."

[6] *Volume for all Libraries*: "am friendly."

[7] Word interlined.

To Caspar Wistar

DEAR SIR   Monticello Aug. 17. 13.

I recieved your favor of June 29. by mr Correa, it's bearer. I found him what you had described in every respect; certainly the greatest collection, and best digest of science in books, men, and things that I have ever met with; and with these the most amiable and engaging character. the only alloy to the pleasure of his society was the reflection that we were never more to enjoy it. it is a partial taste of that death which is to separate us from all things.—not knowing his address I take the liberty of placing under your cover a letter put into my hands for him.

The world as well as myself will readily excuse the delay of your observations on the Mammoth bones, in favor of the more interesting work on our own structure, which has occasioned the delay; and our country will rejoice to see her capable sons at length entering the field of science and emulating the European quarter in it's brightest ornament. for indeed, excepting their science, they have little worthy of emulation.

I thank you sincerely for your kind offers[1] respecting my grandson. our purpose in sending him to Philadelphia was that he should lay a foundation there in those branches of useful[2] science which he could not acquire at home; and on his return apply to those which could be acquired here. for some time after he came home he pursued this plan with assiduity. but at the beginning of the present year, he was put into possession of a farm, and has become so much attached to it's management as to make his studies now a[3] secondary concern. they are therefore now but irregularly attended to. and as farming will be the business of his life, a calling yielding to none in happiness, independance and respectability, we must be contented with the superstructure which his leisure will permit him to raise of himself on the foundation of the sciences already laid. towards this he has no one to thank so much as yourself. of this I can assure you he retains the most lively sense; altho from a want of habit in epistolary correspondence he is remiss in expressing his gratitude to those to whom it is due. to myself your kind offers increase the obligations for which I was so much your debtor before. I can only express to you my sincere sense of them, & assure you that occasions only, and not the will, are wanting to prove it by every thing in my power. among the valuable intimacies, scattered here and there thro' a long life, and which interest both the heart and the head, there are none I look back to with warmer feelings, than yours; nor one to whom I can with more truth than to yourself repeat the assurances of affectionate friendship and respect.   TH: JEFFERSON

PoC (DLC); at foot of first page: "Doct[r] Wistar"; endorsed by TJ. Enclosure not found.

Earlier this year TJ passed the bulk of his farm at Shadwell to his GRANDSON Thomas Jefferson Randolph (Conveyance of Part of Shadwell to Thomas Jefferson Randolph, 26 Mar. 1813).

[1] Reworked from "offices."
[2] Word interlined.
[3] Manuscript: "a a."

Biography of
Meriwether Lewis

I. THOMAS JEFFERSON TO PAUL ALLEN, 18 AUG. 1813
II. UNIDENTIFIED AUTHOR'S SHORT BIOGRAPHY OF
MERIWETHER LEWIS, [BEFORE 18 AUG. 1813]
III. PAUL ALLEN TO THOMAS JEFFERSON, 18 AUG. 1813

EDITORIAL NOTE

Thomas Jefferson had long advocated sending an American-sponsored expedition to explore the region between the Missouri River and the Pacific Ocean. Although frustrated by the inability of George Rogers Clark in 1783–84, John Ledyard in 1788, and André Michaux in 1793 to fulfill this mission, Jefferson finally saw his dream become a reality with the dispatch in 1804 and safe return two years later of Meriwether Lewis and William Clark's Corps of Discovery. The trip itself proved to be only half the battle, however. From almost the moment of their return, Jefferson hoped and expected that an authorized version of Lewis's detailed journals would soon be published. In this he was to be greatly disappointed. Lewis contracted in 1807 with the Philadelphia firm of C. & A. Conrad & Company to have the work printed, but he never submitted a manuscript and, in consequence, nothing was accomplished prior to his suicide in 1809.

After Jefferson helped facilitate the conveyance of the orphaned documentation to Washington, D.C., Lewis's former colleague and current executor William Clark took up the task of transporting it to Philadelphia and finding an editor. He eventually chose Nicholas Biddle, an intelligent young man who proved well-suited to the task. The outbreak of the War of 1812 and collapse of Conrad & Company in that same year delayed publication, but with the assistance of Paul Allen and a new publisher, Bradford & Inskeep of Philadelphia (aided by Abraham H. Inskeep of New York), the work was issued in two volumes in 1814 as a *History of the Expedition under the command of Captains Lewis and Clark to the Sources of the Missouri, thence across the Rocky Mountains and down the River Columbia to the Pacific Ocean. Performed during the years 1804–5–6. By order of the Government of the United States.* For the next ninety years it would remain the only printed account based on Lewis's journals.

Jefferson's letter to Allen of 18 Aug. 1813, which he had originally composed as a stand-alone biographical essay, was placed just after the preface to the first volume of the work and entitled the "Life of Captain Lewis." It has been cited and quoted on numerous occasions by historians, most often as evidence of Jefferson's high regard for Lewis's abilities and of the "depressions of mind" that beset the famed explorer throughout his adulthood. Indeed, the widespread unwillingness to lend credence to the possibility that Lewis might have been murdered is at least in part attributable to Jefferson's interpretation of Lewis's mental condition as unstable, both earlier and at the time of his death. Though saddened, Jefferson was clearly not surprised by reports that Lewis had died by his own hand, and the scholarly community has, by and large, followed suit (*PTJ*, 6:371, 13:382, 25:624–6; Jackson, *Letters of Lewis and Clark*, 2:392–7, 494–6; John Brahan to TJ and James Neelly to TJ, both 18 Oct. 1809; C. & A. Conrad & Company to TJ, 13 Nov. 1809; TJ to James Madison, 26 Nov. 1809; TJ to Bernard McMahon, 13 Jan. 1810; Vardis Fisher, *Suicide or Murder? The Strange Death of Governor Meriwether Lewis* [1962], esp. 179–82; Stephen E. Ambrose, *Undaunted Courage: Meriwether Lewis, Thomas Jefferson, and the Opening of the American West* [1996], esp. 476–81; James P. Ronda, *Jefferson's West: A Journey with Lewis and Clark* [2000]).

I. Thomas Jefferson to Paul Allen

SIR   Monticello. Aug. 18. 1813.

In compliance with the request conveyed in your letter of May 25. I have endeavored to obtain,[1] from the relations & friends of the late Governor Lewis, information of such incidents of his life as might be not unacceptable to those who may read the Narrative of his Western discoveries. the ordinary occurrences of a private life, and those also while acting in a subordinate sphere in the army, in a time of peace, are not deemed sufficiently interesting to occupy the public attention; but a general account of his parentage, with such smaller incidents as marked early character are briefly noted; and to these are added, as being peculiarly within my own knolege, whatever related to the public mission, of which an account is now to be published. the result of my enquiries & recollections, shall now be offered, to be enlarged or abridged as you may think best;[2] or otherwise to be used with the materials you may have collected from other sources.[3]

Meriwether Lewis, late Governor of Louisiana,[4] was born on the 18th of Aug. 1774. near the town of Charlottesville, in the county of Albemarle, in Virginia, of one of the distinguished families of that state. John Lewis, one of his father's uncles, was a member of the king's council, before the revolution. another of them, Fielding Lewis, married a sister of Gen¹ Washington. his father William Lewis, was the youngest of five sons of Col° Robert Lewis of Albemarle, the fourth of whom, Charles, was one of the early[5] patriots who stepped forward in the commencement of the revolution, and commanded one of the regiments first raised in Virginia, and placed on Continental establishment. happily situated at home, with a wife and young family, and a fortune placing him at ease, he left all, to aid in the liberation of his country, from foreign[6] usurpations, then first unmasking[7] their ultimate end & aim. his good sense, integrity, bravery, enterprize and remarkable bodily powers, marked[8] him as an officer of great promise.

but he unfortunately died early in the revolution. Nicholas Lewis, the second of his father's brothers, commanded a regiment of militia in the succesful expedition of 1776. against the Cherokee Indians; who, seduced by the agents of the British government, to take up the hatchet against us, had committed great havoc on our Southern frontier, by murdering and scalping helpless women and children, according to their cruel and cowardly[9] principles of warfare. the chastisement they then recieved closed the history of their wars, prepared them for[10] recieving the elements of[11] civilisation, which, zealously inculcated[12] by the present government of the United States, have rendered them an industrious, peaceable and happy people. this member of the family of Lewises, whose bravery was so usefully proved on this occasion, was endeared to all who knew him by his inflexible[13] probity, courteous disposition, benevolent heart, & engaging modesty & manners. he was the[14] Umpire of all the private differences of his county, selected always by both parties. he was also the guardian of Meriwether Lewis, of whom we are now to speak, and who had lost his father at an early age.[15] he continued some years under the fostering[16] care of a tender mother, of the respectable family of Meriwethers of the same county; and was remarkable even in infancy for enterprise, boldness & discretion. when only eight years of age, he habitually went out, in the dead of night,[17] alone with his dogs, into the forest to hunt the raccoon & opossum,[18] which, seeking their food in the night, can then only be taken. in this exercise, no season or circumstance could obstruct his purpose, plunging thro' the winter's snows and frozen streams, in pursuit of his object. at thirteen he was put to the Latin school, and continued at[19] that until eighteen, when he returned to his mother, and entered on the cares of his farm, having, as well as a younger brother,[20] been left by his father with a competency for all the correct and comfortable[21] purposes of temperate life. his talent for observation, which had led him to an accurate knoledge of the plants & animals of his own country, would have distinguished him as a farmer; but at the age of twenty, yielding to the ardor of youth, & a passion for more dazzling pursuits, he engaged as a volunteer in the body of militia which were called out by Gen[l] Washington on occasion of the discontents produced by the Excise-taxes in the Western parts of the United States; and from that situation he was removed to the regular service as a lieutenant in the line. at twenty three he was promoted to a Captaincy; and, always attracting the first attention, where punctuality & fidelity were requisite, he was appointed paymaster to his regiment.   about this time a circumstance occurred which, leading to the transaction which is the subject of this book,[22] will justify a recurrence to it's original idea.   while I resided in Paris, John Ledyard of Connecticut arrived there, well known in the United States for energy of body & mind. he had accompanied Capt[n] Cook on his voyage to the Pacific ocean, and distinguished himself on that voyage by his intrepidity. being of a roaming disposition, he was now panting for some new enterprize.[23] his immediate object at Paris was to engage a mercantile[24] company in the fur-trade of the Western coast of America, in which however he failed. I then proposed to him to go by land to Kamschatka, cross in some of the Russian vessels to Nootka sound, fall down into the latitude of the Missouri, and penetrate to, and[25] thro', that, to the United States. he eagerly siesed the idea, & only asked to be assured of the permission of the Russian government. I interested, in obtaining[26] that, M. de Simoulin M.P. of the Empress at Paris, but more especially the Baron de Grimm, M.P. of Saxe-Gotha, her more special agent, & correspondent there, in matters not immediately diplomatic.[27] her permission was obtained, & an assurance of protection, while the course of the voyage should be thro' her territories. Ledyard set out from Paris, & arrived at S[t] Petersburg after the Empress had left that place, to pass the winter, I think, at Moscow. his finances not permitting him to make unnecessary[28] stay at S[t] Petersburg, he left it with a passport from one of the ministers; and, at 200. miles from Kamschatka, was obliged to take up his winter quarters. he was preparing, in the spring, to resume his journey, when he was arrested by an officer of the Empress, who by this time[29] had changed her mind, and forbidden his proceeding. he was put into a close[30]-carriage, & conveyed day & night, without ever stopping, till they reached Poland, where he was set down, & left to himself. the fatigue of this journey broke down his constitution, and when he returned to Paris, his bodily strength was much impaired.[31] his mind however remained firm, & he after this undertook the journey to Egypt. I recieved a letter from him, full of sanguine hopes, dated at Cairo, the 15th of Nov. 1788. the day before he was to set out for the head of the Nile, on which day however he[32] ended his career and life. and thus failed the first attempt to explore the Western part of[33] our Northern continent.

In 1792. I proposed to the American Philosophical Society that we should set on foot a subscription to engage some competent person to explore that region in the opposite direction, that is, by ascending the Missouri, crossing the Stony mountains, and descending the nearest river to the Pacific. Cap[t] Lewis being then stationed at Charlottesville, on the recruiting service, warmly sollicited me to obtain for him the execution of that object. I told him it was proposed that the person engaged should be attended by a single companion only, to avoid exciting alarm among the Indians. this did not deter him. but mr André Michaux, a professed botanist, author of the Flora Boreali-Americana, and of the Histoire des chesnes d'Amerique, offering his services, they were accepted. he recieved his instructions, and when he had reached Kentucky in the prosecution of his journey, he was overtaken by[34] an order from the Minister of France, then at Philadelphia, to relinquish the expedition, and to pursue elsewhere the Botanical enquiries on which he was employed by that government. and thus failed the 2$^\text{d}$ attempt for exploring that region.[35]

In 1803. the act for establishing trading houses with the Indian tribes being about to expire, some modifications of it were recommended to Congress by a confidential message of Jan. 18. and an extension of it's views to the Indians on the Missouri. in order to prepare the way, the Message proposed the sending an exploring party to trace the Missouri to it's source, to cross the Highlands, and follow the best water-communication which offered itself from thence to the Pacific ocean. Congress approved the proposition, and voted a sum of money for carrying it into execution. Cap$^\text{t}$ Lewis, who had then been near two years with me as private Secretary, immediately renewed his sollicitations to have the direction of the party. I had now had opportunities of knowing him intimately. of courage undaunted, possessing a firmness & perseverance of purpose which nothing but impossibilities could divert from it's direction, careful as a father of those committed to his charge, yet steady in the maintenance of order & discipline, intimate with the Indian character, customs & principles, habituated to the hunting life, guarded,[36] by exact observation of the vegetables and animals of his own country, against losing time in the description of objects already possesd, honest, disinterested, liberal, of sound understanding, and a fidelity to truth so scrupulous that whatever he should report would be as certain as if seen by ourselves; with all these qualifications, as if selected & implanted by nature in one body, for this express purpose, I could have no hesitation in confiding the enterprize to him. to fill up the measure desired, he wanted nothing but a greater familiarity with the technical language of the natural sciences, and readiness in the Astronomical observations necessary for the geography of his route. to acquire these he repaired immediately to Philadelphia, and placed himself under the tutorage of the distinguished Professors of that place, who with a zeal & emulation, enkindled by an ardent devotion to science, communicated to him freely the information requisite for the purposes of the journey. while attending too, at Lancaster, the fabrication of the arms with which he chose that his men should be provided, he had the benefit of daily communication with mr Andrew Ellicot, whose experience in Astronomical observation, and practice of it in the woods, enabled him to apprise Capt Lewis of the wants & difficulties he would encounter, and of the substitutes & resources offered by a woodland and uninhabited country.

Deeming it necessary he should have some person with him, of known competence to the direction of the enterprise, in the event of accident to himself, he proposed William Clarke, brother of General George Rogers Clarke, who was approved, and, with that view recieved a commission of Captain.[37]

In April 1803. a draught of his instructions was sent to Capt Lewis, and on the 20th of June they were signed in the following form.[38]

[*TJ's instructions to Meriwether Lewis of 20 June 1803 will be dealt with at that date by PTJ, and the text that TJ included at this point is accordingly omitted here.*]

While these things were going on here, the country of Louisiana, lately ceded by Spain to France, had been the subject of negociation at Paris between us and this last power; and had actually been transferred to us by treaties executed at Paris, on the[39] 30th of April. this information, recieved about the 1st day of July, increased infinitely the interest we felt[40] in the expedition, & lessened the apprehensions of interruption from other powers. every thing in this quarter being now prepared, Capt Lewis left Washington on the 5th of July 1803. and proceeded to Pittsburg, where other articles had been ordered to be provided for him. the men too were to be selected from the military stations on the Ohio. delays of preparation, difficulties of navigation down the Ohio,[41] & other untoward obstructions, retarded[42] his arrival at Cahokia until the season was so far advanced as to render it prudent to suspend his entering the Missouri before the ice should break up in the succeeding spring.

From this time his journal, now published, will give the history of his journey to and from the Pacific ocean, until his return to St Louis on the 23^d of Sep. 1806. never did a similar event excite more joy thro' the United States. the humblest of it's citizens had taken a lively interest in the issue of this journey, & looked forward with impatience for the information it would furnish—their anxieties too for the safety of the corps had been kept in a state of excitement by lugubrious rumors, circulated from time to time, on uncertain authorities, and uncontradicted by[43] letters, or other direct information from the time they had left the Mandan towns, on their ascent up the river, in April of the preceding year 1805. until their actual return to St Louis.

It was the middle of Feb. 1807. before Capt Lewis, with his companion Clarke, reached the city of Washington, where Congress was then in session. that body granted to the two Chiefs and their followers the donation of lands which they had been encoraged to expect[44] in reward of their toil & dangers. Capt Lewis was soon after appointed Governor of Louisiana, and Capt Clarke a General of it's militia, and Agent of the US. for Indian affairs in that department.

A considerable time intervened before the Governor's arrival at St Louis. he found the territory distracted by feuds & contentions among the officers of the government, & the people themselves divided by these into factions & parties. he determined at once to take no side with either; but to use every endeavor to conciliate and harmonise them. the even-handed justice he administered[45] to all soon established a respect for his person & authority; and perseverance and time wore down animosities, & reunited the citizens again into one family.

Governor Lewis had, from early life, been subject to hypocondriac affections. it was a constitutional disposition in all the nearer branches of the family of his name, and was more immediately inherited by him from his father. they had not however been so strong as to give uneasiness to his family. while he lived with me in Washington, I observed at times sensible depressions of mind; but knowing their constitutional source, I estimated their course by what I had seen in the family. during his Western expedition[46] the constant exertion, which that required, of all the faculties of body & mind, suspended[47] these distressing affections; but after his establishment at St Louis in sedentary occupations, they returned upon him with redoubled vigor, & began seriously to alarm his friends. he was in a paroxysm of one of these, when his affairs rendered it necessary for him to go to Washington. he proceeded to the Chickasaw bluffs, where he arrived on the 16th of Sep. 1809. with a view of continuing his journey thence by water. mr Neely, agent of the US. with the Chickasaw Indians, arriving there two days after, found him extremely indisposed,[48] and betraying, at times, some symptoms of a derangement of mind. the rumors of a war with England, & apprehensions that he might lose the papers he was bringing on, among which were the vouchers of his public accounts, & the journals & papers of his Western expedition, induced him here to change his mind, and to take his course by land thro' the Chickasaw country. altho' he appeared somewhat relieved, mr Neely kindly[49] determined to accompany & watch over him. unfortunately, at their encampment, after having passed the Tennisee one day's journey,[50] they lost two horses; which obliging mr Neely to halt for their recovery, the Governor proceeded, under a promise to wait for him at the house of the first white inhabitant on his road. he stopped at the house of a mr Grinder, who not being at home, his wife, alarmed at the symptoms of derangement she discovered, gave him up the house, & retired to rest herself in an outhouse, the Governor's and Neely's servants lodging in another. about three aclock in the night, he did the deed which plunged his friends into affliction, and deprived his country[51] of one of her most valued citizens,[52] whose valour and intelligence would have been now employed in avenging the wrongs of his country, and in emulating by land the splendid deeds which have honored her arms on the ocean. it lost too to the nation[53] the benefit of recieving from his own hand the Narrative now offered[54] them of his sufferings & successes, in endeavoring to extend for them the boundaries of science, and to present to their knolege that vast & fertile country, which their sons[55] are destined to fill with arts, with science, with freedom & happiness.[56]

To this melancholy close of the life of one, whom posterity will declare not to have lived in vain, I have only to add that all the facts I have stated are either known to myself, or communicated by his family or others,[57] for whose truth I have no hesitation to make myself responsible; and I conclude with tendering you the assurances of my respect & consideration.   TH: JEFFERSON

RC (Andalusia Foundation, Andalusia, Pa.; photocopy in DNT); at foot of text: "Mr Paul Allen. Philadelphia." Dft (DLC). Enclosed in TJ to Allen and TJ to Nicholas Biddle, both 20 Aug. 1813. Printed in Biddle, *Lewis and Clark Expedition*, 1:vii–xxiii.

Parts of the second paragraph of this letter draw on the Unidentified Author's Short Biography of Meriwether Lewis, document no. II below.

M.P.: minister plenipotentiary. STONY MOUNTAINS: Rocky Mountains. The DISTINGUISHED PROFESSORS of Philadelphia who instructed Lewis in science included Benjamin Smith Barton, Robert Patterson, Benjamin Rush, and Caspar Wistar (Jackson, *Letters of Lewis and Clark*, 1:16–9, 21, 51–2). Under the 3

Mar. 1807 "Act making compensation to Messrs. Lewis and Clarke, and their companions," the TWO CHIEFS of the expedition each received land warrants for 1,600 acres, while their compatriots got 320 acres apiece. In addition, everyone was awarded double pay (*U.S. Statutes at Large*, 6:65–6).

[1] In Dft TJ here canceled "collect."

[2] Preceding five words interlined in Dft in place of "according to your better judgment."

[3] In Dft TJ added text to this point, including dateline and salutation, in left margin.

[4] Preceding four words interlined in Dft.

[5] Word interlined in Dft in place of "first."

⁶ In Dft TJ here canceled "bondage."
⁷ Word interlined in Dft in place of "betraying."
⁸ Word interlined in Dft in place of "made."
⁹ Preceding three words interlined in Dft in place of "known."
¹⁰ In Dft TJ here canceled "entering on."
¹¹ Preceding two words interlined in Dft in place of "those elements."
¹² Preceding three words interlined in Dft in place of "so humanely bestowed."
¹³ Reworked in Dft from "remarkably distinguished by a severe."
¹⁴ In Dft TJ here canceled "universal."
¹⁵ Reworked in Dft from "a very tender age."
¹⁶ Preceding three words interlined in Dft in place of "in the."
¹⁷ Preceding five words interlined in Dft.
¹⁸ Preceding four words added in margin of Dft in place of "these animals."
¹⁹ Preceding two words interlined in Dft in place of "engaged in."
²⁰ Preceding six words added in margin of Dft.
²¹ Preceding two words added in margin of Dft.
²² Preceding eight words interlined in Dft in place of "most remarkable transaction of his life."
²³ Word interlined in Dft in place of "expedition."
²⁴ Word interlined in Dft.
²⁵ Preceding two words interlined in Dft.
²⁶ Word interlined in Dft.
²⁷ In Dft TJ here canceled "she not only permitted."
²⁸ Word interlined in Dft in place of "any."
²⁹ In Dft TJ here canceled "from the caprice or wim."
³⁰ Word interlined in Dft.
³¹ Preceding three words interlined in Dft in place of "appeared gone."
³² Preceding five words interlined in Dft.
³³ Preceding four words interlined in Dft.
³⁴ Preceding three words interlined in Dft in place of "recieved."

³⁵ In Dft TJ here canceled "when in 1803. Louisiana was <*acquired*> ceded to the US. a knolege of the Missouri was no longer an object of mere geographical curiosity, but was become highly interesting to the nation, all the country covered by the waters running into the Misipi constituting the extent of their new acquisition in the upper country. Capt Lewis was now become my private Secretary, and on the first mention of the subject he renewed his sollicitations to be the person employed. my knolege of him, now become more intimate, left no hestitation on my part. I had now had opportunities of knowing his character intimately."
³⁶ Word interlined in Dft in place of "familiarized."
³⁷ Paragraph interlined in place of "It being deemed necessary also to provide an associate properly qualified to succeed to the direction of the enterprise in the event of accident to Capt Lewis, he proposed Capt William Clarke of Ohio, brother to Genl George Rogers Clarke, who was approved without hesitation." In Dft TJ first interlined and added in the margin the earlier version, then canceled it and replaced it in the margin with the later rendition.
³⁸ Sentence interlined in Dft in place of "In June 1813. the following instructions were given him." In Dft TJ added "here insert the instructions verbatim," with the instructions there inserted by him being the original Dft (DLC: TJ Papers, 199:35393–4).
³⁹ In Dft TJ here canceled "1st day of May."
⁴⁰ Reworked in Dft from "our interest."
⁴¹ Preceding three words interlined in Dft.
⁴² Word interlined in Dft in place of "prevented."
⁴³ In Dft TJ here canceled "any."
⁴⁴ Preceding three words interlined in Dft in place of "promised."
⁴⁵ Word interlined in Dft in place of "dealt out."
⁴⁶ Word interlined in Dft in place of "enterprize."
⁴⁷ Word interlined in Dft in place of "exempted him from."

[48] Reworked in Dft from "in extremely ill health."

[49] Word interlined in Dft.

[50] Reworked in Dft from "a day's journey on this side of the Tenissee."

[51] Remainder of Dft written perpendicularly in right margin.

[52] In Dft TJ here canceled "who, if now living, would."

[53] Preceding six words interlined in Dft in place of "and lost to the world."

[54] Word interlined in Dft in place of "presented."

[55] Preceding two words interlined in Dft in place of "they."

[56] Remainder of Dft added in a different ink.

[57] Preceding two words interlined in Dft.

II. Unidentified Author's Short Biography of Meriwether Lewis

[before 18 Aug. 1813]

M Lewis, born August 18, of[1] 74 in Albemarle. he first went to common day schools, learning to read, to write & Arithmetic with ordinary facility,[2] he was early remarkable for intrepidity, liberality & hardihood, at eight years of age going alone with his dogs at midnight in the depth of winter, hunting wading creeks where the banks were covered with ice & snow. he might be tracked through the snow[3] to his traps by the blood which trickled from his bare feet. at eleven years old he was taken from his mother and remained untill thirteen with his gaurdian, when he was put to Latin schools kept by D[r] Everett Parson Maury[4] &[5] Parson Wardell. From eighteen to twenty he remained on his farm an affectionate son and[6] an assiduous and attentive[7] farmer, observing with minute attention all plants and insects which he met with. In his twentieth year he joined a volunteer corps as a private under T. Walker against the insurgents. during the same year he was appointed Lieutenant in the US army. in his twenty third year he was promoted to a captaincy and returned to Albemarle to recruit, he again joined the army and acted as paymaster untill he was made private secretary to the President

MS (DLC: TJ Papers, 148:25877); in an unidentified hand; undated; endorsed by TJ: "Lewis Meriwether."

Matthew MAURY and James Waddell (WARDELL) were Episcopal and Presbyterian clergymen, respectively.

[1] Manuscript: "o."

[2] Preceding three words interlined.

[3] Preceding three words interlined.

[4] Manuscript: "Parson, Maury."

[5] Author here canceled "finally to."

[6] Preceding four words interlined.

[7] Word interlined in place of "active."

III. Paul Allen to Thomas Jefferson

DEAR SIR   Philadelphia Aug. 18 1813—

I have in consequence of the reception of Your letter & the prospect which it gives Me of rendering the work more compleat by the addition of Gov. Lewis biography prevailed upon the Booksellers[1] to delay the publication of the first volume as it was not originally contemplated to have done.[2] Their plan was to publish the first volume as soon as it was struck off & to have the second published with all possible expedition afterwards. But Sir I apprehend Your delay has done Me a benefit, as a publication in the manner contemplated would unquestionably have done an essential injury to the work. I am now authorized by the Booksellers to say that they will wait four weeks for the commu[nica]tion which You have obligingly condescended to promise [me. T]he work will now all be published at once, & your communication will be placed in the front of the Narrative. If Sir it would not suit amidst the multiplicity of your other engagements to finish the biography at the time which the Booksellers have stipulated I think that I might venture to add a procrastination of three or four weeks on my own responsibility. You would confer an essential obligation by informing Me at an early period whether either & which of these portions of time would best enable You to fulfill Your benevolent engagement. I am not apprehensive that the fulness of Your Biography will be an obstacle to its publication now that I have prevailed upon the Booksellers to procrastinate the volumes. I wish very much to enliven the dulness of the Narrative by something more popular splendid & attractive. The publick taste has from a variety of adventitious[3] causes been gorged to repletion on fanciful viands & the most nutritive & invigorating aliments will not be relished unless seasoned with something of that character. Biography partakes to a certain extent of this quality, &[4] is essentially connected with subjects dear to every heart

I am Sir with sentiments of esteem Yours &c   P ALLEN

RC (DLC); mutilated at seal; at foot of text: "His Ex Thomas Jefferson Esqr Monticello"; endorsed by TJ as received 14 Sept. 1813 and so recorded in SJL.

The BOOKSELLERS Samuel F. Bradford and John Inskeep, of Philadelphia, and Abraham H. Inskeep, of New York, subsequently published Biddle, *Lewis and Clark Expedition.*

[1] Manuscript: "Boossellers."
[2] Reworked from "as it was originally contemplated to have done before the second."
[3] Manuscript: "adventious."
[4] Allen here canceled "were it only from motives of a wish to see."

From Lucy Cooley

DEAR SIR   Troy Athens County August 18. 1813
M[r] Jabez Cooley Inform[d] me by letter that he had been to work for
you and M[r] Randolph but was now in the service of the united States
as A substitute[1] for your head Miller I wish you to be so kind as to
forward the Inclosed letter to him if you know where he is he wrote
to me that he belong[d] to Cap[t] Wood[s] Company of Infantry from the
88th Reg[mt] of Albemarle County your Compliance with the above
Request will much Obliege your
      most Obedient servant   LUCY COOLEY

RC (MHi); addressed: "M[r] Thomas Jefferson"; franked, with stamp deleted; endorsed by TJ as received 14 Sept. 1813 and so recorded in SJL. Enclosure not found.

Lucy Calkins Cooley (ca. 1777–ca. 1835) was the wife of JABEZ COOLEY. He reputedly died during wartime military service. In 1820 Lucy Cooley was a resident of Carthage Township, Athens County, Ohio, and three years later she married John Calkrill in the same county (William W. Hough, "Lucy Calkins and Jabez Cooley of Connecticut, Massachusetts and Ohio," *Connecticut Nutmegger* 36 [June 2003]: 23–32; DNA: RG 29, CS, Ohio, Athens Co., 1820; Athens Co. Marriage Book, 23 Aug. 1823).

On 2 Apr. 1813 TJ "Gave Jabez Cooley an ord. on Gibson & Jefferson for 30.D. being a moiety for 88. days work on the road for Mr. [Thomas Mann] Randolph & myself." This road ran along the north bank of the Rivanna River from Secretary's Ford to just opposite Milton (*MB*, 2:1287–8). During Randolph's absence on military service, a Mr. Gilmer and Randolph's own son Thomas Jefferson Randolph served successively as HEAD MILLER for TJ at the Shadwell Mills (TJ to Thomas Mann Randolph, 14 Nov. 1813).

[1] Manuscript: "substitue."

From Samuel H. Smith

SIR   Washington, Aug. 18. 1813.
    I take the liberty of enclosing the following trifle delivered here on
the late anniversary of our Independence, which I ask you to receive
entirely as a tribute of respect. I hope your contemplated improvements have kept pace with your wishes,[1] and that the calm delights
of retirement are enhanced by the finish, which art, under the direction of taste, knows how to bestow on the finest natural scenery. M[rs]
Smith begs me to communicate her affectionate remembrance to
yourself and all the members of your family.
    I am, with great consideration & regard—Yo. ob. S[t]
                                                    SA. H. SMITH

RC (DLC); at foot of text: "Th. Jefferson Esqr."; endorsed by TJ as received 20 Aug. 1813 and so recorded in SJL. Enclosure: Smith, *Oration pronounced by Samuel H. Smith, Esquire, in the City of Washington, on Monday, the Fifth of July, 1813* (Washington, D.C., 1813; Sowerby, no. 4690), in which Smith recalls the spirit of unity and common purpose that predominated in America during the Revolutionary War and at the 1787 Federal Convention; argues that those who oppose the war with Great Britain should not be allowed to thwart the will of the majority; underscores the importance of the conflict to the survival of the nation and the preservation of the liberties enjoyed by its citizens; suggests that "one of the best means of prosecuting with vigor the arduous contest in which we are engaged, as well as of insuring permanent security and defence" is "to lay the foundations of a navy commensurate with the present, and increasing with the expanding resources of the nation" (p. 15); compares the country's prospects to those of Rome during its wars with Carthage; favors the construction of more roads, canals, and manufacturing establishments; invokes Joel Barlow as a supporter of such policies, all of which, according to Smith, will serve to "cement our union, increase our enjoyments, ensure to us longer periods of peace, and render us invulnerable to the inevitable wars in which we may be involved" (p. 23); and concludes that, while cultivating a love of peace, the United States should "proclaim to the world our resolution, to receive no wrongs without redress, no insults without atonement" (p. 24).

[1] Reworked from "hopes."

To Paul Allen

SIR   Monticello Aug. 20. 13.

In my letter of the 5th inst. I requested what time you could give me for further enquiry on the subject of the life of Govr Lewis. I have since satisfied myself that there is no more matter within my reach, and being about to set out on a journey, on which I shall be absent three weeks, I have concluded it best to forward you without delay the sketch I have been able to prepare. Accept with it the assurance of my great respect.   TH: JEFFERSON

P.S. not knowing who is to print the work, I will ask the favor of you to desire the printer, when the work is compleat, to send me thirteen copies, 3 of them neatly bound, the rest in boards (for transmission to Europe) the best conveyance is by the stage, addressed to Gibson & Jefferson, merchants of that place, who will pay the transportation and forward them to me. they would be still safer, if any passenger to Richmond would take them under his care. the amount shall be remitted on reciept of the printer's bill.

PoC (DLC); postscript added in a different ink; adjacent to signature: "Mr Paul Allen"; endorsed by TJ. Enclosure: TJ to Allen, 18 Aug. 1813. Enclosed in TJ to Nicholas Biddle, 20 Aug. 1813.

The PRINTER of Biddle, *Lewis and Clark Expedition*, was James Maxwell, of Philadelphia (Benjamin Kite and Thomas Kite, *Kite's Philadelphia Directory for 1814* [Philadelphia, 1814]).

To Nicholas Biddle

In a letter from mr Paul Allen of Philadelphia, I was informed that other business had obliged you to turn over to him the publication of Govr Lewis's journal of his Western expedition; and he requested me to furnish him with any materials I could for writing a sketch of his life. I now inclose him such as I have been able to procure, to be used with any other information he may have recieved, or alone, if he has no other, or in any way you & he shall think proper. the part you have been so good as to take in digesting the work entitles you to decide on whatever may be proposed to go out under it's auspices; and on this ground I take the liberty of putting under cover to you, and for your perusal, my letter to mr Allen, which I will request you to seal & hand on to him. I am happy in this occasion of expressing my portion of the thanks all will owe you for the trouble you have taken with this interesting narrative, and the assurance of my sentiments of high esteem and respect.   TH: JEFFERSON

RC (Andalusia Foundation, Andalusia, Pa.; photocopy in DNT); mutilated, with missing text supplied from PoC; addressed: "Mr N. Biddle Chesnut Street opposite the State House Philadelphia"; franked; endorsed by Biddle. PoC (DLC). Enclosures: TJ to Paul Allen, 18, 20 Aug. 1813.

To Youen Carden

SIR   Monticello Aug. 20. 13.

I did not know till yesterday that mr Randolph intended to give up the lease of my toll-mill. I shall now be glad to employ you there upon our former terms. I shall be glad to know by the return of the bearer whether you will engage to come. if you say so, this letter binds it on my part. I am to set out for Bedford in a day or two & shall be absent about three weeks, and on my return I will send to you, as I expect you will be wanting about that time. Accept my best wishes.

                                        TH: JEFFERSON

RC (MHi); addressed: "Mr Yewen Carden." PoC (MHi); endorsed by TJ.

Carden, who had worked at TJ's toll mill from 1808 to 1811, returned to his employ on 12 Sept. 1813 at his FORMER salary of $40 a year (TJ's Agreement with Carden, 29 Nov. 1809; TJ's Account with Randolph & McKinney, [ca. 10 June 1812]; TJ's Account with Carden, 26 Dec. 1814–14 June 1824).

From James Leitch

SIR,   Charlottesville Aug. 20ᵗʰ 1813

At your request I take the liberty of Sending you your account with Samˡ: & Jaˢ Leitch to the 1ˢᵗ Insᵗ at which time our partnership expired—you will not consider this as an application at this time for the Ballance but will consult your own Convenience in dischargeing the Same—your Draft on Gibson & Jefferson was duly paid for which I consider myself under Obligations to you—

I expect in the course of this week & next a general Supply of Groceries together with other articles Should you do me the favour to continue your Custom I should be happy at all times to furnish you on the best terms I can afford

respectfully your Oblgᵈ Friend   JAˢ LEITCH

P.S. owing to your being debited with Principle & Inᵗ on yʳ note to Dinsmore at the time it was assigned to us & Inᵗ calculated on that amt untill paid you will observe a Difference which if you will be good enough to inform me shall be placed to your Credit

RC (MHi); endorsed by TJ as received 20 Aug. 1813 and so recorded in SJL. Enclosure not found.

TJ noted on 2 Aug. 1813 that, of his $1,000 draft on Gibson & Jefferson, $618.40 was to be used to pay off the "principal of my note to Jas. Dinsmore," $159 was to settle the "interest from 1809. Apr. 7. to 1813. July 31," and $222.60 was to be placed to his CREDIT in his account with Samuel & James Leitch (*MB*, 2:1291).

From James Martin (of New York)

SIR   Treasury Department Washington Augᵗ 20 1813

So many years have Elapsed since I had the Honour of a line from you that you have probably altogether forgotten me, as well as the Occasion which procured me that favour. I have no other Justification in recalling either than the wish to keep a place in your recollection, and, in a manner similar to my former Effort, to contribute an hour towards the Amusement of one to whom I feel more than the common Obligation. I sent you in 1796 an Oration I had spoken at Jamaica Long Island and received from you a very polite Acknowledgment of the present. Some late political events here brought one of its predictions into my mind which tho frequently Impressed on the subject, had Solaced itself in the vulgar hope that at least the fear would not be Realized in my day—At the close of this Oration I find the Sentences Copied on the other Side—the Opinion must have been Occasioned by Jay's Treaty and the Theoretic dread I had of one day seeing that power still more perniciously Exercised. As I was abroad during the discussion of the Constitution I was Unaware of the Arguments, my Observations therefore were purely the result of my own reflections on the subject and I can now look upon them with the more Satisfaction as the Unbiassed result of my own Information—It is perhaps fortunate for us that our youthful Habits have not yet been so completely corrupted but that we are within the Reach of a remedy which I am Confident we shall one day want and which one, not very remote day we may be very Averse to take. I kno[w]¹ not whether that part of the Constitution met your approbation—if it did, with all my reverence for you I cannot agree in Sentiment. You perhaps think more favorably of England than I do, but, as I accquired part of my Education and Studied my profession there, I have had more Opportunitys of Knowing that that Corruption which has ruined them at home is almost as pervading abroad and if you can trace to other Sources the Conduct upon which the enclosed Letter to Quincy Comments you have more Charity than I pretend to—you will readily perceive that my last present to you is influenced by the same Sentiment which was the Ground work of the first. I am not known nor intend to be as its Author but merely Sound the Tocsin in hopes some abler Champion, if it should become necessary, may be ready to Combat what seems to me the most preposterous and Abominable of all Doctrines—

The place from which I date my Letter may Surprize you—the fact is that wearied of Farming (tho merely from want of Society) and incommoded by a 20 years dispute with my native State in which, pyrrhus like, I am ruined by my Victories I came to close my days in Washington And my friend Mʳ Gallatin having lef[t] with me his Arduous task of Judging of petitions for remissions of forfeitures I am submitting my Opinions on the Cases to the Acting Secretary and thus discharging my Duty to my friend and the public with Approbation I hope, and with Integrity I know. Accept, Sir, my long continued wishes for all the Happiness, as you close your Life, which your great Services to your Country make the hope of every republican and of no one more Cordially than

Your faithful & obedᵗ humble Servant—   JAˢ MARTIN

RC (MHi); torn at seal; addressed: "Thoˢ Jefferson Esqʳ Monticelli Virginia"; franked; postmarked Washington, 20 Aug.; endorsed by TJ as received

14 Sept. 1813 and so recorded in SJL; notation by TJ on address leaf: "mine of 98. Feb. 23. his of 1801. Feb. 22."

James Martin (ca. 1753–1831), attorney, was born in Boston, the son of Anne Gordon Martin, a Massachusetts woman from a prominent mercantile family, and William Martin, a British artillery officer who remained loyal to the Crown during the American Revolution. He received his legal education in England, was admitted to the Massachusetts bar in 1773, left the colony soon thereafter, and spent much of the next two decades in the West Indies. Martin returned to America in 1791 and began the lengthy but ultimately successful process of reclaiming his parents' property in Massachusetts, which had been confiscated during the Revolutionary War. After joining the New York bar in 1792 and briefly working in Aaron Burr's law office, Martin acquired an estate in Jamaica, Long Island. He lived on Long Island thereafter except for a stint from 1813–15 at the Treasury Department reviewing forfeiture cases for Albert Gallatin (*PTJ*, 29:156–7; Maeva Marcus and others, eds., *The Documentary History of the Supreme Court of the United States, 1789–1800* [1985–2007], 6:199–211; Linda K. Kerber, "The Paradox of Women's Citizenship in the Early Republic: The Case of *Martin vs. Massachusetts*, 1805," *American Historical Review* 97 [1992]: 349–78, esp. 349, 362, 372; DNA: RG 29, CS, N.Y., Queens Co., 1800, 1820, 1830; Martin to Gallatin, 12 Sept. 1815 [NHi: Gallatin Papers]; *New-York Spectator*, 20 Dec. 1831).

On the verso of the address leaf of the RC, Martin quoted as follows from his 4 July 1796 oration SPOKEN AT JAMAICA LONG ISLAND, a speech he had previously enclosed in full to TJ on 20 July 1796 and which TJ had deposited in his library (Sowerby, no. 3179): "The people of England suffered their parliament 80 years ago to prolong their own Existence from three years to Seven—with that Act commenced the Æra of their destruction—A Seven Years Legislator became an object worth corrupting and we are too well accquainted with their History not to see how their Government has availed itself of the infirmity—A Similar disease grows with our Growth and must Subdue at Length—At least the poetry looks prophetic—Supreme Laws of the Land can be made by twenty people some of whom are <u>Legislators for Six Years</u>!—It is the duty of those whose profession, as has been well said, teaches them to Snuff the Approach of Tyranny in every tainted Breeze to suggest such things to you and it is your Duty to consider them Happy people! that can say quietly We the people having conferred an Authority by mistake or which has been abused by design think proper to revoke it &c &c." The phrase on sensing "the Approach of Tyranny in every tainted Breeze" came from Edmund Burke's famous 22 Mar. 1775 parliamentary speech on conciliation with the American colonies.

Martin disapproved of the six-year terms to which United States senators were elected and had a THEORETIC DREAD of the constitutional right of the United States president and Senate to create binding law without the approval of the House of Representatives by making treaties with foreign powers. The enclosed LETTER TO QUINCY, presumably addressed to the prominent Massachusetts Federalist Josiah Quincy, has not been found. The ACTING SECRETARY of the treasury was William Jones (*DAB*).

¹ Word stained.

From William C. C. Claiborne

DEAR SIR,   New Orleans 21st Augt 1813

Since my letter of the 14th Instant, it has been deemed expedient to proceed against mr Livingston before the Parish court of New

Orleans, by way of information, and of <u>which</u> a copy is herewith enclosed. Mr Livingston and his friends (I learn) are clamorous on the occasion;—They represent the procedure as unprecedented, and affect to consider it as a Wicked (but feeble) attempt to justify opposition to the Tribunals of the United States. To me the Subject presents a very different aspect;—the care of our Rivers & Ports, appertain exclusively to the State authorities, and the means resorted to, Seem to me the best calculated, to preserve the Public Rights.— The case is to be argued on the 24th instant, and the result is anxiously awaited.—

I have the honor to be Sir with the greatest respect Your faithful friend
                                        WILLIAM C. C. CLAIBORNE

RC (DLC); in a clerk's hand, with closing, signature, and internal address by Claiborne; at foot of text: "Mr Thomas Jefferson Monticello Virginia"; endorsed by TJ as received 22 Sept. 1813 and so recorded in SJL.

On this day Claiborne wrote a nearly identical letter to his congressman, Thomas B. Robertson (Claiborne, *Letter Books,* 6:261).

ENCLOSURE

François Xavier Martin's Motion for an Injunction against Edward Livingston

The State of Louisiana Parish of Orleans SS } To the Honble the Judge of the Parish of orleans aforesaid

Francis X. Martin Attorney general for the Said State comes hereinto Court and gives the Court to understand and be informed, that the River mississipi is an ancient navigable River and Publick high way used and to be used of Right by all the people of this State in common with all the people of the united states, in its whole width, breadth and length; and that the Banks, Battures, Beaches, and Shores of the Said River are and from time immemorial hath been known and used as a common high way by all the persons, sailing upon, and navigating their Ships, Boats Barges and vessels, and on which they might freely anchor, unload, moor, make fast to, and lie at. and that, portion of the Bank and shore of the Said River, forming the Port of the city of new orleans and its Suburbs has been always heretofore bounded by an embankment, Dyke and Levee and that all the Land lying in front of the Said Levee, Dyke and embankment forming the shore and Batture of the River, has always heretofore been and now is a part of the Common high way. and that the Said embankment, Dyke and Levee extending along the margin of the Said River from the ancient limits of the City in front of the Suburb S^t mary as far as and to the former plantation of madam Delor, has been erected and kept up and maintained at the public costs and Labour, and has ever heretofore been known to be, and now is the Boundary and dividing line between the land and water, and to which embankment and Levee So as aforesaid made, kept up and maintained at the Public Cost and labour, the high water flows as a part of the River and Port aforesaid, and that all that part of the said River flowing up to the Said Levee at high water, in front of the Suburb S^t mary in the Parish aforesaid constitutes and forms a part of the Public and common port of the Said City and is part of the Said navigable River and as Such has always heretofore been used and known—and that at the time of low waters in the Said River there is left bare, a large Bar, Beach or Shoal of Land commonly called the Batture lying below the Levee in front of the Said Suburb S^t mary, and that the Same is part of the Public high way of this State, and upon which, all the good people of the State have been heretofore used to pass and repass, to unload their boats and vessels upon, and temporarily to lay their cargoes of whatsoever kind, and wood and Lumber—brought into the Said Port for Sale there—And further that no one[1] person, can have any exclusive right to occupy permanently any part of the Said Port, and high way, without annoying and obstructing the rights of the public, and violating the fundamental Laws of the State and acts of the General assembly. And further that no[2] works, buildings, embankment and fixtures can be made on the Said Batture, but which in their effects must occasion great damage to the navigation of the Said River by filling and causing to be filled up the Said Port and harbour, by the deposits of mud and Sand which Such works will occasion to the common nusance of the Public—And the Said attorney general further gives the Court to understand and be informed, that Edward Levingston of the Said Parish attorney and Counsellor at Law on the twenty-fourth day of august one thousand Eight hundred and Seven in the Parish aforesaid with a great number of labouring men with Spades, Shovels, hoes, axes and other impliments did unlawfully, wickedly and injuriously enter into and upon the Said Batture So as aforesaid being part of the Public high way and port of the said City and Suburb S^t mary, he the Said Edward Levingston well knowing all and Singular the premises, and with the labouring men aforesaid did unlawfully employ them for the Space of one month and longer in digging into the ground, and heaving up large mounds of Earth across the Said Batture, and did dig a large Canal and Basin, and Surrounded the Same by a high mound and embankment across the Said Batture, and did with the Said Labouring men cause to be erected divers works on the Said Batture, and did plant, logs of wood, and Posts for an enclosure of a large part of the Said Batture being a part of the public high way and Port of the Said City to the common nuisance of all the citizens of this State passing and repassing and Sailing and navigating in the Same Port, and the Said works So erected the Said Edward Levingston from the day aforesaid until the day of exhibiting this present information has caused to remain to the great obstruction of the Said Port and high way by which the Port and Harbour of the city of new Orleans is in a great degree choaked and filled up with the deposits[3] of mud and Sand, and the currents and eddies of the Said River in and about the Said Port greatly changed and altered and parts of the port so filled up with mud and Sand that it cannot be any longer navigated with Safety, and the harbour and Quay opposite to and lying immediately in front of the Said Suburb S^t mary is So obstructed and filled up by reason of the works aforesaid that the good people of this State cannot navigate, sail, pass and repass with their Boats and vessels nor can they moor and anchor their Said vessels in parts of the Said Quay, harbour and Port as conveniently as they before were used and accustomed to do and Still of right ought to do—and the Said Attorney general further gives to the Court to understand and be informed that the Said Edward Levingston has Said, and declared, and So the truth is that he means and intends again to enter unto and upon every part of the Said Batture, and then and their to occupy and exclusively appropriate to his own use every part and parcel thereof in its whole extent from opposite to the upper end of the city line, to some place above Julia Street in the Suburb S^t mary in the Parish aforesaid—and thereon to erect Such works and edifices as he from time to time may please to direct and order, thereby wholly Shutting up the Said Port, destroying the Harbour and entirely obstructing the Said high way to the great injury and nusance of the publick and all the good people of this State and others resorting to and wishing to pass and use the Said Port and Harbour as formerly they did and as of right they now ought to do, to the evil example of all others in like cases offending and contrary to the act of assembly in Such case made and provided—and against the peace and dignity of the state of Louisiana, all which the Said attorney general is ready to verify and prays may be inquired into by a Jury—wherefore and in consideration of the before alledged facts, all of which will be proved in due Season by inquestionable evidence, the Said attorney general in behalf of the State of Louisiana, prays that your honor will be pleased, the premises considered to grant an injunction against the Said Edward Levingston injoining and restraining him and all other persons for him in whatever character or capacity they may presume to act, from entering into and upon the Said Batture, for the purpose of possessing exclusively the Same or any part thereof, and from causing the Same or any part thereof to be enclosed, and from making any buildings[4] or works thereon of any kind to the prejudice of the public in the enjoyment of the Same as a port Quay, harbour and public high way as they have heretofore been used to enjoy in passing and repassing Sailing with their vessels, unloading and loading the Same in the Said port in the Customary places and of anchoring, mooring, and landing their vessels as formerly and in the accustomed places and manner in the Said Port in front of the Said Suburb S^t mary—and to cause Such other proceedings to be had herein as the nature of the case may require and the Laws of the Land Justify; and that all the works on the Same Batture, So as aforesaid injuriously and unlawfully made and erected may be abated, demolished, and removed—

Signed F. X. MARTIN.

We maketh oath that the material facts in the above information are true—

Signed DEJEAN AINÉ.

Sworn to before me
this 14th of August 1813.
Signed N. GIROD. Juge de Paix.

Signed PAUL LANUSSE.
Signed F^D PERCY JEUNE

Tr (DLC); in a clerk's hand, with a few emendations, possibly by Martin; at foot of text, in Thomas S. Kennedy's hand and signed by him: "A true Copy from the original"; additional notation at bottom of last page by transcriber of above document: "103. The State vs Edwd Levingston} Information Let an Injunction

issue as is herein prayed for, to remain in force till the further order of the Court New Orleans August 14th 1813. Signed J^s Pitot Judge. Filed August 14th 1813. Signed Thos S. Kennedy clk."

The ACT OF ASSEMBLY may refer to section one of the 1812 act granting

Louisiana statehood (*U.S. Statutes at Large*, 2:703). JUGE DE PAIX: "justice of the peace." AINÉ: "the elder." JEUNE: "the younger."

On 4 Sept. 1813 Governor William C. C. Claiborne reported to Thomas B. Robertson that "the Judge of the Parish, Mr. Pitot, thought proper to dessolve the injunction, which he had previously awarded;—It seems the Judge was under an impression; that until Mr. Livingston, had done some act to deprive the Citizens of the use of the Batture, or erected some works thereon, which might obstruct the Navigation of the Mississippi, the interference of the Court was premature and improper.—Thus the case rests for the present, nor has Mr. Livingston yet thought proper to prosecute the Mayor of New Orleans, or the inhabitants who are in the habit of taking as formerly *Dirt* from the Batture;—I am extremely desirous to have the right to tittle [title] to the Batture finally settled; But feel some difficulty in determining the best manner of bringing the question fairly before our Courts.—The subject however is submitted to the consideration of the Attorney General (Mr. Martin) and the course he advises will be pursued" (Claiborne, *Letter Books*, 6:264).

[1] Manuscript: "one one."
[2] Word interlined, possibly by Martin.
[3] Manuscript: "deposists."
[4] Manuscript: "buidings."

To Abigail Adams

DEAR MADAM   Monticello Aug. 22. 13.

A kind note at the foot of mr Adams's letter of July 15. reminds me of the duty of saluting you with friendship and respect; a duty long suspended by the unremitting labors of public engagement, and which ought to have been sooner revived, since I am become proprietor of my own time. and yet so it is, that in no course of life have I been ever more closely pressed by business than in the present. much of this proceeds from my own affairs; much from the calls of others; leaving little time for indulgence in my greatest of all amusements, reading. Doct[r] Franklin used to say that when he was young, and had time to read, he had not books; and now when he had become old and had books, he had no time. perhaps it is that, when habit has strengthened[1] our sense of duties, they leave no time for other things; but when young, we neglect them, and this gives us time for any thing. however I will now take time to ask you how you do, how you have done? and to express the interest I take in whatever affects your happiness. I have been concerned to learn that, at one time you suffered much & long from rheumatism. and I can sympathise with you the more feelingly, as I have had more of it myself latterly than at any former period; and can form a truer idea of what it is in it's higher degrees. excepting for this, I have enjoyed general health; for I do not consider as a want of health the gradual decline & increasing debility which are the natural diathesis of age. this last comes on me fast. I am not able to walk much; tho' I still ride without fatigue; and take long & frequent journies to a distant possession.　　I have compared notes with mr Adams on the score of progeny, and find I am ahead of him, and think I am in a fair way to keep so. I have $10\frac{1}{2}$ grandchildren, and $2\frac{3}{4}$[2] great-grand-children; and these fractions will ere long become units. I was glad to learn from mr Adams that you have a grandson far enough advanced in age and acquirements to be reading Greek. these young scions give us comfortable cares, when we cease to care about ourselves. under all circumstances of health or sickness, of blessing or affliction, I tender you assurances of my sincere affection and respect; and my prayers that the hand of time and of providence may press lightly on you, till your own wishes shall withdraw you from all mortal feeling.　　Th: Jefferson

RC (MHi: Adams Papers); addressed: "Mrs Adams Quincy." PoC (DLC).

The DISTANT POSSESSION was TJ's Poplar Forest estate in Bedford County. The comparison ON THE SCORE OF PROGENY took place in TJ to John Adams, 21 Jan. 1812, and John Adams to TJ, 3 Feb. 1812. TJ's $\frac{1}{2}$ grandchild was Septimia Anne Randolph (Meikleham), who was born on 3 Jan. 1814, and his $\frac{3}{4}$ great-grandchild was Ellen Monroe Bankhead, who was born on 3 Sept. 1813 (Shackelford, *Descendants*, 1:128, 2:48 [with Bankhead's birth year mistakenly given as 1812]; *Richmond Whig & Public Advertiser*, 19 Jan. 1838). The Adams grandson able to read GREEK was George Washington Adams.

[1] Manuscript: "strengthed."
[2] Integer reworked from "3."

To John Adams

Dear Sir　　　　　　　　　　　　　　　Monticello Aug. 22. 13.

Since my letter of June 27. I am in your debt for many; all of which I have read with infinite delight. they open a wide field for reflection; and offer subjects enough to occupy the mind and the pen indefinitely. I must follow the good example you have set; and when I have not time to take up every subject, take up a single one.　　Your approbation of my outline to Dr Priestly is a great gratification to me; and I very much suspect that if thinking men would have the courage to think for themselves, and to speak what they think, it would be found they do not differ in religious opinions, as much as is supposed. I remember to have heard Dr Priestly say that if all England would candidly examine themselves, & confess, they would find that Unitarianism was really the religion of all: and I observe a bill is now depending in parliament for the relief of Anti-Trinitarians. it is too late in the day for men of sincerity to pretend they believe in the Platonic mysticisms that three are one, & one is three; & yet the one is not three, and the three are not one: to divide mankind by a single letter into ὁμοουϛιans, and ὁμοιουϛιans. but this constitutes the craft, the power and the profit of the priests. sweep away their gossamer fabrics of factitious religion, and they would catch no more flies. we should all then, like the quakers, live without an order of priests, moralise for ourselves, follow the oracle of conscience, and say nothing about what no man can understand, nor therefore believe; for I suppose belief to be the assent of the mind to an intelligible proposition.

It is with great pleasure I can inform you that Priestly finished the comparative view of the doctrines of the Philosophers of antiquity, and of Jesus, before his death; and that it was printed soon after. and, with still greater pleasure, that I can have a copy of his work forwarded from Philadelphia, by a correspondent there, and presented for your acceptance, by the same mail which carries you this, or very soon after.   the branch of the work which the title announces is executed with learning and candor, as was every thing Priestley wrote: but perhaps a little hastily; for he felt himself pressed by the hand of death. the Abbé Batteux had in fact laid the foundation of this part, in his Causes premieres; with which he has given us the originals of Ocellus, and Timaeus, who first committed the doctrines of Pythagoras to writing; and Enfield, to whom the Doctor refers, had done it more copiously. but he has omitted the important branch, which in your letter of Aug. 9. you say you have never seen executed, a comparison of the morality of the old testament with that of the new. and yet no two things were ever more unlike. I ought not to have asked him to give it. he dared not. he would have been eaten alive by his intolerant brethren, the Cannibal priests. and yet this was really the most interesting branch of the work.

Very soon after my letter to Doct^r Priestley, the subject being still in my mind, I had leisure, during an abstraction from business, for a day or two while on the road, to think a little more on it, and to sketch more fully than I had done to him, a Syllabus of the matter which I thought should enter into the work. I wrote it to Dr Rush; and there ended all my labor on the subject; himself & Dr Priestley being the only depositories of my secret. the fate of my letter to Priestley, after his death, was a warning to me on that of Dr Rush; and at my request his family was so kind as to quiet me by returning my original letter & Syllabus. by this you will be sensible how much interest I take in keeping myself clear of religious disputes before the public; and especially of seeing my Syllabus disembowelled by the Aruspices of the modern Paganism. yet I inclose it to you with entire confidence, free to be perused by yourself and mrs Adams, but by no one else; and to be returned to me.

You are right in supposing, in one of yours, that I had not read much of Priestley's Predestination, his No-soul system, or his controversy with Horsley. but I have read his Corruptions of Christianity, & Early opinions of Jesus, over and over again; and I rest on them, and on Middleton's writings, especially his letters from Rome, and to Waterland, as the basis of my own faith. these writings have never been answered, nor can be answered, by quoting historical proofs, as they have done. for these facts therefore I cling to their learning, so much superior to my own.

I now fly off in a tangent to another subject. Marshal, in the 1st vol. of his history, c. 3. pa. 180. ascribes the petition to the king of 1774. (1. Journ. Congr. 67.) to the pen of Richard Henry Lee. I think myself certain it was not written by him, as well from what I recollect to have heard, as from the internal evidence of style: his was loose, vague, frothy, rhetorical. he was a poorer writer than his brother Arthur; and Arthur's standing may be seen in his Monitor's letters, to ensure the sale of which they took the precaution of tacking to them a new edition of the Farmer's letters; like Mezentius who 'mortua jungebat corpora vivis.' you were of the committee, and can tell me who wrote this petition: and who wrote the Address to the inhabitants of the colonies ib. 45.　　　of the papers of July 1775. I recollect well that mr Dickinson drew the petition to the king, ib. 149. I think Robt R. Livingston drew the address to the Inhabitants of Great Britain. ib. 152. am I right in this? and who drew the Address to the people of Ireland, ib. 180.? on these questions, I ask of your memory to help mine. ever and affectionately your's　　　　　Th: Jefferson

P.S. Miss Lomax, daughter of one of our friends of 1776. lately dead, now here on a visit, asks permission to consign to you a memorial of the family respect for you:[1] not done with the pencil, the burine or the chissel, but with the only instrument habitual to her, the humble scissars. you will find it inclosed.

RC (MHi); right margin of second page trimmed, with missing text supplied from PoC; endorsed by Adams as answered 14 Sept. 1813; docketed by Charles Francis Adams. PoC (DLC); postscript added separately. Enclosures: enclosures 1–2 to Richard Rush to TJ, 12 Aug. 1813. Other enclosure not found.

ὁμοουϛιANS and ὁμοιουϛιANS: "homoousians" and "homoiousians." The COMPARATIVE VIEW was Priestley, *Heathen Philosophy*. TJ's CORRESPONDENT in Philadelphia was Nicolas G. Dufief. Despite the publication of works attributed to them in Charles BATTEUX, *Ocellus Lucanus, De la Nature de l'Univers, avec la traduction françoise & des remarques* (Paris, 1768; Sowerby, no. 1293; Poor, *Jefferson's Library*, 8 [no. 417]), *Timee de Locres, De l'Ame du Monde, avec la traduction françoise & des remarques* (Paris, 1768; Sowerby, no. 1293; Poor, *Jefferson's Library*, 8 [no. 417]), and *Histoire des Causes Premières, ou Exposition Sommaire des Pensées des Philosophes sur les Principes des Êtres* (Paris, 1769; Sowerby, no. 1293), the supposed Pythagoreans OCELLUS, AND TIMAEUS are now believed to have left no writings that can definitively be called their own (*OCD*, 1058, 1526). Haruspices (ARUSPICES), the plural of haruspex or aruspex, were soothsayers of ancient Rome who prophesized by inspecting the entrails of sacrificial animals (*OED*). The 1774 petition to the king was attributed to Richard Henry Lee in John Marshall (MARSHAL), *The Life of George Washington* (Philadelphia, 1804–07; Sowerby, no. 496; Poor, *Jefferson's Library*, 4 [no. 133]), 2:180, not the 1ST VOL. An EDITION combining *The Farmer's and Monitor's Letters to the Inhabitants of the British Colonies*

was published in Williamsburg in 1769 (Sowerby, no. 3076), the Pennsylvania FARMER'S LETTERS being the work of John Dickinson. The Etruscan ruler Mezentius devised a method of execution in which he tied the living and the dead together (MORTUA JUNGEBAT CORPORA VIVIS) (Virgil, *Aeneid*, 8.485 [Fairclough, *Virgil*, 2:94–5]).

In a 14 Sept. 1813 letter Adams thanked Judith LOMAX for her gift: "My antient Friend, Mr Jefferson has presented me, in your name, with a Compliment more grateful to my heart, than the most costly monument of Art and Adulation could be, It is admired by all the Ladies of my Family, old and young, as the most exquisite production of the kind, they have ever Seen. It will be preserved with care, by my grand daughters and I hope, very soon by my great grand daughters: but by none will it be more highly esteemed, than by your obliged Friend and Servant" (Lb in MHi: Adams Papers).

[1] Preceding two words not in PoC.

To Nicolas G. Dufief

D[EAR S]IR   Monticello Aug. 22. 13.

I am desirous of sending to mr John Adams late Presidᵗ of the US. at Quincy, Mass. a copy of Priestley's 'Doctrines of heathen philosophy compared with those of revelation' printed at Northumberland Pensva in 1804. will you be so good as to procure one, and inclose it to him by mail 'de ma part.' be so good as to chuse the best binding you find ready prepared, and to place the article to my account. I would wish it to go on without delay, as I give him reason to expect by a letter which goes by this mail. Accept the assurance of my esteem & respect.   TH: JEFFERSON

[*Note by TJ at foot of text:*] added P.S. for 6. leaves from pa. 433. to 444. of his Fr. & Eng. dict:

PoC (DLC); salutation faint; adjacent to signature: "M. Dufief"; endorsed by TJ.

DE MA PART: "from me."

To Peter Derieux

Monticello Aug. 23. 13.

Th: Jefferson presents his respects to mr Derieux, and incloses him a letter he has lately recieved from a mr Dutasta, now at New york which it may be interesting to mr Derieux to answer. as Th:J. is just now setting out on a journey & to be absent some time, he supposes mr Derieux' answer had better go to New York direct.

PoC (DLC); dateline at foot of text; endorsed by TJ as a letter to Derieux, corrected from "Dutasta." Enclosure: Dutasta to TJ, 1 July 1813, recorded in SJL as received 30 July 1813 from New York, but not found.

From James McKinney

SIR   North Milton Augst 23rd 13.

I am apprehensive I have left the draft of the hemp break amongst some papers I left in charge of my Son at the city of Washington, I hunted diligently for it here, but contrary to my expectation cannot find it, however, I can draw or explain the model from memory So as to make you perfectly understand the principal on which it works, I will Send it to you on Saturday

Be pleasd to accept my Sincere Esteem   JAMES McKINNEY

you will See by the scrap enclosd Something of the principal on which it works he scratched it off withe the pen & from that took his draft   J McK

RC (DLC); postscript on address verso; addressed: "Thomas Jefferson Esquire Monticello." Enclosure not found.   A brake (BREAK) is a toothed tool or machine for breaking or crushing flax or hemp (*OED*).

To James Madison

DEAR SIR   Monticello Aug. 23. 13.

I have been prevented setting out to Bedford as early as I had counted. I depart tomorrow. in the mean time I have consulted with as many as I could of the leading men of our county on the subject of the Principal assessor, as I proposed in my letter of the 15th. of those consulted who are known to yourself were mr Divers, the mr Carrs, mr Randolph, Bankhead Etc. one character has struck all of these in the very first instance, that of Peter Minor. he is the son of Colo Garrett Minor of Louisa, married to a daughter of Dr Gilmer, and settled about 4. miles up the river from Charlottesville. he is a farmer, an excellent one, a man of sound judgment, honest, independant, and well acquainted with the value of the taxable subjects. he was brought up to the law, but declined entering into the practice, clear of any passions which might produce bias and the strict justice of his character so well known that his decisions will satisfy those submitted to them. I observe the quota of our county is something under 10,000.D. this is to be divided among the owners of taxable property first by the sub-assessors, & then to be equalised by the principal assessor. this is what makes him important. the most abominable and barefaced partialities under the former real tax by Congress have excited attention here on the revival of a similar measure. I suppose the appointment will be made in this county or Nelson, as being the middle of the 4. counties lying in a string along James River. I am not acquainted in Nelson. if they offer a better man than Minor we shall be glad to be under his agency, I hope you continue to gain strength and that on my return I shall find you in good health. affectionate salutations

Th: Jefferson

P.S. I shall see mr Nicholas, Patterson E^{t}c tomorrow. if they suggest a better person than Minor, I will write to you from Warren

RC (DLC: Madison Papers). PoC (DLC); endorsed by TJ: "Madison Presid^t Aug. 23. 13."

The MR CARRS were Peter Carr and Samuel Carr. In 1806 Peter Minor married Lucy Walker Gilmer, a DAUGHTER of George Gilmer (*Tyler's Quarterly Historical and Genealogical Magazine* 2 [1920]: 133; *WMQ*, 1st ser., 9 [1901]:

181). By the FORMER REAL TAX BY CONGRESS, TJ apparently meant the Direct Tax of 14 July 1798 (*U.S. Statutes at Large*, 1:597–604). Madison ultimately appointed William Armistead, not Minor, as the principal assessor for Albemarle, Amherst, Fluvanna, and Nelson counties (*JEP*, 2:441, 443 [21, 23 Dec. 1813]).

To Richard Rush

Monticello Aug. 23. 13.

Th: Jefferson acknoleges the reciept from mr Richard Rush of the originals of his letters of Apr. 21. and 23. 1803. and of Jan. 16. 1811. to his father, and begs him to recieve his sincere thanks and to convey the same with his friendly respects to mrs Rush & the family for this mark of attention to his feelings. he knew they would be safe while kept with the family; and was satisfied afterwards in the belief of their having been destroyed. he cannot be less so on their being put into his own hands. mr Rush will see the grounds of his anxieties when a like letter to D[r] Priestley, published in England[1] after his death, shall be dragged into our papers by those whose craft it attacks. he salutes mr Rush with the friendship which he bears to all the family of his deceased friend.

PoC (MHi); dateline at foot of text; endorsed by TJ.

[1] Preceding two words interlined.

To Samuel H. Smith

Monticello Aug. 23. 13.

Th: Jefferson presents his compliments to mr Sam[l] H. Smith, & his thanks for the oration he has been so kind as to send him. he has read it with great pleasure, and sympathises in all it's sentiments sincerely, one excepted, respecting the exhausting our resources on a navy. our strength is on the land, & weakness on the water. our enemies' strength is on the water, at land nothing. and however capriciously fortune has hitherto disposed of events, he apprehends that to transfer the war to the scene where we are nothing and they omnipotent, is exactly what they must wish. considering however the votes of Congress as indicating the will of the majority to be in favor of the experiment, he substitutes acquiescence for conviction, and will go chearfully with the nation. if they are wrong, events will soon correct them: if right no man on earth will rejoice more sincerely than himself[1] at being corrected in an error, and on seeing a re-establishment of that right which nature has given in common to all nations over an element purposely interposed to bring the most distant of them together. he seises with great pleasure every occasion of recalling himself to the memory of mr & mrs Smith.

RC (DLC: J. Henley Smith Papers); dateline at foot of text; addressed: "Samuel H. Smith esq. Washington Col."; franked; postmarked Milton, 25 Aug. PoC (DLC); endorsed by TJ.

Early in 1813 congress passed several laws authorizing expenditure of a total of $3.5 million to expand the United States Navy (*U.S. Statutes at Large*, 2:789, 821 [2 Jan., 3 Mar. 1813]).

[1] Preceding two words interlined.

To Alexander H. Stevens

Monticello Aug. 23. 13.

Th: Jefferson presents his compliments to mr Alexander H. Stevens, acknoleges the reciept of the 2. vols of the Code Criminel & du Commerce which he has been so kind as to bring him from mr Warden, and he prays him to accept his thanks for his care and trouble, with the assurances of his respect.

PoC (MHi); dateline at foot of text; endorsed by TJ.

To Augustus B. Woodward

DEAR SIR   Monticel[lo Aug]. 24. 13.

Your favor of the 16th is put into my hand in the moment I was getting into my carriage to set out on a journey, on which I shall be absent 3. or 4. weeks. I stop a moment merely to mention this fact, lest the pleasure of your visit should be lost to me and the trouble of it to yourself. should your stay in Washington be so long I shall be very happy to see you on my return. the circumstance now explained will be a sufficient apology for saying nothing on the principal subject of your letter.
Accept the assurance of my esteem and respect.

TH: JEFFERSON

PoC (DLC); dateline faint, with month enhanced by an unidentified hand; at foot of text: "Judge Woodward"; endorsed by TJ.

From Josiah Meigs

Cincinnati, Ohio, Aug. 25, 1813.

Mr. Meigs having noticed an attempt of the Enemy to throw the blame of his late atrocities at Hampton on Foreign Troops in his service, is led to state the following facts, and he communicates them to Mr. Jefferson, presuming that it will be ascribed to a wish that the truth may be not concealed.—

Mr Meigs resided in the Island of Bermuda from December 1789 to May 1794—He was during that period a Counsellor at Law, and was in habits of intimacy with the Governor Henry Hamilton, & a number of the officers of the British Navy & Army. At the table of Bridger Goodrich Esq., formerly of Portsmouth in Virginia, who joined Lord

Dunmore in the commencement of the revolutionary war, he heard the following recitals—

Major Andrew Durnford of the Corps of Engineers, related that he had the command of the detachment which was intended to surprise and capture Major General Putnam, at Horseneck;—that the General having escaped by descending a dangerous precipice on horseback, his men took the wife of the Minister of the Parish, Mrs. _____ into the School House in that Village, and that to his knowledge about twenty-eight of them _____ passed over her. Goodrich exclaimed, "You and your men ought to have been d—d" Durnford laughed it off as a mere bagatelle. Goodrich observed that the British had in many cases disgraced themselves, and the human character by similar atrocities, and to confirm it, said, that while he was serving on board the Roebuck Frigate commanded by Sir Andrew Snape Hammond, in Chesapeake Bay, a canoe, with two persons on board was seen passing a small river or inlet; that a boat from the Frigate having brought the Canoe along side of the ship, it appeared that a young man was conveying his sister, a handsome, neatly dressed young woman to the other side of the water to be married to her lover that day—The young man was ordered off with his canoe,—the young woman was taken into the Cabin by the Officers, where she was kept about three weeks, and then sent ashore ruined, humbled and lost.—

Henry Hamilton, who was then Governor of Bermuda was formerly Governor of Upper Canada and was taken, (in 1777—I think), by George Rogers Clarke, whose Nephew, the gallant Major Croghan has nobly signalized himself in the late bloody repulse given the Enemy at Fort Stephenson on the River Sandusky—

After having written the foregoing Mr. M. doubts whether it will not be deemed improper to transmit it to Mr Jefferson—but the truth ought to be known—

Mr M. is certain that Mr Jefferson will hear with pleasure that he and his family enjoy health, and has the honour to be

with Esteem, Affection & high Respect

his obliged & obedient servant   JOSIAH MEIGS.

RC (DLC); addressed: "The honourable Thomas Jefferson, Esquire Monticello Virginia"; franked; postmarked Cincinnati, 26 Aug. 1813; endorsed by TJ as received 14 Sept. 1813 and so recorded in SJL.

British admiral Sir John Borlase Warren largely blamed the ATROCITIES committed during the 26 June 1813 sack of Hampton on a unit made up of French prisoners-of-war, the so-called Canadian Chausseurs or Chausseurs Britanniques (Heidler and Heidler, War of 1812, 225). In February 1779 General Israel Putnam barely escaped capture by a force of British cavalry at HORSENECK (now part of Greenwich), Connecticut (William

Farrand Livingston, *Israel Putnam: Pioneer, Ranger, and Major-General, 1718–1790* [1901], 388–92). Henry Hamilton had been taken at the fall of Vincennes early in 1779, not 1777 (*PTJ*, 2:256–8, 286–7). Forces under the command of

Major George Croghan repulsed a British attack on FORT STEPHENSON (present-day Fremont, Ohio) on 2 Aug. 1813 (Heidler and Heidler, *War of 1812*, 489–90).

From William Canby

B. Wine Mills 27th 8mo 1813

Esteemed friend, I have for years at times felt affection toward thee, with a wish for thy Salvation; to wit the attainment while on this stage of time (in the Natural Body) of a sutable portion of divine life, for otherways we know little more than the life of Nature, & therein are in danger of becoming inferior to the Beasts which perish, in consequence of declining the offers of divine life, made to every Rational being.—But I have long had better hope of thee, & have thought (particularly in our little quiet meeting yesterday), "that thou had been faithful in (at least) a few things, & wish thou mayst be made Ruler over more, & enter into the Joy of thy[1] Lord & into his Rest."— & it occurred in order thereto we shou'd becom Christians, "for he that hath not the spirit of Christ is none of his,"—& this knowledg & belief is strongly[2] insisted on I think by divers of his apostles, who had personally seen, & were eyewitnesses of his majesty; particularly in the Mount, & of others who had not that View; which however was insufficient to perfect them, & was[3] taken away, that they might be more effectually turned to that spirit which leadeth into all Truth, whose power alone is able to Reduce the spirit of Nature to sutable silence & submission. W^M CANBY

RC (MHi); dateline at foot of text; addressed (clipped): "[…] Virginia"; endorsed by TJ as received 14 Sept. 1813 and so recorded in SJL. Tr (on deposit ViU: TJP); misdated 29 Aug. 1813; on verso of Tr of TJ to Canby, 18 Sept. 1813, which concludes with the note that "The originals of the foregoing letters were in the possession of the late Timothy Pickering." Printed in Wilmington *Delaware Gazette*, 1 Nov. 1814 (misdated 29 Aug. 1813), and elsewhere, following wording of Tr.

William Canby (1748–1830), miller, lived his whole life in the vicinity of

Wilmington, Delaware. He was a Quaker who opposed war, slavery, and the slave trade, favored the education of free African-Americans and, in his zeal for peace, even seems to have blamed British impressment of American seamen on his own countrymen. During TJ's presidency, Canby implored him on several occasions to earn salvation by deepening his Christian faith (Wilmington Monthly Meeting of Friends, birth and death register, 1713–1860, p. 3 [PSC-Hi]; Henry S. Canby, *Family History* [1945], 33–4; *EG*, 350–1n; DNA: RG 29, CS, Del., New Castle Co., 1800, 1810, 1820; Canby to TJ, 27 May 1802, 1 Feb. 1803, 24 Mar.

1808 [all in DLC]; *Niles' Weekly Register*, 8 May 1830).

Canby's biblical allusions are: THE BEASTS WHICH PERISH (Psalms 49.12); THAT THOU HAD BEEN FAITHFUL . . . INTO HIS REST (Matthew 25.23); FOR HE THAT HATH NOT THE SPIRIT OF CHRIST IS NONE OF HIS (Romans 8.9);

Jesus's sermon on the MOUNT (Matthew 5–7); and THAT SPIRIT WHICH LEADETH INTO ALL TRUTH (John 16.13).

[1] Tr: "our."
[2] RC: "stronly." Tr: "Strongly."
[3] Tr here adds "to be."

To Archibald Robertson

DEAR SIR   Poplar Forest Aug. 27. 13.

I inclose you an order on Messrs Gibson & Jefferson for 600.D. I had hoped to have done more & sooner: but unfortunately no part of my crop of flour got to market until the blockade commenced, and after keeping it on hand[1] in hopes of some reasonable price, until there was danger of it's spoiling I have been obliged at last to sell, getting for the greater part of it 4.D. only, which after paying for the grinding & transportation neats me 47. cents the bushel for my wheat. in addition to the loss of last year's labor, the prospect of the current one is worse. in Albemarle the drought has been such that I literally make nothing; the ground having never been even moistened since the 27th of May. I am glad to find it something better, tho' not very well here. I will thank you to send me by the bearer the articles below mentioned. Accept the assurance of my esteem & respect

TH: JEFFERSON

2. loaves white sugar.
20. ℔ brown d^o
2. ℔ tea.
2. or 3. gall^s molasses
a clamp for a dry rubbing brush

PoC (ViU: TJP); adjacent to signature: "Mr Robertson"; postscript added in a different ink; endorsed by TJ as a letter to Brown & Robertson and so recorded in SJL.

The enclosed ORDER has not been found, but TJ noted the transaction the following day (*MB*, 2:1292). NEATS: an obsolete form of "nets" (*OED*).

[1] TJ here canceled "long."

From Horatio G. Spafford

My Hon^d & much esteemed Friend— Albany, 8 Mo. 27, 1813.

Thy favor of the 15. inst., is duly received, & I hasten to send the book, by the Mail. I hope it will arrive safe, & find thee enjoying good health, & all the consolations that belong to a liberal benefactor to his country, in the evening of a well spent life. After thou shalt have examined the Gazetteer, I should be glad to hear thy opinion of its merits. The preface tells of the expense & magnitude of the labor; & as the plan of the Work is new, I want thy opinion of its comparative merit. My intention is to pursue the plan of writing, & form Gazetteers of the several States; then separate the parts, & form a Geography, & Gazetteer, of the United States, in separate volumes. An arduous & expensive undertaking; but I am young, ambitious, & formed to habits of industry, adapted to such a Work. The writings of Dr. Morse, are not of the right character for this Nation; & when the Government shall have duly examined & contrasted mine with his, I hope for some patronage from the National Administration. Indeed, wast thou at Washington, I should even now solicit it; for[1] a strong predilection for Washington City, & am waiting for events to call me there. In this state, I have experiencd a very liberal patronage. Could I have the same from the General Government, I should immediately remove to its seat. During the years of my youth, I studied 4 years in Virginia, & I believe they have inclined my mind to an attachment to the habits & manners of that country, rather than to those of the Northern States.

It has always appeared to me that our Government ought to have a Department of Geography, or at least some Secretaryship, with a small salary. I wish I could converse with thee on this subject. But, devoted as I am to the project which I have opened to thee, perhaps my views may be misled by my wishes & interests. During 3 years past, my postage, & every expense of communication by Letter, has incurred an expense of seven hundred dollars—a heavy tax on an individual, neither poor nor rich. And did I not hope for some relief by & by from Government, I should not[2] risk so heavy expenses, with such an uncertainty of remuneration. Thy thoughts on these suggestions would be very gratefully received, & perhaps might guide my future destiny.   Would it be unjust, or impolitic, or in any way improper, for the Nation to grant me a right of frankage? This would be a noble patronage;—& I am vain enough to believe I merit the distinction: Is it solely interest, or does my reason justly conclude that the Post Master General's Department could profitably patronise my Works?—The Dead Letters returned to Washington from this State, lost for the want of more correct & extensive information, as I am informed by several Post-Masters, amount to a large Sum every year. And these Post-Masters assure me that they believe it would be profitable to distribute a copy to each office.

In a Letter from President Madison,[3] some time since, he intimates the propriety of forming [Gazet]teers of all the States, & seems to express a friend[ly good] will toward my efforts. This Mail also bears a copy of my Gazetteer to him.　　　I regret that motives of delicacy seem to forbid my communicating as freely with him, as with thee, an intermediate friend, in private life. In this State, the best men, of all parties, are my friends & Correspondents, the latter description of which embrace a large majority of the intelligence[4] of this State. Their initials are printed in the Gazetteer, subjoined to the articles which they furnished. With the highest sentiments of esteem & respect, thy friend,　　　　　　HORATIO GATES SPAFFORD.

RC (MHi); torn at seal; addressed: "Thomas Jefferson, Esqr, Monticello, Virginia. with a packet"; franked; postmarked Albany, 28 Aug.; endorsed by TJ as received 14 Sept. 1813 and so recorded in SJL.

Spafford sent his BOOK, *A Gazetteer of the State of New-York* (Albany, 1813; Sowerby, no. 4172), to TJ separately through the mail. The PREFACE to this work asserts (p. 3) that he spent three years and $7,000 preparing it for publication. In his library TJ had copies of two works by Jedidiah MORSE, *The American Universal Geography* (Boston, 1796; Sowerby, no. 3963) and *The American Gazetteer* (Boston, 1797; Sowerby, no. 3964). The United States Congress ap-

parently never awarded Spafford the RIGHT OF FRANKAGE that he requested of President James Madison in July 1810. The latter commended his EFFORTS, wished him success with his gazetteer, and commented that "An extension of it to all the States would proportionally extend the value of the Work." Spafford's endorsement indicates that he sent Madison "2 Gazetteers" in a missing letter of 28 Aug. 1813 (Madison, *Papers, Pres. Ser.*, 2:413–6, 435–6).

[1] Thus in manuscript. Spafford may have omitted "I have."
[2] Word interlined.
[3] Reworked from "Jefferson."
[4] Reworked from what appears to be "best."

From Brown & Robertson

D SIR　　　　　　　　　　　　Lynchburg Aug. 28th 1813.

Yours of yesterday we have received, covering a draft upon Messrs Gibson & Jefferson for Six hundred Dollars which will be passed to your order—

The whole of the articles ordered are sent except the Molasses which the servant could not carry

Yrs Respy
B. & ROBERTSON
⚘ […]. GARLAND.

RC (ViU: TJP); entirely in Garland's hand; initial in signature illegible; addressed: "Thomas Jefferson Esqʳ Poplar Forrest"; endorsed by TJ as received 28 Aug. 1813 and so recorded in SJL.

To Francis Eppes

MY DEAR FRANCIS   Poplar Forest Aug. 28. 13

After my return from this place to Monticello in May last I recieved the letters which yourself and your cousin Baker wrote me. that was the first information I recieved of your being at school at Lynchburg, or I should certainly have sent for you to come and see me while I was here. I now send 2. horses for yourself and your cousin and hope your tutor will permit you both to come and stay with me till Monday morning when I will send you back again. I left your aunt and all your cousins well in Albemarle. in hopes of seeing you here immediately I remain affectionately yours

TH: JEFFERSON

PoC (CSmH: JF); at foot of text: "Francis Eppes"; endorsed by TJ.

Eppes's AUNT in Albemarle County was Martha Jefferson Randolph.

To Thomas A. Holcombe

Poplar Forest Aug. 28. 13

Th: Jefferson presents his compliments to the Principal of the Lynchburg academy with whom Francis Eppes[1] a grandson of his is, the only child of a deceased daughter, whom he has but rare opportunities of seeing. there is with him also another connection, master Baker. it will be a gratification if they can be permitted to come and stay with him till Monday morning when they shall be sent back again. if the principal himself could at any time make it convenient to come and take a plantation dinner with Th:J. he would be very happy to see him. he salutes him with esteem and respect.

PoC (MHi); dateline beneath closing; at foot of text: "Mʳ Halcomb"; endorsed by TJ.

Thomas Anderson Holcombe (1785–1843), teacher, attorney, and merchant, was born in Prince Edward County and, according to one source, educated at Hampden-Sydney College. He resided in Amelia County in 1810, spent some time in Georgia, and then settled permanently in Lynchburg. Holcombe ran a classical school in his adopted hometown for several years and later worked as a lawyer and a commission merchant. He organized a temperance society and gave speeches, distributed tracts, and traveled the state in aid of this cause. Holcombe also served as Lynchburg's mayor, 1823–24, as a Presbyterian elder, and as a director of the local branch of the Bank of Virginia. He owned twelve slaves in 1840 (Margaret Anthony Cabell, *Sketches and Recollections of Lynchburg by the Oldest Inhabitant (Mrs. Cabell) 1858* [1858; repr. with additional material by Louise A. Blunt, 1974], 247–53; William Asbury Christian, *Lynchburg and Its People* [1900], 79, 105, 134–5; Ruth H. Early, *Campbell Chronicles and Family Sketches Embracing the History of Campbell County, Virginia, 1782–1926* [1927], 427–8; DNA: RG 29, CS, Amelia Co., 1810, Lynchburg, 1820, 1840; *Richmond Enquirer*, 5 Jan. 1832, 7 Aug. 1835, 7 Nov. 1843; Lynchburg Hustings and Corporation Court Will Book, C:91–2, 319–23; gravestone inscription in Presbyterian Cemetery, Lynchburg).

Maria Jefferson Eppes was TJ's DECEASED DAUGHTER.

¹ Preceding two words interlined.

James McKinney's Description of a Hemp Brake

[ca. 28 Aug. 1813]

1ˢᵗ It works like a Sawmill that as it the¹ same frame & Crank—The proportion is that the gate is one third the Size or hight of the frame in which it works & is Six feet in width with 5 breakers 3 below & 2 Above with the Same flare & rake as hemp brakes commonly worked by hand—To explain myself better it is nothing more or less than like a double Saw gate working up & down in the Same Manner as your Saw Mill with 2 grooves in the fender posts in Stead of one their is also a pitman exactly like a Saw Mill as thus—

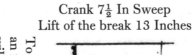

Crank 7½ In Sweep
Lift of the break 13 Inches

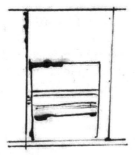

To be drawn on a Scale of an inch to the foot as you will See by the inclosᵈ drafts

MS (DLC: TJ Papers, 199:35413); in McKinney's hand; conjecturally dated on the basis of McKinney's promise of 23 Aug. 1813 that he would send a drawing or explanation of the hemp brake to TJ on the following Saturday, 28 Aug. 1813; endorsed by TJ: "Hemp breaker"; with unrelated notations on verso in several different hands. Enclosures not found.

[1] Thus in manuscript. McKinney may have intended "that has the."

From Isaac McPherson

RESPECTED FRIEND   Baltimore 28th aug. 1813

I duly reciev'd thy verry able letter of the 13th In[s], and have greatly to regret that the public had not been possessd of the views thou hast there taken of the subject, before the late trial of O Evans v[s] Sam[l] Robinson in the circuit court at Baltimore—had it been the case, the result of that trial must have terminated the question between[1] Evans and the public—perhaps there never was a trial conducted in any of the superior Courts of the u.s, where it was more evident to every person present, that the whole subject was wraped in obscurity, and from which the council for the defendant were wholy unable to draw it—though esteemed sound Lawyers, they were not mechanicks, and the jury were mere merchants—I shall certainly hold myself bound, not to make any use of thy letter that can be the means of giving inquietude to thyself, yet I deem it to be so clear, concise, and conclusive, upon the subject of the Elevators, that I must beg thy permission to make that use of it, that its merits deserve, and which cannot fail to be so beneficial to the public—In the prosecution of the trial and since, of Evans v[s] Robinson, several circumstances have transpired to induce me to believe, that so much merit was not due to Evans, as had been by common consent awarded him—Sam[l] Strouds deposition proves that Evans was not the first to apply the Elevator to raising of flour, and Marshall and Strouds deposition proves that, an incomplete Hopper-boy was made and in use before Evans claimed to be the inventor of that machine—Lewis Evans deposition proves that Jonathan Ellicott was the first to apply the spiral screw to removing flour horizontally, by which the whole system is connected and, that Evans acknowleged himself not to have made that discovery[2]—How much of the "improvement in manufactoring flour" is really owing to Oliver Evans will probably never be known, owing to the difficulty in procuring testimony from distant parts—he will certainly claim the merit of having been instrumental in combining several usefull inventions for that purpose; But as they were all seperate and complete machines, of themselves, I can never

[453]

suppose that he would be entitled to recover under a pattent, for being the first person to let the public know, that they could all be employd in the same mill House!—It appears of importance in the investigation of this subject, that we should know the time at which the Gentleman in Caroline County first invented and applyd the Elevator in his drill, if it was before Evans obtained his patent from the State of Maryland in 1787 it would seem conclusive that he had no right to the benefit of a patent under the Law, if thee can bring this to thy recollection, thee will oblige me by communicating it, or if not to advise me how to direct a letter to him—Seeing the situation in which the public are placed, by the continuation of Evans patent, with the influence of a judicial decision in his favour, and the exorbitant damages allowd, it is found to be a verry embarrassing question[3] to decide, as to what steps to recommend, in the many Suits now depending for damages in the circuit court of Maryland—I have enclosed with the depositions of Strouds and Marshalls a coppy of a Letter written by Jonathan Ellicott to a member of the senate during the time the subject was under considerati[on by] a committee of that body last winter—

The verry frank and candid manner which thee treated my first communication, and a full persuasion that thou art desirous that no obstruction shall be thrown in the way of usefull manufacturs, is the only appology I can render for intruding on thy time and attention—

With sentiments of great respect I am thy friend

ISAAC M^cPHERSON

RC (DLC); mutilated at seal; addressed: "Thomas Jefferson Esquire Monticello Virginia"; endorsed by TJ as received 15 Sept. 1813 and so recorded in SJL.

McPherson summarized depositions of Samuel Stroud and of Edward MARSHALL and James Stroud, both dated 5 Jan. 1813, and of LEWIS EVANS, dated 8 Dec. 1812, all of which had been submitted to Congress early in 1813 (*Memorial to Congress on Evans' Patent*, 16–8, 28). With the letter above McPherson enclosed the second and probably the first of the 5 Jan. 1813 depositions, but the versions transmitted to TJ have not been found. The GENTLEMAN IN CAROLINE COUNTY was Thomas C. Martin. Evans obtained the exclusive right to use the elevator and hopper-boy from Delaware, MARYLAND, and Pennsylvania in 1787, three years before receiving a federal patent for these inventions (*Annals*, 13th Cong., 2d sess., 641 [25 Feb. 1814]; *List of Patents*, 4). A select COMMITTEE of the United States Senate looked into the public outcry against Evans's patent pretensions between 11 Jan. and 23 Feb. 1813 (*JS*, 5:227, 272).

[1] Manuscript: "betwen."
[2] Manuscript: "discovey."
[3] Manuscript: "qustion."

Extract of Jonathan Ellicott to
Thomas Worthington

[ca. Jan.–Feb. 1813?]

"I was at Baltimore the other day, and heard many persons speaking of the verry grevious law passed by congress extending a pattent right to Oliver Evans for what he calls his Mill Improvements for an other term of fourteen years; under which law he has obtained a judgement for the extraordinary fine of Eighteen hunerd and fifty Dollars against a certain Sam¹ Robinson of this state, who erected the machinery in his mill during the period in which Evans had no pattent—His mill, I understand, is capable of manufactoring about twelve Barrels of flour per day; a quantity that I have experiensd may be made by one miller with ease, without the use of what he calls his machinery; or in other words in the old way—This alarming decision, together with a number of others, which it is unnesscessary here to ennumerate, but which are also verry extravagant in Evans' favour, I hope thou wilt accept as my appology for troubleing thee at this time—It is suspected by some persons, I find, that Evans is not the original inventor of the greater part of the machinery which he has pattented; but that he has artfully obtained this Law (while those interested made no opposition to it) for renewing his pattent for his Improved Elevator, &C and his council at the late trial contended, as I understood, that if no originality whatever belonged to Evans, or even no improvement, in the diffrent machines yet for the mere combination of the diffrent parts of the machinery for the purpose of improvement in the manufactory of flour, that this alone entitled him to recover under the act of Congress, and this being admitted by the opposite council, and the court, we are obliged to admit it as the construction of the Law—   For thy information I will mention some things that have come to my own knowlege, respecting a part of what he calls his improved machinery—Sometime previous to the year 1786 I had invented several methods of removing meal, wheat, or other substances, in an horizontal, ascending or descending direction, Viz. by a screw revolving in a box, trough, or chest, one of which I had afterwards executed by two persons by the name of Evans, who were then working for me; I found it to answer the purpose well—Sometime afterwards hearing that Oliver Evans had machinery for Elevating meal, I went to see it, and found an Elevator placed in a slanting direction in his mill, near the meal spout, at the lower end and terminating at the uper end, so as to discharge its flour, if I recollect right, into or near the bolting hopper—It imediately struck me that an application of the screw would enable him to place the Elevator in a more convenient way by bringing the work of several pair of stones to one point; and I then informd him, accordingly,—I returnd home; and sometime afterwards he came to our mills on Patapsco, and part of what passed at that time on the subject will appear by the within copies of depositions, taken since the termination of Evans' suit against Robinson—I also invented a method of removing flour, wheat, or other substance, by means of a Band or strap with wooden Blocks, fastened on it, revolving round two rollers or pulleys to be put in motion by the gears of the mill; and an other method by placing two rollers or pullys, one of which to be situated higher than the other, so that the Substance to be removed falling near the highest roller, by its own gravity would descend to the lowest end of the band and fall off; the under side of the band returning empty to the upper roller— these I explained to Oliver Evans before the publication of his "mill wrights guide"; and I think he saw them in actual opperation. I also informed him previous to obtaining his permission to use the Elevator and hopper-boy that I had invented a method to raise both flour and wheat; and had actually raised them by means of wind, produced[1] both by a fan and a common bellows—many years since this a poor man in Chester County, Pennsylvania, whose name is Baily, has obtained a pattent for the same thing; and verry possibly the idea may be original with him as well as myself; Evans has commencd a Suit against him which I expect is to be supported on his sweeping privilege for the combination of machinery applyd to the manufactory of flour—Thou wilt find those improvements on which I claim origenality described in Evans' "mill wrights guide" and in his specification as his improvements; but two of them with their names changed, the screw he calls a conveyor; the band revolving on rollers he calls a drill, I called it a drag, the descender not being so material an implement he has brought forth without even altering its name—The Elevation of wheat and flour by means of wind he has not brought forth at all, possibly least it might get into use, and lead to a discovery that by taking out a pattent for it I might injure the[2] money-making part of the business—I think it will be found in his specification, said that he knows of diffrent ways of effecting the diffrent duties of his machinery in the manufactory of wheat into flour; but he claims under all, or to that import—I have not been solicitous to be considerd an inventor; and as thou wilt percieve not anxious to make money out of the public as a pattentee; otherwise I should have taken out pattents not only for those things but for a number of others to which I consider myself, in point of originality, entitled: otherwise I should have done it at least at the expiration of Evans' first term of fourteen years, which he had granted by a Law of the state of Maryland— If his pattent had not been renewed and the public again placed in his power for an other term of fourteen years, without any limitation as to price, I should not have troubled myself to inquire whose, originally, the inventions were; my only wish is that the public may have the best machinery they can obtain on reasonable and iquitable terms; and this I think them entitled to— Evans also claims merrit for the improvements, because (as he alledges) they enable the miller to make a Barrel of flour out of half a Bushel of wheat less than it could be made from in the old way;—That there has been an improvement in the milling business within the last twenty-five years, must be known to every person who has made any observation on the subject, but to suppose the whole people employed in the business to have remained idle spectators and Oliver Evans to have been the sole improver and combiner of machinery for that purpose, is absurd; these improvements must have proceeded from the combined efforts of many millers, mill wrights, Blacksmiths, and other mechanicks, employd in the art and aided also by the improvement in agriculture, in producing better wheat more pure and clean; but that a Barrel of flour can[3] be made out of a pound less of wheat with the use of this machinery, than without it, must be evident to the dullest apprehension, the mill stones and Bolting cloths being the sole agents in extracting the flour from the bran, without any pretended magic of the machinery—all that can be said in favour of the Elevators, conveyors and hopper-boys, is, that they save manuel labour—

It may be observed, that when I saw the mill in which Oliver Evans had an Elevator there was one pair of Small stones in her the Elevator and every part of the works, to me appeard rude and trifling, compared with the mills which I had been accustomed to; there were few mills which I had ever seen that pretended to do merchant work that were not superior to his; Thence it would appear, that if Oliver Evans has been of benefit to the community in the milling art, it has proceeded more from his method of riding from mill to mill and communicating the improvements of one to an other than from any inventions of his own; for nothing, except the idea of an Elevator, was to be gained by viewing his mill as far as I recollect. And although on my first acquaintance with Oliver Evans I was induced to believe he was the inventor of the Elevator, yet at the present time, on a fair investigation of the subject, I think it extremely doubtfull whether he will prove to be the real inventor, or improver, of the machinery, or any part of it—

To conclude, I sincerely wish every justice to be done to Oliver Evans, which in truth and honesty he is entitled to; but if it shall appear, that he has arrogated to himself the right of inventions that in reality never belonged to him, or if he is actually extending his claim beyond the proper limits, either in point of time or in exacting from individuals sums of money that are in themselves exorbitant, I feel particularly desirous that equal justice may be done to the public"

Signed JONATHAN ELLICOTT

Tr (DLC: TJ Papers, 200:35597–600); in Isaac McPherson's hand; conjecturally dated based on comment in covering letter; at head of text: "Extract of a letter from Jonathan Ellicott to Thomas Worthington Esqr."

Jonathan Ellicott (1756–1826), miller and manufacturer, joined other members of his family in managing the famed Ellicott's Mills on the Patapsco River near Baltimore for more than a quarter-century. The Ellicotts added an ironworks to their flour-milling operation in 1806, after which they manufactured iron, copper, and nails on a large scale (Martha E. Tyson, *A Brief Account of the Settlement of Ellicott's Mills* [1871], 38–47; Oliver Evans, *The Young Mill-Wright & Miller's Guide* [Philadelphia, 1795; Sowerby, no. 1180], 125; Charles Varle, *A Complete View of Baltimore* [1833], 100; tombstone in Ellicott family graveyard, Ellicott City, Md.).

Thomas Worthington (1773–1827), public official, was born near Charles Town, Virginia (now West Virginia) and worked as a surveyor before marrying well and moving in 1798 to Chillicothe in the Northwest Territory. There he prospered as a farmer, miller, and land speculator. Worthington served several terms in the territorial legislature, was a prominent member of the convention that drafted Ohio's 1802 constitution, and sat in the new state's General Assembly in 1803, 1807–08, 1821–23, and 1824–25. He also represented Ohio as a Republican in the United States Senate, 1803–07 and 1810–14, including service as chair of the Indian Affairs, Military Affairs, and Public Lands committees. During two terms as governor, 1814–18, Worthington acquired a reputation as a supporter of banking interests, internal improvements, and public education (*ANB*; *DAB*; Alfred Byron Sears, *Thomas Worthington: Father of Ohio Statehood* [1958]; Chillicothe *Scioto Gazette*, 5 July 1827).

Congress's VERRY GREVIOUS "Act for the relief of Oliver Evans" was enacted on 21 Jan. 1808 (*U.S. Statutes at Large*, 6:70–1). Evans held NO PATTENT for his supposed improvements in the manufacture of flour and meal between the expiration of his first patent on 18 Dec. 1804 and the receipt of his second on 22 Jan. 1808 (*List of Patents*, 4, 62). The TWO PERSONS BY THE NAME OF EVANS were Lewis Evans and Joseph Evans (*Memorial to Congress on Evans' Patent*, 28). Jeremiah BAILY patented his "Ma-chine for raising grain, by blowing" on 5 Mar. 1810 (*List of Patents*, 79).

[1] Manuscript: "produed."
[2] Manuscript: "the the."
[3] Thus in manuscript, but in the context "cannot" appears to have been intended.

From Destutt de Tracy

MONSIEUR   a paris ce 29 aoust 1813.

j'ai eu le Bonheur de recevoir la lettre dont vous m'avez honoré en datte du 26 janvier 1811., et le commentaire anglais Sur Montesquieu que m'a remis de votre part Mr Warden.

le 21 octobre de cette meme année 1811., je vous ai fait mes re-merciments de cet ouvrage; je vous ai exprimé autant qu'il m'a été possible combien j'étois reconnoissant de vos bontés et flatté des eloges que vous vouliez bien donner a mes foibles essays dont vous n'aviez que le commencement; et j'ai pris la liberté de vous adresser mes trois volumes d'idéologie, en vous annonçant un manuscript Sur l'economie politique que j'esperois me procurer bientot.

enfin le 15 novembre 1811., la fregatte americaine qui devoit porter ma lettre n'etant pas encor partie, j'ai eu l'honneur de vous en ecrire une Seconde en vous envoyant le manuscript que je vous avois annoncé.

par cette meme fregatte j'ai aussi ecrit le meme jour a la Societé philosophique americaine pour lui faire hommage de quelques livres, la remercier d'avoir bien voulu m'admettre dans Son Sein, et la prier de m'expedier un duplicata du diplôme que l'on me disoit qu'elle m'avoit envoyé mais qui ne m'est jamais parvenu.

j'ai reçu, il y a environ un an, une reponse de Son Secretaire M^r james en datte du 19 May 1812. dans la quelle il m'accuse la reception de ma lettre, et me mande qu'il vous envoye pour moi un nouveau diplôme en vous priant de le Signer et de me le faire passer.

j'esperois, Monsieur, a tous moments le recevoir de vous; et je de-sirois vivement d'aprendre en meme tems Si vous aviez reçu mes let-tres et mes envoys de la meme datte. rien jusqu'a present ne m'est arrivé de votre part. j'en Suis affligé. vos bontés me Sont cheres. vous m'y avez accoutumé. je Souffre d'en etre privé. je vous prie de me consoler et de me dire Si vos lettres Se Sont egarées, ou Si vos occu-pations vous ont empeché de vous occuper des miennes.

je vous prie Surtout d'agréer toujours les assurances de mon attachement, de mon admiration, et de mon respect.

Le C^{TE} DESTUTT-TRACY

P.S. je prends la liberté de donner cette lettre a Mrs Barlow.

EDITORS' TRANSLATION

SIR   Paris 29 August 1813.
I have had the happiness of receiving the letter with which you honored me, dated 26 January 1811, and the English Commentary on Montesquieu, which Mr. Warden delivered to me on your behalf.

On October 21 of that same year of 1811, I thanked you for this book and expressed to you as best I could how grateful I was for all of your kindnesses and how flattered I was by the praise you so kindly bestowed on my feeble essays, of which you had only the first. I also took the liberty of sending you my three volumes on ideology and informing you of a manuscript on political economy that I hoped to get to you soon.

Finally, on 15 November 1811, the American frigate that was to take my letter having yet to depart, I had the honor of writing you a second letter and sending the manuscript I had described to you.

By this same frigate I wrote on the same day to the American Philosophical Society, offering it some books, thanking it for kindly admitting me into its bosom, and asking it to send me a duplicate of the membership diploma that had never reached me, although I was informed that it had been sent.

About a year ago I received a reply from its secretary, Mr. James, dated 19 May 1812, in which he acknowledged my letter and indicated that he was sending a new diploma through you, having asked you to sign it and pass it along to me.

I have been hoping, Sir, to receive it from you at any moment. At the same time I am also anxious to learn whether you received the letters and packages I sent you on the same date. Nothing has yet arrived from you. This distresses me. Your kindnesses are dear to me. You have accustomed me to them. I suffer by being deprived of them. I beseech you to console me and let me know whether your letters got lost or if your own pursuits have prevented you from attending to mine.

Above all, please accept my regards, attachment, admiration, and respect.

Le C^{TE} DESTUTT-TRACY

P.S. I take the liberty of giving this letter to Mrs. Barlow.

RC (DLC); endorsed by TJ as received 5 Nov. 1813 and so recorded in SJL. Translation by Dr. Genevieve Moene.

The American Philosophical Society admitted Destutt de Tracy to membership on 17 Jan. 1806. At its 1 May 1812 meeting the SOCIÉTÉ announced his gift of two of his own works and three by Pierre Jean Georges Cabanis, all but one of which TJ also owned (APS, Minutes [MS at PPAmP]; Sowerby, nos. 861–2, 1239, 1246). SJL records no retirement-era correspondence between TJ and society secretary Thomas C. JAMES, and none has been found. More than two years later Destutt de Tracy was still complaining that his NOUVEAU DIPLÔME had not yet reached him (see enclosure to Lafayette to TJ, 17 Feb. 1816).

From William P. DuVal

DEAR SIR   At my Fathers, aug^t 29th 1813 Buckingham County
my father presented me your letter of April last, in which you say you have occasion for the services of a friend in the neighbourhood of Shelbyville, Kentucky, The high opinion I have always entertained of you both, as a statesman, and gentleman, would at all times, induce me to serve you, with elacrity and pleasure, and I assure if any circumstance could add to this disposition, the old friend of my father would be the first,[1]   I shall not return to Kentucky untill next spring, if your business will not admit of this delay, I will after receiving your instructions, write to some friend of mine in Kentucky, on whom I can depend, to do the business for you, I intend to do myself the pleasure of visiting your residince this fall.
            I am with respct & Esteem   W^M P. DuVal

RC (MHi); endorsed by TJ as received 4 Nov. 1813 and so recorded in SJL.

William Pope DuVal (ca. 1784–1854), attorney and public official, was the son of TJ's old friend William DuVal. A native of Henrico County, he moved in his teens to Kentucky, settled in Bardstown, was admitted to the bar in 1804, and commanded a company of mounted rangers during the War of 1812. DuVal represented Kentucky in the United States House of Representatives, 1813–15, supporting the War Hawks and favoring the revival of the Bank of the United States. President James Monroe chose him as federal judge for East Florida in 1821 and, with a recommendation from John C. Calhoun, he became Florida's first civil governor the following year, serving until Andrew Jackson removed him in 1834. Renowned for his storytelling skills, DuVal was also the model for Washington Irving's fictional character, Ralph Ringwood. DuVal chaired the committee on the executive department at an 1838–39 state constitutional convention, and he sat in the territorial senate, 1839–42. He lost a bid to return to Congress in 1848, soon moved to Texas, and there defended slavery and states' rights and opposed the Compromise of 1850. DuVal died on a business trip in Washington, D.C. (*ANB*; *DAB*; Robert L. Meriwether and others, eds., *The Papers of John C. Calhoun* [1959–2003], 5:406–7, 633; *Terr. Papers*, vols. 22–26; *JEP*, 3:293, 294, 295, 4:378 [15–17 Apr. 1822, 26 Mar. 1834]; Frank L. Snyder, "William Pope DuVal: An Extraordinary Folklorist," *Florida Historical Quarterly* 69 [1990]: 195–212; Washington *Daily National Intelligencer*, 31 Mar. 1854).

[1] Manuscript: "frist."

From Samuel H. Smith

Your favors of the 15th & 23^d Inst. afford me unfeigned satisfaction from that natural feeling of the human heart that is always gratified at living in the recollection & esteem of those we respect, & by the opportunity they furnish of reciprocating with earnestness the liveliest wishes for your felicity. The world will have it, particularly that portion of it who see things thro' the jaundised medium of disappointed ambition, that you are still our political Palinurus, participating in all the cares & anxieties of gov^t. It is in vain that I laugh at their folly, and tell them that you have formed too true an estimate of happiness to suffer the calm delights of retirement to be disturbed by public cares not called for by a sense of duty; judging of others by themselves, they adhere to their conviction that you have only fled from the pagentry of power, to enjoy the more securely the substance. They have never realised, they are incapable of realising the proud satisfaction & happy light-heartedness with wch a sound & pure mind, after having done its duty, flies from public honors. They feel not that the only legitimate ambition of a correct mind is in the evening of life to command that independence wch leisure alone can confer.

Proceeding from great to little things I can assure you with perfect truth, that I enter on the office assigned me by the partiality of the President, with no flushed expectations of happiness. Had personal considerations altogether guided my decision I should not have accepted it. when in town I have always sighed for the country; and settled in the country I have been happy & contented; and it has greatly added to my happiness that Mrs S. concurred with me in all these sentiments. Here we were anchored, as we believed, for life, looking for nothing else, contented with a moderate independence.

Mr Dougherty had spoken to me before I received Your favor. I felt then a strong desire to serve him, wch has been greatly strengthened by Your interposition. But, as I told him then, the field of my authority does not, I fear, offer any place for wch he is Qualified that is worthy his acceptance. For clerical duties he does not seem fitted; the Messenger had been previously fixed; & there only remain one or two hands to be employed in the stamping with little higher compensation than that of common mechanical labor. Under these circumstances I can only say that the subject shall not be lost sight of, & that if any thing offers by wch he can be served I will embrace the occasion with much pleasure.

With regard to Your subn to the Nat. Intel. the whole concern was long since transferred to Mr Gales, whom I will desire to forward Your account. While the establishment was under my direction, Your punctuality always kept pace with the assigned periods of payment.

There remains untouched the great topic of a Navy. In principle we concur. It is only in the application of that principle we differ, if indeed we differ at all. The true original policy of this nation was the vigorous cultivation of its internal resources, connected with an inflexible purpose to forbear, at least until they were expanded, from any attempt to protect commerce by forcible means. To this end our course should have been firm, consistent, undeviating. Roads, canals & fortifications should have been boldly urged, & a militia, fully competent to defence, been organised; and war, in defence of our rights on the ocean, should not have been gone into. This was the original ground of our political friends. It was the true ground. It should have been maintained. To maintain it, the Embargo was resorted to; & so great was then the stake, I think now, as I thought then, that measure ought to have been enforced, if necessary, even by the bayonet. Unfortunately it was abandoned, & we all know the consequences. We are involved in war with England. If this war deprived us merely of our foreign trade, we might, perhaps, find an indemnity in the rapid growth of manufactures, wch now annually exceed 240 millions of dollars. But it does more. It blockades our ports & harbours; it destroys the utility of our rivers, converting them into the facilitating instruments of aggression; it stops the great arterial circulation; industry & enterprise become its victims. Even the great internal interests demand that the enemy should be driven from our bays, rivers, harbors & coasts. For this a strong naval force is essential, sufficiently strong to retort upon the enemy at a distance from our shores the injuries inflicted upon us. For I need not remind you, that to render a war short-lived, <u>offensive</u> measures are the most decisive. But there is no end to this topic.

Mrs S. begs me, with mine, to tender you and Your family, her most affectionate remembrances. It would, indeed, afford us heartfelt pleasure once more to breathe Your[1] mountain air & mingle in Your domestic circle. Should an occasion offer, we shall seize it with delight.

I am, with the greatest respect and esteem   Sa. H. Smith

RC (DLC); at foot of text: "Thomas Jefferson Esqr."; endorsed by TJ as received 14 Sept. 1813 and so recorded in SJL.

A palinurus is the pilot or helmsman of a ship, from the pilot of Aeneas (*OED*).

[1] Manuscript: "Yours."

Judith Lomax's Poem: "Monticello"

[ca. Aug. 1813]

Monticello.—Composed[1] while viewing the Clouds gathering
and rolling about the Mountain.—

> A cloud rests on the Mountain's brow,
> And through it "dim seen forms" appear,
> Floating in air, or station'd now,
> In gloomy grandeur near.
>
> ———————
>
> These forms fantastic bring along,
> To Fancy's mental eye;
> Those times when Ossian, "Son of song,"
> Awaked the tender sigh.
>
> ———————
>
> And still the vision'd scene untrue,
> My Mind with rapture[2] fills;
> For still methinks I seem to view,
> The "Spirit of the hills."
>
> ———————
>
> And Fancy too, in Selma's hall,
> Awakes the Hero's name;
> Methinks I hear the Bard recall,
> The deeds of Fingal's fame.
>
> ———————
>
> But why should thus my entranced[3] Soul,
> In "other times" delight;
> When o'er the present age there[4] roll,
> Beams of more vivid light?
>
> ———————
>
> Yes, Monticello sheds a ray,
> O'er each dark gath'ring cloud;
> And proudly owns a blaze of day,
> Which malice ne'er can shroud.
>
> ———————
>
> Here Virtue, Taste, and Science dwell,
> This is their fav'rite Seat;
> They mark the spot they love so well,
> And guard[5] their sweet retreat[6].—

MALVINA, alias, JUDITH LOMAX.—

MS (DLC: Randolph Family Manuscripts); entirely in Lomax's hand. Printed in Lomax, *The Notes of an American Lyre* (Richmond, 1813; Sowerby, no. 4452), 49.

Judith Lomax (1774–1828), author, was the unmarried eldest daughter of Thomas Lomax and Ann Lomax, of Port Tobago in Caroline County. She was a fervent evangelical Episcopalian and supporter of the American Colonization Society. TJ reported to John Adams on 22 Aug. 1813 that she was then at Monticello, while James Hunter recorded in loose sheets for a diary on 30 Aug. 1813 that he "visited, by invitation of C Bankhead monticello.—I was very much pleased with the place.—m^r Jefferson not at home.—m^rs Randolph there.—a very polite agreeable woman. met with miss Judith Lomax <*there*>" (MS in ViHi: Hunter Family Papers; in Hunter's hand). Lomax continued to reside in Caroline County after the sale in 1816 of her family's plantation but relocated to Fredericksburg in the winter of 1826–27. She was impoverished and living with her mother at the time of her death, when her personal estate was valued at $161.35 (Edward L. Lomax, *Genealogy of the Virginia Family of Lomax* [1913], 19, 24; Laura Hobgood-Oster, ed., *The Sabbath Journal of Judith Lomax, 1774–1828* [1999; based on MS at ViHi]; *Alexandria Gazette, Commercial and Political*, 9 Jan.

1816; DNA: RG 29, CS, Caroline Co., 1820; Fredericksburg *Virginia Herald*, 23 Jan. 1828; Fredericksburg Hustings Court Will Book, B:362–3, C:121).

Later in 1813 Lomax dedicated *The Notes of an American Lyre*, her slim volume of poetry and prose, to TJ. In addition to the poem printed above, the book contained a second celebrating TJ's election as president, "A Prophecy, on the 11th of February, 1801"; a third "To Miss R******h" thanking one of TJ's grandchildren for giving her a copy of William Godwin's *St. Leon: A Tale of the Sixteenth Century*; and a fourth "Written immediately on my return home from the South West Mountains," in which Lomax recalls her visit and invites Ellen Wayles Randolph (Coolidge) to reciprocate by calling on her (pp. 12–3, 50–1).

James Macpherson's poetry written in the guise of the alleged ancient Gaelic author OSSIAN (the BARD) contains the hero Fingal, his palace named Selma, and the songstress MALVINA.

[1] Text to this point in *American Lyre* reads "*Written at Monticello, Albemarle county, and composed.*"
[2] *American Lyre*: "transport."
[3] *American Lyre*: "raptur'd."
[4] *American Lyre* substitutes "æra" for preceding two words.
[5] MS: "gaurd." *American Lyre*: "*guard.*"
[6] Text in *American Lyre* ends here.

Deposition of Martin Dawson in *Jefferson v. Michie*

on the 10th day of March in the year 1804 as appears from a referance to the agreement and Contract for a deed filed in the office of the County of Albemarle At the request of John Henderson I drew an[1] agreement between the said John Henderson & David Michie for the purpose and intent of erecting a merchants mill and other water works near the town of Milton when the said Michie saw the agreement he made some alterrations in it and then said Henderson & Michie put their names to it and desired me to keep it till applied for, the agreement remained in my hands from that time till the spring

before last as well as my memory serves me when it was applied for and delivered, there was no injunction by the parties when the agreement was left with me to keep the Contents secret, and nothing said to me about the said agreement by either of the parties from the time it was deposited till applied for—these facts stated at the request of David Michie   MARTIN DAWSON
milton 1 Sep[t] 1813.

Tr (ViU: TJP-LBJM); in George Carr's hand.

5 July is recorded in SJL as received 10 July 1813 from Milton.

A missing letter from Dawson to TJ of

[1] Manuscript: "and."

From John Adams

Quincy Sept. 2. 1813

Οὐδὲ γυνὴ κακοῦ ἀνδρὸς ἀναίνεται εἶναι ἄκοιτις
πλουσίου· ἀλλ' ἀφνεὸν βούλεται ἀντ' ἀγαθοῦ.
Χρήματα γὰρ τιμῶσι, καὶ ἐκ κακοῦ ἐσθλὸς ἔγημε,
καὶ κακὸς ἐξ ἀγαθοῦ. πλοῦτος ἔμιξε γένος.

Grotius renders this into latin, thus.

Nec dedignatur ditemque malumque maritum
femina: divitiæ præ probitate placent.
In pretio pretium est: genus et prænobile, vili,
obscurum claro, miscet avaritia.

I Should render the Greek into English thus.

Nor does a Woman disdain to be the Wife of a bad rich Man. But She prefers a Man of Property before a good Man. For Riches are honoured; and a good Man marries from a bad Family, and a bad Man from a good one. Wealth mingles all races.

Now please to tell me, whether my translation has not hit the Sense of Theognis, as exactly as that of Grotius.

Tell me also, whether Poet, Orator, Historian or Philosopher can paint the Picture of every City, County or State in our pure, uncorrupted, unadulterated, uncontaminated federal Republick; or in France England Holland, and all the rest of Christendom[1] or Mahometanism, in more precise Lines or Colures.?[2]

Another translation of the whole Passage of Theognis.

Arietes quidem et Asinos quærimus, Cyrne, et Equos
Generosos, et quisque vult ex bonis,:
Admittere: ducere autem malam (filiam) mali non renuit
Generosus Vir, Si ei pecunias multas dederit.

Nulla (femina) mali viri recusat esse Uxor
Divitis; Sed divitem vult pro bono
opes quidem æstimant, et ex malo (natam) bonus ducet
Et malus ex bono ortam. Divitiæ mixent genus.

Now, my Friend, who are the αριϛοι.? Philosophy may Answer "The Wise and Good."[3] But the World, Mankind, have by their practice always answered, "the rich the beautiful[4] and well born."[5] And Philosophers themselves in marrying their Children[6] prefer the rich[7] the handsome[8] and the well descended to the wise and good.

What chance have Talents and Virtues in competition, with Wealth and Birth? and Beauty?[9]

Haud facile emergunt, quorum Virtutibus obstant
Res Angusta Domi.
one truth is clear,; by all the World confess'd
Slow rises worth, by Poverty oppress'd.

The five[10] Pillars of Aristocracy, are Beauty Wealth, Birth, Genius and Virtues.[11] Any one of the three first, can at any time over bear any one or both of the two last.

Let me ask again, what a Wave of publick opinion, in favour of Birth has been Spread over the Globe, by Abraham, by Hercules, by Mahomet, by Guelphs, Ghibellines, Bourbons, and a miserable Scottish Chief Steuart? By Zingis by, by, by, a million others? And what a Wave will be Spread by Napoleon and by Washington? Their remotest Cousins will be Sought and will be proud, and will avail themselves of their descent. Call this Principle, Prejudice, Folly Ignorance, Baseness, Slavery, Stupidity, Adulation, Superstition or what you will. I will not contradict you. But the Fact, in natural, moral, political and domestic History I cannot deny or dispute or question.

And is this great Fact in the natural History of Man? This unalterable Principle of Morals, Philosophy, Policy domestic felicity, and dayly Experience from the Creation; to be overlooked, forgotten neglected, or hypocritically waived out of Sight; by a Legislator? By a professed Writer upon civil Government, and upon Constitutions of civil Government?

Thus far I had written, when your favour of Aug. 22 was laid on my table, from the Post Office. I can only say at present that I can pursue this idle Speculation no farther, at least till I have replied to this fresh proof of your friendship and Confidence. Mrs A. joins in cordial Thanks, with   JOHN ADAMS

you may laugh at the introduction of Beauty, among the Pillars of Aristocracy. But Madame Barry Says Le veritable Royauté est la

Beauté,[12] and there is not a more certain Truth, Beauty, Grace, Figure, Attitude, Movement, have in innumerable Instances prevailed over Wealth, Birth, Talents Virtues and every thing else, in Men of the highest rank, greatest Power, and Sometimes, the most exalted Genius, greatest Fame, & highest Merit:

RC (DLC); at foot of text: "President Jefferson"; endorsed by TJ as received 17 Sept. 1813 and so recorded in SJL. FC (Lb in MHi: Adams Papers); partially in Adams's hand.

For the passage from Theognis immediately preceding that quoted here and Adams's source, see Adams to TJ, 9 July, [ca. 14] Aug. 1813. A modern rendition of the GREEK INTO ENGLISH of the current section, consisting of lines 187–90, reads "and a woman does not refuse to be the wife of a base man who is rich, but she wants a wealthy man instead of one who is noble. It is money people honour; one who is noble marries the daughter of one who is base and one who is base marries the daughter of one who is noble. Wealth has mixed up blood" (Gerber, *Greek Elegiac Poetry*, 200–1). The additional Latin translation, ARIETES QUIDEM . . . MIXENT GENUS, appears in Ralph Winterton, ed., *Poetæ Minores Græci* (London, 1700, and other eds.; Sowerby, no. 4382; Adams's copy at MBPLi), 376. αρίϛτοι: "best men; nobles." HAUD FACILE . . . ANGUSTA DOMI: "It's not easy anyway

to climb the ladder when cramped personal resources block your talents" (Juvenal, *Satires*, 3.164–5, in *Juvenal and Persius*, trans. Susanna Morton Braund, Loeb Classical Library [2004], 180–1). ONE TRUTH IS CLEAR . . . POVERTY OPPRESS'D is a free quotation from Samuel Johnson, *London: A Poem, In Imitation of the Third Satire of Juvenal*, 2d ed. (London, 1738), 14. ZINGIS: Genghis Khan. LE VERITABLE ROYAUTÉ EST LA BEAUTÉ: "Beauty is the true royalty."

[1] RC: "Chritendom." FC: "Christendom."
[2] FC: "Colours."
[3] Omitted closing quotation mark editorially supplied.
[4] Preceding two words interlined.
[5] Omitted closing quotation mark editorially supplied.
[6] RC: "Childen." FC: "Children."
[7] RC: "riich." FC: "rich."
[8] Preceding two words interlined.
[9] FC to this point in Adams's hand.
[10] Reworked from "four."
[11] FC: "Virtue."
[12] RC: "Bautee." FC: "Beutee."

From Thomas Voigt

HONORED SIR,   Phila[d] September 3[d] 1813

I Received yours of the 16th of July—and have sent according to your Orders a Gold Watch which I beleive to be a suitable one, and has bin Originally intended for a Lady, which is a plain, neat and verry Exquisite peace of workmanship, and am in hopes that it will meat your approbation—

The Gentleman,[1] M[r] Short, which was to give me directions about the Chane & Seal has Left this Citty and has gone to Boston, but have ventured to send such a Chane as our Ladyes ware in Phia[d] and I bleive nearly such as you discribe in your Letter,—there are no such

Seals as you discribe, in Phila[d] at presant,[2] but verry probable I shall be able to procure one for you before Long, the Lapedary that formerly did that kind of work for Me has gone on to Pitsburg to the Glass Manufactory, and on that account I am [not][3] enabled to get one at presant—

I Shall be verry happy to transact any buisiness for you at any time in my Line—your Clock at the University performs Remarckaby well—

I am very Respectfully yours &[c]   THO[s] VOIGT

RC (MHi); dateline at foot of text; adjacent to closing: "Tho[s] Jefferson"; endorsed by TJ as received 14 Sept. 1813 and so recorded in SJL.

TJ ordered a gold watch for his granddaughter Ellen Wayles Randolph (Coolidge) in a letter dated 30 July 1813, not the 16TH OF JULY. The astronomical case clock that Voigt had made for TJ was at this time (and would for several years remain) in the possession of Robert Patterson, a longtime professor of mathematics at the UNIVERSITY of Pennsylvania (Patterson to TJ, 10 May 1809 [note], 25 Aug. 1815).

[1] Manuscript: "Gentlemam."
[2] Manuscript: "peesant."
[3] Omitted word editorially supplied.

From José Corrêa da Serra

SIR   Philadelphia 6 Sept[ber] 1813
Together with this Letter i forward to you by the post office the book of Senator Fossombroni. The 1st part of the book is wholly antiquarian, and though highly curious to Italian readers, is of Little interest to any other; the second part will give you an idea of that ingenious and experimented practice. If it was judged proper to familiarize the Americans with it then it would be necessary to extract and translate what relates to it, in Fossombroni's memoir on this matter (which is printed in the 3[d] vol. of the transactions of the Italian society) and in the tracts of the Florentine collection of hydraulic books.

Permit me to expose an idea which came to my memory in reading the unlucky accident of the two schooners upset in Lake Ontario in these Last cruizes of Com[re] Chauncey. In the time of Suwarow's campaign, the English assisted the house of Austria in building a flotilla of war in the Lake of Constance, and sent an English officer of the name of Williams to command it. As it was the first instance of a Lake navy in the actual state of naval improvement, i heard many interesting observations, made by competent judges, and particularly on the necessity of making alterations in the construction, because sea water being considerably heavier than fresh water, seemed to indicate that at Least the prominence of the Keel ought to be in an inverse ratio to the weight of the water, in order to give steadiness to the ship, and safety to its navigation. That a merchant ship had not the same necessity of hazardous manoeuvres, and consequently Less occasion of feeling the necessity of such an alteration. Has this been attended to, by your naval constructors in the Lakes?

When i returned to Washington with Col. Randolph we missed to meet Mr Madison. I write to him as is my duty in Leaving this continent, but i remember you of Mr Warden's title of Consul general, about which you were so good as to promise me your interest. I have Learned since i am in Philadelphia that Mr Sylvanus Bourne had the same title in Holland when that country enjoyed a government of its own.

In a few days i go to the northern ports in order to find embarkation for the Peninsula. Whatever occasions there or elsewhere may occur of obeying your commands, Mr Vaughan will forward them to me. I will profit of the Leave i obtained of writing to you if i meet with, or think any thing worth your notice, but do not exact any answer but what you will think fit. I hope you will find me always

Most sincerely yours   JOSEPH CORRÊA DE SERRA

P.S. I enclose Mr Cuvier's paper, and write to him, that if it is possible to have the objects, it will be by your means and care.

RC (DLC); endorsed by TJ as received 17 Sept. 1813 and so recorded in SJL. Enclosure: Vittorio Fossombroni, *Memorie Idraulico-Storiche sopra la Val-di-Chiana* (Florence, 1789; Sowerby, no. 3921). Other enclosure printed below.

The 1ST PART of Fossombroni's enclosed book, which was a hydrographic history of Tuscany's Chiana Valley, deals with its ancient state, while the SECOND PART concerns the transformation of its marshy and malarial regions into arable land through the creation of an integrated, artificial drainage system. Fossombroni published an article "Sopra la Distribuzione delle Alluvioni" ("On the Distribution of Alluvion") in the *Memorie di matematica e fisica della Società Italiana delle scienze* (TRANSACTIONS OF THE ITALIAN SOCIETY) 3 (1786): 533–52. United States naval commodore Isaac Chauncey lost two schooners in a storm on LAKE ONTARIO in August 1813

(*Albany Argus*, 17 Aug. 1813). James Ernest Williams commanded the Austrian flotilla on Lake Constance during Russian general Aleksandr Suvorov's (SUWAROW'S) 1799 Italian campaign (Lawrence Sondhaus, *The Habsburg Empire and the Sea: Austrian Naval Policy, 1797–1866* [1989], 6, 8; Chandler, *Campaigns of Napoleon*, 256; New York *Commercial Advertiser*, 8 June 1799; *Philadelphia Gazette & Daily Advertiser*, 24 July 1800). Corrêa da Serra wrote President James Madison on 9 Sept. 1813 to recommend that David Bailie Warden be given the title of CONSUL GENERAL, adding that "At Monticello I asked Mr. Jefferson on the propriety of speaking to you, about a concern of Mr. Warden your Consul at Paris, he not only approved of it, but kindly promised to interfere in it" (Madison, *Papers, Pres. Ser.*, 6:605). Corrêa da Serra was bound for the Iberian PENINSULA.

Georges Cuvier to José Corrêa da Serra

M. Cuvier prie M. Corréa de vouloir bien s'employer, pour procurer au Museum

Un cràne du bison d'amerique, (<u>Buffalo</u>) <u>bos bison</u>. L.
et S'il est possible une peau et un squelette.
Idem, du boeuf musqué du canada (<u>bos moschatus</u>. L.)
un exemplaire de l'animal nommé <u>Mink</u> ou <u>minx</u> à la caroline; s'il est possible dans l'esprit de vin. C'est une espèce de loutre ou de putois.

Si M. Corréa va au brésil, ou s'il peut y avoir des correspondances nous lui demanderons

le squelette du <u>gnouroumi</u> ou grand fourmilier (myrmé cophaga jubata.)
celui du <u>tamanduaï</u> ou fourmilier moyen.

Il suffit que les os soient grossierèment décharnés, et enfermés pèle mèle dans un sac pour chaque espèce.

Mr. Cuvier begs Mr. Corrêa to try to procure for the Museum

a skull of the American bison (<u>Buffalo</u>) <u>bos bison</u>. L.
and if possible a hide and a skeleton.
Idem, of the Canadian musk ox (<u>bos moschatus</u>. L.)
a specimen of the animal called the <u>mink</u> or <u>minx</u> in Carolina; if possible preserved in spirit of wine. It is a kind of otter or skunk.

If Mr. Corrêa goes to Brazil, or has contacts there, we will ask him for

the skeleton of the <u>gnouroumi</u> or giant anteater (myrmecophaga jubata.)
and that of the <u>tamandua</u> or medium-sized anteater.

It suffices if the bones are roughly cleaned and placed pell-mell in separate bags for each species.

RC (DLC: TJ Papers, 195:34722–3); undated. Translation by Dr. Roland H. Simon.

Georges Cuvier (1769–1832), zoologist and paleontologist, was born and educated in the French-speaking portion of Württemberg. In 1795 he moved to Paris, where his skills as a scholar and teacher facilitated his rapid rise within the scientific community. Cuvier was soon teaching zoology at the Écoles Centrales and animal anatomy at the Muséum d'Histoire Naturelle, and he became a professor at the Collège de France in 1800, perma-nent secretary of the physical sciences at the Institut de France in 1803, a counsellor of state in 1814, and a baron in 1819. During his long career Cuvier took a special interest in the Muséum's anatomical collections. With his assistance its holdings grew from a few hundred skeletons in the 1790s to thirteen thousand specimens at the time of his death. Although TJ owned several of Cuvier's works, the two men apparently never met nor corresponded personally (*DSB*; Sowerby, nos. 423, 999, 1020; Poor, *Jefferson's Library*, 5, 7 [nos. 174, 304]).

From Nicolas G. Dufief

Monsieur,   A Philad^e ce 6 Septembre 1813

J'ai eu l'honneur, Mardi dernier, 31 dernier, d'envoyer <u>de votre part</u> à Mr J. Adams le Seul exemplaire qu'il y eût en ville de l'ouvrage du Dr Priestley. Il le recevra <u>cartonné</u> n'ayant pas eu le temps de le faire relier puisque vous désiriez qu'il lui parvînt <u>without delay</u>: Dans la lettre qui accompagnait l'envoi, je n'ai pas manqué de mentionner cette circonstance

Dans deux ou trois jours, je vous adresserai la feuille qui manque au 1er vol. de mon dictionnaire qui par la faute du Relieur Se trouve incomplet

Agreez les assurances de mon profond respect, & de mon parfait devouement   N. G. Dufief

EDITORS' TRANSLATION

Sir,   Philadelphia 6 September 1813

This past Tuesday the 31st, I had the honor of sending to Mr. J. Adams <u>on your behalf</u> the only copy of Dr. Priestley's work to be found in this city. He will receive it <u>in boards</u>, as you desired it to reach him <u>without delay</u>, and I did not have time to get it bound. In the letter accompanying the package I did not fail to mention this circumstance

Within two or three days I will send you the sheet that is missing from the first volume of my dictionary, which was omitted by the binder

Please accept the assurances of my profound respect and perfect devotion

N. G. Dufief

RC (DLC); endorsed by TJ as received 15 Sept. 1813 and so recorded in SJL. Translation by Dr. Roland H. Simon.

Dufief's lettre to John Adams is dated 30 Aug. 1813 (MHi: Adams Papers).

From Nathaniel H. Hooe

Sir   King George C^t Forest Hill Sep^t 6th 1813

Your favor of the 21st of july I have reced after lying in the post office at Fredericksburg upwards of one month. at the same time I reced a letter from Messrs Gipson & Jefferson which had also been in the office for some time, covering a check on the Farmers Bank of Fredericksburgh for 76. D 60 c in my favor on your Accp^t which they requested I would inform you <u>of when</u> I reced it, which sum is in full with the Interst, I am sorry to learn by your favor that you ware among the unfortunate farmers who were caught with their Flour on hand after Such a very high price had been offering, But the distance you are from market accounts for it, the last years crop of wheat about me has been sold at a very high price and I beleive the money all gone, & we are regreting very much the present low prices of wheat & corn, In this quarter I beleive we are all most a half year before you in the disposal of our crops which is generally I beleive an advantage in quantity, & sometimes the use of money ariseing from early sales   yours Very Respectfully   NATH^L H. HOOE

RC (MHi); addressed: "Thomas Jefferson Esqr Monticello," with postmaster's note: "mail to—Milton"; stamped; postmarked King George Court House, 7 Sept. 1813; endorsed by TJ as received 15 Sept. 1813 and so recorded in SJL.

David Michie's Plea and Answer in *Jefferson v. Michie*

[by 6 Sept. 1813]

The plea of David Michie the Def^t named in the bill of Complaint of Thomas Jefferson Complainant exhibited in the County Court of Albemarle

The said Defendant by protestation not Confessing or acknowledging all or any of the matters and things in the Complainants said bill of Complaint Contained to be true in such manner and form as the same is therein declared and set forth, but avering that the same are untrue, malicious and unfounded, for plea thereto saith that heretofore and before the said Complainant exhibited his bill in this worshipful Court to wit on the 12^h day of May in the year 1804 Craven Peyton in the Complainants now bill mentioned admitted to be his the said Complainants agent, did exhibit his bill of Complaint in the superior Court of Chancery holden at the Capital in the City of Richmond against the said John Henderson also in the now Complainants bill named under whom this Def^t Claims lands, premises, rights and previledges also in the now Complainants[1] bill mentioned, to which bill the said John Henderson filed his answer and on the 2^d day of June in the same year 1804 the said Craven Peyton by leave of the said Court filed his amendment to his said Original bill against the said John Henderson, Eliz^h James L, Charles, Isham, Bennett Hillsborough, Elizabeth, Frances Lucy and Nancy Crawford Hendersons for the same matters to the same effect as to the title, as the now Complainant doth state insist and rely on by his present bill set forth, to which amended bill the said John Henderson did also put in

[472]

his Answer, and the said then Complainant thereto, as also to his first Answer replied, and sundry depositions and exhibits were duly taken & filed and the suit was so proceeded in that the said bill in Chancery was on the 8ʰ day of June in the year 1805 by the Judge of the said Superior Court of Chancery dismissed and he ordered to pay to the said Defendant John Henderson his Costs—from which decree of dismission the said then Complainant by petition to the then Judge of the said Supʳ Court of Chancery obtained an appeal to the honourable Court of Appeals where on the 7ʰ day of January in the year 1812 by the Consideration and decree of the said Court of Appeals, the said decree of the Superior Court of Chancery as by an attested Copy of the said record and proceedings in the said suit hereto annexed Nᵒ 1 will more fully and at large appear, and which said record and proceedings are prayed to be taken as a part of this plea

And therefore this deft doth plead the said decree in bar to the said now Complainants said present bill.

And to so much of the said bill as this Deft has not pleaded unto, he in no Sort waveing the benefit of his said plea but wholy relying and insisting thereon for Answer to the residue of the Complainants said bill or to so much thereof as he is advised it is material for him to Answer unto, Answereth and saith that he admits that Bennett Henderson died intestate seized of the tract of land in the bill mentioned leaving a widow & eleven Children as is therein stated, and that one of them shortly thereafter likewise dying intestate, an assignment of dower to the widow and partition among the Survivors took place under the Sanction of this Court and after the mode specified in said bill.—From the latitude which the Complainant has allowed himself in his bill aforesaid, so far from it being deemed irrevolent it may be Considered as tending to elucidate the Controversy between the parties that this respondent should take a transiant view of some important incidents which took place anterior to the period at which the Complainant Commences its history. The late Colᵒ Bennett Henderson in his life time some where about the year 1780 while the Courts of law in this Commonwealth were occluded by the pressure of the war in which we were then engaged being seized of lands in fee simple bordering on the South side of the river Rivanna, erected a mill on said river at a place called the mountain falls, which said mill was extremely profitable to him dureing his life & after his death his personal estate being swept away by his debts it formed the principal Source of Revenue & Subsistance to his aged widow & helpless Children. This respondent believes that the father of this Complainant upwards of a half a Century² ago had erected a water grist mill, some distance above the mountain falls, which was destroyed by the flood of 1771 long subsequent to the erection of the said mill by said Henderson somewhere about the year ___ the Complainant obtained leave of this Court to rebuild the said mill; and soon after the death of the said Col° Bennett Henderson the said Complainant exhibited his bill in Chancery a Copy of which and the proceedings thereon is hereto annexed N° 2 and prayed to be taken as a part of this answer, from which it does appear that the said Henderson was impeached for illegal proceedure in the original erection of said mill as well with a Certain depredation on the property of the Complainant at the same time. To this bill Complaining as aforesaid and praying that the dam of the said mill might be prostrated as a nusance, notwithstanding these serious Charges and the magnitude of interest at stake, there appears to have been made no defence by the widow and the orphans. And as the reasons assigned for this failure as well as the Cause why the exhibition of the bill was defered until the death of Col Henderson have no immediate bearing upon the points now litigated, this respondent refrains from any notice of them. In Consequence of the exhibition of the said bill and the omission on the part of the widow & orphans to defend the same, the mill dam erected by the said Henderson was pronounced by the decree of the then high Court of Chancery to be a nusance and ordered to be abated; which said Order was immediately Carried into execution by the said Complainant, which act, and the manner in which it was performed Altho they excited a strong sensation in this section of the Country & proved fatal to the interests of the widow and the orphans[3] are foreign from the present subject; But as the Comp^t has wandered[4] out of his way to make an impression unfavourable to the reputation of this respondent he Considers himself imperitively Called on to repel by every fair means the attempt, and should the Conduct of either the respondent or Comp^t in these transactions with the Hendersons merit odium, the reproach[5] thereof may devolve upon him who may have justly incurred it. With this view this respondent begs leave to state that the mill site at the mountain falls had long been Considered as a desideratum by the Complainant either to preclude Competition or for other purposes. He is led to this opinion from a belief of the Complainants haveing solely formed the scheme of the division of the late Bennett Hendersons real estate a Copy of which will be found among the exhibits N° 1 and prayed to be admitted as a part of this answer from which it will be seen that human ingenuity Could not have devised a better plan by which the many parcels into which it is Cut should fall a prey to an opulant neighbour. To shew that the foregoing Idea is not a visionary one, a Certain Craven Peyton (then ostensibly acting for himself, but now known to have been the agent of the said Comp^t) availing himself of suitable opportunieties to purchase of the heirs of said Henderson both here and in Kentucky, to which state he many times went for that purpose and in all the Conveyances of said property altho the ancient mill site is Cautiously reserved, it is but too obvious that <u>that</u> formed the primary object. The Complainant has inveighed against this respondent for the privacy and Concealment which marked his negotiations with John Henderson, and does not perceive that he is liable in a more eminent degree to a similar accusation. why Charge this Respondent with Chicanery & occult practices when, he himself is forced to shroud in darkness and go behind the scenes? It is not a Sufficient answer that the Complainant was in public service & Compelled to act by another; because the avowal of the agency would have answered every rational purpose without the assumption on the part of Peyton of the Charecter of a real purchaser. Deeds executed to the Complainant himself or to the said Peyton as his agent would have been valid in law & more economical. It must then have been to Attain some misterious end. Perhaps if it had been known to the parties that the purchases were made for the Complainant, the object and the benefit being palpable, higher expectations would have been formed and greater demands have been made or perhaps the injury already received by the delapidation of their mill reduced As they were in their Circumstances,[6] wounded pride, or indignant feeling might have inclined them to preclude the Complainant from the gratification of his wishes. But what were their motives or the motives[7] of the Complainant in acting thus Ambigiously we will leave to Conjecture This respondent further answering saith that in the year 1804 he entered into a Contract with John Henderson Contained in two Seperate instruments (Copies of which numbered 3 & 4 are hereto annexed & requested to be incorporated with this answer) to erect a water grist mill in partnership, after the s^d Henderson had obtained leave from this Court to that effect tho' streniously opposed by the said Craven Peyton. To which Contract in the hand writing of Mr Martin Dawson this respondent refers for proof as to the liberality of his views in relation to the said Jno Henderson. It will appear from the said Contract (whose legal operation it is Contended from the date of its execution vested the possession) that for a moiety of lots N° 8. 9 & 10 and a moiety of his interest in the dower land, this respondent was to advance to the said Henderson £1000 in the way therein designated. This is an important fact in vindication of this respondents purity of intention and rectitude of

Conduct, for it will be seen that he estimated the mill site and the lands appertenant thereto not exceeding 10 acres at a sum not greatly inferior to that which, from the evidence of the Complainants agent, he paid for the whole tract Containing $1126\frac{1}{4}$[8] acres, and as this respondent has been informed in [rubish?] of property of little value. To prove to your worships that this respondent intended no fraud or Circumvention but wished to have possessed this property at a fair price, he begs leave to refer the Court to an extract of his letter to the Complainant dated July 20[h] 1812 "I am greatly averse to litigation on account of the manifold perplexities it superinduces, but having removed from Louisa & expended money not only in the purchase of this, but other property, with a view solely to the advantages to be derived from such an establishment, I am loth to relinquish any benefit that Can arise to me from my original Contract with Henderson, which I have always been ready to execute in its fullest extent without regarding to whom the interest secured thereby to Henderson might be transferred." How in the face of this avowal Could the Complainant Charge this respondent with Confederating with the said Henderson to injure him "by Clandestine & fraudulent bargains and deeds on false Considerations never actually paid?"—Viewing the establishment originating out of his Contract with Henderson as a source of future Comfort and wealth without recuring to the manuel labour of slaves this respondent had intended to devote his best energies and to have applied his principle resources[9] towards it, as a proof of which he purchased a well improved lot in the town of Milton and removed his family & Store to that place. Shortly after this event, to his great astonishment when on the eve of Commencing[10] his operations, in acting under the Authority of this worshipful Court, the said John is arrested in his progress by an Injunction from the High Court of Chancery. Here this respondent Cannot refrain from remarking the evident disingenuousness which charectirized the Conduct of the Complainant himself. It is understood to have been the uniform practice of that Court never to award Injunctions where they have been previously dissolved in the County Courts except in Cases of the most flagrant and palpable oppression and for reasons almost too manifest to require explenation, for after a Subject has undergone discussion under all its aspects and in all its ramifications before a Court of Competent jurisdiction in the County where the parties litigent and their witnesses are individually well known, and been solemnly decided, it would appear presumptious in another Court at a distance from the Scene of action and an utter Stranger to all Concerned to reverse the same. Why then let it be asked was a Communication of the previous question and desicion thereon in this Court not made to the Chancellor? There however after another severe ordeal the efforts of the Complainant shared the same fate. This respondent Calls them the efforts of the Complainant, for the bill itself Carries internal evidence of himself being the Author. Here then Scepticism itself, it might reasonably have been presumed, would have been satisfied. Far from it an appeal is taken and again on Solemn argument the decree of the Chancellor is affirmed as will be seen from the record N° 1 which is also prayed to be taken as a part of this Answer While the subject was pendente lite this respondent admits that doubts existed in his own mind as to the result, and taught a lesson by the Complainant he was silent as to his pretentions, for notwithstanding the mystery in which this affair was attempted to be enveloped, he had strong suspicions that the Complainant was behind the Curtain and that he had to Contend against his Colossal strength. But wherein is the great Criminality of not promulgating to the world a transaction the event of which was dubious and uncertain. Besides, this respondent is naturally of a taciturn disposition, of Solitary habits, and fond of those studies which are best adapted to such propensities. If further reasons are required to expulpate him from the enormous guilt[11] of silence, one may be superadded which will satisfy the Complainant himself. It is this; this respondent knew that he stood on impregnible grounds, he well knew that Peyton, the recognized agent of the Complainant was apprized of his title, and it is a principal too well established and too often repeated in the books to have escaped his observation, that a knowledge of a title of another to property in the agent, is evidence of a possession of the same knowledge by the principal.

To elucidate this point, (as this respondent has been informed most of the bar has been forestalled by the Complainant) he begs leave to refer your Worships to 1 atk 265. 3 atk 646. 1 Ves. 64 & Sugd 492. To prove that the said Peyton agent of the Comp^t possessed information of this respondents equitable lien, he begs leave to refer to an original letter from Col° Ch^s L Lewis brother in law of said Complainant and father in law of said Peyton which is numbered 5 and which he also prays may be received as a part of this his Answer. Where then was the necessity, let it be again asked, for this respondent to have promulgated to the world his intentions or to Complain of the grievancies already sustained, or which might still assail him. But to remark further on this head this respondent does not dispare of being able to put a final Close to this Controversy by proveing that the Complainant himself was not ignorant of his title. Hendersons

[477]

title being ratified by the Court of dernear resort in this Commonwealth and that title being transferred for valuable Consideration to this respondent by deed proved by one witness and Continued for further proof in this Worshipful Court, a Copy of which is hereto annexed numbered 6 and prayed to be taken as a part of this his Answer; And the original Contract being known to all the parties Concerned, to Peyton and the Comp^t as well as to James Lewis & Matthew Henderson before any Conveyance of the said John to them, as this respondent believes he Can establish; Closes the door as he is advised to all future investigation. It was on this ground principally that this respondent was induced through sound advice to decline any extrajudicial arbitration and as evidence of such advice he begs leave to refer to the plea prefixed to this answer which will Shew that he has Consulted Counsel learned in the law on the occasion, and that his said Counsel wished the subject to be regulated by the strict principles of law alone. He Cannot therefore take shame or Confusion to himself for withdrawing the proposition made by himself and acceeded to by the Complainant. For independant of the legal right and the many instances on record of honorable persons acting in the same way where important interests are at Stake and want of Candor is indicated by the adversary it must appear obvious that no assential injury Can arise to either party from the Step thus taken. For as it now stands the Cause will Come farely before the tribunals of the Country and experiance a full[12] according to its intrinsic merits. To justify however the Conduct of this respondent, to the most censorious, in the adoption of the foregoing measure he will prove that he has not been treated with that expansive liberality by the Complainant, which he had reason to have expected And for evidence whereof he begs leave to refer to the whole of the Correspondance between the agent of the Complainant, the Complainant himself, and this respondent, and not to garbled parts thereof a Copy of which N° 7 will be found among the exhibits in this Cause, and prayed to be taken as a part of this answer. From which among other things it will appear that the Complainant wished to embarrass the submission to Arbitration with all the refinements of Special pleading, and notwithstanding this respondent had fully opened to him the Nature of his Claim the said Complainant withheld from him any information on the points on which he rested his pretentions. In addition hereto he Considers himself as unfarely dealt with by the Complainant in the affair of the forceable entry & detainer alluded in the Comp^{ts} bill, the particular incidents of which he will not now detail, as that Cause remains yet to be determined by a Court of Competent Authority, one remark however he Cannot forbear making that the Justices before whom the Cause was tried refused to award a veniere facias in a traverse tendered, and the Comp^t accepted of a warrent of restitution when a book in the hands of his attorney of high authority Viz. Hawkins pleas Cro., and believed to belong to the Comp^t, shewed that in such a Case it was mandatory on them to have a jury summoned to determine the question of force. whereby this respondent expressly avers that the Comp^t either[13] Connived at, or wantonly deprived him of a <u>Constitutional right</u>, that of a <u>trial</u> by his <u>Peers</u>. The Comp^t has stated that $750 were given by him to James Lewis for his interest in Jno Hendersons title to all the Lands about Milton, and that that was but a pretenced bill purchased by him. Why would the Comp^t disburse such a Sum in the purchase of a mere shadow, when in doing this he knew he was violating a positive law of the Country. The depositions of Richard Price and James L Henderson were taken and used at the trial in the High Court of Chancery between Peyton & Henderson, altho the Comp^t for reasons best known to himself avers to the Contrary in his bill aforesaid, and which said bill according to the best authorities ought to have been Sworn to, and it is Conceived that where the same rights are at issue, they will be admissible testimony, but with what propriety the Comp^t Could have obtruded on the Court the deposition of James L Henderson this respon^t is at a loss to devine, when it appears he is most materially interrested. Nor Can this respondent Conceive that the evidence of James Lewis in the event of any future litigation Can be received as legal, in as much as he the said Lewis Contrary to law executed a trust Conveyed to himself for his own benefit and must be amenable when Called on to repair any injury which may have accrued.

As for the evidence of Craven Peyton when it is Considered how deeply he was affected at the opening of the Correspondance on the subject of this respondents title under Henderson, herein before referred to, it is a matter of some surprise, that the Comp^t who professes to wish <u>nothing</u> but what the law <u>will Sanction</u> should attempt to introduce it. The Suspicious situation in which he was found at the interview with this respondent on the Island of the honble M^r nelson, the extremity to which he then seemed Solicitous of pressing the affair, and the expression of his feelings contained in his letter, ought to induce the Comp^t to forego any benefit that might accrue to him from the testimony of such a witness.

But this respondent flatters himself that the Comp^t in tenderness to his agent will, on seeing the letter of Col^o Charles L Lewis herein referred to, and on recollecting the oath taken by the said Peyton on the trial of the warrent of forcible entry & detainor, Not be inclined to bring him forward again. What is the evidence this bill prays to have perpetuated? The depositions of Richard Price, James L Henderson Elizabeth Henderson, Dabney Carr Benjamin Brown & Craven Peyton all of which as the Comp^t shews go, either to the nullification of Hendersons Claim, or to prove Concealment on the part of this respondent of the one derived by him of s^d Henderson. Now this respondent respectfully Conceives, that Hendersons title being established by a decision of the Court of Appeals Cannot[14] be invalidated by any subsequent evidence whatever, and if it Can be established that either the Comp^t or his agent was privy to the Contract between the respondent and the said Jno Henderson, the other mass of evidence is equally nugatory and unavailing. It would then be not only preposterous but oppressive to Carry this respondent from the Rivanna to the Ohio and from the Ohio to the Washita to Attend to the Collection of evidence which in no aspect of the Case, Can subserve the purpose of the Complainant. on Col^o Lewis' letter this resp^t relies as Conclusive proof that he Can establish Mr Peytons knowledge of his Contract with Henderson, for how Could he in 1807 assign as a motive for Peytons Hostility to this respondent, his transactions with Henderson relative to the mill Site at milton without its being self evident that Peyton was then apprized thereof And afterwards in 1808 formed his Contract with a full view of their nature. This respondent might here rest his Case with the Court under a thorough Conviction that the prayer of the Comp^{ts} bill ought not to be granted, but he feels himself[15] Constrained to Notice either an intervertant[16] or deliberate error on the part of the Comp^t in his bill aforesaid.—He therein states that he was deprived at the trial between Peyton and Henderson in the High Court of Chancery of the evidence Comprized in the depositions of James Lewis Henderson & Richard Price by the failure of Comm^s to return them, or by some other Circumstance[17] preventing them being known to the Court, or to the Comp^{ts} Counsel, at the date of the decree; Whereas it is apparent from the record of the Case that he was fully availed of their benefit,—a transcript of which record he was informed by the clerk of the Court of Appeals, the Comp^t had in his possession. Charged, menaced & proscribed as this respondent has been both by the principle and agent, he has Considered it as an insuperable obligation on him to Come forward thus independtly in his own defence and in this as well as in all other Cases where his honor or his interest is at stake, he must speak in the bold & energatic language of truth; when however the whole Circumstances attendant on this Contraversy are deliberately weighed, he flatters himself that it will be found that he has not overleaped the limits of ordinary decorum, or the indispensible obligations of self defence.

When charges of moral turpitude are exhibited to the world according to the Solemnities and forms of juducial proceedings by a person of the first standing in Society against any individual however obscure, they ought to be well founded, for they remain as monuments of either the guilt or innocence of him against whom they are levelled. He who impeaches the rectitude of another, should be covered himself with an impenatrable shield. He should examine well the ground he occupies, and be Confident that both his Conduct & pretensions will stand the severest test of Criticism, because well founded recrimination by a law, which no human statute Can repeal must excite the most painful Sensations. It will be truly unfortunate for him if in accuseing his Antagonist with insidiousness and Chicane, the charge should with ten fold force recoil on himself. Above all it must inflict a deep and Corroding wound on the feelings of one who has held in his hands the destinies of a great and free people, to be suspected of a Conspiricy against the dearest rights and best interests of any portion of that Community over which he was Called to preside.

With this remarks this respondent Closes this his Answer and prays to be hence dismissed with his reasonable Costs &ᶜ

Albemarle County to wit

This day appeared before me a Justice of the peace for the County aforesaid David Michie and made oath that this his Answer Contains the truth so far as it relates to his own acts and doings, and so far as it relates to the acts and doings of others, he believes it to be true. Given under my hand this 6ʰ day of Sepᵗ 1813   JNO HARRIS

Tr (ViU: TJP-LBJM); in George Carr's hand; undated; one word illegible; at head of text: "at Rules held in the Clerks office of Albemarle County Court in October 1813 Came the Defendant David Michie and filed his plea & answer to the Plaintiffs bill—and on his motion a rule is entered against the Plaintiff for replication thereto The plea & answer follows in these words." Enclosures (all of which are transcribed in ViU: TJP-LBJM): (1) Virginia Court of Appeals, Court Record [1804–12] in *Peyton v. Henderson* (for a summary of this case, see note to Craven Peyton to TJ, 6 Aug. 1809, and Haggard, "Henderson Heirs"). (2) TJ's 1795 bill of complaint regarding the Henderson milldam and related documents, all of which have been printed or noted above at *PTJ*, 28:471–4, 477, 480–5, 520, 31:208. (3) Articles of agreement between John Henderson and Michie, 10 Mar. 1804. (4) Memorandum of agreement between Henderson and Michie, 10 Mar. 1804 (preceding two enclosures, witnessed by Martin Dawson, summarized above at note to Michie to TJ, 18 June 1812). (5) Charles L. Lewis to Michie, Buck Island, 22 Apr. 1807, stating that the recent removal of the boat allowing for communication across the Rivanna River was due to Craven Peyton's dislike of Michie, which grew out of "the transactions between you & John

Henderson respecting the mill seat at Milton, as he has often spoke against you Concerning that affair in the family"; asking Michie to have a small boat constructed, with Lewis promising to pay half the cost; and calling for secrecy until the vessel was actually "in the water." (6) Michie and Henderson's indenture of 12 June 1812, confirming their 10 Mar. 1804 contract, summarized above at note to Michie to TJ, 18 June 1812. (7) transcripts of letters between Michie, TJ, and Peyton, all of which have been printed or noted above at Michie to TJ, 18, 21, 27 June, 20 July 1812, 23 Apr., 30 May 1813, and TJ to Michie, 20, 22, 27 June 1812, 20 Apr., 30 May 1813.

John Harris (d. 1832) had been an Albemarle County justice of the peace since 1807. At the time of his death he owned seven large estates and more than two hundred slaves and was believed to be the county's wealthiest citizen (Woods, *Albemarle*, 220, 377, 402; Lay, *Architecture*, 48; DNA: RG 29, CS, Albemarle Co., 1830; Albemarle Co. Will Book 11:162–81). The JUDGE OF THE SAID SUPERIOR COURT OF CHANCERY was George Wythe. TJ OBTAINED LEAVE OF THIS COURT to rebuild his mill on 8 Oct. 1778 (ViU: TJP-LBJM). BY CLANDESTINE & FRAUDULENT BARGAINS . . . NEVER ACTUALLY PAID quoted from TJ's Bill of Complaint in *Jefferson v. Michie*, 16 June 1813. PENDENTE LITE: "during the proceeding or litigation; contingent on the outcome of the case" (*Black's Law Dictionary*). ATK: John Tracy Atkyns, *Reports of Cases Argued and Determined in the High Court of Chancery in the time of Lord Chancellor Hardwicke*, 3 vols. (Lon-

don, 1765–68; Sowerby, no. 1754). VES.: Francis Vesey, *Cases Argued and Determined in the High Court of Chancery in the time of Lord Chancellor Hardwicke, from the year 1746–7, to 1755*, 2 vols. (London, 1788; Sowerby, no. 1756). SUGD: Edward Burtenshaw Sugden, *A Practical Treatise of The Law of Vendors and Purchasers of Estates* (Philadelphia, 1807). The COURT OF DERNEAR RESORT (dernier or last resort) was the Virginia Court of Appeals. The EXTREMITY to which Peyton seemed disposed to press Michie in June 1812 was a duel (see note to Michie to TJ, 21 June 1812; Statement of Joseph Jones Monroe, 22 June 1812).

In October 1813 "the Complainant by his Counsel" replied "generally,—and the plea of the Defendant on motion of the Comp^t" was "set down for argument" (Tr in ViU: TJP-LBJM; in George Carr's hand; partially dated).

[1] Manuscript: "Complaimants."
[2] Manuscript: "Centry."
[3] Manuscript: "orphan."
[4] Manuscript: "wondered."
[5] Manuscript: "reproah."
[6] Manuscript: "their Cir Circumstances."
[7] Manuscript: "moties or the moties."
[8] The correct figure is 1,162¼.
[9] Manuscript: "recouses."
[10] Manuscript: "Conmencing."
[11] Manuscript: "gult."
[12] Thus in manuscript, with "hearing" or "trial" possibly omitted.
[13] Manuscript: "eather."
[14] Manuscript: "Canmot."
[15] Manuscript: "himmself."
[16] Thus in manuscript, with "inadvertent" possibly intended.
[17] Manuscript: "Circumistance."

To Charles Johnston

DEAR SIR   Poplar Forest Sep. 7. 13.

I am really afflicted by the use mr Griffin makes of my bonds, passing them off into the hands of those who are unacquainted with the views under which they were given, and particularly their dates arranged. when I was here last I told mr Griffin this bond could not be paid until the ensuing winter, & desired him not to dispose of it. altho' no promise was made, he was to take no measure till my present visit to this place, & I have been every day expecting he would call on me. however with these things you ought not to be troubled. it is not in my power to pay the bond now, and the funds out of which it is to be paid are now in my barn. they are to be got to Richmond & disposed of to enable me to pay it. I am sorry to be able to give you no better prospects, but any others would be delusive. with this apology to which I am constrained with reluctance, accept the assurance of my great esteem & respect   TH: JEFFERSON

PoC (ViU: TJP-ER); at foot of text: "Charles Johnston esq."; endorsed by TJ.

For the two notes or BONDS with which TJ settled his debt on 11 Sept. 1812 with Burgess Griffin, his former Poplar Forest overseer, see note to TJ to Patrick Gibson, 7 Mar. 1813. TJ did not pay his debt to Griffin until the spring of 1815 (*MB*, 2:1309). TJ had LAST visited Poplar Forest late in April and early in May 1813 (*MB*, 2:1288).

A missing letter from Johnston to TJ of 7 Sept. 1813 is recorded in SJL as received the same day.

From John Sen Trescot

HONOURED SIR   Charleston S° Carolina September 7th 1813.

The members of the Antiquarian Society from whom you received a letter through Dr Shecut their secretary, soliciting your junction with them, (having extended the views and changed the name of the society to that of the Literary and Philosophical society of South Carolina) have by a resolve ordered the above information to be communicated to your excellency; and your acceptance of Honoury membership in the society under it's present form be solicited.

I have the honour of subscribing myself your most Obdt & Humbl Servt   JOHN SEN TRESCOT M. D.
                                            Corresponds Secretary.

RC (MoSHi: TJC-BC); endorsed by TJ as received 19 Sept. 1813 and so recorded in SJL.

John Sen Trescot (d. ca. 1821), physician, was described as a resident of Charleston, South Carolina, when he entered the freshman class of Yale College in 1804. He did not graduate. In 1810 Trescot received a medical degree from the University of Pennsylvania, and he practiced medicine in Charleston for at least a decade starting by 1809. He was a founder of the Antiquarian Society of Charleston in 1813, and he sometimes served as an attending physician at the city dispensary. Trescot owned fourteen slaves in 1820 (*Catalogue Of the Officers and Students in Yale-College, November, 1804* [n.d.]; *Directory for the District of Charleston* [Charleston, 1809], 102; *Pennsylvania Magazine of History and Biography* 31 [1907]: 380–1; Charleston *City Gazette and Commercial Daily*

Advertiser, 5 Oct. 1810, 6 Oct. 1812, 25 Oct. 1821; Joseph Folker, *A Directory of the City and District of Charleston; and Stranger's Guide . . . for the year 1813* [Charleston, 1813], 78; *The Directory and Stranger's Guide, for the City of Charleston . . . For the Year 1819* [Charleston, 1819], 91; John L. E. W. Shecut, *Shecut's Medical and Philosophical Essays* [Charleston, 1819], 48; DNA: RG 29, CS, S.C., Charleston Co., 1820).

On this day Trescot sent a similar letter to President James Madison (Madison, *Papers, Pres. Ser.*, 6:601).

From Pierre Samuel Du Pont de Nemours

CHER ET RESPECTABLE AMI,   Paris. 8 Septembre 1813.

J'ai l'honneur de vous envoyer imprimé l'ouvrage dont je vous ai l'obligation, car c'est vous qui m'y avez fait Songer.

Il a Subi plusieurs corrections pour le rendre plus digne de vous et de votre Patrie.[1]

Je vous demande en retour, avec les plus vives instances,[2] un exemplaire de votre excellent <u>Commentaire Sur Montesquieu</u>. J'en avais commencé la traduction, et je ne Saurais l'achever par ce qu'il a fallu rendre à Mr Warden celui qu'il m'avait prêté.—Je n'ai ôsé le lui redemander. Il ne convenait pas que je le visse depuis qu'il S'est mal conduit[3] envers Madame Barlow qui a la tête d'un homme et le coeur d'un Ange, et qui approuvait[4] Son Neveu remplissant un devoir Sacré.[5]

Je ne Sais quand nous pourrons imprimer votre livre en Français; mais il faut qu'il y soit mis, et par un Homme dont le coeur et l'esprit Soient d'accord avec les vôtres.—notre Langue est encore plus universelle que l'anglaise; et les Peuples qui la parlent Sont ceux qui ont le plus besoin de vos instructions.

Envoyez moi donc ce livre précieux.[6] Faites moi ajouter cette reconnaissance à toute celle que je vous dois et à l'attachement aussi tendre que respectueux que je vous ai voué pour la vie.

DUPONT (DE NEMOURS)

EDITORS' TRANSLATION

DEAR AND RESPECTABLE FRIEND,   Paris. 8 September 1813.

I have the honor of sending you a printed copy of a work for which I am obliged to you, because you inspired me to write it.

It has undergone several revisions to make it more worthy of you and your country.

In return I ask you very earnestly for a copy of your excellent <u>Commentary on Montesquieu</u>. I had begun to translate it but was unable to finish it before

I had to return Mr. Warden's copy to him.—I did not dare ask him for it again. I would have thought it improper to see him again after he behaved badly toward Mrs. Barlow, who has the head of a man and the heart of an angel, and who approved of her nephew fulfilling a sacred duty.

I do not know when we will be able to print a French translation of your book, but it must be done, and by a man whose heart and mind are in tune with yours.—Our language is in even more universal use than English; and the people who speak it are the ones most in need of your instruction.

Send me, therefore, this precious book. Allow me to add this favor to all of my other debts to you and to the tender and respectful attachment which I have dedicated to you for the rest of my life.

DuPont (de nemours)

RC (Gallery of History, Las Vegas, 1994); dateline at foot of text; at head of text: "a Monsieur Jefferson"; mistakenly endorsed by TJ as a letter of 18 Sept. 1813 received 14 Dec. 1813 and so recorded in SJL. Dft (DeGH: Pierre Samuel Du Pont de Nemours Papers, Winterthur Manuscripts); unsigned; containing substantial differences from the RC, only the most important of which are noted below. Tr (DeGH: Eleuthere Smith Papers, Winterthur Manuscripts); wording generally follows Dft. Translation by Dr. Genevieve Moene. Enclosure: Du Pont, *Sur l'éducation nationale dans les États-Unis d'Amérique* (Paris, 1812; Poor, *Jefferson's Library*, 5 [nos. 207, 209–10]).

Following Joel Barlow's death in December 1812, the American chargé d'affaires at Paris, David Bailie WARDEN, attempted to assume his duties on an interim basis and began styling himself United States consul general. Ruth Baldwin BARLOW, however, refused to turn her husband's official papers over to him and tried unsuccessfully to have her nephew Thomas Barlow appointed instead, actions which led to considerable friction between the two parties. As United States minister plenipotentiary to France, William H. Crawford removed Warden from office in June 1814, at least in part because of his actions with respect to the Barlows (Francis C. Haber, *David Bailie Warden, A Bibliographical Sketch of America's Cultural Ambassador in France, 1804–1845* [1954], 16–8; Madison, *Papers, Pres. Ser.*, 6:5, 87–90; Clara Baldwin to Dolley Madison, 16 Feb. 1813

[ViU]; Providence *Rhode-Island American, and General Advertiser*, 16 Apr. 1813).

[1] Dft here adds "Mr Paterson m'avait promis de le traduire. Je voudrais qu'il ne l'est pas achevé ou publié avant que cette édition française lui Soit parvenue" ("Mr. Patterson promised me that he would translate it. I intended that he would not perfect or publish it before this French edition reached him").

[2] Preceding five words not in Tr.

[3] Dft omits "mal" before this word and then adds "avec imprudence, de raison et entier défaut de respects" ("with imprudence of mind and a complete lack of respect").

[4] Word replaced in Dft with "défendait les droits de la légation americaine en Soutenant" ("defended the rights of the American legation in supporting").

[5] Preceding four words replaced in Dft with "Secretaire de cette légation chargé des chiffres dans le devoir qu'il avait de ne les remettre qu'au nouveau ministre plenipotentiaire envoyé par M^r le President" ("fulfilling his responsibility as secretary of this legation in charge of ciphers by remitting them to no one but the new minister plenipotentiary sent by the president").

[6] Dft here adds "par duplicata, par triplicata, dans les paquets, de votre gouvernement à votre digne Ambassadeur jusqu'à ce que je vous en aies accusé la reception" ("in duplicate, triplicate, and in the packages sent by your government to your worthy ambassador, until I have acknowledged the receipt of it to you").

To Henry Flood

Dear Sir   Poplar Forest Sep. 8. 13.

I am very much indebted to you for helping my cart on with the loan of a wheel. my people set out this morning and I hope will return it safe. but I must beg the additional favor of you to have their broken one repaired. I think there is a wheelwright at your neighbor Swiney's. in the mean time they will have to ask quarters of you. according to present appearances I think I can get away on Saturday morning, ask a dinner of you, and a bed at mr Noah Flood's. accept the assurance of my great esteem & respect.   Th: Jefferson

PoC (MHi); at foot of text: "Maj^r Henry Flood"; endorsed by TJ.

TJ actually left Poplar Forest on Sunday, 12 Sept. 1813, not SATURDAY. He dined at Henry Flood's tavern, where he settled an earlier account and paid $9.62½ "for having cart wheels mended" before traveling on to NOAH FLOOD'S establishment (MB, 2:1293).

Memorandum to Jeremiah A. Goodman

1813. Sep. 8.

Mr Goodman's crop for the next year 1814. will be as follows.

Corn in McDaniel's field; but as this turns out to be but 50. acres, we must add other grounds to it; and there are none but what belong to some other field, except those over the S. Tomahawk,[1] & above the lower corn field. we must of necessity then give the tobacco ground, & the stubble ground there to corn, and put the upper corn grounds into oats to help out. some of the strongest spots in the Fork field may be in corn.

Peas in the Fork field.

wheat in the Tomahawk Cornfield and in the Ridge field.

tobacco, in such meadow grounds on S. Tomahawk as can be cleaned up, and in a new clearing to be made on the S. side of the S. Tomahawk. I should be glad to have 80. thousand tob° hills tended. the clearing to extend ¼ mile from the branch[2]

sow from half an acre to an acre in hemp.

sow timothy in the meadow ground ready for it, this month.

in all your fields of corn or small grain, reserve the galled & poor spots and put peas into them.

let the ox-cart be employed in winter in carting out any manure you may have, and straw. generally speaking this ought to be put on the galled & poor places of the field turned out to rest for 2. years, because that would give time for the straw to rot. but as that would be, for the present year, the Belted field which needs it least, I would give it to the galled & poor spots of the Ridge field, which needs it most, and I would leave them without putting any thing into them.

take for your own use one eighth of the peach or apple brandy which will be made, & put the rest into the cellar of the house.

let the people have hereafter a fixed allowance of salt; to wit, give to their bread maker a pint a month for each grown negro to put into their bread; and give besides to each grown negro a pint a month for their snaps, cymlins & other uses. this will be a quart a month for every grown negro.

the people have asked for a little flour for their labors in harvest. give half a peck to each grown person.

I accept mr Mitchell's terms for grinding my flour this year. let all the wheat be delivered to him in the course of this & the next month, and sent down in all October & November to Richmond.[3]

MS (NN: George Arents Tobacco Collection); written entirely in TJ's hand on one side of a single sheet. Not recorded in SJL.

GALLED: "eroded" (*OED*).

TJ evidently prepared this memorandum to guide Goodman in his management of the Tomahawk Plantation at Poplar Forest. A missing letter from Goodman to TJ of 9 Sept. 1813 is recorded in SJL as received 14 Oct. 1813 from Poplar Forest.

[1] Manuscript: "Tomohawk."

[2] Preceding nine words added in a different ink.

[3] Paragraph apparently added at a different sitting.

To Randolph Jefferson

DEAR BROTHER   Poplar Forest Sep. 8. 13.

The cart sets out this morning with your spinning Jenny in perfect order, and will deliver it I hope safe from accident. according to present appearances I may leave this on Saturday morning, and if in time to get to Noah Flood's I may be with you to dinner on Sunday,[1] but if I get only to Henry Flood's I shall dine at Gibson's & be with you on Sunday evening; and it is yet possible I may be detained here till Sunday. my best affections to my sister & yourself.

TH: JEFFERSON

PoC (ViU: TJP-CC); at foot of text: "Randolph Jefferson esq."; endorsed by TJ.

During his return trip to Monticello from Poplar Forest, TJ had breakfast on 13 Sept. 1813 at GIBSON'S ordinary in northern Buckingham County before proceeding to Randolph Jefferson's Snowden estate for what turned out to be his last visit to his brother's home (*MB*, 2:1187n, 1293; TJ's Deposition Regarding Randolph Jefferson's Estate, 15 Sept. 1815). MY SISTER: TJ's sister-in-law Mitchie Pryor Jefferson.

[1] Preceding two words interlined.

To Joseph Slaughter

DEAR SIR   Poplar Forest Sep. 8. 13.

By the help of your survey, I am now enabled to lay off my fields to my mind. but there are 3. or 4. dividing lines to be run with a compass & chain. I stay to see this done, in the hope that the day after you get[1] back from Albemarle court, you will be so good as to come & run them for me. it will take a few hours only, and the moment they are run, so that my overseers may know where to begin their fallows, I depart. Accept the assurance of my respect & esteem

TH: JEFFERSON

PoC (MHi); at foot of text: "Cap[t] Slaughter"; endorsed by TJ.

At some point during the previous year TJ composed a memorandum apparently asking Slaughter to SURVEY "Tomahawk branch from where the Ridge branch enters it to where it crosses my line below & recieves a small branch from the South. Survey the Ridge branch, Middle branch, Machine branch, Prize branch, and a branch below that, without a name, from where they enter Tomahawk to their headsprings, & from each head spring run to the Lynchburg road, & mark the course & distance to it. let the offset from the spring of the Machine branch to the road, strike it at the barn. from different points of the survey, take the bearing of the dwelling house, that we may know the position of that with respect to the fields the ground between the Ridge branch & Machine branch is to be divided into two equal fields by a line or lines from Tomahawk up. the back line of the cleared lands, from where the present road crosses the Machine branch, North-Eastwardly to the North Easternmost corner of what is called the 3. years old ground, & then down along the Eastern side of the same cleared land to Tomahawk.

the quantity of open land between branch & branch to be ascertained, as these branches are to be the divisions of fields.

the whole on a scale of 10. po. to $\frac{1}{4}$ of an Inch

when at the place where Tomahawk crosses my line, fix the position of the county line by a large marked poplar near there which Ben Johnson shewed me" (MS in ViU: TJP, TB [Thurlow-Berkeley] no. 1136 [532-06]; entirely in TJ's hand; undated; with drawing by TJ showing the Mountain and Lynchburg roads, Tomahawk Creek and the branches flowing into it, and a part of Poplar Forest's eastern boundary). Slaughter's surviving field notes are located on the back of a letter he had written to an unidentified correspondent on 10 Nov. 1812 (ViU: TJP, TB 1136 [532-n1]). The completed survey, which is in Slaughter's hand and signed by him, contains notes by TJ giving the names of several streams and eight cultivated fields, the acreage of various parts of Tomahawk plantation, the date "Septemb. 1813," and the scale of the map as "40. po. to the inch." In addition to depicting the six fields present on Jefferson's Map of Tomahawk plantation published as an illustration to Vol. 4, Slaughter's survey reveals three new fields on the north branch of Tomahawk Creek: an 81½-acre Upper field, a 60-acre Middle field, and an 80-acre Lower field (MS in ViU: TJP-ER).

[1] TJ here canceled "here."

From Isaac Doolittle

SIR—   Washington 11th Septr 1813

I have the honor to enclose herewith two letters that I was charged with in France—one of which from the respectable Mr Dupont de Nemours—and which a long detention in England, as a prisoner of War has prevented me from forwarding sooner;

At the same time I take the liberty to request to be informed whether the Eloge Historique de François Péron—which Mr Barnet—American Consul for Havre de Grace addressed to you some time since—came safe to hand—

and remain—Sir,

With the most profound respect your most obedient Servant

I, DOOLITTLE—
of New Haven—

RC (MHi); at foot of text: "Thomas Jefferson late President of the United States Monticello"; endorsed by TJ as received 17 Sept. 1813 and so recorded in SJL. Enclosures: (1) Pierre Samuel Du Pont de Nemours to TJ, 10 Feb. 1813. (2) Tadeusz Kosciuszko to TJ, 1 Dec. 1812, noted below at TJ to John Barnes, 18 Sept. 1813.

Isaac Doolittle (1784–1852) was a Connecticut native who was detained in France by 1809 and lived there off and on for more than a decade. During his sojourn in Paris he was befriended by Isaac Cox Barnet, United States minister plenipotentiary Joel Barlow, and Pierre Samuel Du Pont de Nemours. Doolittle lived with Barnet, received instruction in the useful arts from Barlow and, with Du Pont's assistance, joined the Société d'Encouragement pour l'Industrie Nationale. He left Europe carrying a packet of American consular dispatches in February 1813 and succeeded in concealing and eventually delivering them despite being captured by a British warship and held for more than three months. Doolittle soon returned to Paris and worked for a time as a clerk under Barnet at the United States consulate, but he failed in two attempts to obtain American consulships elsewhere in France. His *Manuel de l'ingénieur mécanicien constructeur de machines a vapeur* (Paris, 1821) was a translation of Oliver Evans, *The Abortion of the Young Steam Engineer's Guide* (Philadelphia, 1805). Shortly after Doolittle's version came out he moved to New York City, where he helped introduce the art of lithography into the United States. From the end of 1822 to about 1846, he was manager of the Bennington Iron-Works in Vermont, where he also wrote for the *American Journal of Science and Arts* and obtained at least three patents. Doolittle died in Rochester, New York (William Frederick Doolittle, *The Doolittle Family in America* [1901–08], 1:303–4; Greville Bathe and Dorothy Bathe, *Jacob Perkins: His Inventions, His Times, & His Contemporaries* [1943],

139–41; New Haven *Connecticut Herald*, 15 Aug. 1809; Madison, *Papers, Pres. Ser.*, 6:6–7, 613; Doolittle to James Monroe, 9 Sept. 1814 [DNA: RG 59, LAR, 1809–17]; Benjamin Silliman to John Quincy Adams, 30 July 1819 [DNA: RG 59, LAR, 1817–25]; Edmund Burke, comp., *List of Patents for Inventions and Designs, issued by the United States, from 1790 to 1847* [1847], 124, 163, 313; DNA: RG 29, CS, N.Y., Rochester, 1850).

HAVRE DE GRACE: Le Havre, France.

To John Wayles Eppes

DEAR SIR   Poplar Forest Sep. 11. 1813.

I turn with great reluctance from the functions of a private citizen[1] to matters of state. the swaggering on deck, as a passenger, is so much more pleasant than clambering the ropes as a seaman, & my confidence in the skill and activity of those employed to work the vessel is so entire, that I notice nothing, en passant, but how smoothly she moves. yet I avail myself of the leisure which a visit to this place procures me, to revolve again in my mind the subject of my former letter; & in compliance with the request of yours of   to add some further thoughts on it. tho' intended as only supplemental to that, I may fall into repetitions, not having that with me, nor paper or book of any sort, to supply the default of a memory on the wane.[2]

The objects of finance in the US. have hitherto been very simple; merely to provide for the support of the government, on it's peace establishment, and to pay the debt contracted in the revolutionary war; a war which will be sanctioned by the approbation of posterity thro' all future ages. the means provided for these objects were ample; & resting on a consumption which little affected the poor, may be said to have been sensibly felt by none. the fondest wish of my heart ever was that the surplus[3] portion of these taxes, destined for the paiment of that debt, should, when that object was accomplished, be continued, by annual or biennial[4] re-enactments, and applied, in time of peace, to the improvement of our country by canals, roads, and useful institutions, literary or others, and, in time of war, to the maintenance of the war. and I believe that, keeping the civil list within proper bounds, the surplus[5] would have been sufficient for any war, administered with integrity & judgment.[6] for authority to apply the surplus to objects of improvement, an amendment of the constitution would have been necessary.[7] I have said that the taxes should be continued by annual or biennial re-enactments; because a constant hold, by the nation, of the strings of the public purse, is a salutary restraint, from which an honest government ought not to wish, nor a corrupt one to be permitted, to be free. no tax should ever be yielded for a longer term than that of the Congress granting it, except when pledged for the reimbursement of a loan.[8] on this system, the standing income being once liberated from the revolutionary debt, no future loan, nor future tax, would ever become necessary; and wars would no otherwise affect our pecuniary interests, than by suspending the improvements belonging to a state of peace.[9] this happy consummation would have been achieved by another eight years administration, conducted by mr Madison, and executed in it's financial department, by mr Gallatin, could peace[10] have been so long preserved. so enviable a[11] state, in prospect for our country, induced me to temporise, and to bear with national wrongs which, under no other prospect, ought ever to have been unresented, or unresisted. my hope was that, by giving time for reflection, and retraction of injury, a sound calculation of their own interests would induce the aggressing nations to redeem their own characters by a return to the practice of right. but our lot happens to have been cast in an age when two nations to whom circumstances have given a temporary superiority over others, the one by land, the other by sea,[12] throwing off all restraints of morality, all pride of[13] national character, forgetting the mutability of fortune, and the inevitable doom which the laws of nature pronounce against departure from justice, individual or national,[14] have dared to treat her reclamations with derision, and to[15] set up force instead of reason, as the umpire of nations. degrading themselves thus from the character of lawful societies, into lawless bands of robbers and pirates, they are abusing their brief ascendancy by desolating[16] the world with blood & rapine. against such a banditti, war had become[17] less ruinous than peace; for their peace was a war on one side only. on the final and formal declarations of England therefore, that she never would repeal her orders of council as to us,[18] until those of France should be repealed as to other nations as well as us, and that no practicable arrangement against her impressment of our seamen could be proposed or devised, war was justly declared, and ought to have been declared. this change of condition has clouded[19] our prospects of liberation from debt, and of being able to carry on a war without new loans or taxes. but altho' deferred, these prospects are not desperate. we should keep for ever in view the state of 1817. towards which we were advancing, and consider it as that which we must attain. let the old funds continue appropriated to the civil list & revolutionary debt, and the reversion of the surplus to improvement during peace; and let us take up this war as a separate business, for which substantive, and distinct provision is to be made.

That we are bound to defray it's expences within our own time and unauthorised to burthen posterity with them, I suppose to have been proved in my former letter. I will place the question nevertheless in one additional point of view. the former regarded their independant right over the earth; this over their own persons.[20] there have existed nations, & civilised & learned nations who have thought that a father had a right to sell his child as a slave, in perpetuity; that he could alienate his body & industry conjointly, and a fortiori his industry separately; and consume it's fruits himself. a nation asserting this Saticide[21] right might well suppose they could burthen with public as well as private debt, their 'nati natorum, et qui nascentur ab illis.' but we, in this age, and in this country especially, are advanced beyond these notions of natural law. we acknolege that our children are born free; that that freedom is the gift of nature, and not of him who begot them; that tho' under our care during infancy, and therefore of necessity under a duly tempered authority, that care is confided to us to be exercised for the preservation & good of the child only; and his labours during youth are given as a retribution for the charges of infancy. as he was never the property of his father, so, when adult, he is sui juris, entitled himself to the use of his own limbs, and the fruits of his own exertions. so far we are advanced, without mind enough it seems,[22] to take the whole step. we believe, or we act as if we believed, that altho' an individual father cannot alienate the labor of his son, the aggregate body of fathers may alienate the labors of all their sons, & of their posterity, in the aggregate, and oblige them to pay for all the enterprises, just or unjust, profitable or ruinous, into which our vices, our passions, or our personal interests may lead us. but I trust that this proposition needs only to be looked at by an American, to be seen in it's true point of view; and that we shall all consider ourselves unauthorised to saddle posterity with our debts, & morally bound to pay them ourselves, & consequently within what may be deemed the period of a generation, or the life of[23] the Majority. in my former letter, I supposed this to be a little over[24] 20. years. we must raise then ourselves the money for this war, either by taxes within the year, or by loans; and if by loans, we must repay them ourselves; proscribing for ever the English practice of perpetual funding; the ruinous consequences of which, putting right out of question, should be a sufficient warning to a considerate nation, to avoid the example.

The raising money by Tontine, more practised on the continent of Europe than in England, is liable to the same objection, of encroachment on the independant rights of posterity; because the annuities not expiring gradatim; with the lives on which they rest, but all on the death of the last survivor only, they will of course over-pass the term of a generation; and the more probably as the subjects, on whose lives the annuities depend, are generally chosen of the ages, constitutions, & occupations, most favorable to long life.

Annuities for single lives are also beyond our powers; because the single life may pass the term of a generation. this last practice is objectionable too, as encoraging celibacy, and the disherison of heirs.[25]

Of the modes which are within the limits of right, that of raising, within the year, it's whole expences, by taxation, might be beyond the abilities of our citizens to bear. it is moreover generally desirable that the public contributions should be as uniform as practicable, from year to year,[26] that our habits of industry & of expence, may become adapted to them; and that they may be duly digested, & incorporated with our annual economy.

There remains then for us but the method[27] of limited anticipation; the laying taxes for a term of years, within that of our right, which may be sold for a present sum, equal to the expences of the year; in other words, to obtain a loan, equal to the expences of the year, laying a tax adequate to it's interest, & to such a surplus as will reimburse, by growing instalments, the whole principal within the term. this is in fact what has been called raising money on the sale of annuities for years. in this way, a new loan, & of course a new tax is requisite every year, during the continuance of the war; & should that be so long as to produce an accumulation of tax beyond our ability, in time of war, the resource would be an enactment of the taxes, requisite to ensure good terms, by securing the lender, with a suspension of the paiment of instalments of principal, & perhaps of interest also, until the restoration of peace. this method of anticipating our taxes, or of borrowing on annuities for years, ensures repaiment to the lender, guards the rights of posterity, prevents a perpetual alienation of the public contributions, & consequent destitution of every resource, even for the ordinary support of government. the public expences of England, during the present reign, have amounted to the fee simple value of the whole island. if it's whole soil could be sold, farm by farm, for it's present market price, it would not defray the cost of governing it, during the reign of the present king, as managed by him.[28] ought not then the right of each successive generation to be guarantied against the dissipations & corruptions of those preceding by a fundamental provision in our constitution? and, if that has not been made, does it exist the less; there being between generation

& generation, as between nation & nation, no other law than that of nature? and is it the less dishonest to do what is wrong, because not expressly prohibited by written law? let us hope that our moral principles are not yet in that stage of degeneracy; and that in instituting[29] the system of finance to be hereafter pursued, we shall adopt the only safe, the only lawful & honest one, of borrowing on such short terms of reimbursement of interest & principal, as will fall within the accomplishment of our own lives.[30]

The question will be asked, and ought to be looked at, what is to be the resource, if loans cannot be obtained? there is but one. 'Carthago delenda est.' Bank-paper must be suppressed, and the circulating medium must be restored to the nation to whom it belongs. it is the only fund on which they can rely for loans; it is the only resource which can never fail them; and it is an abundant one for every necessary purpose. treasury bills, bottomed on taxes, bearing, or not bearing interest, as may be found necessary, thrown into circulation, will take the place of so much gold & silver, which last, when crouded,[31] will find an efflux into other countries, and thus keep the quantum of medium at it's salutary level. let banks continue if they please; but let them discount for cash alone, or for treasury notes. they discount for cash alone[32] in every other country on earth, except Great Britain, &, her too often unfortunate copyist, the US. if taken in time, they may be rectified by degrees, & without injustice; but if let alone till the alternative forces itself on us, of submission to the enemy for want of funds,[33] or the suppression of bank paper, either by law, or by a convulsion, we cannot foresee how it will end.

The remaining questions are Mathematical only. how are the taxes & the time of their continuance, to be proportioned to the Sum borrowed, & the stipulated Interest?

The Rate of interest will depend on the state of the money market; & the duration of the tax on the will of the legislature. let us suppose that (to keep the taxes as low as possible) they adopt the term of 20. years for reimbursement, which we call their maximum; & let the interest they last gave of $7\frac{1}{2}$ p.c. be that which they must expect to give. the problem then will stand in this form. Given the Sum borrowed (which call s.) a million of dollars for example: the rate of interest .075 or $\frac{75}{1000}$ (call it r − 1.) & the duration of the annuity or tax, 20. years (= t.) what will be (a) the annuity or tax, which will reimburse principal & interest within the given term? this problem, laborious, & barely practicable to common arithmetic, is readily enough solved Algebraically, &[34] with the aid of Logarithms.

The theorem applied to the case is $a = \dfrac{\overline{r - 1} \times s}{1 - \frac{1}{r}t}$ the solution of which gives

a = 98,684.2 D; nearly 100,000.D. or $\frac{1}{10}$ of the Sum borrowed.

It may be satisfactory to see stated in figures the yearly progression of reimbursement of the million of Dollars, & their interest at $7\frac{1}{2}$ p.c. effected by the regular paiment of €M D. annually. it will be as follows.[35]

	D			D
Borrowed	1,000,000.			
balance after 1st paimt	975,000	balance after 11th paiment	594,800.
2d	948,125.	12th	539,410.
3d	919,234.	13th	479,866.
4th	888,177.	14th	415,850.
5th	854,790.	15th	347,039.
6th	818,900.	16th	273,068.
7th	780,318	17th	193,548.
8th	738,841	18th	108,064.
9th	694,254.	19th	16,169.
10th	646,324.		

If we are curious to know the effect of the same annual sum on loans at lower rates of interest, the following process will give it.

from the Log. of a. subtract the Log. $\overline{r - 1}$.

and from the N° of the remaining Logarithm, subtract s.

then subtract the Log. of this last remainder

from the difference between the Log. a. & Log. $\overline{r - 1}$. as found before.

divide the remainder by Log. r. the Quotient will be t.

It will be found thus that €M D. will reimburse a million

	years	D
at $7\frac{1}{2}$ p.c. interest in	19.17. costing in the whole	1,917,000.
7.	17.82	1,782,000.
$6\frac{1}{2}$	16.67	1,667,000.
6.	15.72	1,572,000.
$5\frac{1}{2}$	14.91	1,491,000.
5.	14.2	1,420,000.[36]
0.	10.	1,000,000.

by comparing the 1st & the last of these articles, we see that if the US. were in possession of the circulating medium, as they ought to be, they could redeem what they could borrow from that, dollar for dollar, & in 10. annual instalments; whereas, the usurpation of that fund by bank paper obliging them to borrow elsewhere at $7\frac{1}{2}$ p.c. two dollars are required to reimburse one. so that it is literally true that the toleration of banks of paper-discount costs the US. one half their war-taxes; or in other words, doubles the expences of every war. now think, but for a moment, what a change of condition that would[37] be which should save half our war-expences, require but half the taxes, and enthral us with debt but half the time.

Two loans having been authorised, of 16. and $7\frac{1}{2}$ millions, they will require for their due reimbursement 2,350,000.D. of the 3. millions expected from the taxes lately imposed. when the produce shall be known of the several items of these taxes, such of them as will make up this sum should be selected, appropriated & pledged for the reimbursement of these loans. the balance of 650,000.D. will be a provision for $6\frac{1}{2}$ millions of the loan of the next year. and in all future loans, I would consider it as a rule, never to be departed from, to lay a tax of $\frac{1}{10}$, and pledge it for the reimbursement.[38]

In the preceding calculations, no account is taken of the increasing population of the US. which we know to be in a compound ratio of more than 3. p.c. per annum; nor of the increase of wealth, proved to be in a higher ratio by the increasing productiveness of the imposts on consumption. we shall be safe therefore in considering every tax as growing at the rate of 3. p.c. compound ratio annually. I say, <u>every tax</u>; for as to those on consumption, the fact is known; & the same growth will be found in the value of real estate, if valued annually; or, which would be better, 3. p.c. might[39] be assumed by the law as the average increase, and an addition of $\frac{1}{33}$ of the tax paid the preceding year, be annually called for. supposing then a tax laid which would[40] bring in 100,000.D. at the time it is laid, & that it increases annually at the rate of 3. p.c. compound, it's important effect may be seen in the following statement.

it yields the	& reduces the D	it yields the D	& reduces D
1st year 103,000,	Milln to 972,000.	9th year 130,470	it to 515,382
2d 106,090	938,810	10th 134,390	419,646.
3d 109,273.	899,947.	11th 138,420.	312,699
4th 112,550.	854,896.	12th 142,580.	193,517.
5th 115,920.	803,093.	13th 146,850.	61,181
6th 119,410.	743,915.	14th 151,260. overpays	85,491.
7th 122,990.	676,719.	1,759,883.	
8th 126,680.	600,793.		
915,913			

this estimate supposes a million borrowed at $7\frac{1}{2}$ p.c. but, if obtained from the circulation without interest, it would be reimbursed within

8. years 8 months, instead of 14. years, or of 20. years, on our first estimate.[41]

But this view being in prospect only, should not affect the quantum of tax which the former calculation pronounces necessary. our creditors have a right to certainty, & to consider these political speculations as make-weights only to that, & at our risk, not theirs.[42] to us belongs only the comfort of hoping an earlier liberation than that calculation holds out; and the right of providing expressly that the tax hypothecated shall cease so soon as the debt it secures shall be actually reimbursed;[43] and I will add that to us belongs also the regret that improvident legislators should have exposed us to a 20. years thraldom of debts & taxes, for the necessary defence of our country, where the same contributions would have liberated us in 8. or 9. years; or have reduced us perhaps to an abandonment of our rights, by their abandonment of the only resource which could have ensured their maintenance.

I omit many considerations of detail, because they will occur to yourself, & my letter is too long already. I can refer you to no book as treating of this subject fully, & suitably to our circumstances. Smith gives the history of the public debt of England, & some views adapted to that, & Dr Price, in his book on annuities, has given a valuable chapter on the effect of a sinking fund. but our business being to make every loan-tax a sinking fund for itself, no general one will be wanting; and if my confidence is well founded that our original impost, when freed[44] from the revolutionary debt, will suffice to embellish & improve our country in peace, & defend it in war, the present may be the only occasion of perplexing ourselves with sinking funds.

Should the injunctions under which I laid you, as to my former letter, restrain any useful purpose to which you could apply it, I remove them; preferring public benefit to all personal considerations. my original disapprobation of bank circulating-paper is not unknown, nor have I since[45] observed any effects either on the morals, or fortunes of our citizens, which are any counterbalance[46] for the public evils produced. and a thoro' conviction that, if this war continues, that circulation must be suppressed, or the government shaken to it's foundation by the weight of taxes, & impracticability to raise funds on them,[47] renders duty to that paramount to the love of ease & quiet.

When I was here in May last, I left it without knowing that Francis was at school in this neighborhood. as soon as I returned on the present occasion, I sent for him; but his tutor informed me he was gone on a visit to you. I shall hope permission for him always to see me, on my visits to this place, which are three or four times a year.— ever affectionately Yours   TH: JEFFERSON

RC (ViU: TJP); at foot of first page: "Mr Eppes." PoC (DLC); lacking closing and signature, with the latter supplied by an unidentified hand. 2d Dft (DLC: TJ Papers, 199:35435–8, 35440); lacking closing and with signature supplied by an unidentified hand. 1st Dft (DLC: TJ Papers, 199:35439); fragment consisting of two pages from middle of letter. Tr (ViU: TJP-Ca, TB [Thurlow-Berkeley] no. 1299); consisting of extracts in Joseph C. Cabell's hand of this letter and of TJ to Eppes, 24 June, 6 Nov. 1813. Enclosed in TJ to James Monroe, 28 Sept. 1813, 3 Aug. 1814, Monroe to TJ, 1 Oct. 1813, 26 Apr. 1815, TJ to Cabell, 17 Jan. 1814, and Cabell to TJ, 6 Mar. 1814.

France enjoyed a TEMPORARY SUPERIORITY on land, while Great Britain controlled the sea. TJ used SATICIDE, a term not in *OED* or *Black's Law Dictionary*, on at least one other occasion to denote the murder of a child by a parent (*PTJ*, 2:494n). NATI NATORUM, ET QUI NASCENTUR AB ILLIS: "children's children and their race that shall be born of them," from Virgil, *Aeneid*, 3.98 (Fairclough, *Virgil*, 1:378–9). GRADATIM: "step by step; gradually" (*OED*). DISHERISON: "disinheritance" (*OED*). The Roman senator Marcus Cato supposedly exclaimed CARTHAGO DELENDA EST ("Carthage must be destroyed") after all of his votes (Plutarch, *Cato*, book 27, in *Plutarch's Lives*, trans. Bernadotte Perrin, Loeb Classical Library [1914–26; repr. 1968], 2:382–3; Charles E. Little, "The Authenticity and Form of Cato's Saying 'Carthago Delenda Est,'" *Classical Journal* 29 [1934]: 429–35). TJ used a method for calculating the time necessary for paying off a debt at varying rates of interest with the AID OF LOGARITHMS, a technique that he had gleaned from a newspaper in 1793 (Philadelphia *General Advertiser*, 2 Mar. 1793; *PTJ*, 25:465–7). Congress authorized borrowing $7\frac{1}{2}$ MILLIONS on 2 Aug. 1813 (*U.S. Statutes at Large*, 3:75–7). Adam Smith

included a chapter on the PUBLIC DEBT OF ENGLAND in the fifth book of his *Inquiry into the Nature and Causes of the Wealth of Nations*, 3d ed. (London, 1784; Sowerby, no. 3546), 3:394–465, while a chapter on the EFFECT OF A SINKING FUND appeared in Richard Price, *Observations on Reversionary Payments; on Schemes for providing Annuities for Widows, and for Persons in Old Age . . . and on The National Debt*, 2d ed. (London, 1772; Sowerby, no. 3688), 135–65. Francis Eppes's TUTOR was Thomas A. Holcombe.

[1] Preceding seven words interlined in 2d Dft.

[2] Letter to this point, including dateline and salutation, added in left margin of 2d Dft in place of "Dear Sir." Tr begins here.

[3] Word interlined in 2d Dft.

[4] Preceding two words interlined in 2d Dft.

[5] Preceding nine words interlined in 2d Dft in place of "it."

[6] Word interlined in place of "wisdom" in 2d Dft.

[7] Tr ends here with "<*I ha*> &^{c} &^{c}."

[8] Sentence interlined in 2d Dft. Tr resumes here.

[9] Tr ends here with comment that "After condemning perpetual annuities, long annuities, Tontines, and annuities for lives, as <*being*> surpassing the term of 19 years, he proceeds."

[10] Word interlined in 2d Dft in place of "war."

[11] Preceding three words interlined in 2d Dft in place of "and this beatific."

[12] From "two nations" to this point reworked in 2d Dft from "two of the most powerful nations of the world, abusing their force and."

[13] Reworked in 2d Dft from "all the bonds of morality, and all regard to."

[14] Preceding three words interlined in 2d Dft.

[15] In 2d Dft TJ here canceled "substitute."

[16] Preceding six words interlined in 2d Dft in place of "ravaging."

[17] In 2d Dft TJ here canceled "preferable."

[18] Preceding three words interlined in 2d Dft.

[19] Preceding two words interlined in 2d Dft in place of "therefore has changed <*disappointed*>."

[20] Sentence interlined in 2d Dft.

[21] Word interlined in 2d Dft in place of "Cannibal."

[22] Preceding two words interlined in 2d Dft.

[23] Reworked in 2d Dft from "the period of life for."

[24] In PoC TJ here keyed a note to the foot of the page: "a lapse of memory, not having the letter to recur to."

[25] Tr resumes here.

[26] Preceding four words interlined in 2d Dft.

[27] Tr: "practice."

[28] Tr ends here with "&c &c."

[29] Word interlined in 2d Dft in place of "setting out in."

[30] Tr resumes here.

[31] Word interlined in 2d Dft in place of "overcharged."

[32] Preceding nine words interlined in 2d Dft in place of "as is the case."

[33] Preceding four words interlined in 2d Dft.

[34] Preceding two words interlined in 2d Dft.

[35] 1st Dft begins here, with the sums in the following table carried to two decimal places. To the right of the table in 1st Dft, instead of the general description of the method given in 2d Dft and RC, TJ included the following example:
"Formula.

from the Log. of annual sum 10.		1.0000000
subtract Log of the ratio − 1 = .075		8.8750613
from the N° of this Log.	133.33	2.1249387
subtract am^t of loan	100.	
& subtract Log. of y^e rem^r	33.33	1.5228353
divide y^t rem^r by Log. 1.075 to wit 0.0314085		0.6021034

the quotient 19.17 is the N° of years requis^{te} for redemptn."

[36] 1st Dft: "1,420,600." 1st Dft ends here, with order of preceding two tables the reverse of sequence in 2d Dft and RC.

[37] TJ here canceled "produce."

[38] 1st Dft resumes here.

[39] 1st Dft: "may."

[40] Word interlined in 1st Dft in place of "will."

[41] 1st Dft ends here.

[42] Tr ends here.

[43] In 2d Dft TJ initially ended the paragraph here before adding remainder to end of line and in left margin.

[44] Word interlined in 2d Dft in place of "liberated."

[45] Word interlined in 2d Dft.

[46] Reworked from "counterpoise" in 2d Dft.

[47] Preceding seven words interlined in 2d Dft.

From John Adams

DEAR SIR   Quincy Sept: 14. 1813

I owe you a thousand thanks for your favour of Aug. 22 and its Enclosures, and for Dr Priestley's "Doctrines of heathen Philosophy compared with those of Revelation." your Letter to Dr Rush, and the Syllabus, I return inclosed with this, according to your Injunction; though with great reluctance. May I beg a copy of both? They will do you no harm: me and others much good. I hope you will pursue your plan; for I am confident you will produce a Work much more valuable than Priestleys; tho' that is curious and considering the expiring powers with which it was written, admirable.

The Bill in Parliament for the relief of Antitrinitarians is a great Event; and will form an Epoch in Ecclesiastical History. The Motion was made by my Friend Smith of Clapham, a Friend of the Belshams. I Should be very happy to hear, that the Bill is passed.

The human Understanding is a revelation from its Maker which can never be disputed or doubted. There can be no Scepticism, Pyrrhonism or Incredulity or Infidelity here. No Prophecies, no Miracles are necessary to prove this celestial communication. This revelation has made it certain that two and one make three; and that one is not three; nor can three be one. We can never be So certain of any Prophecy, or the fullfillment of any Prophecy; or of any miracle, or the design of any miracle as We are, from the revelation of nature i.e. natures God[1] that two and two are equal to four. Miracles or Prophecies might frighten Us out of our Witts; might Scare us to death; might induce Us to lie; to Say that We believe that 2 and 2 make 5. But We Should not believe it. We Should know the contrary.

Had you and I, been forty days with Moses on Mount Sinai and admitted to behold, the divine Shekinah, and there told that one was three and three, one: We might not have had courage to deny it; but We could not have believed it. The thunders and Lightenings and Earthquakes[2] and the transcendant Splendors and Glories, might have overwhelmed Us with terror and Amazement: but We could not have believed the doctrine. We Should be more likely to Say in our hearts, whatever We might Say with our Lips, This is Chance. There is no God! No Truth. This is all delusion, fiction and a lie or it is all Chance. But what is Chance? It is motion; it is Action; it is Event; it is Phenomenon, without cause. Chance is no cause at[3] all. it is nothing. And Nothing has produced all this Pomp and Splendor; and Nothing may produce Our eternal damnation in the flames of Hell fire and Brimstone for what We know, as well as this tremendous Exhibition of Terror and Falshood.

God has infinite Wisdom, goodness and power. He created the Universe. His duration is eternal, a parte Ante, and a parte post. His presence is as extensive as Space. What is Space? an infinite, Spherical Vaccuum. He created this Speck of Dirt and the human Species for his glory: and with the deliberate design of making, nine tenths of our Species miserable forever, for his glory. This is the doctrine of Christian Theologians in general: ten to one.

Now, my Friend, can Prophecies, or miracles convince you, or me, that infinite Benevolence, Wisdom and Power, created and preserves, for a time, innumerable millions to make them miserable, forever; for his own Glory? Wretch! What is his Glory? Is he ambitious? does he want promotion? Is he vain? tickled with Adulation? Exulting and tryumphing in his Power and the Sweetness of his Vengeance? Pardon me, my Maker, for these Aweful Questions. My Answer to them is always ready: I believe no such Things. My Adoration of the Author of the Universe is too profound and too Sincere. The Love of God and his Creation; delight, Joy, tryumph, Exultation in my own existence, 'tho but an Atom, a Molecule organique, in the Universe; are my religion. Howl, Snarl, bite, ye Calvinistick? ye Athanasian Divines, if you will. ye will Say, I am no Christian: I Say ye are no Christians: and there the Account is ballanced.

yet I believe all the honest men among you, are Christians in my Sense of the Word.

When I was at Colledge I was a mighty Metaphisian. At least I thought myself Such: and Such Men as Lock, Hemenway, and West thought me So too: for We were forever disputing, though in great good humour.

When I was Sworn as an Attorney in 1758, in Boston, 'tho I lived in Braintree; I was in a low State of Health; thought in great danger of a Consumption; living on Milk, Vegetable Pudding and Water. Not an Atom of Meat or a drop of Spirit. My next Neighbour, my Cousin my Friend Dr Savil was my Physician. He was anxious for me, and did not like to take upon himself the Sole Responsability of my recovery. He invited me to a ride. I mounted my Horse and rode with him to Hingham, on a visit to Dr Ezekiel Hersey, a Physician of great fame: who felt my pulse, looked in my Eyes, heard Savil describe my regimen and course of Medicine; and then pronouned his oracle "Persevere, and as Sure as there is a God in Heaven you will recover." He was an everlasting Talker, and ran out, into History, Philosophy Metaphysicks, &c and frequently put questions to me, as if he wanted to sound me, and See if there was any thing in me, besides Hectic fever. I was young, and then very bashful: however Saucy I may have Sometimes been Since. I gave him very modest and very diffident Answers. But when he got upon Metaphysicks, I Seemed to feel a little bolder, and ventured into Some thing like Argument with him. I drove him up, as I thought, into a Corner, from which he could not[4] escape. Sir, it will follow from what you have now advanced, that the Universe, as distinct from God is both infinite and eternal. "Very true, Said Dr Hearsey:

your inference is just; the Consequence is inevitable; and I believe the Universe to be, both eternal and infinite." Here I was brought up! I was defeated. I was not prepared for this answer. This was 55 years ago.

When I was in England from 1785, to 1788 I may Say, I was intimate with Dr Price. I had much conversation with him at his own House, at my houses, and at the houses and Tables of many Friends. In some of our most unreserved Conversations, when We have been alone, he has repeatedly Said to me "I am inclined to believe that the Universe, is eternal and infinite.[5] It Seems to me that an eternal and infinite Effect, must necessarily flow from an eternal and infinite Cause; and an infinite Wisdom Goodness and Power, that could have been induced to produce a Universe in time, must have produced it from eternity." "It Seems to me, the Effect must flow from the Cause."

Now, my Friend Jefferson, Suppose an eternal Self existent Being existing from Eternity, possessed of infinite Wisdom, Goodness and Power, in absolute total Solitude, Six thousand years ago, conceiving the benevolent project of creating a Universe! I have no more to Say, at present.

It has been long, very long a Settled opinion[6] in my Mind that there is now, never will be, and never was but one being who can Understand the Universe. And that it is not only vain but wicked for insects to pretend to comprehend it.   JOHN ADAMS

RC (DLC); at foot of text: "President Jefferson"; endorsed by TJ as received 27 Sept. 1813 and so recorded in SJL. FC (Lb in MHi: Adams Papers). Enclosures: enclosures 1–2 to TJ to Adams, 22 Aug. 1813.

William Smith's bill for the relief of British ANTITRINITARIANS was passed by Parliament and received the royal assent on 21 July 1813 (Richard W. Davis, *Dissent in Politics, 1780–1830: The Political Life of William Smith, MP* [1971], 148, 190–4; London *Times*, 22 July 1813). PYRRHONISM: a form of skeptical philosophy predicated on the impossibility of attaining certain knowledge of anything (*OED*). A PARTE ANTE, AND A PARTE POST: "that which is in the past, and that which is to come."

[1] Preceding three words interlined.
[2] RC: "Earthques." FC: "earthquakes."
[3] RC: "att." FC: "at."
[4] Word interlined.
[5] Superfluous closing quotation mark here editorially omitted.
[6] Phrase reworked from "long, very long Settled."

From "A Man of Years & A Citizen"

FRIEND,—   [received 14 Sept. 1813]

thou wert wise in thy Administration:—thou didst Reward thy Officers generally,—but this unpresuming Young man, thou did cruelly overlook.—Use thy unfluence to do him essential Service.—thou art rich,—he is poor and deserving, and in disgust I am afraid will soon throw up his commission.—Be humane & generous as thy nature I know will prompt.   A MAN OF YEARS & A CITIZEN

RC (DLC: TJ Papers, 199:35443); undated; endorsed by TJ as an "Anonymous" letter covering an "Address of Capt Jas B. Wilkinson," received 14 Sept. 1813 and so recorded in SJL. The printed enclosure, not found, was addressed to the citizens of Mobile and dated 4 July 1813 (*Bulletin of the Bureau of Rolls and Library of the Department of State* 10 [1903]: 35).

United States Army captain James Biddle Wilkinson, a son of General James Wilkinson, was probably the UN-PRESUMING YOUNG MAN mentioned above. He was still in the service when he died in Louisiana a week before TJ received this letter (New York *National Advocate*, 25 Oct. 1813; Heitman, *U.S. Army*, 1:1037).

From John Adams

DEAR SIR   Quincy Septr 15. 1813

My last Sheet, would not admit an Observation that was material to my design.

Dr Price was "inclined to think" that infinite Wisdom and Goodness, could not permit infinite Power, to be inactive, from Eternity: but that, an infinite and eternal Universe, must have necessarily flowed from these Attributes.

Plato's System was "Αγαθος" was eternal, Self existent &c. His Ideas, his Word, his Reason, his Wisdom, his Goodness, or in one Word, his "Logos," was omnipotent and produced the Universe from all Eternity.

Now! As far as you and I can understand Hersey[1] Price and Plato, are they not of one Theory? of one mind? What is the difference? I own, an eternal Solitude of a Self existent Being infinitely wise, powerful and good, is to me, altogether incomprehensible, and incredible. I could as Soon believe the Athanasian Creed.

you will ask me "What conclusion, I draw from all this"?[2] I answer, I drop into myself, and acknowledge myself to be a Fool. No Mind, but one, can See through, the immeasurable System. It would be Presumption and Impiety in me to dogmatize, on Such Subjects.

My duties, in my little infinitessimal Circle I can understand and feel. The Duties of a Son, a Brother, a Father, a Neighbour, a Citizen, I can See and feel: But I trust the Ruler with his Skies.

Si quid novisti rectius, istis

Candidus imperti, Si non, his Utere mecum,

This World is a mixture of the Sublime and the beautiful, the base and contemptible, the whimsical and ridiculous, (according to our narrow sense; and triffling Feelings). It is a Riddle and an Enigma. you need not be Surprised then, if I Should descend from these Heights, to an egregious Trifle. But, first let me Say. I asked you in a former Letter, how far advanced We were in the Science of Aristocracy, Since Theognis's Stalions Jacks and Rams? Have not Chancellor Livingston and Major General Humphreys introduced an hereditary Aristocracy of Merino Sheep? How shall We get rid of this Aristocracy? It is intailed upon Us forever. And an Aristocracy of Land Jobbers and Stock jobbers, is equally and irremediably entailed upon Us, to endless generations.

Now for the odd; the whimsical; the frivolous. I had Scarcely Sealed my last Letter to you, upon Theognis's doctrine of well born, Stallions, Jacks and Rams; when they brought me from the Post Office a Packett, without Post Mark, without Letter, without name date or place. Nicely Sealed, was a printed Copy of Eighty or Ninety Pages in large full Octavo, intitled

Section first

Aristocracy. I gravely composed my risible Muscles and read it through. It is, from beginning to End an Attack upon me by name for the doctrines of Aristocracy in my 3 Volumes of "Defence" &c. The Conclusion of the whole is that an Aristocracy of Bank Paper, is as bad as the Nobility of France or England. I, most assuredly will not controvert this point, with this man. Who he is, I cannot conjecture; The Honourable John Taylor of Virginia, of all men living or dead first occurred to me.

Is it Oberon? Is it queen Mab, that reigns and Sports with Us little Beings? I thought my Books as well as myself were forgotten. But behold! I am to become a great Man in my expiring moments. Theognis and Plato, and Hersey, and Price and Jefferson and I, must go down to Posterity together;—and I know not, upon the whole, where to wish for better company. I wish to add Vanderkemp, who has been here to See me, after an interruption of 24 years. I could and ought to add many others but the catalogue would be too long,

I am, as ever,   JOHN ADAMS

P.S. why is Plato associated with Theognis &c.? Because no Man ever expressed So much terror of the Power of Birth. His Genius could invent no remedy or precaution against it; but a Community of Wives; a confusion of Families, a total extinction of all Relations of Father, Son and Brother. Did the French Revolutionists contrive much better, against the influence of Birth?

RC (DLC); at foot of text: "President Jefferson"; endorsed by TJ as received 30 Sept. 1813 and so recorded in SJL. FC (Lb in MHi: Adams Papers); with postscript incorporated into body of letter.

Αγαθος: "good." SI QUID NOVISTI . . . UTERE MECUM: "If you know something better than these precepts, pass it on, my good fellow. If not, join me in following these," from Horace, *Epistles*, 1.6.67–8 (Fairclough, *Horace: Satires, Epistles, and Ars Poetica*, 290–1). Adams had received an unbound and uncut advance copy of John Taylor of Caroline's work, *An Inquiry into the Principles and Policy*

of the Government of the United States (Fredericksburg, 1814; TJ's copy documented in his MS Retirement Library Catalogue, DLC: TJ Papers, ser. 7, p. 88 [no. 656]). It contained neither the title page nor the author's introductory letter "To The Public." Plato proposes a COMMUNITY OF WIVES; A CONFUSION OF FAMILIES in *The Republic*, 5.7 (*Plato*, trans. Paul Shorey, Loeb Classical Library [1930; repr. 1969], 5:452–5).

[1] Word interlined.
[2] Ending single quotation mark editorially regularized to double quotation mark.

From Gales & Seaton

SIR,   Office of the National Intelligencer Sept. 15. 1813

In compliance with your request, communicated through Mr Saml H. Smith, we enclose a statement of your acct for the Intelligencer, from the commencement of your subscription.—The dates of the credits, we cannot give, not finding them on the books, as kept by Mr Smith's clerk.

Very respectfully Your Obt Servts   GALES & SEATON

RC (DLC); in the hand of Joseph Gales; at foot of text: "Hon. Thomas Jefferson"; endorsed by TJ as received 22 Sept. 1813 and so recorded in SJL.

The printing partnership of Gales & Seaton, publishers of the Washington *National Intelligencer*, lasted from 1812 until 1860. The *National Intelligencer* was an organ of Jeffersonian Republicanism during TJ's lifetime and published the most authoritative version of the congressional debates for many years. TJ began taking the paper in 1800 from

Samuel H. Smith, its first proprietor, and he continued his subscription until 1818. Gales & Seaton also published the Washington *Universal Gazette*, 1812–14, and an enormous quantity of public records through its *Register of Debates in Congress* (1825–37), *American State Papers* (1832–61), and *Annals of Congress* (1834–56). The firm's partners eventually became Whigs and lost lucrative government printing contracts when Andrew Jackson's Democratic party came to power late in the 1820s (William E. Ames, *A History of the National*

Intelligencer [1972]; Brigham, *American Newspapers*, 2:1416, 1479; *MB*, 2:1031, 1294, 1349).

Joseph Gales (1786–1860) was born in England and immigrated to America in 1795 with his father of the same name, who was also a prominent journalist. He spent his youth in Philadelphia and in Raleigh, North Carolina, and he attended the University of North Carolina. In 1807 Gales became a reporter for the *National Intelligencer*. Smith took him into partnership two years later, and he became sole proprietor in 1810. Gales served briefly in the local militia during the War of 1812, became active in the American Colonization Society, and was mayor of Washington, 1827–30 (*ANB*; *DAB*; Washington *Constitution*, 24 July 1860).

William Winston Seaton (1785–1866), Gales's brother-in-law, was a native of King William County. The two men collaborated harmoniously as co-editors and owners of the *National Intelligencer* until Gales's death. Seaton then issued the paper by himself until rising debts forced him to sell it in 1864. He was also a War of 1812 veteran and shared his partner's interest in the American Colonization Society. Seaton served in his turn as mayor of Washington, 1840–50 (*ANB*; *DAB*; Josephine Seaton, *William Winston Seaton of the "National Intelligencer": A Biographical Sketch* [1871]; Washington *Daily Constitutional Union*, 16 June 1866).

ENCLOSURE

Account with the *National Intelligencer*

[ca. 15 Sept. 1813]

Thomas Jefferson Esq   D^r

Dolls

For the National Intelligencer, from Oct 31. 1800
to Oct 31. 1813, @ $5 per ann   }   65.—

Cr.

By cash, Oct 31. 1800	$5.—
By do through J. Barnes[1]	5.—
By do through Capt Lewis	5.—[2]
By do	5.—
By do thro J. Barnes	5.—
By do	10.—
By do	5.—

40.—
Balance due $25.—

MS (DLC: TJ Papers, 199:35494); in the hand of Joseph Gales; undated.

TJ's own records document only five payments: $5 each in 1800 and 1801 and $10 each in 1804, 1808, and 1809, with BARNES named in connection with the 1801 and 1808 payments and with no mention of LEWIS (*MB*, 2:1031, 1046, 1133, 1230–1, 1240; Account with Samuel H. Smith, 16 Nov. 1807 [MHi]).

[1] Manuscript: "Banes."
[2] TJ wrote in left margin next to this line: "1803. Feb. 12."

To William D. Meriwether

Sir   Monticello Sep. 17. 13.

I lent you some time ago the London & Country brewer and Combrun's book on the same subject. we are this day beginning, under the directions of Capt Millar, the business of brewing Malt liquors, and if these books are no longer useful to you I will thank you for them, as we may perhaps be able to derive some information from them. Accept the assurance of my respect & consideration.

                                                      Th: Jefferson

PoC (MHi); at foot of text: "Capt Meriwether"; endorsed by TJ.

Capt millar: Joseph Miller. Although Martha Wayles Skelton Jefferson had brewed beer at Monticello during the early years of their marriage, TJ did not continue the practice after his wife's death in 1782. During the last dozen years of TJ's life, however, the Monticello brewery, under the direction of Peter Hemmings, produced as much as two hundred gallons of ale per annum for home consumption (Ann Lucas, *The Philosophy of Making Beer* [1995; keepsake for Spring Dinner at Monticello, 12 Apr. 1995]; TJ to James Barbour, 11 May 1821). The books TJ was seeking were William Ellis, *The London and Country Brewer*,

6th ed. (London, 1750; Sowerby, no. 1204) and Michael Combrune, *The Theory and Practice of Brewing*, rev. ed. (London, 1804; Sowerby, no. 1206).

On this day TJ received a letter dated Philadelphia, 10 Sept. 1813, from Jonathan Williams, the president of the United States Military Philosophical Society, announcing that the society would hold its next annual meeting in New York City on 1 Nov. 1813, at which time it was to receive reports, examine its finances, elect new members and officers for the coming year, and "devise the best means of promoting the future usefulness of the Institution" (printed circular in DLC; endorsed by TJ as a "Circu[lar]" [edge trimmed] from Williams received 17 Sept. 1813 and so recorded in SJL).

To John Barnes

Dear Sir   Monticello Sep. 18. 13.

I have just recieved a letter of Dec. 1. from Genl Kosciuszko, in which he says 'I have recieved a bill of exchange of 5500 francs from mr Barnes, and I have been punctually paid by the house of mr Morton. I pray you to continue to remit me my interest thro' the same channel; if mr Morton will have the goodness to permit it'

This putting out of all doubt the preferable channel of remittance, will enable you to adopt the same means without further delay. ever affectionately Yours   Th: Jefferson

PoC (DLC); at foot of text: "Mr Barnes"; endorsed by TJ.

Tadeusz Kosciuszko's letter to TJ of

1 Dec. 1812, not found, is recorded in SJL as received 17 Sept. 1813, having been enclosed in Isaac Doolittle to TJ, 11 Sept. 1813.

To William Canby

S<small>IR</small>   Monticello Sep. 18. 13.

I have duly recieved your favor of Aug. 27.[1] am sensible of the kind intentions from which it flows, & truly thankful for them, the more so as they could only be the result of a favorable estimate of my public course. during a long life,[2] as much devoted to study, as a faithful transaction of the trusts committed to me would permit, no subject has occupied more of my consideration than our relations with all the beings around us, our duties to them, and our future prospects. after reading &[3] hearing every thing which probably can be suggested respecting them, I have formed the best judgment I could as to the course they prescribe, and in the due observance of that course, I have no recollections which give me uneasiness. an eloquent preacher of your religious[4] society, Richard Motte, in a discourse of much unction and pathos, is said to have exclaimed aloud to his congregation, that he did not believe there was a Quaker, Presbyterian, Methodist or Baptist in heaven. having paused to give his audience time to stare and to wonder, he added, that, in heaven, God knew no distinctions, but considered all good men as his children, and as brethren of the same family. I believe, with the Quaker preacher, that he who steadily[5] observes those moral precepts in which all religions concur, will never be questioned, at the gates of heaven, as to the dogmas in which they all differ. that on entering there, all these are left behind us, and the Aristideses & Cato's, the Penns & Tillotsons, Presbyterians and Papists, will find themselves united in all principles which are in concert with the reason of[6] the supreme mind. of all the systems of morality antient or modern, which have come under my observation, none appear to me so pure as that of Jesus. he who follows this steadily need not, I think, be uneasy, altho' he cannot comprehend the subtleties & mysteries erected on his doctrines by those who, calling themselves his special followers & favorites, would make him come into the world to lay snares for all understandings but theirs. these metaphysical heads, usurping the judgment seat of god, denounce as his enemies all who cannot percieve the Geometrical logic of Euclid, in the demonstrations of St Athanasius, that three are one, and one is three; and yet that the one is not three, nor the three one.[7] in all essential points, you and I are of the same religion; and I am too old to go into enquiries & changes[8] as to the unessential. repeating therefore my thankfulness for the kind concern you have been so good as to express, I salute you with friendship and brotherly esteem.[9]   T<small>H</small>: J<small>EFFERSON</small>

RC (PHC: Charles Roberts Autograph Collection); addressed: "Mr William Canby Brandywine mills. near Wilmington Del."; franked; postmarked Milton, 22 Sept. PoC (DLC). Tr (NjP: Straus Autograph Collection); endorsed: "Religion. creed of the wise." Tr (ViU: TJP); at foot of text: "The originals of the foregoing letters were in the possession of the late Timothy Pickering"; on verso of Tr of Canby to TJ, 27 Aug. 1813. Printed in Wilmington *Delaware Gazette*, 1 Nov. 1814, and elsewhere.

THAT THREE ARE ONE, AND ONE IS THREE refers to the Christian doctrine of the Trinity.

[1] *Delaware Gazette*: "29."
[2] Preceding four words not in *Delaware Gazette*.
[3] Preceding two words not in *Delaware Gazette*.
[4] Word not in Tr at ViU.
[5] Word not in *Delaware Gazette*.
[6] Preceding three words not in *Delaware Gazette*.
[7] Preceding twelve words not in *Delaware Gazette*.
[8] Tr at ViU: "charges." Preceding three words not in *Delaware Gazette*.
[9] *Delaware Gazette* substitutes "love" for this word.

To Isaac Doolittle

SIR   Monticello Sep. 18. 13.

I thank you for your care of the two letters from France which you have been so kind as to forward me. the Eloge historique de François Peron from mr Barnet came safely to hand, and I am only waiting a safe conveyance for the return of my thanks to him, as also for transmission of[1] a book which M. Dupont desires me to send him. with my thanks be pleased to accept the assurance of my respect.

                                       TH: JEFFERSON

PoC (MHi); at foot of text: "Mr I. Doolittle"; endorsed by TJ.

[1] Preceding two words interlined.

To William Duane

DEAR SIR   Monticello Sep. 18. 13.

Repeated enquiries on the part of Senator Tracy what has become of his book (the MS. I last sent you) oblige me to ask of you what I shall say to him.   I congratulate you on the brilliant affair of the Enterprize & Boxer. no heart is more rejoiced than mine at these mortifications of English pride, and lessons to Europe that the English are not invincible at sea. and if these successes do not lead us too far into the navy-mania, all will be well. but when are to cease the severe lessons we recieve by land, demonstrating our want of competent officers? the numbers of our countrymen betrayed into the hands of the enemy by the treachery, cowardice, or incompetence of our high officers, reduce us to the humiliating necessity of acquiescing in the brutal conduct observed[1] towards them. when, during the last war, I put Governor Hamilton & Maj[r] Hay into a dungeon & in irons for having themselves personally done the same to the American prisoners who had fallen into their hands, and was threatened with retaliation by Philips, then returned to N. York, I declared to him I would load ten of their Saratoga prisoners (then under my care & within half a dozen miles of my house) with double irons for every American they should misuse under pretence of retaliation: and it put an end to the practice. but the ten for one are now with them. our present hopes of being able to do something by land seem to rest on Chauncey. strange reverse of expectations that our land-force should be under the wing of our little navy. Accept the assurance of my esteem & respect. TH: JEFFERSON

RC (NNGL, on deposit NHi); addressed: "General Duane Philadelphia"; franked; postmarked Milton, 22 Sept. PoC (DLC).

On 5 Sept. 1813 the USS *Enterprise* captured HMS *Boxer* after a sharp fight off Portland, District of Maine (*Boston Daily Advertiser*, 8 Sept. 1813). In 1778–79 General William Phillips (PHILIPS) was the ranking officer in the Convention Army, a force of British and Hessian soldiers who had been taken by the Americans at the Battle of Saratoga in 1777 and marched south to Albemarle County a year later. He was allowed to leave for N. YORK in the autumn of 1779. Governor Henry Hamilton and Major Jehu Hay were captured at Vincennes in April 1779 and paroled against TJ's wishes on 10 Oct. 1780 (*PTJ*, 2:256–8, 287n, 3:44–9, 86n, 227, 333, 664–6, 4:24–5; Philander D. Chase, "'Years of Hardships and Revelations': The Convention Army at the Albemarle Barracks, 1779–1781," *MACH* 41 [1983]: 9–53).

[1] Word interlined.

To Nicolas G. Dufief

DEAR SIR   Monticello Sep. 6. [for 18][1] 13.

Your favor of the 6th has been recieved & I thank you for having forwarded the book to mr Adams as desired. in the Aurora of Sep. 7. I see a book advertised as under publication at N. York under the title of 'the American brewer & malster' which, as teaching the method of malting Indian corn I should be very glad to get. could you procure it for me if published or when published. I would also thank you for 2. copies, if to be had, of the little French work Du bonheur et de la morale. it was published in Paris in petit format, without the author's name. it is the best general treatise on Morals, either antient or modern, which I have ever seen, & deserves well a good translation into our language. I think it would be a work of great sale.

I salute you with esteem & respect.   Th: Jefferson

PoC (DLC: TJ Papers, 199:35448); misdated; at foot of text: "M. Dufief"; endorsed by TJ as a letter of 18 Sept. 1813 and so recorded in SJL.

Although it was ADVERTISED in the Philadelphia *Aurora General Advertiser*, 7 Sept. 1813, the AMERICAN BREWER & MALSTER was not published until years later, as Joseph Coppinger's *The American Practical Brewer and Tanner* (New York, 1815). "Malster" is a variant spelling of maltster (*OED*). The work DU

BONHEUR ET DE LA MORALE published in PETIT FORMAT was Jean Zacharie Paradis de Raymondis's *Traité élémentaire de Morale et du Bonheur* (Paris, 1795; Sowerby, no. 1249).

[1] Initially using the date of the letter to which he was responding, TJ wrote "6." He left it uncanceled, which suggests that he sent the letter before catching this mistake, but on the PoC he interlined "for 18."

To Harry Innes

Dear Sir   Monticello Sep. 18. 13.

Your information is correct that we possess here the genuine race of Shepherd dogs. I imported them from France about 4. years ago. they were selected for me by the Marquis Fayette, and I have endeavored to secure their preservation by giving them, always in pairs, to those who wished them. I have 4. pair myself at different places, where I suffer no other dog to be; and there are others in the neighborhood. I have no doubt therefore that from some of these we can furnish a pair, or perhaps two, at any time when Judge Todd can send for them; he giving me some notice to seek out a litter in a proper state for travelling. there are so many applications for them that there are never any on hand, unless kept on purpose. their extraordinary sagacity renders them extremely valuable, capable of being taught almost any duty that may be required of them, and the most anxious in the performance of that duty, the most watchful & faithful of all servants. but they must be reasonably fed; and are the better for being attached to a master. if they are forced by neglect & hunger to prowl for themselves, their sagacity renders them the most destructive marauders imaginable. you will see your flock of sheep & of hogs disappearing from day to day, without ever being able to detect them in it. they learn readily to go for the cows of an evening, or for the sheep, to drive up the chickens, ducks, turkies every one into their own house, to keep forbidden animals from the yard, all of themselves and at the proper hour, and are the most watchful house-dogs in the world. I shall be happy in an occasion of being useful to you by putting you in stock with them, and avail my self of this occasion of renewing to you the assurance of my high esteem and respect.   TH: JEFFERSON

RC (DLC: Innes Papers); addressed: "The honble Judge Innes Frankfort Kentucky"; franked; stamped; postmarked Milton, 21 Sept. PoC (MHi); endorsed by TJ. Tr (DLC: John Jordan Crittenden Papers); posthumous copy.

From George Logan

DEAR SIR   Stenton Sep[r] 18th: 1813

Retired to my farm, I frequently contemplate with pleasure, the happiness and prosperity of the United States, under your administration. Your persevering exertions to civilize and comfort the Indians, on our extensive frontier. and your prompt attention to the abolition of the slave trade; will be recorded by the faithful pen of the historian to your immortal honor—Would to God; that whilst you had the power; you had concluded a treaty of commerce and friendship with Great Britain—Then would our country have escaped the direful calamities with which it is now overwhelmed.

One of the greatest evils of War, is to destroy the moral character of the people. To rend from its settled rectitude this principle; and so to environ it with tumult and confusion,[1] that its refined dictates can be no longer heard; is to break down the fortress of a republican government; and to invite the destructive horrors of anarchy—The certain prelude to military despotism and national slavery. Such being my opinion founded on calm and deliberate reflection. I made use of every effort in my power to prevent a war with France in 1798, as I have done to prevent a war with England. I am satisfied this great evil would have been avoided had M[r] Madison been left to his own judgment—But he was influenced by men as devoid of principle, as of genuine patriotism: by the councils of whom, he was precipitated into this ruinous measure

You are considered the particular friend of the President. As you value his reputation, and the happiness of your country; engage him to come forward decisively, with such just and honorable proposals for obtaining peace with Great Britain, as if not accepted, will place that government completely in the wrong. On this momentous occasion—all half way measures should be avoided.

Much has been said, and variously asserted respecting the disposition of the British nation towards the United States. I wish that disposition to have another fair trial. From my own observation when last in England, as well as from information derived from men of every party, and in every situation of life I am confident a treaty of peace and commerce may yet be made with that nation, equally honorable and beneficial to both countries. A renewed effort of the President to restore peace with Great Britain, may meet the obloquy of a few infuriated, or self interested individuals—But it is the province of a great[2] statesman to consider the utility of a measure, and not to shrink from the path of known duty.

Should the war continue, owing to the apathy or neglect of M[r] Madison, in embracing any favorable opportunity of terminating it— The history of his administration, will be the history of the calamities and miseries of his country.

Accept assurances of my friendship   GEO LOGAN

ps
I have lately sent to the President—an appeal to the nations of Europe by madam de Stael Holstein published at Stockholm by authority of Bernadotte.

It merits your attention.

RC (DLC); at foot of text: "Tho[s] Jefferson Esq[r]"; endorsed by TJ as received 27 Sept. 1813 and so recorded in SJL. FC (PHi: Logan Papers); in Logan's hand; endorsed by Logan, with his additional notation: "N⁰ 14."

George Logan (1753–1821), scientific farmer, public official, and amateur diplomat, was born at Stenton, his family's estate near Germantown, Pennsylvania, and received a medical degree from the University of Edinburgh in 1779. He returned from Europe the following year and turned his attention to improving his landholdings. Logan experimented extensively with crop rotation and sheep raising, helped found the Philadelphia Society for Promoting Agriculture in 1785, and was elected to the American Philosophical Society in 1793. In the latter year TJ called him "the best farmer in Pensylva. both in theory and practice." The two men struck up a friendship during TJ's tenure as secretary of state and kept up a fairly regular correspondence thereafter. Logan represented Philadel-phia County in the Pennsylvania House of Representatives, 1785–89, 1796–97, and 1798–1801, and he sat in the United States Senate, 1801–07. A firm Jeffersonian Republican, he opposed indirect taxes and the slave trade and supported internal improvements and the establishment of a national university. Logan is best remembered today for his private diplomatic peace mission to France in 1798. TJ, who had provided his friend with a certificate of introduction prior to his departure, was later obliged to explain that he had had no knowledge of Logan's intentions. One result of the enterprise was the passage the following year of what became known as the Logan Act, which still prohibits American citizens from engaging in diplomatic negotiations with a foreign country without the consent of the United States government. Undeterred, Logan made a similar trip to England in 1810 (*ANB*; *DAB*; Deborah Norris Logan, *Memoir of Dr. George Logan of Stenton*, ed. Frances A. Logan [1899]; Frederick B. Tolles, *George Logan of Philadelphia* [1953]; *PTJ*,

20:734, 25:650–1, 26:576, 30:386–7, 644, 645; APS, Minutes, 18 Jan. 1793 [MS in PPAmP]; *U.S. Statutes at Large,* 1:613; *New-York Columbian,* 12 Apr. 1821).

The APPEAL was Madame de Staël Holstein, *An Appeal to the Nations of Eu-*

rope against the Continental System: Published at Stockholm, by Authority of Bernadotte, In March, 1813 (Boston, 1813).

¹ FC: "commotion."
² FC: "genuine."

To Isaac McPherson

SIR   Monticello Sep. 18. 13.

I thank you for the communication of mr Jonathan Ellicot's letter in your's of Aug. 28. and the information it conveys. with respect to mine of Aug. 13. I do not know that it contains any thing but what any man of Mathematical reading may learn from the same sources. however if it can be used for the promotion of right, I consent to such an use of it. your enquiry as to the date of Martin's invention of the drill plough with a leathern band & metal¹ buckets I cannot precisely answer: but I recieved one from him in 1794 & have used it ever since for sowing various seeds, chiefly peas, turnips & Benni. I have always had in mind to use it for wheat; but sowing only a row at a time I had proposed to him some years ago to change the construction so that it should sow 4. rows at a time, 12 I. apart; and I have been waiting for this to be done either by him or myself; & have not therefore commenced that use of it. I procured mine at first thro' Colº John Taylor of Caroline who had been long in the use of it, & my impression was that it was not then a novel thing. mr Martin is still living, I believe. if not Colº Taylor, his neighbor, probably knows it's date.   if the bringing together under the same roof, various useful² things before known, which you mention as one of the grounds of mr Evans's claim, entitles him to an exclusive use of all these either separately or combined, every utensil of life might be taken from us by a patent. I might build a stable, bring into it a cutting knife to chop straw, a handmill to grind the grain, a curry comb & brush to clean the horses, & by a patent exclude every one from ever more using these things without paying me. the elevator, the conveyer, the hopper boy are distinct things, unconnected but by juxta-position. if no patent can be claimed for any one of these separately, it cannot be for all of them. several nothings put together cannot make something. this would be going very wide of the object of the patent laws. I salute you with esteem & respect   TH: JEFFERSON

PoC (DLC); at foot of text: "Mr Isaac McPherson."

TJ suggested to Thomas C. Martin through John Taylor of Caroline in 1798 that the DRILL PLOUGH be altered to allow the sowing of 4. ROWS AT A TIME, 12 I. APART (*PTJ*, 30:252, 347, 387; *MB*, 2:976).

¹ Word interlined.
² Word interlined.

To Josiah Meigs

DEAR SIR   Monticello Sep. 18. 13.
I thank you for the information contained in your letter of Aug. 25. I confess that when I heard of the atrocities committed by the English troops at Hampton, I did not believe them; but subsequent evidence has placed them beyond doubt. to this has been added information from another quarter which proves the violation of women to be their habitual practice in war. mr Hamilton, a son of Alexander Hamilton, of course a federalist and Angloman, and who was with the British army in Spain some time, declares it is their constant practice, and that at the taking Badajoz, he was himself eye-witness to it in the streets, & that the officers did not attempt to restrain it. the information contained in your letter proves it is not merely a recent practice. this is a trait of barbarism, in addition to their encoragement of the savage cruelties, & their brutal treatment of prisoners of war, which I had not attached to their character.   I am happy to hear that yourself & family enjoy good health & tender you the assurance of my great esteem & respect.   TH: JEFFERSON

PoC (DLC); at foot of text: "Mr Josiah Meigs"; endorsed by TJ.

Alexander Hamilton, the namesake son of America's first secretary of the treasury, was present at the bloody siege of BADAJOZ. Following its capture on 6 Apr. 1812 by forces under the command of Arthur Wellesley, Viscount Wellington, the city was sacked for two full days (New York *Frank Leslie's Illustrated Newspaper*, 21 Aug. 1875; Ian C. Robertson, *Wellington at War in the Peninsula, 1808–1814* [2000], 10, 196–8).

To Thomas Ritchie

DEAR SIR   Monticello Sep. 19. 13.
The inclosed biographical Notice of our late minister mr Barlow was prepared for some of the public papers of Europe, and has been forwarded to me by one of it's authors. you will see subscribed to it as much of their names as they chuse to communicate. I inclose it to you

supposing it possible you might think it worthy of translation and of publication in your paper. when done with I shall be glad to recieve the original again. I avail myself with pleasure of the occasion of assuring you of my great esteem and respect.   TH: JEFFERSON

PoC (DLC); at foot of text: "Mr Ritchie"; endorsed by TJ.

The INCLOSED BIOGRAPHICAL NO-TICE had been sent to TJ by ONE OF IT'S AUTHORS, Pierre Samuel Du Pont de Nemours, on 10 Feb. 1813. It was translated and published in the Richmond *Enquirer* on 29 Oct. 1813.

To Caspar Wistar

DEAR SIR   Monticello Sep. 19. 13
    The inclosed letter from mr Brackenridge on the subject of the mounds & remains of fortifications in the Western country, came to me without any indication whether meant, or not, for communication to the Philosophical society. considering it's subject and the information it contains as meriting the attention of the society, I take the liberty of requesting your communication of it to them; and tender you the assurance of my great esteem & respect.
                                              TH: JEFFERSON

PoC (DLC); at foot of text: "Dr Wistar"; endorsed by TJ. Enclosure: Henry M. Brackenridge to TJ, 25 July 1813.

Brackenridge's LETTER was presented to the American Philosophical Society at a meeting held on 1 Oct. 1813 and referred to a committee composed of Benjamin Smith Barton, Robert Patterson, and John Vaughan (APS, Minutes, 2 [i.e. 1] Oct. 1813 [MS in PPAmP]).

From Abigail Adams

DEAR SIR   Quincy Sepbr 20th 1813
    your kind and Friendly Letter found me in great affliction for the loss of my dear and only daughter, mrs smith
    She had been with me only three weeks having undertaken a journey from the State of N york, desirious once more to See her parents, and to close her days under the paternal roof
    She was accompanied by her Son and daughter, who made every exeertion to get her here, and gratify what Seemd the only remaining wish She had, so helpless and feeble a State as She was in, it is wonderfull how they accomplishd it, two years Since, She had an opper-

ation performed for a Cancer in her Breast, this She Supported, with wonderfull fortitude, and we flatterd ourselves that the cure was effectual, but it proved otherways. it Soon communicated itself through the whole mass of the Blood, and after severe sufferings, terminated her existance.

you sir, who have been called to Seperations of a Similar kind, can sympathize with your Bereaved Friend.   I have the consolation of knowing, that the Life of my dear daughter was pure, her conduct in prosperity and adversity, exemplary, her patience and Resignation becomeing her Religion—   you will pardon my[1] being so minute, the full Heart loves to pour out its Sorrows, into the Bosom of sympathizing Friendship.

A Lovely only daughter of her Mother, lives to console me
"who in her youth, has all that Age requires
And with her prudence; all that youth admires"
you call,d upon me to talk of myself, and I have obey,d the Summons from the assureance you gave me, that you took an interest in what ever affected my happiness.

"Greif has changed me since you saw me last,
And carefull hours, with times deformed hand
hath written Strange defeatures o'er my face"
But altho, time has changed the outward form, and political "Back wounding calumny" for a period interruped the Friendly intercourse and harmony which Subsisted, it is again renewed, purified from the dross.

with this assurance I beg leave To Subscribe myself
Your Friend   ABIGAIL ADAMS

RC (DLC); endorsed by TJ as received 6 Oct. 1813 and so recorded in SJL.

WHO IN HER YOUTH . . . YOUTH ADMIRES: George Crabbe, "Arabella," in his *Tales, 1812, and other selected poems*, ed. Howard Mills (1967), 222. GREIF HAS

CHANGED ME . . . DEFEATURES O'ER MY FACE: William Shakespeare, *The Comedy of Errors*, act 5, scene 1. BACK WOUNDING CALUMNY: Shakespeare, *Measure for Measure*, act 3, scene 2.

[1] Manuscript: "by."

From Charles L. Bankhead

MY DEAR SIR   [20 Sept. 1813]
I must beg you for a hamper of charcoal to dry our malt. Capt Miller apologises for not comeing up befor this—his excuse is the dampness of the weather, which he does not urge on his own account,

but in consideration of our malt, thinking that in his absense it might grow too fast in this weather—

affectionately Yours   CHAS: L BANKHEAD

RC (ViU: TJP-ER); undated; addressed: "Mr: Jefferson Monticello"; endorsed by TJ as a letter of 20 Sept. 1813.

To Henry M. Brackenridge

SIR   Monticello Sep. 20. 13.

Your favor of July 25. is just now recieved: and I have read with pleasure the account it gives of the antient mounds & fortifications in the Western country. I never before had an idea that they were so numerous. presuming the communication was meant for me in my relation with the Philosophical society, and deeming it well worthy their attention, I have forwarded it to them, and with my thanks for the information it contained, I pray you to accept the assurance of my great respect   TH: JEFFERSON

PoC (DLC); at foot of text: "Mr H. M. Brackenridge. Baton rouge"; endorsed by TJ.

To James Martin (of New York)

SIR   Monticello Sep. 20. 13.

Your letter of Aug. 20. enabled me to turn to mine of Feb. 23. 98. and your former one of Feb. 22. 1801. and to recall to my memory the oration at Jamaica which was the subject of them.[1] I see with pleasure a continuance of the same sound principles in the address to mr Quincy. your quotation from the former paper alludes, as I presume, to the term of office of our Senate; a term, like that of the judges, too long for my approbation. I am for responsibilities at short periods; seeing neither reason nor safety in making public functionaries independant of the nation[2] for life, or even for long terms of years. on this principle I prefer the Presidential term of 4. years, to that of 7. years which I myself had at first suggested, annexing to it however ineligibility for ever after; and I wish it were now annexed to the 2d quadrennial election of President.

The conduct of Massachusets, which is the subject of your address to mr Quincy, is serious, as embarrassing the operations of the war, & jeopardising it's issue; and still more so, as an example of contumacy against the Constitution. one method of proving their purpose would be to call a Convention of their state, and to require them to declare themselves members of the Union, and obedient to it's determinations, or not members, and let them go. put this question solemnly to their people and their answer cannot be doubtful. one half of them are republicans, and would cling to the union from principle. of the other half, the dispassionate part would consider 1.[3] that they do not raise bread sufficient[4] for their own subsistence, and must go to Europe for the deficiency if excluded from our ports, which vital interests would force us to do. 2. that they are a navigating people without a stick of timber for the hull of a ship, nor a pound of any thing to export in it which would be admitted at any market. 3. that they are also a manufacturing people, and left by the exclusive system of Europe without a market but ours. 4. that as the rivals of England in manufactures, in commerce, in navigation, and fisheries, they would meet her competition in every point. 5. that England would feel no scruples in making the abandonment & ruin of such a rival the price of a treaty with the producing states; whose interest too it would be to nourish a navigation beyond the Atlantic, rather than a hostile one at our own door.[5] and 6. that in case of war with the Union, which occurrences between coterminous nations frequently produce it would be a contest of 1. against 15.   the remaining portion of the Federal moiety of the state would, I believe, brave all these obstacles, because they are monarchists in principle, bearing deadly hatred to their republican fellow citizens, impatient under the ascendancy of republican principles, devoted in their attachment to England, and preferring to be placed under her despotism, if they cannot hold the helm of government here. I see, in their separation, no evil but the example: and I believe that the effect of that would be corrected by an early and humiliating return to the Union, after losing much of the population of their country,[6] insufficient in it's own resources to feed numerous inhabitants and inferior in all it's allurements to the more inviting soils, climates, and government of the other states.[7]   whether a dispassionate discussion before the public, of the advantages & disadvantages of separation to both parties would be the best medecine for this dialytic fever, or to consider it as sacrilege ever to touch the question, may be doubted. I am myself generally disposed to indulge, & to follow reason; and believe that in no case would it be safer than in the present. their refractory course however will not be unpunished by the indignation of their co-states, their loss of influence with them, the censures of history, & the stain on the character of their state.[8]   With my thanks for the paper inclosed accept the assurance of my esteem and respect.

TH: JEFFERSON

PoC (DLC); at foot of first page: "Mr James Martin." Tr (ViU: TJP); in Nicholas P. Trist's hand. Enclosure: enclosure to Martin to TJ, 20 Aug. 1813.

TJ FIRST SUGGESTED, in 1787, that American presidents be allowed to serve only one four-year term in office. By the following year, however, he was willing to support a seven-year term, as long as the incumbent was ineligible for reelection (*PTJ*, 12:351, 13:619). TJ got his wish for limits to presidential service long afterward with the enactment in 1951 of the twenty-second amendment to the United States Constitution, under which no one is eligible to run for president after their 2^D QUADRENNIAL ELECTION to that office. DIALYTIC: of or pertaining to dissolution (*OED*), with TJ here alluding to attempts to separate from or dissolve the bonds of national union.

[1] Tr begins here.
[2] Preceding three words interlined.
[3] Tr ends here.
[4] Word interlined in place of "necessary."
[5] Tr resumes here.
[6] Tr ends here.
[7] Tr resumes here.
[8] Tr ends here.

From John Adams

DEAR SIR   Quincy Sept^r [22] 1813

Considering all things, I admire Dr Priestleys last Effort for which I am entirely indebted to you. But as I think it is extreamly imperfect, I beg of you to pursue the investigation, according to your promise to Dr Rush, and according to your Syllabus. It may be presumptuous in me to denominate any Thing of Dr Priestley imperfect: but I must avow, that among all the vast Exertions of his Genius, I have never found one, that is not imperfect; and this last is egregiously So. I will instance at present in one Article. I find no notice of Cleanthes: one of whose Sayings alone ought to have commanded his Attention. He compared "Philosophers to Instruments of Musick, which made a Noise, without Under Standing it, or themselves." He was ridiculed by his Brother Philosophers, and called "An Ass." He owned, he was the "Ass of Zeno: and the only one, whose back and Shoulders were Stout enough to carry his Burthens." Why has not Priestley, quoted more from Zeno, and his Disciples? Were they too Christian? though he lived two Centuries[1] and an half before Christ?

If I did not know, it would be Sending Coal to Newcastle, I would, with all my dimness of Eyes and trembling of Fingers copy in Greek the Hymn of Cleanthes and request you to compare it, with any Thing of Moses of David of Soloman.

Instead of those ardent oriental Figures, which are So difficult to understand We find that divine Simplicity, which constitutes the Charm of Grecian Eloquence in prose and verse.

Pope had read, if Priestley had not the
ΚΛΕΑΝΘΟΥΣ ΥΜΝΟΣ ΕΙΣ ΔΙΑ.
Κύδιστ' ἀθανάτων, πολυώνυμε, παγκρατὲς αἰεὶ
Ζεῦ, φύσεως ἀρχηγὲ, νόμου μέτα πάντα κυβερνῶν,
Χαῖρε.

"Most glorious of immortal beings! though denominated by innumerable names and titles, always omnipotent,! Beginning and End of Nature! governing the Universe by fixed Laws![2] Blessed be thy name!" What think you, of this translation? Is it too Jewish? or too Christian? Pope did not think it was either: for the first Sentence in his Universal prayer is more Jewish and more christian Still. If it is not a litteral translation, it is a close paraphrase, of this Simple Verse of Cleanthes.

Father of all! in every Age,
In every clime ador'd
By Saint by Savage and by Sage
Johovah, Jove, or Lord.

But it may be Said, for it has been Said, that Pope, was a Deist and Swift too, as well as Bolingbroke. What will not Men Say? But is the Existence, the Omnipotence, the Eternity, the Alpha and Omega, and the Universal Providence of one Supream Being, governing by fixed Laws, asserted by St John in his Gospel, or in the Apocalypse, whether his or not, in clearer or more precise terms?

Can you conjecture, a reason why Grotius has not translated this Hymn? Were Grotius and Priestley both afraid that The Stoicks would appear too much like Unitarian Jews and Christians.

Duport has translated, the Sentence thus
Magne Pater Divûm, cui nomina multa, Sed una
Omnipotens Semper Virtus, tu Jupiter Auctor
Naturæ, certa qui Singula lege gubernas,
Rex, Salve!
Bougainville, has translated it
Pere, et Maitre des Dieux, Auteur de la Nature,
Jupiter, O Sagesse! O loi sublime et pure!
Unite Souveraine à qui tous les mortels
Sous mille noms divers elevent des Autels;
Je t'adore, nos cœurs te doivent leur homage,
Nous Sommes tes enfans, ton ombre, ton image:
Et tout ce qui respire animé par tes mains,
A celébrer ta gloire invite les humains.
Beni-Sois a jamais!

I am so awkward in Italian, that I am ashamed to quote that Language to you: but Pompeius a Gentleman of Verona, [has] translated it thus: and you will understand it.

O glorioso fra gli eterni, in guise

Molte nomato, onnipossente ognora,

Tu che, tutto con legge governando,

De la natura Sei principio e duce,

Salve, O Giove.

It appears to me, that the great Principle of the Hebrews was the Fear of God: that of the Gentiles, Honour the Gods, that of Christians, the Love of God. Could the quiveration of my nerves and the inflammation of my Eyes be cured and my Age diminished by 20 or 30 years: I would attend you in these researches, with infinitely more Pleasure, than I would be George the 4th Napoleone, Alexander, or Madison. But only a few Hours; a few moments remain for

your old Friend   JOHN ADAMS

RC (DLC: TJ Papers, 199:35460–1); mutilated at seal, with one word supplied from FC; partially dated; addressed: "Thomas Jefferson Esquire late President of U.S Monticello Virginia"; franked; postmarked Quincy, Mass., 22 Sept.; endorsed by TJ as a letter of Sept. 1813 received 6 Oct. 1813 and so recorded in SJL. FC (Lb in MHi: Adams Papers); fully dated.

At TJ's behest Adams had recently received a copy of Joseph Priestley's LAST EFFORT, *The Doctrines of Heathen Philosophy, compared with those of Revelation* (Northumberland, Pa., 1804; Sowerby, no. 1528). Adams's anecdotes of Cleanthes comparing PHILOSOPHERS TO INSTRUMENTS OF MUSICK and describing himself as the ASS OF ZENO derive from the brief biography by Diogenes Laertius in his *Lives of Eminent Philosophers*, trans. Robert D. Hicks,

Loeb Classical Library (1925; repr. 1970), 2:274–7, 278–9. SENDING COAL TO NEWCASTLE is an idiomatic allusion to sending something literally or figuratively to a place where it is already amply available. Adams quotes the opening lines of the *Hymn to Zeus* by Cleanthes (ΚΛΕΑΝΘΟΥΣ ΥΜΝΟΣ ΕΙΣ ΔΙΑ), of which a modern translation reads "Noblest of immortals, many-named, always all-powerful / Zeus, first cause and ruler of nature, governing everything with your law, / greetings!" (Johan C. Thom, ed., *Cleanthes' Hymn to Zeus* [2005], 34, 40). Adams's source for the Greek original and the Latin, French, and Italian translations of this work was Brunck, *Gnomici Poetæ Græci*, 141–9.

[1] Manuscript: "Conturies." FC: "centuries."

[2] RC follows this word with a question mark, FC with an exclamation point.

To William Champe Carter

DEAR SIR   Monticello Sep. 23. 13.

I was in hopes, after recieving the reacknolegement of your deed to mr Short that all further trouble was at an end. but a more serious one arises. Col° Monroe called on me two days ago and stated that the deed to mr Short had run in upon his prior one, and included some of the land, which he claims now to have settled. as he does not state this error of the lines as of his own knolege, but from the information of others, I am not without hopes he may be mistaken; because you conducted the Surveyor yourself in laying off mr Short's land, which was so soon after your conveyance to Col° Monroe, that you could hardly have forgotten his lines. he is very fair, candid, and accomodating and will let it be settled in the most amicable way, but, Sir, the settlement will require your presence. we propose that yourself, mr Short & Col° Monroe shall each name an Arbitrator, who shall go on the lines with a surveyor, and determine on the spot the right and the damages, if any. it is left to you to fix on the day of meeting most convenient to yourself. this cannot be till the fall of the leaf; but the sooner after that the better; and the rather as I shall go to Bedford the first week of November, and not return till the middle of December. some time in the 3^{d} or 4th week of Oct. if convenient to you, would be suitable. I subjoin the description of his land taken from his deed to refresh your memory, and tender you the assurances of my great esteem & respect   TH: JEFFERSON

'containing 1000. a^{s} be the same more or less & bounded as followeth to wit on the South by a run on the Eastern side of Dick's plantation & running thence to the source of the said run: & thence in a strait line to the top of the S.W. mountains: North to the lands of mr Jefferson, & thence by the lands of Mazzei to the road; and along the road South to the beginning.'

PoC (DLC); at foot of text: "W. Champe Carter esq."; endorsed by TJ. Enclosed in TJ to James Monroe and Monroe to TJ (first letter), both 23 Sept. 1813.

On 20 Sept. 1793 Carter and his wife, Maria Byrd Farley Carter, sold Monroe 1,000 acres just south of Monticello, a property that Monroe dubbed Highland (Albemarle Co. Deed Book, 11:163–5). Just over three years later, on 8 Dec. 1796, the Carters conveyed Indian Camp to William Short, an adjoining property situated farther south and consisting of roughly 1,330 acres. William Champe Carter's REACKNOLEGEMENT of the latter agreement is dated 1 Feb. 1813 (note to TJ to Carter, 16 Jan. 1813). The subjoined DESCRIPTION is taken from the Carters's 1793 indenture with Monroe. DICK'S PLANTATION formed a part of the Indian Camp Quarter tract inherited by Carter from his father in 1792 (*VMHB* 44 [1936]: 353; TJ to Carter, 16 Jan. 1813).

To James Monroe

Monticello Sep. 23. 13.

Th: Jefferson incloses to Col° Monroe the copy of a letter he proposes to send to mr Champe Carter, if the contents meet his approbation; which he asks the favor of him to signify to him, with the return of the letter.   he sets out to mr Madison's early tomorrow morning, weather permitting, which he does not mention to have any influence on Col° Monroe's movements. perhaps indeed their meeting at mr Madison's should rather be avoided, as the newspapers might announce it, as on former occasions, as portending some great conspiracy. he salutes him with affectionate respect.

PoC (MHi); dateline at foot of text; endorsed by TJ. Enclosure: TJ to William Champe Carter, 23 Sept. 1813.

From James Monroe

DEAR SIR   23–Sepr 1813.

I intended calling on you to day, which I still hope to be able to do in the afternoon. Your letter to Mr Carter is in all respects what it should be. I intend also to write him, & will bring my letter to him to show you.

I think it most adviseable that we should avoid a meeting at Mr Madisons, for the reason that has occured to you. I had intended to set out back to washington, in the commencement of this week, with intention to return here early in oct^r for Mrs Monroe, but the interruption by the rain & rise of the waters, has been such, as to incline me to delay rather longer here, & take her with me, at once.

I send you a letter recd. by the private mail, & the note which I recd., of the naval victory on Lake Erie

very respectfully & sincerely your friend   JA^s MONROE

RC (MHi); dateline at foot of text; endorsed by TJ as received 23 Sept. 1813 and so recorded in SJL. Enclosure: TJ to William Champe Carter, 23 Sept. 1813.

The enclosed letter received by PRIVATE MAIL has not been identified. The NOTE might have been Secretary of the Navy William Jones's letter to President James Madison of 18 Sept. 1813 confirming Oliver Hazard Perry's NAVAL VICTORY ON LAKE ERIE, which was apparently forwarded to Monroe about this time (Madison, *Papers, Pres. Ser.*, 6:639–40, 653–4).

From James Monroe

Thursday eveng. [23 Sept. 1813]

Jaˢ Monroe's best respects to Mʳ Jefferson—He hastens to communicate to him the very interesting intelligence recᵈ this evening from the Secry of the navy, on which he gives him his most sincere congratulations

RC (DLC: TJ Papers, 199:35463); partially dated at foot of text; endorsed by TJ as a letter of 23 Sept. 1813 received the following day.

Monroe probably enclosed a note from SECRY OF THE NAVY William Jones, dated 21 Sept. 1813 and sent from the Navy Department, asking Monroe to "Accept my hearty congratulation We shall have good news from Chauncey tomorrow" (RC in MHi; addressed: "Hon. James Monroe Milton Vᵃ").

From Donald Fraser

VENERABLE SIR— New York Septʳ 24ᵗʰ 1813.

Being advanced in Years (63) I find my former profession, of a Teacher, rather irksome—Hence, I am desirous of obtaining the appointment a Chaplain to one of the Brigades of the U. States Army— My son Donald Fraser Junʳ now at "Fort George" writes me that a Chaplain's office is now vacant in the first Brigade of Infantry—My Son was a great favorite of the late Genˡ Pike,[1] to whom he was Aide camp, & is now in the family of Genˡ Boyde

I was not bred a regular Clergymen, But have in the Years 1775 & 6, Preached occasionally, in New England, when a Teacher there— I humbly conceive, that I am qualifyed to compose, & to Deliver a Practical & moral Discourse tho' not a Theological or Doctrinal Sermon—My moral character, thank God, is I trust, irreproachable.

I have been informed, that Some persons have been appointed to the office of Chaplain, who were not clergy men; Indeed, I know two Such in the Navy—I am Sorry to intrude upon your time, in Your retirement: After a Summer's-day of arduous exertions in the cause of your country—Permit me to request Your having the goodness to write a few lines to the Secretary of State, in my behalf—As a line from you will, as it ought, have great weight with him. I have had the honor, of being once or twice in company with Genˡ Armstrong—: He knows my character—

That the Unerring Ruler of the Universe may preserve your life, in health & much Do[m]estic happiness for 15 or 20 Years longer in the

[525]

full use of your mental faculties—Is, the Sincere wish of one, whom You have repeatedly favoured—& is, with gratitude &[2] great respect Sir, your humble Servant.   DONALD FRASER SEN[R]

RC (MHi); torn at seal; addressed: "Thomas Jefferson Esq[r] Late President of the United States. Montacello"; franked; postmarked Baltimore, 3 Oct.; endorsed by TJ as received 6 Oct. 1813 and so recorded in SJL.

With this letter Fraser may have enclosed a testimonial dated New York, 31 Aug. 1813, in which Garret Sickels, George McKay, William Mooney, John Remsen, and Clarkson Crolius attested "To all whom it may concern, we the Subscribers, do hereby certify that we have been personally acquainted with the Bearer; Mr. D. Fraser Sen[r]—& believe him to be a genuine Republican." Fraser

added a postscript describing Mooney and Crolius as "fervent friends to Government, & Staunch Reppublicans— They were both for Some Years Grand Sachems of the 'Tammany Society' in New York" (MS in DLC; in an unidentified hand except for signatures by Sickels, McKay, Mooney, Remsen, and Crolius and postscript by Fraser).

American forces captured the British outpost of FORT GEORGE at the northern end of the Niagara Peninsula in May 1813 (Stagg, *Madison's War*, 333). Fraser did not secure an army chaplaincy.

[1] Word added in margin.
[2] Manuscript: "& &."

From William Duane

DEAR AND RESPECTED SIR,   Phil[a] Sep[r] 26, 1813

I have the pleasure of receiving yours of the 18th this day—the work of Tracy, is going forward but slowly, as I cannot devote from my present engagements the time I should wish to see it pushed forward. I have put it in the hands of one of Neef's assistants, a sensible and liberal young man; and Neef is able to render the abstruseness of Tracy's metaphysis[1] a little more comprehensible than my young friend or myself should—I did not calculate upon accomplishing it before the close of the present fall, and I think it will be ready for a full perusal by the end of October.

The affair of the Enterprize & Boxer, has been followed by another triumph still more signal in manner and consequences. The victory on Lake Erie has laid the foundation for the Security of the western countries, which ought to have been long since achieved by the enormous means of every kind money, men, and stores furnished, but which have been wasted in a manner the most shameful and with effects corresponding in disgrace. It is deplorable, with the experience of ages and of our own times, with common sense to resort to, how unfortunate has been the manner in which the military operations were c[omm]enced and the hands in which they were placed. Poor Pike when I last saw him in this city said to me at parting—

"I shall go to Canada probably never to return, but I shall go; for the generals we have are all generals of the Cabinet, and it is only after several of us who have some knowlege of military business are Sacrificed, that men will be placed to lead who are now in the ranks or in obscurity—you shall then see our cabinet generals retire and fighting generals brought forward."

It was a great calamity that such a man as Eustis should have had the appointments of the army at his discretion, since his errors have been a burthen to the country and an obstacle to his successor; that is however now in some measure correcting itself. no man esteems gen Dearborne more than I do, but it was a great mistake to place him in these times at the head of a raw army—and it was still worse to give him coadjutors incompetent from various causes to supply any of his deficiencies. He had Morgan Lewis for Q^r master General, who if it could procure him a diadem could not give an instruction nor define the duties of one of his deputies, in fact, it was sending a vessel to Sea without raising her anchors to put such a man in such a station, and yet the expedient resorted to was to make him a Major General who could not execute the duties of Q^r master! Another of poor Dearbornes props was Alexander Smythe, a man who to this hour is incapable of exercising a company, and this is the man who was to organize a raw army! General Bloomfield had some experience and was wounded at Brandywine, and his knowlege of details in the old forms is perhaps equal to any one of his cotemporaries; but he has not the remotest idea of modern principles, nor of that distribution of the duties which renders ten thousand men as manageable as one thousand he is a man of [rote?]² —and independent of the effects of a[ge] which is already dotage, he was not competent to any service in action, and especially in Canada; while Pike was in his brigade it was well because Pike saved him the trouble of every sense but hearing— and at last the organization of the Staff, afforded an opportunity to place him where no military service was required, but where it required the greatest patience and a Sentiment of generosity to keep matters out of confusion—a Volunteer association composed of the Sons of Tories and Aristocrats in this city were called into Service by him at the very moment they were defaming the government—they were sent to camp and were a curse to the neighborhood—on their march they entered peacable houses and carried away provisions by violence, tho' amply supplied by public providence; they practised in common various acts of violence on the public arms in their hands and damed them as Democratic Arms and returned them totally unfit for service; yet these men received <u>public thanks in a General order</u>

[527]

for their exemplary conduct and discipline! As adjutant General I declined signing and refused to publish such an order—but it is only a
Specimen of what was doing on the frontiers

I speak of this matter more fully because it comes under my own
Eyes and knowlege—I have no motive of a personal kind to be
dissatisfied with Gen. B. and he has more than once said he was
fortunate in having me as his adj. Gen. But it goes to shew what unhappy misconceptions governed the choice of officers. Winder was a
younger man, but before he was appointed he knew no more of military affairs than his horse; and I am satisfied he could not put a company in motion now after two Years experience. Chandler was not a
whit better as to intelligence. The consequences have been Seen, but
it has cost the country much treasure and much more precious blood,
which might have been saved. But if I were to go into the enumeration of all that might be truly said and deplored on this Subject, you
would be tired and I should be ashamed to exhibit a picture so inconsistent with the virtue of a republic and So fatal to its character for
talents and public spirit The refusal of Gen. Davie and Governor
Ogden of rank in the army, they pretend to justify upon such grounds
as those, tho' I am perfectly aware that their refusal was actuated
by different motives. Their nomination however is very characteristic of the fatal policy which has too long prevailed, and which your
goodness will excuse me for saying was too much countenancd by
yourself; it is too plain that we are not all <u>republicans nor all federal-
ists</u>—and the spirit of faction in the East, I apprehend has been too
much encouraged by the mistakes which they perceived we ran into,
and which they attributed to a fear of their power instead of that
benignity in which it originated

It will be found true I believe in all times that men who are indifferent to social and moral obligations, can be governed by no other
means than by their fears or interests; to place men of such a character on a level with men of principle or virtue is to reduce virtu
and vice, patriotism and perfidy to a common standard of merit! The
effects have been felt in our political affairs—and in our military operations—the army has exhibited a theatre of dissention, and the
sword which was sent to the field to assail the Enemy has been too
frequently unsheathed to assault the vindicator of his countrys rights
and government. The late General Pike told me, that until he witnessed the treasonable and Seditious discourses in the field, he had
considered himself a federalist, but that he was not only cured, but
astonished how the government ever appointed one of them to a place
of honor or confidence. I fear that the policy of <u>courting enemies</u> and

<u>sacrificing friends</u> prevails too much in political affairs, and remote and small as its beginnings were, that it has been carried to such a height as if not speedily put a stop to by some generous and magnanimous rallying of the republicans, it will end in the frustration of all the good that has arisen out of the triumph of 1800. I could Say a great deal on this topic if I were not afraid of tiring you or giving you pain—and I have not written on politics so much as I have now written since March last.

The sentiments you express concerning the unhappy men in the hands of the enemy, have warmed my most affectionate feelings towards you—Would to God that M[r] Madison felt as you do, and would act upon it; he would glorify himself and it would do more than ten sail of the line or twenty thousand men in prosecuting the war to a peace, and in elevating our country in the eyes of the World. Can it be possible that M[r] Madison does not converse with you or is his health such as to render him unable; surely M[r] Monroe would think and act with your thoughts. It would be rendering a most honorable Service to M[r] Madison and to humanity to point out this glorious path to Justice and national Dignity

I have never had the confidence or personal knowlege of M[r] Madison with which you have honored me, or I should have written him on such subjects often. A man has been lately Sent from Halifax to England in Irons who has been a citizen of the U.S. 20 years and with a family!

You may expect very soon to hear of something very decisive and brilliant by our land forces—the orders for operations have been issued for movements at four points on the same day; the Erie business will favor Harrisons operations, if he has only prudence to consult some man of talents as to his operations; but Proctor must evacuate Michigan and Malden to prevent being cut off; if Harrison possessed[3] either talents or enterprize he would by throwing 2000 men across the Lake to <u>Long Point</u>, compel him to Surrender at Discretion.

The operations going on[4] lately have had in view to deceive the enemy, and it has succeeded admirably for I find Sir Geo. Prevost has forsaken Kingston, where he ought to have made his stand in order to go up to the head of the Lake, to meet those demonstrations which were making there for no purpose in the world, as I believe but to delude him into a snare.

The division under Gen. Hampton has proceeded down Champlain; the troops with him are select and excellent; he has some able men near him, and he has discretion enough to depend on them more

than on himself, which is no bad quality in such a responsible station—being in it. I presume that he will be, (as he ought to be) in
montreal at least before the 1st of October; in that event our whole
force must be brought below. Kingston will I suppose be taken by
Wilkinson. Quebec will be left for the end of may & June next—
when it must fall—a siege of four weeks ought to bring Quebec under
the American banner.

But I have tired you—if it is not interesting it will be at least an
evidence of my unabated respect and confidence in Your continued
liberality & friendship WM DUANE

RC (DLC); hole in manuscript; endorsed by TJ as received 6 Oct. 1813 and
so recorded in SJL.

The WORK of Destutt de TRACY was the
manuscript of the fourth volume of his
Élémens d'Idéologie. The SENSIBLE AND
LIBERAL YOUNG MAN was William T.
Woodman, who wrote Duane on 23 Dec.
1813 from Falls of Schuylkill, Pennsylvania, that "When I commenced the translation of the manuscript you sent me, it
was my intention, after having once gone
over it, to transcribe the whole of it, and
correct the language, which I am conscious is far from being as pure and per-
spicuous as it ought to be. But situated as
I was, so much of my attention was engrossed by the school, that I had very little time to devote to the translation, in
consequence of which it was so long on
hand that I have been unable to accomplish my original design. I am fearful my
present indispensable engagements, will
for a considerable length of time prevent
me from giving it the necessary corrections. As I send it to you it is almost a literal version from the original, and for this

reason it abounds with Gallicisms, and
awkward constructions. You will of
course make every alteration and amendment that you may think proper, and if
you find it too inaccurate to be corrected,
as it comes from the press, I will endeavour to find time to amend it as soon as
possible" (RC in ViU: TJP; addressed:
"Col. Wm Duane No 98. Market Street
Philadelphia").

The American naval commander Oliver Hazard Perry had scored an important VICTORY ON LAKE ERIE on 10 Sept.
1813 (Heidler and Heidler, War of 1812,
413). TJ famously declared in his first
inaugural address that "We are all republicans: we are ALL FEDERALISTS" (PTJ,
33:149). LONG POINT is on Lake Erie.
KINGSTON is on Lake Ontario.

[1] Thus in manuscript, a rarely used
word meaning "transformation, meta-
morphosis" (OED). Duane may have intended "metaphysics."
[2] Word illegible.
[3] Manuscript: "possed."
[4] Manuscript: "only."

From John Wayles Eppes

DEAR SIR, Mill Brook Sep. 26th[1] 1813

I met with Doctr Flood at Buckingham court house on the second
monday of the present month. From him I had the pleasure of hearing you were in good health and that a letter from you to me had been
put into the mail at his Fathers on that morning—The letter has
not been received and I am unable to account for its failure—Even

if it had gone on to Richmond it ought to have reached me on Tuesday last—

From Mr Holcombes being called out with the militia Francis left Lynchburg rather sooner than I had expected—I have preferred keeping him at home to sending him back during the sickly season— He was just prepared to visit you previous to his return to school when the heavy Rains and rise of water courses induced me to detain him a week—Nothing but the uncertainty whether he would find you in Bedford or at Monticello prevented my sending him up in August, as he might at that time have passed several weeks with you without postponing the period of his return to school—

The account of commodore Perrys success on the Lake reached us by the mail last Evening. It will have a happy effect on public sentiment which has been greatly depressed by our various misfortunes.

The late Rains have produced great injury on the branches of Roanoke. I have not heard from the main river but the whole crop of every description is destroyed on Staunton—

Present me to the family and accept for your health and happiness every wish

from yours sincerely.   JNO: W: EPPES

RC (MHi); endorsed by TJ as received 27 Sept. 1813 and so recorded in SJL.

DOCTR Joel Walker Flood's FATHERS establishment was the Buckingham County ordinary of Henry Flood (H. Edgar Hill, "Descendants of John Flood" [2005 typescript in ViCMRL]; Eclectic

Repertory, and Analytical Review, Medical and Philosophical 1 [1811]: 518). The STAUNTON River is the name given to the section of the Roanoke River that flows from what later became the city of Roanoke to Clarksville.

[1] Reworked from "27th."

From Nicholas Biddle

SIR,   Andalusia On the Delaware Sepr 28. 1813

My residence in the country during the Summer has prevented me from answering sooner your very polite note of the 20th of August covering a communication to Mr Allen which was immediately transmitted to him. It is now a long time since I was tempted by the request of Genl Clark & other friends as well as by the natural interest of the subject to undertake the composition of the narrative part of the travels of Mssrs Lewis & Clark, whilst Dr Barton took charge of the objects of natural history connected with the work. I had written off roughly nearly the whole when other occupations interposed, and on Genl Clark's visit here last spring I gave up the manuscripts to Mr

Allen, who was to take the rude outline as I had left it, add from the original journals whatever had been omitted in the first rapid sketch, mould the whole as he thought best and superintend the publication. He informs me that about one half of the second & last volume of the narrative is printed & that the whole will appear shortly. The introductory notice of Gov[r] Lewis is very interesting and the account of the previous projects for exploring the country west of the Mississipi contains new & curious information. you mention the assistance of the Baron de Grimm. you may not perhaps have seen the correspondence of that gentleman which was published last year at Paris. I have received it & if I thought the perusal of it would gratify you, would forward it to you at Monticello, the more willingly, as I know that you regard with interest the literary occurrences of France. This correspondence however, tho' in five large Octavo volumes does not reach lower than the year 1782, a circumstance which diminishes in some degree its value to us.

My estimable friend M[r] Correa spent a short time with me on his way northward to embark for Europe. I am delighted at his visit to Monticello, since the sentiments with which he returns from it, have raised our country in his estimation, & will do us much honor abroad. They have also added greatly to the respectful consideration with which I am

Sincerely Yrs   NICHOLAS BIDDLE

RC (DLC); at foot of text: "Thomas Jefferson Esq. Monticello"; endorsed by TJ as received 10 Oct. 1813 and so recorded in SJL. FC (DLC: Biddle Papers); entirely in Biddle's hand; endorsed by Biddle.

A total of eleven volumes of the *Correspondance littéraire, philosophique et critique* of Friedrich Melchior, Freiherr von Grimm, covering the period from 1753 to 1782 were published in Paris in 1812. Another five volumes published in 1813 brought the edition down to 1790, and a final supplementary volume appeared in 1814. TJ acquired the first sixteen volumes, and probably the final one as well, through Robert Walsh and Joseph Milligan early in 1818 (Walsh to TJ, 27 Jan. 1818; Milligan to TJ, 6 Feb. 1818; Poor, *Jefferson's Library*, 14 [no. 918]).

To James Monroe

TH:J. TO COL[o] MONROE   Sep. 28. 13.

I inclose you the letters on finance, for perusal. I had not an opportunity of proposing the reading them to the President, there being much company with him. when will the ladies & yourself do us the favor of a visit?

RC (NN: Monroe Papers); dateline at foot of text; addressed: "The Secretary of State"; with endorsement and notes by Monroe on verso. Not recorded in SJL. Enclosures: TJ to John Wayles Eppes, 24 June, 11 Sept. 1813.

Monroe summarized portions of TJ's letter to Eppes of 24 June on verso: "200.000.000. the am[t] which may circulate—this gone into the hands of banks—

Let bills, as requird, be issued, on a tax redeeming them in 15. years on an interest of 6. pr cent—

Their credit being establishd issue others not bearing interest bottomed on a tax & if their credit faulterd, open public loans in w[h] these alone sho[d] be rec[d] as specie; a sinking fund—

The states should grant to congress the exclusive right to issue paper for ever, with a saving of charterd rights—all s[o] of connecticut river do it at once, except delaware, Congress wo[d] begin, by compelling uncharterd banks to wind up soon—

These bills would make their way & supplant unfunded paper of banks, by their solidity, universality, being rec[d] in taxes & duties—By taking bank paper & running the banks confine them to their specie

between war & war all this called in."

From Nicolas G. Dufief

MONSIEUR,   A Philad[e] ce 29 Septembre 1813

Vous trouverez, ci-Inclus, la feuille que par La faute de mon relieur vous n'avez pas reçu beaucoup plutôt. Je vous prie, d'avoir pour lui & pour moi beaucoup d'Indulgence

The "American Brewer & Malster" n'a point encore paru. Je veille cet ouvrage pour vous l'envoyer aussi tôt qu'il sera Imprimé. J'ai deux ouvrages <u>on brewing</u> l'un intitulé "the philosophical principles of the Science of Brewing,"[1] by Richardson & l'autre the Theory & practice of brewing by Combrune

Le traité du Bonheur & de la Morale ne Se trouve, à Philad[e] chez aucun libraire. Vous Serait-il égal de l'avoir de hasard? Car, je crois pouvoir vous en procurer un exemplaire. Je serais charmé de voir un aussi bon ouvrage traduit en Anglais, avec quelques notes

J'ai l'honneur d'être, très-respectueusement votre très-dévoué Serviteur   N. G. DUFIEF

EDITORS' TRANSLATION

SIR,   Philadelphia 29 September 1813

You will find enclosed the sheet that, due to a mistake by my binder, you did not receive much sooner. I beg you to forgive both him and me

The "American Brewer & Malster" has not come out yet. I will watch for this work, so as to be able to send it to you as soon as it is printed. I have two books <u>on brewing</u>, one entitled "the philosophical principles of the Science of Brewing," by Richardson, and the other the Theory & practice of brewing by Combrune

The Traité du Bonheur et de la Morale is not to be found in any Philadelphia bookstore. Would a secondhand copy suffice? I believe I can find you
one. I would be delighted to see so fine a work translated into English and
provided with a few notes

I have the honor to be, very respectfully, your most devoted servant

N. G. DUFIEF

RC (DLC); endorsed by TJ as received
6 Oct. 1813 and so recorded in SJL.
Translation by Dr. Roland H. Simon. En-
closure: Dufief, *A New Universal and
Pronouncing Dictionary of the French and
English Languages* (Philadelphia, 1810;

Sowerby, no. 4822; Poor, *Jefferson's Library*, 14 [no. 881]), 1:433–44.

[1] Omitted closing quotation mark editorially supplied.

From Thomas Law

D^R SIR   Wa[shing]ton Octo^r [1]st 1813.

Enclosed I submit to your perusal, what I trust will be deem'd
worth the trouble—If after a Year, these Treasury notes (become
due), were rec^d as Cash in paym^t of Subsⁿ to the loan, it would give
them full credit & enable Gov^t to issue more—The loan would also be
obtain'd on more advantageous terms, as these note holders would
encrease the number of competitors for the loan—

I remain With esteem Y^{rs} unfeignedly   T LAW—

RC (DLC: TJ Papers, 199:35472);
dateline mutilated; addressed: "To
Thomas Jefferson Esqr Monticello";
franked; postmarked Washington, 2
Oct.; endorsed by TJ as a letter of 1 Oct.

1813 received five days later and so
recorded in SJL. Enclosure not found.

The ENCLOSED memorial, not found, is
described in TJ to John Wayles Eppes
and TJ to Law, both 6 Nov. 1813.

From James Monroe

DEAR SIR   oct^r 1st 1813.

I have read with great interest & satisfaction your remarks on
finance, which I return by the bearer. we are now at the mercy of
monied institutions, who have got the circulating medium into their
hands, & in that degree the command of the country, by the adventurers in them, who without mu[ch] capital are making fortunes out
of the public and individuals. many of these institutions are hostile to
the gov^t, and the others have already gone far in loans made to it.
Hamiltons plan, was a reliance on monied institutions, aided by
taxes, at the head of which he had plac'd a national bank, since

extinct; and Gallatins has been the same, in respect to a national bank, having proposed to reinstate it, & in respect to any[1] species of taxes. Yours appears to me to be more simple, more consistent with original principles & with those of the constitution, much more œconomical, and certain of success, in both its parts, if it could be got into operation. I fear however that that has become difficult if not impracticable, by the ascendancy gaind by the existing institutions, & the opposition they would be sure to make, to its introduction in the radical form proposed, on which its success would principally depend. These corporate bodies would make a great struggle, before they would surrender—either their power, or the profit they are making by the use of it. Something however ought to be done to relieve the nation from the burthens & dangers inseparable from the present plan.

The fatiguing process of my concerns here, has kept me constantly at home and engaged. we will have the pleasure to dine with you to morrow if the weather permits, and mr Hay who joind us last night, indisposed, will accompany us, if his health should improve.

with great respect & esteem I am Dear Sir your friend

JA[s] MONROE

I find among my papers a bond of yours which came into my hands, while you were in Europe, & your aff[rs] in those of Colonel Lewis which is enclosed.

RC (DLC); edge frayed; endorsed by TJ as received 1 Oct. 1813 and so recorded in SJL. Enclosures: TJ to John Wayles Eppes, 24 June, 11 Sept. 1813. Other enclosure not found.

TJ's close friends Francis Eppes (ca. 1747–1808) and Nicholas Lewis man-aged his business affairs while he was in EUROPE serving as United States minister plenipotentiary in France, 1784–89 (MB, 1:23, 225; PTJ, 6:210; Malone, Jefferson, 2:203–4).

[1] Preceding four words interlined in place of "the."

From Edmund M. Blunt

SIR,   New-York, Oct. 2, 1813

May I beg your acceptance of a copy of the Nautical Almanac for 1814?

Respectfully, your very obt sert   EDM M BLUNT

RC (DLC); endorsed by TJ as received 10 Oct. 1813 and so recorded in SJL. Enclosure: Blunt, Blunt's Edition of the Nautical Almanac and Astronomical Ephemeris, for the year 1814 (New York, 1813; Sowerby, no. 3810).

To Andrew Moore

Dear Sir   Monticello Oct. 2. 13.

I take the liberty of troubling you on behalf of a Capt Joseph Millar, stationed at Charlottesville as an Alien; and will state his case as represented to me, and as believed by me. his father & mother came over about 1768. to Maryland to settle there. he was born there soon after their arrival, and the father dying, the mother thought it safest to return to her friends in Ireland where this son was brought up. he took to the seafaring business which he has followed all his life, except 4. years that he was engaged in a brewery in England. his voyages have been chiefly between England, the US. and the Baltic. a brother of his settled in Norfolk was a citizen[1] and died there not long since, possessed of 9 houses, and a plantation. the Capt hearing of it, left England the 1st of Nov. last to come and look after the property. he says it had been reported then in Liverpool, but was not believed that we had declared war. he had a passage of 105. days & therefore did not arrive in the Chesapeak till Feb. 8. was taken possession of by the English squadron, detained 10. days, ordered back, and attempting to get into the Delaware was ship wrecked. this is his case, and his birth in Maryland, as soon as he can get the proofs, will establish him a citizen. he asks permission to go in the mean time, gather up his property and put it into a course of being taken care of. his conduct here has been such as to acquire the esteem of all the neighbors insomuch that he is the inmate of all their houses & is looking out for a piece of land to settle here, never intending to leave the state again. in his principles he is as much an Anti-Anglican, and as fully with us in feelings as any one of us, and I am not afraid to make myself answerable that he shall have no communication with the British during the stay in Norfolk with which you may be so good as to indulge him. he thinks he could not arrange his affairs there in less than from a fortnight to a month, so as to take up his final residence here. after he shall have recieved the proofs of his birth in Maryland, he is advised to proceed to establish his citizenship by taking out a Habeascorpus, returnable before some federal judge, who may decide on it. the answer which you may be pleased to give, or the formal permission will probably come more certainly if directed to me; and he is anxious to set out immediately to look to his affairs. for coming from the north to Norfolk by water, he was permitted to stay there only two days to get his linen washed, & advised to keep within doors, so that he did not even see his property while there. having become intimate in my family, and much with us, I feel an interest for his success, and have the most perfect confidence in his honesty and sincere dispositions towards our country, and shall therefore be gratified by any indulgence which your duty may permit you to extend to him; and I avail myself with pleasure of this opportunity of assuring you of my great & friendly esteem & respect.   TH: JEFFERSON

PoC (DLC); at foot of first page: "General Moore"; endorsed by TJ.

Andrew Moore (ca. 1748–1821), attorney and public official, was born near Staunton and educated at Augusta Academy (later Washington and Lee University). After studying law under George Wythe in Williamsburg, he was admitted to the bar in 1774 and established a legal practice in Augusta County. Moore took part in Lord Dunmore's War in 1774. During the Revolutionary War he served in the 9th Virginia Regiment of the Continental army, 1776–78, fighting at the Battle of Saratoga and rising from lieutenant to captain. Moore represented Rockbridge County in the Virginia House of Delegates, 1780–83, 1785–88, and 1799–1800, and in the 1788 state convention that ratified the new United States Constitution, which he supported. He was a member of the United States House of Representatives, 1789–97 and 1804, the Senate of Virginia, 1800–01, and the United States Senate, 1804–09. During his long political career Moore proved to be a staunch Republican and a strong supporter of James Madison. He favored the disestablishment of the Episcopal Church in Virginia and opposed excise taxes, the Bank of the United States, and the Alien and Sedition Acts. By TJ's appointment, he was federal marshal for the Western District of Virginia from 1801 until it was merged into one statewide district the following year. Madison appointed him federal marshal for the Virginia District in 1810 and he held that position until shortly before his death. Moore was also a general in the state militia and a trustee of his alma mater, 1782–1821 (*ANB*; *DAB*; Charles W. Turner, "Andrew Moore—First U. S. Senator from West of the Blue Ridge Mountains," *Filson Club History Quarterly* 28 [1954]: 354–70; Heitman, *Continental Army*, 398; Leonard, *General As-*

sembly; *PTJ*, 2:549n, 32:360n; *JEP*, 1:402, 405, 2:156, 3:144, 153 [6, 26 Jan. 1802, 10, 11 Dec. 1810, 27 Nov., 9 Dec. 1818]; Joseph A. Waddell, *Annals of Augusta County, Virginia* [1902; repr. 1958], 232–3; *Richmond Enquirer*, 5 June 1821).

Joseph Miller (1776–1824), brewer, was born in Chestertown, Maryland, but his widowed mother carried him back to Ireland as an infant. During the years that followed he worked as a sea captain and in a London brewery. Miller decided to return to America after learning that a naturalized American half brother of his had died in Norfolk in November 1809 and left him property there. He left England in the autumn of 1812 but was delayed repeatedly by French and English vessels patrolling the Atlantic. Miller finally arrived in Norfolk early in April 1813 but was ordered inland and went to Albemarle County, where he struck up a friendship with TJ, helped establish a brewery at Monticello, and taught the former president's slave Peter Hemmings how to malt and brew beer. With TJ's assistance Miller returned to Norfolk in the autumn of 1813, but he visited Monticello several times thereafter. At the end of the War of 1812 Miller confirmed his American citizenship, established himself as a brewer in Norfolk, corresponded with TJ until at least 1819, and occasionally sent him corks for his beer bottles (Moore to TJ, 8 Oct. 1813; Petition from Joseph Miller to the Virginia General Assembly, 15 Dec. 1815; TJ to James Barbour, 11 May 1821; Joseph Miller Jr. to TJ, 20 Aug. 1825; Ann Lucas, *The Philosophy of Making Beer* [1995; keepsake for Spring Dinner at Monticello, 12 Apr. 1995]; *MB*, 2:1318–9n, 1331, 1351).

Under the general authority of a 1798 Alien Act, Moore as federal marshal for Virginia was required to move any enemy ALIEN found near the coast to a point at least forty miles from tidewater. He also had the authority to grant individuals monthly permits waiving this require- ment (*U.S. Statutes at Large*, 1:577–8; New York *Western Star, and Harp of Erin*, 6 Mar. 1813).

¹ Preceding three words interlined.

To George Logan

DEAR SIR   Monticello Oct. 3. 13.

I have duly recieved your favor of Sep. 18. and I percieve in it the same spirit of peace which I know you have ever breathed, and to preserve which you have made many personal sacrifices. that your efforts did much towards preventing declared war with France, I am satisfied. of those with England I am not equally informed. I have ever cherished the same spirit with all nations from a consciousness that peace, prosperity, liberty & morals have an intimate connection. during the eight years of my administration there was not a year that England did not give us such cause as would have provoked a war from any European government. but I always hoped that time and friendly remonstrances would bring her to a sounder view of her own interests, and convince her that these would be promoted by a return to justice and friendship towards us. continued impressments of our seamen by her naval commanders, whose interest it was to mistake them for theirs, her innovations on the law of nations to cover real piracies, could illy be borne; and perhaps would not have been borne, had not contraventions of the same law by France, fewer in number but equally illegal, rendered it difficult to single the object of war. England, at length, singled herself and took up the gauntlet, when, the unlawful decrees of France being revoked as to us, she, by the Proclamation of her Prince-regent, protested to the world that she would never revoke hers, until those of France should be removed as to all nations. her minister too, about the same time, in an official con- versation with our Chargé, rejected our substitute for her practice of impressment; proposed no other; and declared explicitly that no ad- missible one for this abuse could be proposed. negociation being thus cut short, no alternative remained but war, or the abandonment of the persons & property of our citizens on the ocean. the last one I pre- sume no American would have preferred. war was therefore declared and justly declared; but accompanied with immediate offers of peace on simply doing us justice. these offers were made thro' Russel, thro Admiral Warren, & thro the government of Canada. and the media- tion proposed by her best friend, Alexander, and the greatest enemy of Bonaparte,[1] was accepted without hesitation. an entire confidence in the abilities and integrity of those now administering the government, has kept me from the inclination, as well as the occasion, of intermedling in the public affairs, even as a private citizen may justifiably do. yet if you can suggest any conditions which we ought to accept, and which have not been repeatedly offered & rejected, I would not hesitate to become the channel of their communication to the administration. the revocation of the orders of council, and discontinuance of impressment appear to me indispensible. and I think a thousand ships taken unjustifiably in a time of peace, and thousands of our citizens impressed, warrant expectations of indemnification; such a Western frontier perhaps given to Canada as may put it out of their power hereafter to employ the tomahawk and scalping knife of the Indians on our women and children; or, what would be nearly equivalent, the exclusive right to the lakes. the modification however of this indemnification must be affected by the events of the war. no man on earth has a stronger detestation than myself of the unprincipled tyrant who is deluging the continent of Europe with blood. no one was more gratified by his disasters of the last campaign; nor wished, more sincerely, success to the efforts of the virtuous Alexander.[2] but the desire of seeing England forced to just terms of peace with us, makes me equally solicitous for her entire exclusion from intercourse with the rest of the world, until, by this peaceable engine of constraint, she can be made to renounce her views of dominion over the ocean, of permitting no other nation to navigate it, but with her licence, and on tribute to her; and her aggressions on the persons of our citizens who may chuse to exercise their right of passing over that element. should the continental armistice issue in closing Europe against her, she may become willing to accede to just terms with us; which I should certainly be disposed to meet, whatever consequences it might produce on our intercourse with the continental nations. my principle is to do whatever is right, and leave consequences to him who has the disposal of them. I repeat therefore that if you can suggest what may lead to a just peace, I will willingly communicate it to the proper functionaries. in the mean time it's object will be best promoted by a vigorous & unanimous prosecution of the war.

I am happy in this occasion of renewing the interchange of sentiments between us, which has formerly been a source of much satisfaction to me;[3] and with the homage of my affectionate attachment & respect to mrs Logan, I pray you to accept the assurances of my continued friendship and esteem for yourself.   TH: JEFFERSON

RC (PHi: Logan Papers); at foot of first page: "Doctor Logan"; endorsed by Logan. PoC (DLC). Tr (MHi: Timothy Pickering Papers); in Logan's hand; enclosed in Logan to Pickering, 1 Jan. 1815. Extract printed in Philadelphia *Poulson's American Daily Advertiser*, 6 Dec. 1813, and other newspapers.

The UNLAWFUL DECREES OF FRANCE were the Berlin and Milan decrees. THE LAKES: the Great Lakes. The UNPRINCI-PLED TYRANT was Napoleon, whose DISASTERS OF THE LAST CAMPAIGN occurred during his ill-fated 1812 invasion of Russia. The ARMISTICE suspending hostilities between Napoleon and his continental adversaries began on 2 June and ended with Austria's 12 Aug. 1813 declaration of war on France (Chandler, *Campaigns of Napoleon*, 898, 900).

[1] Word interlined in place of "Alexander."

[2] Newspaper extract consists of preceding two sentences.

[3] Tr ends here.

From John Adams

Quincy Sept [ca. 4 Oct.] 1813

σὲ γὰρ πάντεσσι θέμις θνητοῖσι προσαυδᾶν.

"It is not only permitted but enjoined upon all Mortals to address you." Why should not our Divines translate it

"It is our duty and our priviledge to address the Throne of thy grace and pray for all needed lawfull Blessings temporal and Spiritual,."

Θέμις was the Goddess of honesty, Justice, Decency, and right; the Wife of Jove, another name for Juno. She presided over all oracles, deliberations and Counsells. She commanded all Mortals to pray to Jupiter, for all lawful Benefits and Blessings.

Now, is not this, (So far forth) the Essence of Christian devotion? Is not this Christian Piety? Is it not an Acknowledgement[1] of the existence of a Supream Being? of his universal Providence? of a righteous Administration of the Government of the Universe? And what can Jews, Christians or Mahometans do more?

Priestley, the heroic Priestley, would not have dared to answer or to ask[2] these questions; tho' he might have answered them, consistently enough with the Spirit of his System.

I regret that Grotius has not translated this Hymn: and cannot account for his omission of it. Duport translates, the above line, only by "Te nempe licet mortalibus ægris cunctis compellare." Where he finds his ægris, I know not. No such Idea, is in the greek. All Mortalls, Sick or well, have a right and it is their duty to pray, as far as I can understand the Greek.

Bougainville translates it

"Et[3] tout ce qui respire animé par tes mains, à celebrer ta gloire, invite les humains. Beni Sois a jamais." This translation is Christian with a witness. None but a Jew, a Mahometan or a Christian, could ever have translated that Simple line in this manner. yet the Idea, the Sentiment translated into Christianity is very well: well enough.

The Gentleman of Verona Gironomo Pompei, translates it thus, After Salve o Giove, for "χαῖρε." "però che gli nomin tutti, dritto è ben, che a te volgan le parole." Now tell me, what resemblanc[e] of the Greek you can find in this Italian Version.

In this manner are the most ancient Greek Theologians rendered and transmitted to our youth, by the Christians.

Ἐκ σοῦ γὰρ γένος ἐσμὲν, ἰης μίμημα λαχοντες

Μοῦνον,[4] ὅσα ζώει τε καὶ ἔρπει θνήτ' ἐπὶ γαῖαν.

"Ἐκ σοῦ γὰρ γένος ἐσμὲν" I presume is the phrase quoted by Saint Paul, when he Says to the Atheneans, "One of your own Poets have Said We are all his Offspring." Acts. 17th 28. "For[5] in him We live and move and have our being; as certain also of your own Poets have Said, for We are also his Offspring.[6] Forasmuch then as We are the Offspring of God, We ought not to think that the Godhead is like unto Silver or Gold, or Stone graven by Mans device." This reasoning is irresistable. For what can be more mad, than to represent the eternal almighty omnipresent Cause and Principle of the Universe, by Statues and Pictures, by Coins or Medals?

Duport renders these two lines by "Omnes tua namque Propago
Nos Sumus, æternæ quasi imago vocis et echo"[7]
Tantum, quotquot humi Spirantes repimus.
Bougainville translates them thus
Nous Sommes tes enfans, ton Ombre ton image:
Et tout ce qui respire animé par tes mains,
A celebrer ta gloire invite les humains.
Beni Sois a jamais.
Pompei renders them
Che Siam tua Stirpe, e solo noi, fra quanti;
Vivon mortali e muovon Su la terra,
lo imitar de la voce abbiam Sortito.

Moses Says. Genesis. 1. 27. "God[8] created man in his own image." What then is the difference between Cleanthes and Moses? Are not the Being and Attributes of the Supream Being: The Resemblance, the Image the Shadow of God in the Intelligence, and moral qualities of Man, and the Lawfulness and duty of Prayer, as clearly[9] asserted by Cleanthes as by Moses? And did not the Chaldeans, the Egyptians the Persians the Indians, the Chinese, believe all this, as well as the Jews and Greeks?

Alexander appears to have behaved to the Jews, as Napoleon did to the Mahometans in the Pyramid of Grand Cairo. Ptolomy the greatest of his Generals, and a greater Man than himself was So impressed with what he learned in Judea, that he employed 70 learned Men to translate the Hebrew Scriptures into Greek, nearly 300 years before Christ. He Sent learned Men to collect Books from all Nations and deposited them in the Alexandrian Library. Will any Man make me believe that Cæsar that Pompey, that Cicero, that Seneca, that Tacitus, that Dionisius Hallicarnassensis, that Plutarch, had never Seen nor heard of the Septuagint? Why, might not Cleanthes, have Seen the Septuagint? The Curiosity of Pompey to See, the interiour of the temple Shews that the System of the Jews, was become an object of Speculation. It is impossible to believe, that the Septuagint, was unknown and unheard of by Greeks or Romans at that time, at least by the great Generals Orators Historians Phylosophers[10] and Statesmen, who looked through the then known World, for information of every thing, on the other hand how do We know how much Moses Samuel Joshua David Solomon and Esdrass, Daniel Ezekiel, Isaiah and Jeremiah learned in Babilon Egypt and Persia? The Destruction of the Library at Alexandria, is all the answer We can obtain to those Questions. I believe that Jews Grecians Romans and Christians all conspired, or connived At that Savage Catastrophy.

I believe Cleanthes to be as good a Christian as Priestley.

But enough of my School Boy criticisms and crude Philosophy, problematical History and heretical Divinity for the present.

JOHN ADAMS

RC (DLC: TJ Papers, 199:35470–1); edge trimmed, with missing text supplied from FC; partially dated, with full date conjectured from location of FC in Lb at MHi; at foot of text: "President Jefferson"; endorsed by TJ as a letter of Sept. 1813 received 13 Oct. 1813 and so recorded in SJL. FC (Lb in MHi: Adams Papers); dated 4 Sept. 1813, but entered in proximity to letters of 4 Oct. 1813 and obviously written after Adams to TJ, [22] Sept. 1813.

In the first two-thirds of this letter, Adams continues the discussion of the opening of the *Hymn to Zeus* by Cleanthes that he began in his previous letter of [22] Sept. 1813. Here he takes up lines 3–5, σὲ γὰρ . . . προσαυδᾶν and Ἐκ σοῦ γὰρ . . . ἐπὶ γαῖαν, of which a modern translation reads "For it is right for all mortals to address you: / for we have our origin in you, bearing a likeness to God, / we, alone of all that live and move as mortal creatures on earth" (Johan C. Thom, ed., *Cleanthes' Hymn to Zeus* [2005], 34–5, 40). As his source Adams used Brunck, *Gnomici Poetæ Græci*, 141–9. Adams was unsatisfied with the Latin, French, and Italian translations of these lines in that work, which can be translated "It is surely permitted for all feeble mortals to address you. For we are all your offspring, as if an image and very great echo of the eternal voice, however many of us animate beings creep upon the ground" (Latin translation by Dr. John C. Miller); "We are your children, your shadow, your image. And all that breathes, brought to life by your hands, invites human beings to celebrate your glory. Be blessed forever" (French translation by Dr. Roland H. Simon); and "It is indeed right, that all men, that they turn their words to you" (Italian translation by Dr. Jonathan T. Hine and Dr. Rosanna M. Giammanco Frongia). Θεμίς: "Themis." ÆGRIS: "feeble; sick." χαῖρε: "Hail." ALEXANDER the Great and Napoleon practiced religious toleration during their respective campaigns in Egypt (Josephus, *Jewish Antiquities*, 11.5, in *Josephus*, trans. Ralph Marcus, Loeb Classical Library [1937; repr. 1966], 6:472–9; Felix Markham, *Napoleon* [1963], 61–2). Gnaeus Pompeius Magnus (Pompey the Great) visited the INTERIOUR OF THE TEMPLE after the fall of Jerusalem to Roman forces in 63 B.C. (Josephus, *Jewish Antiquities*, 14.4, in *Josephus*, 7:481n, 482–5). Most of the specifics surrounding the destruction of the ancient LIBRARY AT ALEXANDRIA in Egypt remain controversial (Roger S. Bagnall, "Alexandria: Library of Dreams," APS, *Proceedings* 146 [2002]: esp. 356–60).

[1] RC: "Acknonowledgement." FC: "acknowledgement."
[2] Preceding three words interlined.
[3] Omitted opening quotation mark editorially supplied.
[4] This word thus in Brunck, giving the phrase the meaning "bearing only a likeness to God." Thom renders the word as "μοῦνοι."
[5] Omitted opening quotation mark editorially supplied.
[6] Extraneous closing quotation mark editorially omitted.
[7] Omitted closing quotation mark editorially supplied.
[8] Omitted opening quotation mark editorially supplied.
[9] RC: "cleary." FC: "clearly."
[10] Word interlined.

From Charles Yancey

D^R SIR   4th october 1813.

I have So far intruded as to give the bearer hereof Joel Walker Esqr[1] this letter of introduction to You he lives in the State of Ohio & has partook of the privations & hordships of a Soldier he merely wishes to see You & Your situation I think him Worthy Your Notice I am Yours Respectfully   CHARLES YANCEY

RC (DLC); dateline at foot of text; addressed [torn]: "[...] Monticello Mr Walker"; with unrelated calculations by TJ on verso; endorsed by TJ as received 5 Oct. 1813 and so recorded in SJL.

TJ was probably being introduced to Joel Walker (1764–1834), who was born near Natural Bridge, reputedly served as a private during the Revolutionary War, and became a surveyor thereafter. He lived in Rockbridge and Greenbrier counties before moving to Ohio in 1803 (Emma Siggins White, *Genealogy of the Descendants of John Walker of Wigton, Scotland* [1902], 228–9; DNA: RG 29, CS, Ohio, Fayette Co., Madison, 1830).

[1] Word interlined.

To Patrick Gibson

DEAR SIR   Monticello Oct. 6. 13.

In my letter of Aug. 10. I informed you I should draw on you from Bedford for 600.D. in favor of Brown & Robertson. this I accordingly did; and from the same place made three other draughts in favor of the sheriff of Bedford for 111.D. Nimrod Darnell 50.D. & Jeremiah A. Goodman 37.50 D it is questionable however whether this last will be called for.   in the same letter I mentioned that I should have occasion to draw in Sep. for about 600.D. and in Octob. for about 300.D. to answer existing calls. accordingly on the 4th inst. I drew in favor of Craven Peyton for 483.34 & of D. Higginbotham for 50.D. and on the 5th for 138.43 in favor of William Garth Dep^y sheriff of Albemarle for taxes; and I have to ask the favor of you to send me by post 300.D. which may be in 2. bills of 100.D each & the rest 20^s & 10^s and also to remit for me 25.D. to Gales & Seaton editors of the National Intelligencer at Washington. some small draughts will still remain to be made which will carry me beyond the estimate of my letter of Aug. 10. and will render it necessary at the next renewal of my note in bank, to add to it 500.D. to cover these draughts.

The unfortunate loss on my flour of the last year by the blockade & consequent fall of price, is seriously felt, and is much aggravated by the calamitous drought of the present year; such an one as has never been seen since the year 1755. we were 5. months from the 14th of April without rain to lay the dust, except a small one in May. this has reduced our crops both of wheat & corn to about a third of an ordinary one, and the latter being insufficient for the subsistence of our families, we shall have to buy, & probably at a high price. in Bedford I have been less unfortunate. tho' they had considerable droughts, they make bread for subsistence, a midling crop of wheat & some tobacco. I suppose I shall have to send you from both places about 400. barrels of flour. that from Bedford is ordered to be got down in all October & November. from this place it will not go so soon; but all will be down before Christmas. I think this the more essential, because, believing that the enemy cannot remain in the bay during the winter, I think all produce, which gets down in time, may be exported in the months of Dec. Jan. & Feb. subject only to the ordinary war-risks of capture, which will still admit it's bearing a reasonable price. there is no fear of their being permitted to lie in Hampton roads, should they even attempt it. this loss of 2. years crops by the blockade & drought is very afflicting to me in it's consequences, in still obliging me to trespass on the indulgence of the bank & of yourself. of the last crop half the price was lost, and in the present year, from 800. bushels of wheat sown, I had a right to expect as many barrels of flour, and am cut short one half by the drought. the remedy must be to make no new money engagements but for bread, and work out the existing ones as fast as the circumstances of the war will permit us. Accept the assurance of my great esteem & respect.

TH: JEFFERSON

PoC (ViU: TJP); at foot of first page: "Mr Gibson"; endorsed by TJ as a letter to Gibson & Jefferson and so recorded in SJL.

TJ issued DRAUGHTS IN FAVOR OF Brown & Robertson on 27 Aug., the sheriff of Bedford County ("for taxes now paiable") and Jeremiah A. Goodman ("for cotton to be used only if he finds a favorable purchase") on 9 Sept., and Nimrod Darnil on 12 Sept. 1813. On 4–5 OCTOB. he settled his corn account with Craven Peyton, returned money he had borrowed from David Higginbotham, and paid his Albemarle County taxes (TJ to Archibald Robertson, 27 Aug. 1813; MB, 2:1292–3).

Presumably about this same time, late in the summer or early in the autumn of 1813, TJ compiled a note summarizing the portions of the Virginia General Assembly's 20 Feb. 1813 "Act imposing Taxes for the support of Government" pertaining to land, slaves, carriages, and mills (MS at MHi; entirely in TJ's hand; undated; based on Acts of Assembly [1812–13 sess.], 3–4).

A missing letter from Higginbotham to TJ of 12 Sept. 1813 is recorded in SJL as received 15 Sept. 1813 from Milton.

From Andrew Moore

SIR   Lexington Octr 8th 1813—

I have Receivd your Letter of the 2^d Ins^t And have inclosd to Capt Miller a Written Permit to Return to Norfolk—He must Consider the Liberty as Subject to be Revoked by any[1] anstance of Misconduct Hostile to the Government—And also In the Event of the Commissary Generals disapprobation—Neither of Which I apprehend—

I congratulate on our late Successes on the Lakes & upper Cannada—The late Attempts to Mutiny By the Marines & Seamen And also by Troops destend for Land Service—As Reported here Will— I am persuaded—Prevent their being Trusted on shore—I think a Premium—in Land—to Deserters—to be laid off at a future day— and not Transferrable before surveyd—If such a Provision could be made known in the British fleet—Would fight all our Battles— On my Return to Richmond—Which will be as soon as I Recover from an Indisposition—I have been under since I left that place—I will Render any Assistance in my Power To promote the Sucess of Capt Miller

I am Sir With Great Respt & Estm Your Obt Ser^t

AND^W MOORE

RC (DLC); addressed: "Thomas Jefferson Esqr Monticello Albemarle County"; franked; postmarked Lexington, 11 Oct., and Charlottesville, 14 Oct.;

endorsed by TJ as received 14 Oct. 1813 and so recorded in SJL.

The LATE SUCCESSES by United States forces included Oliver Hazard Perry's naval victory on Lake Erie, the recapture of Detroit and, three days before the date of this letter, the American triumph at the Battle of the Thames (Stagg, *Madison's War*, 329–30). Recent British raids on Maryland's Eastern Shore had been foiled, at least in part, by the desertion of nearly one hundred of their servicemen and "a sort of a MUTINY, or pretty general determination of the troops to desert, while in *Kent* Island" (*Albany Argus*, 10 Sept. 1813).

[1] Word interlined.

From John Barnes

DEAR SIR— George Town 10th Octr 1813—

Your very Acceptable favour—tho dated, the 18th Ulto did not reach, me before last[1] evening—conveying the ageeable intilligence—Genl Kosciuskos receiving—your last years Remittance for ƒ5,500 franc's—with order to remit his Annual Int thro same Convenint Channel—in consequence, I instantly Addressed a few lines to Mr Geo Williams—at Baltimore on the subject of an immediate Remittance exchange &c—and if Necessary—I would wait upon him—to compleat the Negociation—in Order to convey as early as possible the 1st 2d & 3d to the good Genl—at Paris—

most Respectfully Dear Sir—your Obedt servt

JOHN BARNES.

PS.—your favr 21 July recd 26h lay unanswerd—daily expecting—to be favourd—with advices from Mr williams Baltimore—but am still without any from that Gentn—

your order of Mr J. Smith—was duly hond—

RC (ViU: TJP-ER); addressed: "Thomas Jefferson Esquire Monticello—Virginia"; franked; postmarked Georgetown, 11 Oct.; endorsed by TJ as received 13 Oct. 1813 and so recorded in SJL.

Jonathan SMITH was the cashier of the Bank of Pennsylvania.

[1] Reworked from "late."

From Frederick Jordy

DR SIR New Orleans 11h octobr 1813

It is with extreme reluctance I trouble you with these lines; I never yet applied to any living being for aid, whilst I could by dint of industry & the help of my talents work my way through the world: neither should I have resorted to this means now, were it not for the sake of my family. the height of Political intolerance made me quit Boston in the fall of 1807 (I had been teaching french there since 1801) possessing a Small Capital the fruit of 15 years close application, I ventured to remove to kentuckey in hopes there to bring up my children in the bosom of peace & plenty. the misfortunes of the times, false friends robbed me of the means of executing my plan; anxious for the wellfare of my young family; I removed to Natchez in 1811 there all my attempts proved abortive in consequence of bad crops, & the war which soon broke out. hither I have removed in hopes a great town, a Numerous population would enable me to rise again, by exerting all my talents, this is my last stake, but I fear I shall Draw a frightful blank. To you Sir I venture to address my self: If it be in your power to relieve from impending want, a father of a family, a man who never deserved the frowns of fortune, Through misconduct; lend a helping hand! to a man of your discernement Six hours conversation must have been sufficient to appreciate my merit, when I was at your house during the summer of 1799. Had I had the honor of being Personally Acquainted with Mr Maddison, I should have taken the liberty of applying to him, but being an utter stranger to that great man I thought an application to you would be more proper, & could not fail of having the desired effect If I had the good fortune of interesting you in my favor.

I now Inhabit a Portion of the union, where a good Citizen, master of the different languages that are spoken here, may be most advantageously employed, & at no time more effectually so as, at present, when the minds of many are alienated by the pressure of privations incident to a necessary war & the machinations of an insidious foe. If you Judge me Competent Sir to afford the least aid to government, I dare request your recommendation, it will not fail of having the good effect it so fully deserves.

If I was yet young & unincumberd with a family; I should prefer entering the Army but at forty Eight it is time for a man to seek the shades of retirement; Especially when his feeble means, compel him to attend to the Education of his children.

with Ardent wishes for your Happiness

I have the Honor to be Dr Sir with sentiments of the most Profound Respect your Very obedient & Humble Servant   FRED JORDY

RC (MHi); endorsed by TJ as received 5 Nov. 1813 and so recorded in SJL.

Frederick Jordy (Jordis) (born ca. 1765), language instructor, was described in one source as "a German." During the 1790s he lived in Salem, Massachusetts, where he reportedly taught French to Nathaniel Bowditch in exchange for instruction in English from the latter. Jordy served as a secretary to the French consul at Boston in 1798 and taught and translated French and German in that city and its environs from about 1801 until at least 1807. He then moved successively to Kentucky, to Natchez, and to New Orleans. In 1814 he asked General Andrew Jackson to help him obtain an appointment at the New Orleans customhouse. Twelve years later Jordy advertised an evening school to teach French and English to New Orleans residents (*Salem Gazette*, 8 Oct. 1793, 24 May 1796; Henry I. Bowditch, *Memoir of Nathaniel Bowditch: prepared for the young* [1841], 22–3; *The Boston Directory* [Boston, 1798], 71; [1805], 76; [1807], 97; *Salem Impartial Register*, 5 Jan. 1801; Boston *Columbian Centinel & Massachusetts Federalist*, 24 Sept. 1803; Jackson, *Papers*, 3:457; New Orleans *Louisiana Advertiser*, 16 Oct. 1826).

To John Adams

DEAR SIR   Monticello Oct. 12. 13.

Since mine of Aug. 22. I have recieved your favors of Aug. 16. Sep. 2. 14. 15. and ___ and mrs Adams's of Sep. 20. I now send you, according to your request a copy of the Syllabus. to fill up this skeleton with arteries, with veins, with nerves, muscles and flesh, is really beyond my time and information. whoever could undertake it would find great aid in Enfield's judicious abridgment of Brucker's history of Philosophy, in which he has reduced 5. or[1] 6. quarto vols of 1000. pages each of Latin closely printed, to two moderate 8^{vos} of English, open, type.

To compare the morals of the old, with those of the new testament, would require an attentive study of the former, a search thro' all it's books for it's precepts, and through all it's history for it's practices, and the principles they prove. as commentaries too on these, the philosophy of the Hebrews must be enquired into, their Mishna, their Gemara, Cabbala, Jezirah, Sohar, Cosri and their Talmud must be examined and understood, in order to do them full justice. Brucker, it should seem, has gone deeply into these Repositories of their ethics, and Enfield, his epitomiser, concludes in these words. 'Ethics were so little studied among the Jews, that, in their whole compilation called the Talmud, there is only one treatise on moral subjects.—[2] their books of Morals chiefly consisted in a minute enumeration of duties. from the law of Moses were deduced 613. precepts, which were divided into two classes, affirmative and negative, 248 in the former, and 365 in the latter.—it may serve to give the reader some idea of the low state of moral philosophy among the Jews in the Middle age, to add, that of the 248. affirmative precepts, only 3. were considered as obligatory upon women; and that, in order to obtain salvation, it was judged sufficient to fulfill any one single law in the hour of death;

[548]

the observance of the rest being deemed necessary, only to increase the felicity of the future life. what a wretched depravity of sentiment & manners must have prevailed before such corrupt maxims could have obtained credit! it is impossible to collect from these writings[3] a consistent series of moral Doctrine.' Enfield B. 4. chap. 3. it was the reformation of this 'wretched depravity' of morals which Jesus undertook. in extracting the pure principles which he taught, we should have to strip off the artificial vestments in which they have been muffled by priests, who have travestied them into various forms, as instruments of riches and power to them. we must dismiss the Platonists & Plotinists, the Stagyrites & Gamalielites, the Eclectics the Gnostics & Scholastics[4] their essences & emanations, their Logos & Demi-urgos, Aeons & Daemons male & female, with a long train of E^{t}c. E^{t}c. E^{t}c. or, shall I say at once, of Nonsense. we must reduce our volume to the simple evangelists, select, even from them, the very words only of Jesus, paring off the Amphibologisms into which they have been led by forgetting often, or not understanding, what had fallen from him, by giving their own misconceptions as his dicta, and expressing unintelligibly for others what they had not understood themselves. there will be found remaining the most sublime and benevolent code of morals which has ever been offered to man. I have performed this operation for my own use, by cutting verse by verse out of the printed book, and arranging, the matter which is evidently his, and which is as easily distinguishable as diamonds in a dunghill. the result is an 8vo of 46. pages of pure and unsophisticated doctrines, such as were professed & acted on by the <u>unlettered</u> apostles, the Apostolic fathers, and the Christians of the 1st century. their Platonising successors indeed, in after times, in order to legitimate the corruptions which they had incorporated into the doctrines of Jesus, found it necessary to disavow, the primitive Christians, who had taken their principles from the mouth of Jesus himself, of his Apostles, & the Fathers cotemporary with them. they excommunicated their followers as heretics, branding them with the opprobrious name of Ebionites or Beggars.

For a comparison of the Graecian philosophy with that of Jesus, materials might be largely drawn from the same source. Enfield gives a history, & detailed account of the opinions & principles of the different sects. these relate to

the gods, their natures, grades, places and powers;
the demi-gods and daemons, and their agency with man;
the Universe, it's structure, extent, production and duration;
the origin of things from the elements of fire, water, air and earth;

the human soul, it's essence and derivation;

the summum bonum, and finis bonorum; with a thousand idle dreams & fancies on these and other subjects the knolege of which is witheld from man, leaving but a short chapter for his moral duties, and the principal section of that given to what he owes himself, to precepts for rendering him impassible, and unassailable by the evils of life, and for preserving his mind in a state of constant serenity.

Such a canvas is too broad for the age of seventy, and especially of one whose chief occupations have been in the practical business of life. we must leave therefore to others, younger & more learned than we are, to prepare this euthanasia for Platonic Christianity, and it's restoration to the primitive simplicity of it's founder. I think you give a just outline of the theism of the three religions when you say that the principle of the Hebrew was the fear, of the Gentile the honor, & of the Christian the love of God.

An expression in your letter of Sep. 14. that 'the human understanding is a revelation from it's maker' gives the best solution, that I believe can be given, of the question, what did Socrates mean by his Daemon? he was too wise to believe, & too honest to pretend that he had real & familiar converse with a superior[5] and invisible being. he probably considered the suggestions of his conscience, or reason, as revelations, or inspirations from the Supreme mind, bestowed, on important occasions, by a special superintending providence.

I acknolege all the merit of the hymn of Cleanthes to Jupiter, which you ascribe to it. it is as highly sublime as a chaste & correct imagination can permit itself to go. yet in the contemplation of a being so superlative, the hyperbolic flights of the Psalmist may often be followed with approbation, even with rapture; and I have no hesitation in giving him the palm over all the Hymnists of every language, and of every time. turn to the 148th psalm in Brady & Tate's version. have such conceptions been ever before expressed? their version of the 15th psalm is more to be esteemed for it's pithiness, than it's poetry. even Sternhold, the leaden Sternhold, kindles, in a single instance, with the sublimity of his original, and expresses the majesty of God descending on the earth, in terms not unworthy of the subject.

'The Lord descended from above
And bowed the heav'ns most high;

And underneath his feet he cast
The darkness of the sky.
On Cherubim and Seraphim
Full royally he rode;
And on the wings of mighty winds
Came flying all abroad.'[6]
Psalm XVIII. 9. 10.

The Latin versions of this passage by Buchanan & by Johnston, are but mediocres, but the Greek of Duport is worthy of quotation.

Ουρανον αγκλινας κατεβη· ὑπο ποςςι δ' ἑοιςιν
Αχλυς αμφι μελαινα χυθη, και[7] νυξ ερεβεννη.
Ῥιμφα ποτᾶτο Χερουβῳ οχευμενος, ὡςπερ εφ' ἱππῳ·
Ἱπτατο δε πτερυγεςςι πολυπλαγκτου ανεμοιο.

the best collection of these psalms is that of the Octagonian dissenters of Liverpool in their printed Form of prayer; but they are not always the best versions. indeed bad is the best of the English versions; not a ray of poetical genius having ever been employed on them. and how much depends on this may be seen by comparing Brady & Tate's XVth psalm with Blacklock's Justum et tenacem propositi virum of Horace, quoted in Hume's history Car. 2. ch. 65. a translation of David in this style, or in that of Pompei's Cleanthes, might give us some idea of the merit of the original. the character too of the poetry of these hymns is singular to us. written in Monostichs, each divided into strophe and antistrophe, the sentiment of the 1st member responded with amplification or antithesis in the second.

On the subject of the Postscript of yours of Aug. 16. & of mrs Adams's letter, I am silent. I know the depth of the affliction it has caused, and can sympathise with it the more sensibly, inasmuch as there is no degree of affliction, produced by the loss of those dear to us which experience has not taught me to estimate. I have ever found time & silence the only medecine, and these but assuage, they never can suppress, the deep-drawn sigh which recollection for ever brings up, until recollection and life are extinguished together.   ever & affectionately yours   Th: Jefferson

P.S. your's of Sep ___ just recieved

RC (MHi: Adams Papers); edge trimmed, with missing text supplied from PoC; at foot of first page: "President Adams"; endorsed by Adams as answered 25 Nov.; docketed by Charles Francis Adams. PoC (DLC). Enclosure: enclosure no. 2 to TJ to Adams, 22 Aug. 1813.

Adams's partially dated letter to TJ with an AUG. 16 postscript is printed above at 14 Aug. 1813, while the partially dated letter from John Adams mentioned last by TJ in the opening sentence above is printed at 22 Sept. 1813.

ENFIELD'S JUDICIOUS ABRIDGMENT: William Enfield, The History of Philoso-

phy, from the earliest times to the beginning of the present century; drawn up from Brucker's Historia Critica Philosophiæ, 2 vols. (Dublin, 1792; Sowerby, no. 1337; Poor, Jefferson's Library, 9 [no. 518]). Johann Jakob BRUCKER's six-volume work was first published in Leipzig, 1742–47. The stagirites (STAGYRITES) were followers of Aristotle, who was a native of the Macedonian city of Stagira (OED). TJ's first attempt to cull Jesus's true teachings VERSE BY VERSE from the Bible is printed in EG, 55–105. The EBIONITES were first-century Christians who denied the divinity of Christ (OED). FINIS BONORUM: "chief good." Socrates discusses his DAEMON, a guardian angel that spoke to him when he was about to make a mistake, in Plato's *Apology*, 31c–d (Plato, *Euthyphro, Apology, Crito, Phaedo, Phaedrus*, trans. Harold North Fowler, Loeb Classical Library [1914; repr. 1990], 1:114–5).

The editions of THE PSALMIST cited by TJ included Nahum Tate and Nicholas BRADY, *A New Version of the Psalms of David, Fitted to the Tunes Used in Churches* (London, 1696); Thomas STERNHOLD and John Hopkins, *The Whole Booke of Psalmes, collected into Englysh metre* (London, 1562); James Duport and George BUCHANAN, *Psalmorum Davidicorum Metaphrasis Graecis versibus contexta . . . Cui in oppositis paginis respondens accessit Paraphrasis Poetica Latina* (London, 1742; Sowerby, no. 4399), with the Greek extract quoted by TJ appearing on p. 44; Arthur JOHNSTON, *Psalmorum Davidis Paraphrasis Poetica et Canticorum Evangelicorum*, ed. William Benson (London, 1741; Sowerby, no. 4398); and *A Form of Prayer, and A New Collection of Psalms, for the use of a Congregation of Protestant Dissenters in Liverpool* (London and Liverpool, 1763; Sowerby, no. 1513). The last-named publication was used by the OCTAGONIAN DISSENTERS, who met at a chapel called the Octagon in Liverpool, England, 1763–76 (Richard Brooke, *Liverpool as it was during the last quarter of the eighteenth century* [1853], 58–60).

Thomas BLACKLOCK's English translation of Horace's poem beginning JUSTUM ET TENACEM PROPOSITI VIRUM is in David Hume, *The History of England, from the Invasion of Julius Cæsar to The Revolution in 1688* (London, 1790–91; Sowerby, no. 370), 7:496. The Latin original is in *Odes*, 3.3 (Horace, *Odes and Epodes*, trans. Charles E. Bennet, Loeb Classical Library [1914; repr. 1995], 178–85). CAR. 2: Charles II, king of England. Girolamo POMPEI's Italian translation of Cleanthes is in Brunck, *Gnomici Poetæ Græci*, 147–9. MONOSTICHS: poems or epigrams of a single metrical line; such lines alternating within in a dialogue (*OED*).

Adams's letter to TJ OF SEP __ referred to in the postscript was received at Monticello on 13 Oct. and is printed above at 4 Oct. 1813.

[1] Preceding two words interlined.
[2] TJ uses this and the following dash to signal his omission of a sentence each from Enfield's *History of Philosophy*, 2:208.
[3] TJ here omits "any thing like" from Enfield's *History of Philosophy*, 2:209.
[4] Preceding two words interlined.
[5] TJ here canceled "power."
[6] Omitted closing quotation mark editorially supplied.
[7] Word editorially expanded. TJ used the Greek ampersand, a lowercase kappa with a tail.

From Patrick Gibson

SIR   Richmond 13th October 1813

I am favord with your letter of the 6th Inst and shall attend to the several dfts as they appear, I now send you inclosed $300 in small notes—as also a note for renewal on the 29th Inst for your signature—I have this moment learnt from Mr Higginbotham that he is going up immediately, and as there is some risk in sending notes by the mail, I have asked the favor of Mr H: to be the bearer of this—New flour is dull sale at $5.—

Your obt Servt   PATRICK GIBSON

I have paid Mr H: $8 for repairing your Watch

RC (ViU: TJP-ER); at head of text: "Thomas Jefferson Esquire"; endorsed by TJ as a letter from Gibson & Jefferson received 17 Oct. 1813 and so recorded in SJL. Enclosure not found.

Contract to Purchase Corn from Craven Peyton, with Subsequent Receipts

M. Bacon & C. Peyton have bargained for all the corn C. Peyton may have to sell—except about Seventy barrells—that is C.P. is to let M. Bacon hav[e] One hundred Barrells if he makes as much to sell aftar deducting the above Seventy; the Corn to be recav^d between the 1st & tenth of Novr On the rivar bank. at Twenty Shilling ⅌ barrell payable on the first day of March 1814—the Corn for the use of M. Jefferson;

Octr. 13–1813—
E Bacon for Th Jefferson
C. Peyton

No^r 12. 1813. Rece^d of C. Peyton for M Jefferson Eighty Four Barrells of the within mentioned corn it being all to spare

E Bacon for Th Jefferson

for value Rece^d pay Martin Dawson & Co the within Eighty Four Pounds

C. Peyton
De^r 13–1813—

Milton 6th March 1814
rec^d of Thomas Jefferson Esqr his Dft on Gibson & Jefferson for two hundred and eighty dollars pay^e at Sight for this consideration—in fav^r Martin Dawson

Martin Dawson & Co

MS (MHi); edge trimmed; contract in Peyton's hand, signed by Edmund Bacon and Peyton; first receipt on verso, in Peyton's hand and signed by Bacon; second receipt written perpendicularly to first, in Peyton's hand and signed by him, adjacent to signature: "M. Jefferson"; third receipt written below second, in Dawson's hand and signed by him; endorsed by Peyton: "Corn contract for 1813—E. Bacon" and by Dawson: "Craven Peyton to Martin Dawson & Co} Dft $280.00 1st March 1814."

TJ recorded this transaction on 13 Oct. 1813 and 6 Mar. 1814 (*MB*, 2:1294, 1298).

Robert B. Sthreshly to Edmund Bacon

SIR   [...] October 13 1813

on reflecting upon your offer considering it to be a good one I have determined to take it That is you may have your choise either to give me the 19/. cash or 20/. on the—160 Days this you can determine me either by the bearer John who is going to mill or by some other opportunity in the course of the Day the corn to be taken from the Stack in the course of November and early in December my head man Seems to think I shall certainly have 100. Blls for sale but in case of an accident we will say from 80 to 100 Blls

I am Sir your most ob^t   ROBERT B. STHRESHLY

RC (MHi); one word illegible; addressed: "Mr Bacon manager for Mr Jefferson"; endorsed by TJ: "Sthreshly Robert."

Robert B. Sthreshly (d. 1835), merchant in Port Royal, Caroline County, owned ten slaves in 1810. He expressed an interest in purchasing William Short's Indian Camp plantation in 1811–12 but settled instead on a property on Moore's Creek about one mile west of Monticello. In 1816 Sthreshly sold this possession to William D. Meriwether and moved to Kentucky. He acquired land near the town of Henderson in the winter of 1816–17 and was still living there in 1830.

Sthreshly died in Louisville (DNA: RG 29, CS, Va., Caroline Co., 1810, Ky., Henderson Co., 1830; TJ to Short, [26] July 1811, 26 Apr. 1812; Albemarle Co. Deed Book, 18:215–6, 20:122–3; Sthreshly to TJ, 24 Feb. 1817, 6 May 1823; Washington *Daily National Intelligencer*, 7 Dec. 1835).

On this day TJ recorded the purchase from Sthreshly of "100. Bar. corn @ 20/ paiable 160. days after delivery." On 2 May 1814 he drew on Gibson & Jefferson "in favr. of John Perry assee. of Rob. B. Sthreshly for corn bought ante Oct. 13. for 230.D. paiable the 10th. inst." (*MB*, 2:1294, 1299).

From William F. Gordon

DEAR SIR   Ch[arlottes]ville 15th Octr 1813.

I have the pleasure to inform you that the Judge this morning gave his opinion in your case of a Forcible entry & detainer v Michie in which the Inquest of the Jury was considered as sufficient on which to issue a warrant of restitution, and that the Justices acted legally in awarding restitution and in refusing the Traverse tendered by Michie, which put nothing in issue—The Case was argued by Mr Johnson Mr Barbour and myself on your part and by Mr Monroe on the part of Mr Michie—I cannot inform you what will be the course of Michie—If he wishes to appeal from the decision of this Court I believe, without Reference to authorities or to the Law, that his correct course will be to apply for a writ of Error to the General Court if he still continues dissatisfied.

With the highest respect I am Yr ob sert   W^M F. GORDON

RC (MHi); mutilated at seal; addressed: "Thomas Jefferson Esqr Monticello"; endorsed by TJ as received 17 Oct. 1813 from Charlottesville and so recorded in SJL.

The JUDGE of the state circuit court sitting in Charlottesville at this time was Archibald Stuart, while the JUSTICES of the peace in question were John Watson

and David J. Lewis. A WRIT OF ERROR directs a lower court to deliver a case to an appellate court for review (*Black's Law Dictionary*).

SJL records missing letters from TJ to Gordon of 4 and 16 June 1813. A letter of 6 Oct. 1813 to TJ from "Gordon & Barbour" (probably William F. Gordon and Philip P. Barbour), not found, is recorded in SJL as received the day it was written.

Archibald Stuart's Decision in
Jefferson v. Michie

[15 Oct. 1813]

David Michie   Plt   } upon a writ of certiorari directed
  against
Commonwealth at the instance of Thomas Jefferson Deft
  to John Watson and David J Lewis commanding them to certify to
  this Court more fully the proceedings had before them in a writ of
  forcable entry and detainer, by the Commonwealth at the instance
  of Thomas Jefferson against David Michie the 30^h day of July
  1812, whereby the said Michie was found guilty of a forcable detainer of the land in the inquisition mentioned, and a writ of restitution awarded and issued
This day came the parties aforesaid by their attornies and thereupon the transcript of the proceedings in the case aforesaid being seen and inspected it seems to the Court that there is no error in the proceedings aforesaid. Therefore it is considerd that the same be affirmed and that the said plaintiff pay to the Defendant Thomas Jefferson his costs by him about his defence in this behalf expended

MS (Albemarle Co. Law Order Book [1809–21], 185); in Alexander Garrett's hand; at head of page and applying to this entry: "Friday October the fifteenth 1813. Present the same Judge as on yesturday," with that judge identified as Stuart on p. 175.

Stuart presided over the Virginia circuit COURT covering Albemarle, Amherst, Augusta, Bath, Nelson, and Rockbridge counties (*ANB*).

To William McClure

Sir   Monticello Oct. 16. 13.

I was just going out on my ride the other day when your son called with your letter, which prevented my doing more than sending an order for the barrel of flour. I have with chearfulness supplied your necessities in consideration of getting my spinners & weavers instructed, informing you always that when this was done, you would have to look to other resources: and desirous that you should do this in time I mentioned to you some time ago[1] that when Dolly should be able to go on by herself, we should take her home. we accordingly propose, as the winter is now setting in, that after finishing the piece of cloth now in her loom, that it shall be set up here, & she come home to weave on it here. you will then have to stand on your own legs, as I formerly observed to you. you shall be welcome to continue in the house and tenement, free of rent, and I shall with pleasure do any thing I can towards promoting your business and it's success, which I am sure if pushed with activity will be a sufficient resource for your maintenance. accept the assurance of my best wishes for your success and of my respect.   Th: Jefferson

SC (MHi); at foot of text: "Mʳ William Mᶜlure"; endorsed by TJ.

No LETTER of October 1813 from Mc-

Clure to TJ is recorded in SJL and none has been found.

[1] Preceding three words interlined.

From John Jacob Astor

Sirr   New york 18 octʳ 1813

From the corect view which you had of the Importancs of my undertaking Relative to the trade in the Indian country and Particularly our establishment near the mouth of Columbia River I am Lead to belive that it would have afortd you pleasure to have heard of our Sucess which I had hopes to have Comunicated to you & which I Should have had in my Power to have Done had we not fallen a Sacrifics to Political events tho the Restrictive Measurs adopted by Congress prevented our oprating from this quater in the Interio yet we ware going on well from the other Side of the Land all our Pepal thare who went by Land across the Country & those who went by watter Round Cape Horn had meet at Columbia River where In 1811 thy Establishd thamselfs thy had build a forte & &. & and had Cliard Some Land from which thy ware Raissing Considerable Suplys—thy found the Indians in the vecenity Peaceble & friendly and thy had in 1811 Send Several parties in the Interior and a Long the coast to explor the country which thy found to abound with fish & game and the quantity of valuable furrs fare exceeding our most Sangguine exspectations thy had Establishd Several trading houses or post in the Interior & all Seemd to Promise well—the north west Compay of Canada became Senicble that in consequece of our arrangemts thy would have to abandon a great part of thire Indian trade made Representation to the British Government which ever being Ready to graps at & to monopolize the commerce of the world readily Listond to thire Representations & thy have Send out a frigate to Destroy our establishment & no Doubt to plunder[1] us of our property from the Information which I have Reced I am Lead to belive that the British government means to take possistion of Columbia River & to protect the north west Company in fixing a post for trade—

I have Long Since ben fearefull of that Such Steeps would be taking & I did Inform our government of it 12 months ago—Soliciting Some protection and Recomending that a Smal Garison might be plaisd there which with what we had and could have Done would have Securd the plaise for at Least Some few years to com I hope yet that government will Do Somethig and if So we may yet hold our possion which if Peace would in 4 or 5 years Prove of very great Importancs

you may have Seen by the publick papers the arrivl of M\ Stuart & others from Columbia the former Gentleman had resited there 15 months & had During that time explord a considerable part of the coumtry he keep a jurnal & of his voyage across the country which he Left with the President should you feel a Desire to read it I am Sure the President will Send it to you you will See that thire are Large & extenive Rivers in that part of the country of which we[2] had no knowladge before—I belive in the cours of 4 or 5 years if we had remaind at Peac we should have Drawn furrs from that coumtry to amount of Some Millions of Dollars ℔ annum—and we should most Certainly have confind the British traders to British Dominions—but as it is unless we have a Speedy Peace & that than we are permitted to carry on a trade to there we must exspect to abandon our plan & loss our Property & the Labour & time which has ben Spent in the undertaking which is very Considerable—in the mean time I am fearfull that our pepal will be Driven off & perhaps Dispers and it may not be easey to get tham to gether again thire number is about 120 and about 30 to 40 Sandwich Islanders who apear to be an excellent pepal Since the war I have Send two ships to Columbia River to give notics of the war and to furnish tham with Suplys—which if thy have arrivd in Safty may be the means to Safe the plais tho I have greate fears—I am with very great Respt

Sir your most obld Servent   JOHN JACOB ASTOR

RC (DLC); at head of text: "Thomas Jefferson Esqʳ"; endorsed by TJ as received 22 Oct. 1813 and so recorded in SJL.

The RESTRICTIVE MEASURS Astor complained of were the United States Non-Intercourse laws of 1 Mar. and 28 June 1809 and James Madison's 2 Nov. 1810 presidential proclamation restricting trade with Great Britain (*U.S. Statutes at Large*, 2:528–33, 550–1;

Madison, *Papers, Pres. Ser.*, 2:612–3). Robert Stuart's journal of his VOYAGE ACROSS THE COUNTRY was printed more than a century later as *The Discovery of the Oregon Trail: Robert Stuart's Narratives of His Overland Trip Eastward from Astoria in 1812–13*, ed. Philip Ashton Rollins (1935; repr. 1995).

[1] Manuscript: "blunder."
[2] Manuscript: "we we."

From John Barnes

DEAR SIR—   George Town Colum 19ᵗʰ Octʳ 1813.

Notwithstandᵍ I wrote Mʳ George Williams the 9ᵗʰ Insᵗ requesting a sett of exchange for same Amoᵗ as last year—at present ex—on the same firm vz Messʳ Russell & Morton—I am as yet most cruely disappointed—in not receiving any Ansʳ   I think it more than probable he is gone to some Eastern Port, in Order to recd some Cargo and dispatch—her back to Boroudeau—for no other than an Eastern port,—can a Vessel Venture to sail from—   I have been for these three weeks Horssed—with a Cold, I cannot get quit off—or I shᵈ ere this, have Ventured on a Journey to Baltimore for the purpose of Purchasing a Sett of Ex—on the best possible term of Safety—it is I hope possible I may yet have a line from Mʳ Williams, at least[1] learn his present place of Residence—I shall again write him—by this Nights Mail—

Most Respectfully—Dear Sir—Your Obedᵗ servᵗ

JOHN BARNES,

RC (ViU: TJP-ER); at foot of text: "Thoˢ Jefferson Esqʳ Monticello"; endorsed by TJ as received 22 Oct. 1813 and so recorded in SJL.

[1] Manuscript: "lest."

To Edmund M. Blunt

Monticello Oct. 19. 13.

Th: Jefferson presents his compliments to mr Blunt, and returns him many thanks for the copy of his edition of the Nautical Almanac for 1814. which he has been so kind as to send him. it is a very acceptable present as his inland situation renders it difficult to procure the English edition, to which mr Blunt's is made entirely equivalent by it's exact conformity with the original. he salutes him with respect & with his best wishes for the continuance of success in this useful publication.

RC (CtY: United States Presidents Collection); dateline at foot of text; addressed: "Mʳ Edmund M. Blunt Nº 202. Waterstreet New York"; franked. PoC (DLC); endorsed by TJ.

To Burgess Allison

Sɪʀ   Monticello Oct. 20. 13.

I had seen the advertisement of your spinning machine some time ago, and wished to know it's principle, as I was certain it would be ingenious. I have just been gratified with it in mr Cooper's emporium, and am as much pleased with it as I expected. it has some valuable improvements on the Jenny which I am in the use of in my family. will you be so good as to inform me what one of them of 12 spindles will ordinarily do in a day, and what is it's price? also, as the blockade, if it continues might render it difficult to get one brought round what is the patent price of permission to make a single one, for I believe my workman who makes the Jennies perfectly well could make one of these by mr Cooper's drawing. if you have information respecting mr Hawkins I should be glad to learn how he has succeeded in England: I hope in a manner worthy of his ingenuity. Accept the assurance of my esteem & respect   Tʜ: Jᴇꜰꜰᴇʀꜱᴏɴ

SC (MHi); at foot of text: "Dʳ Allison"; endorsed by TJ.

Burgess Allison (1753–1827), educator, Baptist clergyman, and inventor, preached in his native Bordentown, New Jersey, from the age of sixteen. He attended Rhode Island College (later Brown University) in 1777, received an honorary D.D. degree from that institution in 1804, and operated a classical boarding school for more than twenty years. A longtime friend of Charles Willson Peale, Allison was elected to the American Philosophical Society in 1789 and served as one of its secretaries in 1801 and 1810–11. Between 1802 and 1818 he patented improved methods of distilling spirits and stove construction. Allison also invented a nail and spike-making machine and, in 1812, a portable spinning machine. He was elected the chaplain of

[559]

the United States House of Representatives in 1816 and held that post for four years. James Monroe nominated Allison as a chaplain in the United States Navy in 1822. The Senate rejected him then, but the president renominated him a year later and secured his confirmation. Allison, who spent the rest of his life as a chaplain at the Washington Navy Yard, died in Trenton, New Jersey (Sprague, *American Pulpit*, 6:121–4; *PTJ*, 33:104–5; *Historical Catalogue of Brown University . . . 1764–1904* [1905], 524; APS Minutes, 16 Jan. 1789, 2 Jan. 1801, 5 Jan. 1810, 4 Jan. 1811 [MS in PPAmP]; Philadelphia *Aurora General Advertiser*, 19 June 1799; Peale, *Papers*, esp. 3:572–4, 4:440; *List of Patents*, 28, 34, 45, 74, 113, 191; *JHR*, 10:31, 13:22 [5 Dec. 1816, 8 Dec. 1819]; *JEP*, 3:265, 272, 337, 338 [14 Jan., 7 Feb. 1822, 28 Feb., 3 Mar. 1823]; Washington *Daily National Intelligencer*, 23 Feb. 1827).

Allison's first ADVERTISEMENT for his new "Portable Machine for Spinning Wool" appeared in 1812 (Philadelphia *Poulson's American Daily Advertiser*, 6 June 1812). Thomas Cooper included a description and DRAWING of the invention in his *Emporium of Arts & Sciences* 1 (1813): 461–3. In December 1802 Allison and John Isaac HAWKINS patented an improved method of manufacturing paper out of corn husks, and they also collaborated in marketing the physiognotrace (*List of Patents*, 31; *Alexandria Advertiser and Commercial Intelligencer*, 25 Jan. 1803; Peale, *Papers*, vol. 2, pt. 1, pp. 652, 653n). Hawkins had impressed TJ with the INGENUITY of the polygraph he developed with Peale, which TJ used to copy his own correspondence (Silvio A. Bedini, *Thomas Jefferson and His Copying Machines* [1984]).

To Gales & Seaton

MESS^{RS} GALE AND SEATON   Monticello Oct. 20. 13

I duly recieved your favor inclosing my account. on turning to my papers I found my last account with mr Saml H. Smith, agreeing with yours in the result, altho' not in the particulars. I send you a copy of it merely that these last may be understood. I have no doubt the result of both is right as they agree. I therefore some time ago desired the house of Gibson & Jefferson, in Richmond my correspondents to remit you the balance 25.D. if you have any person who recieves for you in Richmond I will give him a standing order to recieve the price of the paper of that house annually and to a day. Accept the assurances of my respect.   TH: JEFFERSON

SC (DLC); endorsed by TJ.

TJ's LAST ACCOUNT with Samuel H. Smith, enclosed herein, has not been found.

To John Sen Trescot

SIR   Monticello Oct. 20. 13.

Your letter of Sep. 7. is just recieved, informing me that the society, heretofore called Antiquarian, had extended it's views, and changed it's name to that of the Literary & Philosophical society of South Carolina, and had named me one of it's honorary members. I am very sensible of the honor done me by this nomination, and beg leave thro' you to return my thanks to the society. my distance from the institution, as well as my time of life will, I fear, render me but an unprofitable member to the society: but I pray you to assure them that I shall with willingness and zeal avail myself of any occasion which may offer of rendering them service. to yourself permit me to offer the assurance of my high respect and consideration.

                                    TH: JEFFERSON

PoC (MoSHi: TJC-BC); at foot of text: "Doctʳ Trescot"; endorsed by TJ.

From Thomas Voigt

DEAR SIR,   Philaᵈ October 20ᵗʰ 1813

I take the Liberty of Writeing you a few Lines Respecting the Watch & Chane, which I have ventured to send to you by post, Early in September Last, as I have not heard from you since, I fear you have not Received it—

I Remain yours Respectfully—   THOˢ VOIGT

RC (MHi); dateline at foot of text; adjacent to closing: "Thoˢ Jefferson Esqr"; endorsed by TJ as received 27 Oct. 1813 and so recorded in SJL.

To Patrick Gibson

DEAR SIR   Monticello Oct. 21. 13.

Your favor of the 13ᵗʰ with 300.D. inclosed is duly recieved, and I now return you the note for the bank filled up with 2000.D. the additional 500 D. being intended to cover my draughts until I shall get some flour down. I am concerned to learn that flour is but at 5.D. in Richmond. I see by the prices current of Philada it is there at 10.D. and some gentlemen now with me & recently from Baltimore assure me wheat was selling there at 1. D 60 presuming from this that there is a prospect of exportation during the winter, I am in hopes it will at length have some effect on the Prices at Richmond. Accept the assurance of my esteem & respect TH: JEFFERSON

PoC (facsimile in catalogue of 24 Mar. 1988 auction at Swann Galleries, New York City, lot 90); at foot of text: "Mr Gibson." Recorded in SJL as a letter to Gibson & Jefferson. Enclosure not found.

To John Adams

DEAR SIR   Monticello Oct. 28. 13.

According to the reservation between us, of taking up one of the subjects of our correspondence at a time, I turn to your letters of Aug. 16. & Sep. 2.

The passage you quote from Theognis, I think has an Ethical, rather than a political object. the whole piece is a moral <u>exhortation</u>, παραινεϛις, and this passage particularly seems to be a reproof to man, who, while with his domestic animals he is curious to improve the race by employing always the finest male, pays no attention to the improvement of his own race, but intermarries with the vicious, the ugly, or the old, for considerations of wealth or ambition. it is in conformity with the principle adopted afterwards by the Pythagoreans, and expressed by Ocellus in another form. 'περι δε της εκ των αλληλων ανθρωπων γενεϛεως Eτc—ουχ ήδονης ένεκα ή μιξις.'[1] which, as literally as intelligibility will admit, may be thus translated. 'concerning the interprocreation of men, how, and of whom it shall be, in a perfect manner, and according to the laws of modesty and sanctity, conjointly, this is what I think right. first to lay it down that we do not commix for the sake of pleasure, but of the procreation of children. for the powers, the organs and desires for coition have not been given by god to man for the sake of pleasure, but for the procreation of the race. for as it were incongruous for a mortal born to partake of divine life, the immortality of the race being taken away, god fulfilled the purpose by making the generations uninterrupted and continuous. this therefore we are especially to lay down as a principle, that coition is not for the sake of pleasure.' but Nature, not trusting to this moral and abstract motive, seems to have provided more securely for the perpetuation of the species by making it the effect of the oestrum implanted in the constitution of both sexes. and not only has the commerce of love been indulged on this unhallowed impulse, but made subservient[2] also to wealth and ambition by marriages without regard to the beauty, the healthiness, the understanding, or virtue of

the subject from which we are to breed. the selecting the best male
for a Haram of well chosen females also, which Theognis seems to
recommend from the example of our sheep and asses, would doubtless improve the human, as it does the brute animal, and produce
a race of veritable αριϛτοι. for experience proves that the moral
and physical qualities of man, whether good or evil, are transmissible
in a certain degree from father to son. but I suspect that the equal
rights of men will rise up against this privileged Solomon,[3] and
oblige us to continue acquiescence under the 'Αμαυρωϛις γενεος
αϛτων' which Theognis complains of, and to content ourselves with
the accidental aristoi produced by the fortuitous concourse of breed-
ers. for I agree with you that there is a natural aristocracy among
men. the grounds of this are virtue & talents. formerly bodily powers
gave place among the aristoi. but since the invention of gunpowder
has armed the weak as well as the strong with missile death, bodily
strength, like beauty, good humor, politeness and other accomplishments, has become but an auxiliary ground of distinction. there is
also an artificial aristocracy founded on wealth and birth, without either virtue or talents; for with these it would belong to the first class.
the natural aristocracy I consider as the most precious gift of nature,
for the instruction, the trusts, and government of society. and indeed
it would have been inconsistent in creation[4] to have formed man for
the social state, and not to have provided virtue and wisdom enough
to manage the concerns of the society. may we not even say that that
form of government is the best which provides the most effectually
for a pure selection of these natural aristoi into the offices of government?   the artificial aristocracy is a mischievous ingredient in
government, and provision should be made to prevent it's ascendancy. on the question, What is the best provision? you and I differ;
but we differ as rational friends, using the free exercise of our own[5]
reason, and mutually indulging it's errors. you think it best to put the
Pseudo-aristoi into a separate chamber of legislation where they may
be hindered from doing mischief by their coordinate branches, and
where also they may be a protection to wealth against the Agrarian
and plundering enterprises of the Majority of the people. I think that
to give them power in order to prevent them from doing mischief, is
arming them for it, and increasing instead of remedying the evil. for
if the coordinate branches can arrest their action, so may they that of
the coordinates. mischief may be done negatively as well as positively.
of this a cabal in the Senate of the US. has furnished many proofs. nor
do I believe them necessary to protect the wealthy; because enough
of these will find their way into every branch of the legislature[6] to

protect themselves. from 15. to 20. legislatures of our own, in action for 30. years past, have proved that no fears of an equalisation of property are to be apprehended from them. I think the best remedy is exactly that provided by all our constitutions, to leave to the citizens the free election and separation of the aristoi from the pseudo-aristoi, of the wheat from the chaff. in general they will elect the real good and wise. in some instances, wealth may corrupt, and birth blind them; but not in sufficient degree to endanger the society.

It is probable that our difference of opinion may in some measure be produced by a difference of character in those among whom we live. from what I have seen of Massachusets and Connecticut myself, and still more from what I have heard, and the character given of the former by yourself, [vol. 1. pa. 111.] who know them so much better, there seems to be in those two states a traditionary reverence for certain families, which has rendered the offices of the government nearly hereditary in those families. I presume that from an early period of your history, members of these families happening to possess virtue and talents, have honestly exercised them for the good of the people, and by their services have endeared their names to them. in coupling Connecticut with you, I mean it politically only, not morally. for having made the Bible the Common law of their land they seem to have modelled their morality on the story of Jacob and Laban. but altho' this hereditary succession to office with you may in some degree be founded in real family merit, yet in a much higher degree it has proceeded from your strict alliance of church and state. these families are canonised in the eyes of the people on the common principle 'you tickle me, and I will tickle you.' in Virginia we have nothing of this. our clergy, before the revolution, having been secured against rivalship by fixed salaries, did not give themselves the trouble of acquiring influence over the people. of wealth, there were great accumulations in particular families, handed down from generation to generation under the English[7] law of entails. but the only object of ambition for the wealthy was a seat in the king's council. all their court then was paid to the crown and it's creatures; and they Philipised in all collisions between the king & people. hence they were unpopular; and that unpopularity continues attached to their names. a Randolph, a Carter, or a Burwell must have great personal superiority over a common competitor to be elected by the people, even at this day. at the first session of our legislature after the Declaration of Independance, we passed a law abolishing entails. and this was followed by one abolishing the privilege of Primogeniture, and dividing the lands of intestates equally among all their children, or other representatives. these laws, drawn by myself, laid the axe to the root of Pseudo-aristocracy. and had another which I prepared been adopted by the legislature, our work would have been compleat. it was a Bill[8] for the more general diffusion of learning. this proposed to divide every county into wards of 5. or 6. miles square, like your townships; to establish in each ward a free school for reading, writing and common arithmetic; to provide for the annual selection of the best subjects from these schools who might recieve at the public expence a higher degree of education at a district school; and from these district schools to select a certain number of the most promising subjects to be compleated at an University, where all the useful sciences should be taught. worth and genius would thus have been sought out from every condition of life, and compleatly prepared by education for defeating the competition of wealth & birth for public trusts.   my proposition had for a further object to impart to these wards those portions of self-government for which they are best qualified, by confiding to them the care of their poor, their roads, police, elections, the nomination of jurors, administration of justice in small cases, elementary exercises of militia, in short, to have made them little republics, with a Warden at the head of each, for all those concerns which, being under their eye, they would better manage than the larger republics of the county or state. a general[9] call of ward-meetings by their Wardens on the same day thro' the state would at any time produce the genuine sense of[10] the people on any required point, and would enable the state to act in mass, as your people have so often done, and with so much effect, by their town-meetings.[11] the law for religious freedom, which made a part of this system, having put down the aristocracy of the clergy, and restored to the citizen the freedom of the mind, and those of entails and descents nurturing an equality of condition among them, this on Education would have raised the mass of the people to the high ground of moral respectability necessary to their own safety, & to orderly government; and would have compleated the great object of qualifying them to select the veritable aristoi, for the trusts of government, to the exclusion of the Pseudalists: and the same Theognis who has furnished the epigraphs of your two letters assures us that 'Ουδεμιαν πω, Κυρν', αγαθοι πολιν ωλεςαν ανδρες.' altho' this law has not yet been acted on but in a small and inefficient degree, it is still considered as before the legislature, with other bills of the revised code, not yet taken up, and I have great hope that some patriotic spirit will, at a favorable moment, call it up, and make it the key-stone of the arch of our government.

With respect to Aristocracy we should further consider that, before the establishment of the American states, nothing was known to History but the Man of the old world, crouded within limits either small or overcharged, and steeped in the vices which that situation generates. a government adapted to such men would be one thing; but a very different one that for the Man of these states. here every one may have land to labor for himself if he chuses; or, preferring the exercise of any other industry, may exact for it such compensation as not only to afford a comfortable subsistence, but wherewith to provide for a cessation from labor in old age. every one, by his property, or by his satisfactory situation, is interested in the support of law and order. and such men may safely and advantageously reserve to themselves a wholsome controul over their public affairs, and a degree of freedom, which in the hands of the Canaille of the cities of Europe, would be instantly perverted to the demolition and destruction of every thing public and private. the history of the last 25. years of France, and of the last 40. years in America, nay of it's last 200. years, proves the truth of both parts of this observation.

But even in Europe a change has sensibly taken place in the mind of Man. science had liberated the ideas of those who read and reflect, and the American example had kindled feelings of right in the people. an insurrection has consequently begun, of science, talents & courage against rank and birth, which have fallen into contempt. it has failed in it's first effort, because the mobs of the cities, the instrument used for it's accomplishment, debased by ignorance, poverty and vice, could not be restrained to rational action. but the world will recover from the panic of this first catastrophe. science is progressive, and talents and enterprize on the alert. resort may be had to the people of the country, a more governable power from their principles & subordination; and rank and birth and tinsel-aristocracy will finally shrink into insignificance even there. this however we have no right to meddle with. it suffices for us, if the moral & physical condition of our own citizens qualifies them to select the able and good for the direction of their government, with a recurrence of elections at such short periods as will enable them to displace an unfaithful servant before the mischief he meditates may be irremediable.

I have thus stated my opinion on a point on which we differ, not with a view to controversy, for we are both too old to change opinions which are the result of a long life of enquiry and reflection; but on the suggestion of a former letter of yours that we ought not to die before we have explained ourselves to each other. we acted in perfect harmony thro' a long and perilous contest for our liberty and independance. a constitution has been[12] acquired which, tho neither of us think perfect, yet both consider as competent to render our fellow-citizens the happiest and the securest on whom the sun has ever shone. if we do not think exactly alike as to it's imperfections, it matters little to our country which, after devoting to it long lives of disinterested labor, we have delivered over to our successors in life, who will be able to take care of it, and of themselves.

Of the pamphlet on aristocracy which has been sent to you, or who may be it's author, I have heard nothing but thro' your letter. if the person you suspect it may be known from the quaint, mystical and hyperbolical ideas, involved in affected, new-fangled and pedantic terms, which stamp his writings. whatever it be, I hope your quiet is not to be affected at this day by the rudeness or intemperance of scribblers; but that you may continue in tranquility to live and to rejoice in the prosperity of our country until it shall be your own wish to take your seat among the Aristoi who have gone before you. ever and affectionately yours.   TH: JEFFERSON

P.S. can you assist my memory on the enquiries of my letter of Aug. 22.?

RC (MHi: Adams Papers); edge trimmed, with missing text supplied from PoC; brackets in original; at foot of first page: "M͏ʳ Adams"; endorsed by Adams as answered 15 Nov. 1813; docketed by Charles Francis Adams. PoC (DLC). Tr (DLC: TJ Papers, 199:35492); in TJ's hand; at head of text: "Extract of a letter from Th: Jefferson to John Adams Oct. 28. 1813"; conjoined with Tr of TJ to Joseph C. Cabell, 2 Feb. 1816, and MS of TJ's Notes on Popular Election of Juries, [after 2 Feb. 1816].

Adams's partially dated letter with an AUG. 16. postscript is printed above at 14 Aug. 1813. παραινεϛις: "advice." TJ is quoting from the opening paragraphs of the fourth chapter of OCELLUS of Lucania's work *On the Nature of the Universe*, which is now believed to be spurious (Ocellus of Lucania, *De la nature de l'Univers* [Paris, 1768], 66–7; Sowerby, no. 1293; Poor, *Jefferson's Library*, 8 [no. 417]; *OCD*, 1058). OESTRUM: "estrus,"

specifically meaning the heat of female mammals (*OED*) but here applied more generally to humans OF BOTH SEXES. αριϛτοι: "best men, nobles." The biblical king SOLOMON allegedly had 700 wives and 300 concubines (1 Kings 11.3). Αμαυρωϛις γενεος αϛτων: "muddying the race of citizens." The citation VOL. 1. PA. 111 is to Adams's *A Defence of the Constitutions of Government of the United States of America* (London, 1787; Sowerby, no. 3004; Poor, *Jefferson's Library*, 11 [no. 650]). The biblical STORY OF JACOB AND LABAN is in Genesis, chapters 29–31. PHILIPISED (philippized): written or spoken by one wrongly or corruptly inspired or influenced, as with those who took the side of Philip of Macedon (*OED*). TJ's drafts of laws ABOLISHING ENTAILS, mandating equal division of the LANDS OF INTESTATES, providing for the MORE GENERAL DIFFUSION OF LEARNING, and protecting RELIGIOUS FREEDOM are printed in *PTJ*, 1:560–2, 2:391–3, 526–35, and 545–53, respectively. Ουδεμιαν πω, Κυρν', αγαθοι πολιν ωλεϛαν ανδρες: "Never yet, Cyrnus, have noble men destroyed a city" (Theognis, 43, in Gerber, *Greek Elegiac Poetry*, 180–1). Adams had suggested that WE OUGHT NOT TO DIE BEFORE WE HAVE EXPLAINED OURSELVES TO EACH OTHER in his letter to TJ of 15 July 1813. For John Taylor of Caroline's recently arrived PAMPHLET ON ARISTOCRACY, see Adams to TJ, 15 Sept. 1813, and note.

¹ Omitted closing quotation mark editorially supplied.
² Manuscript: "subservivient."
³ In PoC TJ here interlined "and his Haram."
⁴ Preceding two words interlined.
⁵ Word interlined.
⁶ Manuscript: "legislation."
⁷ Word interlined.
⁸ Tr begins here, preceded by a short introductory passage, portions of which appear earlier in the RC and PoC: "the

law for religious freedom having put down the Aristocracy of the clergy and restored to the citizen freedom of the mind; & those of entails & descents sapped at the root the great inequality of conditions existing among us, it was thought necessary to give to Aristocracy it's coup de grace by diffusing education thro' the mass of the people in order to qualify them generally for those civil functions they would now be called to perform, and especially for the judicious selection & superintendance of those whom they were to entrust with the care of their rights of liberty, property & conscience, and with the faithful administration of the government. with this view a law was <*proposed*> prepared by the Revisors."
⁹ Word interlined.
¹⁰ Manuscript: "of of."
¹¹ Tr ends here.
¹² Preceding four words interlined in place of "we have."

From Horatio Turpin

DEAR SIR   Richmond 28ᵗʰ October 1813.
    This will be handed you by my friend Capᵗ Ross a young gentleman on a visit to the United States from Hamburg a nephew to Mʳ David Ross, who wishes to pay his respects to you, your politeness & Attention to him will confer an Obligation on
        Sir Yʳ Mᵒ Obdᵗ   HOR. TURPIN

RC (MHi); endorsed by TJ as received 12 Nov. 1813 and so recorded in SJL.

Writing from Richmond the preceding day, Edward Ross advised his friend David Parish that "After I have gone, all the diversions through at the Oxford Iron Works, I shall proceed on from thence to Monticello; for my Uncle [DAVID ROSS], intends giving me a letter of Introduction to Mʳ Thoˢ Jefferson, who is a very intimate friend and School Mate of his and where I am promised to meet with a very hospitable Reception. My Uncle will also give me letters of Introduction to Mʳ Madison and Monroe" (RC at NCaS; ad-

dressed: "David Parish Esquire. &c Philadelphia"; stamped; postmarked 28 Oct.; endorsed by Parish as received 1 Nov. 1813 and answered the same day). No letter of introduction from David Ross to TJ for Edward Ross is recorded in SJL and none has been found.

On 23 Nov. 1813 Ross again wrote Parish, this time from Mount Ida in Buckingham County, to inform him that he had just returned "from Monticello, where I have been some time and was much delighted with the very friendly & hospitable Reception I met with from Mʳ Jefferson; what strong impression his amiable Grand Daughter Miss Randolph has made upon my Heart is impossible to describe and between you and me, I have some reason to believe, she is not alltogether indifferent to what regards me. . . . I have not rode ever since my return from Monticello, where I intend very soon making another long Visit as Mr Jefferson particularly begged me so to do and appears to have taken a great liking to me, for he did ride every day out with me, did show me all his Mills, farms, Machineries, Curiosities &c &c he conversed with me about Politicks all day long, about Europe and many other Countries" (RC at NCaS; addressed: "David Parish Esqre &c &c &c Philadelphia Pennsilvania"; stamped; postmarked New Canton, 23 Nov.; endorsed by Parish as received 29 Nov. 1813 and answered the following day).

To Thomas Voigt

SIR   Monticello Oct. 29. 13.

The watch had arrived safe and was entirely approved. I should have acknoleged it, but expected you would forward a seal and deferred my answer that I might at the same time remit you for that & the balance of 3.D. which I observe due on your bill. to remove suspence I now mention this with the assurance of my respect.

TH: JEFFERSON

PoC (MHi); at foot of text: "Mr Thos Voigt"; endorsed by TJ.

Voigt never sent TJ a SEAL for the watch, and TJ does not seem to have remitted him the outstanding BALANCE OF 3.D. Voigt's BILL, which came to $133 and had apparently been mailed to TJ along with the timepiece, has not been found.

From Samuel K. Jennings

DEAR SIR,   30th Octo^r 1813

I have satisfied myself, by a great number of experiments, that the influence of cold upon the skin, is the most universal cause which places the system in a state of predisposition to disease. I have also ascertained by experiment hundreds of times repeated, that a timely application of intense heat to the surface, will correct the predisposition, and prevent disease, even when sternly threatened. I have also further ascertained, that the same application, with the addition of some evacuations when necessary, will produce the same effect, in all seasons of the year. Indeed I hesitate not to say, that, <u>heat</u> may be used in this way to prevent Pleurisies and Rheumatisms in the Winter and Spring, and Intermittent, Remittent and continued fevers in the Summer and Autumn. I will include also every grade of bilious fever, which is not excited by an agent of power sufficient to destroy before it gives an alarm. I will not except typhus or Slow-fever as it is commonly called in this country.—

After fever is formed, so as to make regular medical attention necessary, I have also ascertained by experience, that heat may be used in the intermission and remission of the paroxisms, as a safe tonic agent.—that it may be so managed as commonly to supercede the necessity of blisters—And that in all cases, by judicious application, the course of disease may be shortened, and convalescence made more speedy and safe.

Your own experience in preventing the accession of threatening disease, by living abstemiously, and covering yourself warmly in bed, will evince to you the practicability of this plan. In your case the skin is warmed, and a balance regained in the course of two or three days—Upon my plan, the same object can be accomplished in one night.

Having ascertained that so much could be effected by the application of heat, I have taken pains to invent some appropriate method for its performance. And have succeeded[1] in the device of a stove by which the heated gas, escaping from burning ardent spirit, may be conveniently and safely conveyed into the patient's bed &c &c. Doctor Hall will give you an exhibition of the apparatus, and the process for using it.

I have thought fit to call it a "portable warm and hot bath."

It would be a valuable acquisition to the Army and Navy of the U States. [Would?] you be so obliging, as to give it a [letter?] of introduction to the Government? If you think well of it, Doctor Hall will be the bearer. He is authorized to transact the business for me. Hoping you will excuse this liberty

I am Dear Sir Your most Obed^t friend & Hum Servt

SAM^L K JENNINGS

RC (MHi); dateline beneath signature; mutilated at seal; addressed: "The Hon^l Thomas Jefferson Esqr Montecello" by "Doctor Hall"; endorsed by TJ as received 6 Nov., but recorded in SJL as received 5 Nov. 1813.

Samuel Kennedy Jennings (1771–1854), physician, teacher, and Methodist minister, was born in Essex County, New Jersey, and graduated from Queen's College (later Rutgers University) in 1790. He taught school in New London, Virginia, was ordained a Methodist deacon in 1805 and an elder in 1814, and edited the *Lynchburg Press* from 1809 until at least October 1813. In January 1814 Jennings received a patent for his "portable warm and hot bath" (renewed by Congress in 1843), which was said to relieve those suffering from rheumatism and other complaints. Later in 1814 the secretary of war ordered him to exhibit his invention in Norfolk, where he apparently remained until moving to Baltimore in 1817. In the latter city Jennings served as president of Asbury College for a number of years and taught at Washington Medical College, 1827–45. He left the Methodist Episcopal Church for the breakaway Methodist Protestant Church in 1828. Jennings's published works included *The Married Lady's Companion, or Poor Man's Friend* (New York, 1808) and *A Compendium of Medical Science* (1847). He moved to Alabama in 1845, later suffered a debilitating stroke, and returned to Baltimore about a year before his death (Thomas H. Stockton, *A Discourse on the Life and Character of the Rev. Samuel K. Jennings, M.D.* [1855]; Sprague, *American Pulpit*, 7:279–81; *A General Catalogue of the Officers and Graduates of Rutgers College* [1855], 18; Margaret Anthony Cabell, *Sketches and Recollections of Lynchburg by the Oldest Inhabitant (Mrs. Cabell) 1858* [1858; repr. with additional material by Louise A. Blunt, 1974], 209–10; Ruth H. Early, *Campbell Chronicles and Family Sketches Embracing the History of Campbell County, Virginia, 1782–1926* [1927], 436; Brigham, *American Newspapers*, 2:1120; *List of Patents*, 135; *JHR*, 38:137, 565–6

[4 Jan., 3 Mar. 1843]; Washington *Daily National Intelligencer*, 29 July 1814; Norfolk *American Beacon and Commercial Diary*, 11 Mar. 1817; *Salem* [Mass.] *Gazette*, 16 Apr. 1824; Harold J. Abrahams, *The Extinct Medical Schools of Baltimore, Maryland* [1969], 20, 22; Nathan Bangs, *A History of the Methodist Episcopal Church* [1840], 3:74–5; Baltimore *Sun*, 20 Oct. 1854).

The BEARER may have been Daniel Hall, who lauded Jennings's invention as "the happiest discovery of the age" in a letter written at Baltimore on 20 July 1814 and printed by Jennings in *A Plain, Elementary Explanation of the Nature and Cure of Disease, predicated upon facts and experience; presenting A View of that Train of Thinking which led to the invention of the patent, portable Warm and Hot Bath* (Washington, 1814), 111–2.

[1] Manuscript: "succeeeded."

From James Cutbush

D^R SIR   Philad^a Oct. 31st 1813.

The work you did me the honor to subscribe for, is nearly complete: the 1st vol. is finished, and the second, nearly So. I have collected, with much pains, a considerable quantity of American matter relative to the arts, manufactures, &c. and will, in a few days, send you a copy for your opinion. In the mean time I subscribe myself your friend & humble Servt   JA^S CUTBUSH

RC (DLC); adjacent to closing: "T. Jefferson Esq."; endorsed by TJ as received 5 Nov. 1813 and so recorded in SJL.

TJ had subscribed to Cutbush's WORK, *The American Artist's Manual, or Dictionary of Practical Knowledge*, 2 vols. (Philadelphia, 1814; Poor, *Jefferson's Library*, 6 [no. 221]).

An undated letter from Cutbush to TJ, not found, is recorded in SJL as received 14 Dec. 1813.

From Joseph Graham

Sir,   Port Republic Rockingham va Nov. 1–1813

Believing that a Reading of the inclosed Pamplett will not be disagreeable to you I have inclosed it to you; if it shall meet my expectation I am gratified if not; I think you will readily not take it in bad
part from your sincere & obt hb¹ S^t   JOSEPH GRAHAM

RC (DLC); dateline beneath signature; at head of text: "Thomas Jefferson
Esqr."; endorsed by TJ as received 13
Dec. 1813 and so recorded in SJL. Enclosure not found.

Joseph Graham (1768–1826) kept a
public house in Port Republic and served
from 1811 until his death as its postmaster. He owned six slaves in 1810 and four
a decade later, with his other holdings including nearby Weyer's Cave. According
to one 1815 visitor, Graham kept "a lock
upon the door of the cave and charges
50 cents to each visitor, which produces
him a considerable revenue" (DNA: RG
29, CS, Port Republic, 1810, 1820; Axelson, *Virginia Postmasters,* 169; *A Description of Wier's Cave, in Augusta
County, Virginia* [Albany, 1815], 8 [with
Graham's name corrupted to "Bing-
ham"]; Charleston, S.C., *City Gazette
and Commercial Daily Advertiser,* 29
July 1820; Rockingham Co. Minute
Book, esp. 6:61, 12:136–7; Rockingham
Co. Administrators' Bonds, 1 Jan. 1827;
Graham family Bible records [photocopy
of typescript in TJ Editorial Files];
gravestone inscription at Port Republic
Cemetery).

To George Hay

Dear Sir   Monticello Nov. 2. 13.

You may remember the case of Peyton & Henderson in the courts
of Chancery & Appeals, in which you acted for Peyton, and that I informed you that I had an interest in it. being in Washington myself
& totally unable to pay any attention to it, it was so wretchedly managed by Peyton as to render failure inevitable. the two only witnesses
who were important to him were not examined till a few days before
the Chancellor pronounced his decree, and were not returned to court
until after the appeal had been taken, & of course they could not have
been read in that court. in the mean time however Henderson def in
appeal, had conveyed all his property to trustees for the paiment of
debts, and Peyton purchased the part in question between him &
Henderson and paid the money to the trustee. having now the rights
both of pl. & def. in himself, I do not believe he gave you notice of it,
for I presume if he had the suit would either have gone off by consent
or there would have been a confession of error by the def. and a re-
versal. so much is said merely to recall the case to your mind; that
which I am now to mention tho concerning the same property depending on a different question. a David Michie had some time

before entered into a secret agreem^t with Henderson for a joint interest & partnership in the mill seat in question by a deed executed before a single witness and kept secret in the hands of that witness until
the decision of the C^t of appeals. I had then been in possession of
the lands some years. Michie considering the judgment of the court
of appeals as reestablishment[1] of Henderson's claim, entered on the
lands with some laborers and began to dig a canal. as soon as I heard
of it I went in person and ordered him off, and on his refusal obtained
a writ of forcible entry and detainer, on which he was removed on the
usual proceedings. altho' the jury were unanimous as to my possession & his forcible[2] detainer, yet as he had entered in my absence
peaceably 2. or 3. of them were squeamish about finding that he entered forcibly with pistols, swords, staves &^c which they said was not
the fact. the finding of the forcible entry therefore was so mollified as
to leave it doubtful whether sufficiently found, but no doubt as to my
seisin & possession & his forcible detainer. he removed the proceedings by Certiorari before the district judge, & there as I understand
insisted that both an entry & detainer forcibly having been alledged
& only the detainer found, it was vicious. it is said that judge Homes
had so decided in some case; but judge Stewart decided otherwise
here: and Michie has this day given me notice that on Friday the 12th
inst. he will move the Genl court for a writ of error. I must ask of
yourself & mr Wirt as usual to appear for me & oppose it. the possession is all important to Michie, because he can set up no other
claim but under the one witnessed, unrecorded deed. but it is important to me also; because these lands were purchased by Peyton of the
widow & 10. children all by separate deeds drawn by himself, and defective some[3] of them in form & substance & also in their probats.
and altho the purchases & paiments have been fair & executed by paiment & delivery, yet the informalities might give rise to chicanery. I
hope therefore the proceedings of the District court will be confirmed
& my possession retained. should it be otherwise would it be a case
where the court above would order a melius inquirendum, or would
they leave me to renew the process of forcible entry? the former
would be preferred. be so good as to consider this letter as intended
for mr Wirt as well as yourself, and drop me a line of information as
to the issue of the motion for the writ. friendly salutations to you
both.   TH: JEFFERSON

PoC (MHi); at foot of first page: "M^r
Hay"; endorsed by TJ.

The ONLY WITNESSES important to

Craven Peyton's case, according to TJ,
were Richard Price and Kemp Catlett.
Their depositions, taken on 17 May and
19 July 1805 respectively, cast doubt on

the legality (and even existence) of the contract giving John Henderson the right to run a millrace through his mother's lands. CHANCELLOR George Wythe issued his decree on 8 June 1805 (*Craven Peyton v. John Henderson* Court Record [ViU: TJP, TB (Thurlow-Berkeley) no. 907]). DEF: defendant. James Lewis and Matthew Henderson, John Henderson's TRUSTEES FOR THE PAIMENT OF DEBTS, received the deed to the mill seat from him in 1806. Lewis (THE TRUSTEE) purchased it at public auction in 1808 and later sold the possession to Peyton for $750 (Deposition by James Lewis, with Queries Posed by Thomas Jefferson and

David Michie, 1 July 1812; Haggard, "Henderson Heirs," 14–5). PL.: plaintiff. Martin Dawson was the SINGLE WITNESS to the agreement between John Henderson and David Michie. JUDGE HOMES: Hugh Holmes. JUDGE STEWART: Archibald Stuart. For Peyton's purchases from the WIDOW & 10. CHILDREN of Bennett Henderson, see Haggard, "Henderson Heirs," 5–9. MELIUS INQUIRENDUM: a writ ordering further investigation (*Black's Law Dictionary*).

[1] Manuscript: "reestabliment."
[2] TJ here canceled "entry, y."
[3] Word interlined in place of "several."

From Burgess Allison

[3 Nov. 1813]

[...] It is now a year since I have had a letter from M[r] Hawkins; he was then, and had been some time engaged as an Engineer, had undertaken two very stupendous works: one of them the constructing a Tunnel under the River Thames about eleven miles below London, which he had nearly compleated. The other was a Tunnel through Shuters hill, about eight miles from London, to level the eastern road. He had brought his Claviol to great perfection, so as to be pronounced one of the most delightsome Instruments ever exhibited in England: but for want of a more perfect knowledge of mankind, he was cheated out of the advantages of that and some other ingenious inventions. By the small Catalogue, which I enclose herewith, you will see the nature of an Institution [he] was about establishing; but being engaged by Govern[ment] in these publick works as an Engineer, he gave up all other pursuits. He still stiles himself an American, and always writes about coming <u>home</u> as soon as he possibly can.—

With sentiments of sincere Esteem, I remain: your Obed[t] Hb[l] Se[t]

B ALLISON

RC (DLC: TJ Papers, 199:35498); incomplete text consisting of last page and address verso; mutilated at seal; addressed: "Tho[s] Jefferson Esq[r] Monticello Virginia"; franked; postmarked Burlington, N.J., 4 Nov.; endorsed by TJ as a letter of 3 Nov. 1813 received seven days later from Burlington and so recorded in

SJL. Enclosure: John Isaac Hawkins, *Catalogue of Hawkins's Museum of Useful and Mechanical Inventions* (London, 1810).

Although Hawkins failed in his attempt to construct a TUNNEL UNDER THE RIVER THAMES, his successor Marc

Isambard Brunel built one that opened to the public in 1843 (Henry Howe, *Memoirs of the Most Eminent American Mechanics* [1856], 428–41; *ODNB*, 8:358). SHUTERS HILL: Shooters Hill, now located within the London borough of Greenwich. In 1800 Hawkins patented a CLAVIOL (claviole), a kind of compact, portable, upright pianoforte (*OED*; *List of Patents*, 21). TJ bought one that same year from the inventor for $264, but he returned the instrument two years later because it would not stay in tune (*PTJ*, 32:xxxv; *MB*, 2:1014, 1016, 1018; TJ to Hawkins, 13 Apr. 1802 [DLC]).

From James Monroe

DEAR SIR   Washington Novr 3^d 1813.

I receivd lately the enclosed letter from ch: Carter in which he proposes to submit the question between m^r Short and me, relating to the boundary of the land purchasd of him, to your decision. I most willingly accede to the proposition, and hope that you will undertake it. It will take you a mornings ride, thro' some rough ground, with a guide, which you may easily procure. You have all the other lights necessary in the case.

We have nothing new from Europe respecting our own particular concerns. nothing from our Envoys directly, or of them, more than what you see in the news papers. mr Crawford's notification of his arrival was acknowledged by the D. of Bassano, in very respectful terms, but there the business rests. Wilkinson is said to have mov'd towards Kingston, & there is a report of a canonade being heard at a distance, which is probable, as it also is, that we shall dislodge them of all the country above Montreal in which city, it is hoped, that our troops will take their winter quarters:

very respectfully your friend & serva[nt]   JA^s MONRO[E]

My affairs particularly the change in their managment require my personal attention in albemarle, for which purpose, I contemplate, making a visit there soon, if possible.

RC (DLC); edge frayed; endorsed by TJ as received 13 Dec. 1813 and so recorded in SJL. Enclosure not found. Enclosed in Monroe to TJ, 23 Nov. 1813.

On 27 July 1813 American minister plenipotentiary William H. Crawford notified the French minister of foreign affairs, Hugues Bernard Maret, duc de BASSANO, of his arrival in Paris. Writing from Dresden five days later, Bassano acknowledged the receipt of Crawford's message IN VERY RESPECTFUL TERMS (*ASP, Foreign Relations*, 3:628; Connelly, *Napoleonic France*, 324).

Albemarle County Court Decision
in *Jefferson v. Michie*

Thomas Jefferson } Comp^t

vs } Upon a bill in chancery to perpetuate testamoney

David Michie } Deft

This cause came on [to]¹ be heard² this fourth day of November 1813 On the bill answer, plea set down for argument and exhibits, and the arguments of council being heard & mature consideration had thereon, It is adjudged ordered and decreed by the court³ that the defendants plea be overruled, and that commissions be and are hereby awarded the complainant to take the depositions de bene esse of the several witnesses as prayed for in his bill, which when taken in pursuence of said commission on reasonable notice to the defendant shall be filed and preserved among the records of this court in perpetuam rei memoriam of the subject matter in the complainants bill contained and to be used in any future controversey touching said subject matter between the complainant and the defendant and any person claiming under them or either of them And it is further adjudged ordered and decreed by the court that the complainant pay to the defendant his costs by him herein expended

MS (Albemarle Co. Order Book [1813–15], 267); in Alexander Garrett's hand; at head of p. 264 and applying to this entry: "At A court of Quarterly Sessions continued and held for the county of Albemarle the 4th day of November 1813 Present } James Old Charles Wingfield John Watson & Joshua Key } Justices." Tr (ViU: TJP-LBJM); in George Carr's hand.

DE BENE ESSE: "in anticipation of a future need"; IN PERPETUAM REI MEMORIAM: "in perpetual memory of a matter" (*Black's Law Dictionary*).

¹ Omitted word editorially supplied.
² Preceeding three words not in Tr.
³ Preceeding three words not in Tr.

From Josiah Meigs

DEAR AND RESPECTED FRIEND,   Cincinnati, Ohio, Nov. 5. 13

I had the honour to receive your letter of Sept. 18 at the usual interval—If this people could but appreciate the real character of Britain, I think she would yield to our claims of Justice.—I have, ever since the year 1794 been satisfied that war or submission to the insolence of our old master made the only alternative. The evil Genius of Mr Hamilton came nearly to paralyse the nation—But we seem now to be encountering with vigour an unavoidable evil.—My feelings since my arrival here on the 22ᵈ of March last have been more awake than at any former period—and events of high interest have taken place, almost under my Eye.—In my youth I saw the thousands of New-England moving to the defence of Boston, New York &c—at that time I could not estimate the object in view so well as I have since my residence here—In the first 10 days of September I saw not less than 5000 mounted Voluntiers from Kentucky swarming around the Arsenal at Newport on the bank opposite to Cincinnati,—the Fleets crossing, and almost sinking with the burden of Men & Horses—and the gallant children of the Country chearfully marching to the North—and I have witnessed a far more pleasing Picture, if possible, viz those brave and right honest men returning to their Wives & Families & Fire Sides after having dashed to irrecoverable ruin the Power of Britain on this great outline of the Nation.

The wretched Savages seem to be now absolutely dependant on the mercy of the United States—and what is to be done relative to them is an interesting Question—Shall we, like the chosen people exterminate them?—I trust we shall not—

But I am occupying your attention with my own feelings—Your time, I doubt not is always agreeably employed—and I will only add that my own Joy is much increased, when I reflect that you and all good men have the same Joy—

I am very respectfully

Yours.   J MEIGS

RC (DLC); at foot of text: "The honourable Thomas Jefferson. Esquir"; endorsed by TJ as received 13 Dec. 1813 and so recorded in SJL.

Meigs evidently concluded that Great Britain's power on the frontier had been DASHED TO IRRECOVERABLE RUIN by the American victory over a force of British regulars and its Indian allies at the Battle of the Thames on 5 Oct. 1813, an action in which volunteers from Kentucky played a decisive part (Stagg, *Madison's War*, 329–30). In the Bible, God repeatedly orders the CHOSEN PEOPLE (the Jews) to exterminate their enemies (e.g., Deuteronomy 7.1–6, 20.16–7; 1 Samuel 15.1–3).

To John Barnes

DEAR SIR   Monticello Nov. 6. 13.

I have just recieved from Genˡ Kosciuzko a duplicate of his letter of May 30. to which he adds this P.S. 'you render me a great service by the arrangement with mr Morton to whom I owe many thanks for the most obliging manner in which I have been treated at Paris, and for the exactitude of his correspondent.' this channel then being so agreeable to the General we had better adhere to it, even if it occasions delay: because besides the justification of his approbation, if the house sees that we make our remittances steadily to them & to them alone, they will not be afraid to advance to the General, if our remittances should be delayed accidentally, knowing that they will come in the end. I thought it well to apprise you of this for your government, and only add my affectionate esteem & respect.

TH: JEFFERSON

PoC (DLC); at foot of text: "Mr Barnes"; endorsed by TJ.

TJ was remitting to Tadeusz Kosciuszko through the merchant HOUSE of Russell & Morton of Bordeaux.

To John Wayles Eppes

DEAR SIR   Monticello Nov. 6. 13.

I had not expected to have troubled you again on the subject of finance; but since the date of my last I have recieved from mr Law a letter covering a memorial on that subject which from it's tenor I conjecture must have been before Congress at their two last sessions. this paper contains two propositions, the one for issuing Treasury notes bearing interest, & to be circulated as money; the other for the establishment of a National bank. the 1st was considered in my former letters; the 2d shall be the subject of the present.

The scheme is for Congress to establish a National bank, suppose of 30. millions capital, of which they shall contribute 10. Millions in new 6. percent stock, the states 10. millions, & individuals 10. Millions, one half of the two last contributions to be of similar stock, for which the parties are to give cash to Congress: the whole however to be under the exclusive management of the individual subscribers, who are to name all the Directors, neither Congress or the states having any power of interference in it's administration. discounts are to be at 5. p.cent, but the profits are expected to be 7. percent. Congress then will be paying 6. p.c. on 20.M. and recieving 7. p.c. on 10.M. being it's third of the institution: so that on the 10.M. cash which they recieve from the states and individuals, they will in fact have to pay but 5. p.c. interest. this is the bait. the charter is proposed to be for 40. or 50. years, and if any future augmentations should take place, the individual proprietors are to have the privilege of being the sole subscribers for that. Congress are further allowed to issue to the amount of 3.M. of notes bearing interest, which they are to recieve

back in paiment for lands at a premium of 5. or 10. p.c. or as sub-
scriptions for canals, roads, and bridges, in which undertakings they
are of course to be engaged. this is a summary of the scheme as I understand it: but it is very possible I may not understand it in all it's
parts, these schemes being always made unintelligible for the gulls
who are to enter into them. the advantages and disadvantages shall
be noted promiscuously as they occur; leaving out the speculation of
canals E^{t}c. which being an episode only in the scheme, may be omitted, to disentangle it as much as we can.

1. Congress are to recieve 5.M. from the states (if they will enter
into this partnership, which few probably will) and 5.M. from the individual subscribers, in exchange for 10.M. of 6. p.c. stock, one percent of which however they will make on their 10.M. stock remaining
in bank, and so reduce it, in effect, to a loan of 10.M. at 5. p.c. interest. this is good: but

2. they authorise this bank to throw into circulation 90.M. of Dollars, (3. times the capital) which increases our circulating medium 50.
p.c. depreciates proportionably the present value of the Dollar, and
raises the price of all future purchases in the same proportion.

3. this loan of 10.M. at 5. p.c. is to be once for all only, neither the
terms of the scheme, nor their own prudence could ever permit them
to add to the circulation[1] in the same or any other way for the supplies of the succeeding years of the war. these succeeding years then
are to be left unprovided for, & the means of doing it in a great measure precluded.

4. the individual subscribers, on paying their own 5.M. of cash to
Congress, become the depositories of 10.M. of stock belonging to
Congress, 5.M. belonging to the states, and 5.M. to themselves, say
20 Millions, with which, as no one has a right ever to see their books,
or to ask a question, they may chuse their time for running away,
after adding to their booty the proceeds of as much of their own notes
as they shall be able to throw into circulation.

5. the subscribers may be 1. 2. or 3. or more individuals (many
single individuals being able to pay in the 5.M.) whereupon this
Bank-Oligarchy or Monarchy enters the field with 90.M. of dollars to
direct & controul the politics of the nation. and of the influence of
these institutions on our politics, and into what scale it will be
thrown, we have had abundant experience. indeed England herself
may be the real, while her friend and trustee here shall be the nominal and sole subscriber.

6. this state of things is to be fastened on us, without the power of
relief for 40. or 50. years. that is to say, the 8. millions of people now

existing, for the sake of recieving 1. Dollar 25 cents apiece at 5. p.c. interest, are to subject the 50.M. of people who are to succeed them within that term, to the paiment of 45.M. of Dollars, principal and interest which will be payable in the course of the 50. years.

7. but the great & National advantage is to be the relief of the present scarcity of money, which is produced and proved by

1. the additional industry created to supply a variety of articles for the troops, ammunition E^{t}c.

2. by the cash sent to the frontiers, and the vacuum occasioned in the trading towns by that.

3. by the late loans.

4. by the necessity of recurring to shavers with good paper which the existing banks are not able to take up; and

5. by the numerous applications for bank charters, shewing that an increase of circulating medium is wanting.

Let us examine these causes and proofs of the want[2] of an increase of medium, one by one.

1. the additional industry created to supply a variety of articles for troops, ammunition E^{t}c. now I had always supposed that war produced a diminution of industry, by the number of hands it withdraws from industrious pursuits, for employment in arms E^{t}c which are totally unproductive. and if it calls for new industry in the articles of ammunition & other military supplies, the hands are borrowed from other branches on which the demand is slackened by the war; so that it is but a shifting of these hands from one pursuit to another.

2. the cash sent to the frontiers occasions a vacuum in the trading towns which requires a new supply. let us examine what are the calls for money to the frontiers. not for clothing, tents, ammunition, arms which are all bought in the trading towns.—not for provisions; for altho these are bought partly in the intermediate country, bank bills are more acceptable there, than even in the trading towns.—the pay of the army calls for some cash; but not a great deal; as bank notes are as acceptable with the military men; perhaps more so. and what cash is sent must find it's way back again, in exchange for the wants of the upper from the lower country. for we are not to suppose the cash stays accumulating there for ever.

3. this scarcity has been occasioned by the late loans. but does the government borrow money to keep it in their coffers? is it not instantly restored to circulation by paiment[3] for it's necessary supplies? and are we to restore a vacuum of 20.M. of D. by an emission of 90. Millions?

4. the want of medium is proved by the recurrence of individuals with good paper to brokers at exorbitant interest; and

5. by the numerous applications to the state governments for additional banks, New York wanting 18. millions, Pensylvania 10. Millions E^{t}c but say more correctly, the speculators and spendthrifts of N. York & Pensylva, but never consider them as being the states of N. York and Pensylvania. these two items shall be considered together.

It is a litigated question whether the circulation of paper, rather than of specie, is a good or an evil. in the opinion of England and of English writers it is a good; in that of all other nations it is an evil: and excepting England, and her copyist the US. there is not a nation existing, I believe, which tolerates a paper circulation. the experiment is going on however, desperately in England, pretty boldly with us, and at the end of the chapter, we shall see which opinion experience approves. for I believe it to be one of those cases where mercantile clamor will bear down reason, until it is corrected by ruin. in the mean time however let us reason on this new call for a National bank.[4]

After the solemn decision of Congress against the renewal of the charter of the bank of the US. and the grounds of that decision, the want[5] of constitutional power, I had imagined that question at rest, and that no more applications would be made to them for the incorporation of banks. the opposition on that ground to it's first establishment, the small majority by which it was overborne, and the means practised for obtaining it, cannot be already forgotten. the law having passed however by a Majority, it's opponents, true to the sacred principle of submission to a majority,[6] suffered the law to flow thro' it's term without obstruction.[7] during this, the nation had time to consider the constitutional question, and when the renewal was proposed, they condemned it, not by their representatives in Congress only but by express instructions from different organs of their will. here then we might stop, and consider the memorial as answered. but, setting authority apart, we will examine whether the legislature ought to comply with it, even if they had the power.

Proceeding to reason on this subject, some principles must be premised as forming it's basis. the adequate price of a thing depends on the capital & labor necessary to produce it. (in the term capital, I mean to include science, because capital as well as labor has been employed to acquire it.) two things requiring the same capital and labor, should be of the same price. if a gallon of wine requires for it's production the same capital & labor with a bushel of wheat, they should be expressed by the same price derived from the application of a common measure to them. the comparative prices of things being thus to be estimated, and expressed by a common measure, we may proceed to observe that were a country so insulated as to have no commercial intercourse with any other, to confine the interchange of all it's wants and supplies within itself, the amount of circulating medium as a common measure for adjusting these exchanges would be quite immaterial. if their circulation for instance were of a million of dollars, and the annual produce of their industry equivalent to ten millions of bushels of wheat, the price of a bushel of wheat might be 1.D. if then by a progressive coinage their medium should be doubled, the price of a bushel of wheat might become progressively 2.D. and without inconvenience. whatever be the proportion of the circulating medium to the value of the annual produce of industry, it may be considered as the representative of that industry. in the first case a bushel of wheat will be represented by 1.D. in the second by 2.D. this is well[8] explained by Hume, and seems admitted by Adam Smith B.2. c.2. 436. 441. 490. but where a nation is in a full course of interchange of wants and supplies with all others, the proportion of it's medium to it's produce is no longer indifferent. ib. 441. to trade on equal terms the common measure of values should be as nearly as possible on a par with that of it's corresponding nations whose medium is in a sound state; that is to say, not in an accidental state of excess or deficiency. now one of the great advantages of specie as a medium is that, being of universal value, it will keep itself at a general level, flowing out from where it is too high, into parts where it is lower. whereas, if the medium be of local value only, as paper money, if too little indeed, gold & silver will flow in to supply the deficiency; but if too much, it accumulates, banishes the gold & silver not locked up in vaults and hoards, and depreciates itself; that is to say, it's proportion to the annual produce of industry being raised, more of it is required to represent any particular article of produce than in the other countries. this is agreed by Smith (B.2. c.2. 437.) the principal advocate for a paper circulation; but advocating it on the sole condition that it be strictly regulated. he admits nevertheless that 'the commerce and industry of a country cannot be so secure when suspended on the Daedalian wings of paper money, as on the solid ground of gold and silver; and that in time of war, the insecurity is greatly increased, and great confusion possible where the circulation is for the greater part in paper.' B.2. c.2. 484. but in a country where loans are uncertain, and a specie circulation the only sure resource for them, the preference of that circulation assumes a far different degree of importance, as is explained in my former letters.

[582]

The only advantage which Smith proposes by substituting paper in the room of gold and silver money, B.2. c.2. 434. is 'to replace an expensive instrument with one much less costly, and <u>sometimes equally convenient</u>':[9] that is to say, pa. 437. 'to allow the gold and silver to be sent abroad and converted into foreign goods' and to substitute paper as being a cheaper measure. but this makes no addition to the stock or capital of the nation. the coin sent out was worth as much, while in the country, as the goods imported & taking it's place. it is only then a change of form in a part of the national capital, from that of gold and silver to other goods. he admits too that while a part of the goods recieved in exchange for the coin exported, may be 'materials,[10] tools and provisions for the emploiment of an additional industry, a part also may be taken back in foreign wines, silks E'c. to be consumed by idle people who produce nothing; and so far the substitution promotes prodigality, increases expence & consumption, without increasing production.' so far also then it lessens the capital of the nation. what may be the amount which the conversion of the part exchanged for productive goods may add to the former productive mass, it is not easy to ascertain, because, as he says, pa. 441. it is impossible to determine what is the proportion which the circulating money of any country bears to the whole value of the annual produce. it has been computed by different authors from a[11] 5th to a 30th of that value.[12] in the US. it must be less than in any other part of the commercial world; because the great mass of their inhabitants being in responsible circumstances, the great mass of their exchanges in the country is effected, on credit, in their merchant's ledger, who supplies all their wants thro' the year, and at the end of it, recieves the produce of their farms, or other articles of their industry. it is a fact that a farmer with a revenue of 10,000 D. a year, may obtain all his supplies from his merchant, and liquidate them at the end of the year, by the sale of his produce to him, without the intervention of a single dollar of cash. this then is merely barter, and in this way of barter a great portion of the annual produce of the US. is exchanged without the intermediation of cash.[13] we might safely then state our medium at the minimum of $\frac{1}{30}$. but what is $\frac{1}{30}$ of the value of the annual produce of the industry of the US? or what is the whole value of the annual[14] produce of the US?[15] an able writer and competent judge of the subject in 1799. on as good grounds as probably could be taken estimated it, on the then population of $4\frac{1}{2}$ millions of inhabitants, to be $37\frac{1}{2}$ millions sterling, or $168\frac{3}{4}$ M. of Dollars. see Cooper's Political arithmetic 47. according to the same estimate for our present population it will be 300.M. of Dollars, $\frac{1}{30}$ of which, Smith's minimum, would be 10.M. and $\frac{1}{5}$, his maximum, would be 60.M. for the quantum of circulation. but suppose that, instead of our needing the least circulating medium of any nation, from the circumstance before mentioned, we should place ourselves in the middle term of the calculation, to wit at 35. millions. one fifth of this at the least, Smith thinks should be retained in specie, which would leave 28. millions of specie to be exported in exchange for other commodities; and if 15 M. of that should be returned in productive goods, and not in articles of prodigality, that would be the amount of capital which this operation would add to the existing mass. but to what mass? not that of the 300.M. which is only it's gross annual produce; but to that capital of which the 300.M. are but the annual[16] produce. but this being gross, we may infer from it the value[17] of the capital by considering that the rent of lands is generally fixed at one third of the gross produce, and is deemed it's nett profit, and twenty times that it's feesimple value. the profits on landed capital, may, with accuracy enough for our purpose, be supposed on a par, with those of other capital. this would give us then for the US. a capital of 2000. millions, all in active employment, and exclusive of unimproved lands lying in a great degree dormant. of this, 15 millions would be the hundred and thirty third part. and it is for[18] this petty addition to the capital of the nation, this minimum of 1.D. added to $133\frac{1}{3}$ or $\frac{3}{4}$ p.c. that we are to give up our gold & silver medium, it's intrinsic solidity, it's universal value, and it's saving powers in time of war, and to substitute for it paper, with all it's train of evils, moral, political and physical, which I will not pretend to enumerate.[19]

There is another authority, to which we may appeal for the proper quantity of circulating medium for the US.[20] the old Congress, when we were estimated at about[21] two millions of people on a long and able discussion, June 22. 1775.[22] decided the sufficient quantity to be two millions of Dollars which sum they then emitted;[23*] according to this it should be 8.M. now that we are 8.M. of people. this differs little from Smith's minimum of 10.M. and strengthens our respect for that estimate.

There is indeed a convenience in paper, it's easy transmission from one place to another. but this may be mainly supplied by bills of exchange, so as to prevent any great displacement of actual coin. two places trading together balance their dealings for the most part, by their mutual supplies, and the debtor individuals of either may,

---

*within 5. months after this they were compelled by the necessities of the war to abandon the idea of emitting only an adequate circulation, and to make those necessities the sole measure of their emissions.[24]

instead of cash, remit the bills of those who are creditors in the same dealings; or may obtain them through some third place with which both have dealings. the cases would be rare where such bills could not be obtained, either directly or circuitously, and too unimportant to the nation to overweigh the train of evils flowing from paper circulation.

From 8. to 35. millions then being our proper circulation and 200.M. the actual one, the Memorial proposes to issue 90.M. more because, it says, a great scarcity of money is proved by the numerous applications for banks, to wit, N. York for 18.M. Pensylvania 10.M. E^tc. the answer to this shall be quoted from Adam Smith B.2. c.2. pa. 462. where speaking of the complaints of the traders against the Scotch bankers, who had already gone too far in their issues of paper, he says 'those traders and other[25] undertakers having got so much assistance from banks wished to get still more. the banks, they seem to have thought, could extend their credits[26] to whatever sum might be wanted, without incurring any other expence besides that of a few reams of paper. they complained of the contracted views and dastardly spirit of the Directors of those banks, which did not, they said, extend their credits in proportion to the extension of the trade of the country; meaning, no doubt, by the extension of that trade, the extension of their own projects beyond what they could carry on, either with their own capital, or with what they had credit to borrow of private people in the usual way of bond or mortgage. the banks, they seem to have thought, were in honor bound to supply the deficiency, and to provide them with all the capital which they wanted to trade with.' and again pa. 470. 'when bankers discovered that certain projectors were trading, not with any capital of their own, but with that which they advanced them, they endeavored to withdraw gradually, making every day greater and greater difficulties about discounting.—these difficulties alarmed & enraged in the highest degree those projectors. their own distress, of which this prudent and necessary reserve of the banks was no doubt the immediate occasion, they called the distress of the country; and this distress of the country, they said, was altogether owing to the ignorance, pusillanimity, and bad conduct of the banks, which did not give a sufficiently liberal aid to the spirited undertakings of those who exerted themselves in order to beautify, improve, and enrich the country. it was the duty of the banks, they seemed to think, to lend for as long a time, and to as great an extent, as they might wish to borrow.' it is probably the good paper[27] of these projectors which the Memorial says the banks being unable to discount, goes into the hands of brokers, who (knowing the risk of this good paper) discount it at a much higher rate than legal interest, to the great distress of the enterprising adventurers who had rather try trade on borrowed capital than go to the plough or other laborious calling. Smith again says pa. 478. 'that the industry of Scotland languished for want of money to employ it, was the opinion of the famous mr Law. by establishing a bank of a particular kind which, he seems to have imagined, might issue paper to the amount of the whole value of all the lands in the country, he proposed to remedy this want of money.—it was afterwards adopted, with some variations, by the Duke of Orleans at that time regent of France. the idea of the possibility of multiplying paper to almost any extent was the real foundation of what is called the Missisipi scheme, the most extravagant project, both of banking & stock jobbing, that perhaps the world ever saw.—the principles upon which it was founded are explained by mr Law himself, in a discourse concerning Money & trade, which he published in Scotland when he first proposed his project. the splendid but visionary ideas which are set forth in that and some other works upon the same principles, still continue to make an impression upon many people, and have perhaps in part contributed to that excess of banking which has of late been complained of both in Scotland and in other places.' the Missisipi scheme, it is well known, ended in France[28] in the bankruptcy of the public treasury, the crush of thousands and thousands of private fortunes, and scenes of desolation and distress equal to those of an[29] invading army burning & laying waste all before it.

At the time we were funding our National debt we heard much about 'a public debt being a public blessing'; that the stock representing it was a creation of active capital for the aliment of commerce, manufactures and agriculture. this paradox was well adapted to the minds of believers in dreams, and the gulls of that size entered bonâ fide into it. but the art & mystery of banks is a wonderful improvement on that. it is established on the principle that 'private debts are a public blessing.' that the evidences of those private debts, called bank notes, become active capital and aliment the whole commerce, manufactures, & agriculture of the US. here are a set of people for instance who have bestowed on us the great blessing of running in our debt about 200.M. of D. without our knowing who they are, where they are, or what property they have to pay this debt when called on. nay, who have made us so sensible of the blessing of letting them run in our debt, that we have exempted them by law from the repaiment of these debts beyond a given proportion (generally estimated at one third.) and to fill up the measure of blessing, instead of paying, they recieve an interest on what they owe from those to whom they owe.

for all the notes, or evidences of what they owe, which we see in circulation, have been lent to somebody on an interest which is levied
again on us thro' the medium of commerce. and they are so ready still
to deal out their liberalities to us, that they are now willing to let
themselves run in our debt 90. Millions more, on our paying them
the same premium of 6. or 8. p.c. interest, and on the same legal ex-
emption from the repaiment of more than 30.M. of the debt when it
shall be called for. but let us look at this principle in it's original form,
and it's copy will then be equally understood. 'a public debt is a public blessing.' that our debt was juggled from 43.[30] up to 80.M. and
funded at that amount, according to this opinion, was a great public
blessing, because the evidences of it could be vested in commerce,
and thus converted into active capital, and then[31] the more the debt
was made to be, the more active capital was created. that is to say, the
Creditors could now employ in commerce the money due them from
the public, and make from it an annual profit of 5. p.c. or 4.M. of D.
but observe that the public were at the same time paying on it an interest of exactly the same amount of 4.M. of D. where then is the gain
to either party which makes it a public blessing? there is no change
in the state of things, but of persons only. **A.** has a debt due to him
from the public, of which he holds their certificate as evidence, and
on which he is recieving an annual interest. he wishes however to
have the money itself, and to go into business with it. **B.** has an equal
sum of money in business, but wishes now to retire, and live on the
interest. he therefore gives it to **A** in exchange for **A**'s certificates of
public stock. now then **A** has the money to employ in business, which
B so employed before. **B** has the money on interest to live on which **A**
lived on before: and the public pays the interest to **B** which they paid
to **A** before. here is no new creation of capital, no additional money
employed, nor even a change in the employment of a single dollar. the
only change is of place between **A.** and **B.** in which we discover no
creation of capital, nor public blessing. suppose again the public to
owe nothing. then **A** not having lent his money to the public, would
be in possession of it himself, and would go into business without the
previous operation of selling stock. here again the same quantity of
capital is employed as in the former case, tho no public debt exists. in
neither case is there any creation of active capital, nor other difference
than that there is a public debt in the first case, and none in the last,
and we may safely ask which of the two situations is most truly a
public blessing. if then a <u>public</u> debt be no public blessing, we may
pronounce, a fortiori, that a <u>private</u> one cannot be so. if the debt
which the banking companies owe be a blessing to any body, it is to

themselves alone who are realising a solid interest of 8. or 10. p.c. on it. as to the public, these companies have banished all our gold and silver medium which, before their institution, we had without interest, which never could have perished in our hands, and would have been our salvation now in the hour of war; instead of which they have given us 200.M. of froth and bubble, on which we are to pay them heavy interest, until it shall vanish into air, as Morris's notes did. we are warranted then in affirming that this parody on the principle of 'a public debt being a public blessing,' and it's mutation into the blessing of private instead of public debts, is as ridiculous as the original principle itself. in both cases the truth is that Capital may be produced by industry, and accumulated by economy; but juglers only will propose to create it by legerdemain tricks with[32] paper.

I have called the actual circulation of bank paper in the US. 200. millions of Dollars. I do not recollect where I have seen this estimate; but I retain the impression that I thought it just at the time. it may be tested however by a list of the banks now in the US. and the amount of their capital. I have no means of recurring to such a list for the present day: but I turn to two lists in my possession for the years 1803. and 1804.[33]

	D
in 1803. there were 34. banks whose capital was	28,902,000.
in 1804. there were 66. consequently 32. additional ones. their capital is not stated, but at the average of the others (excluding the highest, that of the US. which was of 10.M.) they would be of 600,000.D each and add	19,200,000
making a total of	48,102,000

or say of 50.M. in round numbers.[34] now every one knows the immense multiplication of these institutions since 1804. if they have only doubled, their capital will be of 100.M. and if trebled, as I think probable, it will be of 150.M. on which they are at liberty to circulate treble the amount. I should sooner therefore believe 200.M. to be far below than above the actual circulation.   In England, by a late Parliamentary document, (see Virginia Argus of Oct. 18. 13. & other public papers of about that date) it appears that 6. years ago the bank of England had 12. millions of pounds sterling in circulation, which had increased to 42.M. in 1812. or to 189 M. of D. what proportion all the other banks may add to this I do not know: if we were allowed to suppose they equal it, this would give a circulation of 378.M. or the double of ours on a double population. but that nation is essentially commercial; ours essentially agricultural, and needing therefore less circulating medium, because the produce of the husbandman comes but once a year, and is then partly consumed at home, partly exchanged by barter. the Dollar which was of 4/6 sterl. was by the same document stated to be then 6/9 a depreciation of exactly 50. p.c.   the average price of wheat on the continent of Europe, at the commencement of it's present war with England, was about a French crown of 110. cents the bushel. with us it was 100. cents, and consequently we could send it there in competition with their own. that ordinary price has now doubled with us, and more than doubled in England; and altho' a part of this augmentation may proceed from the war demand, yet from the extraordinary nominal rise in the prices of land and labour here, both of which have nearly doubled in that period, and are still rising with every new bank, it is evident that were a general peace to take place tomorrow, & time allowed for the reestablishment of commerce, justice and order, we could not afford to raise wheat for much less than 2.D. while the continent of Europe, having no paper circulation, & that of it's specie not being augmented, would raise it at their former price of 110. cents. it follows then that, with our redundancy of paper, we cannot, after peace, send a bushel of wheat to Europe unless extraordinary circumstances double it's price in particular places, and that then the exporting countries of Europe could undersell us.

It is said our paper is as good as silver, because we may have silver for it at the bank from which it issues. this is not true. one two or three persons might have it: but a general application would soon exhaust their vaults, and leave a ruinous proportion of their paper in it's intrinsic worthless form. it is a fallacious pretence for another reason. the inhabitants of the banking cities might obtain cash for their paper as far as the cash of the vaults would hold out: but distance puts it out of the power of the country to do this. a farmer having a note of a Boston or Charleston bank, distant hundreds of miles, has no means of calling for the cash. and while these calls are impracticable for the country, the banks have no fear of their being made from the towns; because their inhabitants are mostly on their books, & there on sufferance only, and during good behavior.

In this state of things we are called on to add 90.M. more to the circulation. proceeding in this career it is infallible that we must end where the revolutionary paper ended. 200.M. was the whole amount of all the emissions of the old Congress, at which point their bills ceased to circulate. we are now at that sum; but with treble the population, and of course a longer tether. our depreciation is, as yet, but at about 2. for 1. owing to the support it's credit recieves from the small reservoirs of specie in the vaults of the banks. it is impossible to say at what point their notes will stop. nothing is necessary to effect it but a general alarm; and that may take place whenever the public shall begin to reflect on and percieve the impossibility that the banks should repay this sum. at present, caution is inspired no farther than to keep prudent men from selling property on long paiments. let us suppose the panic to arise at 300.M. a point to which every session of the legislatures hastens us by long strides. nobody dreams that they would have 300.M. of specie to satisfy the holders of their notes. were they even to stop now, no one supposes they have 200.M. in cash, nor even the $66\frac{2}{3}$ M. to which amount alone the law obliges them to repay. $133\frac{1}{3}$ M. of loss then is thrown on the public by law: and as to the $66\frac{2}{3}$ which they are legally bound to pay, and ought to have in their vaults, every one knows there is no such amount of cash in the US. and what would be the course with what they really have there? their notes are refused. cash is called for. the inhabitants of the banking towns will get what is in the vaults, until a few banks declare their insolvency; when, the general crush becoming evident, the others will withdraw even the cash they have, declare their bankruptcy at once, and leave an empty house and empty coffers for the holders of their notes. in this scramble of creditors, the country gets nothing, the towns but a little. what are they to do? bring suits? a million of creditors bring a million of suits? against John Nokes and Robert Stiles wheresoever to be found? all nonsense. the loss is total. and a sum is thus swindled from our citizens of[35] seven times the amount of the real debt and 4. times that of the factitious one of the US. at the close of the war. all this they will justly charge on their legislatures; but this will be poor satisfaction for the 2. or 300.M. they will have lost. it is time then for the public functionaries to look to this. perhaps it may not be too late. perhaps, by giving time to the banks, they may call in and pay off their paper by degrees. but no remedy is ever to be expected while it rests with the state legislatures. personal motives can be excited thro' so[36] many avenues to their will that in their hands it will continue to go on from bad to worse, until the catastrophe overwhelms us.   I still believe however that on proper representations of the subject a great proportion of these legislatures would cede to Congress their powers of establishing banks, saving the charter rights already granted. and this should be asked, not by way of amendment to the constitution, because until three fourths should consent nothing could be done; but accepted from them one by one singly as their consent might be obtained. any single state, even if no other should come into the measure, would find it's interest in arresting foreign bank paper immediately, and it's own by degrees. specie would flow in on them as paper disappeared. their own banks would call in and pay off their notes gradually, and their constituents would thus be saved from the general wreck. should the greater part of the states concede, as is expected, their power over banks to Congress, besides ensuring their own safety, the paper of the non-conceding states might be so checked and circumscribed by prohibiting it's reciept in any of the conceding states, and even in the non-conceding as to duties, taxes, judgments or other demands of the US. or of the citizens of other states, that it would soon die of itself, and the medium of gold & silver be universally restored. this is what ought to be done. but it will not be done. Carthago non delebitur. the overbearing clamor of merchants, speculators and projectors, will drive us before them with our eyes open until, as in France, under the Missisipi bubble, our citizens will be overtaken by the crush of this baseless fabrick, without other satisfaction than that of execrations on the heads of those functionaries, who from ignorance, pusillanimity, or corruption have betrayed the fruits of their industry into the hands of projectors and swindlers.

When I speak comparatively of the paper emissions of the old Congress & of the present banks, let it not be imagined that I cover them under the same mantle. the object of the former was a holy one; for if ever there was a holy war, it was that which saved our liberties and gave us independance. the object of the latter is to enrich swindlers at the expence of the honest & industrious part of the nation.

The sum of what has been said is that, pretermitting the constitutional question on the authority of Congress, and considering this application on the grounds of reason alone, it would be best that our medium should be so proportioned to our produce as to be on a par with that of the countries with which we trade, and whose medium is in a sound state: that specie is the most perfect medium because it will preserve it's own level, because, having intrinsic and universal value it can never die in our hands, and it is the surest resource of reliance in time of war: that the trifling economy of paper as a cheaper medium, or it's convenience for transmission weigh nothing in opposition to the advantages of the precious metals; that it is liable to be abused, has been, is, and for ever will be abused in every country in which it is permitted: that it is already at a term of abuse in these states which has never been reached by any other nation, France excepted, whose dreadful catastrophe should be a warning against the instrument which produced it; that we are already at 10. or 20. times the due quantity of medium, insomuch that no man knows what his property is now worth, because it is bloating while he is calculating, and still less what it will be worth when the medium shall be relieved from it's present dropsical state: and that it is a palpable falsehood to say we can have specie for our paper whenever demanded. instead then of yielding to the cries of a scarcity of medium set up by speculators, projectors and commercial gamblers, no endeavors should be spared to begin the work of reducing it by such gradual means as may give time to private fortunes to preserve their poise, and settle down with the subsiding medium; and that for this purpose the states should be urged to concede to the general government, with a saving of chartered rights, the exclusive power of establishing banks of discount for <u>paper</u>.

To the existence of banks of <u>discount</u> for <u>cash</u>, as on the continent of Europe, there can be no objection, because there can be no danger of abuse, and they are a convenience both to merchants and individuals. I think they should even be encouraged by allowing them a larger than legal interest on short discounts, and tapering thence, in proportion as the term of discount is lengthened, down to legal interest on those of a year or more. even banks of <u>deposit</u>, where cash should be lodged, and a paper-acknolegement taken out as it's representative, entitled to a return of the cash on demand would be convenient for remittances, travelling persons E^{t}c. but, liable as it's cash would be to be pilfered & robbed, and it's paper to be fraudulently re-issued, or issued without deposit, it would require skilful & strict regulation. this would differ from the bank of Amsterdam in the circumstance that the cash could be re-demanded on returning the note.

When I commenced this letter to you[37] my dear Sir, on mr Law's memorial, I expected a short one would have answered that. but as I advanced the subject branched itself before me into so many collateral questions that even the rapid views I have taken of each have swelled the volume of my letter beyond my expectations, and I fear beyond your patience. yet on a revisal of it I find no part which has not so much bearing on the subject as to be worth merely the time of perusal. I leave it then as it is, and will add only the assurance of my constant and affectionate esteem and respect.   TH: JEFFERSON

RC (ViU: TJP); at foot of first page: "John W. Eppes esq." PoC (DLC). Tr (ViU: TJP-Ca, TB [Thurlow-Berkeley] no. 1299); consisting of extracts in Joseph C. Cabell's hand of this letter and of TJ to Eppes, 24 June, 11 Sept. 1813. Tr (MHi); incomplete. Enclosed in TJ to Wilson Cary Nicholas, 6 Nov. 1813, TJ to Cabell, 17 Jan. 1814, Cabell to TJ, 6 Mar. 1814, TJ to James Monroe, 3

Aug. 1814, and Monroe to TJ, 26 Apr. 1815.

Congress chartered the BANK OF THE US. on 25 Feb. 1791 but did not renew it once its twenty-year term had expired (*U.S. Statutes at Large*, 1:191–6). TJ is citing David HUME, *Political Discourses* (Edinburgh, 1752), esp. 46–7, and the first volume of ADAM SMITH, *An Inquiry into the Nature and Causes of the Wealth of Nations*, 3d ed., 3 vols. (London, 1784; Sowerby, no. 3546). Although TJ's quotations from Smith are not always exact, he accurately conveys the author's meaning. French comptroller-general John Law's overly ambitious MISSISIPI SCHEME collapsed in 1720, leading to his dismissal from office and financial ruin for many investors (*ODNB*). Robert MORRIS'S NOTES, which were backed by his own fortune, played an important role in public finance during the final years of the American Revolution, but he later went bankrupt (*ANB*). Alexander Hamilton included a variation of the phrase A PUBLIC DEBT IS A PUBLIC BLESSING in his January 1790 report on public credit (Harold C. Syrett and others, eds., *The Papers of Alexander Hamilton* [1961–87], 6:106). The names JOHN NOKES AND ROBERT STILES, like John Doe, were used in court and legal documents to refer to imaginary or unknown persons (*Black's Law Dictionary*). CARTHAGO NON DELEBITUR (correctly, "deleretur"): "Carthage should not be destroyed." The Roman senator Publius Scipio Nasica supposedly added this exclamation to the end of his speeches (Plutarch, *Cato*, book 27, in *Plutarch's Lives*, trans. Bernadotte Perrin, Loeb Classical Library [1914–26; repr. 1968], 2:382–3; Charles E. Little, "The Authenticity and Form of Cato's Saying 'Carthago Delenda Est,'" *Classical Journal* 29 [1934]: 432–3). BASELESS FABRICK: William Shakespeare, *The Tempest*, act 4, scene 1.

¹ RC: "circulalation."
² MHi Tr begins here.
³ RC: "paimemt."
⁴ TJ originally placed the following paragraph just after the opening paragraph of this letter. He then canceled it

(although the text remains fully legible) and appended a marginal note to the PoC stating that the deleted material had been "inserted afterwards."

⁵ The canceled version reads "and the known grounds of that decision to have been the want."

⁶ The canceled version reads "true to the principle that the will of the Majority is to prevail."

⁷ The canceled version has "further difficulties" instead of this word.

⁸ MHi Tr: "will be."

⁹ Omitted closing quotation mark editorially supplied.

¹⁰ Omitted opening quotation mark editorially supplied, with passage that follows taken from Smith, *Wealth of Nations*, 1:438.

¹¹ In PoC TJ here placed an asterisk keyed to a note running perpendicularly along the right margin: "the real cash or money necessary to carry on the circulation and barter of a state is nearly one third part of all the annual rents of the proprietors of the said state: that is one ninth of the whole produce of the land. Sr Wm Petty supposes $\frac{1}{10}$th part of the value of the whole produce sufficient. Postlethwait. voce ["word"] 'Cash.'" This note also appears in MHi Tr.

¹² Unmatched closing quotation mark editorially omitted.

¹³ ViU Tr begins here.

¹⁴ Word interlined.

¹⁵ Text from "of the US? or what" to this point not in ViU Tr.

¹⁶ Word interlined.

¹⁷ TJ here canceled "profit."

¹⁸ Text from "but this being gross" to this point interlined in RC in place of a heavily canceled passage.

¹⁹ ViU Tr ends here.

²⁰ ViU Tr resumes here.

²¹ Word interlined.

²² Date added in margin.

²³ Preceding five words interlined, with extraneous period at end of addition editorially omitted.

²⁴ ViU Tr ends here.

²⁵ Word interlined.

²⁶ MHi Tr: "creditors."

²⁷ MHi Tr: "people."

²⁸ Preceding two words interlined.

²⁹ MHi Tr: "any."

30 Preceding two words added in margins.

31 MHi Tr ends here.

32 Word interlined in place of "on."

33 ViU Tr resumes here.

34 ViU Tr ends here, with concluding comment by Cabell that "200 m. Mr J. thinks would be a moderate estimate of the am^t of Bank paper in circulation at the date of this letter."

35 TJ here canceled "eight."

36 Word interlined in place of "too."

37 Preceding two words interlined.

To Thomas Law

DEAR SIR   Monticello Nov. 6. 13.

Your favor of Oct. 1. came duly to hand, and in it the Memorial which I now return. I like well your idea of issuing treasury notes bearing interest, because I am persuaded they would soon be withdrawn from the circulation and locked up in vaults & private hoards. it would put it in the power of every man to lend his 100. or 1000.D. tho' not able to go forward on the great scale and be the most advantageous way of obtaining[1] a loan.   the other idea of creating a National bank, I do not concur in, because it seems now decided that Congress has not that power, (altho' I sincerely wish they had it exclusively) and because I think there is already a vast redundancy, rather than a scarcity of paper medium. the rapid rise in the nominal price of land and labor (while war & blockade should produce a fall) proves the progressive state of the depreciation of our medium. ever with great esteem and respect

Your's   TH: JEFFERSON

RC (NNGL, on deposit NHi); at foot of text: "Thomas Law esq."; addressed (torn): "Thomas [...]"; franked; postmarked Charlottesville, 10 Nov. PoC (DLC); endorsed by TJ. Enclosure not found.

1 Word interlined in place of "making."

To Wilson Cary Nicholas

DEAR SIR   Monticello Nov. 6. 13.

You took the trouble of reading my former letters to mr Eppes on the subject of our finances, and I therefore inclose you a third letter to him on an important branch of the same subject, banks, for your perusal, if the volume does not appear too formidable. be so good as to stick a wafer into the letter and put it into the shortest post-line for Ça-ira which is his nearest post-office.—I expect within 10. or 12. days to set out for Bedford, and may have the pleasure of seeing you for a moment en passant, as the season requires me to make Gibson's my first day's stage. with great esteem & respect:

Your's

TH: JEFFERSON

PoC (DLC); at foot of text: "Col° W. C. Nicholas"; endorsed by TJ. Enclosure: TJ to John Wayles Eppes, 6 Nov. 1813.

En route to Poplar Forest, TJ spent the night of 21–22 Nov. 1813 at GIBSON's ordinary in Buckingham County (*MB*, 2:1295).

To Joseph C. Cabell

DEAR SIR   Monticello Nov. 7. 13.

As the meeting of our legislature approaches, and I shall be absent in Bedford from the 17th inst. to about the 8th of Dec. within which period you will possibly be passing, I have thought it best to inform you that the Rivanna co. & myself consent that the bill concerning us which was before the legislature at their last session, should pass verbatim as amended by the Senate. this was stated to me three days ago by mr Minor their Secretary, and had before been expressed to me by mr Divers, and that Col° Branham's opposition at the last session was against their sense. it proceeded from his timidity & sheer want of understanding. I consider this matter then as so settled, as far as respects the parties: and I inclose you an abstract of the bill, shewing what we understand it to be. I have suggested two verbal alterations in it in red ink. the 1st is to avoid making the act extend their power, by a side wind, over the whole river, which is neither agreeable to the title of the act, nor to the wishes of the company or the consent of the people either above or below their portion of the river. the 2d is to prevent the demand of toll for <u>vessels</u> either loaded or empty, which I mentioned to mr Minor, and he assured me they wished nothing to be taken for <u>vessels</u>, but only the <u>articles</u> they carried. I have not the least interest in either of these amendments, and only mention them on account of their general propriety.   I make no opposition to the duration of the act, at the same time thinking it longer by 20. years than the legislature ought to make it, and 7. years longer than they have a power to make it. this last assertion depends on the question whether one generation has a power to bind a succeeding one? a question which I think I have demonstrated in the negative in a late correspondence with the chairman of the Committee of ways and means of Congress, on the subject of a financial plan for the war. this, should you have the curiosity to enter into it, I shall willingly communicate to you on any convenient occasion. should you not be passing until my return from Bedford I shall be very happy to see you here, and to take that occasion for the communication: and should you be done with Say, I should be glad to recieve him then, as I wished to consult him on a part of the subject, and particularly on that of banks, a very important member of the discussion. Accept the assurance of my friendly attachment & respect.

TH: JEFFERSON

RC (ViU: TJP); addressed: "Joseph C. Cabell esquire <Warminster> Williamsburgh," with the correction made in an unidentified hand; franked; postmarked Milton, 12 Nov., and Richmond, 25 Nov.; endorsed by Cabell, with his notation: "Enclosing an abstract of the Rivanna Bill." PoC (DLC); endorsed by TJ.

TJ's son-in-law John Wayles Eppes was the CHAIRMAN OF THE COMMITTEE OF WAYS AND MEANS of the United States House of Representatives. The work by Jean Baptiste SAY was his *Traité d'Économie Politique, ou Simple Exposition de la manière dont se forment, se distribuent, et se consomment les richesses,* 2 vols. (Paris, 1803; Sowerby, no. 3547; Poor, *Jefferson's Library,* 11 [no. 697]).

ENCLOSURE

Thomas Jefferson's Abstract of the Rivanna Company Bill

A bill to amend the act intituled an act incorporating a company to open E^{t}c the Rivanna river from Milton to Moore's ford E^{t}c

§.1. Be it enacted by the General assembly that instead of the tolls E^{t}c [this section goes on to fix the tolls.]

§.2. And be it further enacted that it shall be lawful for the court of Albemarle county E^{t}c [after reimbursem^t of the company, to appoint directors to take toll sufficient to rebuild the locks E^{t}c.] and keep the same in repair, as well as to keep open the navigation of the said portion[1] of the said river in other respects E^{t}c

Amendm^t of the Senate

Be it further enacted that so long as the company aforesaid shall continue to use the navigation of the canal leading to the Shadwell mills, no toll shall be demanded or recieved on their behalf unless the same shall be demanded & recieved at the locks which now are, or hereafter may be erected by them on said canal, and shall be demanded & recieved only on articles[2] passing the sd locks.

All acts & parts of acts coming within the purview of this act are hereby repealed. Provided nevertheless that nothing in this act contained shall be construed to affect the private right of any person or persons whatsoever.

amendmt of the Senate

This act shall be in force from[3] [and after the time when the assent of the company aforesd hereto shall have been given by the Directors thereof, & duly certified to the court of Albemarle county, & there recorded, and shall thereafter continue in force until the 1st day of Feb. in the year 1840. and no longer.]

MS (ViU: TJP, TB [Thurlow-Berkeley] no. 1257); undated; entirely in TJ's hand; brackets in original.

For the drafting of this bill concerning the Rivanna Company and its movement through the Virginia legislature during its 1812–13 session, see Petition of Rivanna Company to Virginia General Assembly, [ca. 5 Oct. 1812], and note. The bill was reintroduced in the House of Delegates on 13 Jan. 1814, and it received its first and second readings and was recommitted four days later. By 24 Jan. the lower house had agreed to the amendments proposed by the Senate of Virginia a year earlier, and the bill passed into law on 31 Jan. 1814. The rough bill from the 1813–14 session and the final text of the act both include the revisions TJ suggested above (Vi: RG 79, House of Delegates, Rough Bills; *JSV* [1813–14 sess.], 28; *Acts of Assembly* [1813–14 sess.], 91–2).

[1] Preceding four words interlined in red ink.

[2] Preceding three words interlined in red ink in place of "on vessels."

[3] TJ here canceled "the passing thereof."

To Nicolas G. Dufief

DEAR SIR   Monticello Nov. 7. 13.

I ought sooner, in answer to your letter of Sep. 29. to have said that I shall be glad to recieve the second hand copy of the Traité du Bonheur et de la morale, which you supposed you could get me. I am anxious to recieve the 'American brewer & malster' as soon as published. I have both Richardson & Combrune which you mention. accept my friendly & respectful salutations.   TH: JEFFERSON

PoC (DLC); at foot of text: "M. Dufief"; endorsed by TJ.

To Chapman Johnson

DEAR SIR   Monticello Nov. 7. 13.

I was unwell during the last session of our district court, or I should have seen you there and delivered to you the inclosed for your kind assistance in the case of Michie's Certiorari on the proceedings of forcible entry; and I was not without a hope that your business might have given you leisure to take a dinner or an evening with us which will always give me pleasure.

I had a conversation with mr Minor, secretary of the Rivanna company a few days ago, in which he told me the company was unanimously of consent that the bill which was before the legislature at the last session should pass verbatim as amended by the Senate. one of the company [mr Divers] had before told me the same, and that the opposition of Col° Branham one of their company, and of our members, was against their intention. it proceeded from timidity and sheer ignorance in him. I mentioned to mr Minor that the use of the words 'on vessels' in the amendment of the Senate instead of 'only on articles' might subject empty <u>vessels</u> to toll. he assured me it was not their[1] understanding that[2] vessels, should pay, but only the <u>articles</u> they carried, and they wished it to be so expressed. the change does not concern me, and I mention it only for the good of those who will be passing the locks.

Accept the assurance of my great esteem & respect.

Th: Jefferson

PoC (MHi); brackets in original; at foot of text: "Chapman Johnson esq."; endorsed by TJ.

TJ enclosed $20 for Johnson's KIND ASSISTANCE in opposing the recently thwarted certiorari motion of David Michie (*MB*, 2:1295).

[1] TJ here canceled "intention."
[2] TJ here canceled "empty."

From Thomas Cooper

Dear Sir   Carlisle Nov. 8–1813

I sent you about a twelve month ago, a copy of my edition of Justinian's institutes, and another copy of my introductory lecture; I presume you received them as I sent them if I do not mistake under Mr Madison's care.

I write at present to say that I have at my disposal Dr Priestley's library and apparatus. The library consists of about 4400 Volumes of all descriptions, some of them very valuable. There are of course many [the]ological works, but they are in a great measure such as a Man of learning would like to possess for consultation. I value his Library at 5000. Dlrs, & his philosophical apparatus at 1000. Do you know any seminary likely to become purchaser? If I could afford it, they should not go out of <u>my</u> possession, but I cannot.

I have offered them to William & Mary College at Williamsburgh in your State, from whence I have received an invitation as Ch[emical][1] professor. I am strongly inclined to accept the invitation, if I thought the place was healthy, and I could have a good apparatus there, f[or] I am looked at with great suspicion and distrust by a body of Parsons who form a large part of the Trustees of this College. I have done and said nothing since my two years residence here, to irritate in the slightest degree this <u>Genus irritabile</u>—I have even gone to Church with tolerable regularity, but I think they hate me with more cordiality because I have furnished them with no ground of complaint.

This makes me uncomfortable here, although with my Professorship and my authorship I make out to live tolerably well.

I have now published 3 Numbers of the Emporium, each number containing about 160 or 170 pages, and coming out every two months. In my next I shall insert a paper on political Economy by Dr Erick Bollman, written with talent, but as I think with very high toned federal feelings. Pray is it a secret who wrote the Commentary on Montesquieu? He ascribes it to you, but I have always understood it to be the work of a frenchman, and written in french. I do not agree with it in toto, but it is a valuable work.

Have you attended to the Opinion of the Judges in answer to Governor Strong's questions in the appendix to 8th Massach. Rep.?

It seems to me, a blow at the Union. I have been attacking it in a new paper published by J. Conrad in Ph^a The American Register, but the federalists chuckle at it. Adieu. Believe me with sincere esteem Dear Sir Your friend   THOMAS COOPER

RC (MHi); holes in manuscript; endorsed by TJ as received 13 Dec. 1813 and so recorded in SJL.

Despite his bouts with the GENUS IRRITABILE ("irritable class"), Cooper remained at Dickinson College until 1815 (*ANB*). Justus Erich Bollman's piece on POLITICAL ECONOMY appeared in the December 1813 issue of the *Emporium of Arts & Sciences*, 119–61. On 1 Aug. 1812 Massachusetts governor Caleb Strong asked his state's supreme court "Whether the commanders in chief of the militia of the several states have a right to determine whether any of the exigencies contemplated by the constitution of the *United States* exist, so as to require them to place the militia, or any part of it in the service of the *United States*" and, if so, whether "the militia thus employed can be lawfully commanded by any officers but of the militia, except by the president of the *United States*." The "exigencies" for federal use of the militia enumerated in Article 1, section 8 of the United States Constitution are "to execute the laws of the union, suppress insurrections and repel invasions." The justices answered affirmatively to the first question and negatively to the second (*Reports of Cases Argued and Determined in the Supreme Judicial Court of the Commonwealth of Massachusetts* [Newburyport, Mass., 1813], 8:549–54). Cooper was apparently "An American," whose pseudonymous contribution on the controversy appeared in the inaugural 25 Sept. 1813 issue of the Philadelphia *American Weekly Messenger; or, Register of state papers, history and politics* (the AMERICAN REGISTER).

[1] Reading supplied from transcription of this text in *Collections of the Massachusetts Historical Society*, 7th ser., 1 (1900): 185.

From Wilson Cary Nicholas

my Dear Sir   Warren Nov. 8. 1813

I am very much obliged to you for allowing me to read your letters to Mr Eppes. I have done it with great satisfaction and attention. Your letters contain the ablest system of finance that I believe cou'd be devised, if the U.S. were now to commence their financial operations, with all the powers of the State and Genl Governments and we were free from prejudices against paper money and the influence of a Bank capital of fifty millions of dollars. The great resource of supplying the circulating medium or substituting public paper for coin, cou'd then be used—To attempt it now, wou'd be to encounter such a host & to interfere with the interest of so great a proportion of the most active of our people that I fear its success wou'd be impracticable—particularly as you seem to admit, that the immense circulation of paper has had an influence upon the price of property and even upon the price of our produce. Circumstances grateful at <u>least</u> to the great body of agriculturists. I presume it will not be denied that Banks have to some degree increased the improvements & the manufactures of the U.S. It is probable few of the Bank Charters will expire during the present war and when they do, I suspect few of the States wou'd be willing to give up the power to renew them. In many of the States a considerable proportion of the stock is state property, in all it is an important source of revenue. Independent of local and personal considerations that wou'd operate in favour of the Banks, The jealousy of the State Gov^{ts} for the preservation of their rights, wou'd have very great influence. The tendency of the government seems to be to lessen and not enlarge the powers of the Genl Gov^t. When some of the most essential rights of that Gov^t are denied to it, can it be expected that new & important powers will be granted? I think not, & shou'd therefore doubt very much, its being practicable ever to put down State Banks with the consent of the States. without that consent, I am sure you are one of the last men in America, that wou'd wish it to be attempted at any time, but particularly at this moment. To a very considerable extent I believe the Banks may be relied upon to aid the government with money either directly or indirectly. They have and will continue to make direct Loans, they lend to individuals who lend to the U.S. (a Bank in N.Y. lately lent Mr Parish a million of dollars for that purpose) & they will unquestionably hold treasury notes to a considerable amount. Perhaps in all these ways, as much money may be derived from the Banks as wou'd equal what you deem an adequate circulation. Your maxim that adequate funds shou'd be provided for the payment of interest and a proportion of the principal, whenever a loan is authorized, I think shoud be limitted by the ability of the people and the importance of the object. Our independence as a nation ought not be lost, let the means of defending it cost what they may. There are few wars that we can be engaged in that will not be as interesting to posterity as to us.[1] If there is a limit to our right to bind them, it wou'd seem that the object of the expenditure, more than any other circumstance, ought to determine who shou'd be the paymaster. For a benefit that was exclusively ours it wou'd be unreasonable to charge the cost to others, but for a great national advantage that wou'd inure to posterity to the latest generations I cannot believe it is a violation of right or of justice to leave to those who are to participate in the benefit the payment of that part of the cost, that wou'd be inconvenient to us. If our power over posterity is limitted, their claims upon us must have some reasonable bounds. The sacrifice of blood, of money that can be conveniently paid & the produce of our lands during a war wou'd seem to be our full contingent, all beyond that shoud be paid by posterity. If this doctrine is admitted, the interest of those who are to succeed us will be better taken care of than it wou'd be if it shall be established that we exceed our rightful power, when we contract debts that cannot be paid within twenty years: we have had the experience of one war with G.B. It is now thirty eight years since its commencement. Perhaps[2] half the debt contracted during that war was sunk by the depreciation of paper money. we had a long interval of peace & prosperity and after all our exertions there remains of that debt somewhere about $40,000000 unpaid. It cannot be unjust that the children of those who achieved the revolution shou'd pay what it wou'd have been not only inconvenient but impracticable for their fathers to have paid. I am sure you wou'd not have consented that our efforts shou'd have ceased, when our debt amounted to the sum we cou'd pay in twenty years. If the present war shou'd continue many years, wou'd it be possible to pay an additional tax every year of two millions? which we must do if we provide for the payment of interest annually and[3] one tenth part of the principal. will the present generation bear this in addition to the other burthens of the war that they cannot escape? If they will not & cannot, is the interest of posterity consulted when the object for which we contend, must be abandoned rather any part of the cost of maintaining their rights shou'd devolve upon them? If as I believe the circulation of Bank paper cannot be arrested (at any rate during this war) the only resources remaining are taxes & loans. The sum we can pay in taxes is very limitted. I doubt if under present circumstances we can pay a greater sum in any year of the war, than that imposed during the last session of Congress, that you suppose will have rather more than 600,000 applicable to new loans, this will go but little way. what then is to be done? I see no resource but to borrow, to pay when we are able. If it requires a sum that we shou'd be fifty years in redeeming, I wou'd have it sooner than abandon the war with disgrace. I have little doubt we can obtain as much money as we shall want; our countrymen will take stock to an immense amount. Foreigners will take what may be over the home demand. If it is necessary or will make the premium less, Let the public lands, the[4] taxes lately imposed & the present or any other rate of impost be pledged until the debt is paid. I wou'd impose no new taxes nor wou'd I have pledged those imposed during the last session, to be collected until peace. I shou'd doubt very much the success of alternate issues of paper that shou'd and shou'd not bear interest. I fear the solicitude to obtain the first wou'd destroy all appetite for the last. The issue of treasury notes, I think a very happy expedient, but that it has not been managed to the most advantage. The time of redemption is too short and the interest too high, as it is used, it is only a means of anticipating revenue for a short time. I think it might have been used so as to answer all the purposes of a war to be paid at a distant day. Notes of this description to a vast amount wou'd have been held by individuals. They wou'd be hoarded by all that description of people who will not trust their money out of their own hands & who by holding it lose the interest.[5] Every man who was collecting a sum for a particular object, and a great proportion of those who now deposit large sums in the Banks not intended for immediate use wou'd gladly hold that sort of paper

FC or unsent RC (DLC: Nicholas Papers); entirely in Nicholas's hand; consisting of one sheet folded to form four pages, with last page fully filled, suggesting that an additional page or pages may be missing; unaddressed, with internal evidence clearly pointing to TJ as the intended recipient. Not recorded in SJL and probably never sent.

Early in April 1813 David parish and Stephen Girard, of Philadelphia, jointly subscribed for just over $7 million of the $16 million war loan authorized by Congress on 8 Feb. of that year. John Jacob Astor, of New York, pledged $2 million at the same time (*U.S. Statutes at Large*, 2:798–9; *ASP, Finance*, 2:647; New York *Commercial Advertiser*, 15 Apr. 1813; Philip G. Walters and Raymond Walters Jr., "The American Career of David Parish," *Journal of Economic History* 4 [1944]: 149–66, esp. 159–61).

[1] Reworked from "that will be as interesting as to us."

[2] Manuscript: "Perhapaps."

[3] Nicholas here canceled "the principal in twenty years."

[4] Nicholas here canceled "direct."

[5] Reworked from "& who lose the interest by so doing."

To John Jacob Astor

DEAR SIR   Monticello Nov. 9. 13.

Your favor of Oct. 18. has been duly rec^d and I learn with great
pleasure the progress you have made towards an establishment on
Columbia river. I view it as the germ of a great, free & independant
empire on that side of our continent, and that liberty & self government spreading from that as well as this side will ensure their compleat establishment over the whole. it must be still more gratifying to
yourself to foresee that your name will be handed down with that of
Columbus & Raleigh, as the father of the establishment and founder
of such an empire. it would be an afflicting thing indeed should the
English be able to break up the settlement. their bigotry to the bastard liberty of their own country, and habitual hostility to every degree of freedom in any other will induce the attempt. they would not
lose the sale of a bale of furs for the freedom of the whole world. but
I hope your party will be able to maintain themselves. if they have assiduously[1] cultivated the interests & affections of the natives, these
will enable them to defend themselves against the English, and furnish them an asylum even if their fort be lost. I hope, and have no
doubt our government will do for it's success whatever they have
power to do, and especially that at the negociations for peace, they
will provide by convention with the English for the safety and independance of that country, and an acknolegement of our right of pa-
tronising them in all cases of injury from foreign nations. but no
patronage or protection from this quarter can secure the settlement if
it does not cherish the affections of the natives, and make it their interest to uphold it. while you are doing so much for future generations of men, I sincerely wish you may find a present account in the
just profits you are entitled to expect from the enterprize.   I
will ask of the President permission to read mr Stuart's journal. with
fervent wishes for a happy issue to this great undertaking which
promises to form a remarkable epoch in the history of mankind, I
tender you the assurance of my great esteem & respect.

TH: JEFFERSON

PoC (DLC); at foot of text: "John
Jacob Astor esq."

TJ is not known to have requested per-
mission to peruse Robert STUART'S
JOURNAL of his ten-month trek across the
North American continent.

[1] Manuscript: "assiduouly."

[603]

To William Champe Carter

Dear Sir   Monticello Nov. 9. 13.

In a letter of Sep. 23. I informed you of a claim of Col° Monroe's to some part of the lands you sold to mr Short, he thinks about 30. acres, and proposed to you a meeting at your convenience to run the lines. Col° Monroe I believe wrote to you at the same time. I was then obliged to limit the time of meeting to some day before the present Date, by the necessity of my visiting Bedford about this time. I shall set out for that place on the 17th inst. and may be a month absent. the earlier you can fix on a time after that for surveying[1] the more acceptable it will be; and I will pray you to notify it to me as soon as you can that notice may be given to Col° Monroe. if you can conveniently make this your head quarters during the operation we shall be very happy to receive[2] you. with sentiments of great esteem & respect I am Dear Sir

Your friend & serv^t   Th: Jefferson

PoC (DLC); at foot of text: "W. Champe Carter esq."; endorsed by TJ.

TJ set out for Poplar Forest on 21 Nov. 1813, not THE 17TH INST., and he re-

mained there for about three weeks (*MB*, 2:1295).

[1] Manuscript: "survying."
[2] Manuscript: "recive."

To William Short

Dear Sir   Monticello Nov. 9. 13.

You have heretofore been apprised of a claim of Col° Monroe to a corner of your tract of land on the top of the mountain, which he supposes included within the lines of his prior deed. some years ago he mentioned this to me; but as mr Carter had conducted your survey in person, I imagined Col° Monroe had been illy informed, and as he never repeated the thing to me, I presumed he had become satisfied. on hearing however of the sale to Higgenbotham, when he was here in Sep. he made his claim formally to him, who communicated it to me. I immediately called on Col° Monroe on the subject. he explained the information on which he supposed we had run on his lines, but without knowing the fact. we agreed at once that a surveyor should be employed to run the lines of his deed (of which he gave me a copy) that we would both desire the attendance of mr Carter, who would be ultimately responsible to you, and so settle the thing at once. I wrote to mr Carter, desiring him to fix any day he pleased, before this present date, and we would all attend with him. Col° Monroe wrote also. I had hoped thus to inform you of the renewal of the claim and[1] it's final settlement at the same time. but I have no answer from mr Carter. I have therefore this day written to him again, informing him that I shall set out to Bedford on the 17th shall be absent a month, and requesting him to fix a day as soon after that as he can, and to attend. Col° Monroe guesses there may be about 30. acres in question; but it is a mere guess. if it proves true, the price you were to recieve for it will be to be deducted from the bonds, and mr Carter will have to refund to you what he recieved and interest, which will probably leave on you a loss of about a dollar an acre. I will not suffer it to rest until it is finally and justly settled, & will accompany the surveyor on the lines.

From the fork of James river, & the falls of the other rivers upwards and Westwardly, we have had the most calamitous year ever seen since 1755. it began with the blockade, so that the fine crops of the last year, made in these upper parts, which could not be at market till after Christmas, were shut up by that and lost their sale. after keeping my flour till the approach of the new harvest, I was obliged to sell it lest it should spoil on my hands, at a price which netted me only 47. cents a bushel for my wheat, of course a total sacrifice. in the year 1755. it never rained from April to Nov. there was not bread enough to eat, & many died of famine. this year, in these upper regions, we had not a single rain from Apr. 14. to Sep. 20. say 5. months, except a slight shower in May. the wheat was killed by the drought as dead as the leaves of the trees now are. the stems fell before the scythe without being cut, & the little grain in the head shattered on the ground. from 500. as sowed here, I have not got in 1500. bushels, not three times the seed. our corn has suffered equally. from 270. acres planted, and which in common years would have yielded me from 800. to 1000 barrels, I shall not get a barrel an acre, and a great portion of that will be what are called nubbings, being half formed ears with little grain on them. corn consequently starts with us at $3\frac{1}{3}$ D. and being the principal food of our laborers, it's purchase will be a heavy tax. I am told the drought has been equally fatal as far as Kentucky. there have been a few local exceptions here from small bits of clouds accidentally passing over some farms. should the little wheat we have made be shut up by a continuance of the blockade thro' the winter, we shall be absolutely bankrupt by the loss of two successive crops. this is really the case for exclaiming 'O fortunati mercatores'!

I found in Correa every thing good and valuable as you had

notified me. the only circumstance of regret was the necessity of part-ing with him. what a misfortune that we cannot liberalize our legis-lators so far as to found a good academical institution. W^m & Mary college, removed to a central and healthy part of our state, it's funds enlarged and constitution amended, with such a man as Correa for it's president instead of the simpleton Bracken, would afford a com-fortable look[2] into futurity. but there is something in the constitution of our legislatures which does not permit a choice of the best wood for that fabric. a parcel of petty fogging academies too, as they pre-sume to call themselves, with one or two masters, barely able to teach the rudiments of Latin, and the use of the chain & compas, fill us with Blackstone lawyers and Sangrado doctors, sufficient to starve out real science, which is accordingly totally extinct in this state.   but war, famine, and ignorance are too much for the subject of one letter. affectionate & respectful salutations therefore.   TH: JEFFERSON

RC (ViW: TJP); at foot of first page: "W. Short esq."; endorsed by Short as re-ceived 15 Nov. 1813.

The TRACT OF LAND was the Indian Camp estate in Albemarle County. O FORTUNATI MERCATORES: "O happy traders!" from Horace, *Satires*, 1.1.4 (Fairclough, *Horace: Satires, Epistles, and Ars Poetica*, 4–5). The fictional Dr. SANGRADO was a quack whose patients

often died while under his care (Alain René Le Sage, *Histoire de Gil Blas de San-tillane*, 4 vols. [Paris, 1715–35; repr. Lon-don, 1769; Sowerby, no. 4346]).

SJL records a missing letter from Short to TJ of 9 Nov. 1813 as received 13 Dec. 1813 from New York.

[1] Preceding six words interlined.
[2] Word interlined in place of "view."

From John Barnes

DEAR SIR,   George Town 10th Nov 1813.—
    since I had the honor of Addressing you the 19 Ult—I had the pleasure of receiving the inclosed from Mr Williams—to which I replied the 28th requesting the fav^r (in Case he should suceed in purchasing a Set of Ex—at New York. (if not too much trouble) he would also engage a Sett in my fav^r for ƒ5000 franc's—and that I would also wish to avail my self of the indulgence—in Case himself or Mr Russell—on his Arrival—should be authorized to draw—to pur-chase a like sum early in the Spring but of this intelligenc I am not yet fav^d with—
    Mr Williams, I presume has not yet recd his expected advices from New York. under these Circumstances we must patiently wait the issue—
    On the 2^d Instant I was gratified—on receiving the good Gen^ls

Acknowledgm^t of his having recd from Mr Morton his ƒ5,500 franc's—dated Paris 30th May (second.)—

with greatest Esteem I am Dear Sir—Your most Obed^t servant.

JOHN BARNES.—

RC (ViU: TJP-ER); at foot of text: "Thomas Jefferson Esqr Monticello—Virginia"; endorsed by TJ as received 20 Nov. 1813 and so recorded in SJL. Enclosure: George Williams to Barnes, Baltimore, 20 Oct. 1813, explaining that he refrained from acknowledging Barnes's letters because he had expected to learn from John A. Morton's nephew in the near future whether Tadeusz Kosciuszko had received his annual payment; lamenting that the younger Morton has been too ill to supply this information; reporting the death of "a fond Brother" of his own; stating that, to the best of his knowledge, no bills on France are available for purchase in Baltimore; hoping that the arrival of Mr. Russell in America will facilitate the payment of Kosciuszko's stipend; and announcing his intention to write to New York to obtain a bill (RC in ViU: TJP-ER, filed with Kosciuszko accounts, 1809–16; addressed: "John Barnes Esquire George Town Dis^t of Columbia"; stamped; postmarked Baltimore, 20 Oct.; endorsed by Barnes as received 22 Oct. 1813 and answered six days later).

Barnes had evidently received a SEC-OND, or Dupl, of Kosciuszko's 30 May 1813 letter to him.

From Samuel Greenhow

SIR.   Richmond 11th Novr 1813.

I [am][1] very unwilling to be considered as impertinent, and have therefore hesitated, before I determined, that, I might, without impertinence, inclose to you a Copy of the Address & Constitution of an Association in Virginia, for the distribution of Bibles gratuitously, to those who are not able to purchase them.—Conscious of the purity of my motive, I have discarded the doubts which at first presented themselves to me as to the propriety of this Act.

This association has no tendency to produce any legal preference of Sects—that, it exists, made up of persons of all the different religious[2] sects known among us, is perhaps (Under God) the result of that perfect toleration secured to us, in all matters relative to religion.—The distribution of Bibles, so far from being calculated to give undue influence to any one sect, will tend to counteract the improper influence of ambitious and worldly men licensed as Preachers & pastors—To me then it seems, that, this Association can not possibly produce evil of a political sort; which, from the devotion of so large a part of your life to the service of our Country, I suppose would be a previous enquiry with you—

If then, no evil will probably result from it, and the possession of the Bible shall, as I am sure it will, add to the Enjoyments of a number of our poor fellow Citizens who can not purchase—If, as I imagine is certain, the System of morals inculcated in the new testament, is the most perfect in existence—

If the most correct principles of Civil liberty are presented in that Book—And if the distribution of Bibles shall excite Citizens of the poorer class, to make greater exertions to teach their children to read, and thus increase the Stock of knowledge in that Class of Society— then without Enquiring whether you or I receive this Book as a work of Inspiration, I shall hope for your patronage of the Association—

We should be much pleased to number you among the members of the Society; But, if you should prefer it, we will thankfully receive any donation that you may be pleased to aid us with—

Should you think this letter worthy of notice, you will please address your reply to me as Treasurer of the Bible Society of Virginia; or to any of the managers, whose names you will find on the last page of the inclosed pamphlett.

I am Very respectfully Y^{rs} &^{c} SAMUEL GREENHOW

RC (DLC); endorsed by TJ as received 16 Nov. 1813 and so recorded in SJL. Enclosure: *Address of the Managers of the Bible Society of Virginia, to the Public* (Richmond, 1813), with subjoined, separately paginated *Constitution of the Bible Society of Virginia.* The former mentions English and American precursors; emphasizes the importance of the Bible to improving the morals of mankind and preparing humanity "for the life that now is, and for that which is to come" (p. 5); stresses the great need to disseminate the scriptures to the ignorant and erring of the world; underscores the nondenominational character of the organization; and states that its work will secure heavenly blessings to the Society and to the nation as a whole. The Society's constitution gives as its object "the distribution of Bibles and Testaments to the poor of our country, and to the Heathen" (p. 1); provides for the election of managers, the replacement of vacancies on the board, and the calling of annual meetings; and declares that "Persons of every religious creed or denomination may become members of this Society, upon paying five dollars subscription money, and binding themselves to pay four dollars annually, so long as they choose to continue in the Society" (p. 2).

[1] Omitted word editorially supplied.
[2] Word added in margin.

To Thomas Hornsby

SIR   Monticello Nov. 11. 13.

Your letter of July 21. was recieved on the 6th of Aug. and should have been answered immediately, but that I was in daily expectation of one from Govr Greenup on the same subject. I accordingly recieved one a fortnight after in which he inclosed a letter from you to him proposing an interview. and in his letter to me he said he should make an appointment with you as soon as he should be well enough. it has been in expectation of the result of this that I have so long omitted answering you. but presuming that something has prevented the interview proposed, I now proceed to acknolege the reciept of yours. I am much gratified by the candor and temper which breathes thro' the whole of it, and with the prospect it offers of a just and honorable adjustment of the difficulties into which I have been unfortunately thrown. your statement shews that the different sentiments we entertain of our rights have been produced by an entirely different view of the facts. my statement of these to Governor Greenup was taken, partly from the depositions in the suit of Peyton & John Henderson, and partly from mr Peyton himself who read and affirmed that statement to be strictly true before it was sent away. it was indeed exactly what he had always and uniformly told me, from the time of the purchase in 1802. to this day: that, altho' he knew that John Henderson here was the legal guardian of the 5. minor children, yet their removal to Kentucky had thrown them necessarily under the tutorage & care of their mother and brothers there, and that he found James L. Henderson in the exercise of that care jointly with the mother, that the proposition to him to purchase their lands was from both, and that it was concluded with their joint approbation, the deed having been written and signed by Jas L. H. alone merely as the acting penman for the family.   on the reciept of your letter, I communicated it to mr Peyton. in this it is supposed that mrs Henderson had no part in the transaction and that it was even without her knolege, or that of the young persons concerned. he not only solemnly attested again the facts he had ever before uniformly stated to me, but added some new circumstances; particularly that the purchase having taken place at the same time with that of the dower, the whole transaction passed in a house of but a single room, in which the family was necessarily together, and the whole of course done in their presence and unavoidably with their knolege. he, immediately on reading your letter wrote one to Jas L. Henderson, which he delivered me open to forward, in which he appeals to him to testify mrs Henderson's joint agency in the case, and that the two daughters Eliza and Frances were present & concurring. this last circumstance, to be sure, of the concurrence of the infants, is not material, because at their age they might not be supposed to understand what was going on, and consequently not now to remember what they did not understand. I inclose you a copy of this letter in which mr Peyton reminds Jas L. H. of the facts with a minuteness and a confidence to which one cannot but give credence; and the more as it is a case in which he has no personal interest to lead him astray. it is merely a question of memory then between mrs Henderson and him; whether it is most likely she should have forgotten things which did happen, or he hold impressed in his memory things which did not happen? the testimony of Ja^s L. H. would decide between them, if we could obtain it; but that is rendered difficult by the slow and uncertain communications between this place and Washita. I am endeavoring however to procure it. altho' they were not the legal, they were the natural guardians of the minor children, in the absence of John, the one legally appointed; and it was natural for a stranger, seeing them live in family together, acting for the minors, and concurring in a measure for their advantage, to give credit to what they undertook to do and to presume it would be settled among themselves. I know nevertheless that the law, to protect the interests of minors, gives them a right to annul such a transaction when of age: yet custom sanctions it, because it would be very injurious to infants if opportunities of obvious benefit to them were to be lost for ever thro' want of power to take advantage of them. on the whole however, I know, Sir, that yourself & mrs Hornsby have a right to chuse whether you will look to those who acted for her in her infancy, and to the mortgage and bond of Ja^s L. Henderson for indemnification, or to annul their act, or to say what compromise you will make with an innocent purchaser who has honestly paid once what was then the full value, & by the decline of the place is now become more than the value, who has been guilty of no fraud, nor other fault than that of over-confidence in what were deemed family transactions. on this subject I must ask the favor of you to confer with Governor Greenup, who is so kind as to undertake to act for me in this business, and I will confirm whatever he does in it. I propose this in order to facilitate a settlement, because it can be so much better adjusted by conversation than in writing at the distance we are apart. and with the dispositions to justice which your letter manifests, I trust that the adjustment will not be difficult. to the circumstances formerly stated, it may be proper to add that the navigation of our river being now extended and daily practised up to Charlottesville, the warehouses at Milton rotted down, and the inspection about to be suppressed, Milton is already nearly, and soon will be entirely abandoned, it's vacant lots now selling merely as arable land. I am in duty bound to thank you for the readiness with which you have stayed the proceedings here, and willingness to enter into friendly explanations leading to a satisfactory settlement of the business; and tender you the assurance of my esteem & respect.   TH: JEFFERSON

PoC (ViU: TJP); at foot of first page: "Thomas Hornsby esquire"; endorsed by TJ. Enclosure not found.

For the DEPOSITIONS recorded in the case of *Peyton v. Henderson*, see Craven Peyton v. John Henderson Court Record (ViU: TJP, TB [Thurlow-Berkeley] no. 907) and Haggard, "Henderson Heirs," 10–2. On 18 Sept. 1802 James L. Henderson signed a MORTGAGE AND BOND stipulating that he would pay Craven Peyton £5,000 if the minor Henderson

heirs failed to transfer the title to their lands when they came of age or married (Haggard, "Henderson Heirs," 7–8; Albemarle Co. Deed Book, 14:520–1). TJ thought of his purchases from the Hendersons as FAMILY TRANSACTIONS because Elizabeth Lewis Henderson was his cousin and the sister-in-law of his sister Lucy Jefferson Lewis (Haggard, "Henderson Heirs," 3, 24; *PTJ*, 28:474).

SJL records a missing letter of 12 Nov. 1813 from TJ to Christopher Greenup.

From Thomas Lehré

DEAR SIR   Charleston Novr 11th 1813

I am sorry to inform you that the great Patriot Peter Freneau Esqr, of this City, departed this life on Monday last.

In him our Country has lost one of its firmest and best friends— He continued to his last moments, one of your greatest friends, and admirers.   The Republican Party here will most sensibly feel his loss.

The enclosed paper will give you but a faint Idea of the high estimation in which he was held by his fellow Citizens here.

That you may continue to enjoy health,[1] a long life, and every other blessing this life affords, is the most fervent wish, of

Dear Sir Your Obedient[2] & very Humble Servt

THOMAS LEHRÉ

RC (DLC); at foot of text: "Thomas Jefferson late President U.S. Montacello"; endorsed by TJ as received 20 Nov. 1813 and so recorded in SJL.

PETER FRENEAU, a dedicated Republican, was the brother of the poet Philip Freneau and a political ally of Charles Pinckney. In 1809 TJ appointed him federal commissioner of loans for South Carolina. Freneau is best known as the longtime publisher of two Charleston newspapers, the *City Gazette and Commercial Daily Advertiser* and the *Carolina Gazette* (*PTJ*, 32:266; *JEP*, 2:110, 111 [17, 18 Feb. 1809]; Brigham, *American Newspapers*, 2:1415). The ENCLOSED PAPER was probably a copy of the effusive obituary of Freneau that appeared this day in the *City Gazette*.

[1] Manuscript: "heath."
[2] Manuscript: "Obedent."

From John Adams

As I owe you more for your Letters of Oct. 12. and 28 than I Shall be able to pay, I Shall begin with the P.S. to the last.

I am very Sorry to Say, that I cannot "assist your memory in the Enquiries of your letter of August 22^d." I really know not who was the compositor of any one of the Petitions or Addresses you enumerate. Nay farther I am certain I never did know. I was so shallow a polititian, that I was not aware of the importance of those compositions. They all appeared to me, in the circumstances of the Country like childrens play at marbles or push pin, or rather like misses in their teens emulating each other in their pearls, their braceletts their Diamond Pins and brussells lace.

In the Congress of 1774 there was not one member, except Patrick Henry, who appeared to me Sensible of the Precipice or rather the Pinnacle on which he Stood, and had candour and courage enough to acknowledge it. America is in total Ignorance, or under infinite deception concerning that Assembly. To draw the characters of them all would require a volume and would now be considered as a caracatura print. one third Tories. another Whigs and the rest mongrels.

There was a little Aristocracy, among Us, of Talents and Letters. Mr Dickinson was primus inter pares; the Bell Weather; the leader of the Aristocratical flock. Billy, alias Governor Livingstone, and his Son in law Mr Jay, were of this priviledged order. The credit of most if not all those compositions was often if not generally given to one or the other of these choice Spirits. Mr Dickenson however was not on any of the original[1] Committees. He came not into Congress till Oct. 17. He was not appointed till the 15th by his assembly. Vol. 1. 30. Congress adjourned 27. Oct. though our correct Secretary has not recorded any final Adjournment or dissolution. Mr Dickenson was in Congress but ten days. The business was all prepared arranged and even in a manner finished before his arrival.

R. H. Lee was the Chairman of the Committee for prepareing "the loyal and dutiful Address to his Majesty." Johnson and Henry were acute Spirits and understood the Controversy very well; though they had not the Advantages of Education like Lee and John Rutledge. The Subject had been near[2] a month under discussion in Congress and most of the materials thrown out there. It underwent another deliberation in committee; after which they made the customary compliment to their Chairman, by requesting him to prepare and report a draught, which was done, and after examination, correction, amelioration or pejoration, as usual reported to Congress. Oct. 3. 4. and 5th were taken up in debating and deliberating on matters proper to be contained in the Address to his Majesty. Vol. 1. 22. October 21. The Address to the King was after debate recommitted and Mr John Dickenson added to the Committee. The first draught was made and all the essential materials put together by Lee, it might be embellished and Seasoned afterward with some of Mr Dickenson piety: but I know not that it was. Neat and handsome as the composition is, having never had any confidence[3] in the Utility of it, I never have thought much about it Since it was adopted. Indeed I never bestowed much Attention on any of those Addresses: which were all but repetitions of the Same Things: the Same facts and arguments. Dress and ornament rather than Body, Soul or Substance. My thoughts and cares were nearly monopolized by the Theory of our Rights and Wrongs, by measures for[4] the defence of the country; and the means of governing our Selves.

I was in a great Error, no doubt, and am ashamed to confess it; for those things were necessary to give Popularity to Our cause both at home and abroad. And to shew my Stupidity in a Stronger light the reputation of any one of those compositions has been a more Splendid distinction[5] than any aristocratical Starr or garter, in the Escutchion of every man who has enjoyed it. Very Sorry that I cannot give you more

Satisfactory information, And more So that I cannot at present give more Attention to your two last excellent Letters I am

as Usual affectionately yours   JOHN ADAMS

N.B. I am almost ready to believe that John Taylor of Caroline, or of Hazel Wood Port Royal, Virginia, is the Author of 630 pages of printed Octavo, upon my Books, that I have received. The Style answers every characteristic, that you have intimated.

Within a Week I have received, and looked into his Arator. They must Spring from the Same brain as Minerva issued from the head of Jove; or rather as Venus rose from the froth of the Sea.

There is however a great deal of good Sense in Arator. and there is Some in his "Aristocracy."[6]

RC (DLC); at foot of third page: "President Jefferson"; above postscript on fourth page: "please to turn over"; endorsed by TJ as received 13 Dec. 1813 and so recorded in SJL. FC (Lb in MHi: Adams Papers); internal address and additional signature beneath postscript in Adams's hand.

PUSH PIN: a simple children's game,

hence anything trivial or childish (*OED*). Caricatura (CARACATURA): "caricature." VOL. 1. was the first volume of the edition of the *Journals of Congress* published in Philadelphia in 1800. The CORRECT SECRETARY of the First Continental Congress was Charles Thomson. Adams's comments notwithstanding, John Dickinson played a central role in drafting the 1774 ADDRESS TO THE KING (Edwin Wolf, "The Authorship of the 1774 Address to the King Restudied," *WMQ*, 3d ser., 22 [1965]: 189–224; Paul H. Smith and others, eds., *Letters of Delegates to Congress, 1774–1789* [1976–2000], 1:228–33). For the full text of the address, which was engrossed and signed on 26 Oct. 1774, see Worthington C. Ford and others, eds., *Journals of the Continental Congress, 1774–1789* [1904–37], 1:113, 115–22.

John Taylor of Caroline was the AUTHOR of *An Inquiry into the Principles and Policy of the Government of the United States* (Fredericksburg, 1814; TJ's copy documented in his MS Retirement Library Catalogue, DLC: TJ Papers, ser. 7, p. 88 [no. 656]), recently RECEIVED by Adams, as well as *Arator; being a series of Agricultural Essays, Practical & Political* (Georgetown, 1813; Sowerby, no. 814).

¹ Word interlined.
² Word interlined.
³ RC: "confidenc." FC: "confidence."
⁴ Preceding eleven words interlined in place of "by."
⁵ Preceding four words interlined in place of "more."
⁶ Omitted closing quotation mark editorially supplied.

To Samuel Brown

DEAR SIR   Monticello Nov. 13. 1813.

On the 24ᵗʰ of April I took the liberty of putting under your cover a letter for James L. Henderson of Washita, and in yours of May 25. you were so kind as to state to me the conveyance you had procured for it, and the probability that an answer might be returned by the same person. none having been recieved, I fear that Henderson¹ does not mean to answer, altho' in that letter I only asked from him some particular information as to facts which he alone possesses, and which might enable me to compromise advantageously, or perhaps defeat the claim set up to the lands he sold me. I asked for nothing but the information he possessed, saying nothing about his responsibility, because I believe it worth nothing as he went off to Washita bankrupt, this of course renders his information the more important to me and therefore I write him another letter & again trouble you with the request to find a conveyance to him. I do not know his particular residence at Washita, nor whether there is a post to that country, or what his nearest post office is, nor even do I know in what state or territory it is. if I could learn these particulars, I might save you the trouble of being the medium of our correspondence. it would be still more important to me if I could find out some good character near him whom I could request to confer with him & communicate the result.

The Capsicum which accompanied your letters recieved in June, was of course too late for that season, but I shall give it a fair trial in the spring. if it proves more equal to our climate than our former kinds it will be a valuable addition to our gardens. I sent some of it to Dʳ Sheecut of S. Carolina, author of the Flora Caroliniensis, and some to mr MᶜMahon of Philadelphia, that it might be tried in those places also.

A medical gentleman called on me a few days ago, on his way to Washington to obtain a patent for a medical machine invented by Dʳ Jennings of Lynchburg, which, after an experience of 6. months they consider almost as a Panacea. it is a tin quadrantal tube, like that in the margin about 3. feet long, 4.I. diameter at the lower end and 2.I. at the upper. into the square aperture at bottom is set a small tin cup of ardent spirits, which are kindled, and the fumes issue at the small end which is introduced into the bed of the patient, under the bedclothes, and the fumes permitted to apply as an atmosphere to the whole body, or to any particular part of it, as the Doctor & patient may chuse. it produces what degree of sweat you desire. he uses it as a substitute for the water bath, but ascribes abundance of other effects to it. of these you will form better conceptions than I can. I was almost tempted to let him try his invention on my chronic rheumatism under which I have been suffering much for some weeks past. but I consider that an old crazy carcase like mine is not a safe subject for new experiments. with every wish for your health & happiness accept the assurance of my great friendship and respect. Tʜ: Jᴇꜰꜰᴇʀꜱᴏɴ

PoC (DLC); at foot of first page: "Doctʳ Samuel Brown." Enclosure: TJ to James L. Henderson, 12 Nov. 1813, recorded in SJL, but not found.

TJ received only one letter from Brown ɪɴ ᴊᴜɴᴇ; that of 13 June arrived at Monticello on 1 July 1813. The ᴍᴇᴅɪᴄᴀʟ ɢᴇɴ-ᴛʟᴇᴍᴀɴ who had recently called on TJ may have been Daniel Hall, of Baltimore.

¹ Word interlined in place of "that man."

From Patrick Gibson

Sɪʀ   Richmond 13ᵗʰ Novʳ 1813

I send you inclosed as requested in yours of the 9ᵗʰ Insᵗ one hundred dollars in small notes—but little change has taken place in the price of flour, it is, if anything more dull, sales have been made on the basin at $4\frac{3}{4}$ and a little at $4\frac{1}{2}$ \$, our mill flour has been sold at 5\$ on 4 months

Very respectfully I am

Your ob^t Servt

PATRICK GIBSON

RC (ViU: TJP-ER); between dateline and salutation: "Thomas Jefferson Esqre"; endorsed by TJ as received 16 Nov. 1813 and so recorded in SJL.

SJL records a missing letter from TJ to Gibson & Jefferson OF THE 9TH INS^T.

From John Adams

DEAR SIR   Quincy Nov. 14: 1813

Accept my thanks for the comprehensive Syllabus, in your favour of Oct. 12.

The Psalms of David, in Sublimity beauty, pathos and originality, or in one Word, in poetry, are Superiour to all the Odes Hymns and Songs in any language. But I had rather read them in our prose translation, than in any version I have Seen. His Morality however, often Shocks me, like Tristram Shandy's execrations.

Blacklocks translation of Horace's "Justum" is admirable; Superiour to Addisons. Could David be translated as well; his Superiority would be universally acknowledged. We cannot compare the Sybbiline Poetry. By Virgils Pollio we may conjecture, there was Prophecy as well as Sublimity. Why have those Verses been annihilated? I Suspect platonick Christianity, pharisaical Judaism, or machiavilian Politicks, in this case; as in all other cases of the destruction of records and litterary monuments. The Auri Sacra fames, et dominandi Sæva cupido.

Among all your researches in Hebrew History and Controversy have you ever met a book, the design of which is to prove, that the ten Commandments, as We have them in our Catechisms and hung up in our Churches, were not the Ten Commandments written by the Finger of God upon tables, delivered to Moses on mount Sinai and broken by him in a passion with Aaron for his golden calf, nor those afterwards engraved by him on Tables of Stone; but a very different Sett of Commandments?

There is such a book by J. W. Goethens Schristen. Berlin 1775–1779. I wish to See this Book.

you will See the Subject and perceive the question in Exodus 20. 1–17. 22–28.   chapter 24. 3 &c   ch. 24. 12.   ch. 25. 31   ch. 31. 18.   ch. 31. 19.   ch. 34. 1.   ch. 34. 10 &c.

I will make a Covenant with all this People. Observe that which I command this day.

1

Thou Shall not adore any other God. Therefore take heed, not to enter into covenant, with the Inhabitants of this country; neither take for your Sons, their daughters in marriage. They would allure thee to the Worship of false Gods. Much less Shall you in any place, erect Images.

2

The Feast of unleavened bread, Shall thou keep. Seven days, Shall thou eat unleavened bread, at the time of the month Abib; to remember that about that time, I delivered thee from Egypt

3

Every first born of the mother is mine; the male of thine herd, be it Stock or flock. But you Shall replace the first born of an Ass with a Sheep. The first born of your Sons Shall you <u>redeem</u>. No Man Shall appear before me with empty hands.

4

Six days Shall thou labour: the Seventh day, thou shall rest from ploughing and gathering.

5

The Feast of Weeks shalt thou keep, with the firstlings of the wheat Harvest: and the Feast of Harvesting, at the end of the year.

6

Thrice, in every year, all male persons shall appear before the Lord. Nobody shall invade your Country, as long as you obey this Command.

7

Thou shall not Sacrifice the blood of a Sacrifice of mine, upon leavened bread.

8

The Sacrifice of the Passover Shall not remain, till the next day.

9

The Firstlings of the produce of your land, thou Shalt bring to the House of the Lord.

10

Thou shalt not boil the kid, while it is yet Sucking.

And the Lord Spake to Moses: Write these Words; as, after these Words I made with you, and with Israel a Covenant.

I know not whether Goethens translated or abridged from the Hebrew, or whether he used any translation Greek, Latin, or German.

But he differs in form and Words, Somewhat from our Version. Exod. 34. 10. to 28. The Sense Seems to be the Same. The Tables were the evidence of the covenant, by which the Almighty attached the People of Israel to himself. By these laws they were Seperated from all other nations, and were reminded of the principal Epochas of their History.

When and where originated our Ten commandments? The Tables and The Ark were lost. Authentic copies, in few, if any hands; the ten Precepts could not be observed, and were little remembered.

If the Book of Deuteronomy was compiled, during or after the Babilonian Captivity, from Traditions, the Error or amendment might come in there.

But you must be weary, as I am at present, of Problems, conjectures, and paradoxes, concerning Hebrew, Grecian and Christian and all other Antiquities; but while We believe that the finis bonorum will be happy, We may leave learned men to this disquisition and Criticism[1]

I admire your Employment, in Selecting the Philosophy and Divinity of Jesus and Seperating it from all intermixtures. If I had Eyes and Nerves, I would go through both Testaments and mark all that I understand. To examine the Mishna Gemara Cabbala Jezirah, Sohar Cosri and Talmud of the Hebrews would require the life of Methuselah, and after all, his 969 years would be wasted to very little purpose.[2] The Dæmon of Hierarchical despotism has been at Work, both with the Mishna and Gemara. In 1238 a French Jew, made a discovery to the Pope (Gregory 9th) of the heresies of the Talmud. The Pope Sent 35 Articles of Error, to the Archbishops of France, requiring them to Seize the books of the Jews, and burn all that contained any Errors. He wrote in the same terms to the Kings of France, England Arragon, Castile Leon, Navarre and Portugal. In consequence of this Order 20 Cartloads of Hebrew Books were burnt in France: and how many times 20 cartloads were destroyed in the other Kingdoms? The Talmud of Babylon and that of Jerusalem were composed from 120 to 500 years after the destruction of Jerusalem. If Lightfoot derived Light from what escaped from Gregorys fury[3] in explaining many passages in the New Testament, by comparing the Expressions of the Mishna, with those of the Apostles and Evangelists, how many proofs of the Corruptions of Christianity might We find in the Passages burnt? JOHN ADAMS

RC (DLC); at foot of text: "President Jefferson"; endorsed by TJ as received 13 Dec. 1813 and so recorded in SJL, although SJL gives the date of composition as 15 Nov. 1813. FC (Lb in MHi: Adams Papers).

A translation of HORACE'S "JUSTUM" (from the *Odes*, 3.3) by Joseph Addison appears in the latter's *Miscellaneous Works, in Verse and Prose* (London, 1726; Sowerby, no. 4546), 1:142–7. Virgil's fourth eclogue is also known as the POLLIO because it was written during the consulship of Caius Asinius Pollio (Fairclough, *Virgil*, 1:48–53). AURI SACRA FAMES, ET DOMINANDI SÆVA CUPIDO: "accursed hunger for gold, and cruel lust for power." The first clause is from Virgil's *Aeneid*, 3.57 (*Virgil*, 1:376–7). The biblical story of Aaron and HIS GOLDEN CALF is in Exodus 32.1–20. J. W. GOETHENS SCHRISTEN: Johann Wolfgang von Goethe, *D. Goethens Schriften*, 4 vols. (Berlin, 1775–79). This work included Goethe's argument that the biblical Ten Commandments inscribed on stone tablets were the "Ritual Commandments" recorded in Exodus 34.11–26, rather than the "Ethical Command-ments" from Exodus 20.2–17 and Deuteronomy 5.6–21 generally accepted as forming the Decalogue (Bernard M. Levinson, "Goethe's Analysis of Exodus 34 and Its Influence on Wellhausen: The *Pfropfung* of the Documentary Hypothesis," *Zeitschrift für die Alttestamentliche Wissenchaft* 114 [2002]: 212–23). FINIS BONORUM: "chief good." The JEZIRAH, Zohar (SOHAR), and COSRI are kabbalistic works. John LIGHTFOOT was an English biblical scholar. George Wythe bequeathed a copy of his works to TJ (*The Works of the Reverend and Learned John Lightfoot D.D.*, 2 vols. [London, 1684; Sowerby, no. 1530]).

[1] RC: "disquisitions and Criticisms." FC: "disquisition and criticism."
[2] Adams here canceled "Accept my thanks for all favors. John Adams."
[3] Preceding five words interlined in place of "them."

To Thomas Mann Randolph

DEAR SIR   Monticello Nov. 14. 13.

Your motions have hitherto put it out of our power to write to you from the uncertainty of the times and places at which a letter could meet you. your last however from Cayuga removes the difficulty, as we presume a letter now written will find you at Headquarters, and that these will be somewhere in the line between Sacket's harbor and Montreal. we have heard of the movements of Genl Wilkinson as far as Grenadier island, and Genl Hampton's to within 4. miles of the hostile camp, and we expect every mail to inform us of their both opening on Montreal, leaving Kingston to be taken at leisure. in short we are rejoicing in the expectation that all Canada above the Sorel is ours, and that the earlier disgraces of the war are now wiped away. this with the execution of Hull, and perhaps the disgrace of 3. or 4. more will satisfy all with the state of the war, the Anglomen excepted. the success of Bonaparte in the battle of Dresden, and repair of the checks given by Bernardotte and Blucher, which I have no doubt he will soon effect, added to the loss of Canada, will produce a melancholy meeting between the Executive of England and it's parliament. and should it overset the ministry it may give us peace with

England, and consequently war with all those arrayed against her in Europe, which will hardly mend our situation.

The family is all well, and has been constantly so since you left us. you will hear this from our Martha herself, and perhaps from others of the family. we are just finishing our wheat sowing, as your people are also, and we are about to begin that of rye to feed us from harvest till the next corn season; for of corn I do not make a barrel to the acre. I believe it is expected you will make enough to serve till harvest at least. I buy largely at 20/ the price at which it starts.   the manufacturing mill is just beginning to recieve wheat and to do something. there have been some discouragements to the bringing it in. the want of a visible and responsible head is supplied to a certain degree by Jefferson's taking that post, which I dare say he will discharge satisfactorily. some flour for neighborhood use, perhaps too closely ground (to wit the barrel from 4 bush.–7 ℔) has discredited the mill for a while. an assistant miller has been engaged by Jefferson on trial, and after a month's trial, the opinion of his skill & good conduct is favorable, and perhaps that he may understand grinding better than Gilmer. but he could not supply Gilmer's place as principal. I am still afraid it will be a losing concern to you as long as you are absent, unless you had a skilful and honest partner, not easy to be found. since our last operations on the dam, altho' the river is now very low indeed so that no boat can go down, we have the greatest abundance of water. I was at the mills yesterday. all were going with full heads, the locks leaking as usual, and a great deal of water running over the waste. I was disappointed in raising the breast of the dam a foot higher by the water becoming extremely cold just as we had got all our logs & stone in place ready to be laid down. this is therefore deferred to the spring, and will remove our difficulties from the dam to the canal bank which will be in danger of overflowing. the Rivanna company have had their works viewed by Commissioners and it is presumed they will be recieved at the next court, and toll begin to be levied. they have agreed that the bill respecting them shall pass as amended by the Senate, which provides that they shall recieve their toll <u>at the locks,</u> and only on <u>what passes thro' them</u>, saving moreover all other private rights. I am not without a hope the Executive is taking measures to prevent the enemy's lying in Hampton road thro' the winter which may give an outlet to our produce. I have proposed to them the building a fort at the mouth of Lynhaven R. to command that bay and be a rallying point for the light horse & infantry kept to scour that coast. as yet prices do not look up. the new wheat is sold here @ 3/6 & 3/9 and at the Buckingham mills & all above them at the same. I have heard of no price at Richmond further than that the new flour is dull @ 5.D. I leave this for Bedford in 2. or 3. days and shall not be back till the middle of December, until which time of course I shall not be able to write to you again. we are all in the hope however of seeing you before that, as in that climate the troops must very shortly go into winter quarters, on which event you have nourished our hopes of your coming and passing the winter at home. not despairing then of finding you here on my return from Bedford I salute you with affection and respect and with every wish for your health and safety. Th: Jefferson

RC (DLC); at foot of first page: "Col⁰ Thoˢ M. Randolph"; endorsed by Randolph. PoC (MHi); endorsed by TJ.

Randolph's letter from CAYUGA, New York, is not recorded in SJL and has not been found. The SOREL is an obsolete name for the Richelieu River in Quebec, Canada (*A Gazetteer of the World, or Dictionary of Geographical Knowledge* [1850–56], 6:671). Although Napoleon won the BATTLE OF DRESDEN, 26–27 Aug. 1813, his subordinates were defeated at Grössbeeren that same month by

Crown Prince Charles John of Sweden, the former Napoleonic marshal Jean Baptiste Jules Bernadotte (BERNADOTTE), and by Gebhard Leberecht von BLUCHER at the Katzbach (Chandler, *Campaigns of Napoleon*, 903–11). TJ alluded to MARTHA Jefferson Randolph and Thomas JEFFERSON Randolph.

Missing letters from Randolph to TJ of 12 and 16 Nov. 1813 are recorded in SJL as received 13 Dec. 1813 from an encampment near Cornwall, Canada, and from French Mills, New York, respectively.

From John Adams

Dear Sir   Quincy November 15.[1] 13

I cannot appease my melancholly commiseration for our Armies in this furious Snow Storm, in any way So well as by Studying your Letter of Oct. 28.

We are now explicitly agreed, in one important point, vizᵗ That "there is a natural Aristocracy among men; the grounds of which are Virtue and Talents."

you very justly indulge a little merriment upon this Solemn Subject of Aristocracy. I often laugh at it too, for there is nothing in this laughable world more ridiculous than the management of it by almost all the nations of the Earth.[2] But while We Smile, Mankind have reason to Say to Us, as the froggs said to the Boys, What is Sport to you is Wounds and death to Us. When I consider the weakness, the folly, the Pride, the Vanity, the Selfishness, the Artifice, the low craft and mean Cunning, the want of Principle, the Avarice the unbounded Ambition, the unfeeling Cruelty of a majority of those (in all Nations) who are allowed an aristocratical influence; and on the other hand, the Stupidity with which the more numerous multitude, not only become their Dupes, but even love to be taken in by their Tricks: I feel a Stronger disposition to weep at their destiny, than to laugh at their Folly.

But tho' We have agreed in one point, in Words, it is not yet certain that We are perfectly agreed in Sense. Fashion has introduced an indeterminate Use of the Word "Talents." Education, Wealth, Strength Beauty, Stature, Birth, Marriage, graceful Attitudes and Motions, Gait, Air, Complexion, Physiognomy, are Talents, as well as Genius and Science and learning. Any one of these Talents, that in fact commands or influences[3] two Votes in Society, gives to the Man who possesses it, the Character of an Aristocrat, in my Sense of the Word.

Pick up, the first 100 men you meet, and make a Republick. Every Man will have an equal Vote. But when deliberations and discussions are opened it will be found that 25, by their Talents, Virtues being equal, will be able to carry 50 Votes. Every one of these 25, is an Aristocrat, in my Sense of the Word; whether he obtains his one Vote in Addition to his own, by his Birth Fortune, Figure, Eloquence, Science learning, Craft Cunning, or even his Character for good fellowship and a bon vivant.

What gave Sir William Wallace his amazing Aristocratical Superiority? His Strength. What gave M[rs] Clark, her aristocratical Influence to create Generals Admirals and Bishops? her Beauty. What gave Pompadour and Du Barry the Power of making Cardinals and Popes? their Beauty. you have Seen the Palaces of Pompadour and Du Barry: and I have lived for years in the Hotel de Valentinois,[4] with Franklin who had as many Virtues as any of them. In the investigation of the meaning of the Word "Talents" I could write 630 Pages, as pertinent as John Taylors[5] of Hazelwood. But I will Select a Single Example; for female Aristocrats are nearly as formidable in Society as male.

A daughter of a green Grocer, walks the Streets in London dayly with a baskett of Cabbage Sprouts, Dandelions and Spinage on her head. She is observed by the Painters to have a beautiful Face, an elegant figure, a graceful Step and a debonair. They hire her to Sitt. She complies,[6] and is painted by forty Artists, in a Circle around her. The Scientifc Sir William Hamilton outbids the Painters, Sends her to Schools for a genteel Education and Marries her. This Lady not only causes the Tryumphs of the Nile of Copenhagen and Trafalgar, but Seperates Naples from France and finally banishes the King and Queen from Sicilly. Such is the Aristocracy of the natural Talent of Beauty. millions of Examples might be quoted from History Sacred and profane, from Eve, Hannah, Deborah Suzanna Abigail, Judith, Ruth, down to Hellen[7] Madame de Maintenon and Mrs Fitzherbert. For mercy's Sake do not compell me to look to our chaste States and Territories, to find Women, one of whom lett go, would, in the Words of Holopherne's Guards "deceive the whole Earth."

The Proverbs of Theognis, like those of Soloman, are Observations on human nature, ordinary life, and civil Society, with moral reflections on the facts. I quoted him as a Witness of the Fact, that there was as much difference in the races of Men as in the breeds of Sheep; and as a Sharp reprover and censurer of the sordid mercenary practice of disgracing Birth by preferring Gold to it. Surely no Authority can be more expressly in point to prove the existence of Inequalities, not of rights, but of moral intellectual and physical inequalities[8] in Families, descents and Generations. If a descent from, pious, virtuous, wealthy litterary or Scientific Ancestors is a letter of recommendation, or introduction in a Mans favour, and enables him to influence only one Vote in Addition to his own, he is an Aristocrat, for a democrat can have but one Vote. Aaron Burr had 100,000 Votes from the Single Circumstance of his descent from President Burr and President Edwards.

your Commentary on the Proverbs of Theognis reminded me of two solemn Characters, the one resembling John Bunyan, the other Scarron. The one John Torrey: the other Ben. Franklin. Torrey a Poet, an Enthusiast, a Superstitious Bigot, once very gravely asked my Brother Cranch, "whether it would not be better for Mankind, if Children were always begotten from religious motives only."? Would not religion, in this Sad case, have as little Efficacy in encouraging procreation, As it has now in discouraging it?—I Should apprehend a decrease of population even in our Country where it increases So rapidly.—In 1775 Franklin made a morning Visit, at Mrs Yards to Sam. Adams and John. He was unusually loquacious. "Man, a rational Creature"! Said Franklin. "Come; Let Us Suppose a rational Man. Strip him of all his Appetites, especially of his hunger and thirst. He is in his Chamber, engaged in making Experiments, or in pursuing Some Problem. He is highly entertained. At this moment a Servant knocks, "Sir dinner is on Table."[9] "Dinner"! Pox! Pough! But what have you for dinner?" Ham and Chickens. "Ham"! "And must I break the chain of my thoughts, to go down and knaw a morsel of a damn'd Hogs Arse"? "Put aside your Ham." "I will dine tomorrow."

Take away Appetite and the present generation would not live a month and no future generation would ever exist. Thus the exalted dignity of human Nature would be annihilated and lost. And in my opinion, the whole loss would be of no more importance, than putting out a Candle, quenching a Torch, or crushing a Firefly, <u>if in this world only We have hope</u>.

your distinction between natural and artificial Aristocracy does not appear to me well founded. Birth and Wealth are conferred on Some Men, as imperiously by Nature, as Genius, Strength or Beauty. The Heir to honours and Riches, and power[10] has often no more merit in procuring these Advantages, than he has in obtaining an handsome face or an elegant figure. When Aristocracies, are established by human Laws and honour Wealth and Power are made hereditary by municipal Laws and political Institutions, then I acknowledge artificial Aristocracy to commence: but this never commences, till Corruption in Elections becomes dominant and uncontroulable. But this artificial Aristocracy can never last. The everlasting Envys, Jealousies, Rivalries and quarrells among them, their cruel rapacities upon the poor ignorant People their followers, compell these to Sett up Cæsar, a Demagogue to be a Monarch and Master, pour mettre chacun a Sa place. Here you have the origin of all artificial Aristocracy, which is the origin of all Monarchy. And both Artificial Aristocracy, and Monarchy, and civil, military, political and hierarchical Despotism, have all grown out of the natural Aristocracy of "Virtues and Talents,."

We, to be Sure, are far remote from this. Many hundred years must roll away before We Shall be corrupted. Our pure, virtuous, public Spirited federative Republick will last for ever, govern the Globe and introduce the perfection of Man, his perfectability being already proved by Price Priestly, Condorcet Rousseau Diderot and Godwin.

"Mischief has been done by the Senate of U.S" I have known and felt more of this mischief, than Washington, Jefferson and Madison altogether.[11] But this has been all caused by the constitutional Power of the Senate in Executive Business, which ought to be immediately, totally and eternally abolished.

your distinction between the αριστοι and pseudo αριστοι, will not help the matter. I would trust one as Soon as the other with unlimited Power. The Law wisely refuses an Oath as a witness in his own cause to the Saint as well as to the Sinner.

No Romance would be more amusing, than the History of your Virginian and our new England Aristocratical Families. yet even in Rhode Island, where there has been no Clergy, no Church, and I had almost Said, no State, and Some People Say no religion, there has been a constant respect for certain old Families.—57 or 58. years ago, in Company with Col. Counsellor, Judge, John Chandler, whom I have quoted before, a Newspaper was brought in. The old Sage asked me to look for the News from Rhode Island and See how the Elections had gone there. I read the List of Wantons, Watsons, Greens, Whipples, Malbones &c. "I expected as much," Said the aged Gentleman, "for I have always been of Opinion, that in the most popular Governments, the Elections will generally go in favour of the most ancient families." To this day when any of these Tribes and We may Add Ellerys, Channings Champlins &c are pleased to fall in with the popular current, they are sure to carry all before them.

you suppose a difference of Opinion between you and me, on this Subject of Aristocracy. I can find none. I dislike and detest hereditary honours, Offices Emoluments established by Law. So do you. I am for excluding[12] legal hereditary distinctions from the U.S. as long as possible. So are you. I only Say that Mankind have not yet discovered any remedy against irresistable Corruption in Elections to Offices of great Power and Profit, but making them hereditary.

But will you Say our Elections are pure? Be it so; upon the whole. But do you recollect in history, a more Corrupt Election than that of Aaron Burr to be President, or that of De Witt Clinton last year. By corruption, here I mean a Sacrifice of every national Interest and honour, to private and party Objects.

I See the same Spirit in Virginia, that you and I See in Rhode Island and the rest of New England. In New york it is a Struggle of Family Feuds. A fewdal Aristocracy. Pensylvania is a Contest between German,[13] Irish and old English Families. When Germans and Irish Unite, they give 30,000 majorities, There is virtually a White Rose and a Red Rose, a Cæsar and a Pompey in every State in this Union and Contests and dissentions will be as lasting. The Rivalry of Bourbons and Noailleses produced the French Revolution, and a Similar Competition for Consideration and Influence, exists and prevails in every Village in the World.

Where will terminate, the Rabies Agri? The Continent will be Scattered over with Manors, much larger than Livingstons, Van Ranselaers, or Phillips's. Even our Deacon Strong will have a Principality among you Southern Folk. what Inequality of Talents will be produced by these Land Jobbers?[14]

Where tends the Mania for Banks.? At my Table in Philadelphia, I once proposed to you to unite in endeavours to obtain an Amendment of the constitution, prohibiting to the seperate States, the Power of creating Banks; but giving Congress Authority to establish one Bank, with a branch in each State; the whole limited to Ten Millions of dollars.

Whether this Project was wise or unwise, I know not, for I had deliberated little on it then and have never thought it worth thinking much[15] of Since. But you Spurned the Proposition from you with disdain.

This System of Banks begotten, hatched and brooded by Duer, Robert and Gouverneur[16] Morris, Hamilton and Washington, I have always considered as a System of national Injustice. A Sacrifice of public and private Interest to a few Aristocratical Friends and Favourites. My Scheme could have had no Such Effect.

Verres plundered Temples and robbed a few rich Men: but he never made Such ravages among private property in general, nor Swindled So much out of the pocketts of the poor and the middle Class of People as these Banks have done. No people but this would have borne the Imposition So long. The People of Ireland would not bear Woods half pence. What Inequalities of Talent, have been introduced into this Country by these Aristocratical Banks!

Our Winthrops, Winslows, Bradfords, Saltonstalls, Quincys, Chandlers, Leonards Hutchinsons Olivers, Sewalls &c are precisely in the Situation of your Randolphs, Carters and Burwells, and Harrisons. Some of them unpopular for the part they took in the late revolution, but all respected for their names and connections and whenever they fall in with the popular Sentiments, are preferred, ceteris paribus to all others. When I was young, the Summum Bonum in Massachusetts, was to be worth ten thousand pounds Sterling, ride in a Chariot, be Colonel of a Regiment of Militia and hold a Seat in his Majesty's Council. No Mans Imagination aspired to any thing higher, beneath the Skies. But these Plumbs, Chariots, Colonelships and counsellorships are recorded and will never be forgotten: No great Accumulations of Land were made by our early Settlers. Mr Baudoin a French Refugee, made the first great Purchases and your General Dearborne, born under a fortunate Starr is now enjoying a large Portion of the Aristocratical Sweets of them.

As I have no Amanuenses but females, and there is So much about generation[17] in this letter that I dare not ask any one of them to copy it, and I cannot copy it my Self I must beg of you to return it to me. your old Friend   JOHN ADAMS.

RC (MHi: Adams Papers); at foot of text: "President Jefferson"; endorsed by TJ as a letter of 16 Nov. 1813 received 13 Dec. 1813 and so recorded in SJL; endorsed by Adams after its return as "My Letter to Jefferson Nov. 15: 1813." Tr (DLC); in TJ's hand; correctly dated but endorsed by TJ as received 15 Dec. Enclosed in TJ to Adams, 24 Jan. 1814.

The story of the FROGGS and the boys is from *Aesop's Fables*. The DAUGHTER OF A GREEN GROCER was Lady Emma Hamilton, the wife of William Hamilton and mistress of Horatio Nelson, the latter of whom won the naval battles of THE NILE OF COPENHAGEN AND TRAFALGAR (*ODNB*, 24:396–410, 40:789–93). DECEIVE THE WHOLE EARTH quotes the Catholic and Eastern Orthodox Bible, Judith 10.19. Paul SCARRON was a French comic author known for his mastery of burlesque. Adams's BROTHER CRANCH was his brother-in-law Richard Cranch. POUR METTRE CHACUN A SA PLACE: "to keep everyone in their place." The United States Constitution, article 2, section 2, gives the Senate some EXECUTIVE influence through its power to reject treaties and presidential nominations. αριστοι: "best men; nobles." During the English War of the Roses of the fifteenth century, the WHITE ROSE symbolized the Yorkists, while the red represented the house of Lancaster. RABIES AGRI: "madness for land." Caleb STRONG was a Federalist and governor of Massachusetts, 1800–07 and 1812–16 (*DAB*). William Wood's receipt in 1722 of an exclusive monopoly to mint HALF PENCE and farthings for Ireland led to a storm of protest and the revocation of the privilege three years later (*ODNB*). Adams's female AMANUENSES during this period included his niece Louisa Catherine Smith, his daughter-in-law Sarah Smith Adams, and his granddaughters Susanna Boylston Adams, Abigail Louisa Adams, and Caroline Amelia Smith.

[1] Reworked from "16."

[2] Word interlined in place of "World."

[3] Preceding two words interlined.

[4] RC: "Velentinois." Tr: "Valentinois."

[5] RC: "Taytors." Tr: "Taylor's."

[6] Word interlined here in place of "<Stopps> Strips."

[7] Word interlined.

[8] RC: "inqualities." Tr: "inequalities."

[9] Omitted closing quotation mark editorially supplied.

[10] Preceding two words interlined.

[11] RC: "altoger." Tr: "all together."

[12] RC: "exluding." Tr: "excluding."

[13] RC: "Germon." Tr: "German."

[14] Sentence interlined.

[15] Word not in Tr.

[16] RC: "Governeur." Tr: "Gouverneur."

[17] TJ here canceled "& procreation" in Tr.

From John E. Hall

SIR   Baltimore 15th Nov. 1813

I was fortunately enabled to procure a copy of "The Proceedings" &c from Judge Cooper, and have Sent it to my printer. It contains a few Ms. notes, which, being in your hand-writing, will be attended to in the new edition. It has just occurred to me that you might wish to avail yourself of such an opportunity to make further alterations & therefore I trouble you with this letter. If you have no further use for the plate, from which your engraving is made, I should be glad to have it, as it would save the expense of a new one. Mr Livingston has given me a reply to your pamphlet. The two will form the first two numbers of the Law Journal—about 300 pp. My friend, Mr Duponceau, has been kind enough to undertake the revision of the proofsheets—the printing being done at Philad: From his great accuracy, I have no doubt your pamphlet will be faithfully copied. The errors in punctuation, I do not think we have a right to meddle with, excepting in very evident cases.

I am, Sir, yr obt Servt   J. E. HALL

RC (DLC); endorsed by TJ as received 13 Dec. 1813 and so recorded in SJL.

The PRINTER of Hall's *American Law Journal* was William Fry, of Baltimore. TJ provided corrections in some of the copies of his 31 July 1810 Statement on the Batture Case that he published in 1812 and distributed to friends and public officials, one particularly comprehensive example being at DLC: Rare Book and Special Collections. The pamphlet and Edward Livingston's REPLY, *An Answer*

to Mr. *Jefferson's Justification of his Conduct in the Case of the New Orleans Batture* (Philadelphia, 1813; Sowerby, no. 3507), were published in the first and second issues, respectively, of the *American Law Journal 5* (1814). TJ wrote in the copy of his batture pamphlet now at DLC: Rare Book and Special Collections that the typesetter had introduced ERRORS IN PUNCTUATION so "innumerable" that "no correction of them will be attempted."

From Peter Minor

DEAR SIR   Ridgeway Nov. 15. 1813

I stated to you the other day in conversations that I believed the directors of the Rivanna Company were entirely satisfied with the Law respecting the navigation of our River, as it was amended last winter[1] by the Senate; A copy of which you have Seen. I have now the pleasure of confirming that statement. The matter has been agitated in full meeting & decided unanimously that the passage of such a law would comprehend every object of their petition to the last assembly: And if you have no objection to it they will petition that the Bill as amended may pass into a Law.

The objects of their late petition to the assembly were Simply these. 1st To get the Tolls reduced, which had been fixed So high as effectually to prohibit the passage of all produce, And as they had built Locks which would require from time to time rebuilding & repairs 2dly to get their charter extended or perpetuated for the purpose of keeping up these locks, after the Company would be dissolved by the provisions of the first law. This was the extent of their petition.

It never was their intention to demand toll any where but at the Locks, nor upon any lading but what passed the locks This I am induced to mention from an Idea that you have been impressed with a contrary belief.

Nor did they ever think of demanding Toll upon your Property, but at all times to grant you a free use of the Locks in consideration of your granting to them the use of your canal.

The amendments proposed by the Senate seem to have been predicated upon a Supposition that the directors would act contrary to the above statement I assure you they never had such an intention.— It remains to be settled, (& on this point the directors have instructed me to consult you) How far you consider Your self bound to grant them the use of Your canal for the purposes of Navigation, a Scite for their Toll House &c. & in what way you will have this obligation expressed; Whether by a contract or [a] Grant as formerly proposed, to be recorded here,[2] or by Some provision which by your consent might be incorporated in the Law. For the satisfaction of those for whom they act, they deem Some act of this Sort on your part necessary   with the highest Esteem & respect I remain &c.   P. MINOR.

RC (MHi); notation by TJ at head of text: "N⁰ 15."; mutilated at seal; addressed: "Mʳ Jefferson Monticello"; endorsed by TJ as received 16 Nov. 1813 and so recorded in SJL.

Under the PROVISIONS of the 30 Dec. 1806 act incorporating the Rivanna Company, "as soon as the subscribers, or their legal representatives, shall be reimbursed the principal sums of money paid by them respectively, with legal interest, the said tolls shall cease, and the said river thenceforth be deemed and taken as a public highway, free from any toll or imposition whatever" (Samuel Shepherd, *The Statutes at Large of Virginia . . . being a continuation of Hening* [1836], 3:320).

[1] Word written over "year," erased.
[2] Preceding four words interlined.

To William F. Gordon

DEAR SIR   Monticello Nov. 16. 13.

The omission of the affidavit to my bill v. Michie was from want of reflection and recollection. I know that in a suit at Common law where depositions are desired lest the witnesses should die before trial, an affidavit is always required and altho ours is a different case, yet it was not worth while to run any risk for want of a mere formality. I have therefore prepared an affidavit stating distinctly the case of every witness, which I shall send to the clerk to-day to file with the papers. but that will not make it a part of the record. the question then is whether it will be best to move the court at it's next session,

& before any advantage taken of the omission, to enter the affidavit nunc pro tunc, as an amendment of the record? or to say nothing about it on the presumption the adversary will not observe it. this last is never safe[1] policy; and if we propose the amendment by an entry nunc pro tunc, perhaps it may be proper to enter with it a new[2] <u>confirmation</u> of the order. all this I leave to yourself & mr Barber to do in it as you see best. I think however one thing certain; that the order to take the depositions is a merely interlocutory step from which there can be no appeal, & that the final decree is only on re-cieving & recording the depositions. in this view, the case being yet pending, the record may certainly be amended.—there is a just an-swer to the def's objections against our taking depositions, which is that it is in his power to render them unnecessary as soon as he pleases, by bringing his suit if he intends one: and we may offer to suspend this proceeding now if he will instantly file his bill or decla-ration so that the depositions may be taken in chief at once. still all this is left to you

your friend & serv[t]   TH: JEFFERSON

PoC (MHi); at foot of text: "M[r] W[m] F. Gordon"; endorsed by TJ.

The affidavit that TJ PREPARED to send to the clerk has not been found. NUNC PRO TUNC: "having retroactive legal effect" (*Black's Law Dictionary*). MR BARBER: Philip Pendleton Barbour. IN CHIEF here refers to that part of a legal proceeding at which the main body of ev-idence is presented (*Black's Law Dictionary*).

A missing letter from Gordon to TJ of 11 Nov. 1813 is recorded in SJL (with note that Gordon had mistakenly dated it "Dec. for Nov") as received 13 Nov. 1813.

[1] Word interlined in place of "good."
[2] Word interlined.

From Chapman Johnson

DEAR SIR,   Staunton 16. Nov[r] 1813

I had the pleasure of receiving your letter of the 7. by the last mail enclosing twenty dollars, my fee in the <u>certiorari</u> case of Michie, in the Albemarle Circuit court—.

I was very sorry to hear that indisposition had deprived us of the pleasure of seeing you, at Charlotte'sville—I hope when at Char-lottesville hereafter, I shall have it in my power, to avail my self of your polite invitation to visit you at Monticello—

It gives me great pleasure to know, that the Rivanna Company are satisfied, of the propriety of the law, proposed last winter in the Sen-ate, by way of amendment to the bill passed in the House of Delegates—. I am fully satisfied myself that justice required the protection of your rights, contained in that amendment, and I hope that no further difficulty will occur in its passage—If I should be present, in the Senate, I will attend to the verbal criticism which you suggest—

Very Respectfully Your Ob^t Sv^t　　　　　　　C. JOHNSON

RC (MHi); endorsed by TJ as received 13 Dec. 1813 and so recorded in SJL.

From Hugh Holmes

DEAR SIR　　　　　　　　　　　　　Winch^r Nov 17th 1813

Shortly after my return the 5th ins^t from the judicial labours of the fall circuit I addressed a note to the manufacturer of y^r merino wool urging the completion of the fabric and desiring to know when I might expect it—he returned the answer enclosed—which is not satisfactory as to the time of finishing it but I hope we shall be able to send it to you by your nephew Judge Carr who intends going to Albemarle about the middle of December—it was with a reluctance almost bordering on refusal that this manufacturer engaged to work the wool on terms of charging for carding, spinning, weaving, fulling dying & dressing because he prefers to <u>buy</u> the wool & <u>sell the Cloth</u> at <u>his own price</u>—I know from experience that including the high price of Merino wool a y^d of broad cloth 6 q^r wide can be made for $5. this cloth the manufacturer can readily sell at $10 by which he makes a clear proffit of $5 per y^d. hence it is that they refuse to the Citizens at large access to their machinery—this monopoly growing out of the war non importation, &c must find reasonable limits on the return of peace or the multiplication of similar establishments—

I merely write you now to shew you that I have not forgotten the Trust & to renew the assurance of my disposition to serve you but more especially of the high respect & esteem of

y^r friend　　　　　　　　　　　　　H^H HOLMES

RC (MHi); at foot of text: "Mr Jefferson"; endorsed by TJ as received 13 Dec. 1813 and so recorded in SJL. Enclosure: Cyrus B. Baldwin to Holmes, Front Royal, 12 Nov. 1813, stating that the wool for TJ and James Barbour is "in work, but I cannot name any time when it will be finish,d"; that he has been disappointed in finishers he expected from the northward; that if some of them arrive next month as expected, the work will be done immediately; that he has the best spinners and weavers and would hate to put their good cloth into the hands of bad finishers, whose inferior efforts would reduce its value by two or three dollars a yard; that he is anxious to supply cloth equal to that of northern manufacturers; and that if Holmes's friends will show "a little or rather good deal of patience & some charity," his industriousness will match it (RC in MHi;

torn at seal, with mutilated words re-copied by Holmes; notation by Holmes keyed to Barbour's name: "Govr Barbour has also a small quantity of wool there";

addressed: "Ho^n Hugh Holmes Winchester").

Q^R: a quarter of a yard, or nine inches.

From James Martin (of New York)

SIR   Washington nov^r 17. 1813

I received with all imaginable Gratitude your Letter from monticello but confess I am Embarrassed by the Condescension on your part in writing it—you have taken however the favorable side to me and relieved me from the apprehension that what was most respectfully designed to Amuse a Vacant half hour might be Construed into a presumption which I was not justified in—no monk ever read any of the Fathers with the Devotion I do the Sentiments you Communicate—they have the Authoritative Stamp that wisdom & Experience give to all you say—And were it not that I know that were one to rise from the dead he could not controul the passions which at present influence that very moral & Religious Set—I believe I should have run the risque of your displeasure and by publishing your Opinion have shamed at least if not Silenced them—the poets have, to be sure, drawn very beautiful pictures of turbulent Crowds awed from Sedition by the Appearance of one man of Superior Sanctity and wisdom but I am certain no modern poet would draw the same picture—Great Britain has found the Art of closing even that Avenue pope's Line 'Huge Bales of British Broad cloth Block the Door' is I am afraid as Embarrassing morally as the poet supposes it would be in reality but for paper money—that I write solely to amuse you in a leisure moment I can now give you a proof because I leave off at that phrase 'paper money' to tell you that having amused myself this morning by turning the whole Amount of the parliamentary Grants of last year into time I find that the national Expenditure of Great B^n was 1000 Dollars per minute and therefore I think the question their politicians so frequently ask each other 'How are we ruined'? is easily Answered—to continue my Efforts I cut from the newspapers two Articles which if they do not Amuse you will at least shew that we do not bear either the naval or Law Oppressions without shewing some resentment—the one was wrote in a moment of Vexation at reading in the papers the Affidavits of poor people on the potomac who had been robbed of those Identical Articles and the other at reading (in the Federal papers) a Character given of a man to whom the Country owes I believe more than half its plagues—and which was so very highly Coloured that with one who knew him it could not be suffered to pass with Impunity—

your Indulgence to me does not make me forget that it is a Trespass, at least upon politeness, to write you long Letters and therefore considering myself now at Liberty to write you when I think I can write you entertainingly I am only to request you not to take the trouble of Answering this but to give me an Annual Certificate of your Health and your permission to continue writing—

I am with the utmost respect your Obliged & Obed^t Servt

JA^s MARTIN

RC (MHi); dateline at foot of text; endorsed by TJ as received 13 Dec. 1813 and so recorded in SJL. Enclosures not found.

In June 1813 a firestorm of controversy resulted when the state senate of Massachusetts approved a resolution by the Federalist ex-congressman Josiah Quincy that "in a war like the present, waged without justifiable cause, and prosecuted in a manner which indicates that conquest and ambition are its real motives, it is not becoming a MORAL & RELIGIOUS people to express any approbation of military or naval exploits, which are not immediately connected with the defense of our sea-coast and soil" (*Salem* [Mass.] *Gazette*, 18 June 1813; Edmund Quincy, *Life of Josiah Quincy of Massachusetts* [1869], 324). As part of a poem making the general point that political corruption is rendered easier when paper money replaces bulkier bribes, Alexander Pope's line, HUGE BALES OF BRITISH BROAD CLOTH BLOCK THE DOOR, appeared with minor variations in his *Of the Use of Riches, an Epistle To the Right Honorable Allen Lord Bathurst* (London, 1732), 3.

To Peter Minor

DEAR SIR   Monticello Nov. 18. 13.

Your favor of the 15th is recieved, notifying me that the Directors of the Rivanna company have had under consideration the bill respecting the navigation of our river, that they have decided unanimously that the passage of that law as it was amended by the Senate, would comprehend every object of their petition to the last assembly, and that they propose to petition that the bill, as amended, may now pass into a law. to this I give my entire consent.

I recieve with satisfaction your assurances that 'it never was their intention to demand toll any where but at the locks, nor upon any lading but what passed the locks.' this assurance would at all times have satisfied me if incorporated into the new law, so as to controul the former one. I acknolege I was under a contrary impression as to their intentions; and that this was not without foundation, as to a part of the

Directors is countenanced by the following facts. 1. that the bill was drawn and passed the lower house without any Proviso to this effect. 2. that when amended in the Senate by the insertion of this proviso, Col⁰ Branham, one of the Directors & a member of the lower house, did not think proper to let it pass. and 3. that Capᵗ Meriwether, another of the Directors, was so displeased with the Senator of our district for the insertion of this proviso, that he endeavored to prevent his reelection by denouncing him in letters to Amherst as having sacrificed the public interest to that of an individual, to which was added his opposition to him in this county; altho' certainly, as our common representative, it was the duty of the Senator to see justice done to all.[1] that a majority of the[2] Directors wished nothing but justice, I have ever believed, and now beg them to accept my sincere assurances of it; and what I have said is merely for my own justification, and to shew that I have made no opposition, but on a point which themselves consider as right; and I hope I may further appeal to themselves to say whether, in every other instance, I have not yielded to their undertaking every aid and facility they have asked. I certainly would not have said thus much but to secure myself against the suspicion of making my private interests an obstacle to a public right, for which I am not conscious of having in my whole life given occasion. however we have now explained, & understand one another, and there is an end of the question.

To the use of my canal, a site for a toll house, & any other necessary conveniences I have always without hesitation consented & now consent: and I am willing to confirm them by grant or contract for a reasonable term of years, and for this I ask no consideration, no use of the locks, for they can never be of any use to me. I only request such provisions by the Directors as may secure my mills against interruptions to which the boatmen have already shewn themselves wantonly prone, and so they will be unless there be some person, or some rules at least, to controul the opening & shutting of the locks. the enormous leakage of the locks too, when either open or shut, is a great evil to be provided against, with such other regulations as reason and experience will call for. I am sure there will be no difficulty in these arrangements, because I ask nothing but protection from injury, which the Directors could have no interest or wish to permit. and there will be the less difficulty in making satisfactory arrangements, as I have raised the water in my dam one foot, and have the materials ready & in place for raising it another foot in the next warm season, so that the surplus of water, beyond what is necessary for the mills, will be sufficient for the locks if used according to reasonable regulations.   I set out tomorrow for Bedford, and immediately on my return shall be ready to enter into such stipulations as may give reasonable security and contentment on all sides. and as the subject is entirely new & untried I think it will be better to leave an opening for amendments from time to time, as experience may shew them necessary.

I have said and say I am willing the bill should pass as amended by the Senate. but I will suggest two other verbal amendments which concern me no more than every other person, and which the Directors would probably desire to have made for the sake of correctness.

In the 2ᵈ section of the bill it is said they are to take such toll as will enable them to keep the locks in repair, and to keep open the navigation 'of the said river.' say rather 'of the sd portion of the river.' otherwise it might be construed to extend power over the whole river from it's source to it's mouth, which is not intended.

In the 1ˢᵗ amending clause of the Senate it is provided that no toll shall be demanded but at the locks, and 'on <u>vessels</u> passing the locks.' this would make the vessels themselves, whether loaded or empty, liable to toll, which I understand is not intended. instead therefore of '<u>vessels passing the said locks</u>' say '<u>articles liable to toll passing thro' the sd locks.</u>' I suggest these amendments merely for the consideration of the Directors, who would doubtless prefer removing uncertainties before circumstances which may not be foreseen shall render them important; and with assurances that I am sincerely disposed to facilitate to them all the objects of their institution and to give as little trouble or impediment as possible to those who may use the navigation of my canal I tender to them & yourself every sentiment of esteem and respect.   TH: JEFFERSON

RC (DLC); at foot of first page: "Peter Minor esq." PoC (MHi); at head of text: "Nᵒ 16."; endorsed by TJ.

The state SENATOR OF OUR DISTRICT was Joseph C. Cabell.

[1] In PoC TJ here inserted an asterisk keyed to a note written perpendicularly in right margin: "to this might have been added a 4ᵗʰ proof that in the letter of the Secretary for the Directors of Nov. 10. 1810 is an objection to the instrument proposed by me in these words '3. an exception is next made to any produce other than of your own lands adjacent passing by water toll-free.'" Minor's missing letter to TJ of 10 Nov. 1810 is accounted for at note to TJ to Minor, 18 Nov. 1810.

[2] TJ here canceled "District."

From Lieutenants Fawcett and Dickonson

Charlottesville Nov[r] 19th 1813—

Lieutenants Fawcett, and Dickonson beg leave to return their kind thanks to M[r] Jefferson for the attention shewn them while at Charlottesville; and whould have done themselves the honor of waiting upon him, had time permitted—

RC (MHi); in an unidentified hand; addressed (edge trimmed): "Thomas Jefferson Esq[ue?] Monticello"; endorsed by TJ as received 13 Dec. 1813 and so recorded in SJL.

From Thomas Lehré

DEAR SIR   Charleston Nov: 23[d] 1813

I have taken the Liberty of sending you a paper, which contains a sketch of the life & Character of the late Peter Freneau Esq[r]—His name will be long revered and remembered by your Political friends in this State. I congratulate you and our Country [on][1] the brilliant successes[2] of our arms both by sea and by Land—They have contributed to make the war very popular, and to defeat the machinations of the enemies of the present administration. I remain with the highest considerations

Dear Sir Your Obedient H. Servant   THOMAS LEHRÉ

RC (DLC); at foot of text: "Thomas Jefferson late President U.S. Monticello Virginia"; endorsed by TJ as received 13 Dec. 1813 and so recorded in SJL.

The enclosed SKETCH OF THE LIFE & CHARACTER OF THE LATE PETER FRE-NEAU was printed this day in the Charleston *City Gazette and Commercial Daily Advertiser.*

[1] Lehré here canceled "on," which is restored editorially to enhance readability.
[2] Manuscript: "succcesses."

From James Monroe

DEAR SIR   washington nov[r] 23. 1813

The enclosed was written before my late visit to Albemarle, and detaind in consequence of it, to be deliverd in person, but afterwards forgotten and left here. I need not add my sincere desire that you will have the goodness to decide the question to which it relates.

we have nothing from abroad, immediately, concerning our own affairs; and no new light as to the result, of the great battles, near dresden. nor do we yet know whether our troops are to take their quarters in montreal, forcing the enemy into Quebec, or to retire within our former limits. the former is still more than probable.

with great respect & esteem I am sincerely your friend

JA[s] MONROE

RC (DLC); endorsed by TJ as received 13 Dec. 1813 and so recorded in SJL. Enclosure: Monroe to TJ, 3 Nov. 1813.

Although Napoleon soundly defeated an Allied army commanded by Prince Karl Philipp Schwarzenberg at DRESDEN on 26–27 Aug. 1813, he was beaten at the subsequent Battle of the Nations, also known as the Battle of Leipzig, 16–19 Oct. 1813 (Chandler, *Campaigns of Napoleon*, 906–36).

From William Cooper

SIR   New York Nov[r] 24th 1813

At a time when our enemy has avowed his intention to prosecute the war with the utmost rigor against our towns, villages, and citizens, it becomes the duty of every American to aid his Government in repelling them. I shall not be deterred by one disaster from respectfully submitting a plan, which I shall, I trust, <u>demonstrate</u> would completely banish them from our waters. Indeed, I am about submitting to M[r] Serrurier a proposal for "carrying the war to Carthage."

Last winter I offered to build, at my own expence, a floating battery for the purpose of aiding our operations against the British in Kingston, and on the S[t] Lawrence, if Government would furnish the arms and ammunition. The offer was accepted, and I, accordingly, undertook the enterprize. I did not think that I could, prudently, appropriate more than $2500 for the object, and, therefore, constructed it but slightly; although I have no doubt but it would have answered its intention, if it had arrived safely in Sackets Harbor, or if I had even completed it before I left Oswego. Impatient to get to the Harbour, I set sail before the decks were caulked, or, indeed, entirely laid: Of course I was not prepared to encounter a heavy gale, which arose as I had every prospect of weathering Stony-point. Having but a dozen soldiers on board, all of whom were seasick, it was impossible to pump out the water as fast as it washed over the bulwarks, and run into the hold. She filled in about an hour and settled on the bottom; where, in the course of an hour and a half, she went to pieces. I state these explanatory circumstances that no prejudice may arise in your mind against floating batteries from the fate of that one. The plan, however, which I shall now propose is no way similar except in its form.

I enclose a sketch, which will be, I think, sufficient to enable you to understand my explanation. The form of my proposed battery is an irregular octagon: The longest sides may be varied as may be deemed expedient: The one I built at Oswego was only 30 feet—its extreme length 70: the angles are 45°, of course allowing 20 feet for the breadth of the boats, the sides l l l l will be about 28 feet. The extremities between o and o are the width of the water way, or 6 feet. I have represented this battery as 100 feet extreme length; of course its longest side is 60 ft.

The only methods of over coming a floating battery must be by sinking, burning, battering to pieces, or capturing by boarding. This, I will show is secure from all, at the same time that it is morally certain that no floating enemy is secur from it.

The battery is intended to draw 6 feet water, the bottoms of the two vessels perfectly flat; in short every part of its surface is right-lined except the roof.

The deck which supports the carronades or mortars being but little elevated above the water, the height of the battery, when ready for service, will not much exceed six feet; except the spring of the arch, which I shall mention.

I ought to have pursued a more regular course of explanation. I, however, know that I shall be understood—

It is unnecessary to enter into the details which form my demonstration of the power of this machine, because, after having furnished you with an account of its form and proportions, you will immediately understand them.

The burthen of each vessel will be 9600 cubic feet: Both, or the buoyancy of the battery below[1] its decks 19200 cubic feet of water = 535 tons. + −

I purpose to move it by a steam engine of 3 feet cylinder

The battery which I constructed had an oak bulwark 4 feet thick, extending one foot below the water line. This was, therefore, liable to be burnt by red-hot shot—although I had pretty well guarded against it, by methods of extinguishment. It could not be sunk by cannon shot[2] because no cannon ball, with any practicable angle of depression, could penetrate, with force, a foot below water, according to the existing mode of warfare—

It might be sunk because it was not bomb-proof. I, however, depended upon its great strength, and the character of its intended armament; willing to run the risques to which I might be exposed.

A common vessel of war is a slave of the winds and tides—my battery is the slave of our will.

Making the vessels which support the bulwarks and superstructure of the dimensions I noticed I will proceed to the bulwarks themselves.

Instead of four feet of solid oak, I will construct the bulwarks, from two feet below the water line, of oak, <u>two</u> feet thick, and enclose it, completely, with three inches of <u>wrought iron</u>. This will be equally as light as my bulwarks, at the same time that it will be <u>impenetrable</u>.

The specific gravity of iron (wrought) is, about, 7645, of oak 925, of course, three inches of iron are not so heavy as two^3 feet of oak: But, to simplify the calculation, we will take the 4 feet of oak. The length of bulwark 244 × by the depth 8 × the thickness 4 = 7808 cubic feet of oak = of our American oak, as I have found by experiment about 7000 cubic feet of water = less than 180 tons—
leaving an excess of 355 tons burthen, deducting the weight of the vessels—these, allowing them to be one foot thick, of solid oak throughout, below the bulwarks, already estimated, will weigh about 70 tons: But all this is specifically lighter than the water, and an extravagant allowance besides.

The roof shall be bomb-proof, about one inch thick of iron, with a gentle curve or arch = to 70 tons. sufficient to change the direction of any **ball** or resist the fall of any bomb. We have now a buoyant power of 195 tons, abundantly sufficient for guns ammunition, steam engine, fuel, &c.

An engine of 3 foot cylinder propells a steam boat of 400 tons, at the rate of 9 miles an hour. This we see daily. Allowing for the shape of my battery; and, particularly, for the <u>direct</u> method in which my propelling power acts, instead of Mr Fultons' oblique, I may reasonably, nay, demonstrably, expect six miles. This is sufficient to change the whole art of maratime warfare, where the hostile parties are as near as the French and English, or as the blocading squadrons of the British and ourselves

Allowing, agreeably to my sketch, 14 ten or twelve inch mortars, or columbiads to each battery. they will equal, <u>of iron</u> to 40 tons. Steam engine 30 tons. I have still sufficient buoyant power for fuel ammunition, mys[elf] and crew, for a week at least—say 200 men

Where are we now? We go when we please: we go where we please; so far as our fuel will carry us. We can <u>always</u> choose our position. Our armament shells must either blow to peices or sink every thing if properly directed

By making the piston work, <u>horizontally</u> instead of <u>vertically</u>, I

compress the Engine within the altitude of the centre of the arch &—
30 ft. in length

To Describe the plan of <u>my engine</u> is unnecessary, because those, in use, are <u>sufficient</u>—and mine far better. I am indeed, surprized that Iron has not been used long since in forming bulwarks. I have allowed three inches for the iron, because I happened to know that no ball could penetrate that thickness: perhaps much less would suffice. The iron necessary, according to that plan, would amount for bulwark & roof

to 160 tons	$24000
Steam engine	20000
Building, at the most	20000
	64000

64000 without the guns—less than the expence of a single sloop of war! and what can oppose it. The guns should be cast on purpose. A ten or 12 inch shell fired into a vessel would injure her much in bursting, & if below the water would sink her inevitably. I have no doubt that Captain Manby's plan for "rending vessells asunder," which I lately saw announced in an English paper, is by firing shells charged with some of the strong fulminating powders.

If we had one of these batteries here no enemy would dare approach the coast, when he knew that a calm would be his certain destruction. Indeed, such is the mighty power of the steam engine, that an ordinary breeze would not secure his escape. One in the Chesapeake would effectually protect its shores from depredations and its trade from annoyance by the British. A smaller one on Lake Ontario would inevitably destroy the British naval force, even in Kingston harbour, and render immense service elsewhere. A half dozen might run over from Calais, or Dunkirk, and burn the East and West India Docks; in fact almost ruin England, if not quite compel her to sue for peace, on any terms

No form of construction admits of such immense strength. The one I was wrecked in was, weak—the water-way was entirely open and wide for the purpose of rowing inside. But here the deck timbers may be continuous: flat bars of iron from bottom to bottom would not much impede it, but would render it very strong. The bulwarks between o & o come to the waters edge nearly, so that the water has a free passage between the boats, and under the engine. By inserting a few tubes into the boiler below the surface of the water[4] the force of the steam would produce fountains of boiling water that would drive an enemy from the roof; and the turning of a cock would regulate the discharge.

What might not a few of these batteries effect! How could England protect her towns on the coast from destruction? The small draught of water would enable the batteries to go any where, and find harbours where not even a sloop of 80 tons could enter.

There would be no great difficulty in destroying Halifax if not Quebec. A transport vessel for wood would be secure in company, and an experienced and prudent commander, in the summer might navigate her without any risque

From France how easy to enter the Thames and ascend to London! Coal could be procured by laying any town under contribution when it was wanted, and the circumnavigation of England, accomplished;—teaching that proud nation that her wooden walls could no longer protect her; and inflicting a just and dreadful punishment for her maratime agressions, and disabling her, forever, from availing herself of her naval superiority—

I have taken the liberty to address you, because I know that your love for the Country will dispose you to give my suggestion a consideration, and because I know that your favorable opinion will ensure its adoption—

The loss of a finger on my right hand, which was torn off when I was wrecked, will be my apology for this scrawl—

I Am, Very Respectfully, Your Excellency's Most Obedient Humble Servant   WILLIAM COOPER

RC (DLC); hole in manuscript; dateline adjacent to closing; at head of text: "His Excellency Thomas Jefferson"; at foot of text: "William Cooper N° 23 North Moore St: New York"; endorsed by TJ as received 13 Dec. but recorded in SJL under 14 Dec. 1813.

William Cooper (1786–1819), the son of Judge William Cooper (1754–1809) and elder brother of the author James Fenimore Cooper, was born in Burlington, New Jersey. From 1800–02 he attended the College of New Jersey (later Princeton University), where his extravagant lifestyle attracted notice even before his expulsion on unproven charges of arson. Cooper then spent five years as a law-office clerk in Cooperstown, New York, and in New York City. Although his father bought him a house in the metropolis and stocked his library with law books, Cooper failed to establish a legal practice or improve his family's steadily

declining financial position (Alan Taylor, *William Cooper's Town: Power and Persuasion on the Frontier of the Early American Republic* [1995], 21, 333–8, 394–5; *New-York Commercial Advertiser*, 2 July 1808; *Longworth's New York Directory* [1813], 105; [1815], 171; Cooperstown *Otsego Herald*, 16 Feb. 1818, 25 Oct. 1819; gravestone inscription in Christ Episcopal Churchyard, Cooperstown).

George Prevost, a British lieutenant general, informed his American counterpart, General James Wilkinson, by way of a much-publicized 17 Oct. 1813 letter that "the commanders of His Majesty's armies and fleets on the coasts of America" were prepared, under certain conditions, "to prosecute the war with unmitigated severity" against the TOWNS, VILLAGES, AND CITIZENS of the United States (*ASP, Foreign Relations*, 3:635). Cooper was casting himself in the role of the ancient Roman general Scipio Africanus, who successfully proposed a direct attack on CARTHAGE, here equated with Great Britain. Robert Fulton preferred to employ steamboat paddle wheels, the boards of which enter the water at an OBLIQUE angle (Robert Routledge, *Discoveries and Inventions of the Nineteenth Century* [1893], 93–4). CO-LUMBIADS are heavy, cast-iron cannon or howitzers (*OED*). During the autumn of 1813, American newspapers published reports from England concerning George William MANBY's method by which "a

ship, within pistol or musket shot, may be *rent asunder* . . . in a very short space of time" (Philadelphia *Poulson's American Daily Advertiser*, 5 Oct. 1813). The large and commercially significant EAST AND WEST INDIA DOCKS were located just outside of London.

[1] Word interlined in place of "above."
[2] Preceding three words interlined.
[3] Word interlined in place of "three."
[4] Preceding six words interlined.

ENCLOSURE

William Cooper's Drawing of a Floating Battery

[ca. 24 Nov. 1813]

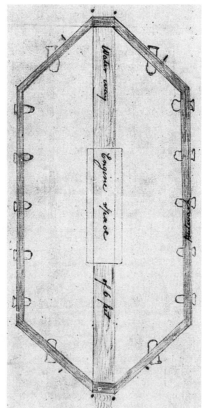

MS (DLC: TJ Papers, 200:35536); entirely in Cooper's hand; undated.

From William F. Gray

SIR,   Fredericksburg Nov. 25ᵗʰ 1813

By this day's stage I send you a small Box that has been sent to my care from J. Milligan & Co of Geo. Town.

Wishing it safe to hand

I am Respectfully Yours &c   Wᴹ F. GRAY

RC (DLC); endorsed by TJ as received 13 Dec. 1813 and so recorded in SJL.

From Walter Jones

DEAR SIR.   Post-office Kinsale novʳ 25. 1813.

A change for the worse, in the aspect of our political Parties, within twenty years, cannot, I think, have escaped your observation.—

Instead of a close adherence & frequent recurrence to first principles, as the invariable Standard by which men & measures should be tried, party has more & more assumed the character[1] of personal Factions. measures are supported or opposed, with little regard, in either Case, to their intrinsic merits, as they happen to be introduced & favoured by particular sets of men.—Language the most gross, brutal, and unsparing is the daily vehicle of calumny & detraction. they invade, like the plagues of Egypt, our innermost dwellings, they spare neither age nor bodily infirmities, they poison the Enjoyments of social Life, and disgrace our national Taste & morality.

If the federal Party transcends its antagonists, in this ignominious Career, candour must nevertheless declare, that the latter are in no Condition to "Cast the first Stone."

amid Such vitiated Elements, republicanism must decline, and we are not now to learn, that its decline, must be followed by Some form of Rule, more acceptable to the federal faction. So that in a contest carried on upon factious ground, the federalists have every thing to gain, and the republicans every thing to lose.—

under these Circumstances, I have thought it very desirable, to introduce a more temperate & rational Style in our political disquisitions. and to contribute my mite to So good an End, I have written the inclosed Essay, which I beg you to peruse—I have striven to preserve as much temper, as the present State of things admits one to exercise.—I wish to be Scrupulously accurate in my account of the federal Party, both in regard to facts & Inference. I have stated both, as a long Course of observation & reflexion have presented them to me. but as I do not entirely confide in my own Judgment, I know not where I could So well Subject it to needful Correction, as to you.— favour me therefore with remarks, that may Serve for the Correction of <u>facts especially</u>, and in as Short a time as may be quite Convenient to you. for should I be disposed to make it public, I could wish to do so, while our Legislature is in Session.—I have encountered two perilous Topics, one in Shewing that our own party is not impeccable & immaculate, the other in taking Gen[1] washington on my Shoulders, to bear him harmless through the federal Coalition.—

It would afford me exceeding pleasure to Say all this to you, instead of writing.—If I accomplish an upland Trip, next Summer, which I am meditating to take, I may once more have the pleasure of taking you by the hand, before we go, "quo Numa devenit & Ancus."—

yours, dear Sir, with much respect and very affectionate Esteem

WALT: JONES

P.S.

be good enough to inclose the paper to me at the P. office of Kinsale, as I have no Copy of it.

RC (DLC); endorsed by TJ as received 21 Dec. 1813 and so recorded in SJL. Enclosure not found.

The ten biblical PLAGUES that befell Egypt are described in Exodus, chapters 7–11. Jesus dispersed a mob gathered to kill a woman accused of adultery by asking whichever of them was without sin to CAST THE FIRST STONE (John 8.7). QUO NUMA DEVENIT & ANCUS: to the land of the dead, "where Numa and Ancus have gone down before," from Horace, *Epistles*, 1.6.27 (Fairclough, *Horace: Satires, Epistles, and Ars Poetica*, 288–9).

[1] Manuscript: "characterr."

To Elizabeth Trist

DEAR MADAM   Poplar Forest Nov. 25. 13.

Being so much more within writing distance here than at Monticello, and with time freer from interruption, I avail myself of it to renew to you the assurances of my constant friendship, and my wishes for your health and happiness. and as brother Jonathan must have become stale and lost his powers of excitement, I send you a little work of a higher order to[1] make you laugh on a gloomy day. it has the merit too of giving us a peep behind the curtain at those contemptible beings composing that government which has forced us by it's wrongs and indignities to become it's enemy, & has subjected us to the mortification and remorse of wishing some success to such a wretch as Bonaparte. that he will fall in time, his ruthless tyrannies and restless endeavors to extend them are a sufficient security. but our peace and safety oblige us to pray that this may not be until the bankruptcy which he is forcing on Great Britain shall have swept her thousand ships from the ocean. for I see no certain term to the continual wars of Britain but in the downfall of her paper credit, and consequent inability to pay, feed, or repair the gigantic navy which enables her to plunder every flag, and to disturb the peace of every shore. the depreciation of her paper medium, acknoleged to be at this moment at 50. p. cent, and the known laws of the acceleration of descending bodies, and of paper medium more than of all others, is an assurance to us that her career is near it's end.[2]

At length, my dear friend, we are getting thro' the afflicting chapter of the Hulls, the Winchesters, Van Raentslaers & Boerstlers, and see our affairs look up under something like fidelity, courage, and talent. and the further we advance in experience, the more talent will start forward from the mass in which it has as yet been undistinguished, and will prove that we have Perries; Decaturs and Hulls of the right sort on the land as well as the ocean. the last news I have from the army was of Hampton's affair with Prevost, and Gen[l] Wilkinson's readiness to strike at either Kingston or Montreal. the latter I hope, because it will give us all Canada above Quebec, and Kingston may be permitted to capitulate at leisure. I have great confidence[3] that the English have not at this moment a post or an army above Quebec. mr Randolph had just joined Wilkinson, at the date of his last letter.

I left all well at Monticello, but Martha expecting very soon to be otherwise, I shorten my stay here that, in the absence of her husband she may have the comfort of other friends around her.[4] be so good as to present me to mr and mrs Gilmer, and to be assured yourself of my affectionate friendship & respect.

TH: JEFFERSON

PoC (MHi); at foot of first page: "M[rs] Trist"; endorsed by TJ. Tr (PPAmP: Catharine Wistar Bache Papers; extracts in RC of Trist to Catharine Wistar Bache, 13 Dec. 1813).

BROTHER JONATHAN: James Kirke Paulding, *The Diverting History of John Bull and Brother Jonathan. By Hector Bull-us* (New York, 1812). Thomas Moore's pseudonymous *Intercepted Letters; or, the Twopenny Post Bag. to which* are added, *Trifles Reprinted. By Thomas Brown, the Younger* (Philadelphia, 1813; Sowerby, no. 4519) was the enclosed LITTLE WORK OF A HIGHER ORDER (Trist to Bache, 13 Dec. 1813 [PPAmP: Bache Papers]). The HULLS OF THE RIGHT SORT took after Isaac Hull, the captain of the USS *Constitution*, rather than his uncle General William Hull, who surrendered Detroit to the British in August 1812 (*ANB*). The 26 Oct. 1813 AFFAIR between General Wade Hampton and a

British force under the command of Lieutenant Colonel Charles de Salaberry, not Sir George Prevost, ended in an American defeat (Heidler and Heidler, *War of 1812*, 88–9, 429).

[1] Tr begins here.
[2] Tr ends here.
[3] Tr resumes here.
[4] Tr ends here.

To Ellen W. Randolph (Coolidge)

MY DEAREST ELLEN   Poplar Forest Nov. 26. 13.

The situation in which I left your dear Mama makes me very anxious to hear of her during my stay here. uncertain whether this may not find her in bed, I address it to you to pray you to write me a line letting me know how she is. if it is done, on the reciept of this letter and put immediately into the post office of <u>Charlottesville</u>, it will still find me here. direct to me at Poplar Forest near Lynchburg. if you have heard any thing from your Papa since I left you, let me know it. indeed, as I shall see no newspaper till I get back, if it be known with you whether a stroke is struck either against Kingston or Montreal the news will be acceptable.   I had a terrible journey up, thro two days of rain, which tho' light, was nearly constant; but the roads dirtier & heavier than I have ever found them on this rout. the 2^d day I was able to get but 25. miles, and on the 3^d which brought me here I was from day-light to dark getting 34. miles. I was so well guarded that I was not at all wet, and my rheumatism is sensibly abated. according to my present prospect I shall be with you after an absence of three weeks. kiss your dear Mama for me, and deliver my affections to all the fireside assuring yourself of my tender love.

TH: JEFFERSON

PoC (MHi); endorsed by TJ.

Ellen (Eleonora) Wayles Randolph (1796–1876), the fourth child of Thomas Mann Randolph and TJ's daughter Martha Jefferson Randolph, shared her name with an elder sister who died in 1794. Born at Monticello, Randolph returned with her family to live there following her grandfather's retirement from the presidency. She became one of TJ's favorite grandchildren, often accompanying him on trips to Poplar Forest and Natural Bridge. In 1816, with his financial assistance, she visited Richmond, Washington, Baltimore, and Philadelphia, winning renown as an intelligent conversationalist. On 27 May 1825 in the Monticello drawing room, she married Joseph Coolidge, a Bostonian who had first visited TJ a year earlier. When the newlyweds settled in Boston, the separation proved difficult for both TJ and his granddaughter. Ellen Coolidge corresponded regularly with those who remained at Monticello but did not return until just after TJ's death. In 1826–28 her mother stayed in Boston near the Coolidges while her two youngest children were educated there. Joseph Coolidge became a successful merchant whose business interests gave his wife several opportunities to live overseas for extended periods of time. By 1847 the

Coolidges had returned to Boston. One of their six children was killed at the battle of Chickamauga in 1863 while serving as a Union army officer (Shackelford, *Descendants*, 1:89–99; Martha Jefferson Randolph to Elizabeth Trist, 31 May 1815 [ViHi: Trist Papers]; ViU: Ellen Wayles Randolph Coolidge Correspondence, including Ellen Randolph [Coolidge] to Martha Jefferson Randolph, 18 Aug. 1817, Virginia Jefferson Randolph Trist to Ellen Randolph Coolidge, 27 June 1825, and [in Coolidge Letterbook, 174–5] Coolidge to Henry Randall, 16 May 1857; Gaines, *Randolph*, 104, 166, 178, 185; Malone, *Jefferson*, 6:16, 458–9, 502; Randall, *Life*, 3:342–4; Thomas Jefferson Coolidge, *Autobiography of T. Jefferson Coolidge* [1923], 3, 5, 7, 42, 51, 82, 87; Joseph Coolidge to TJ, 13 Oct. 1824; *Richmond Enquirer*, 24 June 1825; Heitman, *U.S. Army*, 1:325; *Boston Daily Advertiser*, 24 Apr. 1876).

From Nicolas G. Dufief

MONSIEUR,   À Philadelphie le 26 Novembre 1813

J'ai l'honneur de vous adresser par le Courrier d'Aujourd'hui un petit paquet contenant "le traite élementaire de la Morale & du Bonheur." S'il arrivait que ce ne fut l'ouvrage que vous attendez, je vous prie d'avoir la bonté de me le renvoyer. Aussitôt que l' "American brewer & Malster" paraîtra je m'empresserai de vous le faire parvenir.

Acceptez les assurances de mon profond respect & de mon parfait devouement   N. G. DUFIEF

EDITORS' TRANSLATION

SIR,   Philadelphia 26 November 1813

By today's mail I have the honor of sending you a small package containing the "Traité élémentaire de Morale et du Bonheur." If it is not the book you are expecting, please be so kind as to return it to me. As soon as the "American brewer & Malster" is published, I will hasten to have it sent to you.

Accept the assurances of my profound respect and my perfect devotion   N. G. DUFIEF

RC (DLC); endorsed by TJ as received 13 Dec. 1813 and so recorded in SJL. Translation by Dr. Roland H. Simon. Enclosure: Jean Zacharie Paradis de Raymondis, *Traité élémentaire de Morale et du Bonheur* (Paris, 1795; Sowerby, no. 1249).

To Francis Eppes

DEAR FRANCIS   Poplar Forest Nov. 26. 13.

I have written to ask the favor of mr Halcomb to permit your cousin Baker and yourself to come and pass tomorrow and next day with me here. I send horses for you both, and will send you back on Monday morning. I left your aunt and cousins well at Monticello, and in the hope of seeing you here this evening, I remain affectionately

Your's   TH: JEFFERSON

PoC (CSmH: W. J. Rheese Papers); endorsed by TJ.

A missing letter from Eppes to TJ of 7 Nov. 1813 is recorded in SJL as received 10 Nov. 1813 from Lynchburg.

Eppes's AUNT in residence at Monticello was Martha Jefferson Randolph.

From Gales & Seaton

SIR,   Office of the Nat^l Intelligencer Nov. 26. 1813

We have the honor to acknowledge your favor of the 20th ult° which came duly to hand; and subsequently thereto we rec^d from Mr P. Gibson of Richmond $25 on your account, which sum pays your subscription to Oct 31. 1813.—In furnishing your bill we had reference only to the newspaper acc^t not understanding that you wished a statement of your printing acc^t—Since your settlement with Mr Smith, in Feb. 1809, there is but a single item charged in the latter acc^t—viz—100 Letters relative to applications for office, printed March 8. 1809.—This can be settled for in your next payment—its amount is $3:50.—We have no agent in Richmond; and must ask you to suffer the mode of payment to stand as heretofore

Very respectfully   GALES & SEATON

RC (DLC); in the hand of Joseph Gales; at foot of text: "Thos. Jefferson, Esq:"; endorsed by TJ as received 13 Dec. 1813 and so recorded in SJL; with notation by TJ: "Newspapers."

TJ paid Samuel H. Smith $33.45 on 6 FEB. 1809 for "printg. & newspap.," which apparently settled his printing account to that point (*MB*, 2:1240). For the 100 LETTERS RELATIVE TO APPLICATIONS FOR OFFICE, see TJ to Smith, 6 Mar. 1809, and enclosure.

To Thomas A. Holcombe

SIR   Poplar Forest Nov. 26. 13.

Presuming that Saturdays & Sundays are vacation days at your school I ask the favor of you to permit my grandson Francis Eppes and his cousin Baker [to]¹ pass them with me at this place. they shall be returned again on Monday morning. and as I shall have to ask the same favor of you again at the end of the ensuing week which I shall stay here, I will conform exactly to the hours of sending for them and returning them, if you will be so good as to prescribe them. should yourself, on those or any other days be able to make it convenient to call on me here, I shall be happy to see you, & pray you to accept the assurance of my great respect.   TH: JEFFERSON

PoC (MHi); at foot of text: "Mʳ Hal-   ¹ Omitted word editorially supplied.
comb"; endorsed by TJ.

From Thomas Law

DEAR SIR—   Philadelphia Novʳ 26. 1813.

I was favored with your accompaniement to my thoughts on banking & have reason to believe that Treasury notes will be issued to a larger Amount—The Banks here took them as Cash for a subsⁿ to Govᵗˢ Loan, as they were glad to obtain them—

The enclosed Petⁿ is rapidly signing & the Corporation is anxious to have the Bank. in Hamburgh a similar bank pays 150000 Crowns to the State see Adam Smith—

I am convinced that a Govᵗ might support several useful Institutions by Banks, the profits of which, monied men already too rich take to themselves—

I remain With sincere esteem & regard Yʳˢ mᵗ Obˢ

                                          T LAW—

RC (DLC); written on sheet folded to form four pages, with enclosure on p. 3; addressed: "To Thomas Jefferson Esqʳ Monticello Virginia"; franked; postmarked Philadelphia, 26 Nov.; endorsed by TJ as received 13 Dec. 1813 and so recorded in SJL.

The CORPORATION was Philadelphia's city government. ADAM SMITH wrote that "The city of Hamburgh has established a sort of public pawn-shop, which lends money to the subjects of the state upon pledges at six per cent. interest. This pawn-shop or Lombard, as it is called, affords a revenue, it is pretended, to the state of a hundred and fifty thousand crowns, which, at four and sixpence the crown, amounts to 33,750 l. sterling" (*An Inquiry into the Nature and Causes of the Wealth of Nations* [London, 1776; Sowerby, no. 3546], 2:416).

Petition to the Pennsylvania Legislature

To the Honourable the Senate and House of Representatives of the
State of Pennsylvania.

MERCHANTS and monied men have obtained Charters for numerous Banks, to facilitate negotiations and to increase profits; but hitherto the NE-CESSITOUS, who are compelled to borrow small sums for immediate relief, have been left, unregarded, to the mercy of Extortioners. The wife, whose husband lays on the bed of sickness unable to support his family; the widow, who has not money to pay the sad expense of committing her dear departed to the dust; the mother, who cannot purchase bread for her infant petition-ers; in short, every description of persons, reduced to distress, is compelled to resort to the usurious Pawn Broker. To him, also, the purloiners of prop-erty repair, and for a trifle secretly dispose of that which was most valuable and precious to the owner.

A long and painful observation of these evils, and a natural desire to mitigate distress and to prevent crime, have prompted us to solicit from the Government of this State a CHARTER OF INCORPORATION, for a Bank Es-tablishment, on principles similar to those in Europe, which have been uni-formly attended with the most beneficial consequences.

Mr. NECKAR, speaking of an Institution of this kind, called *Le Mont de Pieté*, in Paris, uses the following expressions:

"Neither the laws, nor the punishments inflicted, were sufficient to stop the progress of Usury in the capital, and it was impossible to be any longer blind to the insurmountable obstacles which opposed a reform; for, in pro-portion as the administration became more vigilant, the usurers increased their precautions to conceal their criminal traffick under forms to appearance legal.

The institution of the Mount of Piety, determined on in December 1777, seemed pointed out by the circumstances of the case. The conditions on loans are nearly equal to ten per cent.; the charges are naturally considerable. The advances made in a year amount to fifteen millions of livres, and the profits over and above the interest does not exceed one hundred and fifty thousand livres: this profit devolves to the general hospital. It has produced the great-est advantages. It provides against those unforeseen and urgent exigencies, which obliged men to have recourse to burthensome expedients, susceptible of an infinity of abuses."

After such a testimony, it were superfluous and mistrustful to endeavour, by affecting phraseology, to excite the sensibility or to awaken the sympathy of an enlightened, patriotick and benevolent legislature. The objects of your consideration supplicate you with anxiety; the advocates of humanity address you with confidence.

Printed broadside (DLC: TJ Papers, 200:35541); on same sheet as covering letter; authorship unstated, with Thomas Law himself as one possibility; undated.

From Nathaniel Ellicott

MY FRIEND THO: JEFFERSON ESQR   Occoquan 27 Nov <u>1813</u>

Those Interested are about to Petition the next Legislature for a Road from this to Normonds ford on the Rapp^k I have had a person out the Two last weeks getting Signers at the last Culpepper and Fauq. Courts &Ct and he has obtained Some hundreds, I Intend to wait on the assembly myself—will you do me the favor to Cover to me in Richmond (during the 1st week in Dec) letters[1] to the members from your and other Counties where Such might be Usefull, Stating the Usefulness and necessity of Such a Road &Ct &Ct in So doing you will Confer a favor on the Public and on no one more than on y^r friend[2]   N ELLICOTT

RC (DLC); endorsed by TJ as received 13 Dec. 1813 and so recorded in SJL.

The abovementioned PETITION and a similar appeal that Ellicott had coauthored the previous year were both received by the Virginia House of Delegates, referred to its Committee of Propositions and Grievances, and rejected (Vi: RG 78, Legislative Petitions, Orange Co. [14 Dec. 1812], Culpeper Co. [13 Dec. 1813]; *JHD* [1812–13 sess.], 54). NORMONDS FORD (Norman's Ford) was located about two miles south of present-day Remington (*MB*, 2:834n).

This day Ellicott also sent a similar letter to President James Madison (DLC: Madison Papers).

[1] Manuscript: "lettes."
[2] Manuscript: "frend."

Appendix
Supplemental List of Documents Not Found

JEFFERSON's epistolary record and other sources describe a number of documents for which no text is known to survive. The Editors generally account for such material at documents that mention them or at other relevant places. Exceptions are accounted for below.

From Joseph Brand, 20 Nov. 1813. Recorded in SJL as received 20 Nov. 1813.

INDEX

Aaron (Hebrew priest; Moses's brother), 616
Abbey (Abby) (TJ's slave; b. *1804*): on Poplar Forest slave list, 308
Abby (TJ's slave; b. *1753*): on Poplar Forest slave list, 308
Abigail (Old Testament figure), 623
Abraham (Old Testament patriarch), 466
Académie Française, 405–7
An Account of Expeditions to the Sources of the Mississippi (Pike), 374, 413
An Act for the assessment and collection of direct taxes and internal duties (*1813*), 397, 398n, 398, 399n, 401, 411
An Act for the better organization of the general staff of the Army of the United States (*1813*), 28n
An Act for the relief of Oliver Evans (*1808*), 353, 354n, 379, 385, 455, 457n
An Act to lay and collect a direct tax within the United States (*1798*), 443
An Act to lay and collect a direct tax within the United States (*1813*), 398–9, 411
Adair, James: on Indians, 137, 138
Adair, John, 189, 190n
Adams, Abigail (John Adams's granddaughter): as J. Adams's amanuensis, 627n
Adams, Abigail Smith (John Adams's wife): correspondence with T. B. Hollis, 228; correspondence with TJ, 437–8, 516–7, 548, 551; and daughter's death, 388, 516–7; family of, 438; health of, 437; house of, xlv, 386 (*illus.*); identified, 298n; letter from, 516–7; letter to, 437–8; sends greetings to TJ, 297, 466; TJ sends greetings to, 437; and TJ's syllabus on Jesus's doctrines, 440
Adams, George Washington (John Adams's grandson), 279, 438
Adams, John: and addresses of Continental Congress, 440, 612–3; and Alien and Sedition Acts, 191, 192n; on aristocracy, 278–9, 286–8, 387, 388n, 466–7, 504, 563, 564; on banks, 626; and T. Belsham's *Memoirs of the Late Reverend Theophilus Lindsey*, 145, 146, 180, 192, 193, 226,

227, 228, 277–8, 367; on A. Burr, 192, 623; on J. Chandler, 284–5, 625; and T. Clark's naval history, 146; and Cleanthes, 520–2, 540–1, 542; on Condorcet, 287; on T. Cooper, 318; and correspondence with TJ, 437; critics of, 255; on daughter's death, 387–8; *Defence of the Constitutions of Government of the United States of America*, 238–9, 278, 287, 288, 296, 388n, 504, 564; defends B. Waterhouse, 38–9, 99–101; on destruction of historical records, 278, 542, 616, 618; *Discourses on Davila*, 287, 288, 296; on election of *1800*, 192, 625; on elections, 625; family of, 146, 300, 438; on B. Franklin, 284, 285n, 287, 622; on French Revolution, 286, 297, 505; on government, 296; Greek handwriting of, xlv, 386 (*illus.*); and A. Hamilton, 254, 284; health of, 183, 501, 522; on P. Henry, 612; on E. Hersey, 501–2, 503, 504; on historians of the American Revolution, 258; house of, xlv, 386 (*illus.*); on human progress, 238–9, 296–7; identified, 4:390–1n; on Indians, 183; on Lafayette, 287; letter of intercepted and published, 233, 234n, 283–4; letters from, 145–7, 180–1, 183–4, 191–3, 226–9, 236–9, 253–6, 258–9, 277–80, 283–5, 286–8, 296–8, 298–300, 301–3, 317–9, 367–8, 386–8, 465–7, 499–502, 503–5, 520–2, 540–3, 612–4, 616–9, 621–7; letters to, 137–9, 193–5, 231–5, 438–41, 548–52, 562–8; and J. Lomax, 440, 441n; mentioned, 38, 89n; on T. Paine, 297; on Plato, 503, 504, 505; and presidential addresses, 180–1, 195n, 237–8, 253–4; on J. Priestley, 145–6, 236–7, 302, 318, 319; and J. Priestley's writings, 302, 317–8, 367–8, 439, 440, 471, 499–500, 510, 520; on Psalms of David, 616; on publication of correspondence, 226–7, 228, 258, 259; and Quakers, 284; reading habits of, 277, 302–3; on religion, 145–6, 227–8, 236–7, 238, 277–8, 297, 298–300, 301–3, 368, 499–502, 503–4, 522, 541, 542, 550, 616–8, 623, 624; resumes correspondence with TJ, 160; on retirement, 192; on Rhode Island,

bacon, 343

Bacon, Edmund: buys corn for TJ, 181–2, 553, 554; identified, 1:52n; letter to from R. B. Sthreshly, 554; Monticello overseer, 136n; orders goods for TJ, 343–8; pays Wayt & Winn, 111n; TJ's promissory note to, 54; witnesses documents, 34, 36, 36

Bacon, Francis: classification system of, 408, 409

Bacon, John, 54

Badajoz, Spain, 515

Baily, Jeremiah: receives patent, 456, 458n

Bainbridge, William, 206, 207n

Baker, Harriet Weissenfels (John Martin Baker's wife): sends greetings to TJ, 165

Baker, John Martin: family of, 164, 165; identified, 1:346n; letter from, 163–5; seeks appointment, 163–5; sends goods to TJ, 163; as U.S. consul, 163–4, 165

Baker, John Wayles (TJ's grand-nephew): on T. Holcombe, 64; identified, 65n; letter from, 64–5; TJ's relationship with, 64–5, 65, 225, 451, 648, 649

Baker, Martin, 19

Baldwin, Cyrus B.: cloth manufacturer, 335, 631–2

Ballard, William: agreement with TJ, 304; identified, 304n; as Tufton overseer, 304

Baltimore, Md.: museums in, 291–2, 374; prices in, 561

Bankhead, Ann (Anne) Cary Randolph (TJ's granddaughter; Charles Lewis Bankhead's wife): gold watch for, 339n; identified, 2:104n

Bankhead, Charles Lewis (Ann Cary Randolph Bankhead's husband): and appointment of principal assessor, 442; identified, 3:188n; letter from, 517–8; requests charcoal from TJ, 517

Bankhead, Ellen Monroe (TJ's great-granddaughter), 438n

Bank of Columbia, 168

Bank of Fredericksburg, 306, 314, 471

Bank of Pennsylvania: drafts on, 156, 258; stock owned by T. Kosciuszko, 168, 307, 546

Bank of the United States: and A. Gallatin, 535; and A. Hamilton, 534; mentioned, 225; opposition to, 581, 594

Bank of Virginia (Richmond): TJ's loan from, 20, 91, 113, 116, 295, 306, 337, 356, 396, 544, 552, 561

Bank of Winchester, 306, 314

banks: J. Adams on, 626; currency issued by, 533n; European, 224–5, 588–9, 592, 649, 650; T. Law on, 578, 594, 649; W. C. Nicholas on, 600; petitions for incorporation of, 649, 650

Banks, Sir Joseph, 252

Barber, Mr. See Barbour, Philip Pendleton

Barbour, James: and appointments, 288–9, 292, 301, 336; identified, 4:415–6n; and W. F. Jones, 126, 127n; letter from, 336; letter to, 288–9; wool cloth manufactured for, 631–2n

Barbour, Philip Pendleton: identified, 5:391–2n; and Jefferson v. Michie, 554, 630; letter from accounted for, 555n; letter to accounted for, 289n

Barlow, Joel: death of, 45, 57, 485n; forwards book manuscript to TJ, 45; identified, 1:589–90n; mentioned, 429n; Obituary by P. S. Du Pont de Nemours and K. E. Oelsner, 515–6; on T. Paine, 297; and J. Wilson, 415n

Barlow, Ruth Baldwin (Joel Barlow's wife): conveys letter, 459; dispute with D. B. Warden, 484, 485n; P. S. Du Pont de Nemours on, 484

Barlow, Thomas, 484, 485n

Barnes, John: on European affairs, 212; health of, 558; identified, 1:32n; and T. Kosciuszko's American investments, 85, 91–2, 118, 166, 167, 168, 211–2, 239–40, 262–3, 307, 507, 546, 558, 577–8, 606–7; letters from, 91, 91–2, 166, 168, 211–2, 262–3, 546, 558, 606–7; letters to, 84–5, 118, 239–40, 307, 507, 577–8; recommends J. Eliason, 91, 166; TJ pays, 117; TJ's account with, 118, 166, 167; as TJ's agent, 506

Barnet, Isaac Cox: identified, 5:463–4n; sends books to TJ, 489, 509

Barney, Joshua: and row galleys, 169–70, 216

Barry, Jeanne du: mentioned, 622; quoted by J. Adams, 466–7

Barton, Benjamin Smith: and American Philosophical Society, 516n; and appointment to U.S. Army medical department, 27, 28n, 46, 64; and history of Lewis and Clark Expedition, 46,

531; identified, 1:521n; on Indians, 137, 138; and instruction of M. Lewis, 424n; on language, 137; letter from, 27–8; letter to, 46; seeks to be treasurer of U.S. Mint, 28n

basins, 348

bass. *See* chub, Roanoke

Bassano, Hugues Bernard Maret, duc de, 575

Batteux, Charles: *Histoire des Causes Premières*, 439

Batture Sainte Marie, controversy over: W. C. C. Claiborne on, 388–9, 394–5, 433–4; and injunction from Orleans Parish court, 433–4, 434–7; F. X. Martin on, 434–6; and New Orleans city council, 388, 390–1, 392–3, 394–5. *See also* Livingston, Edward; *The Proceedings of the Government of the United States, in maintaining the Public Right to the Beach of the Missisipi* (Thomas Jefferson)

Baudouin, Pierre, 626

Bayard, James Ashton: and election of *1800*, 192, 193n; J. W. Eppes on, 313; as peace negotiator, 74, 103, 105n, 313

beans: chickpea, 188, 293; frijole, 188; haricots, 44, 45; snap, 44–5, 487

Bear Creek plantation (part of TJ's Poplar Forest estate): blankets and beds for slaves at, 310; clothing for slaves at, 309

Beauclerk, Amelius: British admiral, 57, 58n

Bec (TJ's slave; b. *1797*): given to T. J. Randolph, 36

Bécourt, Regnault de: *La Création du Monde*, 133, 134n, 213, 368; health of, 368; identified, 5:467–8n; letters from, 133–4, 368–9; letter to, 213; proposed book by, 133, 134n, 368–9

beef: mentioned, 187

beer: brewed at Monticello, 507

Bélidor, Bernard Forest de: *Architecture Hydraulique*, 381

Bellinger, Joseph: identified, 317n; introduced to TJ, 317

Bellona (schooner), 45, 152

Belmont tract: sale of, 20

Belsham, Thomas: *Memoirs of the Late Reverend Theophilus Lindsey, M.A.*, 145, 146, 180, 192, 193, 204, 219, 226, 227, 228, 277, 278, 280, 367; mentioned, 227, 317–8, 500; TJ on, 233

Belsham, William: mentioned, 227, 500

benne (benni; sesame; *Sesamum indicum*). *See* sesame

Bennett, Thomas: identified, 89–90n; letter from, 88–90; letter to, 124–5; and Seventy-Six Association, 88–90, 124–5

benni (benne; sesame; *Sesamum indicum*). *See* sesame

Benson, Thomas: *Vocabularium Anglo-Saxonicum*, 406, 407n

Berlin and Milan decrees: revocation of, 142, 538, 540n

Bernadotte, Jean Baptiste Jules, crown prince of Sweden: book sanctioned by, 513; in *1813* campaign against Napoleon, 619, 621n; as peace broker, 241

Bernard, Sir Francis: correspondence of published, 258

Bess (TJ's slave; b. *1747*). *See* Betty (Bess) (TJ's slave; b. *1747*)

Betty (Bess) (TJ's slave; b. *1747*): on Poplar Forest slave list, 308, 309

Betty (Island Betty; Old Betty) (TJ's slave; b. *1749*): on Poplar Forest slave list, 308, 309

Betty (TJ's slave; b. *1801*): on Poplar Forest slave list, 308

Bible: Acts referenced, 541; Corinthians referenced, 284, 285n; Daniel referenced, 236, 302; Deuteronomy referenced, 98, 100n, 618; Ecclesiastes referenced, 192–3; Exodus referenced, 616–9, 643, 644n; Genesis referenced, 21, 23n, 541; Genesis referenced by TJ, 564, 567n; John referenced, 302, 447, 521, 643, 644n; Judith referenced, 623, 627n; Leviticus referenced, 98, 100n; Luke referenced, 183, 184n, 287, 288n; Matthew referenced, 237, 239n, 447; miracles in, 236; Proverbs referenced, 623; Psalms referenced, 22, 23n, 447, 616; Psalms referenced by TJ, 67, 68n, 402, 407n, 550–1; Revelation referenced, 521; Romans referenced, 447; Samuel referenced, 37, 40n; societies for distribution of, 607–8; Ten Commandments, 616–8

Bible Society of Virginia, 607–8

Bibliothecae Historicae Libri Quindecim de quadraginta (Diodorus Siculus), 382

Biddle, Nicholas: American Philosophical Society membership diploma for, xliv–xlv, 115n, 116n, 386 (*illus.*); and

INDEX

Declaration of Independence: mentioned, 564; signers of, 137, 183

Defence of the Constitutions of Government of the United States of America (Adams), 238–9, 278, 287, 288, 296, 388n, 504, 564

Dejean, Jean B., 436

DeLacy, John Devereux: identified, 62–3n; and inland navigation, 268–9n, 319–20; letter from, 268–9; letter from accounted for, 63n; letters to, 62–3, 319–20; solicits TJ's patronage, 268; and steamboats, 62, 63

Delaplaine, Joseph: identified, 3:51n; letter from, 125–6; letter to, 148–9; publishes engraved portraits, 125–6, 148; *Repository of the Lives and Portraits of Distinguished Americans,* 149n

Delaware River: British blockade of, 31, 61; defense of, 217

Delor, Mrs., 434

Dennis, George (TJ's slave; b. *1808*): on Poplar Forest slave list, 309, 310

Denniston, David, 255

Derieux, Maria Margherita Martin (Peter Derieux's wife): financial situation of, 335; and P. Mazzei's Richmond property, 269, 295, 334; as schoolteacher, 269, 270, 334–5; stepdaughter of P. Mazzei, 305

Derieux, Peter (Justin Pierre Plumard): and Dutasta, 442; financial situation of, 320, 332; identified, 3:395–6n; letters from, 269–71, 332–3; letters to, 320–1, 442; and P. Mazzei, 269, 270, 320–1, 332; and P. Mazzei's Richmond property, 269, 295, 305–6, 321, 334, 335, 337; money sent to by French relatives, 337; requests assistance from TJ, 269, 270; TJ forwards letter to, 442

Desaguliers, John Theophilus: *A Course of Experimental Philosophy,* 381

Destutt de Tracy, Antoine Louis Claude: and American Philosophical Society, 458–60; *Commentary and Review of Montesquieu's Spirit of Laws,* 52, 458, 484, 509, 599; economic theories of, 53; *Élémens d'Idéologie,* 52, 458, 526, 530n; identified, 1:262n; letter from, 458–60; sends manuscript to TJ, 45, 458; *A Treatise on Political Economy,* 509

Detroit, Mich. Territory: W. Hull's surrender at, 54n, 112, 171, 645n; recaptured by U.S. forces, 546n

Dick (Yellow Dick) (TJ's slave; b. *1767*): on Poplar Forest slave list, 308

Dickinson, John: and J. Adams's intercepted letter, 233, 234n, 283–4; and Continental Congress, 232, 440, 612–3, 614n; *The Farmer's and Monitor's Letters,* 440

Dickinson, Rodolphus: *A Geographical and Statistical View of Massachusetts Proper,* 44, 82; identified, 44n; letter from, 44; letter to, 82

Dickinson College: trustees of, 598–9

Dickonson, Lieut.: letter from, 636; thanks TJ, 636

Dictionarium Saxonico et Gothico-Latinum (Lye), 406, 407n

A Dictionary of the English Language (Johnson), 387, 404, 406

Diderot, Denis: and *Encyclopédie,* 381; mentioned, 624

Dinah (TJ's slave; b. *1766*): on Poplar Forest slave list, 308, 309

Dinsmore, James: accounts with TJ, 338n, 431; identified, 1:136n

Diodorus Siculus: *Bibliothecae Historicae Libri Quindecim de quadraginta,* 382

Diogenes Laertius: quoted by J. Adams, 520, 522n

Diogenes of Sinope ("the Cynic"), 229, 230n

Dionysius Halicarnasseus: mentioned, 542; *On Literary Composition,* 277

Discourses on Davila (Adams), 287, 288, 296

Dismal Swamp Canal, 92–3, 94

Disney, John: English Unitarian, 145–6, 227, 228–9

Disquisitions Relating to Matter and Spirit (Priestley), 302, 440

Divers, George: and appointment of principal assessor, 411–2, 412, 442; health of, 110; identified, 1:157–8n; invites TJ to dinner, 412; letter from, 412; letter to, 411–2; and Rivanna Company, 595, 597–8; and wool manufacture, 114

Divers, Martha Walker (George Divers's wife): health of, 110, 266

The Diverting History of John Bull and Brother Jonathan (Paulding), 110, 264, 644, 645n

INDEX

INDEX

INDEX

Perry, Reuben (*cont.*)
for, 163n; TJ's carpenter, 107, 162,
257
Peruvian bark (*cinchona*): used to treat
J. Madison, 241
Peter (F. Smith's slave), 378
Petersburg, Va.: schools in, 269, 332,
334–5
Petty, Sir William: economic theory of,
593n
Peyton, Bernard: identified, 51–2n; introduced by I. A. Coles, 51, 52n
Peyton, Craven: account with TJ, 372,
544; conveys Henderson lands to TJ,
198; corn contract with TJ, 553; and
Henderson case, 50–1, 78, 79, 153,
196, 197, 198, 200, 201n, 315, 316,
367, 472–3, 475, 572, 573, 609–10,
611n; identified, 1:415n; *Jefferson v.
Michie*, 199, 200, 477–82; letters from
accounted for, 367n, 372n; letters to,
50–1, 367, 372; and proposed duel
with D. Michie, 479
Peyton v. Henderson: court costs in,
338n; decision in, 473, 477–8, 480,
572; depositions in, 200, 479, 480,
572, 609; and J. Henderson, 153, 197,
472–3, 475; TJ on C. Peyton's role in,
572
Philadelphia: *Aurora*, 83, 510; banks,
649; directory, 220, 280; and Genet
riots, 254; Museum, 291; newspapers
in, 83, 510, 599; price of flour at, 561;
scarlet fever outbreak in, 74; yellow
fever epidemic (*1793*), 254
Philadelphia, USS (frigate), 206, 207n
Philippe II, Duke of Orléans: and paper
currency, 586
Phill (Phil) (TJ's slave; b. *1801*): on
Poplar Forest slave list, 309
Phill (Phil) (TJ's slave; b. *1808*): on
Poplar Forest slave list, 308
Phillips, William: British general, 510
philology: TJ on, 403–6
*The Philosophical Principles of the Science
of Brewing* (Richardson), 533, 597
Philpotts, Oakley: and unpaid tobacco
bill, 356
Pickering, Timothy: mentioned, 254,
298n; possesses TJ-Canby letters,
447n, 509n; as secretary of state, 194,
195n; on G. Washington's cabinet se-
lections, 259
pigs: killed by dogs, 511
Pike, Zebulon Montgomery: *An Account
of Expeditions to the Sources of the*

Mississippi, 374, 413; mentioned, 209,
525; and War of *1812*, 526–8
Pindar (Greek poet): mentioned, 403
Pitot, James, 434–7
Pitt, William (the Younger): mentioned,
141
Pittsburgh, Pa.: glass factory at, 468
Plato: J. Adams on, 503, 504, 505
Pleasants, Samuel: and books for TJ,
122, 374, 412–3; *A Collection of all
such Acts of the General Assembly of
Virginia, of a public and permanent
nature, as are now in force*, 122; identified, 5:253–4n; letter from, 412–3;
letter from accounted for, 122n; letters
to, 122, 374; Richmond printer, 32
plows: mentioned, 344, 347
Plumard de Bellanger, Marie Françoise,
337, 338n
Plutarch: mentioned, 542; TJ quotes,
494, 498n, 591, 593n
poetry: in America, 297; dedicated to
TJ, 464n; written at Monticello, 463
Poindexter, George: carries letter, 26;
identified, 27n; and seed for TJ, 26,
66
Poland: partitions of, 212
Political Arithmetic (Cooper), 583
political economy: J. W. Eppes asks TJ
for outline of, 312; TJ's letters on
finance, 220–5, 490–7, 578–92
politics: books on, 374, 413, 504, 505n,
613. *See also* Federalist party; Republican party
polygraph: and J. I. Hawkins, 560n
Pompadour, Jeanne Antoinette, mar-
quise de, 622
Pompei, Girolamo: as translator, 280n,
522, 541, 551, 552n
Pompeius Magnus, Gnaeus (Pompey
the Great), 542, 625
Pope, Alexander: and Cleanthes's *Hymn
to Zeus*, 521; quoted, 632, 633n; religious beliefs of, 521; *The Universal
Prayer*, 521; on women, 259
Poplar Forest (TJ's Bedford Co. estate):
barns at, 488n; beds and blankets for
slaves at, 308–9; chimney backs for,
109, 349, 350; clothing for slaves at,
308; corn grown at, 486; and F.
Eppes, 71–3; flour from, 3, 487; hemp
grown at, 486; invitations to visit, 451,
648, 649; livestock at, 366; main
house at, 71, 72, 129, 162, 488n; overseers at, 4, 5, 24–5, 25–6, 486–7; peas
grown at, 486; sheep at, 6; spinning

INDEX

in the High Court of Chancery
(Atkyns), 477
Reports of Cases Argued and Determined in the Supreme Judicial Court of the Commonwealth of Massachusetts, 599
Repository of the Lives and Portraits of Distinguished Americans (Delaplaine), 149n
Republican party: and human progress, 194; W. Jones on, 643, 644; in S.C., 317, 611, 636
Reuben (TJ's slave; b. *1793*): on Poplar Forest slave list, 309
Revolutionary War: mentioned, 429n, 577
Rhea, John: identified, 2:358–9n; letter from, 358–9; sends constituent circulars to J. Madison, 359n; sends constituent circulars to TJ, 358
Rhode Island: J. Adams on, 625; deference to certain families in, 625; elections in, 625
Rhody (TJ's slave; b. *1811*): on Poplar Forest slave list, 309, 310
rice: mentioned, 187
Richardson, John (English author): *The Philosophical Principles of the Science of Brewing*, 533, 597
Richardson, Robert: identified, 5:485–6n; letters from accounted for, 110n, 349n; letters to, 109–10, 349; and Oxford Iron Works, 109–10, 349, 350
Richmond, Va.: Bank of Virginia, 20, 91, 113, 116, 295, 306, 337, 356, 396, 544, 552, 561; British destroy public records in, 371–2; chancery court at, 362, 472–3, 474, 479, 480; Eagle Tavern, 334; flour prices at, 21, 91, 93, 94, 113, 147, 169, 295, 306, 314, 544, 552, 561–2, 615–6, 621; flour shipped to, 331, 487, 544; P. Mazzei's property in, 4, 21, 43, 90–1, 106, 108, 113, 115, 116, 147, 168–9, 185–6, 268, 269, 294, 295, 305–6, 320–1, 321, 332, 334, 335, 337, 396; TJ's lot in, 304–5, 365–6, 371, 372n. *See also* Enquirer (Richmond newspaper); Gibson & Jefferson (Richmond firm); Gibson, Patrick
Ritchie, Thomas: identified, 1:214n; letter to, 515–6; TJ forwards article to, 515–6
Rivanna Company: act establishing, 596, 628, 629n; bill regarding, 595, 596, 597n, 597–8, 620, 628, 629, 630–1,

633–4, 635; directors of, 596, 628, 629, 633–4, 635; petition to General Assembly, 628, 633
Rivanna River: navigation of, 610; water level low, 290, 620. *See also* Henderson case; Shadwell mills
Robbins, Jonathan: case of, 255
Roberts, Thomas (of Virginia): seeks military appointment, 42
Robertson, Archibald: account with TJ, 92, 94; identified, 4:94–5n; letter from, 94; letters to, 92–3, 448; TJ orders groceries from, 448; TJ pays, 448. *See also* Brown & Robertson (Lynchburg firm)
Robertson, John: Albemarle Co. school of, 73, 131
Robertson, Thomas Bolling: and batture controversy, 434n, 437n; identified, 2:351n
Robertson, William (*1721–93*): *History of America*, 326
Robespierre, Maximilien François Marie Isidore de: leader of French Revolution, 140, 228, 293
Robinson, Samuel: and O. Evans's patent machinery, 353, 354n, 453, 454, 455
Rochefoucault. *See* La Rochefoucauld, François de
Roebuck, HMS (frigate), 446
Rogers, Charles: letter from, 21–3; solicits aid for S. Rogers, 22–3
Rogers, Sarah: aid for, 22–3; as artist, 22, 23n; identified, 23n
Romaine, Benjamin: identified, 219n; letter from, 218–9; letter to, 282–3; *Tammany Society, No. 1, Twenty Fourth Anniversary Address*, 218–9, 282
Romans, Bernard: on Indians, 137, 138
Rome, ancient: Christianity in, 367; military service in, 209; Punic wars, 429n
Ronaldson, James: identified, 1:18–9n; sends seeds to TJ, 7n
rope, 343, 345, 348
Ross, David: health of, 350, 364–5; identified, 350n; letter from, 364–5; letter to, 350; and H. Marks's estate, 135; and memories of youth, 364; and nephew E. Ross, 568; payments to, 109–10, 337, 349, 350, 364
Ross, Edward: infatuated with TJ's granddaughter, 568–9n; letters of introduction for, 568; and Oxford Iron

INDEX

Sugden, Edward Burtenshaw: *A Practical Treatise of The Law of Vendors and Purchasers of Estates*, 477

suicide: plants used to commit, 293; TJ on, 293; venesection, 293

Sullivan, James: correspondence with T. Pickering, 259

Sullivan, John: Revolutionary War general, 207

A Summary of the Principal Evidences for the Truth and Divine Origin of the Christian Revelation (Porteus), 15, 61

Superior Court of Chancery for the Richmond District, 362, 472–3, 474, 479, 480

Superior Court of Chancery for the Winchester District, 268

Supreme Court, U.S.: and batture controversy, 392–3, 394–5

Susanna (Suzanna) (biblical figure), 623

Suvorov, Aleksandr: Russian general, 468

Swift, Jonathan: correspondence with Lord Bolingbroke, 267; religious beliefs of, 521; *Travels into several Remote Nations of the World . . . by Lemuel Gulliver*, 70n

Swiney, Mr., 486

Systema Naturæ (Linnaeus), 408, 409

A System of Universal Science (Woodward), 411n

tabasco (*Capsicum frutescens*), 252

Tableau du Climat et du Sol des États-Unis d'Amérique (Volney), 322–3, 327

Tacitus, Cornelius: *C. Cornelii Taciti opera cum varietate lectionum selecta novisque emendationibus*, 93, 94; lost works of, 278; mentioned, 402, 542; *Tacitus C. Cornelii Taciti Opera quae supersunt*, 157; TJ quotes, 402, 407n; tyrants condemned in works of, 53; *The works of Cornelius Tacitus* (trans. Murphy), 93; *The Works of Tacitus* (trans. Gordon), 93

Tacitus C. Cornelii Taciti Opera quae supersunt (Tacitus), 157

Taggart, F. B.: seeks naval appointment, 170–1, 211

Taggart, John: and appointment for son, 170–1, 211; identified, 1:55n; letter from, 170–1; letter to, 211

Tammany societies: of N.Y., 218–9, 526n; TJ elected member of, 218,

219n; TJ on, 282–3; and wearing Indian garb, 218, 219n

Tammany Society, No. 1, Twenty Fourth Anniversary Address (Romaine), 218–9, 282

Tate, Nahum: as translator of Psalms, 550–1, 552n

Tatham, William: surveys of, 120, 122n, 216

taxes: auction sales, 311; on banknotes and negotiable paper, 311; on carriages, 311; customs, 358n; direct, 311–2, 358n, 545n; indirect, 312; on land, 311; on retailers, 311; on stills, 311; on sugar, 311; TJ on, 220–5, 490–7; TJ pays, 544, 545n

Tayloe, John: forwards letter to TJ, 333; identified, 333–4n; letter from, 333–4

Taylor, Bennett (Edmund Randolph's son-in-law), 12

Taylor, George: forwards letters to W. Short, 277

Taylor, John (of Caroline): *Arator: being a series of Agricultural Essays, Practical & Political*, 122, 613; *An Inquiry into the Principles and Policy of the Government of the United States*, 504, 505n, 567, 613, 622; and T. Martin's drill plow, 514, 515n; TJ on writings of, 567

Taylor, Thomas: and P. Mazzei's Richmond property, 4, 21, 43, 90–1, 106, 115, 116, 147, 168, 185–6, 294, 295, 305–6, 320, 321, 396

tea: gunpowder, 348; Imperial, 346; ordered for Monticello, 343, 344, 345, 347, 348; ordered for Poplar Forest, 448

Teach, Edward (Blackbeard), 53

Tennessee: J. Rhea's letter to constituents in, 358–9

Terril, Mr. (of Albemarle Co.): takes boarders, 73

Texas (Spanish colony): American filibustering expeditions against, 188–90, 293; use of bird pepper in, 128, 195

textiles: cambric, 343; coating, 345; cotton, 346, 347; dyeing of, 114, 314, 335; ferret (fabric tape), 345, 346; flannel, 345; hemp, 345; holland, 345, 346; homespun, 308, 309; humhums, 349n; linen, 344, 347; Osnaburg, 347, 349n; plain cloth, 308, 309, 310, 344, 345; shirting, 308, 309, 310, 348; silk, 345; Ticklenburg, 344, 345, 346;

THE PAPERS OF THOMAS JEFFERSON are composed in Monticello, a font based on the "Pica No. 1" created in the early 1800s by Binny & Ronaldson, the first successful typefounding company in America. The face is considered historically appropriate for The Papers of Thomas Jefferson because it was used extensively in American printing during the last quarter-century of Jefferson's life, and because Jefferson himself expressed cordial approval of Binny & Ronaldson types. It was revived and rechristened Monticello in the late 1940s by the Mergenthaler Linotype Company, under the direction of C. H. Griffith and in close consultation with P. J. Conkwright, specifically for the publication of the Jefferson Papers. The font suffered some losses in its first translation to digital format in the 1980s to accommodate computerized typesetting. Matthew Carter's reinterpretation in 2002 restores the spirit and style of Binny & Ronaldson's original design of two centuries earlier.

✧